JAZZ

11/2009

*"You got to be in the sun to feel the sun.
It's that way with music, too."*

—Sidney Bechet

JAZZ

GARY GIDDINS
&
SCOTT DeVEAUX

W.W. NORTON & COMPANY
NEW YORK • LONDON

For information about permission to reproduce selections from this book,
write to Permissions, W. W. Norton & Company, Inc.,
500 Fifth Avenue, New York, NY 10110

For information about special discounts for bulk purchases, please contact
W. W. Norton Special Sales at specialsales@wwnorton.com or 800-233-4830

Manufacturing by Courier Westford
Book design by Lissi Sigillo
Production manager: Julia Druskin

Library of Congress Cataloging-in-Publication Data

Giddins, Gary.
Jazz / Gary Giddins & Scott DeVeaux.
p. cm.
Includes bibliographical references and index.
ISBN 978-0-393-06861-0 (hardcover)
1. Jazz—History and criticism. I. DeVeaux, Scott Knowles. II. Title.
ML3508.G54 2009
781.65—dc22
2009024880

W. W. Norton & Company, Inc.
500 Fifth Avenue, New York, N.Y. 10110
www.wwnorton.com

W. W. Norton & Company Ltd.
Castle House, 75/76 Wells Street, London W1T 3QT

1 2 3 4 5 6 7 8 9 0

To Deborah Halper, Lea Giddins, and Alice Giddins.
—Gary Giddins

To the women in my family: my grown-up daughters Amelia
and Flora Thomson-DeVeaux; my newborn twins, Lena and
Celia; and most of all, my wife, Nancy Hurrelbrinck.
—Scott DeVeaux

CONTENTS

INTRODUCTION

One of the great pleasures of looking into jazz—beyond the excitement and variety of the music itself—derives from its relative historical newness. To the generations born after the Vietnam War, it may seem like an old story that predates rock and hip-hop and their grandparents. But following its contours today, in the early years of the twenty-first century, is like what it might have meant to pursue Shakespeare in 1650, when you could still meet people who saw the plays as originally produced and even worked or hung out with the guy who wrote them. The pioneers of jazz, including its preeminent soloist (Louis Armstrong) and composer (Duke Ellington), worked into the 1970s and beyond. Innovators of later jazz styles and schools are with us now. Young musicians, creating tremendous excitement at this moment, will be acclaimed as tomorrow's masters. In other words, the dust of history has by no means settled on jazz. The canon of masterpieces, far from fixed, remains open to interpretation, adjustment, and expansion.

Jazz is designed to impart a narrative arc that traces the development of jazz from nineteenth-century musical precursors to the present, while offering a few ways to understand that arc. It differs from most jazz histories on at least three counts. First, we do not treat jazz as music in a vacuum, perpetuating itself as a baton passed from genius to genius; we see it, rather, as a reflection of broader cultural, political, social, and economic factors, and attempt to line up the crucial moments in its progress with historical events that it reflected and influenced.

Second, this book requires neither musical knowledge nor ability (only a predisposition for the enjoyment of music and the imagination to feel its expressive power), but it always keeps one eye firmly cocked on illustrative jazz masterworks. To that effect, we include seventy-eight Listening Guides that analyze a broad range of recordings with mostly nonmusicological descriptions of what happens from one passage to the next. Most of these records are recognized classics, while others are fairly or very obscure. We have programmed all seventy-eight selections on four CDs, which can be ordered from the Norton website (www.wwnorton.com/books/recordings -for-jazz). We strongly recommend this collection, not least for the new transfers, which in most instances are superior to those in commercial release.

Third, we emphasize a rudimentary understanding of basic jazz techniques and structures as a corrective to the intimidation many people feel when confronted with improvisation. Toward that goal, we have front-loaded the book with two chapters on basic musical elements and how they function in jazz. The idea is to provide a musician's-eye view of what happens on the bandstand, and to enable the listener to participate more knowingly in the now of jazz creativity. These facets, which are amplified in the glossary, are demonstrated with four classic recordings (part of the CD set and analyzed more closely in succeeding chapters): Louis Armstrong's "West End Blues" (1928), Billie Holiday's "A Sailboat in the Moonlight" (1937), Charlie Parker's "Now's the Time" (1953), and Miles Davis's "So What" (1959).

Finally, a word about what this book is not: it's not an encyclopedia of jazz—such works exist and they are invaluable. A book like this makes choices every step of the way. Just how many choices are possible became especially evident to us as we spent more than a year choosing our musical examples and debating which aspects of the story to emphasize and which to omit, usually for reasons of space or coherence—including most jazz made beyond the borders of the continental United States. If you have a love of jazz, some of your favorites are not mentioned at all or only in passing. We know that of a certainty, because some of our own favorites were relegated to limbo. Mea culpa, Carmen McRae, Art Pepper, et al.!

Acknowledgments

We are privileged to have the participation of the brilliant Herman Leonard, considered by many the greatest photographer ever to focus his camera on jazz. A protégé of Yousuf Karsh, Leonard is distinguished in his work by his total control of light. In the late 1940s, the peak of his jazz period, Leonard brought his equipment to clubs, blocked out the natural light, and created his own chiaroscuro effects, emphasizing the excitement of the music and the milieu through reflected highlights and his signature use of cigarette smoke. Leonard's New Orleans studio was destroyed by

Hurricane Katrina; he now lives and works in California. He shot most of the portraits that introduce each chapter. The photographs in the insert represent various sources and several other great photographers.

Only two names are listed on the cover of *Jazz*, but this book could not exist without the contributions of many others. Chief among them is Norton editor Maribeth Payne, who shepherded the project through several years and over many obstacles. She brought the two writers together, and kept us fixated on the big picture, playing to our strengths individually and as a team. Every writer craves a good line editor and we are blessed with one of the best, Susan Gaustad, who shaved our excesses, pounced on our repetitions, and emended our solecisms. Quite simply: without Maribeth and Susan, no *Jazz*.

Our work was also immeasurably aided by the rest of the staff at Norton: Imogen Howes, editorial assistant; Trish Marx, director of photography; David Botwinik, music typesetter; Julia Druskin, production manager; and Nancy Palmquist, managing editor of trade books. Lissi Sigillo designed the book with dedication and creativity, and Donna Ranieri gathered the illustrations from which the final selection was made. Gary Giddins would like to thank Georges Borchardt, and we are also grateful to the experts who generously commented on early drafts of the manuscript, absolving them of our failings.

Gary Giddins
Scott DeVeaux

JAZZ

Musical Orientation: Elements and Instruments

EMPATHY

Almost every jazz lover has had an experience like this one. You take your seat at a concert, as a quintet—trumpet player, saxophonist, pianist, bassist, and drummer—takes the stage. After a brief piano introduction, which sets the pace and feeling for the first piece, the trumpeter and saxophonist play a melody, supported by the accompaniment of piano, bass, and drums. The tune may or may not be familiar to you, but because it is played simultaneously by the two wind instruments and repeats certain melodic

◀ Charlie Parker—blindingly fast virtuoso, bluesman, romantic ballad player—with his fellow 1949 Metronome All-Stars Lennie Tristano (piano), Eddie Safranski (bass), and Billy Bauer (guitar).

phrases, you can at least be sure that it is a written melody, or theme. Then the theme ends. As the trumpeter steps back, the saxophonist begins to improvise a solo. In a short while, you find yourself totally lost; while similar solos in previous concerts have caught and stimulated you right away, tonight it's all a tangle and you can't find a footing.

All music—all art, all entertainment—requires empathy, but jazz requires empathy of a particular sort. Jazz musicians are inventing a musical statement (improvising) in that space and in that moment. In order to share in their creativity, you have to follow the twists and turns of their musical ideas while simultaneously registering their interaction with other musicians; only then can you evaluate whether a solo is a success—the soloist may be a spellbinder or a bore, inspired or aloof—and the band coherent. Sidney Bechet, the great soprano saxophonist of jazz's early years, once remarked, "You got to be in the sun to feel the sun. It's that way with music too."

One way to gain a deeper understanding is to learn some of the fundamental rules and techniques of music. Obviously, at a basic level you can simply listen to a performance and be amused, amazed, shaken, moved— you don't need anyone to tell you that you like it, or why. A great deal of jazz functions on just such a visceral level. Most fans can recall their first exposure to jazz, whether it was a performance in a nightclub or concert hall, or on a classic recording by Louis Armstrong, Billie Holiday, or John Coltrane. Often, just one encounter is enough to encourage a desire to hear more of that artist and other jazz artists—and, by extension, to learn more about the intricacies of this exciting and passionate art.

Yet only by pressing deeper into the music, to the point where you listen like a musician, can you penetrate jazz's most rewarding mysteries. As a child, you may enjoy your first baseball game knowing only that one player pitches to another while teammates in the field strive to foil any hits. But soon you want more than that: a team to root for, understanding of rules, appreciation for tactics, statistics of varying relevance—all to intensify your involvement in the game. Jazz is similarly most rewarding to a listener conversant with its rules.

This chapter and the next deal with basic musical elements. Some of them will seem incredibly obvious, others not so much. They are offered as a prologue to the history that follows. By understanding what the musician is up against—in terms of structure; or the competing claims of melody, rhythm, and harmony; or the challenge in mastering a particular instrument—you are better able to empathize with and evaluate his or her work. Happily, this kind of preparation may be acquired with virtually no musical ability or training. Most jazz is based on two structures and is performed on a limited number of instruments. If you can feel "time," which is how jazz musicians refer to a rhythmic pulse, and can count to four (most jazz is based on patterns of four beats), you have already mastered its essential principles.

TIMBRE

Timbre refers to quality of sound, or tone color. All instruments, including the human voice, have distinct qualities—timbres—that set them apart, even when they play the same pitch. The gross differences are easy to hear: a violin sounds noticeably different from a trumpet. A tenor saxophone sounds less noticeably different from an alto saxophone. An appreciation of timbre is basic to our ability to recognize voices as well as music. If a friend telephones, we recognize that person's identity by the timbre of his or her voice. But timbre also has an aesthetic component. If two vocalists of the same age and background are equally adept at carrying a tune, hitting every note precisely, it's likely that the one with an appealing sound will be the more pleasing singer.

Further, timbre is something we control. Sometimes we deliberately manipulate our voices to whisper or shout, to command or console. Such manipulation also reveals our emotions—fear, love, anger, exhaustion. Jazz musicians try to lend their instruments the same qualities of human speech, though this is not as easy with a piece of metal as it is with the larynx. Some horn players use mutes—physical devices inserted into the bell of the instrument to distort the sounds coming out. The use of unusual sounds for expressive purposes, known as timbre variation, came to jazz through African American folk culture, but it lies deep within the idea of all folk traditions. Jazz musicians, much more than their classical counterparts, use timbre to attain stylistic individuality. The tenor saxophonist Buddy Tate, known for his many years with the Count Basie Orchestra, once said that the first crucial step for young musicians is to find their own sound. That is a pretty radical notion. Tate didn't mean to suggest that an unfledged musician had to find a sound unlike anyone else's, just for the sake of novelty. Rather, the young musician needs to know who he is in order to find a sound he knows to be his own. The task is only partly a conscious one.

Louis Armstrong had an ebullient personality that's reflected in his trumpet sound. Miles Davis had a more introverted personality that's reflected in his. This kind of individuality can't be taught.

THE ENSEMBLE

Instruments are usually classified by the way they make sounds. In jazz, the largest category consists of those that produce sound by moving air—all referred to in jazz (unlike classical music) as wind instruments, or horns. The physics of wind instruments is fairly simple. Blowing on or into a tube sets a column of air in vibration, producing a particular sound. (Most wind players produce a slight wobble in pitch, known as vibrato.) There are two options for modifying that sound. The first is changing the length of the tube. The second is blowing with increased intensity, which forces the vibration to suddenly jump to a new level, raising the pitch.

Both concepts can be demonstrated on the flute, perhaps the simplest wind instrument in Western music. The flute is blown sideways against a hole placed in the instrument's top, which has an edge that stops and divides the air so that some of it passes into the tube—an effect similar to blowing across the opening of a bottle. The player's fingers cover holes that run lengthwise along the flute. To change the length of the air column, you simply lift a finger to open one of the holes, shortening the vibrating column of air. In effect, the flute behaves as if it were an instrument of continuously changing length.

Increasing the speed of air is more dramatic: by changing the embouchure—the shaping and positioning of the lips and other facial muscles—and applying more pressure, an experienced player can push the pitch significantly higher than before (just how high depends on the instrument). This sets in motion an acoustic phenomenon known as the overtone series: higher pitches caused by secondary vibrations of the main sound wave.

Brass instruments, like trumpet and trombone, use a cuplike mouthpiece, which cradles the performer's lips. But the crucial feature is how air is set into motion. The vibration of the lips, creating a kind of buzz, moves the column of air and produces tones. Because brass instruments require an exceptional amount of pressure to get a sound, there are no external holes: fingers can't be counted on to completely seal them. Instead, most players use a clever technology developed in the nineteenth century, when three valves (usually shaped like pistons) were added to the basic cylindrical tube. These valves serve as controls that shunt the air into a passageway of tubing of various lengths. By depressing different combinations of valves, the trumpet player alters the lengths, thereby producing most of the necessary tones. Changing the speed of air produces the rest. The musician is required to make two calculations before playing each note: the valve setting and the intensity of blowing.

The trumpet has an unmistakable timbre: a brittle, crisp attack with brilliant overtones. Its vibrating tube is entirely cylindrical until it reaches the end, where it flares into a bell. Other instruments feature a tube that increases as it goes along, known as a conical bore. The cornet is a partially conical instrument, flaring toward the end; it's usually found in marching bands and was transplanted to early jazz bands. Another trumpet-like instrument, the flugelhorn, is entirely conical.

The similarity between the trumpet and the cornet causes much confusion in discussions of early jazz. The two instruments look and sound alike, but the cornet has an extra layer of tubing and a deeper mouthpiece, producing a slightly mellower timbre. They are so similar that it is often impossible to distinguish which one is heard on recordings made in the 1920s. Adding to the confusion is the inclination of some commentators and musicians to refer to the trumpet as a cornet, and vice versa. Although the cornet dominated jazz at first, by 1926 it began to lose favor to the trumpet, with its brighter, more piercing sound.

To vary their timbre, many trumpet players carry with them a small arsenal of mutes, each with distinctive possibilities. The straight mute, inserted directly into the bell of the instrument, quiets the sound without too much distortion. The cup mute adds an extension that more or less covers the bell, further attenuating the sound while rounding it out. The Harmon mute is a hollow mute with a hole in the center; originally the hole was

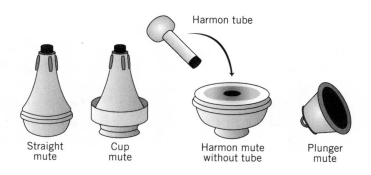

Harmon tube

Straight
mute

Cup
mute

Harmon mute
without tube

Plunger
mute

filled with an adjustable sliding tube, suitable for comic effects, but most jazz musicians simply discarded the tube, creating a highly concentrated sound. Finally, the plunger mute is as simple as the name suggests: it is simply the rubber end of a sink plunger. By moving the plunger in various positions away from the bell, the player can adjust the sound so expertly that it resembles human speech.

Often these mutes are used in combination. Bubber Miley, a soloist with the early Duke Ellington band, developed an unearthly sound by modifying his trumpet, already muted with a tiny, straight pixie mute, with a plunger—all the while growling in his throat. A trumpet player can also vary his timbre by half-valving: depressing one or more of the valves only halfway. The restricted flow of air produces an uncertain pitch, often with a nasal sound. Yet another technique is the shake, a quick trill between two notes that mimics a wide vibrato.

The trombone, with its occasionally comical slide, appears to be an exception to the brass norm; but in fact the use of a slide to adjust the column of air was something of a warm-up for the valve system. Like the trumpet, the trombone has been part of jazz since the beginning. Given how difficult it is to play pitches by pumping a single slide, the achievement of virtuoso jazz trombonists is remarkable. The slide enables the player to glide seamlessly from one note to another, an effect known as a glissando or smear.

With reed instruments, the whole procedure of setting air into vibration is reversed: instead of pressing lips against the mouthpiece, as with brass instruments, the mouthpiece is inserted between the lips. The mouthpiece is rigid—made of ebonite, hard rubber, or metal—with an open back to which a thin cane reed is attached by a metal clamp. The player blows a stream of air into the narrow passageway between the limber reed and the hard part of the mouthpiece, causing the reed to vibrate and producing a sound less biting and more subtle than the brass instruments'.

Virtually all jazz instruments use a single reed—double-reed instruments, such as the oboe and bassoon, are rarely heard except in large orchestrations. The reed is delicate, easily broken, and can be bought or custom-designed in gradations of thickness. The thicker it is, the harder it is to control. Musicians expressed amazement at Benny Goodman's clarinet reeds, which were so thick they were once described as "diving boards."

The particular sound on a reed instrument can be easily manipulated, resulting in a wide diversity of saxophone and clarinet sounds. A player usually presses the tongue lightly against the reed; the shape and quality of pitches is varied by pressing harder with lips or tongue or flicking the tongue against it to emphasize a note. Blowing intensely can result in complicated sounds, often containing more than one pitch, known as multiphonics.

The clarinet is a slim, cylindrical, ebony-colored wooden tube that produces a thin, occasionally shrill sound. A standard member of the New Orleans jazz ensemble, it achieved greater renown during the Swing Era of the 1930s, when two of the most popular bandleaders, Benny Goodman and Artie Shaw, offered an inadvertent clarinet rivalry that excited fans. The clarinet later declined in popularity, though some composers, most notably Duke Ellington, maintained its centrality to their music. Beginning in the early 1960s, thanks chiefly to Eric Dolphy, the bass clarinet (pitched lower than the regular clarinet) found acceptance by musicians and is still often heard.

The saxophone is the one wind instrument jazz can claim as its own. Adolphe Sax invented it in the 1840s in Paris as a family of instruments, deriving their individual names from parts in vocal choirs. The most common kinds of saxophone used in jazz are the alto, tenor, soprano, and baritone saxophone. Because Sax patterned his key system after the clarinet, musicians already familiar with that instrument could readily master the saxophone.

After the Indiana-based Conn Company began to manufacture saxophones in the United States in 1904, American dance bands and vaudeville performers embraced the instrument as much for its comic potential as musical versatility. The saxophone looked funny, with its gooseneck and curved bell, necessitated by the extended tubing. Some early masters of the instrument tongue-flicked the reed on every note, producing a droll, rigid virtuosity. As jazz musicians began to master it, they uncovered another quality—a çozy, seductive timbre that some moral guardians found dangerously sexy. A San Francisco newspaper editorial called it the "Siren of Satan" and demanded its banishment.

By 1930, thanks to such premier players as Sidney Bechet (soprano), Coleman Hawkins (tenor), Johnny Hodges and Benny Carter (alto), and Harry Carney (baritone), the saxophone had become the soul of American music: an all-purpose instrument able to play sweet or hot while suggesting tenderness or aggression. The tenor and alto are by far the most important solo saxophones. By contrast, the baritone is best known for anchoring big-band reed sections. The soprano virtually disappeared between 1930 and 1960, but became hugely fashionable in the 1970s, and has remained so: many established saxophonists "double" on it, and some have made it their primary instrument.

The members of the rhythm section have changed over time, as jazz has changed, but they usually number three or four, and their functions have remained stable: to provide harmony, bass, and percussion. Some instruments are naturally designed to play chords, including the vibraphone, organ, synthesizer, electric piano, guitar, and banjo. The most important, though, is the piano. The acoustic piano (to distinguish it from its electric counterpart) had already gone through a full century of technological changes before the first jazz musicians discovered it. Pianists may use the wide range of the keyboard (over seven octaves) to imitate the sound of a full orchestra or pound on the keys like a drum.

In some bands, two instruments combine to play harmony—for example, piano and vibraphone or, more frequently, piano and guitar. Today we think of the guitar as a solo instrument, but before 1940 its function in jazz was chiefly harmonic and rhythmic. Many bands had four-man rhythm sections—piano, guitar, bass, drums—in which the guitar existed solely to strum chords, one for each beat of a measure. The pianist can, of course, accompany himself, playing chords with the left hand and improvising with the right.

The bass is the rock on which the jazz ensemble is built. In a performance, we are naturally inclined to pay attention to the trumpet or saxophone soloist, while also registering the drums and pianist. The bass can get lost in the undercurrent unless we focus on it. Musicians are always focused on it. It has, roughly speaking, two crucial functions: playing notes that support the harmony, and providing a basic underlying rhythmic foundation. There are several instruments that can fill this role. The most common is the string bass (also known as double bass), the same instrument used in symphony orchestras. Classical musicians usually bow the bass, drawing a horsehair bow across the strings. Jazz musicians also use the bow, but they prefer the technique known as pizzicato: plucking the strings with their fingers. The plucked string has a percussive power that is much better suited to jazz's rhythmic nature.

In the past half century, the string bass has often been supplanted by the guitar-like electric bass. It lacks the powerful natural resonance of the string bass, but has the advantages of loudness and portability. The role of bass can also be filled by the tuba, a low-pitched brass instrument with an intricate nest of tubing ending in an enormous bell. The tuba, which came to jazz from the marching band, was used in some early jazz groups because of its powerful volume, which musicians felt was needed as ballast for the other instruments in the ensemble. In fact, though, the string bass can be played with enough volume; and these days, you almost never hear the bass without amplification—usually a pickup, or small microphone, on the bridge.

The drum kit, or traps (short for "contraption"), is a one-man percussion section within the rhythm section within the band. One seated individual operates it, using all four limbs to manipulate the various components with sticks (or brushes, mallets, or hands) and foot pedals. The traps developed in the 1890s out of marching bands, which were then commonplace throughout the United States. In any parade, the most conspicuous drum is the huge bass drum, strapped to the player's chest and jutting out two to three feet, struck with mallets. Another musician plays the much smaller snare drum, hanging around the neck and named after the metal snare attached to the lower drumhead, which adds a penetrating, rattling sound to each stroke of the drumstick. A third musician holds two large cymbals with handles, and crashes them noisily together.

Some smart musical inventor made the drum set possible by equipping the bass drum with a foot pedal attached to a mallet; this got the bass drum off the player's chest and freed up his hands. It was a logical step to add the snare drum, either on its own legs or attached to the rim of the bass drum, and a freely hanging cymbal, suspended from a stand or also attached to the bass drum. In effect, a new instrument and new kind of musician were born.

While every jazz drummer configures the drum set in his own manner, the basic arrangement is fairly stable. The drummer sits on a stool in the center of a semicircular assembly of drums and cymbals, with the bass drum front and center. The snare drum stands on an adjustable stand at knee-level. Spreading out from it are two or more middle-size drums without snares, called tom-toms, which are tuned according to taste and come in various sizes.

A forest of cymbals provides a steely contrast to the drums below them. Two of them are suspended. The medium-size ride cymbal has a clear, focused timbre and is played more or less continuously—the band "rides" on its lithe rhythmic pulse. The slightly smaller crash cymbal has a splashy, indeterminate pitch, not unlike a small gong, and is used for dramatic punctuations. The third essential cymbal is actually a device with two cymbals, recalling the pair held by the musician in the marching band, but to entirely different effect. It's called the high-hat and consists of two shoulder-level (remember, the drummer is seated) cymbals on an upright pole with a foot pedal at its base. The pedal brings the top cymbal crashing into the lower one with a distinct *chunk*.

In all, a jazz drummer is responsible for at least a half-dozen instruments. Typically, he will use his right foot on the bass drum pedal, his left on the high-hat pedal, his right hand wielding a stick on the ride cymbal, and his left holding a stick to play the snare drum or tom-tom. This description applies to the playing of any conventional drum set in rock, soul, and most other genres of popular music. What distinguishes jazz drumming is the sheer virtuosity—the flexibility and subtlety—that keeps other musicians and the listener involved, a task very different from merely keeping the beat. The drummer is free to respond to whatever the soloist plays and is expected to be attentive and quick-witted enough to fill in the empty spaces or to know when not to.

Drummers also contribute to the overall texture by altering timbre. Cymbals are often renovated to suit personal taste, sometimes with strips of tape on the underside to control the sizzle. The use of various sticks radically changes the sound of drumming. After wooden sticks, the most commonplace are wire brushes, used to strike or literally brush the drumheads with wire strands protruding from (usually) hollow handles. Early drummers realized that brushes, played hard or soft, produce a subtle, swishing sound ideal for gentle accompaniment. Mallets originally used to thump the giant bass drum are now preferred for conveying a soft, quiet rumble.

Some drummers don't play the traps at all. These are the masters of Latin percussion. Congas are tall drums of equal height but different diameters, with the smaller one assigned the lead role. The much smaller bongos have two drumheads, one larger than the other, compact enough to sit between the player's knees. The timbales consist of two drums mounted on a stand along with a cowbell and are played with sticks by a standing musician. Among other percussion instruments are shakers (the maraca is a gourd filled with beans) and scrapers (the guiro is a gourd with ridges). In recent decades, jazz bands often include—in addition to the regular drummer— a percussionist who works with dozens of instruments: shakers, scrapers, bells, blocks, and noisemakers of every description. Percussion, like music, is a world without end.

In any ensemble, some instruments are inherently louder than others—

a trumpet produces more volume than a flute. But each instrument has the ability to play loud and soft within its own range, another indispensable aid to expression. The terms used to indicate volume, or dynamics, come from the Italian. The most common (with their abbreviations) are *pianissimo* (*pp*) and *piano* (*p*) to indicate the softest dynamics; *mezzo piano* (*mp*) and *mezzo forte* (*mf*) to indicate medium dynamics; and *forte* (*f*) and *fortissimo* (*ff*) to indicate the loudest dynamics. The piano, originally called the pianoforte, was named for its ability to play both soft and loud, which earlier keyboard instruments like the harpsichord could not do.

RHYTHM AND METER

Rhythm in music is directly related to biology. The beating of our hearts and the intervals of our breathing are the foundations from which we developed dance and music. Heartbeats are relatively stable and articulate time with a steady thump-thump-thump of the pulse. This "pulse rhythm," moving at a given tempo, or speed, is the basic approach to jazz rhythm.

"Breath rhythm" is more elusive. Although we breathe continuously, we can speed it up or slow it down, or briefly suspend it altogether. In music, this can be called free rhythm, and it is often heard in an introduction, as in the opening of Louis Armstrong's "West End Blues." This cadenza (or unaccompanied passage of brilliant virtuosity) begins with a basic pulse, four even beats you could count as 1, 2, 3, 4. But as the phrase continues, nothing is that simple again. Although the passage is played with tremendous drive, we don't feel like tapping our feet. We are suspended in air until, finally, at 0:15, Armstrong returns to a steady, calm pulsation.

Sonny Rollins's "Autumn Nocturne," on the other hand, begins with an unaccompanied tenor saxophone solo that for nearly five minutes refuses to yield to any kind of regularity. The uneven, continually varying rhythms sound something like "speech rhythm." Through his saxophone, Rollins is talking to us. A still different technique occurs at the beginning of Art Tatum's "Over the Rainbow," where the familiar melody sometimes speeds up and sometimes slows down. This technique is known as rubato, from the Italian for "stolen": the performer "steals" from one part of the rhythmic flow to make another part longer, creating a rhythmic elasticity.

In most conventional jazz performances, a pulse rhythm is firmly in control. A good example is Miles Davis's "So What," as the theme kicks in (0:34). If you tune in to the pulse, or beat, and count along with the music, you will likely come up with a recurring pattern: either "1-2, 1-2" or "1-2-

3-4, 1-2-3-4." No one counts "1-2-3-4-5-6-7-8-9-10." That's because we *automatically* group pulses into patterns that constitute a meter. In jazz and most other kinds of music, the predominant meter is duple, which means that the beats are patterned in twos or fours. Every measure, or bar, has either two or, as in "So What," four beats. Counting with these patterns in mind, you can hear and feel the music through the meter.

Some pieces are in triple meter—groups of three, as in the 1-2-3, 1-2-3 rhythm of the waltz. In recent years, jazz musicians have adopted irregular meters: a pattern, for example, of 1-2-3, 1-2. We normally consider this a meter of five beats per measure, as in Dave Brubeck's performance of "Take Five." Many other metrical combinations are possible, adding together odd groups of twos and threes to make complex meters of seven, nine, eleven, and so forth. Meter is an open-ended resource for creativity, one more way for jazz musicians to make their performances rhythmically challenging.

Another rhythmic landmark is the downbeat—the place where we agree to begin our counting. Musicians typically make the downbeat clear through rhythmic accents, harmonic patterns, and the phrasing of their melodies. At the beginning of the trumpet solo on "So What," Miles Davis plays two preliminary notes (the first is long, the second very short), and then places the third precisely on the downbeat, reinforced by accents on the cymbal and the bass. Count along with him for a while, and you will soon register the downbeat—the **1-2-3-4 | 1-2-3-4**—as second nature. The distance between downbeats is a measure. In notation, musical time runs from left to right, and the bar lines parcel time out, measure by measure.

From Polyrhythm to Swing

The technical vocabulary presented to this point applies equally to standard European classical music. But jazz must also be understood as a music that derives, in a fundamental sense, from Africa. Within the repetitive cyclic structures of jazz, the music is organized by rhythmic layers: highly individualized parts that contrast with one another, even as they serve to create a unified whole. This simultaneous use of contrasting rhythms is known as polyrhythm, or rhythmic contrast. In a piece of African (and African American music), there are *always* at least two different rhythmic layers going on at the same time.

The most basic rhythms are the foundation layers—continuous, unchanging patterns whose very repetition provides a framework for the whole. In "So What," the bass plays a steady stream of evenly spaced notes. High above it, the drummer reinforces this pattern on the ride cymbal.

In this instance, the foundation layers are represented by the lowest- and highest-sounding instruments, the extremes of register. In Billie Holiday's "A Sailboat in the Moonlight," by contrast, a steady, dance-like pulse of two beats to the measure comes from the bass line, the pianist's left hand, and the cymbals. In both instances, rhythm instruments are providing the essential task of keeping time.

In African music (and also Latin jazz), the foundation layer is often a complex rhythm known as a time-line pattern. In the excerpt from the Ghana field recording, analyzed in the first listening guide (available on the Norton website), it's impossible *not* to hear the time-line pattern, played continuously by the bells. Another foundation layer is provided by a drum (A) playing a fixed pattern of two notes. Above the foundation, variable layers add contrasting parts; in African music, these are generally improvised. In the Ghanaian example, two other drums (B and C) supply these variable layers. When they play together (especially at the end of the excerpt), the music arises out of their complex interaction.

Another device you'll hear in the Ghanaian example is call and response, a pervasive principle in folk, pop, and art music. A statement by one musician (or group of musicians), the "call," is immediately answered by a counterstatement, the "response"—as in a conversation. Here, we can easily hear the call and response between a male singer and chorus, and, less easily, between drums A and B.

AKUAPIM PERFORMANCE*

Ghana Field Recording

DATE: 1983
STYLE: African music
FORM: cyclic

0:00	The recording fades into a performance already in progress. The meter is duple: four beats to the cycle. There are two unchanging foundation layers: a time-line pattern played on a pair of metal bells, and a drum (A) sounding a pair of notes. Another drum (B) plays a pattern in a tight call and response with drum A. Above this, we hear a call and response between a male singer and a chorus.
0:13	While drum A remains stable, drum B begins to change, altering its rhythm and timbre.
0:27	Drum B switches to a polyrhythmic pattern, superimposing a meter of three over the basic duple meter.

*To access: www.media.wwnorton.com/cms/music/akuapim.mp3.

0:38	A spoken phrase by the vocal leader signals the end to the call and response. He starts a new pattern.
0:50	A new drum (C) enters—a large wooden box with a resonating hole, hit on its sides with the hands and fists. In the background, someone claps the basic four beats. While drum B remains in its polyrhythmic pattern (in three), drum C plays complex phrases.
1:01	Drum B takes the lead by varying its part.
1:20	Drum B returns to the call and response with drum A heard at the beginning.
1:33	Drum C adds complex patterns.
1:48	As the excerpt fades out, drums B and C enter into a more intense conversation.

In jazz, good examples of call and response are easy to find. In the melody of "So What," the two notes played first by piano and later by the horns answer the string bass's call. In "West End Blues," Louis Armstrong creates new melodies by singing responses to Jimmy Strong's clarinet. Max Roach's drums react to Charlie Parker's opening melody in "Now's the Time." Indeed, you could say that call and response is built into the very fabric of jazz. Musicians are always listening intently, ready to respond to any rhythmic gesture at a moment's notice.

Variable rhythmic layers are constant within the rhythm section. The pianist's chords may fall on the beat (as they do in the first chorus of "West End Blues"), or in between beats. As the drummer keeps time on the ride cymbal with his right hand, his other limbs play accents on the rest of the drum kit that comment on or contradict that pulse. As in the African example, these layers dance above the foundation, sometimes sticking close to the beat, at other times diverging sharply from it. Every time a strong accent contradicts the basic meter, syncopation occurs. In most classical music, syncopation is an occasional rhythmic disruption, a temporary "special effect" injected for variety. In jazz, syncopation is not an effect—it is the very air jazz breathes.

Consider, for example, what happens when you snap your fingers to "So What." More likely than not, your snap does not align with the downbeat. If you count along, the beats you emphasize are not **1**-**2**-**3**-**4**, but 1-**2**-3-**4**. This crucial layer in the music, the backbeat, offers a simple way for listeners to contribute. Whether we actually snap on the backbeat or silently respond to it in the course of listening, we add our own contrasting layer and become part of the music.

If you combine the steady, four-beat rhythm in the bass and cymbal with a backbeat, you end up with a groove, the overall framework within which rhythmic things happen. There are many kinds of grooves. The one we've been describing is known generically as swing, and it's basic to jazz. Within the swing groove, jazz musicians use varied means to divide the main beat. In Miles Davis's solo on "So What," he plays four quick notes in succession (1:45): the notes are not the same length. Davis usually divides the beat by holding the first note of the beat slightly, compensating by compressing the second note. This practice is generally known as swing eighth notes—eighth notes being the division of a standard beat (or quarter note) into two parts.

It is through such subtleties that musicians speak of swinging. This is a term that is impossible to define precisely. But when all the rhythms interlock smoothly, something magical takes place and everyone in the vicinity (musicians, dancers, listeners) feels it. The band is swinging or is "in the groove" or "jumping" or "feeling it together." All those clichés mean basically the same thing. Swinging spreads sunlight on everyone it touches, beginning with the members of the band.

The score of a Beethoven symphony includes all the information a conductor needs to perform it with an orchestra. A score prepared for a jazz orchestra may include the same kind of notation, but musicians unfamiliar with jazz practices, no matter how proficient, might play every note correctly and still turn out a plodding, unrecognizable performance. Similarly, if an operatic soprano who had never sung jazz sang "A Sailboat in the Moonlight," she might sing every note correctly yet capture nothing of Billie Holiday's lithe grace. An inability to swing (and the impossibility of notating swing) has been the ruination of many gifted instrumentalists who have tried to play jazz and failed.

MELODY, SCALES, AND MODES

A sound's pitch is determined by measuring its frequency, or vibrations per second. For example, the note that today's orchestras tune up to—A—is measured at 440 vibrations per second. As the vibrations increase, the sound goes higher; as they decrease, it goes lower.

The pitch spectrum is theoretically limitless. Fortunately, we can think of it in a much more finite manner. If a group of men and women were asked to sing an A, more than likely the notes they sing would not be the same: the women may be able to produce the precise pitch of A=440, but the men's deeper voices would automatically choose a corresponding note with half (220) or even a quarter (110) as many vibrations. These are all A's: the distance, or interval, between them is an octave. The octave has a simple mathematical ratio of 2:1 (which translates into 440:220).

At some point in life, almost everyone in the Western world learns that the center key on a piano keyboard is called "middle C" (256 vibrations per second). From C, count seven white notes from left to right: C, D, E, F, G, A, and B. The next note, another C, is an octave higher, with exactly twice as many vibrations (512). Similarly, the black keys, with their groups of twos and threes, repeat a constant pattern over and over again. All we need for an understanding of the world of pitch is to grasp the patterns within the octave.

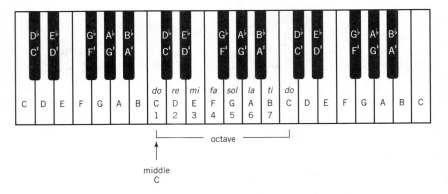

The basic unit of melody is the scale—the pitches within the octave. The twelve notes in an octave (counting white and black keys) make up the chromatic scale, with a half-step interval separating each note. But it is hardly the most common scale. The most basic scale in Western music is the major mode, the white key pitches from C to C: *do, re, mi, fa, sol, la, ti, do.* (For our purposes, "scale" and "mode" are synonyms.) Each note is a degree of the scale: *do* is the first degree, *re* the second degree, and so on.

A crucial aspect of this scale is that the first degree—C (*do*) in the C major scale—is more important than the others. Melodies may not necessarily begin on *do*, but they are very likely to end on it. If you sing the first phrase of "Happy Birthday" ("Hap-py birth-day to you"), you end up floating in mid-air. That's because the last note, "you," falls on a note just short of *do*. The next phrase releases the tension, bringing the melody to its inexorable goal of *do* (on the second "you"). We call *do* the tonic, and music that insists on returning to the tonic (most of the music we listen to) is known as tonal music. The tension and release is like the use of gravity in dance. It is possible to escape the pull of gravity, but not for long.

It doesn't matter what note you choose as the tonic, because scales represent patterns of pitches that can be moved (or transposed) up or down as you like. The pattern is made up of half and whole steps: C to D is a whole step because there's a black key in between. D to E is another whole step, and E to F is a half step. So the complete pattern for a major scale starting on C is W (whole step), W, H (half step), W, W, W, H.

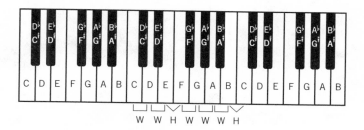

W = whole step
H = half step

The scale is named after its tonic: a C major scale begins on C, and the Eb major scale begins on Eb. (The Eb scale, following the same pattern, is Eb, F, G, Ab, Bb, C D, Eb.) Only C major stays on the white keys. For any other tonic, the patterns will inevitably involve the black keys, usually notated by sharps (♯) or flats (♭) at the beginning of a piece.

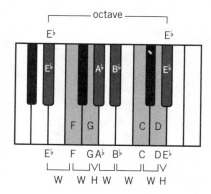

The converse of the major mode is the minor mode, with a different half-step / whole-step pattern. The most important difference is in the third degree of the scale. In minor, the interval between *do* and *mi* (known as a third) is a half step lower: instead of moving from C to E (on the white keys), you move from C to Eb. This difference may not seem like much, but it carries great emotional power. In general, minor sounds sad, moody, angry, or even tragic, while major sounds happy, peaceful, or triumphant. You need only listen to Beethoven's Fifth and Ninth Symphonies to hear the emotional upheaval that comes when the minor mode is thunderously replaced by the major mode at the end. The seven pitches that make up the major and minor modes (the eighth note is the octave) are diatonic scales—the basis of melody in Western music.

Jazz musicians also make much use of another scale, the pentatonic, a five-note scale that often evokes the simplicity of folk music and is, in fact, the platform for much of the world's music. You can get a sense of its sound by rolling your hand along the black keys of the piano keyboard. Since the 1950s, jazz musicians have favored other diatonic scales, some of them steeped in European traditions but abandoned long ago in favor of the major/minor dichotomy. These scales, or modes, have names derived from ancient Greek practice, such as Phrygian, Lydian, and Mixolydian. Miles Davis's "So What" is based on the Dorian mode, which you can hear by playing the white keys (not the major scale) on the piano running from D to D. The Dorian mode has a pattern that falls curiously between major and minor. Jazz thus blurs the major/minor dichotomy of classical music, creating its own shades of emotional nuance.

Other scales are relatively intricate. A scale made up entirely of whole steps may seem to have inherent logic, for example, but the sound it produces is relatively unsettling. Only well-trained musicians can sing the whole-tone scale with any accuracy, but in the hands of composers like Thelonious Monk (or Claude Debussy), it creates a musical effect easily recognized. Suffice it to say that scales are an infinite resource.

THE BLUES SCALE

This brings us to the scale most central to the development of jazz. The blues scale is not merely a collection of pitches, but an avenue into an African American cultural world. All American music—jazz, blues, gospel, pop, rhythm and blues, country and western, rock and roll, hip-hop—is influenced by its sound. We recognize the blues scale when we hear it. Defining it is more difficult.

The blues scale exists somewhere between major and minor. It's actually not so much a scale as a system for creating melody. It's impossible to pin down because it uses a different approach to intonation, which in Western usage means "playing in tune." In the Western world of fixed intonation, where pitches are set at precise frequencies, performing slightly higher or lower is seen as a mistake, indicating that a musician is out of tune. As with other cultures across the globe, African American music takes a more relaxed approach. Certain notes are played with a great deal of flexibility, sliding through infinitesimal fractions (microtones) of a half step for expressive purposes—a system we might call variable intonation. Closer to home, jazz musicians refer to blue notes, or bent notes. These notes cannot be signified in Western notation. On the piano keyboard, they are notes that would fall between the cracks.

Some of the greatest blues musicians play instruments—guitar, bass, trumpet, trombone, clarinet, saxophone—that are capable of producing subtle gradations between proper notes. The piano has no way to vary pitch like this, but it *can* approximate the sound of the blue note by playing two neighboring keys at the same time. Normally, playing both E♭ and E on the piano is a mistake. In jazz, this clash can spice up an improvisation; Thelonious Monk frequently used simulated blue notes to enliven his piano solos with expressive passion. In a sense, the blues is a mildly off-kilter way of looking at musical possibilities.

HARMONY AND TEXTURE

Making harmony—the simultaneous sounding of pitches—is not unlike mixing colors in painting. Combine red and yellow and you get a new shade, orange; combine three notes and you get a chord, a new sound, different from and richer than any of its component pitches. Unlike painting, however, where the original colors disappear into the new one, each individual tone in a chord is still distinct and audible.

The basic chord is a triad, combining three pitches, and takes its name from the bottom note, or root: a C major triad consists of C, E, and G; a D major triad consists of D, F♯, and A. Jazz musicians can do whatever they want with harmony. The three pitches in a C major chord may be arranged as freely as the musician desires, producing particular "voicings" of notes. Additional pitches can be placed in the upper reaches of the chord, producing the more elaborate harmonies known as extended chords.

Jazz musicians improvise over a harmonic progression, a series of chords placed in a strict rhythmic sequence. As the term "progression" suggests, the movement from chord to chord conveys a feeling of moving forward. This is a quintessential jazz process, and is perhaps best understood if you remember that chords, like individual notes, are classified by how they relate to basic diatonic scales. The chord built on the first degree (*do*) is given the Roman numeral I, and the chord built on the fifth degree (*sol*) is designated V. Just as the tonic (*do*) served as a center of gravity for melody, the I chord (or tonic triad) is the focal point of harmony. The I chord is stable: it doesn't want to move. A chord with this stability is considered consonant. Other chords are unstable, or dissonant. The V chord—G, B, D in C major—also known as the dominant, provides the classic example. When you add the fourth degree of the scale to it (producing a seventh chord, G7: G, B, D, F), it sounds as though the entire chord were begging to move, or resolve, to the tonic. This sense of forward movement—dissonant chords pulled as if by gravity toward consonant chords—provides the underlying rhythmic drive of a harmonic progression.

Jazz musicians work within whole networks of chords, usually notated as strings of letters and numbers: in "A Sailboat in the Moonlight," for example, the chords for the first few measures are G C B7 E7 A7 D7 G. The end of a phrase, where a chord progression comes to rest, is called a cadence. Take "Happy Birthday" again. The first line ("Hap-py birth-day to you") ends on an inconclusive note (*ti*), which would be harmonized with a V chord. Although it marks the end of the phrase, it sounds incomplete. The music couldn't end at this point, on what is known as a half cadence. Just as commas and semicolons indicate intermediate stopping points in a sentence, the half cadence serves as a temporary resting place. Not surprisingly, the next phrase ends with the melody resting on *do* and the harmony on the tonic triad. This is a full stop—a full cadence.

The effect of a half cadence and full cadence can be heard in the opening of "A Sailboat in the Moonlight." There are two long phrases, each beginning with the same melody on the tonic but veering off to different conclusions. The first ending is a half cadence ("just for two") and sounds incomplete. The second phrase ("A soft breeze") begins like the first, but moves inexorably toward a full cadence ("come true"), with the melody and the harmony converging on the tonic. The first phrase poses a question that is answered by the second.

Jazz musicians don't stick with the chords written in a book. The creative process often demands the use of harmonic substitutions: replacing chords with ones they prefer, inserting more chords to enliven a slow spot, making chords more complex, or even omitting them to simplify the progression. These things are usually done spontaneously, or they can be worked out in advance as part of an arrangement. One common way to increase the complexity of chords, besides extending them, is to base them on the chromatic scale—chromatic harmony is invariably more complex than diatonic harmony.

Of course, not all music operates according to these rules of tonality. Atonal music recognizes no key center, and often doesn't acknowledge the triad as the basic form of chord. But most jazz doesn't embrace a rigorous atonality. There is plenty of jazz that loosens the grip of tonality, creating free-floating chord progressions but not entirely banishing their pull toward tonal centers. Jazz musicians have a word for it (jazz musicians have a word for everything). When they play tonal harmonic progressions, they speak of playing "inside"; when they step outside of tonality, they play "outside." This language suggests, accurately enough, that a musician can easily move from one extreme to the other, even in the course of a solo.

The balance between harmony and melody produces texture, of which there are three basic types: homophony, in which a melody is supported by harmonic accompaniment; monophony, in which a melody exists on its own, without harmonic accompaniment; and polyphony, in which two or more melodies of equal interest are played at the same time. (Note: These terms do not apply to percussion.)

Most music in and out of jazz is homophonic. We are accustomed to hearing a strong main melody supported by a harmonic accompaniment. When Charlie Parker improvises on "Now's the Time," the pianist and bassist play the harmonies beneath him. While some of the things the pianist and bassist play are also melodic, we never feel they are competing for attention with Parker's saxophone. Homophony is usually performed with the melody and the harmony in separate rhythmic layers: a guitar accompanying a singer, for example. But in one important sub-category of homophonic music, the melody and harmony exist in a single layer: two or more instruments play the same phrase with the same rhythmic patterns, but with different pitches filling out the harmony, as in small vocal groups like barbershop quartets. In jazz, this is called block-chord texture. Big bands depend on block chords. When the entire trumpet section plays, one trumpet states the main melody, while the others play the same rhythm with harmonically complementary notes. Such passages are often called *soli*, since they sound like one improvised solo. The two-note harmonized figure played by three wind instruments in the theme of "So What" is an example of block-chord texture.

Another sub-category is countermelody, or obbligato, where the subordinate instruments have melodic interest of their own, but not enough to compete with the main melody. In the opening theme of "West End Blues," the trombonist and clarinetist play independent melodic lines, yet they merely supplement Louis Armstrong's trumpet lead. A more typical example occurs in "A Sailboat in the Moonlight," where Billie Holiday sings the main melody and tenor saxophonist Lester Young accompanies her, creating melodic ideas so rich they race shoulder to shoulder with her. Still, Young knows his place, emerging at full volume only in the rests (silences) between Holiday's vocal phrases.

When you sing in the shower, play a flute in the woods, or pick out a tune on the piano with one hand, you're creating monophony: a melody with no harmonic accompaniment. If 50,000 people sing "The Star-Spangled Banner" in a baseball stadium without a band, it's still monophonic texture. In jazz, monophony usually occurs in solo breaks or cadenzas, when the rest of the band briefly stops playing. Short breaks, usually two or four bars long, are a commonplace in early New Orleans jazz. An ongoing use of monophonic texture involves stop-time rhythm, created when the ensemble plays a short chord at brief intervals—say, three times a bar or once every bar or once every other bar—and the soloist improvises with just these interruptions from the band prodding him on. Unlike the break, which rarely lasts more than two or four bars, stop-time is open-ended, lasting as long as the musicians want.

And monophonic texture is often used to begin or end a piece. Armstrong begins "West End Blues" with what many regard as the single most significant monophonic outburst in jazz history—a radiant trumpet fanfare that keeps us on the edge of our seat until the rest of the band finally enters. In "Autumn Nocturne," Sonny Rollins extends his unaccompanied introduction long enough to make his audience roar with delight. In "Body and Soul," the monophonic texture comes toward the end, as Coleman Hawkins lets the band drop out, leaving him with an unaccompanied passage that allows a heated performance to cool down. In George Russell's "Concerto for Billy the Kid," pianist Bill Evans extends his solo into a stop-time episode, revving up the tension.

In polyphonic texture, two or more melody lines compete for our attention simultaneously. Polyphony is a special province of classical music, where J. S. Bach epitomizes the art of counterpoint (the intertwining of several equal voices). In jazz, polyphony is treated more casually. New Orleans jazz often features polyphonic passages in which three instruments—trumpet, trombone, and clarinet—improvise at the same time, with no one melody standing out. Polyphony faded from jazz once New Orleans style was replaced by big-band swing, with its homophonic textures. Then in the 1950s, many musicians tried to revive this technique, often by imitating models from classical music. And in avant-garde jazz, musicians go to great lengths to institute equality between all the members in a band.

LICKS, MOTIVES, AND RIFFS

All great jazz soloists have their own way of communicating a personal style through phrasing. Miles Davis favors short, terse phrases—a few notes surrounded by silence (or more precisely, by the rhythm section's response). Charlie Parker prefers long, sinuous, virtuoso phrases that boldly fly from one point to the next. Some melodic phrases, called licks, are simple and basic, part of the common lore of jazz. Budding jazz musicians learn licks by listening closely to experienced soloists. The fast lick in Parker's "Now's the Time" solo (0:46–0:47), for example, pops up in many of his other solos. A different lick turns up, with slight variations, in different passages of "Now's the Time" (0:56–0:58, 1:25–1:26, 1:38–1:39). Although it may be disconcerting to discover that even a player as brilliant as Parker repeats the same licks, this is how improvisation works. You might compare it to speech—another improvised act—where a relatively limited vocabulary creates an infinity of sounds and meaning.

At the beginning of John Coltrane's solo in "Acknowledgement" (1:04), he plays a simple three-note motive (a small musical idea) that jumps upward, then falls back a step, and then varies over the next several seconds. Another motive, a quick six-note fragment that first emerges at 1:16, is used by Coltrane throughout the solo that follows. Later, he introduces a four-note motive (eventually sung as "a love supreme"), taking it on an extended chromatic journey through all the keys (4:55–5:50).

Finally, a riff is a repeated fragment of melody. In the theme of "So What," the bass plays a phrase that is answered by a two-note piano riff—barely long enough to count as a musical thought. The horns then take up the riff, continuing the repetition. Another riff is found in the opening melody of "Now's the Time." In classical music, any melody that repeats insistently is known as an ostinato (Italian for "stubborn"), and these examples are sometimes called ostinato riffs. Tunes such as Count Basie's "One O'Clock Jump" are made of riffs—sometimes in the background, sometimes as the main melody. At their best, riffs are jazz gems: so simple anyone can play them, yet so fully capable of generating emotional and physical exultation.

CHAPTER 2

JAZZ FORM AND IMPROVISATION

TWO STRUCTURES

In jazz, unlike classical music, musical form is relatively straightforward, usually involving short and clearly defined structures and a single melodic framework, taken from either the blues or popular song. It may not be necessary to know the difference between one song form and another—many jazz lovers and even a few critics don't—but after you've come to terms with the basics of jazz form, something magical happens. You find yourself listening with greater insight, riding alongside the musicians and observing the choices they make as they make them.

◄ Percy Heath, best known for his four decades with the Modern Jazz Quartet, also appeared on recordings and in performances with Charlie Parker, Thelonious Monk, Miles Davis, and others.

Jazz concepts of form are derived from African music, where improvisation happens within a cycle. In Africa, the cycle is rhythmic. In jazz, the cycle is known as the chorus, and it involves two dimensions: rhythm and harmony. Each tune is a fixed rhythmic length (twelve or sixteen measures, for example) and has its own harmonic progression. Moreover, the two are interlinked. A harmonic progression can be any size, with chord changes occurring at specific times within the chorus. The ending of a piece is often imposed arbitrarily, after the musicians have played as many or as few choruses as they deem appropriate. If the great symphonic works of classical music may be viewed as cathedrals, with buttressed foundations building heavenward to a spire, great jazz works are more often like modern skyscrapers that rise as many floors as the builder determines yet are basically the same at top and bottom.

A distinguishing feature of jazz is the African principle of rhythmic contrast. There are two distinct layers in a jazz performance, one fixed and one variable. The chord progression (played by the rhythm section) is the foundation, played in an unchanging and potentially endless circle of repeated choruses. The variable part is represented by a soloist (instrumental or vocal) embellishing or improvising over the fixed progression. Both parts are necessary. Although jazz choruses may, in theory, range widely in length and design, in practice musicians tend to focus on codified formats derived from the blues and popular song. Sometimes, blues and pop song are one and the same (W. C. Handy's "St. Louis Blues," for instance); usually not.

Blues form has its origin in African American folk poetry, featuring a distinctive, asymmetric three-line stanza, as in Bessie Smith's "Reckless Blues":

When I wasn't nothing but a child,
When I wasn't nothing but a child,
All you men tried to drive me wild.

Each line takes up four measures—to be precise, two and a half measures for the singer, followed by one and a half measures by an accompanist (an example of call and response). Basic math baptized this form as the twelve-bar blues, with each twelve bars constituting a single chorus. In the early years of the twentieth century, a blues was most often sixteen or eight bars long, but by 1915 the twelve-bar version had won out as a perfect harmonic scheme derived from folk practice. Basically, it requires only three chords, beginning on the tonic, or I chord. The first big change comes at the beginning of the second line. Perhaps because this line is verbally identical to the first, its arrival is signaled by a shift to a IV chord, based on the scale's fourth degree. After two bars, it returns to the tonic. Finally, the third line is underscored with the V chord, the dominant, before also returning by line's end to the tonic.

When I wasn't   nothing but a   child,
| I | I | I | I |

When I wasn't   nothing but a   child,
| IV | IV | I | I |

All you men   tried to drive me   wild.
| V | V | I | I |

This is the blues in its most elemental form, and rarely is it performed so simply. Musicians use harmonic substitutions to add variety to the long stretches of unchanging harmony—for example, moving to IV in the second measure. In "Reckless Blues," the second measure adds a V chord (0:19–0:20), as does the sixth:

When I wasn't   nothing but a   child,
| I | I—V | I | I |

When I wasn't   nothing but a   child,
| IV | IV—V | I | I |

All you men   tried to drive me   wild.
| V | V | I | I |

In Louis Armstrong's "West End Blues." the substitutions are more complicated and more spontaneous. One spot is especially notable: in the last two bars of each chorus, the musicians play a particularly complicated progression of chords known as a turnaround—to lead back to the I chord and the next chorus. The turnaround, also called a turnback, is the transitional passage between choruses or between the distinct parts of a chorus. In a twelve-bar blues, measures 11 and 12 constitute the turnaround. Still, the piece follows the *same basic form*, although each chorus is configured differently in terms of instrumentation and interaction.

WEST END BLUES*

Chorus I

0:16	The full ensemble begins with a I chord.
0:24	The ensemble adds a seventh to the chord, making it want to move on to IV.
0:27	The harmony moves to IV.
0:33	The harmony resolves back to I.
0:39	The band plays a V chord.
0:44	The harmony arrives on I, followed by a turnaround.

Chorus 2 (trombone accompanied by woodblocks)

0:50	I chord
1:02	IV chord
1:07	I chord
1:13	V chord
1:19	I chord and turnaround

Chorus 3 (duet by clarinet and wordless vocal)

1:24	I chord
1:36	IV chord
1:41	I chord
1:47	V chord
1:53	I chord and turnaround

Chorus 4 (piano solo)

1:59	I chord
2:10	IV chord
2:16	I chord
2:21	V chord
2:27	I chord and turnaround

Chorus 5

2:32	I chord
2:44	IV chord
2:50	I chord

Coda (tag ending)

| 2:56 | V chord (piano, rubato) |
| 3:12 | I chord (full cadence) |

*Louis Armstrong and His Hot Five: Armstrong, trumpet, vocal; Fred Robinson, trombone; Jimmy Strong, clarinet; Earl Hines, piano; Mancy Cara, banjo; Zutty Singleton, drums. OKeh 8597 (1928); *Louis Armstrong: The Complete Hot Five & Hot Seven Recordings*, vol. 3 (Columbia/Legacy CK 87011). Recording data for the other pieces discussed in this chapter is given in each piece's respective Listening Guide, later in the book.

The harmonic progression is only one of several dimensions that jazz musicians can alter. They can play a blues chorus in any rhythmic groove—swing, funk, or Latin—and at any tempo. "It's All Right, Baby," a live performance by blues singer Big Joe Turner and pianist Pete Johnson, recorded at Carnegie Hall, is a good example of a fast blues, with each chorus compressed to only fifteen seconds. This performance is shorter than "West End Blues," yet it contains twice as many choruses. At this speed, most listeners will find that the harmonic progression takes a back seat to the rhythmic exhilaration.

IT'S ALL RIGHT, BABY

Chorus 1

0:00   The singer (Big Joe Turner) is accompanied by piano (Pete Johnson): *"Well, it's all right then!"*

Chorus 2

0:14   *"That's all right, baby."*

Chorus 3

0:29   *"Well, you're so beautiful . . ."*

Chorus 4

0:44   *"Baby, what's the matter now?"*

Chorus 5

0:59   *"Roll 'em, boy."*

Chorus 6

1:14   The pianist takes two solos.

Chorus 7

1:28

Chorus 8

1:43   The singer returns (*"Yes, yes!"*) in call and response with the piano.

Chorus 9

1:57   *"Well, all right, then!"*

Chorus 10

2:12   *"Bye . . . bye!"*

Coda

....

2:24   *"Bye bye, baby, bye bye!"*

Charlie Parker's "Now's the Time," recorded in 1953, twenty-five years after "West End Blues" and fifteen years after "It's All Right, Baby," exemplifies blues playing in a more modern context. You can't miss the changes that have taken place: that sizzling cymbal in the first measure tells a very different story from the clip-clopping hand cymbals of 1928. Yet for all its volatility, its radically transformed rhythm, and its increase in dissonance and harmonic complexity, this is still a twelve-bar blues, relying on the same underlying pattern that guided Armstrong and Turner. Each musician takes a solo that fits precisely within the twelve-bar structure: Parker, the group's leader, has the longest solo at five choruses, followed by the pianist (two choruses) and the bass and drums (one chorus each).

In addition to harmonic and rhythmic alterations, each of these recordings is distinguished by a different theme, or head: a composed section fitting securely in the twelve-bar format and usually played at or near the outset of a performance. The head announces the form as well as the melody, and returns at the end, framing the piece. It can be simple—a riff made up of only two notes—or so complicated that it all but disguises the underlying blues structure. In "Now's the Time," the head is built on a six-note riff that Parker frequently amends: compressing it (0:08), adding dissonant notes (0:19), or abandoning it to insert a short improvised phrase (0:22). The harmonic progression may seem more elusive here than in its predecessors, because the pianist plays the chords irregularly and the rapid-fire solos and forceful drumming distract attention from the blues format. But it's there unmistakably in the rhythmic structure: you can *feel* when one chorus is about to end and the next is about to begin.

NOW'S THE TIME

Chorus 1

....

0:05   Charlie Parker (alto saxophone) plays the head.

Chorus 2

....

0:20   Parker repeats the head with slight variations.

Chorus 3

....

0:35   Parker takes a five-chorus solo.

Chorus 4

0:49

Chorus 5

1:03

Chorus 6

1:18

Chorus 7

1:32

Chorus 8

1:46   The pianist, Al Haig, takes a two-chorus solo.

Chorus 9

2:00

Chorus 10

2:14   The bassist, Percy Heath, takes a one-chorus solo.

Chorus 11

2:28   The drummer, Max Roach, takes a one-chorus solo.

Chorus 12

2:42   Parker returns to the head.

The twelve-bar blues may be packed with extended chords and fanciful substitutions, and its structure interrupted by composed transitions and contrasting sections, yet the same basic form remains—and has remained mother's milk in jazz to this day. It has withstood countless musical fashions to become the bedrock for rhythm and blues (in the 1940s) and rock and roll (in the 1950s). There is no such thing as a jazz musician who can't make something of a twelve-bar blues.

The other key structural form for jazz improvisation is the thirty-two-bar AABA popular song. During the golden age of American popular songwriting, roughly from 1925 to 1960, tunes were written mostly by professional songwriters such as George Gershwin, Jerome Kern, Irving Berlin, Cole Porter, Richard Rodgers, Harold Arlen, Spencer Williams,

Johnny Mercer, Jimmy Van Heusen, and many others, including such jazz compatriots as Duke Ellington, Fats Waller, James P. Johnson, and Edgar Sampson. The tunes often originated in scores for movies and Broadway shows and were widely dispersed over the radio and on sheet music.

These songs were often conceived in two sections: an introductory verse, which helped bridge the gap between spoken dialogue and song in musical theater; and the thirty-two-bar section known as the refrain, or chorus—the melody that made the song successful if, as the songwriters hoped, members of the audience left the theater humming it. Verses can still be found in the sheet music, but, with rare exceptions (some songs—"Star Dust," "But Not for Me"—have famous verses that audiences expect to hear), were hardly ever performed outside the original theatrical context. Jazz musicians never played them: they preferred to concentrate on the refrain, turning it into a continuous repeating cycle, not unlike the African tradition.

The idea behind the form is pretty basic. Compose an eight-bar phrase. Repeat it. Contrast it with a new eight-bar phrase (known as the bridge or release or middle section), ending with a half cadence to drive the piece forward. Then repeat the original phrase one last time.

A   statement (8 bars)

A   repetition (8 bars)

B (bridge)   contrast (8 bars)

A   return (8 bars)

This structure does not refer to the words, which can be written in any number of poetic forms. It refers only to the melody and harmonic progression—the parts of the tune that most interest jazz musicians (including singers). The AABA pop song differs profoundly from blues. Unlike the blues, it does not retain a basic chord progression—composers can choose any harmonies they like. The words may change from the first A to the next, but musically, the A sections are alike, though the final cadences will sometimes differ, as in "A Sailboat in the Moonlight," where the first A ends on a half cadence and the second ends with a full cadence.

"Sailboat," a 1937 song by Carmen Lombardo and John Jacob Loeb, is by no means a first-rate example of popular songwriting: it's sentimental, rhythmically staid, and melodically predictable, and for these reasons has not endured as a standard. Yet Billie Holiday's 1937 recording is a true jazz classic, which tells us something essential about jazz. To paraphrase another 1930s song lyric: It ain't what you do, it's how you do it. Her version begins with a four-bar introduction before the AABA song kicks in. Note that she leaves long spaces, or rests, filled in by tenor saxophonist Lester Young (who quietly hovers behind her vocal line all along), and that she does not sing the different A sections exactly the same: she adds subtle rhythmic variations throughout, creating a powerful momentum. Nor does she ever sing the melody exactly as it was written. Real melodic and harmonic contrast comes at the bridge, which she swings in a way that the songwriters never intended.

Three musicians solo in the second chorus, with the pianist Jimmy Sherman playing the first two A sections, the trumpeter Buck Clayton the bridge, and Lester Young the final A. The brief playing time of 78-rpm recordings (usually running under three minutes) and the jukebox market for which these records were manufactured mandated short solos. Accordingly, the third chorus is abbreviated (BA), with Holiday entering on the bridge. Her rhythmic drive pulls all the other musicians along, leading to a grand climax.

A SAILBOAT IN THE MOONLIGHT

Chorus 1 (Billie Holiday, vocal)

A	0:08	*"A sailboat in the moonlight..."*
A	0:24	*"A soft breeze on a June night..."*
B	0:40	*"A chance to sail away..."*
A	0:57	*"The things, dear..."*

Chorus 2

A	1:12	Jimmy Sherman, piano
A	1:28	
B	1:44	Buck Clayton, trumpet
A	2:00	Lester Young, tenor saxophone

Chorus 3 (abbreviated)

| B | 2:16 | *"A chance to sail away..."* |
| A | 2:32 | *"The things, dear..."* |

From 1926 on, jazz musicians constantly interpreted popular songs that, good or bad, provided material to embellish. Some songs proved inspiring, others provoked parody. In most instances, however, a general familiarity with the melody offered listeners a convenient gateway into the performance. The cyclical nature of the pop song chorus created an additional security, even though the average radio fan did not know how many measures were involved or what a bridge was. The ubiquity of the AABA form, in thousands of songs, year after year, with its reliable repetitions and comforting cadences, created a musical lingua franca that was easily appreciated by everyone.

Jazz musicians frequently adapt a popular song without using its melody. The most commonly played popular song in jazz is "I Got Rhythm," written in 1930 by George Gershwin and his lyric-writing brother Ira for the Broadway show *Girl Crazy*. Musicians loved the harmonic progression more than they did the tune. Also, the tune and lyrics were covered by copyright, not the harmonies, on which a new melody could be configured. By focusing exclusively on the chords, they created the second most frequently explored chord progression after the blues, fittingly known as rhythm changes—*changes* being slang for harmonic progression. They also altered the form slightly. As composed by the Gershwins, "I Got Rhythm" includes a final two-bar tag, making the song thirty-four measures. These two bars were rejected by jazz musicians, who preferred the symmetry of the thirty-two-bar form. Having stripped the song to its essentials, musicians fashioned thousands of melodies while modifying the chord progressions to their taste and that of the times. A great many of these spin-offs, such as Duke Ellington's "Conga Brava," Dizzy Gillespie's "A Night in Tunisia," and Thelonious Monk's "Rhythm-a-ning," became jazz standards in their own right. The changes of dozens of other songs, like Fats Waller's "Honeysuckle Rose" or Jerome Kern's "All the Things You Are," have similarly been adapted for completely different rhythmic and melodic approaches.

Musicians have found numberless ways to use the AABA song form as a fount for original compositions. Miles Davis's "So What" is among the best known. As we've seen, the head is made up of a bass line answered, in call-and-response fashion, by a two-note riff. In each eight-bar section, this mini-dialogue is played four times. In the first A section, the bass is answered by the piano; in the next A section (and for the rest of the chorus), the bass is answered by the three horns. At the bridge, there is a subtle but significant difference: the riff moves up a half step to a new key, an easily appreciated modulation—as is the return to the original key in the final A section. Once you hear the half-step change, the shape of the AABA chorus is easy to follow, allowing you to focus on the more significant action: how the players deal with it.

Davis on trumpet and John Coltrane on tenor saxophone negotiate the form according to their distinct styles: Davis with simple, taut phrases, Coltrane with lengthy gusts of notes. They and the listener are warned of the approaching bridge when the pianist, Bill Evans, signifies it with the appropriate chord. At the close of Davis's second bridge (2:56), he signals the changeup himself with a sudden, forceful note. Listening to a performance the way the musicians listened when they created it brings out details, subtle or obvious, that are at the heart of jazz improvisation.

Songwriters, no less than jazz musicians, have also explored various ways of configuring the popular song. Just as the twelve-bar blues won out over the eight- and sixteen-bar variants, the thirty-two-bar AABA song became the standard format after years of experimentation that produced songs of sixteen, twenty-eight, thirty-six, and forty-four bars, among others. Long after AABA became dominant, songwriters continued to create variations. Cole Porter broke the song-form bank with his 1935 standard "Begin the Beguine," which has 104 bars parsed in a structure of AABACCD, all but one section sixteen bars long. The song was considered so complicated that many music business professionals were surprised when it became a huge hit, and were astonished when it became a jazz blockbuster in Artie Shaw's 1938 recording. What they failed to realize was that the public doesn't worry about sheet-music complexity—it looks for repetition to breed familiarity, and "Begin the Beguine" has plenty of that, including an AABA beginning.

Thirty-two-bar forms other than AABA have sustained consistent popularity, particularly the elegant variation ABAC, or AA'. Instead of the bridge providing contrast at the midway point, ABAC uses that moment to reprise the opening melody.

A (8 bars)   statement
B (8 bars)   contrast
A (8 bars)   return of statement
C (8 bars)   conclusion

This form can also be seen as two sixteen-bar sections, the first ending with a half cadence, and the second steering the harmony firmly home with a full cadence:

A (16 bars)   statement
A' (16 bars)   statement with full cadence

Tunes constructed with this form include "Star Dust" and "Embraceable You," as well as original jazz compositions from the early days in New Orleans until now. No less than AABA, the ABAC form serves as a template, suitable for different harmonic progressions. Another template based on AABA, combining pop song form and the blues, is called blues with a bridge. Here the format substitutes a twelve-bar blues for the three A sections; the bridge is usually eight bars and is often based on the bridge in rhythm changes. Lester Young's "D. B. Blues" is a well-known example; another is the Beatles' "Can't Buy Me Love." This form was especially popular during the rhythm and blues and early rock and roll eras, and continues to crop up in jazz.

IMPROVISATION

How can ensemble music made up on the spot make sense? How do musicians manage to keep together? In short, what is improvisation and how does it work? As usual with jazz riddles, the place to begin is in the rhythm section, where each instrument fills multiple roles while working to create a supple and unified underpinning.

Traditionally, the bass has the most restricted role. It provides a rhythmic foundation layer, keeping steady time in a swing groove with a continuous and even string of notes. Because this sound is the neutral backdrop for every other rhythmic gesture, the bassist has little choice but to stick to the basic pattern. But at the same time, the bass plays a crucial harmonic role. Whenever a new chord appears on the chart (the musical score that serves as the basis for jazz performance), the bassist is responsible for playing that chord's root. This creates a daunting challenge: he or she must produce a steady and consistent beat while fitting into a harmonic puzzle. Today's bassists function with ease, unlike those before World War II, who did little more than contribute a "walking bass," marking four even beats to the bar. The walking bass remains an essential ingredient in jazz, but now it invites its own manner of virtuosity.

During Miles Davis's solo on "So What," Paul Chambers's bass line lies underneath, never calling attention to itself and never failing to fulfill its basic rhythmic and harmonic duties. Yet the line has a graceful melodic shape, a product of Chambers's creative imagination. A good bass line is a subtle form of improvisation, constantly supporting and sometimes inspiring the soloist. Davis's spare style gives Chambers a lot of leeway. Other musicians may play so many notes that they present the bassist with a problem of finding notes that don't clutter the performance. An experienced bassist can make the right choices at a split second's notice.

Sometimes the bass line does not move, creating a pedal point. The term derives from pipe organs, where the lowest pipes are sounded on a pedal keyboard played with the feet. During an improvisation, an organist can hold down a pedal for an extended period of time, allowing the chords to drift on top of this foundation. In jazz, pedal points occur whenever the bass refuses to move. A good example occurs during Ronald Shannon Jackson's "Now's the Time" (1:47–1:55), when the bassist freezes the harmony for a full eight bars.

The patterns bassists use in playing Latin or funk rhythms may be more syncopated and complex, while still serving as a rhythmic foundation. At the very beginning of Dizzy Gillespie's "Manteca," the bassist repeats a two-measure riff while the horns add sharply contrasting layers of polyrhythm. In John Coltrane's "Acknowledgement" (starting at 0:32), the bass is the only stable element in the ensemble. Few people notice the bass or give it credit, but it is the rock on which most of jazz stands.

The primary harmony instrument in the rhythm section—usually a piano, but sometimes guitar, organ, vibraphone, or electric keyboards—has a different role. Every chart specifies the chords that must be played, with musical shorthand: Cmaj7, for example, means a C major triad with a major seventh (B) added. But exactly how the chords are to be played is left open. At any given moment, the pianist can play the chord in any voicing (arrangement of notes) or add extra notes. He or she can also use harmonic substitutions—harmonies that replace the existing chord progression. Compare the first and fourth choruses of Armstrong's "West End Blues." In the first, pianist Earl Hines sticks to the script, playing basic chords on the beat. By the fourth, where he is the featured soloist, he replaces these chords with a dense harmonic thicket, carving his own path through the blues form with his broad knowledge of harmony.

The pianist also contributes to the rhythmic foundation, but, unlike the bassist, provides a variable layer, constantly adding to the rhythms to enliven the groove. The pianist listens closely to the rhythmic gestures of the drummer while "feeding" chords to the soloist. This irregular, unpredictable manner of playing chords is known as comping, jazz slang for "accompanying." Done well, comping will inspire a soloist; done unsympathetically, it will drive him out of his mind.

In a typical swing groove, the drummer will play a more or less constant "ride" pattern with his right hand, while accenting the backbeat on the high-hat cymbal with his left foot. The right foot, controlling the bass drum pedal, plays thunderous accents (during and just after the Second World War, this was referred to as "dropping bombs"), while the left hand swoops over the rest of the drum kit, adding sharp responses on the snare drum, tom-tom, or crash cymbal. This is the default rhythm. When the drummer wants to add an improvised passage, or fill, he can use both feet and hands to create more complicated patterns. A good drummer can play many kinds of rhythm, shifting from swing to funk to Latin to a soft ballad to free jazz.

Listening to the rhythm section ought to be a delight in itself. You can take it in as a team, or focus on each member's ability to negotiate his or her role in a constantly changing context, or attend to the various interactions (piano and bass or bass and drums). Still, the limelight in a jazz performance shines most on the soloist, at which point the success of a rhythm section is best measured by its ability to spur and back the saxophonist or trumpet player, filling in the blanks, responding to and offering cues, and never getting in the way.

And what is the soloist doing? The simplest method of improvisation takes a preexisting melody—a song known by millions or an original composition by a member of the band—and varies it. This method, melodic paraphrase, typically adds notes and distorts the rhythm into something that swings, but does not disguise the source material. Jazz musicians often use melodic paraphrase at the beginning and end of a performance. Many jazz classics consist entirely of paraphrase. Art Tatum's 1939 radio broadcast version of "Over the Rainbow" is exemplary in that regard. Throughout the performance, Tatum makes sure you can hear the melody. In the first chorus, he states the AABA tune directly, while cloaking it in intricate harmonies and brilliant runs. During chorus 2, the tune recedes into the background but you can hear it at crucial points, such as the opening of the second A section (1:36) and the start of the bridge (1:55). Tatum is one of those rare jazz musicians who use the original melody to make his improvisation coherent at all times.

In the 1930s and 1940s, people knew the melodies (and words) to countless pop songs by heart, just as we do our favorite hits of today. Relatively few of us are conversant with many songs from what we now call the Classic American Songbook, so in discovering jazz we find ourselves discovering those songs as well as the interpretations by great jazz stylists. It's worth noting, in this context, that Tatum's "Over the Rainbow" reversed that situation. The song, a standard that most of us do know, was generally unfamiliar to the audience that tuned in to his 1939 broadcast. *The Wizard of Oz* had opened only days before.

Of course, most jazz improvisers quickly discard the original melody, which is probably the key reason many people find jazz incomprehensible. Musicians prefer to rely on the changes, the chord progression—a technique known as harmonic improvisation. As we have seen, each chord is made up of only a handful of notes. An E♭ triad features the chord tones E♭, G, and B♭; it excludes all the other notes, such as E, A, or B, which sound horribly dissonant when played next to an E♭ chord. In their earliest training, jazz musicians analyze the chords in a tune and learn to play the consonant chord tones in their improvisation, avoiding notes that sound "wrong." Every decision must be made quickly as one chord changes to another, because melody notes that are consonant with one chord can become painfully dissonant in the next. When chords move fast, as they do in John Coltrane's notorious harmonic labyrinth "Giant Steps," playing them correctly becomes a superhuman task. Even Tommy Flanagan, one of jazz's most accomplished pianists, made mistakes on the original Coltrane recording—a sore point for him that he addressed years later in a radiant trio elaboration of the piece. Running changes can be like running hurdles, with a new barrier to leap every few steps.

Another technique, modal improvisation, solves the hurdle dilemma by replacing a forest of chords with a stable scale or mode. In "So What," the improvisers are expected to create their melodies from the Dorian scale, shifting up a half step on the bridge. Musicians who want to sound bluesy interpolate the blues scale, superimposing it over a passage as if it had no chords. In Charlie Parker's third chorus in "Now's the Time," we hear a highly skilled harmonic improviser ignore the chords and play bluesy licks that contradict the underlying harmony—even though the tune itself is a blues. A similar sensibility can be heard in the last chorus of "West End Blues," where Louis Armstrong follows Earl Hines's dense piano solo with a single note held for a breathtaking four bars, and followed by descending blues phrases. Modal improvisation shows that for jazz musicians, simplicity is just as important as complexity.

IN PERFORMANCE

Jazz can be played by bands of any size or by solo musicians, but—as in classical music, with its symphonic orchestras and chamber groups—there are two dominant ensembles: big bands and small combos. In the 1930s, dance orchestras usually employed about sixteen musicians. These orchestras began to fade after World War II, but big bands have never completely disappeared; they switched their focus, however, from ballroom dancing to concert music. A few "ghost bands" carry on the memory of long-deceased bandleaders from the Swing Era. But most of the contemporary big bands, such as New York's Vanguard Jazz Orchestra (which plays on Monday nights at the Village Vanguard), or the orchestras occasionally organized by musicians like Dave Holland and David Murray, perform a new and modern repertory. The vast majority of big bands, however, are found at universities, where they serve as part of the jazz curriculum. As these bands are educational enterprises and not restricted by payroll, they often climb in size to twenty-five musicians.

The musicians in big bands are grouped by instrument, as they are in symphony orchestras. The sections are often designated as brass (trumpets and trombones), reeds (usually alto, tenor, and baritone saxophones, with an occasional clarinet), and rhythm (piano, bass, drums, and occasionally guitar, electric or acoustic). Although a few bandleaders, like Gil Evans and Butch Morris, developed methods of spontaneous conducting (Morris coined the word "conductioning") that create music spontaneously, 99.9 percent of all big bands use written arrangements, or charts, and music stands. These arrangements often employ block-chord texture, and play one section against another in call-and-response fashion. Improvisation happens only at designated moments, when limited blocks of time (from four measures to several choruses) are set aside for soloists. In this way, the big band balances composition and improvisation.

Jazz is usually played by small groups: a few horns plus rhythm section. The reasons are obvious: small groups are less expensive to maintain, they are a lot more mobile, they fit easily on the cramped bandstands that are fixtures in jazz clubs, and they are more accommodating to the modern jazz template of extended, free-wheeling improvisations. The luxurious sound of big bands, with their vocalists and spiffy uniforms, suited the tastes of Depression audiences; contemporary audiences prefer their jazz to be lean and mean. Ornette Coleman coined a phrase to describe the changeover when he titled an album *Dancing in Your Head*.

Small combos reflect the informal tradition of the jam session, an after-hours phenomenon at which musicians gathered to play for their own enjoyment. The earliest jam sessions typically took place in out-of-the-way venues, far from the public eye. The music was meant as a form of recreation, but it also served an important function within the jazz community. Through open-ended improvisation, musicians could be heard, tested, and judged. By the 1940s, the jam session went public, becoming another way

to hear jazz. Its atmosphere was different from that of a big band—no uniforms, casual bandstand behavior, a milieu of open rehearsal.

The musical format is purposefully kept casual. The head is the only
composed part of the performance. The rest of the tune is improvised—as
many choruses as the soloists want. A typical order of solos begins with the
horn players, then proceeds through the rhythm section: piano (and/or guitar), bass, and drums. Under the bass solos, the accompaniment lightens:
the drummer plays quietly and the piano plinks out a few chords. Drum
solos are a different matter. They can be completely open-ended, in which
case the band waits for a verbal or musical cue to come in. Many drummers prefer to play solos that fit within the cycle, counting bars—as do the
rest of the musicians, who have to remain alert to recognize the point of
reentry. Drum solos can disrupt a mood, however, and some combo leaders
limit them to the exchange of short solos between drummer and soloists,
usually four bars each and called trading fours, though the exchanges may
be eight bars or two or an entire chorus. The trades, which can also be
between soloists, usually occur toward the end of the performance, after
the extended solos have already been played.

Even small groups that are carefully regimented in terms of repertory
and procedure leave more to chance than do big bands. One of the things
left to chance is the audience's reaction. The dance bands measure their
success by the action on the dance floor. A jazz club is essentially a concert
hall that permits drinking and (sometimes) eating. Serious fans act as they
would at a concert, but others assume that any music played in a room that
serves alcohol is there as aural wallpaper. The high cost of admittance, and
the inevitable shushing, tends to keep them at bay, but that same cost also
keeps out many others—including budding young jazz enthusiasts. Those
who do come may be puzzled by the nearly universal ritual of applauding
every solo. Applause is like tipping. You do so as a matter of politesse after
a number, but you ought to cheer a particular solo only when it knocks
your socks off. When that happens, you are firmly situated in the sunshine
of jazz, and ready to peruse its long and tangled history.

3

CHAPTER

The Roots of Jazz

JAZZ AND ETHNICITY

Jazz developed as a convergence of multiple cultures. The primary factor was the importation of African slaves to a world dominated by warring European colonists—particularly the French, Spanish, and English. In striving to keep African musical traditions alive, the slaves eventually found ways to blend them with the abiding traditions of Europe, producing hybrid styles in North and South America unlike anything in the Old World. Miraculously, jazz and other forms of African American music (including spirituals, blues, and

◀ African-Caribbean rhythms, imported into New Orleans as a result of the slave trade, played a powerful role in the birth of jazz. One of its later masters, the Cuban-born conguero Chano Pozo (seen here in 1949), gained prominence during the bebop era.

ragtime) not only overcame subjugation, but assumed dominant roles in American music.

So what kind of music is jazz? In 1987, the U.S. Congress passed a resolution declaring it a "valuable national American treasure," but the full text sums up the confusion sown by the music's contradictory qualities. Jazz is an "art form," brought to the American people through well-funded university courses and arts programs; but it is also a "people's music" that bubbled upward from the aspirations of ordinary folk. It is "an indigenous American music," but also international, having been "adopted by musicians around the world." Although jazz is a "unifying force" that erases ethnic gulfs, it is nevertheless a music that comes to us "through the African American experience."

Three different categories situate jazz within our society. The first is jazz as an art form—as "America's classical music," which can now be found in or near the heart of the cultural establishment, from concert halls and television documentaries to public grants and university curricula. Jazz has not always been accepted as art, but it has always been created by skillfully trained musicians, even if their training took place outside the academy. Certainly, their unique achievement demands and rewards the respect and care routinely brought to classical music.

At the same time, jazz is a popular music. This may seem a more exaggerated claim in a day when jazz recordings comprise 3 percent of the market. But jazz—before, during, and after the Swing Era of the 1930s, when vast audiences heard Duke Ellington, Benny Goodman, Count Basie, and other bandleaders on records, radio, jukeboxes, and movie screens—is a commodity, something bought and sold. So, for that matter, is classical music, never more so than in years of desperation, when its artists are obliged to perform pop tunes and collaborate with pop stars. Jazz musicians continue to sell their services in the commercial marketplace, its artists constantly negotiating with public tastes, however far removed from those tastes their instincts take them.

Finally, jazz is also folk music. Not in the usual sense of music performed in rural isolation: jazz is distinctly urban, at home on the street corner and comfortable on the cutting edge of technology. Yet on a basic level, the qualities that mark jazz as different from other musical genres stem directly from its folk origins, which, more often than not, are African American. We can therefore make the straightforward yet provocative assertion: Jazz is an African American music.

This is the kind of statement that seems designed to make some people apoplectic. Doesn't jazz belong to everybody? Calling it African American (or black or Negro) suggests that only people who have been identified as such in this increasingly mixed-breed society can produce or discern jazz in any meaningful way. Whites ought not to mess with it, except as acolytes and customers. In fact, jazz musicians—including the very best of them—may be black, white, or any shade in between, just as they may be of any age, either gender, and from any part of the world. As Miles Davis once observed, if a jazz musician can play, he didn't "give a damn if he was green and had red breath." John Steinbeck found Davis's attitude to be one of jazz's signal virtues. "Great reward can be used to cover the loss of honesty [among other artists]. But not with jazz players," he said: "Let a filthy kid, unknown, unheard of and unbacked, sit in—and if he can do it—he is recognized and accepted instantly. Do you know of any other field where this is true?"

We usually construe "African American" as an indication of race, a genetic fact to be dutifully reported on census forms. But African American also tells us about ethnicity, which helps to explain how culture makes us who we are. The difference is crucial. Race can't be changed. But because it is learned behavior, ethnicity can. We acquire it in our youth so unconsciously that our cultural habits become second nature. To learn another's culture can be more difficult, but talented and determined people can do it through diligent effort. In the past hundred years, since the advent of recording technology, the primary way diverse peoples have shared their culture is through music. Through jazz, the whole country, the whole world, becomes more African American.

Much of the musical grammar of jazz can be traced ultimately to Africa, including the idea of polyrhythm created within a short rhythmic cycle, and spontaneous interaction as defined by call and response. Jazz melodies use blue notes to alter pitch, and its instrumentalists and vocalists use timbre variation as an expressive device. Jazz often melts away the boundaries separating music from dance and musician from audience. None of these elements by itself is uniquely African. Call and response can be found everywhere, while polyrhythm crops up in such diverse places as Indonesia and India. But the particular combination of sounds that characterize jazz is uniquely African American. Its folk elements are not a fixed list of items that might be lost over the centuries, but flexible principles that can absorb and transform whatever music its performers encounter. Jazz can never completely abandon its folk origins.

FOLK TRADITIONS

Black folk culture accomplished two things. First, it established an African American musical identity that, having survived centuries of slavery, the tumultuous decades after the Civil War, and the transition from rural to urban centers in the early twentieth century, became a means of ethnic fortitude. Jazz musicians drew on the folk tradition to ensure that the music they played was somehow congruent with what it meant to be black. At the same time, the popularity of black music transformed what had previously been white culture. Through music and dance, notions of "blackness" and "whiteness" became thoroughly mixed together, producing what Albert Murray has described as the "mulatto" nature of American customs.

The folk tradition developed in several genres. One was the retelling of local history through lengthy ballads. The blasting of a railroad tunnel on the Virginia-West Virginia border, for example, inspired "John Henry," in which the hard-muscled, steel-driving hero fights a losing battle against modern machinery. Other ballads, like "Staggerlee" and "Railroad Bill," celebrated the exploits of bad men—heroes of resistance who shrugged off society's constraints through their disrespectful and usually violent behavior. The taste for braggadocio and exaggeration, with its emphasis on sexual exploits and one-upmanship, remains prominent in the precincts of hip-hop. Another kind of secular music was the work song, which thrived on railroads, levees, and anywhere else music was needed to pace manual labor. And in the lonely corner of the field where the former slave continued to work, one could hear an unaccompanied field holler, a rhythmically loose vocal line that expressed his or her lonesome individuality.

A different folk tradition emerged in the spiritual, which transformed call-and-response songs into religious poetry. This music was passed on in two ways. The Fisk Jubilee Singers, a vocal group from a new and impoverished black college, performed a polished, carefully arranged version of spirituals before the general public in 1871. But this music was also passed on orally from parents to children and transmuted through performance in "sanctified" Pentecostal churches that were often nothing more than converted storefronts. By the 1920s, it had turned into gospel music, a rich and vibrant tradition that has never ceased to influence American music. When early jazz musicians say they learned music in the church, we may assume they acquired many of the basic skills of musical interaction from this oral tradition.

"THE BUZZARD LOPE" ("THROW ME ANYWHERE, LORD")

A fount of African-influenced folk culture exists on the sea islands of Georgia. Here, slaves brought directly from rice-growing West Africa worked the rice and cotton plantations; during the summer, when white residents fled inland to avoid malaria, there were only a few white overseers in charge. After Emancipation, the slaves, known as Gullahs, were left to eke out a living on their own. The result was a culture rich in African traditions, isolated from the mainland by swamps and salt marshes.

In the 1920s, bridges were built to the mainland, flooding Gullah culture with white capitalism. Lydia Parrish, a Philadelphia-bred Quaker who lived on St. Simons Island, studied the island's music closely and took it upon herself to save it from extinction. She published her findings in 1942, in *Slave Songs of the Georgia Sea Islands*. Earlier, she had used her resources to start a group eventually established as the Georgia Sea Island Singers. Zora Neale Hurston brought the folklorist Alan Lomax to hear the singers in 1935. Twenty-five years later, he returned to the island with recording equipment, determined to preserve their music.

"The Buzzard Lope" is a spiritual dance with African origins. At death, slaves were often thrown into a field, where their bodies were devoured by buzzards. In the dance, singers gathered in a circle, leaving a piece of cloth in the center to represent the body. As they danced, individual singers would enter the ring, imitating a circling buzzard and snatching the carrion. The text is defiant: the superior power of "King Jesus" will protect the slaves, even under the most horrific conditions. The song is done in call-and-response style, with the venerable folk singer Bessie Jones taking the lead, answered by a chorus of seven men. Each separate call and response makes one cycle, with the refrain (the same words) recurring in several of them. The singers clap two rhythms: a backbeat and a polyrhythmic background (counted 3 + 3 + 2), underneath the chorus:

But when Jones enters with her call slightly ahead of the beat, the clappers extend the polyrhythm (3 + 3 + 3 + 3 + 3):

Through intense repetition and syncopation, the music moves irresistibly forward until the singers abruptly cut it off.

THE BUZZARD LOPE (THROW ME ANYWHERE, LORD)

Georgia Sea Island Singers

Bessie Jones, song leader; Joe Armstrong, Jerome Davis, John Davis, Peter Davis, Henry Morrison, Willis Proctor, Ben Ramsay, chorus

LABEL: *Georgia Sea Island Songs* (New World Records, NW278); *Southern Journey,* vol. 13: *Earliest Times—Georgia Sea Island Songs for Everyday Living* (Rounder 1713)
DATE: 1960
STYLE: African American folk
FORM: cyclic

Cycle 1 (refrain)

0:00	Jones begins her first phrase with a rising melody, accompanied by a quiet foot stomp: *"Throw me anywhere, Lord."*
0:03	A chorus sings the response: a simple three-note melody, loosely harmonized: *"In that old field."* The hand clapping begins in earnest.
0:05	Jones repeats her call, this time with a falling phrase.
0:08	The response descends to a full cadence.

Cycle 2

0:10	Jones sings the same melody to new text: *"Don't care where you throw me/Since my Jesus own me."*
0:12	The chorus sings the response, *"In that old field"* (which remains constant throughout the song).

Cycle 3 (refrain)

0:19	Jones returns to the refrain, this time varying the melody with a plaintive blue note. The hand claps follow the syncopated rhythm of her melody.

Cycle 4

0:29	Jones sings a new couplet: *"You may beat and burn me/Since my Jesus save me."*

Cycle 5 (refrain)

0:38	Behind her, you can hear a bass humming a dissonant note.

Cycle 6

0:47	As Jones adds new text, the rhythm becomes more driving: *"Don't care how you treat me/Since King Jesus meet me."*

Cycle 7

0:56	New claps (recorded more distantly) are added to the overall texture: *"Don't care how you do me/Since King Jesus choose me."*

Cycle 8 (refrain)

1:05	

Cycle 9 (refrain)

1:13	Jones changes the melody, moving it triumphantly upward. The performance begins to accelerate slightly.

Cycle 10 (refrain)

1:22	She repeats the refrain, keeping the new melodic variation.

Cycle 11

1:31	The clapping becomes more intense. Jones drives the melody upward in response: *"Don't care where you throw me/Since King Jesus own me."*

Cycle 12

1:40	*"Don't care how you treat me/Since King Jesus meet me."*

Cycle 13

1:49	*"Don't care how you do me/Since King Jesus choose me."*
1:54	One member of the choir enters a beat early—perhaps by mistake, or perhaps as a signal to conclude.
1:57	Jones silences the hand clapping by sustaining her last note.

BLUES: COUNTRY AND VAUDEVILLE

The blues, a new poetic genre, began to emerge at the dawn of the twentieth century, marked by its unusual three-line stanza. Its name evoked a centuries-old synonym for enervating depression: Thomas Jefferson wrote that "we have something of the blue devils at times." Earlier forms of folk poetry usually fell into stanzas of two or four lines, but the blues took the two-line couplet and repeated the first line. It became a musical form through its distinctive chord progression in the accompaniment to ballads such as "Frankie and Johnnie," a story of romantic betrayal from St. Louis that falls roughly into a twelve-bar pattern.

Unlike the ballad, which is a coherent, chronological account of an event usually told in the third person, the blues is personal—a window into the singer's mind. This change in perspective matched the new mood of the times. As the historian Lawrence Levine observed, African American society had recently shifted from the communal confines of slave culture to the cold, terrifying realities of freedom in an unfriendly land. The blues served as an apt and sobering metaphor for the contemplation of those realities.

The earliest blues combined old folk elements with modern instrumental technology. Blues melodies borrowed their rhythmic flexibility from the field holler, prompting some musicians to observe that the blues was "as old as the hills." At the same time, they were accompanied by the guitar, which became widely available for the first time in the rural South in the late nineteenth century. Musicians used guitars as a blank slate for their creativity: they tuned them in unexpected ways and pressed knives, bottlenecks, and other implements against the strings to create haunting blue notes and shivery slides. This early style, later called country blues, was performed chiefly by solitary male musicians throughout the rural South, from the Carolinas to the Mississippi Delta into Texas. The form was loose and improvisatory, suiting the needs of the moment.

"SOON ONE MORNING" ("DEATH COME A-CREEPIN' IN MY ROOM")

Mississippi Fred McDowell was actually born in Tennessee, in 1904. In his thirties, he moved about forty miles south of Memphis to Como, Mississippi, where he worked on cotton farms and played guitar at country dances and juke joints. "I wasn't making money from music," he said. "Sometimes they'd pay me, and sometimes they wouldn't." In 1959, he was rediscovered by Alan Lomax, who recorded his music and launched his career as a professional blues artist. Like other musicians brought to public light during the 1960s folk revival, McDowell was cherished for his archaic acoustic guitar sound; yet he thought of himself as a modern artist. He liked playing electric guitar and was delighted by the ensuing recognition and royalties when the Rolling Stones recorded one of his songs on *Sticky Fingers* (1971).

"Soon One Morning" is not a blues: its poetic shape is a quatrain, not a three-line stanza. And though its text is religious, it is too personal to be a spiritual. It falls somewhere in between, a spiritual reflection informed by blues musical habits. "It's just like if you're going to pray, and mean it, things will be in your mind," he explained. "Songs should tell the truth."

McDowell plays bottleneck guitar: he damps the strings with a glass slide placed over a finger, allowing him to slide from one note to the next. The effect often sounds noisy, as other strings resonate alongside the desired melodic line. McDowell uses the guitar less as accompaniment than as a partner: "If you pay attention, what I sing, the guitar sings, too." When he seems unable to complete his phrases, the guitar serves as an extension of his voice. Though largely ignored by jazz musicians, country blues experienced a huge revival in rock, as musicians like Eric Clapton and the Rolling Stones absorbed recordings by blues musicians from the Mississippi Delta—Son House, Charley Patton, and especially Robert Johnson, who died in 1938 yet sold half a million copies of a two-CD set in 1990.

SOON ONE MORNING (DEATH COME A-CREEPIN' IN MY ROOM)

Mississippi Fred McDowell, guitar, vocal

LABEL: *Southern Journey 10: Yazoo Delta Blues and Spirituals* (Prestige 25010); *The Story of American Music* (Columbia/Legacy CK 61433-61437)
DATE: 1959
STYLE: African American folk music
FORM: four-line stanza (**ABAC; C** is the refrain)

Introduction

0:00	The recording starts abruptly, as if someone had just turned on a microphone. A preliminary note escapes from the guitar.

Chorus 1

0:04	A	With a few louder notes, McDowell begins the first phrase of the four-phrase tune. His line includes blue notes, created by damping the strings with a glass slide. To keep time, he taps quietly but insistently on the downbeat, playing a single low guitar string on the upbeat.
0:13	B	The second phrase parallels the first, but starts on a higher pitch.
0:16		As the melody reaches its highest point, McDowell plays more intensely.
0:20	A	The third phrase also parallels the first, returning to a quieter volume.
0:27	C	The last phrase opens with a different rhythm.
0:32		The last note falls with an accent in the middle of a measure. It sounds as though McDowell has shortened the meter by two beats; but a few seconds later, he makes up the time by entering two beats early with his vocal.

Chorus 2

0:35	A	McDowell sings the first line, doubling the melody on guitar: *"It was, soon one morning, death come creepin' in [my room]."*

In the middle of the word "morning," his voice trails off; the guitar finishes the phrase.

0:41   Again, he fades out before the end of the phrase, leaving the guitar to
carry out the musical thought.

0:43   **B**

0:50   **A**   The third melodic phrase begins with the guitar; the voice enters a few
seconds later.

0:57   **C**   The last line is a refrain, with these words heard in every stanza:
"Oh my Lord, oh my Lord, what shall I do to be [saved]?"

Chorus 3

1:05   **A**   On the next stanza, McDowell's words are almost too faint to be intel-
ligible: *"Well hurry, children, hurry, hurry when my Lord calls."*

1:12   **B**

1:19   **A**

1:26   **C**   He sings the refrain, fading off on the last word.

Chorus 4

1:34   **A**   McDowell moves his guitar accompaniment down an octave, to a lower
register. *"I'm gonna stand right here, I'm gonna wait until Jesus [comes]."*

1:41   **B**

1:48   **A**

1:54   **C**

Chorus 5

2:00   **A**   Over a sharply chopped backbeat, the guitar takes a solo chorus.

2:08   **B**   McDowell's playing causes other strings to resonate, creating a complex,
clanging timbre.

2:14   **A**   The tempo begins to increase noticeably.

2:20   **C**

Chorus 6

2:26   **A**   McDowell returns to the opening stanza:
"Well, soon one morning, death come creepin' in [my room]."

2:32   **B**

2:38   **A**   The guitar takes the remainder of the stanza by itself.

2:44   **C**

Chorus 7

2:50   **A**   The last chorus again features solo guitar, with the melody down an
octave.

2:56   **B**

3:01   **A**

3:07   C
3:10   The guitar stops, ending the piece.

Jazz musicians began to encounter the blues when it crossed the boundary line into popular music. The transition began virtually as soon as the country blues caught the ear of professional entertainers. Gertrude Pritchett, a black stage singer who later became better known as "Ma" Rainey (1886–1939), heard it from a young woman in St. Louis around 1904. Asked about her peculiar style of music, she told Rainey, "It's the blues." Rainey promptly adopted the new style, and went on to fame as one of the most popular singers of what became identified as vaudeville blues, or classic blues—a theatrical form featuring female singers, accompanied by a small band, on the stages of black entertainment circuits in the 1910s and 1920s.

Known as the "Mother of the Blues," Rainey was a short woman with a commanding voice that could be heard in the back rows of crowded theaters or in the unfriendly acoustics of outdoor tent shows. A country bluesman, playing alone, could hasten or retard a passage, so that a blues chorus might turn out to be eleven or thirteen and a half bars. In the hands of artists like Rainey and her ensembles, the blues became more codified, falling into strict twelve-bar stanzas with written harmonic progressions. Many soon-to-be jazz musicians entered show business as backup for singers like Rainey, learning through trial and error how best to match the sound of their instruments to the singer's bluesy strains.

Around the same time Ma Rainey first heard the blues, a wandering cornet player named W. C. Handy (1873–1958) encountered what he later described as "the weirdest music I had ever heard," in a Mississippi railroad station: a guitarist repeating the same line of poetry endlessly ("goin' where the Southern cross' the dog") while scraping notes on the strings with a knife. Struck by how eagerly Southern audiences responded to this sound, Handy studied the music and began transcribing it for his own nine-piece dance ensemble. Soon, Handy—later self-apotheosized as the "Father of the Blues"—began publishing blues-related popular songs, including "Memphis Blues" (1912), "Beale Street Blues" (1917), and the smash hit "St. Louis Blues" (1914). "St. Louis Blues" was recorded at least 135 times over the next thirty years—more than any other tune. In his autobiography, Handy vividly described his first encounter with a blues band:

+ + +

They were led by a long-legged chocolate boy and their band consisted of just three pieces, a battered guitar, a mandolin and a worn-out bass. The music they made was pretty well in keeping with their looks. They struck up one of those over-and-over strains that seem to have no very clear beginning and certainly no ending at all. The strumming attained a disturbing monotony, but on and on it went, a kind of stuff that has long been associated with cane rows and levee camps. Thump-thump-thump went their feet on the floor. Their eyes rolled. Their shoulders swayed. And through it all that little agonizing strain persisted. It was not really annoying or unpleasant. Perhaps "haunting" is a better word, but I commenced to wonder if anybody besides small town rounders and their running mates would go for it.

The answer was not long in coming. A rain of silver dollars began to fall around the outlandish, stomping feet. The dancers went wild. Dollars, quarters, halves—the shower grew heavier and continued so long I strained my neck to get a better look. There before the boys lay more money than my nine musicians were being paid for the entire engagement. Then I saw the beauty of primitive music. They had the stuff the people wanted. It touched the spot. Their music wanted polishing, but it contained the essence. Folks would pay money for it. . . .

That night a composer was born, an *American* composer.

+ + +

The shower of coins increased throughout the 1910s and early 1920s, as the blues became a hot commercial property. Pop song publishers achieved major blues hits, and recording companies followed suit. Recording outfits initially catered to a white audience and recorded only white performers, among them vaudeville stars who specialized in mimicking blacks (as well as white immigrant groups, like the Irish and Dutch). But in 1920, Perry Bradford, an African American songwriter and tune plugger, convinced OKeh Records to try a black artist, Mamie Smith. As sales of her recording "Crazy Blues" soared into the hundreds of thousands, recording companies realized that African Americans represented a serious market.

By this time, blacks were crowding into Northern cities. Although eager to claim themselves as newly urbanized, they were still hungry for music from back home. The blues—a genre that had itself crossed over from folk to popular—became their music. To satisfy their tastes (and to augment profits), record companies offered a new product: "race records," black music created for black people. The phrase sounds offensive today, as it did in the 1940s, when the trade magazine *Billboard* changed the name of its sales sheet of black recordings from "Race" to "Rhythm and Blues." But in the 1920s, the phrase was intended as respectful and accepted as such: African American newspapers frequently described their readers as "the race." The treatment of black performers, on the other hand, was far from respectful. They were paid a modest performing fee but often denied a copyright royalty, and were pressured by executives to record only blues, locking them into a musical ghetto. Yet the discs sold, stimulating a small boom in the musical economy and leaving us with a treasure of incomparable recordings.

Bessie Smith (1894–1937)

The most popular blues diva of the era, the "Empress of the Blues," Bessie Smith, possessed an extraordinarily powerful voice that she had learned to project in crowded halls long before microphones were introduced onstage. If her brassy attack was matched by a stormy temperament, she also displayed a rare sensitivity in adapting her style to the demands of the recording studio. In a career that lasted only fourteen years, Smith made nearly two hundred records, establishing the standard by which other blues singers were measured.

Born in Chattanooga, Tennessee, Smith began her career as a stage professional, singing and dancing in black theaters controlled by the Theater Owners Booking Association—better known as TOBA, an acronym that its exclusively Negro clientele liked to interpret as Tough on Black Asses. TOBA became synonymous with inferior bookings, lodgings, and travel accommodations. Smith was soon established as a favorite in theaters and tent shows, and as a volatile drinker and occasional brawler in her romantically indefatigable private life. Her brief but successful recording career began at OKeh Records in 1923. Some of her accompanists, most notably Louis Armstrong, were already familiar with the blues. For others, recording with Bessie amounted to a crash course in the music, with accompanists scurrying to match her nuances in phrasing and tone. Jazz musicians enjoyed working with her, though, and she enjoyed them and the metropolitan areas in which they flourished, emphasizing her star status with necklaces made of gold coins and bursting onstage through a replica of one of her recordings.

Smith's career peaked in 1929, the same year she made her only film appearance as a downhearted lover in the seventeen-minute short *St. Louis Blues*. Thereafter, the Depression curtailed her audience and her earnings. By the mid-1930s, conceding that her blues style had slid from fashion, she agreed to update her sound by recording pop tunes with younger up-

and-coming jazzmen. But her attempt at a comeback was cut short, in 1937, as she rode to a gig on the back roads of the Mississippi Delta. Her car plowed into the back of a truck; her arm was torn loose and she went into shock. By the time she reached a hospital, she had lost too much blood. John Hammond, who had launched his own career by producing her final recording session, angrily wrote an erroneous account (dramatized in Edward Albee's 1961 play *The Death of Bessie Smith*), claiming that Smith was taken first to a white hospital, where she died shortly after being refused admission. Actually, no one in Mississippi would have thought of taking a black woman to a white facility. Hammond may have invented the story, but the message—that her death was attributable to the casual violence that was the fabric of life for black musicians in the Deep South—rang true.

"RECKLESS BLUES"

Louis Armstrong was not Smith's favorite accompanist: she preferred the cornetist Joe Smith (no relation), who allowed that the great singer deserved a more subservient and discreet accompanist. But on "Reckless Blues," Armstrong shows how thoroughly the language of blues had expanded by 1925 under the influence of singers like Smith.

"Reckless Blues" is a duet by two great artists, competing for our attention. Backed by Fred Longshaw's stolid chords on reed organ—as unswinging a setting as one could imagine—Smith is in command from the start, singing each line of the stanza with simplicity and control. As the "responder" to her "call," Armstrong is alert to every gesture, filling in even the smallest spaces she provides him. His timbre is modified by two mutes: a straight mute to reduce the sound and a plunger to produce *wa-wa* effects. With each stanza, their intensity grows. Smith's lines stick to the melodic outline, but grow more opulent in timbre and more unpredictable in rhythm.

RECKLESS BLUES

Bessie Smith

Bessie Smith, vocal; Louis Armstrong, trumpet; Fred Longshaw, reed organ

LABEL: Columbia 14056-D; *St. Louis Blues*, vol. 2: *1924–1925* (Naxos 8.120691)
DATE: 1925
STYLE: vaudeville blues
FORM: 12-bar blues

Introduction

0:00	Over Longshaw's organ, Armstrong plays an extended blues line, his timbre distorted by a plunger mute. Throughout the piece, Longshaw remains in the background, playing a stable series of chords.

Chorus 1

0:14	*"When I wasn't nothing but a child,"* Smith begins her first blues chorus with a descending melody.
0:17	She pauses briefly, leaving room for a quick Armstrong response.
0:28	*"When I wasn't nothing but a child,"*
0:35	The end of the line is marked by a brief melodic idea, falling and rising through the blue third, seeming to underscore her girlish sauciness.
0:42	*"All you men tried to drive me wild."*

Chorus 2

0:56	*"Now I am growing old,"* Smith's melody follows the same basic pattern as chorus 1. On the word "now," her line is melismatic—several notes for a single syllable.
1:04	Armstrong's response begins with a striking blue note.
1:10	*"Now I am growing old,"* Smith holds out the second "now" with a single note, quavering slightly at the end.
1:23	*"And I've got what it takes to get all of you men told."*

Chorus 3

1:37	*"My mama says I'm reckless, my daddy says I'm wild,"* As if responding to the emotional quality of the lyrics, Smith bursts in a few beats early.
1:50	*"My mama says I'm reckless, my daddy says I'm wild,"* Her line is intensely syncopated, dragging against the beat.
1:58	Armstrong lets a blue note fall agonizingly for three seconds.
2:04	*"I ain't good looking but I'm somebody's angel child."*

Chorus 4

2:18	*"Daddy, mama wants some loving, Daddy, mama wants some hugging,"* Smith interrupts the usual three-line stanza with a repeated call to "Daddy." Armstrong's response mimics the word with a two-note pattern.
2:33	*"Darn it pretty papa, mama wants some loving I vow,"* Smith's emotions are signaled by changes in timbre.
2:40	Mirroring Smith, Armstrong's response is also more emotionally involved.
2:46	*"Darn it pretty papa, mama wants some loving right now."*

Coda

....

2:54   In the last two measures, Armstrong and Longshaw signal the end by
            slowing down slightly. Longshaw's last tonic chord adds a blue seventh
            note.

_____

POPULAR MUSIC: MINSTRELSY AND DANCE

While the black community reveled in its own music, a good many black
musicians moved toward the larger and more affluent audience of white
Americans. "Mighty seldom I played for colored," recalled one violinist.
"They didn't have nothing to hire you with." Long before Reconstruction,
black entertainers realized they could cash in on the exoticism associated
with their color. In the early nineteenth century, in racially mixed areas
on the Lower East Side of Manhattan, loose-limbed black men entranced
crowds of whites by dancing on a shingle placed on the ground. A few performers managed to earn a living this way: on one of his American tours,
Charles Dickens acclaimed William Henry Lane, also known as Master
Juba, as "the greatest dancer known."

Still, the deep imbalance of power between the races made it difficult
for black performers to succeed. Popular culture was shaping up in the
other direction. Attentive white performers studied their black counterparts, adopting their comedic and dance styles and accompanying themselves on banjo (an instrument with African lineage) and "the bones" (a
primitive form of homemade percussion). In the process, they created the
most popular and influential form of entertainment in nineteenth-century
America, minstrelsy.

In New York, in 1843, a quartet of white musicians called the Virginia
Minstrels (after an Austrian group that had recently visited the city) presented an evening's amusement that claimed to depict the culture of plantation slaves. They performed in blackface—a mask of burnt cork, with
grotesquely exaggerated eyes and mouths. Their success was astonishing,
prompting numerous imitators. Within a decade, the "minstrel show" had
become the most beloved theatrical production in the country, touring
everywhere on both sides of Mason-Dixon.

Minstrels invented new and sadly lasting stereotypes of blackness, influencing the perception of blacks particularly in areas were there were none.
As "Ethiopian delineators," their wigs were mops of unruly curls, wild and

woolly, and their stage clothes tattered and outrageously loud in style and color. One of the main minstrel stereotypes, Zip Coon, was an overdressed dandy whose foppish behavior savagely parodied upper-class whites. But the most memorable characterizations were based on a poisonous racial contempt. These happy-go-lucky plantation "darkies" combined savvy musical talent with foolish, childlike behavior that no adult could take seriously. A crippled stable hand known as Jim Crow, whose dance and ditty had inspired the first blackface performer, Daddy Rice, morphed into a character so thoroughly identified with racial exploitation that the phrase "Jim Crow" became shorthand for the entire Southern legal system of post-Reconstruction segregation.

True, abolitionists often claimed that minstrelsy had a positive effect, presenting blacks as human and amusing. But the negative caricatures outlasted any positive aspects of antebellum blackface acts. Similarly, the phrase "natural rhythm," a backhanded compliment paid black musicians, was intended to express a delight in black musical abilities, but was also interpreted to mean that those abilities were not learned but, rather, genetically given, perhaps in compensation for not being as fully human as whites. If talent comes naturally, it is unearned and of only modest value. Along with "natural rhythm" came far less desirable stereotypes: thieving, lying, and childish idiocy. If blacks, as portrayed by minstrels, did not understand what they were doing, they were incapable of behaving otherwise. Perhaps they were better off as chattel.

After the Civil War, something happened that caught white minstrel troupes unprepared. Major white producers organized black minstrel troupes, offering competing tours of racially segregated shows. White audiences soon began favoring black troupes, which were often judged more authentic, even though the black performers were obliged to play the same characters that the white imitators had created. By this point, minstrelsy was as rigorously structured as the circus, and audiences demanded the usual characters, including Tambo and Mr. Bones, the so-called endmen who made leering yet oddly impotent jokes. Blacks were pleased to get work and to travel the country, but they had to wear the burnt cork masks, wigs, and clothing, disguising their individual talents (and complexions) behind characters as fixed as the clowns in commedia dell'arte. Of course, commedia dell'arte satirized all mankind, not a particular ethnic group.

Even under these conditions, black minstrelsy created genuine stars— like Billy Kersands, a comedian whose facial muscles were so malleable he could hold a cup and saucer in his mouth. James Bland, a Howard-educated performer and songwriter, wrote several standard minstrel songs (an area dominated by the great white melodist Stephen Foster), including "O Dem Golden Slippers" and the ballad "Carry Me Back to Old Virginny," which served as Virginia's state song until 1997, when the song's racial dialect ("There's where the old darkey's heart am long'd to go") finally prompted its removal. The state might better have followed the example of Ray Charles, whose vigorous 1960 version of the song simply revised the distasteful lyrics.

As jazz made its first inroads into popular culture, the minstrel show was on its last legs. Genuine stars like the immensely versatile comedian, mime, and songwriter Bert Williams and the majestically inventive tap dancer Bill "Bojangles" Robinson moved their acts to the vaudeville stage. Yet the minstrel show's key stereotypes lingered on and on, winning a new audience in the late 1920s after the first sound film, *The Jazz Singer*, brought Al Jolson's blackface act to audiences who had never seen him onstage. For Jolson's character, blackface represents his devotion to America's vernacular culture and a break with his liturgical Jewish past. Radio comics used "blackvoice" dialect to keep a new generation laughing at minstrel stereotypes—the most popular radio show of the 1930s was *Amos 'n' Andy*. Through the early 1950s, film actors such as Mickey Rooney, Judy Garland, Bing Crosby, and Joan Crawford were occasionally willing to put on cork. Minstrelsy had become a show-biz staple; entertainers felt they could indulge it without acknowledging its racial slurs.

Perhaps the most unnerving aspect of minstrelsy was that it trained white audiences to expect all black entertainers, including those who came to fame long after minstrelsy's heyday, to enact characteristics of the performing fool. Many black artists, most famously the dancer Josephine Baker, moved to Europe to escape those expectations. Jazz musicians generally averted them by focusing on their job, which was to play music. But those who were seen as mainstream entertainers had to play the game. The supremely sophisticated Duke Ellington made his motion picture debut in a cameo appearance with Amos and Andy. Louis Armstrong mugged his way through a notorious 1930s one-reeler, performing the minstrel song "Shine" in heaven, wearing a leopard skin and standing ankle-deep in soap bubbles. Ironically, few whites saw these films. They were distributed almost exclusively to black theaters, where audiences were delighted to see geniuses like Ellington and Armstrong on the screen. Those audiences had no trouble getting beyond the masks, and laughed at Armstrong's inventive humor, knowing that the sound of his trumpet and the authority of his vocal delivery dispelled racist clichés, even turning them into an act of defiance. If stereotypes could not be dispelled, they could certainly be undermined.

Dance Music

The first slave musicians realized they had a knack for inspiring dance with their music. Black fiddlers roamed the South, relying on their abilities to earn money while enjoying a measure of physical liberty. Most were anonymous artisans, and some—like the character Fiddler in Alex Haley's 1976 novel *Roots*—saved their earnings in order to buy their freedom. A few became celebrities. In early nineteenth-century Philadelphia, the free black bandleader and composer Frank Johnson used his knowledge of African American music to "distort a sentimental, simple, and beautiful song into a reel, jig, or country-dance." He eventually toured London, earning a silver bugle by performing for Queen Victoria.

Careers like Johnson's were rare. But at a time when most black people were pushed toward manual labor, music was one of the few skilled professions open to them. Still, like a butler, cook, or maid, a musician hired to play tunes for dancing became a domestic servant, wearing livery (or a conventional black tuxedo) as a symbol of his role. His position in society was relatively elegant and profitable, if clearly subservient. This situation held until the turn of the century, when a revolution shook the world of dance.

In late nineteenth-century America, respectable people danced at balls restricted by invitation to a small, exclusive social circle. Their favorite dances, including the quadrille and the lancer, were formal and elaborate. The waltz placed couples in close physical contact, but the speed of the dance countered anything resembling intimacy. All that began to change early in the twentieth century. When restaurants and cabarets threw open their dance floors to middle-class couples, a slew of new dances entered the mainstream. Sometimes known as "animal dances" (the turkey trot, bunny hug, and grizzly bear were especially popular), they were, to some, shockingly uninhibited and physical, requiring vigorous movement from the hips and lower body. Dancing was now taken up by married couples as well as young people. Women shed their corsets, finding dance a means of physical exercise and personal expression. The advent of the phonograph enabled people to learn these snappy new dances in the privacy of their living rooms.

The most fashionable of the new steps were African American in origin. The Charleston derived its name and syncopations from the highly Africanized islands of South Carolina. The quintessential Charleston theme was composed by the black pianist James P. Johnson. Yet these dances were introduced to middle-class audiences by white experts—most famously Vernon and Irene Castle, who offered graceful interpretations that carefully removed lower-class (and lower-body) excesses. In an interview, Irene explained the origins of the "shimmy shake" with a casual racism typical of its time:

◆ ◆ ◆

We get our new dances from the Barbary Coast. Of course, they reach New York in a very primitive condition, and have to be considerably toned down before they can be used in the drawing-room. There is one just arrived now—it is still very, very crude—and it is called "Shaking the Shimmy." It's a nigger dance, of course, and it appears to be a slow walk with a frequent twitching of the shoulders. The teachers may try and make something of it.

◆ ◆ ◆

While the Castles transformed those "primitive" dances into cool, middle-class elegance, the subversively syncopated music was inescapably black, and derived from the contemporary piano (and, eventually, orchestral) style known as ragtime. "When a good orchestra plays a 'rag,'" Vernon Castle said, "one has simply *got* to move."

The Castles' ragtime was performed by a remarkable black bandleader, James Reese Europe (1881–1919). Born in Alabama, Europe moved to New York at twenty-two to perform in and conduct black musical theater. He quickly shifted his focus to dance music. Most of the good dance jobs in New York were held by white orchestras playing gypsy music. Determined to use black musicians, Europe created the Clef Club—part talent agency, part orchestra. In 1912, as the dance/ragtime craze was nearing its peak, the Clef Club showed its strength with a massive concert in Carnegie Hall. This was not a jazz band: the 125-piece orchestra was made up primarily of string instruments, including mandolin and harp-guitar. Playing arrangements that highlighted Negro syncopation, the Clef Club Orchestra reaffirmed the black musician's place at the center of the dance world. Having caught the attention of the Castles, Europe formed a society orchestra to accompany them.

When the United States entered the First World War, Europe enlisted, eager to show that black men were willing to die for their country. He fought bravely in the trenches and formed the 369th Infantry Band, known as the "Hellfighters," recruiting dozens of his best formerly civilian musicians (including clarinet players from Puerto Rico). Europe, who made his most interesting and prophetic records in 1914, did not approve of improvisation or the jazz mania that ensued in 1917. Nor did he live to see jazz mature into something he might well have embraced. In 1919, shortly after his triumphant return to New York, he was stabbed in the neck by a disgruntled drummer and died at age thirty-eight. Today, his long-neglected recordings seem startlingly prescient, if only because his military band instrumentation favored the brasses and reeds and allowed for short breaks. Europe also pointed to the future in devising bands of different sizes: a small combo ideally suited for jazz, given its size and flexibility, and an orchestra, exemplified by Europe's Hellfighters and such rival bands as Will Marion Cook's Southern Syncopated Orchestra and Tim Brymn's Black Devil Orchestra, ideally suited for ballrooms.

ART MUSIC: BRASS BANDS AND RAGTIME

Having learned during slavery that literacy meant power—why else would it be systematically denied to them?—musically inclined African Americans were drawn to the mysteries of notation and theory. In the all-black schools and universities that sprouted throughout the South after Emancipation, music became a central part of formal education, an outcome not universally praised. Booker T. Washington disdained the usefulness of musical skills: visiting a poor family, he was disgusted to find that people who dined with a single eating utensil had spent their meager income on an expensive reed organ. But many African Americans saw music as an inextricable part of becoming full-fledged citizens.

Through public education, children learned to play string instruments like the violin, and some became skilled performers, including Joseph Douglass, grandson of the abolitionist Frederick Douglass and a brilliant violinist. Soprano Sisserietta Jones was so renowned that she billed herself professionally as "the Black Patti" (after the Italian soprano Adelina Patti). Yet even the most talented of these performers could not support themselves professionally. White audiences refused to hear them, and black audiences were not affluent enough to support them. Barred from opera houses, Jones had to tour with a troupe known as Black Patti's Troubadours, her operatic performances stuck in the middle of minstrel entertainment.

As classically trained youngsters became old enough to worry about employment, jazz absorbed their talents. Classical education brought standards of execution and music theory into jazz, and musicians brought up in the concert tradition carried with them a social ambition that led them to dream of becoming something more in the world. If the symphony orchestra proved a remote goal for most classically trained musicians, the brass band provided a more practical alternative. An import from Britain, the brass band was originally a military institution that in peacetime became a local "people's" orchestra. New brass instruments like the sousaphone were designed for ease in marching, while reed instruments like the clarinet and flute were often added to make the overall sound more fluid and flexible.

The sousaphone was inspired by John Philip Sousa (1854–1932), a conductor and composer whose name was synonymous with brass band excellence. Sousa took over the U.S. Marine Band in 1880 and transformed it into a top-notch concert orchestra, mounting ambitious programs that featured European music as well as his own concert marches. In 1892, he formed his first ensemble. For the next forty years, the Sousa Band toured the world, bringing to brass band music the highest level of virtuosity and precision. Sousa also inspired thousands of lesser ensembles, ranging in size from large professional bands (often led by former Sousa soloists) to small, local amateur groups. Indeed, it was said that "a town without its brass band is as much in need of sympathy as a church without a choir." Staffed by townspeople who mastered as much notation as necessary, local bands played for dances, concerts, and parades. On such occasions, the local butcher, policeman, and lawyer traded their work clothes for uniforms, with the band's name proudly displayed on the front of their caps. We imagine them in a small town on a summer's evening, delighting a crowd from a gazebo on the city square.

Not surprisingly, towns with a significant African American population had their own brass bands, no less eager to display their skills than their white counterparts. For black musicians, bands provided more than a friendly, supportive environment in which to create music. They were also social organizations, offering insurance to members and guaranteeing a decent, brass-led send-off to the graveyard. As the dance craze gathered steam, brass bands thinned their ranks to small dance ensembles, often led by a violinist but featuring wind instruments central to jazz: cornet, clarinet, and trombone. Cymbals, bass drum, and snare drum were combined into the modern drum set. Duple-meter marches—sometimes in a straight 2/4, at other times in a jauntier meter (6/8) with the beat divided into threes—were easily adapted for dancing. The lively rhythms of Sousa's "The Washington Post," written in 1889, accompanied the two-step, a popular dance recently introduced.

The brass band's primary contribution to jazz turned out to be its compositional structure. The defining unit of a march is a sixteen-bar strain, which marries a dominant melody to an equally identifiable chord progression. Marches are made up of a succession of strains, each usually repeated before passing on to the next. A typical march with four strains could be diagrammed as AABBCCDD or AABBACCDD (with the returning A offering a hint of closure and transition). No attempt is made to round things off at the end by reprising the first strain.

The third or trio strain (C) is particularly significant. For one thing, it modulates to a new key (the subdominant, or IV), sometimes with the aid of a short introductory passage, and is often twice as long, lasting thirty-two bars instead of sixteen. Composers used the trio to change the piece's dynamics, texture, or orchestration. Many marches concentrate on the trio at the end, repeating it several times after dramatic interludes—among them Sousa's indelible classic, "The Stars and Stripes Forever."

"THE STARS AND STRIPES FOREVER"

Sousa wrote this march on Christmas Day, 1896, reportedly to commemorate the recent death of his manager, David Blakley. Thanks to America's entry into world affairs in the Spanish-American War two years later, it achieved immense and lasting success as a radiant display of patriotism. Sousa performed "The Stars and Stripes" at every concert. It remains an ideal example of march form. The forceful four-bar introduction is followed by two sixteen-bar strains, each repeated. The trio strain offers, at first, a peaceful respite: a pleasant, hummable melody in a new key. Sousa later set it to the words "Hurrah for the flag of the free," though it became better known for the lyric "Hurray for the red, white, and blue." The trio is twice interrupted by a tumultuous passage, one of the most dramatic that Sousa ever wrote. After twenty-four bars, this interlude leads back to the trio, this time with countermelodies: first a sparkling part for piccolo, then a triumphant one for the trombone section.

THE STARS AND STRIPES FOREVER

Gunther Schuller and the Incredible Columbia All-Star Band

LABEL: *Footlifters: A Century of American Marches* (Columbia M 33513; Sony SK94887)
DATE: composed 1896
STYLE: concert march
FORM: march (**AABBCCC**)

Introduction (4 bars)

0:00	The band opens at full volume, moving forcefully to a half cadence.

Strain A (16 bars)

0:03	Strain **A** begins with a brisk tune in E♭ major played by the cornets and clarinets. The melody is accompanied by percussion (snare drum and cymbals).
0:10	Halfway through, the tune becomes quiet, occasionally interrupted by short bursts from the lower instruments.
0:16	The strain ends on a half cadence.

Strain A

0:17	Strain **A** is repeated.

Strain B (16 bars)

0:30	The melody of strain **B** features a steady rhythm, accented by offbeat "hiccups" from the flutes.
0:43	The strain ends on a full cadence.

Strain B

0:44	Strain **B** is repeated.

Strain C (trio) (32 bars)

0:58	The winds serenely play the trio's melody, now in a new key (A♭ major). Accompanying them are the cornets and horns, playing rhythmic background chords. The trio is 32 bars, twice as long as the previous strains.
1:12	The melody repeats, moving through more distant harmonies before finally ending on a full cadence.

Interlude (24 bars)

1:25	The lower brass instruments (trombones and horns) enter with a tumultuous descending melody, suddenly pulling us out of the key.
1:28	The melody is repeated at a higher pitch.

1:32	Dissonant chromatic chords dissolve into a descending chromatic scale.
1:36	The chords are repeated at a higher pitch.
1:39	The harmony begins to settle on the dominant.
1:43	A descending chromatic scale leads to a repetition of the trio.

Strain C

| 1:46 | The trio is repeated with a countermelody: an elaborate line, decorated with trills, played by the piccolo flute. |

Interlude

| 2:14 | The interlude is repeated. |

Strain C

| 2:36 | A final repetition of the trio with a new trombone countermelody, played at full volume. The drums and cymbals strongly mark each beat. |

While Sousa enjoyed international renown, another kind of music was coming to the fore, one that embodied—as jazz itself would, in the long run—the collision of African American music with the white mainstream, absorbing and combining the disparate aspects of folk music, popular music, and art music. Ragtime probably got its name from the phrase "ragged time," a colorful description of African American polyrhythm.

At the time of the Civil War, "ragged time" would have been heard chiefly on the banjo, the black instrument par excellence. But over the next half century, black performers were able to take up piano—the very symbol of middle-class gentility, and yet sturdy enough to find a home in the lower-class saloons on the fringe of every urban community, white or black. Musicians who stumbled onto this instrument found that the same polyrhythms that enlivened banjo playing fit naturally under a pianist's fingers. The left hand kept a steady, two-beat rhythmic foundation: low bass notes alternating with higher chords. Against this background, the right hand was free to add contrasting rhythms that contradicted the duple meter. To "rag" a piece meant to subject it to this process of rhythmic complication.

Like other pop culture terms (blues, swing, rock, hip-hop), ragtime meant different things to different people. For some, it was a type of song; for others, a dance; for still others, a piano style. These varied associations help to explain how ragtime saturated American music at the turn of the century. One of the earliest commercial forms of ragtime was the coon song, yoking polyrhythmic accompaniments to racial stereotypes. Coon songs were a direct extension of the minstrel show, sold as sheet music with outrageously racist cover illustrations, titles, and lyrics, all designed to further abusive caricatures that remained a stubbornly ingrained part of American life. (The caricatures were by no means limited to blacks; the Irish and Chinese were also popular targets.) One hit song, "All Coons Look Alike to Me," was written by a renowned black minstrel, Ernest Hogan, who simply amended the title of a prostitute's lament, "All Pimps Look Alike to Me." While the song's rhythms conveyed the joys of ragtime, its subject matter was so odious that whistling the melody within sight of black men was enough to start a fight. As coon songs became increasingly offensive, the popular song industry felt the need to retreat, toning them down and calling them "ragtime songs."

The first dance closely associated with blacks to become a national sensation was called the cakewalk, a comic high-stepping parody that may have originated in the later stages of slavery. On the plantations, slaves amused themselves and their white masters by imitating the ballroom finery of a formal dance. The cakewalk satisfied both sides: blacks felt they were ridiculing their masters' social revels, while whites enjoyed the vigorous and exaggerated terpsichore. On the minstrel stage, it was an "exhibition dance," a strutting two-step with elaborate costumes and twirling canes. The most creatively outlandish dancers won a cake.

At the turn of the century, the cakewalk became a public competition with the valued prize of a week's theatrical booking. Its syncopated rhythms charmed people of all social origins, at home and abroad. In France, Claude Debussy sought to capture the dance in a piano piece, "Golliwog's Cakewalk." Through the cakewalk, white people became comfortable with ragtime syncopations and initiated the still-ongoing process of adapting black dance as their own.

Scott Joplin (1868–1917) AND
Wilbur Sweatman (1882–1961)

If coon songs and cakewalks have slipped into the dustbin of history, ragtime has achieved an apparent immortality as a piano style and piano repertory, endlessly reinterpreted from sheet music. The first "rags," translations of improvised piano techniques into written form, appeared in 1897. These pieces adopted the march form, employing rhythmic contrast in a succession of distinct melodic strains. (March form, as it applies to jazz, is perhaps better understood as march/ragtime form.) Over the next two decades, thousands of rags were published—many of them by piano virtuosos who tailored their extraordinary technique to the level of the ordinary pianist. Those that have proved most durable, however, were painstakingly notated by pianist-composers from the hinterland, none more celebrated or gifted than Scott Joplin.

Joplin was born in the backwaters of East Texas, a child of Reconstruction who believed in the power of literacy to lift black people out of poverty. In Texarkana (on the Texas-Arkansas border), he received a sound musical education from a sympathetic German music teacher who gave him free piano lessons and spurred his imagination with excerpts from German operas. (Joplin expressed his appreciation with his only surviving opera, *Treemonisha*, for which—like Richard Wagner—he wrote libretto and music.) Joplin left home as a teenager to become a professional pianist, touring up and down the Mississippi River. In 1893, he performed at the Midway, the rowdy entertainment venue adjacent to the World's Columbia Exposition in Chicago.

The following year, Joplin settled in Sedalia, Missouri, a small but bustling railroad town. He took a leading role in the musical affairs of the black community, organizing a brass band (he also played cornet) while studying music theory at the local black college. Joplin had begun to compose in earnest, and in 1899 published the "Maple Leaf Rag" (named after a Sedalia saloon), a piece that wedded an irresistible melody to polyrhythm and to the harmonies and structure of a concert march. Joplin was shrewd enough to insist on royalty payments rather than the usual flat fee; the income from that one piece, which eventually sold hundreds of thousands of copies, supported him for the rest of his short-lived career. Spurred by his success, Joplin moved to St. Louis and then to New York City. He wrote more than fifty rags (published in a definitive edition by the New York Public Library in 1971), some in collaboration with other pianist-composers, as well as a ballet and two operas.

Joplin did not live to witness the Jazz Age. Having caught syphilis as a youth, he deteriorated slowly and painfully, spending his last few years in a mental home. By the time he died, in 1917, recordings had displaced sheet music as the most effective way to market ragtime; Joplin made no records per se, but did cut several piano rolls that were later released as records. His death was little noted: the ragtime sensation had subsided and Joplin, largely forgotten, had devoted his final years to *Treemonisha*, his semi-autobiographical opera about an impoverished Texas town saved from superstition by an enlightened young woman. Except for an unsuccessful read-through in 1915, it was never produced during his lifetime. True recognition came much later. In 1970, he was inducted into the Songwriters Hall of Fame; in 1972, *Treemonisha* debuted to great fanfare at Morehouse College; in 1976, he was awarded the habitually tardy Pulitzer Prize, and so on. Most surprisingly, he reached No. 3 on the Billboard pop chart in 1974, after his melodious 1903 rag "The Entertainer" was featured in the movie *The Sting*.

Joplin was one of hundreds of ragtime pianists, most of them known to us only through oral history: Joe Jordan, Tom Turpin, Blind Boone, Louis Chauvin. The best of them could improvise confidently within the confines of ragtime harmony, and competed against each other in legendary contests of keyboard skill. A wealth of music that might have illuminated the transition from composed music to improvised jazz was lost, as few could or cared to notate those informal performances. But we can witness one facet of that transition by attending to one of Joplin's closest friends, the neglected clarinetist and saxophonist Wilbur Sweatman, whom Joplin named as executor of his will and heir to his papers.

Jazz supplanted ragtime as a new generation of musicians began to favor recordings over sheet music. Sweatman's career parallels the tumultuous changes in the ragtime era. He began playing professionally in minstrel shows and circus bands, where he developed the exuberant showmanship that catapulted him onto the theatrical stage in the 1910s. His signature gimmick involved playing three clarinets simultaneously—a visually impressive trick much imitated in vaudeville but not in jazz, until Rahsaan Roland Kirk worked out his own method in the 1950s. Musicians admired Sweatman's know-how and showmanship—the saxophonist Garvin Bushell called him "my idol. I just listened to him talk and looked at him like he was God."

Sweatman composed several rags, of which the most successful was "Down Home Rag" (1911), a multistrain piece in march/ragtime form built around a type of polyrhythm known as secondary ragtime. While the meter of the piece is duple, the main melody insistently repeats a pattern of three notes, implying a cross-rhythm. (This device, also called "novelty ragtime," produced a rhythmically tricky sub-category carried on by pianists such as Zez Confrey and George Gershwin.) "Down Home Rag" was widely recorded, not least by James Reese Europe's string-based Society

Orchestra in 1913. Yet not until Sweatman recorded his own version, in 1916, did the piece hint at a new era of blues-inspired improvisation. He chose Emerson Records, a small company that used a soon-to-be-obsolete technology for cutting grooves into a disc or cylinder. Emerson recordings were playable on a handful of machines, which became difficult to find after dominant companies like Victor established a different recording technology. Accordingly, Sweatman's version of "Down Home Rag" is almost entirely forgotten. Yet it survives as crucial evidence of the transition between ragtime and jazz.

"DOWN HOME RAG"

"Down Home Rag" has four strains. The first two (A and B) are nearly identical: they share a chord progression and end with the same melodic fragment. As usual, the trio (strain C) offers contrast by modulating to a nearby key; this trio, however, is the same length as the other strains. In between repetitions of C, the fourth strain (D) moves to the minor mode. Throughout this short, exuberant recording, Sweatman is the focus of attention, performing his composed melodies with unmistakable enthusiasm. But when repeating a strain, he is just as likely to take off in unpredictable directions. His ad-libs don't qualify as genuine improvisation: as with many early jazz artists, his variations have limited range. Still, the swooping blues notes and the piercing timbre of his clarinet suggest what many ragtime musicians may have been doing in live performance at that time.

DOWN HOME RAG

Wilbur Sweatman

Wilbur Sweatman, clarinet, with the Emerson Trio (piano, clarinet, and trombone)

LABEL: Emerson 2377-1, 7161; *Recorded in New York, 1916–1935* (Jazz Oracle 8046)
DATE: 1916
STYLE: ragtime/early jazz
FORM: march/ragtime

Introduction

0:00   The entire band plays an introductory figure, ending with a half cadence.

Strain A

0:04   On clarinet, Sweatman plays the main melody, with a second clarinet distantly in the background. It features a kind of polyrhythm known as secondary ragtime: against the duple meter, Sweatman's line implies a meter of three.

Behind Sweatman, the trombone plays a composed countermelody.

Strain A

0:12   Strain **A** is repeated.

Strain B

0:20   Sweatman plays a new melody over the same chord progression.

0:26   The last two bars of strain **B** are identical to those of strain **A**.

Strain B′

0:28   Sweatman plays a variation on the melody of **B**, which at times features blue notes (0:31, 0:35).

Strain A

0:36   After a brief pause, the band repeats strain **A**.

Transition

0:44   In a four-bar chordal passage, the band modulates to a new key.

Strain C (trio)

0:48   Sweatman plays a new melody, constantly returning to the same high note. Once again, the trombone plays a countermelody.

Strain C′

0:56   While the background clarinet continues with the melody, Sweatman plays a variation, again featuring blue notes.

Strain D

1:05   The new strain changes mode from major to minor.

Strain D′

1:12   Sweatman's variation again features secondary ragime.

Strain C′

1:20   Returning to major mode, Sweatman plays his blue note variation (heard at 1:00).

Strain C'

1:28   The band repeats the strain.

Coda

1:36   A single additional note ends the piece.

Sweatman's high-voltage attack indicates that before the Armistice and the so-called Jazz Age, the basic elements for jazz were in place. For several decades, popular entertainment had been deeply affected by the rhythms and sounds of African American music. Now, despite an abiding racism so onerous it spawned the reawakening of the Ku Klux Klan, the country was ready for a genuinely new phenomenon. It came by way of the remote, dilapidated, and exotic deep-South city of New Orleans.

CHAPTER 4

New Orleans

THE CITY ON THE GULF

The world thinks of jazz as American and Americans think of it as a national phenomenon, like the Mississippi, snaking through one state after another, fed by numerous tributaries such as blues, ragtime, marches, and dance bands, not to mention the overall traditions of Africa, Europe, and the Caribbean, which combined to shape the African American musical perspective before and after Emancipation. But in the beginning, jazz was local, even provincial—a performing tradition unique to the port city of New Orleans,

◀ Jelly Roll Morton, the seminal New Orleans pianist, composer, and bandleader, at a 1926 recording session.

which took its distinctive character from the ever-changing social conditions of that metropolis. The style known as New Orleans jazz (or Dixieland) proved irresistible enough to attract the attention of the whole country, but only in increments as it wandered north of its home base. New Orleans jazz ultimately became the foundation of jazz itself. The reasons lie in the city's geographical, racial, political, cultural, and musical peculiarities.

Southeastern Louisiana slips into the Gulf of Mexico like a well-curved shoe. New Orleans has always been the principal city on the shoe's tongue, cradled in a crescent-shaped bend of the Mississippi River, which flows down through the sole and empties into the Gulf. To the north, New Orleans faces Lake Pontchartrain, the largest inlet in the South, some forty miles wide.

This watery setting not only allowed the city to grow as a major port before the railroad replaced shipping as the primary vehicle for trade, but gave New Orleans a distinct cultural character, blending elements of American commerce with those of a Caribbean island. Founded by France in 1718 and then relinquished as unprofitable to Spain in 1763, New Orleans was reclaimed for the French in 1803 by Napoleon, who almost immediately sold it to the United States as part of the Louisiana Purchase. Many people continued to speak French and Spanish, infusing the city with traditions of European Catholicism and culture. During a time when the South was almost entirely agricultural, it was the largest city of the region. While Atlanta, its nearest rival, was little more than an undeveloped railroad junction, New Orleans rapidly expanded as a lively, advanced urban center with a distinct architectural look, discrete neighborhoods, and a level of sophistication associated with European capitals.

From the early eighteenth century, New Orleans was a hub for the highlife. Although grand opera struggled to gain a foothold in New York and Boston, it thrived in New Orleans. Yet these same opera lovers also celebrated the coming of Lent with Mardi Gras, an uninhibited revelry resembling the carnivals in Latin countries but unlike anything else in the United States. New Orleans relished dances and parades, and mounted balls and celebrations to suit everyone—the rich and poor, the cultured and debauched.

The city's attitudes toward race, unsurprisingly, differed from general practices in Protestant North America, especially during slavery. Elsewhere in the United States, the slaves were forced to discard their connection to Africa and accept most aspects of Western society—they were required to learn English and become Christian (and therefore Protestant). The goal was a more efficient interaction between slaves and masters, who often worked together on small landholdings. New Orleans, however, was oriented toward the Caribbean and South America. In places like Cuba and Brazil, where the slave trade remained constant until well into the nineteenth century, Africans were allowed to retain their own languages, beliefs, and customs. And those retentions carried over to New Orleans, where nearly half the population was black, whether slave or free. When Haiti declared its independence through revolution in 1804, white masters and their slaves fled to New Orleans. In this growing metropolis at the edge of the Caribbean slave world, old-world religious rites (voodoo) and musical traditions thrived.

CONGO SQUARE, CREOLES OF COLOR, AND UPTOWN NEGROES

Nowhere was the conservation of African musical and dance practices more apparent than in a large field behind the French Quarter, popularly known as Congo Square. The square, used in the eighteenth century as a market for merchants of every stripe, was enlarged after the Louisiana Purchase for the use of slave traders, and eventually became the site of a whites-only circus, complete with carousel. In protest, the free black community set up its own market across the way, and by 1817 slaves and free blacks were permitted to congregate there to dance and play music on Sunday afternoons.

Whites were shocked by what they saw: intricate vocal choirs, massed groups of musicians playing drums, stringed gourds, and other homemade instruments; dances that ranged from the rhythmic slapping patterns called juba to the slow sensual gyrations known as bamboula. Benjamin Latrobe, writing in 1819, described one such slow dance: two women, each holding the end of an outstretched kerchief, swayed slowly to the rhythm, "hardly moving their feet or bodies."

The Congo Square events ended before the Civil War, probably in the mid-1840s, by which time few young slaves had personal recollections of Africa. The important thing is that they were permitted to continue as long as they did—a consequence, argues writer Jerah Johnson, of a large African population, abiding tolerance on the part of the French, the proximity of the Caribbean, and the remoteness from other major cities in the United States. Here, African music enjoyed an untrammeled exposure that assured it a role in the developing culture of New Orleans.

The same tolerance that allowed the Congo Square exhibitions influenced racial dynamics in New Orleans before and after the Civil War. North of the Gulf of Mexico, race was divided into two distinct legal spheres—black and white. Anyone within the wide spectrum of browns, tans, and beiges (literally anyone believed to possess a "single drop" of black blood) was technically considered "black," whether slave or free, and forced to live on that side of the racial division. The Caribbean world took a more pragmatic view. While continuing to enforce a barbarous society in which whites owned blacks, it acknowledged a mulatto culture and allowed that culture an intermediary social status, to the benefit of free blacks with lighter skins.

New Orleans adhered to that mulatto conception of race, producing a caste of mixed-race Negroes known as Creoles of Color. (The full description was *les gens de couleur libres*, or free people of color.) These Creoles—usually the result of black and French or black and Spanish alliances—evolved into a significant social group that was accorded many legal and social liberties. By 1860, they had acquired civic power and are thought to have owned about $15 million in New Orleans property. Some even participated in the slave trade. Most Creoles had French surnames, spoke French as well as English, attended Catholic churches, enjoyed a decent education, and worked at skilled trades—cigar making, cobbling, carpentry—that Creoles, as a group, virtually monopolized.

Their superior standing began to dissipate after the Civil War, when Reconstruction generated an increasingly intolerant racism. In 1894, Louisiana and other Southern states adopted the "Jim Crow" laws, which imposed and enforced a rigid color line. Two years later, the U.S. Supreme Court issued its infamous verdict in *Plessy v. Ferguson*, deciding against a light-skinned man (one-eighth black and seven-eighths white) who had insisted on his right to ride a streetcar in the area reserved for whites. When he lost that case, which essentially legalized segregation, the Creoles lost the last threads of their shabby aristocracy.

As their social standing fell, the Creoles, who had not lost their pride, attempted to reserve a geographical separateness from the "corn and field Negroes" pouring into New Orleans from the countryside. For a time, the dividing line was Canal Street, a large thoroughfare that begins at the Mississippi Riverfront and provides a western border for the French Quarter, home to most of the Creoles. On the other side of Canal, moving upward on the river, was the area known as Uptown, which included some of the grimmest neighborhoods in the United States. Each side had its own musical tradition; yet as Jim Crow forced the integration between Creoles and "black blacks," the two traditions collided.

The Uptown Negroes, largely uneducated and unskilled, played a loud, upbeat, impassioned music combining elements of late-nineteenth-century marching bands, ragtime, and folk music with an ad-libbed and often idiosyncratic vitality. Many could not read music, and "faked" their performances by relying on an oral tradition that employed variable intonation (blue notes), rhythmic contrast, and improvisation. To Creoles, who were educated in the European manner and favored a more genteel approach, they failed to meet the minimum standards of professional musicianship.

As long as the Creoles remained on top, socially and musically, they landed the better-paying jobs, and were able to augment their incomes through teaching. However, their students included black Uptown players as well as downtown Creoles, and the bringing together of these two groups ultimately favored the Uptown musicians, who were onto something new: an artistry relying on improvisation, quick thinking, the ability to blend with other improvising musicians, and a rhythmic sharpness that appealed to dancers and listeners. For its part, Creole music contributed French quadrilles, Spanish habaneras, and an insistence on high professional standards.

We can see a microcosm of the Creole role by looking at one of the more notable careers that figured in this cultural mix. Manuel Perez (1878–1946) was born in New Orleans, attended a French-speaking grammar school, trained as a cigar maker (his father's profession), and studied classical music, focusing on the cornet. He soon established a local reputation, and throughout his teen years played with marching bands, dance bands, and ragtime bands, all requiring written music.

For thirty years, beginning at the dawn of the new century, Perez worked with and led the Onward Brass Band, an ensemble with as many as a dozen musicians and a great favorite at picnics along Lake Pontchartrain and at the downtown dance halls. He also led small groups, including one that played on riverboats. Dozens of musicians came under his influence, whether they worked with him or took individual lessons (for which he is said to have refused payment)—among them, clarinetists Albert Nicholas and Barney Bigard, trumpeter Natty Dominique, and drummer Paul Barbarin. The jazz guitarist Danny Barker remembered Perez as "the idol of the downtown Creole colored people. To them, nobody could master the cornet like Mr. Perez." Jelly Roll Morton considered him the finest trumpeter in New Orleans (until the advent of a young jazz player, Freddie Keppard), but noted that he was a Creole from a good family and played "strictly rag time"—syncopated music, but with no improvisation.

Perez himself realized that improvisation, as practiced by the Uptown musicians, was essential for a successful band in the 1910s, and he hired Joe Oliver (the future King Oliver) as his band's improviser. Despite his prodigious technique, though, Perez found it increasingly difficult to find work for his kind of parade music, and in 1937 he returned full time to cigar making until his death nine years later. Some thought that he resented the historical fixation on Uptown jazz at the expense of the Creole contribution, while others said that he was simply uncomfortable with English-speaking interviewers. (He gave his only interview to a French writer.) He had lived to see the kind of parade music at which he excelled reduced to a tourist attraction and jazz transfigured into a worldwide phenomenon that no one in 1910 could have imagined. Significantly, Manny Perez was born fifteen months after the Uptown cornetist and bandleader Charles Joseph Bolden.

Buddy Bolden (1877–1931) AND THE BIRTH OF JAZZ

In the realm of jazz myths, no one stands taller or blows louder than King Buddy Bolden. Some frequently reported "facts" about Bolden are simply untrue: that he attended the exhibitions in Congo Square (they ceased thirty years before he was born), that he owned a barbershop (he worked as a plasterer until he turned to music), and that he edited a scandal sheet called *The Cricket* (no such journal existed). What remains, however, is a myth that astutely connects Bolden's superlative musicianship with the racial realities of turn-of-the-century New Orleans. Bolden is generally acknowledged as the first important musician in jazz, and his rise to fame directly augurs the triumph of African American culture.

Bolden was born in New Orleans, and took up the cornet in his middle or late teens. He began working at parades and other functions in 1895, and turned to music full time in 1901 or 1902. Fighting alcoholism and depression, he suffered a mental breakdown in 1906, and was incarcerated in the state hospital for the insane, where he remained until his death in 1931. His career as musician and bandleader lasted no more than eleven years, in which time he earned the respect of almost every black and Creole musician in the city (few whites were aware of him), as well as a large public following.

The most frequent boasts concerning Bolden's prowess relate to the loudness of his playing and the snake-charmer seductiveness of his approach to slow blues. Jelly Roll Morton claimed that "on a still night," Bolden's cornet could be heard as far away as twelve miles, the distance between the Mississippi Riverfront and Lake Pontchartrain. On the stillest of nights, that would not be possible. Yet it is a fact that Bolden would sometimes step outside the hall his band was working and play a few phrases to attract customers in adjacent neighborhoods. He often played in Johnson Park, a fenced picnic and baseball grounds directly across the road from the theatrical complex in Lincoln Park, where his primary Creole rival, the Joseph Robichaux Orchestra, performed. By blowing his horn in the direction of Lincoln Park, he attracted audiences who preferred his livelier, raunchier brand of music.

The unmistakable implication of these stories is that Bolden was not only loud, but also distinctive in timbre and attack. Other musicians of his generation, like Manny Perez, were remembered for their overall musicianship, the bright clarity of their sound. Only Bolden is consistently recalled in terms of a personal style—establishing him as the first figure whose individuality was a decisive element, the first for whom the "how you do it" is more important than the "what you do." That made him the first jazz celebrity: the father figure on which the New Orleans story (and by extension, the jazz story) is grounded. Combine that distinction with the brevity of his career, the excesses he indulged, his competitive spirit and Pied Piper charisma, and we have a template for American jazz and popular music legends from Bix Beiderbecke, Charlie Parker, and John Coltrane to Elvis Presley, Jimi Hendrix, and Kurt Cobain.

Did Bolden invent jazz? We can't know for certain, but a qualified yes seems reasonable. He was the only musician in that era commonly regarded as an innovator of the new kind of music that evolved into jazz. Eyewitnesses to the musical life of New Orleans at the dawn of the twentieth century fail to cite a precursor to Bolden, or a significant rival to him during his glory days. Even the incurably boastful Jelly Roll Morton recalled Bolden, respectfully, as a stand-alone figure of mythic resonance.

By all accounts, Bolden was the kind of artist on whom little is lost, and he arrived at the right time, amid a musical cornucopia in which schooled and unschooled musicians worked together to provide a broad range of functional music—for picnics, concerts, dances, funerals, parades, and publicity events. Bolden, who could read music (he had studied with a neighbor), played in every kind of setting. The demand for music was so

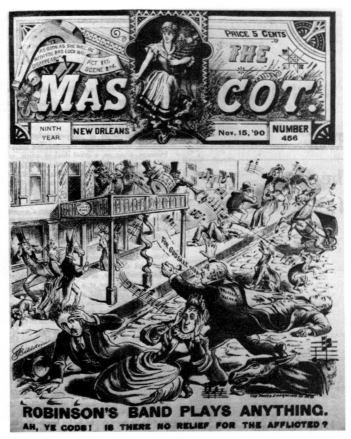

An 1890 issue of the *New Orleans Mascot* depicts white citizens pleading for mercy as a black band, hired to advertise a museum, performs some kind of new, raucous music without the aid of sheet music.

great that musicians were obliged to devise ways to perform that were not reliant on written scores.

In this respect, it's worth looking at a notorious illustration that appeared on the cover of the weekly newspaper the *New Orleans Mascot* in November 1890, five years before Bolden ever performed in public. It depicts four Negro musicians, three playing brass instruments and one a bass drum, all wearing top hats and producing a raucous music that has the power to send the white citizens into a panic, cupping their ears, swooning in pain, imploring the band to stop, or fainting dead away. The musicians, who have no music stands, are performing on a balcony as a publicity stunt, to attract customers to Robinson's Dime Museum; an accompanying editorial attacks Robinson for inflicting such cacophony on the city. Is the band playing something we might recognize as jazz? We can't know, but three things are clear: the musicians are Uptown blacks, not trained Creoles; the music is unusual enough to provoke outrage and confusion; and it is performed without sheet music. Whatever they played was part of an incomparable musical mix in turn-of-the-century New Orleans. Musicians who worked in parades (brass bands) by day and in saloons and dance halls by night had to master the technical know-how required for the former as well as the looser, earthier, ad-lib style necessary for the latter.

Of the musicians who did both, Bolden was the one everyone talked about and remembered. Pops Foster, a jazz bassist, saw him once as a young man and characterized his blues repertory as "stink" music, emphasizing its funky or low-down quality. George Baquet, a Creole clarinetist, recalled seeing Bolden once at the Odd Fellows and Masonic Hall—a "plenty tough" place where customers kept their hats on and interacted with the music through encouraging shouts or sexually provocative dancing. Suddenly Bolden stomped his foot, marked a few beats by banging his cornet on the floor, and began playing the rowdy ballad "Make Me a Pallet on the Floor":

♦ ♦ ♦

Everybody got up quick, the whole place rose and yelled out, "Oh, Mr. Bolden, play it for us, Buddy, play it!" I never heard anything like that before. I'd played "legitimate" stuff. But this! It was somethin' that pulled me! They got me up on the stand that night, and I was playing with them. After that, I didn't play "legitimate" so much.

♦ ♦ ♦

One tune frequently associated with Bolden was called "Funky Butt" or, more politely, "Buddy Bolden's Blues," a melody played by Bolden at an insinuatingly slow tempo, almost a crawl, inviting improvised (often risqué) lyrics with plenty of space for seductive cornet effects. Other pieces he played that have remained a part of jazz include "Tiger Rag," "Didn't He Ramble," "Panama," "Careless Love," and "Bucket's Got a Hole in It." He also performed spirituals ("Ride On, King Jesus," "Go Down, Moses"), sentimental pop fare ("Home, Sweet Home"), and waltzes. A trombonist of the period, Bill Matthews, suggested the diversity of Bolden's repertory:

♦ ♦ ♦

He was one of the sweetest trumpet players on waltzes and things like that and on those old slow blues, that boy could make the women jump out the window. On those old, slow, low down blues, he had a moan in his cornet that went all through you, just like you were in church or something. Everybody was crazy about Bolden when he'd blow a waltz, schottische, or old low down blues.

✦ ✦ ✦

Although Bolden played in different venues, legend invariably ties him to the saloons in or near Storyville, or "the district," as New Orleans locals called it—a zone of legalized prostitution nicknamed for Sidney Story, the alderman who wrote the bill that brought it into existence. Some of the women working in Storyville were housed in elaborate mansions, proudly depicted on city postcards and operated by renowned madams, but most labored in brutal and disease-ridden shacks.

A pernicious myth links jazz to Storyville, according to which jazz musicians were happily employed by brothels until 1917, when the murder of four sailors on shore leave caused the federal government to shut down the district. Yet except for a few pianists, jazz musicians didn't play in bordellos. Many worked in cabarets within Storyville's precincts, but they found much of their work in parks, excursions, parades, advertising wagons, riverboats, and dances throughout the city. The dismantling of Storyville had little effect on the exodus of jazz musicians from New Orleans, which had begun as early as 1907. As Danny Barker remarked, "You never had to figure on getting work in the district, so it wasn't so important when it closed."

Still, it would be a mistake to dismiss Storyville as a factor in the development of New Orleans jazz. The very funkiness of its saloons undoubtedly contributed to the adoption of rhythmic blues as a central part of the repertory, along with expressive techniques that emphasized the music's seductive passion. The achingly slow "snake-hips" dancing encouraged by Bolden and the "talkative" timbre later introduced by King Oliver likely found more traction in this environment than at other social events. In rough precincts like Storyville, where white social arbiters did not breathe down their necks, musicians could explore their bonds with dancers and listeners, and let loose with the kind of artistic transgression typical of outcast communities.

At his peak, Bolden led several different bands, depending on the kind of music required. His best-known jazz ensemble, in place by 1905, consisted of his cornet, a valve trombonist, two clarinetists, a guitarist, a bassist, and a drummer. On occasion, he added a second cornet—some said this was because he was drinking and needed a reliable backup player.

Whatever the motivation, Bolden's use of two cornets would enjoy a historic payoff nearly two decades later in King Oliver's Creole Jazz Band. By the time Oliver began to establish himself, Bolden had been hospitalized as alcoholic and schizophrenic. When he died in 1931, jazz was on the verge of international acclaim, but King Bolden probably know nothing about it. Except in New Orleans, where old-timers still reminisced about him, he was long forgotten.

NEW ORLEANS STYLE

In the decade from Bolden's heyday until the success of recorded jazz in 1917, New Orleans musicians continued to develop their own distinctive style. We can't know precisely what their music sounded like, but by extrapolating backward from later recordings, and by drawing information from photographs and interviews, it's possible to offer a general portrait of early New Orleans jazz. Its instrumentation derived from two sources. Brass band societies, which spawned smaller dance groups, gave the music its melody instruments: trumpet or cornet, trombone, and clarinet. Together, these instruments are called the front line, reflecting their position at the head of a marching band. (Fans who loyally followed a parade band came to be known as the second line.) Brass bands also, inadvertently, fostered the drum set, combining the elements of parade percussion—bass drum, snares, cymbals. The other source was string ensembles, which featured violin, banjo, mandolin, and other instruments—including guitar and bass, which became indispensable to the jazz rhythm section. The piano began to find a stable role in jazz bands with the advent of ragtime.

Originally, the earliest New Orleans bands also included a lead violinist, whose job was to play the melody straight, without improvisation or ornamentation. Against this, the cornet probably improvised a syncopated or ragged version of the melody. By 1917, the cornet had simply displaced the violinist, offering the tune in a more compact, spontaneous form, while the clarinet played a countermelody to *him*—an improvised accompaniment (mostly in eighth notes) that danced around and between the sharply articulated cornet notes. When the Creole influence was still prominent, the clarinet part was often drawn directly from published arrangements; an immortal phrase from the march "High Society," mastered by virtually every New Orleans clarinetist (and many other musicians, too) originated as a written obbligato for piccolo. As clarinetists learned to create their own lines, they drew increasingly from the underlying chord progressions.

Similarly, the trombone originally played parts written for cello or baritone horn, but soon found its own role in filling out the ensemble. The trombone played fewer notes than the clarinet, many of them exaggerated slurs or glissandos facilitated by the slide. (Musicians called this tailgate trombone; when bands toured the streets in a horse-drawn wagon, the trombonist sat in front on the tailgate, to minimize the risk of his slide cracking another musician's skull.)

By the time they began recording, New Orleans bands had already attained an unmistakable ensemble style. Instead of featuring a stand-out soloist like Bolden, the front line improvised a dense, polyphonic texture—a collective improvisation, with each instrument occupying its own musical space (clarinet on top, cornet in the middle, trombone at the bottom), rhythm (clarinet is fastest, trombone slowest), and timbre. Collective improvisation was not the only texture in New Orleans jazz. During the trio section of a piece, the band often played in block-chord texture or, more rarely, presented a single horn plus accompaniment. Breaks and stop-time gambits were common and necessary, revving up the pleasure for audience and band alike. Extended solos, however, were rare. In this sense, New Orleans jazz stabilized the folk aspect of music, in which the group almost always subsumes the individual. This was especially true of the rhythm section, which provided a steady, unrelenting pulse.

Formally, New Orleans bands usually relied on ragtime-type compositions with multiple strains. At the beginning of a number, each strain would be repeated only once before moving to a new strain with its own harmonic progression. The trio offered a point of contrast: modulating to a new key, dynamic level, or texture. The musicians' performances were tied to the composition, with little opportunity to break loose from it to play improvisations (solo or collective). Only toward the end, when the band had hit a groove with itself and with the audience that no one wanted to stop, would a strain be repeated with various embellishments, until the leader called a halt. Greater improvisational freedom came with the twelve-bar blues, but even blues tunes were often arranged to include contrasting sections, suggesting the shape and complexity of a ragtime piece.

THE GREAT MIGRATION

Jazz began to leave New Orleans in the years of the Great Migration, the largest internal relocation of people in the history of the United States. It started in the late nineteenth century, when former slaves began to drift away from their agricultural labors toward cities like New Orleans. With the coming of the First World War, the movement became a torrent, as blacks pushed northward and ended up isolated in the ghettos of Chicago and New York.

The migration, a long time coming, was inevitable. Very few Southern blacks owned land. Under the system of sharecropping, black farmers would work a plot of land, relying on white landowners for plow, seed, housing, and provisions. At year's end, the two sides would "share" the proceeds, though whites routinely manipulated the accounting to leave black families permanently in debt. They were living a life of agricultural peonage, while enduring, at every turn, reminders of their second-class status. They were forced to use segregated transportation, waiting rooms, water fountains, lavatories, doorways, stairways, and theaters, as well as schools and housing. Politically powerless, they were subject to the double standards of white laws. Outside the law, the iniquity extended to murder and torture.

We don't know precisely how many blacks were brutalized and killed in the years between Reconstruction and the Second World War, but more than 3,400 lynchings are documented, and thousands more people simply disappeared. No one was arrested for these crimes, despite photographic evidence of participants (including postcards made as souvenirs). The federal government refused to intervene with legislation. The nation's first anti-lynch activist, Ida B. Wells-Barnett, herself the daughter of slaves, estimated in 1900 that as many as 10,000 blacks had been murdered in the latter part of the nineteenth century alone.

The issue was decided by economics. The United States entered the First World War, in 1917, on the heels of Henry Ford's introduction of the automobile assembly line, producing a crisis in the labor market of Northern industrial cities. The war snatched millions of men away from the workforce, and put a hold on immigration. The manpower shortage was so severe that railroads paid fares to encourage blacks to move. Newspapers like the black-owned *Chicago Defender* encouraged Southerners to leave by listing the contact numbers of people in churches and other organizations who would provide them with financial help. Agricultural interests in the South tried to stop the exodus through intimidation (they delayed travelers until their trains left and disregarded prepaid tickets). But they could not defeat the lure of decent wages and a more humane way of life.

JAZZ MOVES ON: FIRST RECORDINGS

Foremost among the black pioneers seeking to escape the South were entertainers—in minstrel troupes, tent shows, bands, and vaudeville. The bassist Bill Johnson, who had been playing in New Orleans bands as early as 1900, was the first to bring a small ensemble, soon known as the Original Creole Band, to the West Coast, in 1908. Johnson had taken bands through Mississippi, Texas, Arizona, and New Mexico before heading for Los Angeles, and then north to Oakland and San Francisco. In 1914, in anticipation of a high-profile tour, he sent to New Orleans for the brilliant cornetist Freddie Keppard, perhaps the first major jazz figure to travel widely.

A hard-drinking, overweight, and temperamental man, Keppard (1890–1933) had led a band with standard New Orleans instrumentation in 1909, and was acclaimed as Bolden's successor. He perfected an aggressive, gruff, at times snarling attack matched by genuine improvisational facility. Sidney Bechet said, "He played practically the same way as Buddy Bolden, but he *really* played!" Keppard quickly became the Creole Band's star attraction, performing in vaudeville theaters in Los Angeles, Chicago, New York, and places in-between—all before 1917. His importance lies in his impact in bringing New Orleans jazz to the rest of the country, and in setting an example for other musicians, including Jelly Roll Morton.

By the time he finally made some records in the 1920s, Keppard had apparently lost much of his technique. He may also have lost the chance to make the first jazz record. In 1916, the Victor Talking Machine Company invited him to make test discs to see how jazz sounded on records. Keppard refused, reportedly because he didn't want to document his music for others to steal. (He was said to play with a handkerchief over his hand so other musicians couldn't see his fingering.) Consequently, the distinction of making the first jazz records went to a white New Orleans group: the Original Dixieland Jazz Band.

◆ ◆ ◆

Spell it Jass, Jas, Jaz or Jazz—nothing can spoil a Jass band. Some say the Jass band originated in Chicago. Chicago says it comes from San Francisco—San Francisco being away off across the continent. Anyway a Jass band is the newest thing in the cabarets, adding greatly to the hilarity thereof.

◆ ◆ ◆

Reading this excerpt from Victor's publicity sheet for the all-white Original Dixieland Jazz Band (ODJB), we may surmise that "jazz"—at the dawn of the "Jazz Age"—was often misspelled, that some people did not know the location of San Francisco, and that no one had heard about New Orleans, though all five members of the ODJB were natives of that city. The reason for Victor's interest was that the band had come to New York to play at Reisenweber's Restaurant in January 1917, causing a sensation. It was the talk of the town, and the record industry wanted some of the action.

Victor's rival, Columbia Records, had actually been first off the bench, but required the band to record a test of two pop songs, which the label then rejected as cacophony and refused to release. Within weeks, Victor signed the band and produced a double-sided blockbuster: "Livery Stable Blues" / "Dixie Jass Band One-Step." Columbia then rushed its "test" into stores, and sold hundreds of thousands of copies. To most listeners, the ODJB had no equal. Many ragtime records had preceded those of the ODJB (from as far back as 1897), and elements of jazz can be detected in records made between 1914 and 1916 by such African American performers as Bert Williams, James Reese Europe, and Wilbur Sweatman, as well as the white "Mammy singer" Al Jolson. But those elements—robust rhythms or embellishments beyond written ragtime—merely hint at the real thing. The ODJB *was* the real thing, a musical eruption genuinely new to the market.

A vital aspect of New Orleans at the turn of the century was that many neighborhoods were integrated. White musicians were soon attracted to ragtime and to jazz, although they don't seem to have had much early influence on the development of the New Orleans style. There were important white ragtime players, composers, and teachers who undoubtedly influenced black jazz musicians in terms of repertory, harmony, and instrumental technique, but they don't figure in written or oral accounts of the evolution of jazz. The widely imitated five-piece instrumentation of the Original Dixieland Jazz Band, for example, originated with Freddie Keppard.

Yet the white New Orleans jazz tradition is significant in its own right. The commonly accepted father of white jazz was a parade drummer named George "Papa Jack" Laine, who led the Reliance Band in the late nineteenth and early twentieth centuries. Unlike Bolden, who was four years his junior, Papa Jack discouraged improvisation; nevertheless, he trained many young men who took jazz north, including trombonists Tom Brown (who brought the first white jazz band to Chicago in 1915) and George Brunies (who made his name with the New Orleans Rhythm Kings, an influential white band, musically superior to the ODJB), as well as most members of the ODJB. By the time the ODJB began to play in New York, its members included cornetist Nick LaRocca, trombonist Eddie Edwards, clarinetist Larry Shields, pianist Henry Ragas, and drummer Tony Sbarbaro.

So great was the band's initial popularity that it established the word "jazz" as part of the international vocabulary—a term, like "okay," that requires no translation anywhere in the world. Some older musicians would continue to call their music ragtime or New Orleans music, but the die had been cast. Within five years, dozens of bands had appropriated the word. (Originally, it was "jass," but the spelling was changed after vandals repeatedly crossed out the J on the ODJB's billboards and posters.) Hotels throughout Europe began to hire what they called jazz bands (basically any kind of dance ensemble that had drums and at least one reed instrument). The 1920s would always be remembered as the Jazz Age.

The ODJB has taken a bad rap in jazz history. True, its individual musicians were not especially talented, and the band freely indulged in vaudeville antics (such as barnyard imitations on "Livery Stable Blues"), but so did Jelly Roll Morton, and it seems unfair to single out the ODJB for courting the audience or attempting comedy. Compared with later records by King Oliver, the New Orleans Rhythm Kings, and Morton, the ODJB often sounds hokey and insincere. An embittered LaRocca did not help the band's reputation by making racist and self-serving remarks in later years. Still, the ODJB played a spirited, unpretentious music, and served jazz well in several ways: its tunes became Dixieland standards; its name signaled a break with a musical past called ragtime; and a visit the band made to Europe in 1919 helped make jazz international. After its European tour, however, the band lost its verve, and finally called it quits in 1922, just in time for Jelly Roll Morton and King Oliver to redefine New Orleans jazz for all time.

"DIXIE JASS BAND ONE-STEP"

"Dixie Jass Band One-Step," a lastingly popular Dixieland tune, retains ragtime's multistrain form; at the same time, the musicians burst through with their embellishments—especially the clarinetist and the drummer, and particularly in the third strain (or trio). From the opening, which juxtaposes sharp staccato chords with collective improvisation, to its triumphant conclusion, this music is very well organized, though it creates the illusion of carefree artlessness.

The trio is the most famous part of the piece, borrowed from one of the leading rags of the day ("That Teasin' Rag," written by pianist Joe Jordan in 1909) and sometimes played alone. It's a thirty-two-bar chorus, played three times. But because the chorus is made up of two similar sixteen-bar sections, we get a sense that the ensemble is playing the same melody six times, and growing increasingly rowdy with each repeat. In 1917, this out-pouring of energy, underscored by repetition, had no parallel in recorded music—and it struck listeners as either exciting and optimistic or unruly and subversive. The Victor engineers did a remarkable job in capturing the sounds of the instruments, including the drummer's cymbal and wood-blocks. The instrumentation allows us to hear polyphonic details as clarinet and trombone swirl around the cornet lead.

DIXIE JASS BAND ONE-STEP

Original Dixieland Jazz Band

Nick LaRocca, cornet; Eddie Edwards, trombone; Larry Shields, clarinet; Henry Ragas, piano; Tony Sbarbaro, drums

LABEL: Victor 18255; *75th Anniversary* (Bluebird/RCA 61098-2)
DATE: 1917
STYLE: New Orleans jazz
FORM: march/ragtime

Strain A

0:00	**a**	The band opens with forceful tonic chords, surrounded by a brief silence.
0:03		A dramatic outburst (a loud trombone glissando, a clarinet shriek) is fol-lowed by a cymbal crash.
0:04		The band breaks into a short polyphonic passage of collective improvisation.
0:08	**a**	The material from 0:00 to 0:08 is repeated.

Strain B

0:16	**b**	A clarinet break introduces the next strain, which modulates to a new key.
0:18		The band follows with a longer passage of collective improvisation.
0:23	**b'**	The clarinet break returns, followed again by collective improvisation.
0:28		The strain comes to a full cadence on the tonic.

Strain A

0:31	Strain **A** is repeated.

Strain B
....

0:46   Strain **B** is repeated.

Strain C (trio)

1:01   c   The trio modulates to yet another key. While the trumpet plays the main
              melody, the clarinet plays a faster countermelody and the trombone
              adds glissandos.
1:09   The drummer adds strong counterrhythms on a woodblock (one of
              the few parts on the drum set easily captured by acoustic recording
              equipment).
1:16   The clarinet marks the first sixteen bars with a high note.
1:17   c′
1:25   As we approach the final cadence, the harmonies begin to change.
1:31   A loud, raucous note on the cornet signals a repetition of the trio.

Strain C
....

1:33   c   As the band repeats the trio, the drummer increases the intensity of the
              polyrhythm.
1:48   c′
1:53   The drummer plays two powerful strokes on the bass drum.
1:56   The clarinet's line often sounds like a shriek.
2:02   Another repetition is signaled by the cornet's note, played alongside a
              clarinet squeal.

Strain C
....

2:03   c   The band plays the trio one last time.
2:18   c′   The drummer signals the second half by hitting the bass drum, followed
              by a cymbal crash.
2:26   The drummer finally uses the full drum set, adding military-style rolls on
              the snare drum and driving the band toward the conclusion.

Coda
....

2:34   The band adds a four-note coda, a common Jazz Age ending.

Jelly Roll Morton (1890–1941)

The development of jazz may be viewed as an ongoing alliance between
improvisers and composers: soloists who spontaneously create music and
writers who organize frameworks for them. They influence each other,
much as Creoles and Uptown blacks did. So it's fitting that the first great

jazz composer was a Creole who endured expulsion from his family in order to learn from and eventually work with the kind of musicians epitomized by Buddy Bolden. Jelly Roll Morton's genius is extensively documented on records: his legacy is not a matter of speculation, unlike Bolden's—though it, too, is encrusted in myths, chiefly of Morton's own devising.

One of the most colorful characters in American music, Morton worked as a bordello pianist, pimp, pool hall hustler, and comedian before establishing himself as a fastidious musician and recording artist—a pianist, singer, composer, arranger, and music theorist. He was also a diamond-tooth dandy, insufferable braggart, occultist, and memoirist. Morton engraved his most infamous boast on his business card: "Originator of jazz - stomp - swing." He claimed that he had invented jazz in 1902, giving his own date of birth as 1885. In fact, New Orleans baptismal records indicate that he was born Ferdinand Joseph Lamothe in 1890. His proud family traced its lineage back to Haiti, and he apparently inherited a strain of arrogance and standoffishness as well as a lifelong fear of voodoo: in his later years, he paid much of his earnings to a practitioner in hope of lifting a curse.

Morton recognized early on that a French surname would be a liability on the show business circuit, so he changed his to an anglicized version of his stepfather's name, Mouton, claiming that he didn't want to be called "Frenchy." A born hustler, he talked himself in and out of work, alienating many in the jazz world of the 1920s, including Duke Ellington, who dismissed him as a boaster. If Morton didn't exactly invent jazz, he certainly helped to define it, propelling the New Orleans style forward at a time when no one knew precisely what jazz was.

Morton studied guitar and trombone before focusing on piano at age ten. His family disowned him when he began sneaking out to the honkytonks in Storyville to hear the vibrant new music. He ran errands for a singer-pianist named Mamie Desdumes just to learn her trademark blues, and he credited his education in the district for his ability to live in style when he left New Orleans and traveled through Memphis, Jacksonville, St. Louis, Kansas City, Chicago, and California, assimilating new musical approaches and combining them with the dances (habaneras, quadrilles), operas, military music, and jazz he had learned at home.

Morton was thirty-two when he settled in Chicago, in 1922. He made his first records a year later, derivative exercises overwhelmed by loud woodblocks. In July 1923, however, he spent two afternoons at the ramshackle Gennett Records studio in Richmond, Indiana, recording with the talented white hometown band, the New Orleans Rhythm Kings—this was the first significant integrated recording session in jazz history. At these sessions, Morton debuted a few of his tunes, the best of which show how he took the multiple-themes structure and syncopated rhythms of ragtime to a new level, emphasizing a foot-tapping beat (he called it a stomp) and tricky syncopations. One of them was "King Porter Stomp," which has four sections, the last of which became a major anthem of the Swing Era.

Over the next few years, Morton achieved success as a songwriter, earning royalties from sheet music sales or selling the rights outright. Hoping to increase interest in his published tunes, Morton's publisher helped convince the Victor Talking Machine Company to offer him a contract. He began recording with ensembles of seven and eight players in the fall of 1926, at the very moment that Victor switched from acoustic to electrical technology, giving his recordings a vivid fidelity. Morton called his group the Red Hot Peppers, and Victor advertised it as "the Number One Hot Band," although it existed solely to record. To many, the Peppers sessions represent the pinnacle of the New Orleans tradition, an ideal balance between composition and improvisation.

"DEAD MAN BLUES"

"Dead Man Blues" is Morton's interpretation of the New Orleans burial ritual, which he traced back to Scripture: rejoice at the death and cry at the birth. It begins with a scene-setting dialogue in the style of black minstrelsy, a comedic way of announcing Morton's intention to invoke a New Orleans funeral. This leads to the first chorus—each chorus is a twelve-bar blues—in which the musicians collectively embellish a melody in familiar New Orleans style: you can almost see the Grand Marshal leading the mourners, gracefully prancing with his parasol. This particular performance (an alternate take) was rejected by Morton for commercial release, probably owing to the obvious gaffes made by the cornetist during his solo. On this take, however, we can hear a nimble elegance in the collective improvisation that the band failed to capture the second time around.

Morton organized his music scrupulously, going so far as to notate the parts for bass (bass lines are usually improvised, rarely composed), and making the most of his musicians. We are always conscious of each instrument: the tailgate smears of the trombone, the snap of the trumpet, the pretty harmonizing of the clarinets, the clanging rhythm of the banjo. For those who think of New Orleans jazz as genial chaos, with simultaneously improvised melody lines tumbling untidily on top of one another, Morton's music may come as a revelation.

While "Dead Man Blues" is a twelve-bar blues, it's also organized like a tune in march/ragtime form: choruses 1 and 2 correspond to the first strain (A); choruses 3 and 4, played by cornet and rhythm, to the second (B). The fifth and sixth choruses serve as the trio, a section of the piece for which Morton often reserved his most melodic ideas. For this recording, he hired two extra clarinetists to blend with Omer Simeon in playing block-chord harmonies—it's the only time they appear in the performance. In the sixth chorus, Morton introduces another of his trademark devices to increase tension: against the clarinetists' lissome melody, the trombonist Kid Ory plays a countermelody, his spare phrases adding an understated touch of drama.

DEAD MAN BLUES

Jelly Roll Morton and His Red Hot Peppers (alternate take)

Jelly Roll Morton, piano; George Mitchell, cornet; Kid Ory, trombone; Omer Simeon, Barney Bigard, Darnell Howard, clarinets; Johnny St. Cyr, banjo; John Lindsay, bass; Andrew Hilaire, drums

LABEL: Victor 20252; *Birth of the Hot* (RCA/Bluebird 66641)
DATE: 1926
STYLE: New Orleans jazz
FORM: 12-bar blues

Spoken dialogue

0:00   Morton and St. Cyr act out a vaudeville scene, with exaggerated minstrel accents, to prepare us for a New Orleans funeral.

Morton: *"What's that I hear at twelve o'clock in the daytime? Church bells ringing?"*

St. Cyr: *"Oh, man, you don't hear no church bells ringing twelve o'clock in the day."*

Morton: *"Don't tell me—somebody must be dead!"*

St. Cyr: *"Ain't nobody dead. Somebody must be dead drunk."*

Morton: *"Don't tell me, I think there's a fyoo-neral!"*

St. Cyr: *"Well, looky here! I believe I do hear a funeral! I believe I hear that tram-bone blowin'!"*

Introduction

0:18   A trombone glissando introduces a somber march, played by the band
            in block-chord texture. The tune comes from the beginning of the tradi-
            tional hymn "Flee as a Bird to the Mountain," usually performed during
            the procession to the cemetery.

Chorus 1

0:33   Suddenly, as if the funeral ceremony were over, the band swings into a
            faster tempo. The texture is polyphonic, with each instrument contribut-
            ing its individual melodic line to the collective improvisation.

            The bass plays a variety of patterns: the relaxed two-beat pattern at the
            opening adjusts at times to four beats to the bar (0:41) or even eight
            beats to the bar (0:48).

Chorus 2

0:55   Simeon plays a clarinet solo marked by variable intonation (or blue
            notes). Underneath, Morton plays a delicate counterpoint on the piano.

Chorus 3

1:18   Mitchell's cornet solo begins roughly, marred by several obvious errors
            (1:19, 1:27).

1:25   Morton continues to play underneath.

Chorus 4

1:40   As Mitchell continues his solo, he plays with more accuracy and
            confidence.

Chorus 5 (trio)

2:03   Two other clarinets (Bigard and Howard) join Simeon, playing a simple
            melody in block-chord texture. The rhythm section responds to each
            line with a loud accent.

Chorus 6

2:26   As the clarinets repeat their block-chord line, Ory adds a subtle bluesy
            countermelody.

| 2:47 | The trumpet and trombone enter loudly to signal the beginning of the next chorus. |

Chorus 7

| 2:48 | The band improvises polyphonically in a climactic chorus of collective improvisation. |

Coda

| 3:11 | In a witty coda, Morton brings back the clarinet trio, only to cut it short with a final accent by the rhythm section. |

"DOCTOR JAZZ"

The surprisingly raucous "Doctor Jazz," recorded in late 1926, exemplifies the kind of vitality that distinguished American music to the rest of the world—a nearly bumptious optimism found not only in jazz but also in pop music, from the theatrical bravura of songs like the Gershwins' "I Got Rhythm" to the big-beat mayhem of rock and roll. Morton engages the wilder side of New Orleans jazz, and yet the piece is assembled with fastidious attention to detail. The structure is a thirty-two-bar ABAC song (by King Oliver, with whom Morton often performed), providing an ideal map for Morton to navigate between New Orleans jazz and popular song.

Morton employs several jazz techniques to vary the texture and heighten the drama, including stop-time and breaks. "Even if a tune hasn't got a break in it," he advised, "it's always necessary to arrange some kind of spot to make a break." One of the most unusual aspects of the performance is that it begins with the last eight bars of the tune—and a stop-time passage to boot. Stop-time usually appears in the middle of a performance to increase interest; here, Morton grabs you by the lapels with his first blunt chord.

The two most memorable passages are the simplest and most blatant. The second chorus opens with the clarinetist (Simeon) holding a single note for eight bars—not unlike the long note in Louis Armstrong's "West End Blues" (recorded two years later), where the steadiness of a single pitch calls attention to the moving harmonies over which it floats. In this instance, Morton signals the changes on piano. That chorus is a hard act to follow, but Morton finds a way. In the only vocal he recorded at the Red Hot Peppers sessions, he blurts the first syllable—it's not a note so much as a holler, demanding attention. He keeps our attention with his rhythmic displacements (note his phrasing of the line "Ah, the more I get, the more I want it seems"), emphasizing unexpected syllables and exaggerating his vibrato.

DOCTOR JAZZ

Jelly Roll Morton and His Red Hot Peppers

George Mitchell, trumpet; Kid Ory, trombone; Omer Simeon, clarinet; Jelly Roll Morton, piano; Johnny St. Cyr, guitar; John Lindsay, bass; Andrew Hilaire, drums

LABEL: Victor 20415; *Birth of the Hot* (RCA/Bluebird 66641)
DATE: 1926
STYLE: New Orleans jazz
FORM: 32-bar popular song (**ABAC**)

Introduction

0:00		The band begins with the last eight bars of the tune, performed in stop-time: short chords by in the band set up two-bar breaks for the clarinet.
0:03		The clarinet plays a blue note.
0:05		The band responds with collective improvisation.

Chorus 1

0:09	**A**	The overall texture is polyphonic. The muted trumpet paraphrases the melody, while the clarinet improvises beneath him.
0:13		The trombone enters with a melody that responds to the trumpet's statement.
0:19	**B**	The trombone's improvised line forms a counterpoint to the trumpet's melody.
0:29	**A**	
0:38	**C**	

Chorus 2

0:47	**A**	For a full eight bars, Simeon holds a single, unchanging high pitch on clarinet. Underneath, we can hear Morton improvising freely on the harmonies.
0:57	**B**	A cymbal crash cuts Simeon short, returning him to normal improvising.
1:07	**A**	Again, the clarinet holds a single note.
1:12		After another cymbal crash, Simeon slowly descends, following a change in harmony.
1:16	**C**	The band stops playing at the beginning of the measure, leaving the clarinet free to improvise over the guitar's chords.
1:22		At the chorus's end, Simeon retreats to his high note.
1:24		Morton begins to sing, his voice breaking on the opening word, "*Oh!*"

Chorus 3

1:25 **A** *"Oh, hello, Central, give me Doctor Jazz! He's got what I need, I'll say he has."*
Each phrase of Morton's melody is followed by the trumpet and clarinet in collective improvisation.

1:35 **B** *"Oh, when the world goes round, and I've got the blues,*
He's the man that makes me get out a-both my pair of shoes!"

1:44 **A** *"Ah, the more I get, the more I want it seems.*
I page ol' Doctor Jazz in my dreams."
Morton begins each phrase with a powerful growl.

1:54 **C** *"When I'm in trouble, bound and mixed, he's the guy that gets me fixed.*
Hello, Central, give me Doctor Jazz!"
In this stop-time passage, the voice is accompanied only by the steady pulse on the bass drum.

Chorus 4

2:03 **A** A brief phrase of clarinet melody is followed by a composed response, featuring the trombone and trumpet playing in harmony.

2:13 **B** Morton plays a brief (eight bars) piano solo.

2:22 **A** Simeon's clarinet solo is interrupted by two breaks for St. Cyr's guitar.

2:31 **C** Stop-time, featuring first Mitchell's trumpet, then Ory's trombone.

Chorus 5

2:41 **A** For the final chorus, the band plays polyphonically in collective improvisation.

2:51 **B**

3:00 **A** The polyphonic texture is interrupted twice by Simeon's clarinet breaks.

3:09 **C** The stop-time breaks highlight short staccato chords by Morton.

Coda

3:19 The band plays collective improvisation for another two measures.

"Dead Man Blues" and "Doctor Jazz" suggest the opposing sides of Morton's music: a gift for lyricism and a penchant for anarchy. He harnessed the potentially chaotic energy of collective improvisation to meet his own exacting standards, with originality, nuance, and humor—in an era when critical and racial disdain were ever present. As Louis Armstrong once remarked, "No matter how much his diamond sparkled, he still had to eat in the kitchen, the same as we blacks." What Morton's music embodies above all is the raw, restless social energy of the early years of the century, when jazz was a new hustle and the rules had to be made before they could be broken.

By the 1930s, Morton's music was dismissed as hopelessly outdated. In 1938, in a series of Library of Congress interviews with Alan Lomax, he narrated his life, sitting at the piano and playing examples of the musical points he wished to make. When he died in 1941, a revival of interest in New Orleans jazz was just getting underway, too late to help Morton, who was broke and largely ignored or belittled. Only later was he acclaimed as one of the guiding figures of early jazz—an innovatively original, thoughtful, sensitive, and permanent artist.

King Oliver (1885–1938)

If New Orleans jazz started out, in the Bolden era, as local gumbo flavored by the great variety of music available in that city, by 1922 the gumbo was traveled and seasoned. Instrumental mastery had increased, hundreds of new pieces had been written, and the New Orleans style had assimilated flavors of the cities in which it prospered. Jazz had become a fad in the late teens, tricked up with comical routines and instrumental gimmicks. In refusing to cheapen or remodel his music, Joseph "King" Oliver brought New Orleans jazz to an enduring plateau.

Born in an unknown area of Louisiana, Oliver moved to New Orleans in early childhood with his mother, a cook. He did yard work and other menial jobs before turning to music (relatively late in life) around 1905, the peak of Buddy Bolden's reign; after briefly taking up the trombone, he focused on the cornet. He served a long apprenticeship in various brass bands and saloon groups, finally achieving local renown in an orchestra led by trombonist Kid Ory, who billed him as King Oliver in 1917, cementing his place as Bolden's heir. Other trumpeters, notably Freddie Keppard, had called themselves King, but the royal moniker stuck only to Oliver.

He presented quite a sight. Self-conscious about his blind and protruding left eye, the result of a childhood accident (some people called him Popeye), Oliver played seated or leaning against a wall, sporting a derby rakishly angled to cover the affliction, and used an arsenal of objects as mutes to vary his timbre. He would insert or hang over the bell of his horn a rubber plunger, pop bottle, bucket, glass, doorknob, or hat. "He could make his horn sound like a holy-roller meeting," said Mutt Carey, a New Orleans trumpet player who imitated him. Oliver's love of muting devices had an immense influence on jazz, and eventually led to the manufacture of professional mutes. Richard M. Jones, a pianist who later became

an important record producer, recalled Oliver's resourcefulness one night
when his band was playing at a Storyville dance hall called Abadie's and his
rival, Keppard, had drawn a larger crowd across the street at Pete Lala's:

◆ ◆ ◆

I was sitting at the piano and Joe Oliver came over to me and commanded
in a nervous harsh voice "Get in B-flat." He didn't even mention a tune, just
"Get in B-flat." I did, and Joe walked out on the sidewalk, lifted his horn to
his lips, and blew the most beautiful stuff I ever heard. People started pouring out of the other spots to see who was blowing all that horn. Before long
our place was full and Joe came in, smiling, and said "Now that SOB won't
bother me no more." From then on, our place was full every night.

◆ ◆ ◆

The similarity of this story to those told of Bolden is a reminder of the
small community in which jazz continued to mature. In his early years,
Oliver, again like Bolden, organized different bands as required for specific
occasions, from casual socials in the black community to formal affairs at
New Orleans's Tulane University. He could be brusque and ill-tempered,
but he was regarded as honest and loyal, and musicians liked working with
him. In 1918, Oliver moved to Chicago (he played in the band that cheered
the White Sox at the fixed 1919 World Series), and after several years on
the road returned there in 1922 to play at Lincoln Gardens, a swanky,
black-owned nightclub on the Southside (Chicago's black district).

With one exception, Oliver recruited musicians who had come north
from New Orleans: trombonist Honore Dutrey, clarinetist Johnny Dodds,
drummer Warren "Baby" Dodds (Johnny's brother), and bassist and banjoist Bill Johnson (who had founded the Original Creole Band and hired
Oliver when he first arrived in Chicago). The ringer was pianist Lil Hardin, from Memphis by way of Fisk University in Nashville. The band was
an immediate success, but Oliver felt it was missing something. Suffering
from pyorrhea, a disease of the gums, he wanted a second cornetist to
punch up the front line and spell him when his embouchure failed. Weeks
into the job, he cabled New Orleans for twenty-year-old Louis Armstrong
to join him. Oliver had mentored Louis, who later remembered him as a
man who "would stop and show the kids in New Orleans anything they
want to know about their music."

With Armstrong on board, respectfully playing second cornet, the great
ensemble was now complete. King Oliver's Creole Jazz Band attracted
black and white musicians alike, who stopped by when their own engage-

ments were finished. They had never heard anything like it. Nor had they seen a dance hall like Lincoln Gardens, one of the largest nightclubs (it could accommodate a thousand dancers) in the Midwest. A mirrored ball refracted the light over dozens of tables ringing the dance floor, where fans and musicians sat riveted by the band's collective power.

Unlike Morton's Red Hot Peppers band, which existed only in the recording studio, Oliver's Creole Jazz Band played for audiences, including many people who, like him, had moved to Chicago from the South. Oliver had to be responsive to the moods and desires of dancers and listeners alike. Despite its name, his band embodied the ascendancy of the Uptown improvised approach over the Creole written tradition. They performed a rigorously collective music, its most salient characteristic a polyphonic attack similar to the style established, albeit more superficially, by the Original Dixieland Jazz Band.

In April 1923, King Oliver's Creole Jazz Band loaded its instruments into a couple of Model T Fords and traveled the short trip to Richmond, Indiana, to make its first recordings for Gennett Records. Gennett, a rather sainted name in early jazz history, was a small label owned by a firm that manufactured pianos. Gennett had been recording jazz since 1919, but only white bands and not very good ones. With Oliver and Morton, it recognized the commercial potential of music aimed at black audiences. Other labels formed subsidiaries to promote race records, but not Gennett, which saw no reason to segregate its product.

The label's studio was, to say the least, unprepossessing. The squat rectangular building was built a few feet from railroad tracks, which meant frequent disruptions as trains bustled through Richmond. The recording space was a room lined with wood planks. From one wall, a megaphone-shaped horn, about eighteen inches in diameter, jutted out through a black curtain. The musicians had to figure out a way to position themselves around the horn so that the music—traveling through the horn into a stylus (an engraving phonograph needle in the adjoining room), which transmitted the sound onto a lateral disc—would be well balanced. In other words, the only audio mixing they could do was in deciding where to stand. This was the acoustic method of recording. No other method was available in 1923, which is the main reason Oliver's Creole Jazz Band records have always been more difficult to listen to than Morton's electrically recorded 1926 sessions. In 2006, however, recording engineers working with state-of-the-art transfer techniques brought unsuspected detail and vibrancy to these inimitable sessions, which were released as *Off the Record: The Complete 1923 Jazz Band Recordings.*

On these selections, Oliver used two-bar breaks, stop-time choruses, and other devices to vary the texture, but the most memorable moments occur when the entire ensemble builds its head of steam. At first, it may be hard to distinguish between the front-line instruments, but as your ears become accustomed to the sound, you begin to isolate the separate voices—the piping clarinet, the trombone skirting the edges, the two cornets buoying each other. Yet the important thing is not the discrete components, but the marvel of a music in which each instrument contributes to the whole as judiciously as if a master composer had plotted every move, instead of leaving the musicians to spontaneously interact.

A useful introduction to the Gennetts is Oliver's trademark number, "Dippermouth Blues," in part because so much of it is given to solos. After the ensemble plays the theme (a twelve-bar blues), clarinetist Johnny Dodds improvises two choruses over stop-time rhythm played by the rest of the band. Armstrong follows with an open-horn chorus, which serves to introduce Oliver's unmistakably muted sound as he steps forward to play a solo of three choruses. (The other musicians play alongside him in polyphonic texture, but they lower their volume to favor Oliver's improvisation.) The vocal timbre he gets from the mute makes his short phrases particularly pungent—they were widely imitated by other trumpeters. During the Swing Era, Fletcher Henderson orchestrated Oliver's solo as "Sugar Foot Stomp." "Snake Rag" is a more typical performance in that the ensemble is the star performer.

"SNAKE RAG"

As its title warrants, "Snake Rag" is a rag, following the march/ragtime structure of several disparate strains. (Note: Oliver recorded this piece twice: for Gennett in April 1923 and for OKeh Records two months later. The more accomplished OKeh performance is discussed here.) This sly piece, disrupted by an unusual series of pungent two-part breaks, takes its name from Oliver's slang for complicated chromatic lines: he called them "snakes," and the snake here is the descending scale played, unaccompanied, by the dual cornets of Oliver and Armstrong at the end of the A and B strains. The last strain, or trio, is twice as long: thirty-two bars instead of sixteen. The fact that it is played three times in succession contributes to the buildup in excitement and ferment. Yet notice how steady the underlying pulse remains.

During the trio, Oliver and Armstrong play quite different two-bar breaks, accompanied by the trombone. These breaks preserve an aspect of the band's presentation at Lincoln Gardens that had become a signature routine, and a mystery to visiting musicians. They couldn't figure out how the two cornetists managed to harmonize perfectly on apparently ad-libbed passages. Armstrong later explained that seconds before each break, Oliver would mime the fingering of the upcoming part on his cornet, which cued him as to which break they would play. The two examples on this recording are exceptionally expressive, and we can imagine the audience cheering them on.

SNAKE RAG

King Oliver's Creole Jazz Band
King Oliver, Louis Armstrong, trumpets or cornets; Honore Dutrey, trombone; Johnny Dodds, clarinet; Lil Hardin, piano; Bud Scott, banjo; Baby Dodds, drums

LABEL: OKeh 4933; *Off the Record: The Complete 1923 Jazz Band Recordings* (Archeophone ARCH OTR-MM6-C2)
DATE: 1923
STYLE: New Orleans jazz
FORM: march/ragtime

Introduction (strain A, abbreviated)

0:00	The band beings polyphonically, in collective improvisation. Dodds on clarinet drops from a high note to play swirling patterns while Dutrey sticks to a slow, unsyncopated line on the trombone. The two cornets (Armstrong and Oliver) improvise on the main melody.
0:05	Break: the cornets play a "snake"—a steady descending line in harmony.
0:07	Using his slide, the trombone answers with simple, comic glissandos, followed by a pair of chords from the band.

Strain A

0:09	The first strain begins on the I chord. Oliver plays the lead cornet, with Armstrong barely audible behind him.
0:22	The band repeats the snake.

Strain B

0:26	The second strain begins on a different harmony (V).
0:33	In a two-bar break, Dutrey plays three upward trombone glissandos, the last accented by a cymbal crash.
0:40	The band repeats the snake.

Strain B

0:46	Strain **B** is repeated, with slight variation.
0:59	Snake.

Strain A

1:03	Strain **A** is repeated, with more variation.
1:17	Snake.

Strain C (trio)

1:21	With no transition, the tune suddenly modulates to a new key. This strain (trio) lasts twice as long as the previous two. Dutrey plays a trombone line with a distinctive rhythmic profile.

1:37	Dodds fills a break with a descending clarinet line.

Strain C

1:58	Strain **C** is repeated, with considerable variation.
2:13	During a break, Oliver and Armstrong play a bluesy and complex riff.

2:32	Break: St. Cyr sings out in full voice, *"Oh, sweet mama!"*

Strain C

2:34	On this third appearance of strain **C**, the collective improvisation becomes freer and more intense.
2:50	For the final break, the cornets play a new passage, ending with a lengthy blue note.

Coda

3:10	The band tacks on an additional two measures before the cymbal finally cuts them off.

As influential as his music proved to be—Louis Armstrong, Bix Beiderbecke, and Duke Ellington all borrowed from him—Oliver enjoyed only a brief time in the sun. As his gums continued to worsen, he tried to modernize the New Orleans sound with larger ensembles, such as the ten-piece Dixie Syncopators (which included three saxophones), but the arrangements failed to find an audience. Increasingly, he had to delegate the trumpet solos to younger musicians. By 1935, he couldn't play at all; plagued by illness and bad business decisions, he settled in Savannah, Georgia, where he worked as a pool-room janitor and ran a fruit stand. He was broke but not broken when Armstrong ran in to him, in 1938:

◆ ◆ ◆

> He was standing there in his shirtsleeves. No tears. Just glad to see us. Just another day. He had that spirit. I gave him about $150 I had in my pocket, and Luis Russell and Red Allen, Pops Foster, Albert Nicholas, Paul Barbarin—they all used to be his boys—they gave him what they had. And that night we played a dance, and we look over and there's Joe standing in the wings. He was sharp like the old Joe Oliver of 1915. . . . And pretty soon he died—most people said it was a heart attack. I think it was a broken heart.

◆ ◆ ◆

Sidney Bechet (1897–1959)

Sidney Bechet, who played clarinet and soprano saxophone, is widely considered to be the first great improviser in jazz history. During the early years of jazz, when the saxophone was on the margins of this music, playing sweet sounds in a dance orchestra or virtuoso novelties on vaudeville bills, Bechet turned the instrument into one of its leading voices. He was a moody, impassioned man whose tendency toward violence occasionally landed him in jail; but his emotions were imparted in the very timbre of his playing. He was one of the music's first global stars: he spent a good deal of the Jazz Age overseas, and was among the first Americans to perform in the Soviet Union in the 1920s.

Bechet was born in New Orleans to a musical Creole family. Although primarily self-taught on the clarinet, he was also instructed by a few renowned Creole teachers, including George Baquet, who heard him playing on a street corner and took him under his wing. As a young man, Bechet played in every important marching band in the city, occasionally doubling on cornet. In 1916, he left to travel with touring bands; one took him up to Chicago, where, three years later, he attracted the attention of Will Marion Cook (1869–1944). A classically trained violinist and conductor (and protégé of Antonin Dvořák), Cook made his name as a songwriter and composer. In later years, he organized the first concerts in New York devoted exclusively to black composers, including jazz musicians. When they met, Cook was about to take his Southern Syncopated Orchestra to London, and he recruited Bechet—a momentous decision on two counts.

In London, Bechet purchased a straight (no bell curve) soprano saxophone, the instrument with which he ultimately made his mark. He also played clarinet in several prestigious halls with Cook's orchestra (they appeared before King George V), inspiring the first serious essay written about jazz. This lengthy review, by the conductor Ernest Ansermet, singled out "an extraordinary clarinet virtuoso who is, so it seems, the first of his race to have composed perfectly formed blues on the clarinet." He concluded:

◆ ◆ ◆

I wish to set down the name of this artist; as for myself, I shall never forget it—it is Sidney Bechet. When one has tried so often to rediscover in the past one of those figures to whom we owe the advent of our art,—those men of the 17th and 18th centuries, for example, who made expressive works of dance airs, clearing the way for Haydn and Mozart who mark, not the starting point, but the first milestone—what a moving thing it is to meet this very black, fat boy with white teeth and that narrow forehead, who is very glad one likes what he does, but who can say nothing of his art, save that he follows his "own way," and when one thinks that his "own way" is perhaps the highway the whole world will travel tomorrow.

◆ ◆ ◆

Bechet's fellow musicians were no less in awe of him. At one performance, Cook's wife, Abby Mitchell, sang an aria from Puccini's *Madame Butterfly*, and Bechet, without warning (and drawing on his own childhood love for opera), left his seat, walked over to her, and improvised an accompaniment. He expected to be rebuked or fired, but after she finished, Mitchell embraced him with tears in her eyes and said, "Ah, Sidney, only you could have done it like that."

By the time Cook left England, Europe had taken American Negro music to its heart, an affection that would continue throughout the twentieth century. Bechet liked the way he was treated there and, with a contingent of musicians from the Southern Syncopated, decided to stay. He played in both Paris and London, clearing the way for an invasion of black entertainers, but his involvement in a violent argument in London ended with his deportation.

Bechet returned to New York in 1921, and a few years later was hired by yet another legendary musical figure, who was virtually unknown at the time. Duke Ellington later wrote of that encounter, "It was a completely new sound and conception to me." He was referring to Bechet's mastery of the soprano saxophone, a difficult instrument to play in tune, but one with a commanding, piercing sound. The volatile Bechet did not like playing second fiddle to anyone; in jazz, that meant playing clarinet in support of the cornet. With the soprano saxophone, he could dominate any ensemble. What's more, he had begun to think of himself not as a member of a fixed group but as a virtuoso soloist—a new category of which he was perhaps the prime example.

Unsuited to the rigors of a big band, Bechet soon parted with Ellington and reunited with an old buddy from New Orleans—the pianist, song publisher, and record producer Clarence Williams (1893–1965), who asked him to participate in a series of recordings billed as Clarence Williams's Blue Five. These records document, for the first time, Bechet's extraordinary stylistic maturity. On the first recordings, Williams paired Bechet with an uninspired cornetist, and Bechet ran roughshod over him. But in 1924, Williams hired Louis Armstrong, recently departed from King Oliver's band and already the most admired, in-demand black musician in New York. Bechet rose to the challenge. On their dynamic recording "Cake Walking Babies (from Home)," Bechet is more than a match for Armstrong. He proved to be the only musician of that era who could stand head to head with the younger man—occasionally, as in this instance, standing a bit taller.

"CAKE WALKING BABIES (FROM HOME)"

Recorded in New York, where jazz and Tin Pan Alley pop songs first became inextricably entwined, "Cake Walking Babies (from Home)" combines New Orleans jazz polyphony with the popular music of the day—specifically, a song celebrating the still-remembered rag-era cakewalk. As a song publisher who put his name on songs he may or may not have worked on, Clarence Williams thought of records as a way to boost sheet music sales, and usually included vocal choruses on them to promote words and music. The vocal chorus of "Cake Walking Babies" underscores the high-stepping cheerfulness of this forty-bar song (singer Alberta Hunter went on to enjoy a long career as an entertainer, mixing blues and standards).

The rest of the performance offers a different kind of excitement, as cornet and soprano saxophone transform the usual New Orleans front line into a battle of wits. The first chorus begins with the usual collective improvisation. Bechet seems to anticipate Armstrong's every rest, filling those spaces with melodic figures. This chorus is followed by a statement of the sixteen-bar verse—a seldom-heard contrasting melody used to introduce the chorus. The vocal (second) chorus is accompanied only by banjo and piano, and is lively if dated: it's hard to imagine a singer today performing in this style, whereas the bravura interpretations by Armstrong and Bechet, especially in choruses 3 and 4, would be impressive in any day.

CAKE WALKING BABIES (FROM HOME)

The Red Onion Jazz Babies

Louis Armstrong, cornet; Charlie Irvis, trombone; Sidney Bechet, soprano saxophone; Lil Armstrong, piano; Buddy Christian, banjo; Clarence Todd and Alberta Hunter, vocals

LABEL: Gennett 5627; *Louis Armstrong and King Oliver* (Milestone MCD-47017-2)
DATE: 1924
STYLE: New Orleans jazz
FORM: verse/chorus; chorus is 40-bar popular song (**ABA'CA''**)

Chorus 1

0:00	A	The three horns (Armstrong on cornet, Bechet on soprano saxophone, Irvis on trombone) play in collective improvisation. While Armstrong plays the melodic lead, Bechet competes for attention with his aggressive, fluid improvisation.
0:08	B	
0:17	A'	
0:25	C	Armstrong closely paraphrases the original melody (which we will hear in its entirety at 0:59).
0:34	A''	

Verse

0:42	Armstrong and Bechet loosely paraphrase the original melody; the trombone adds a lively response.
0:47	While Armstrong sticks close to the tune, Bechet improvises with more freedom.

Chorus 2 (song)

0:59	A	Hunter sings the song, harmonized by Todd (his extra lyrics are in parentheses); the two are accompanied by banjo and piano. *"Here they come (oh, here we come!), those strutting syncopators! Going some (oh, going some!), look at those demonstrators!"*
1:08	B	*"Talk of [the] town, Green and Brown, picking 'em up and laying 'em down!"*
1:16	A'	*"Prancing fools (oh, prancing fools!), that's what we like to call 'em, They're in a class all alone!"*
1:24	C	*"The only way for them to lose is to cheat 'em, You may tie 'em, but you'll never beat 'em!"*

1:33   **A''**   *"Strut that stuff, they don't do nothing different,*
              Cake walking babies from home!"

1:39   Underneath the vocalists' last notes, the horns begin playing.

Chorus 3

1:41   **A**   The instruments resume their collective improvisation. Armstrong
              plays more freely and with greater intensity. Bechet's timbre is hard and
              penetrating.

1:49   **B**

1:56   Bechet plays a two-bar break in triplets, a rhythm that srongly divides
              the beat into threes.

1:58   **A'**

2:06   **C**   Stop-time: Armstrong improvises a complex syncopated line in his
              upper register.

2:14   At the end of the passage, Armstrong plays his last note with a growl.

2:15   **A''**

2:22   The horns sustain a long note, a signal that another chorus is coming.

Chorus 4

2:24   **A**   The two soloists differ dramatically in style: Armstrong plays sparsely,
              with intense syncopation, while Bechet smoothes out into lengthy
              strings of eighth notes.

2:32   **B**

2:38   Irvis plays a gruff trombone solo during the break.

2:40   **A'**

2:49   **C**   Stop-time: Bechet begins with a rough series of slurs and impro-
              vises a rhythm that shifts unpredictably between triplets and jazzy
              syncopation.

2:58   **A''**   To signal the end of the piece, both Armstrong and Bechet play
              repeated riffs.

In 1925, Bechet returned to Europe with the musical *Revue Negre*, starring singer and dancer Josephine Baker. He played in Berlin, Amsterdam,
and Moscow, where he met up with his most important partner, Louisiana-
born trumpet player Tommy Ladnier. Together, in New York in the early
1930s, the two formed the New Orleans Feetwarmers and made records
that confirmed Bechet's uniquely florid yet exacting style. Bechet continued

to make dozens of memorable records ("Summertime" and "Blue Horizon" are high-water marks of the 1940s New Orleans revival), demonstrating a broad repertory, advanced sense of harmony, and adventurous spirit. His 1932 "Shag" was the first jazz original based on the chords to "I Got Rhythm," and in 1941 his version of "The Sheik of Araby" employed over-dubbing to allow him to play all the parts: clarinet, soprano saxophone, tenor saxophone, bass, and drums—a neat trick, especially at a time when audio tape didn't exist.

Bechet's dominance of the soprano saxophone was so complete that he remained its chief exponent until his death in 1959. By then, he had become one of the most beloved musicians in Europe, especially France, where he settled in 1951. His records graced every café jukebox (one of his compositions, "Petite Fleur," became a national phenomenon), and a memorial bust was unveiled in Nice.

New Orleans jazz has never disappeared, though generations of modern jazz enthusiasts have done their best to ignore it. The tradition is kept alive, quite naturally, at New Orleans's Preservation Hall, a popular tourist attraction located in a small eighteenth-century building in the French Quarter, a few blocks from the Mississippi River. Bands and societies devoted to New Orleans or Dixieland jazz can be found all over the world, from New Jersey to Brazil, Denmark, and Japan. It has become a kind of feel-good folk music, often played by amateurs. No matter where it is played, the repertory, instrumentation, polyphonic front line, and marchlike rhythm section remain essentially the same. So does the attitude, which ranges from happiness to exultation, and is usually nostalgic though rarely senti-mental. Dixieland musicians often wear straw hats and sleeve garters as if to announce that they are part of a musical tradition sufficient unto itself, a thing apart from the evolution of jazz, complete in its own right.

5

CHAPTER

New York in the 1920s

ARABIAN NIGHTS

New York City, particularly the borough of Manhattan, has served as the focus for jazz's maturity and evolution from the late 1920s to the present. But it never quite carried the mythological resonance of places that enjoyed intense associations with specific eras in jazz. The parishes of New Orleans sparked the first great fomenting of jazz; then Chicago proved to be the primary magnet that drew Southern musicians to the North. The wide-open nightlife of Kansas City would inspire countless musicians in the 1930s, and the laid-back

◀ Duke Ellington conducts his orchestra from the piano at the Olympia Theater in Paris, 1958.

temper of Los Angeles would take up the "cool" style of the 1950s. In the end, however, no matter where they came from, no matter how much local renown they achieved, nearly all the great jazz musicians had to make their way to New York to cement a genuine, enduring success.

New York's centrality may be explained in part by cultural inertia, as each generation of its musicians lured the next. Yet as we look more closely at the development of jazz in New York, especially in the early years, we find three interlocking spheres of influence: commercial, sociological, and musical.

The country's entertainment infrastructure—concert halls, theaters, museums, galleries, radio and television, newspapers and magazines, book publishers, and record labels, not to mention managers, agents, bookers, and publicists—took root in New York in the closing years of the nineteenth century and never left. New York media spoke for the nation, and as jazz became a commercial entity, it needed access to that media and to the stimulating atmosphere forged by a powerful industry designed to match performers with audiences.

The years of the Great Migration from South to North coincided with a massive East-to-West emigration from Europe to the United States. Jazz is unusual as an art form in that a majority of its performers belong to ethnic minorities. Most of the major figures in jazz history who were not African American derived from immigrant families that originated in Italy, Ireland, Germany, and Russia. Middle European Jews, whose music involved a blues-like use of the pentatonic scale and a feel for improvisation, were especially drawn to jazz. This confluence of ethnicities proved particularly profound in New York, which in the 1920s accounted for America's largest urban communities of blacks and Jews. An alliance between black musicians and Jewish songwriters replicated, in part, the give-and-take between New Orleans blacks and Creoles, and helped to define jazz for three decades.

It is often said that in encompassing all of jazz, New York produced no specific style of its own. This isn't entirely true. Stride piano originated on the Eastern Seaboard and flowered in New York in the 1920s and 1930s; New York's receptivity then advanced the innovations of modern jazz (or bebop) in the 1940s and avant-garde (or free) jazz in the 1950s and 1960s. The city's most significant contribution to jazz, though, was the development of large bands and orchestrations: the influx of jazz musicians in the 1920s from New Orleans, Chicago, and elsewhere overlapped with the growing enthusiasm for ballroom dancing, generating a demand for elegant orchestras. These were jazz's first important big bands, and some of them would later fuel the Swing Era.

Small wonder that when a young, untested, and unknown Duke Ellington arrived in New York for the first time in 1923 and surveyed the bright lights that extended from one end of Manhattan to the other, he exclaimed, "Why, it is just like the Arabian Nights!" The possibilities were limitless and the soundtrack was jazz—or soon would be.

TRANSFORMATIONS

The twentieth century unfurled in an unceasing progression of technological marvels, from the airplane to cellphones. In the field of entertainment, three periods stand out: the 1920s, for radical transformations in recordings, radio, and movies; the 1940s, for television; and the 1980s, for digitalization. All three media in the first period, the one that concerns us here, had been introduced in the later part of the nineteenth century, but were refined in the 1920s in ways that changed the way Americans lived their lives.

In 1925, the development of electrical recording as a replacement for the primitive technology of acoustical recording meant that records, formerly inadequate for reproducing certain instruments and vocal ranges, now boasted a startling fidelity that especially benefited jazz, with its drums and cymbals and intricately entwined wind instruments. The recording industry, in a slump since 1920, came back to life with dramatically reduced prices in phonographs and discs.

Radio, which had been little more than a hobby for most people, blighted by static and requiring headphones, sprang to life as a broadcast medium in 1921 (KDKA in Pittsburgh), achieving a lifelike clarity with the invention of the carbon microphone and, subsequently, the much-improved condenser microphone. The first radio network, the National Broadcasting Company, debuted in 1926, followed a year later by the Columbia Broadcasting System, uniting the nation with unparalleled powers of communication. The advances in radio and recording gave entertainment seekers a kind of permission to stay at home—a permission that quickly became a national habit, as people grew emotionally attached to broadcasts or obsessed with collecting records. The cinema responded to these technological challenges with an innovation of its own. In 1927, Warner Bros. introduced the first feature film with synchronized dialogue—an adaptation of a Broadway play significantly, if deceptively, called *The Jazz Singer*.

Historically, music had evolved at a pace no faster than human travel. A symphony by Mozart, written in Vienna, might not reach England for months or years; the music of New Orleans could spread only as fast as the musicians moved from one place to another. The rapid growth in radio and records changed all that. It meant that a recording manufactured in New York could reach California the same day over the air and within a week through the mail. Speed affected everything. Earlier, a vaudeville comedian might work up an evening of jokes that he could deliver for an entire year, city after city. On radio, those jokes were depleted in one night. Similarly, pop songs and musical styles wore out as fast as hemlines and hairdos.

As technology encouraged people to stay at home, nightlife received an unintended boost. In 1920, a Republican Congress passed—over President Wilson's veto—the Eighteenth Amendment to the Constitution, prohibiting the manufacture, transporting, and sale of alcohol. Under Prohibition, it was legal to drink and even purchase alcoholic beverages, but since no one could legally sell (or manufacture) it, the amendment's principal effect was to create a vast web of organized crime, catering to a generation that often drank to excess simply to prove that the government could not dictate its level of intoxication.

By 1921, the country was pockmarked with tens of thousands of illicit saloons, memorably tagged as speakeasies. Their gangster owners competed for customers by hiring the most talented musicians, singers, comedians, and dancers around. In mob-controlled cities like Chicago, Kansas City, and New York, many of these nightspots stayed open through breakfast, and jazz was perfectly suited to an industry that required music to flow as liberally as beer. All the composers in town could not have written enough music to fill the order, but improvisers could spin an infinite number of variations on blues and pop songs. Musicians follow the lure of work, and—until it was repealed in 1932—Prohibition provided a lot of work.

DANCE BANDS AND SYMPHONIC JAZZ

A cursory look at early jazz suggests a long dry spell between the 1917 triumph by the Original Dixieland Jazz Band and the classic recordings of King Oliver and others in 1923. Yet the interim was a period of great ferment, especially in New York, where jazz came face to face with a simmering pot of musical styles: Tin Pan Alley popular songs, ragtime, New Orleans jazz, marching bands (especially popular after 1918, in the aftermath of World War I), and vaudeville, which featured anything that could keep an audience attentive during a fifteen-minute act—including comical saxophones, blues divas, and self-styled jazz or ragtime dancers. Jazz musicians freely borrowed and transformed elements from every type of music. Jazz also found its way into elaborate ballrooms and concert halls—oddly enough, two leading figures in this process, Art Hickman and Paul Whiteman, came east from San Francisco.

Hickman (1886–1930), a pianist, drummer, and songwriter, encountered jazz in the honky-tonks of the Barbary Coast, where he believed jazz originated: "Negroes playing it. Eye shades, sleeves up, cigars in mouth. Gin and liquor and smoke and filth. But music!" In 1913, Hickman organized a dance band in San Francisco, which soon included two saxophonists. Though he did not harmonize them in the manner of a reed section (where two or more reed instruments play in harmony), he did assign them prominent roles, creating a smoother sound than the brass-heavy ensembles associated with New Orleans jazz and marching bands. The dual saxophones gave an appealing character to a band that otherwise consisted of trumpet, trombone, violin, and a rigid rhythm section with two or three banjos (a remnant from minstrelsy). Hickman's success served to establish saxophones as an abiding component in the jazz ensemble.

In 1919, the Victor Talking Machine Company brought Hickman's band to New York with great fanfare, partly as an antidote to the boisterousness of the Original Dixieland Jazz Band. But Hickman disliked the city and hurried back to San Francisco, leaving room for a successor—a far more formidable figure. It may be difficult now to appreciate how incredibly popular bandleader Paul Whiteman (1890–1967) was in the 1920s. Tall and corpulent, with a round and much caricatured face, he was the first American pop-music superstar of the twentieth century, a phenomenon at home and abroad—as celebrated as Charlie Chaplin and Mickey Mouse.

Whiteman, more than anyone else, embodied the struggle over what kind of music jazz would ultimately be. Would it be a scrappy, no-holds-barred improvisational music built on the raw emotions and techniques of the New Orleans style, or a quasi-symphonic adaptation, with only vestigial elements to suggest the source of inspiration? Was jazz merely a resource, a primitive music from which art music could be developed, or was it an art in itself? By the late 1920s, almost everyone, including Whiteman, recognized jazz as an independent phenomenon, destined to follow its own rules and go its own way. Yet the question had been passionately argued.

Born in Denver, Whiteman was the son of an influential music teacher,

Wilberforce J. Whiteman, who despised jazz and Paul's association with it. (Ironically, his students included two major figures of the Swing Era, Jimmie Lunceford and Andy Kirk.) Paul studied viola and joined the Denver Symphony Orchestra while in his teens. He began to attract attention when, after moving to San Francisco to play in the San Francisco Symphony Orchestra, he organized a Barbary Coast ragtime outfit in his off hours. He formed his first ballroom band in 1919, achieving success in Los Angeles, Atlantic City, and finally New York, where he became an immediate favorite at the self-consciously ritzy Palais Royal.

Up to this point, Whiteman had been thoroughly outshone by Hickman. The tables turned in 1920, when Victor released Whiteman's first recordings, "Whispering" and "Japanese Sandman," which sold well over a million copies. Whiteman and Hickman had begun with similar instrumentation, but Whiteman built a much larger band, producing a more lavish and flexible sound, with considerable help from composer-arranger Ferde Grofé. Whiteman himself rarely played viola anymore, but he conducted with a graceful if oblivious pomp, demonstrating an appealing personality and making news by fiercely arguing the merits of American music.

In 1924, Whiteman formalized his argument with a concert—he called it "An Experiment in Modern Music"—at New York's Aeolian Hall, a fabled event in twentieth-century musical history. Whiteman had set out to prove his contention that a new classicism was taking root in lowborn jazz. He opened with a crude performance of the Original Dixieland Jazz Band's "Livery Stable Blues," played for laughs as an example of jazz in its "true naked form," and closed with a new work he had commissioned from the ingenious Broadway songwriter George Gershwin (1898–1937), *Rhapsody in Blue*, performed with the composer at the piano. No jazz was heard at that concert, but the response to Whiteman's singular Americana was so fervent that he was promoted as the "King of Jazz" and originator of symphonic jazz, a phrase he coined.

Symphonic jazz represented a fusion of musical styles—in this instance, between Negro folk art and the high-culture paradigm of European classical music. Speaking to a distinctly urban sensibility, it attempted to incorporate the hurry and clatter of the big city in an age of skyscrapers, technology, and fast living. It was also an attempt to democratize high art by giving it an American twist. Much as Joseph Haydn had found profundity in simple folk songs in the late eighteenth century, Claude Debussy and Igor Stravinsky sought inspiration from ragtime in the early twentieth. With symphonic jazz, which was under way before Whiteman's concert, a new group of classically trained composers in both Europe and America hoped to redefine modern music by accenting African American elements. Such symphonic works as Darius Milhaud's *La creation du monde* (1923), George Antheil's *Jazz Symphony* (1925), John Alden Carpenter's *Skyscrapers* (1926), and Grofé's *Metropolis* (1928) all depicted the frenzy of the modern city, specifically New York. Gershwin went so far as to replicate the sound of automobile horns in his 1928 *An American in Paris.* Symphonic jazz lost steam during the Depression, but found new champions in the 1950s, with the advent of Third Stream music, which combined techniques of modern classical music with postwar jazz—another boomlet of marginal importance.

Meanwhile, hardly anyone—certainly no one in the media—noticed that in the very year of Whiteman's Aeolian Hall triumph, a relatively unknown Louis Armstrong had arrived in New York to take a seat in Fletcher Henderson's orchestra. Whiteman, however, did notice, and in 1926 he decided it was time for the King of Jazz to hire a few jazz musicians. Initially, he wanted to recruit black musicians, but his management convinced him that he couldn't get away with a racially integrated band: he would lose bookings, and the black musicians would be barred from white hotels and restaurants. Whiteman countered that no one could stop him from hiring black arrangers; he traded orchestrations with Henderson and added the prolific African American composer William Grant Still to his staff.

Whiteman's first important jazz hire came from vaudeville: singer Bing Crosby (1903–1977) and his pianist and harmonizing partner Al Rinker. Never before had a popular bandleader hired a full-time singer; in the past, instrumentalists had assumed the vocal chores. During his first week with the Whiteman band, in Chicago in 1926, Crosby heard Armstrong, and was astonished by his ability to combine a powerful art with bawdy comedy, ranging from risqué jokes to parodies of a Southern preacher. Crosby became the most popular singer in the first half of the twentieth century, a decisive force on records and radio and in the movies—and a major link between jazz and the mainstream. He helped to make Armstrong's musical approach accessible to the white public by adapting rhythmic and improvisational elements of Armstrong's singing style to his own. In turn, Crosby inspired Armstrong to add romantic ballads to his repertory—they often recorded the same songs within weeks of each other. They would work together, on and off, for the next four decades.

Whiteman then signed up the most admired young white jazz instrumentalists in the country, including cornetist Bix Beiderbecke, saxophonist Frank Trumbauer, guitarist Eddie Lang, and violinist Joe Venuti. An especially influential new recruit was the stubbornly original arranger Bill Challis, who had an uncanny ability to combine every aspect of Whiteman's orchestra—jazz, pop, and classical elements alike. Thanks to Challis and the other new additions, Whiteman was able to release innovative jazz records in the years 1927–29, until financial considerations exacerbated by the Depression obliged him to return to a more reliably profitable pop format.

"CHANGES"

In 1927, the Whiteman band served as a microcosm of the three-way battle involving jazz, symphonic jazz, and pop. Bill Challis favored Crosby and the jazz players, but when the band's old (symphonic) guard complained of neglect, he found ways to bring everyone into the mix. His arrangement of Walter Donaldson's "Changes" opens with strings, incorporates pop and jazz singing, and climaxes with a roaring Beiderbecke solo, the sound of his cornet tightened by a straight mute inserted into the bell of his horn.

The title itself is significant, suggesting changes in the band, changes in taste as ballroom music assimilated the vitality of jazz, and changes in improvisation techniques as harmonic progressions (noted in the lyrics) took the place of polyphonic elaborations of the melody. The title also signifies broader cultural changes that were transforming the United States. In the several months before the recording was made, Charles Lindbergh had flown the Atlantic Ocean, Babe Ruth had hit sixty home runs, and talking pictures had premiered. The national mood was optimistic, as reflected in songs like "Good News," "Hallelujah," "'S Wonderful," "Smile," "There'll Be Some Changes Made," and others in that vein.

Challis emphasizes the changes between new and old with contrasting rhythms and two vocal groups. Rhythmically, he alternates a Charleston beat (two emphatic beats followed by a rest), usually enunciated by the trumpets, with the more evenly stated rhythms of the violins. The performance never sticks to any one sound, preferring to cut back and forth between strings, brasses, saxophones, and voices, with solo spots interspersed. Although six vocalists are listed among the personnel, they never sing in tandem. Three of them, representing Whiteman's old guard, were full-time instrumentalists (trombonist Jack Fulton and violinists Charles Gaylord and Austin Young) who were occasionally deputized to sing pop refrains. Shortly after Crosby and Rinker joined Whiteman, they recruited singer-pianist Harry Barris to form a novelty trio called the Rhythm Boys. Accordingly, Challis divided the vocal chorus into sections, employing both vocal trios and Crosby as soloist. The chorus begins with the old guard ("Beautiful changes"), then—with Barris signaling the change by imitating a cymbal ("pah")—switches to the Rhythm Boys, who blend high-pitched harmonies and a unified scat break. This is followed by the old guard setting up a solo by Crosby, who mimics a trombone slide on the words "weatherman" and "Dixieland." Crosby's solo leads to the record's flash point: Beiderbecke's improvisation.

CHANGES

Paul Whiteman

Paul Whiteman, director; Henry Busse, Charlie Margulis, trumpets; Bix Beiderbecke, cornet; Frank Trumbauer, C-melody saxophone; Wilbur Hall, Tommy Dorsey, trombones; Chester Hazlett, Hal McLean, clarinets, alto saxophones; Jimmy Dorsey, Nye Mayhew, Charles Strickfaden, clarinets, alto and baritone saxophones; Kurt Dieterle, Mischa Russell, Mario Perry, Matt Malneck, violins; Harry Perrella, piano; Mike Pingitore, banjo; Mike Trafficante, brass bass; Steve Brown, string bass; Harold McDonald, drums; Bing Crosby, Al Rinker, Harry Barris, Jack Fulton, Charles Gaylord, Austin Young, vocals

LABEL: Victor 21103; *Paul Whiteman and His Dance Band* (Naxos 8.120511)
DATE: 1927
STYLE: early New York big band
FORM: 32-bar popular song (**ABCA′**), with interlude and verses

Introduction

0:00   The brass section rises through unstable chromatic harmonies until it finally settles on a consonant chord.

Song (D♭ major)

0:10   **A**   The saxophones play the melody, decorated above by short, syncopated trumpet chords and supported by the strings. Underneath, the banjo and piano play four beats to the bar, while the bass plays two beats.

0:19   **B**   The melody shifts to the violins.

0:28   **C**   The trumpets play a jaunty Charleston rhythm, ♩. ♪♩ ‿ | ♩. ♪♩ , answered first by the saxophones, then by the strings.

0:38   **A′**   The saxophones return to the opening melody, which moves toward a full cadence.

Interlude

0:45   The rhythmic accompaniment temporarily stops. Over changing orchestral textures (including a violin solo), the piece modulates to a new key.

Verse 1 (16-bar AABA)

0:52   **A**   The trumpets and strings return to the Charleston rhythm, underscored by the trombones' offbeat accents. The phrase begins in minor but ends in major.

0:56   **A**

1:01   **B**   For the bridge, the saxophones quietly sustain chords.

1:05   **A**

Song (E♭ major)

1:10   **A**   *"Beautiful changes in different keys, beautiful changes and harmonies."* The "sweet" vocal trio harmonizes the melody in block-chord harmony, accompanied by the rhythm section (string bass, banjo, drums).

1:19   **B**   *"He starts in C, then changes to D. He's foolin' around most any old key."* The harmonies shift away from the tonic, matching the intent of the words.

1:28   Break: Barris introduces the "jazz" vocal trio (Rhythm Boys) by imitating a quiet cymbal stroke ("pah").

1:29   **C**   *"Watch that—hear that minor strain! Ba-dum, ba-dum,"* The Rhythm Boys adapt to the new style by singing a more detached and "cooler" series of chords.

1:35   *"Bada(ba)da-lada(bada-lada)-la-dum!"* During a break, the vocalists imitate scat-singing, changing the dynamics to match the rhythm.

1:38   **A′**   *"There's so many babies that he can squeeze, and he's always changing those keys!"* The first trio returns to set up Crosby's solo.

1:46   The voices retreat to background chords.

Verse 2

1:47   *"First, he changes into B, changes into C, changes into D, changes into E, As easy as the weatherman! Now, he's getting kinda cold, getting kinda hot, Listen, I forgot, since he was a tot, he's been the talk of Dixieland!"* Crosby sings the verse with ease, ending each phrase with a rich, resonant timbre.

Song

2:05   **A**   While the voices continue their background harmony, Beiderbecke takes a cornet solo with a sharp, focused sound. Underneath him, the bass switches to a four-beat walking bass.

2:14	**B**	
2:24	**C**	The full band returns with the Charleston rhythm.
2:33	**A'**	In full block-chord texture, the band plays a written-out version of the melody with syncopations.

Coda

| 2:40 | The tempo moves to free rhythm. Over sustained chords, a saxophone plays a short solo. |
| 2:49 | As the chords dissipate, all that's left is the sound of a bell. |

Fletcher Henderson (1897–1952)

Like every other bandleader in New York, black and white, Fletcher Henderson initially looked to Whiteman for inspiration, seeking to emulate his opulent sound and diverse repertory as well as his public success. Yet he would ultimately take big-band music down a very different, far more influential route as he developed into an outstanding arranger.

An unassuming, soft-spoken man who initially had no particular allegiance to jazz, Henderson, like Whiteman, grew up in a middle-class home with parents who disdained jazz. Born in Cuthbert, Georgia, he studied classical music with his mother but seemed determined to follow in the footsteps of his father, a mathematics and Latin teacher, when he graduated from Atlanta University with a chemistry degree. Soon after traveling to New York in 1920 for postgraduate study, he switched from chemistry to music, overcoming his class resistance to the blues by learning how to play piano well enough to record with Ethel Waters and Bessie Smith. He went on to organize dance bands for nightclubs and ballrooms.

In 1924, Henderson began a lengthy engagement at the luxurious Roseland Ballroom at 51st Street and Broadway, New York's preeminent dance palace. As a black musician working in midtown venues with exclusively white clienteles, Henderson offered polished and conventional dance music: fox-trots, tangos, and waltzes. At the same time, he had access to the best black musicians, including an attention-getting young saxophonist named Coleman Hawkins, and, again like Whiteman, kept up with the ever-changing dance scene.

Henderson's band grew in confidence, stature, and size over the next several years. By 1926, it was widely regarded as the best jazz orchestra anywhere, a standing it began to lose in 1927, with the rise of Duke Ellington and other bandleaders who elaborated on the approach pioneered by Henderson and his chief arranger, Don Redman. Although Henderson never achieved a popular renown equal to that of Ellington, Count Basie, Benny Goodman, and other big-band stars, his influence among musicians increased during the 1930s, as he produced a stream of compositions and arrangements that helped to launch big-band music in the Swing Era.

At first, Henderson relied primarily on stock arrangements, anonymous versions of standard popular songs made available by publishing companies, which tended toward basic harmonies with no jazz content. As his pioneering arranger Don Redman (1900–1964)—a child prodigy from West Virginia, who received a degree in music from Storer College at age twenty—began revising them, making increasingly radical changes, the arrangements took on a distinct and exciting character. Ellington would later recall that when he came to Manhattan with the dream of creating an orchestra, "[Fletcher's] was the band I always wanted mine to sound like."

Redman also played all the reed instruments, sang, and composed songs and instrumental novelties often characterized by a wry sense of humor. His most famous work, "Chant of the Weed," was a hymn to marijuana. Redman's great achievement as arranger was to treat the band as a large unit made up of four interactive sections: reeds (saxophones and clarinets), trumpets, trombones, and rhythm section. Over the decade 1924–34, the orchestra grew to an average of fifteen musicians: typically three trumpets, two to three trombones, up to five reeds, and four rhythm (piano, bass or tuba, banjo or guitar, drums). This basic big-band instrumentation, notwithstanding numerous variations, remains unchanged even now.

Redman and Henderson closely studied jazz records coming out of Chicago, and adapted these tunes to their orchestral style. Redman especially liked the New Orleans custom of short breaks, which allowed him to constantly vary the texture of a piece. Yet he avoided the anarchy of New Orleans jazz: when he used polyphony, it was usually not collectively improvised but composed in advance. His principal organizing technique, derived from the church, was a call-and-response interchange, pitting, say, the saxophone section against the trumpets. His best arrangements retained the vitality of a small jazz band, but were scrupulously prepared.

When, in that banner year of 1924, Henderson decided to add a third trumpet player, he sought the hottest soloist he could find. After several long-distance discussions with Lil Hardin Armstrong, Louis's wife, he convinced her to persuade her husband to take his offer. At first, Henderson's well-paid, spiffily dressed musicians didn't know what to make of a country boy like Louis. Customers were also confused: the first time Armstrong stood up to play a solo at Roseland, the audience was too startled to applaud. But Armstrong brought with him essential ingredients that the band lacked: the bracing authority of swing, the power of blues, and the improvisational logic of a born storyteller.

The standard had been raised, and no one understood that better than Redman, who later acknowledged that he changed his orchestration style to accommodate Armstrong's daring. In recordings like "Copenhagen" and "Sugar Foot Stomp" (an ingenious adaptation of King Oliver's "Dippermouth Blues," with Armstrong playing Oliver's solo), Redman's writing began to take on a commanding directness and sharper rhythmic gait. Nor was his fanciful use of breaks and popular melodies lost on Armstrong, who employed them in the Hot Five sessions he initiated after his year with Henderson. Redman's writing not only launched big-band jazz, but also served to link Oliver's Creole Jazz Band (1923) and Armstrong's seminal Hot Five (1925).

"COPENHAGEN"

Several historic threads come together in Fletcher Henderson's 1924 recording of "Copenhagen," a multistrain composition by a Midwestern bandleader (Charlie Davis), named not for the capital of Denmark but after a favorite brand of snuff. The Wolverines, a scrappy little band featuring Bix Beiderbecke, had recorded it in May, and its publisher issued a stock arrangement of the song. To this Don Redman added his own variations, employing aspects of New Orleans jazz (orchestrated polyphony), block-chord harmonies (standard for large dance orchestras), brief breaks, hot solos, old-fashioned, two-beat dance rhythms, and sectional call and response. The piece combines twelve-bar blues with sixteen-bar ragtime strains.

Louis Armstrong's jolting blues chorus is an undoubted highlight in a performance also notable for the spirit of the ensemble and of individual contributions such as Charlie Green's trombone smears and Buster Bailey's whirling clarinet. Henderson hired Bailey around the same time as Armstrong, extending the New Orleans tradition of clarinet obbligato into big-band jazz a decade before the clarinet came to symbolize the Swing Era. Redman, characteristically, came up with contrasting trios, featuring three clarinets in the B strain and three trumpets in the D strain, and opposing approaches to polyphony—notated in the A strain, improvised (against block-chord trumpets) in the E strain. The harmonically surprising finish inclined listeners to shake their heads in wonder and move the needle back to the beginning.

COPENHAGEN

Fletcher Henderson

Fletcher Henderson, piano; Elmer Chambers, Howard Scott, Louis Armstrong, trumpets; Charlie Green, trombone; Buster Bailey, clarinet; Don Redman, clarinet and alto saxophone; Coleman Hawkins, clarinet and tenor saxophone; Charlie Dixon, banjo; Ralph Escudero, tuba; Kaiser Marshall, drums

LABEL: Vocalion 14926; *Fletcher Henderson* (Columbia Legacy/Sony 61447)
DATE: 1924
STYLE: early big band
FORM: march/ragtime

Strain A (16 bars)

0:00	The saxophones and trumpets move up and down through the chromatic scale in block-chord harmony.
0:04	Led by a trombone, the entire band responds with a cleverly written-out imitation of collective improvisation.
0:09	The opening passage is now given to clarinets playing in their lowest register. The response, once again, is scored collective improvisation.

Strain B (12-bar blues)

0:17	A high-pitched clarinet trio plays a bluesy melody. Underneath, the rhythm section (piano, banjo, drums, tuba) plays a lively two-beat accompaniment, with the drummer and banjo player adding a strong backbeat.

Strain B

0:29	A repetition of the previous twelve bars.

Strain B

0:42	Armstrong plays a well-rehearsed solo (the same solo can be heard on another take). His playing is hard-driving, with a swing rhythm and a bluesy sensibility.

Strain C (16 bars)

0:54	The full band plays a series of syncopated block chords, punctuated by cymbal crashes. Again, the response is scored polyphony.

1:02   The previous eight-bar section is repeated.

Strain D (16 bars)

1:11   A trio of trumpets plays a melody in a simple three-note rhythm.

1:17   During a two-bar break, the trumpets are interrupted by the clarinet trio
            performing a disorienting, rising glissando.

Strain A

1:28   The opening of strain **A** is played by the clarinet trio in its highest
            register.

1:36   The same passage is played by the saxophones.

Strain E (12-bar blues)

1:44   The trombone plays an introductory melody.

1:48   While the trumpets play in block-chord harmony, the clarinet and trom-
            bone improvise in New Orleans style.

Strain E

1:57   The repetition of strain **E** has a looser, more improvised feeling: the
            trombone plays with more glissando, while the clarinet sustains its high
            pitch for four measures.

Strain F (16 bars)

2:09   As the trumpet trio plays block-chord harmonies, the clarinet improvises
            busily underneath.

2:16   The break is divided between the banjo and the tenor saxophone.

Coda

2:26   The band returns to strain **A**.

2:34   Without pause, the band suddenly shifts to the beginning of strain **C**.

2:38   A high-pitched clarinet trio reintroduces strain **A**.

2:45   The band moves to block chords that descend precipitously outside the
            piece's tonality. With this bizarre gesture, the piece abruptly ends.

Throughout his career, Henderson continued to provide a showcase for the finest black musicians in New York. A short list of major jazz figures who worked with him includes, in addition to the remarkable trinity of Armstrong, Hawkins, and Redman and others already mentioned, trumpet players Rex Stewart, Tommy Ladnier, Henry "Red" Allen, Roy Eldridge; trombonists Jimmy Harrison, Benny Morton, J. C. Higginbotham, Dicky Wells; clarinetists and saxophonists Benny Carter (also a major composer-arranger), Lester Young, Ben Webster, Chu Berry, Russell Procope, Omer Simeon; bassists John Kirby, Israel Crosby; drummers Kaiser Marshall, Sidney Catlett; and arranger Horace Henderson (his brother). No other big-band leader can lay claim to such a roll. And this is to say nothing of his association with Benny Goodman and the Swing Era.

Don Redman left Henderson's band in 1927 to become director of McKinney's Cotton Pickers, an inventive big band in which he proved himself a charming vocalist—speaking his interpretations with a light, high-pitched voice—and a productive composer. He wrote pop standards ("Cherry," "Gee Baby, Ain't I Good to You," "How'm I Doin'?") and blues ("Save It, Pretty Mama"), as well as instrumental masterpieces like "Chant of the Weed" (1931). As a freelance arranger, he wrote for Armstrong, Whiteman, Jimmy Dorsey, Jimmie Lunceford, and many others, but by the middle 1930s his style was considered passé and he began to recede from jazz. In 1951, Redman became music director for the singer-actor-comedienne Pearl Bailey, an association that lasted more than a decade and took him far from his roots as a jazz visionary yet kept him firmly in the lap of New York entertainment.

THE ALLEY AND THE STAGE

Like New Orleans with its parishes and Chicago with its Southside and Northside, the island of Manhattan consists of diverse neighborhoods ruled by racial and ethnic divisions. In the 1920s, the downtown section, below 14th Street, encompassed the Lower East Side, a populous Jewish area (home to the Yiddish theater) as well as the site of Little Italy and Chinatown; and the West Side, with its business district (Wall Street) and an enclave that attracted artists and bohemians, Greenwich Village. Downtown Manhattan included countless working-class saloons and theaters that presented every kind of entertainment, from vaudeville bills to bar pianists, singers, and small bands. These musicians created variations on ragtime, opera, and pop songs, often combining them with European folk traditions. One of the most important of the ethnic importations came to be known as klezmer, a Jewish dance music (named after the Hebrew phrase for "musical vessel") that shared several elements with jazz, such as variable pitch and blues-like melodies that were embellished through improvisation.

In New York's midtown section, the wealthy homes and establishments

on the East Side were divided from the mostly white ghettos of the West
Side (like Hell's Kitchen) by Broadway, the thoroughfare running north
to south where theaters, cabarets, and dance halls (like the Roseland Ballroom) offered a constant, ravenous market for new songs and entertainers.
On Broadway, you could see plays, musicals, ballet, opera, revues, movies,
vaudeville, and every other kind of show business. More than a dozen
newspapers competed in reporting on the nightlife of the "guys and dolls"
(columnist Damon Runyon's phrase) who frolicked in the most fabled
playground of the Jazz Age.

Midtown was also home to Tin Pan Alley, the first songwriting factory
of its kind. The name has come to represent the popular music written
for the stage and cinema from the 1890s through the 1950s, when rock
and roll began to change the business. Originally, it was the nickname
for buildings on 28th Street between Broadway and Sixth Avenue, where
music publishers had their offices and passersby could hear the cacophony
of a dozen or more competing pianos—songwriters demonstrating their
wares. The Alley introduced the idea of the professional songwriter, who
wrote specific songs to order: ballads, novelties, patriotic anthems, rhythm
songs, and so forth, as commissioned by performers or to meet a public
demand. In the 1920s, for example, thanks to the enormous popularity of
Al Jolson, there was an appetite for "Mammy songs," Southern-themed
ditties that were dutifully turned out by songsmiths who had never been
south of 14th Street.

By the middle 1920s, the most sophisticated generation of songwriters
ever assembled was in place. Rejecting the sentimental formulas that had
dominated the Alley during the previous thirty years, they wrote music
and words that were original, intelligent, expressive, and frequently beautiful, with advanced harmonic underpinnings that gave them a particularly
modern and enduring appeal. The songs this generation wrote remain
the core of the classic American songbook, and were vital to the development of jazz. The songwriters, influenced by jazz rhythms and blues scales,
came of age with Armstrong-inspired improvisers who required new and
more intricate material than the blues and ragtime strains that had served
their predecessors. The two groups were ideally matched: a composer like
George Gershwin actively tried to capture the jazz spirit, and an improviser like Coleman Hawkins found inspiration in Gershwin's melodies and
harmonies.

Among the most masterly and prolific of the new Tin Pan Alley songwriters, the veteran but resourceful and adaptable street-smart Irving Berlin (from New York) and the younger Yale-educated, well traveled and smart-set Cole Porter (from Indiana) were unusual in writing both words and music. For the most part, pop songs were contrived by teams. In the 1920s, those teams included composers George Gershwin, Jerome Kern, Harold Arlen, Richard Rodgers, Vincent Youmans, and Hoagy Carmichael, and lyricists Ira Gershwin, Lorenz Hart, Oscar Hammerstein II, Dorothy Fields, and E. Y. Harburg.

Although whites, and especially Jews, dominated the Alley, black song-writers made important contributions from the start. In addition to the immensely successful W. C. Handy, any account of pantheon songwriters in the 1920s would have to include composers Duke Ellington and Fats Waller and lyricist Andy Razaf. Yet while white entertainers often per-formed songs by black songwriters, black artists were segregated from the-atrical revues and struggled for recognition on the Great White Way—a phrase meant only to designate Broadway's glittery marquee lights, cutting a glowing swath through midtown Manhattan. Their struggle had had ups and downs since the beginning of the century.

During Reconstruction and after, a stage show with a black cast usu-ally meant minstrels. Then in 1898, Will Marion Cook presented *Clo-rindy, or the Origin of the Cakewalk*, the first black production to play a major Broadway theater (the Casino Roof Garden), and one that went a long distance in breaking with minstrelsy, in songs like "On Emancipation Day." More important, *Clorindy* popularized the cakewalk and was the first musical to incorporate ragtime melodies and rhythms. During the next decade, black musicals were often seen on Broadway. Cook also wrote the music—and poet Paul Lawrence Dunbar the lyrics—for the smash hit *In Dahomey* (1903), starring the legendary team of Bert Williams and George Walker. Williams went on to enjoy an astonishing career as the first African American to sign an exclusive recording contract (with Victor, in 1901), the first to star in the Ziegfeld Follies (1910–19), and the first featured in a movie (1910).

Despite Williams's popularity, many white producers and performers resented the success of blacks on Broadway, and by 1910 the bubble had burst. The black presence all but disappeared, until Eubie Blake and Noble Sissle produced their runaway success of 1921, *Shuffle Along*, launching a renaissance of sophisticated black entertainment. A younger generation of black songwriters, publishers, and performers now flourished, including, for the first time, sexy women who had been liberated from any hint of the Aunt Jemima stereotype—among them Ethel Waters, Florence Mills, Nina Mae McKinney, and Josephine Baker, a chorus girl in the years before she wowed Paris dancing naked but for a belt of bananas around her waist.

In 1923, the New Orleans pianist and songwriter Clarence Williams moved to New York, where his song-publishing company encouraged black composers to write a stream of new tunes for black musical revues and white vaudeville stars who needed "rhythmical" numbers. Black song-writers responded by turning out some of the best-known classics in the American songbook; among them were Spencer Williams ("I Ain't Got Nobody," "Basin Street Blues," "I Found a New Baby"), Maceo Pinkard ("Sweet Georgia Brown," "Sugar"), Henry Creamer and Turner Layton ("Way Down Yonder in New Orleans," "After You've Gone"), Shelton Brooks ("The Darktown Strutters' Ball," "Some of These Days"), Chris Smith ("Ballin' the Jack," "Cake Walking Babies [from Home]"), James P. Johnson ("If I Could Be with You One Hour Tonight," "Charleston"), and Noble Sissle and Eubie Blake ("Memories of You," "I'm Just Wild About Harry"), in addition to Ellington and Waller.

While blacks managed to make their mark on Broadway and Tin Pan Alley, they positively dominated uptown Manhattan, or Harlem, which became an entertainment haven with dozens of nightclubs and theaters. Until the close of the nineteenth century, the largest African American community in New York had lived in Greenwich Village (where Fats Waller was born). As whites moved in and landlords raised the rents, blacks were driven into the worst sections of Hell's Kitchen and similar districts. In those years, Harlem, a vast and, until the advent of mass transportation, isolated set-tlement stretching from 110th Street to 155th Street, was mostly white and upper class—regal townhouses still stand on 139th Street, known as Striver's Row. By 1915, most Harlemites were lower- and middle-class Jews, Germans, and Italians, with blacks occupying a few pockets.

Yet a gradual demographic change had begun in 1904, when the Afro-American Realty Company organized a campaign—not unlike the *Chicago Defender*'s crusade to bring Southern blacks to Chicago—to lure African Americans to Harlem. The movement accelerated over the next fifteen years, producing a massive migration involving especially large numbers of Southern and West Indian Negroes. The simultaneous exodus of whites resulted in a nearly complete racial reversal. By 1920, central Harlem had become what poet and memoirist James Weldon Johnson described as "not merely a Negro colony or community, [but] a city within a city, the greatest Negro city in the world." In 1925, philosopher and critic Alain Locke edited a book of essays called *The New Negro*, one of the most influential manifestos ever published in the United States. Locke's anthology argued that African American artists represented a political and cultural force in literature, art, dance, and theater—it was the foundation for the Harlem Renaissance.

The leaders of this renaissance had an ambiguous relationship to jazz, which too often reminded them of coarse stereotypes they preferred to leave behind. In one *New Negro* essay, "Jazz at Home," J. A. Rogers celebrated jazz as "a balm for modern ennui" and a "revolt of the emotions against repression," but argued that jazz's "great future" lay with bandleaders (including Will Marion Cook, Paul Whiteman, and Fletcher Henderson) who "sublimated" those emotions and displayed "none of the vulgarities and crudities of the lowly origin." By contrast, the influential white critic and Harlem nightclub habitué Carl Van Vechten romanticized the more squalid aspects of the "city within a city" in a best-selling novel, *Nigger Heaven* (1926), which made uptown an attraction for thousands of downtown whites.

Unhappily, the very forces that turned Harlem into a cultural carnival also turned it into a slum and a profit center for organized crime. The crammed residents, unable to spread out to racially restricted neighborhoods, fell victim to landlords who increased the rents while partitioning apartments into ever-smaller units. As an added insult, mobsters financed ornate nightclubs—including the Cotton Club, which featured top black performers and sexy floor shows—that refused entrance to black patrons. In these Harlem getaways, the New Negro was banned from witnessing the fruits of his own renaissance.

James P. Johnson (1894–1955) AND STRIDE

Fittingly, the city that established orchestral jazz also encouraged the ripening of the most orchestral brand of jazz piano, initially known as "Harlem style" but eventually recognized internationally as stride piano. Here was an aggressive, competitive, joyous way of playing piano that directly reflected the musical vigor of New York. Imagine ragtime taken for a ride down Tin Pan Alley and then revved up to reflect the metropolitan noise and bustle. Where ragtime was graceful, polished, and measured, stride was impetuous, flashy, and loud. Where ragtime produced a contained repertory, stride was open to anything. The evolution from one to the other occurred gradually.

Like ragtime, stride began as a composed music made up of multiple strains. Then, just as ragtimers had competed in contests of virtuosity, the East Coast stride players began to add their own flourishes and rhythms, eventually developing an offshoot that was livelier, faster, and more propulsive. Perhaps the most remarkable parallel between ragtime and stride is that each style gave birth to the foremost African American composers of its time. Ragtime's pedigree from Scott Joplin to Jelly Roll Morton was more than equaled by stride pianists of the 1920s, who, through their disciples, shaped jazz piano and jazz composition for decades to come—a lineage that includes James P. Johnson, Fats Waller, Duke Ellington, Art Tatum, and Thelonious Monk.

The name "stride" describes the motion of the pianist's left hand, striding back and forth from low in the bass clef to the octave below middle C. On the first and third beats, the pianist plays either a single low note or a chord, usually involving a tenth—an octave plus a third (for example, a low C together with an E, ten white keys higher). Tenths require large hands, so resourceful pianists without the necessary reach perfected "broken tenths": the notes played in rapid succession instead of simultaneously. On the second and fourth beats, the pianist plays a three- or four-note chord in the upper part of the bass clef.

The masters of stride created intricate harmonic and rhythmic patterns that kept the left hand from becoming a mechanical rhythm device. They also developed tricks for the right hand that allowed it to embellish melodies with luscious glissandos, producing a richer texture than traditional ragtime. Many stride pianists studied classical music, and incorporated keyboard techniques of the nineteenth-century virtuosos, particularly Franz Liszt and Frédéric Chopin. They were obliged to keep up with the latest tunes, which also brought modern harmonic splendor to their music.

Stride pianists found they could earn a livelihood by hiring out for Harlem "rent parties." These get-togethers, a social phenomenon of the 1920s, arose from people's need to meet ever-higher rents. Friends and neighbors would congregate for food and music, making contributions to a communal kitty. As the average living room could not accommodate a band, the pianist had to be loud and steady enough to suit dancers and be heard over the volume of conversation. Inevitably, stride pianists achieved a high social standing. They competed with each other pianistically and in personal style—with tailored suits, rakish derbies, expensive cigars, and colorful personalities.

James P. Johnson, the "Father of Stride Piano" with his rhythmic brio and improvised variations, perfected the East Coast style as a progressive leap from its ragtime roots. Almost every major jazz pianist who came along in the 1920s and 1930s—not just Waller, Tatum, and Ellington, but also Earl Hines, Count Basie, and Teddy Wilson—learned from him. Although he never achieved the fame of his protégés, stride revivalists regard him as the most creative artist in the idiom.

Johnson was born in New Brunswick, New Jersey, where his mother sang in the Methodist Church and taught him songs at the piano. He later credited the ring-shout dances (the earliest known African American performing tradition, combining religious songs and West African dances) and brass bands he heard as a child as important influences. After the family moved to New York in 1908, he studied classical piano and encountered like-minded ragtimers—especially Eubie Blake and the short, rotund Luckey Roberts, who was regarded by his colleagues as the best pianist in New York.

Johnson and the others found jobs playing in Jungle's Casino, a Hell's Kitchen dive where black laborers from the Carolinas danced to piano music and managed to impart Southern melodies to Johnson's receptive ears. Beginning in 1918, he punched out a series of influential piano rolls, including an early version of "Carolina Shout," which became an anthem and a test piece—a kind of "Maple Leaf Rag" for New York's piano elite. As ragtime had become popular through widely distributed sheet music, stride found a smaller but dedicated audience through piano rolls.

Of all the technological marvels that changed music in the early years of the twentieth century, the player piano (or pianola), patented in 1897, is the most neglected and underestimated. A hugely popular entertainment apparatus in middle- and upper-class American homes, it served two functions: as a regular piano and as a machine capable of playing music inscribed on piano rolls. These were rolls of paper perforated with tiny squares representing the notes; as the squares rolled over a "tracker bar," they triggered a suction device that, in turn, controlled a lever of the keyboard. Piano rolls could be purchased like records, and were often made by celebrated musicians—Igor Stravinsky wrote an etude for pianola, and pianists as prominent as Joplin, Sergei Rachmaninoff, Gershwin, and Waller introduced original music on rolls. As there was no limit to the number of squares that could be cut into a roll, some pianists (notably Gershwin) would secretly cut the same roll twice, adding accompanying notes the second time—the first instance of overdubbing. (Stymied customers trying to imitate such a roll complained that Gershwin had four hands; turns out, he did.) The player piano operated as a teaching tool: you could play the roll at any speed, and slow it down enough to study the depressed keys. Ellington and Waller, among others, learned to emulate Johnson's vibrant attack by slowing down a roll of "Carolina Shout" and placing their fingers on the depressed keys.

In 1921, Johnson finally initiated a series of sensational disc recordings, including a definitive "Carolina Shout," "Keep Off the Grass," "Worried and Lonesome Blues," and other piano milestones. His career took a whole new direction in 1922, when he was appointed music director of the revue *Plantation Days*, which traveled to London. A year later, he and lyricist Cecil Mack wrote the score for the Broadway smash *Runnin' Wild*, which toured the country and produced two standards: "Old Fashioned Love," which, thanks to a Bob Wills recording in the 1930s, became a country-music favorite; and "Charleston," perhaps the single most widely recognized melody of the 1920s.

While continuing to write songs, produce shows, and play piano (he recorded often as a sideman), Johnson also composed classical pieces that combined nostalgic folk melodies with his own urbane techniques—notably *Yamekraw: Negro Rhapsody*, which W. C. Handy debuted at Carnegie Hall in 1928. He wrote *Harlem Symphony* and *Symphony in Brown* in the 1930s and *De-Organizer*, in collaboration with the poet Langston Hughes, in 1940. Illness slowed him down, and a stroke incapacitated him in 1951, a time when Thelonious Monk and Erroll Garner were extending Johnson's keyboard style into modern jazz.

"YOU'VE GOT TO BE MODERNISTIC"

The transition from ragtime to stride, from formal composition to jazz variations, is illuminated in Johnson's dazzling 1930 recording of "You've Got to Be Modernistic." Consider two aspects of its modernism. First, the introduction and first two strains are ornamented by advanced harmonies, drawing on the whole-tone scale, that keep the listener in a state of perpetual surprise. Second, Johnson switches midway from the formalism of ragtime to the theme and variations of jazz: the structure consists of three sixteen-bar strains (with a four-bar interlude), but with the introduction of strain C, the piece romps through seven choruses of variations with no reprise of strains A or B.

Significantly, the C strain, unlike the virtuosic A and B strains, has the most traditional melody. It begins with a two-bar riff (which Johnson later set to the words "You've got to be modernistic!"), yet suggests a simple Scott Joplin–style ragtime harmony in measures 7 and 8. Johnson, for all his flashing speed and hairpin changes, always exercises a composer's control. Each strain is so distinct from the others (and in the C series, one chorus accents blue notes, another bass notes, another an insistent triple-chord pattern) that the listener is never lulled by repetition or familiarity. The entire performance is a well-ordered whirlwind.

YOU'VE GOT TO BE MODERNISTIC

James P. Johnson, piano

LABEL: Brunswick 4762; *Snowy Morning Blues* (GRP GRD-604)
DATE: 1930
STYLE: Harlem stride
FORM: march/ragtime (**ABAC**)

Introduction

0:00	After an opening left-hand chord, Johnson's right hand plays a series of descending whole-tone chords (triads derived from the whole-tone scale).

Strain A

0:04	Johnson plays the main melody in stride style, with the left hand alternating between bass notes and chords.
0:07	The end of the first phrase is marked by a syncopation in the left hand.
0:10	The melody leads to a chromatic passage featuring whole-tone harmonies.
0:12	The opening melody is repeated.
0:16	A rising series of whole-tone chords resolves in a full cadence.

Strain A

0:20	Following march/ragtime form, Johnson repeats the strain.

| 0:29 | He shifts the pattern in his left hand, playing the bass note one beat early and temporarily disrupting the accompaniment with a polyrhythm. |

Strain B

| 0:35 | The next strain begins with left-hand bass notes alternating with right-hand chords. The pattern descends chromatically. |

Strain B

| 0:50 | Johnson repeats the strain an octave higher, adding a bluesy figure. |

Strain A

| 1:05 | The right hand is even higher, near the top of the piano keyboard. |

Interlude

| 1:20 | To modulate to a new key, Johnson brings back the whole-tone harmonies and texture of the introduction. |

Strain C (trio)

| 1:24 | The trio is built around repetitions of a short riff. |

Strain C

| 1:39 | As before, the repetition is played an octave higher. The end of the riff pattern is reduced to an emphatic blue note, achieved by playing two adjacent notes at the same time. |

Strain C

| 1:54 | The melody is now in the bass line, with the left hand playing each note twice. |
| 2:01 | The rhythmic pattern in the left hand intensifies to three notes in a row. |

Strain C

| 2:09 | The right hand plays widespread chords in a polyrhythm against the basic meter. |

| 2:17 | Here (and again at 2:23), Johnson disrupts the accompaniment by shifting the position of the bass note. |

Strain C

| 2:24 | Against the same harmonic background, Johnson improvises a new riff. |

Strain C

| 2:39 | Johnson begins his riff pattern with a held-out chord. |

| 2:45 | For two measures, the right and left hands play together rhythmically. |
| 2:47 | The riff pattern shifts to the downbeat, changing the groove. |

Strain C

| 2:54 | Johnson plays his right-hand chords in a quick three-note repetition (similar to what we heard in the left hand at 2:03). |
| 3:07 | With a few short chords, he brings the piece to an end. |

Duke Ellington BEGINS (1899–1974)

As the most important composer that jazz—and arguably the United States—has produced, Duke Ellington played a vital role in every decade of its development, from the 1920s until his death in 1974. His music is probably more widely performed than that of any other jazz composer. Ellington achieved distinction in many roles: composer, arranger, songwriter, bandleader, pianist, producer. He wrote music of every kind, including pop songs and blues; ballets and opera; theater, film, and television scores; suites, concertos, and symphonies; music for personal homages and public dedications; and, most significantly, thousands of instrumental miniatures. All of his music contains decisive elements of jazz, even where there is no improvisation. He made thousands of recordings, more than any other composer or bandleader, some inadvertently (he rarely discouraged fans with tape recorders) and others privately and at his own expense, to be released posthumously.

Ellington's early breakthrough, in the late 1920s and early 1930s, advanced four aspects of New York's musical culture. The first three were strictly musical. (1) He clarified the nature of big-band jazz, demonstrating potential beyond Whiteman's imagination or Henderson's achievement. (2) He solidified the influence of stride piano as a jazz factor, employing it not only as a pianist himself but also as a foundation in orchestrations. (3) He proved that the most individual and adventurous of jazz writing could also be applied to popular songs.

The fourth area concerned his persona and proved no less vital to the standing of jazz and especially its relationship to the Harlem Renaissance. Ellington, a handsome, well-mannered, witty, and serious man, violated assumptions about jazz as a low and unlettered music. A largely self-taught artist, Ellington earned his regal nickname with an innate dignity that musicians, black and white, were eager to embrace. He routinely disconcerted critics, but never lost the adoration and respect of fellow artists. In his refusal to accept racial limitations, he became an authentic hero to black communities across the country for nearly half a century.

Edward Kennedy Ellington was born in Washington, D.C., to a middle-class family who encouraged his talent for music and art. He is said to have acquired his nickname as a child, by virtue of his proud bearing. In school (Armstrong High School, as it happens), Ellington's painting won him a scholarship to study at the Pratt Institute. Instead, he pursued and studied the stride pianists who visited the capital. His first composition, "Soda Fountain Rag," written at fourteen, mimicked James P. Johnson's "Carolina Shout."

As a high school senior, Ellington organized a five-piece band and found enough work to keep him going for several years, until he readied himself to try New York, in 1923. He quickly found a job at the Hollywood Club, which after two incidents of insurance-motivated arson returned as the Kentucky Club, where he enlarged the band, focusing on growling, vocalized brasses and finding a creative ally in Bubber Miley, an innovative trumpet player from South Carolina who enlarged on King Oliver's muting effects. Ellington called his new band the Washingtonians, and made a few records between 1924 and 1926 that show little distinction.

By late 1926, Ellington began to reveal a style of his own, influenced by Miley, whose almost macabre, blues-ridden mewling—quite unlike Armstrong's open-horn majesty—was ideally suited to Ellington's theatrical bent. In crafting pieces with and for Miley, Ellington ignored Don Redman's method of contrasting reeds and brasses, and combined his instruments to create odd voicings, thereby creating a new sound in American music. As presented in his first major works, "East St. Louis Toodle-O" (Ellington's version of a ragtime dance), "Black and Tan Fantasy," and two vividly different approaches to the blues, "The Blues I Love to Sing" and "Creole Love Call" (in which he used wordless singing as he would an instrument), the overall effect was mysterious, audacious, and carnal.

Ellington's career took a giant leap on December 4, 1927, when he opened at Harlem's Cotton Club. Although this segregated citadel was thought to represent the height of New York sophistication, it actually exploited tired minstrel clichés. The bandstand design replicated a Southern mansion with large white columns and a painted backdrop of weeping willows and slave quarters. A mixture of Southern Negro and African motifs (featuring capering light-skinned women) encouraged frank sexuality. For Ellington, though, the whole experience was enlightening. He learned much about show business by working with other composers (including the great songwriter Harold Arlen), choreographers, directors, set designers, and dancers.

As the headliner for the next three years, Ellington became a major celebrity in New York and—through the Cotton Club's radio transmissions—the country. His reputation quickly spread to Europe. The club's erotic revues had inspired him to perfect a wry, insinuating music in which canny instrumental voices were blended into an intimate and seductive musical tableau. Inevitably, it was described as "jungle music," a phrase Ellington found amusing. In truth, he was up to something quite radical.

Ellington was finding legitimate musical subjects in racial pride, quite a turn from Tin Pan Alley's coon and Mammy songs, and sexual desire, an equally sweeping break with the Alley's depictions of romantic innocence. He was not a Broadway composer who borrowed from jazz, like Gershwin, but a true jazz composer—with enormous vitality and humor, and a gift for sensuous melodies, richly textured harmonies, and rollicking rhythms that reflected his love of stride piano. As the band grew in size, it gathered a cast of Ellingtonians, musicians who stayed with him for years, decades, and in some instances entire careers—stylists such as alto saxophonist Johnny Hodges, baritone saxophonist Harry Carney, trumpeter (and successor to Miley) Cootie Williams, trombonist Joe "Tricky Sam" Nanton, clarinetist Barney Bigard, and bassist Wellman Braud. Upon leaving the Cotton Club in 1931, the fifteen-piece band now known as Duke Ellington and His Famous Orchestra traveled the world, and in the process augured the future of jazz with a 1932 song title: "It Don't Mean a Thing (if It Ain't Got That Swing)."

"BLACK AND TAN FANTASY"

A great deal of Ellington's music is programmatic, attempting to describe specific places, people, or events. The tongue-in-cheek attitude of Ellington's arresting "Black and Tan Fantasy" can be appreciated without a back story, but it's perhaps more compelling if the satirical point is taken into account. Unlike the Cotton Club, which refused to admit blacks, other Harlem clubs catered exclusively to African Americans. And some, which were regarded as a pinnacle of liberality, invited members of both races. These were known as the "black and tan" clubs. Ellington's piece works as a response to the idea that these small, overlooked speakeasies absolved a racially divided society. "Black and Tan Fantasy" contrasts a characteristic twelve-bar blues by Miley with a flouncy sixteen-bar melody by Ellington. Miley's theme, the black part of the equation, was based on a spiritual he had learned from his mother. Ellington's, the tan part, draws on the ragtime traditions that lingered in the 1920s. As the two strains merge in a climactic evocation of Chopin's "Funeral March," the piece buries the illusions of an era. Yet while black and tans disappeared, the "Fantasy" remained a steady, much revised number in Ellington's book—an American classic.

BLACK AND TAN FANTASY

Duke Ellington and His Orchestra

Duke Ellington, piano; Bubber Miley, Louis Metcalf, trumpets; Joe "Tricky Sam" Nanton, trombone; Otto Hardwick, Rudy Jackson, and Harry Carney, saxophones; Fred Guy, banjo; Wellman Braud, bass; Sonny Greer, drums

LABEL: Victor 21137; *The Best of the Duke Ellington Centennial Edition* (RCA 63459)
DATE: 1927
STYLE: early New York big band
FORM: 12-bar blues (with a contrasting 16-bar interlude)

Chorus 1 (12-bar blues)

0:00	Over a steady beat in the rhythm section, Miley (trumpet) and Nanton (trombone) play a simple, bluesy melody in the minor mode. The unusual sound they elicit from their tightly muted horns is an excellent example of timbre variation.
0:25	A cymbal crash signals the appearance of new material.

Interlude (16 bars)

0:26	The harmonic progression suddenly changes with an unexpected chord that eventually turns to the major mode. The melody is played by Hardwick (alto saxophone) in a "sweet" style, with thick vibrato, a sultry tone, and exaggerated glissandos.
0:38	During a two-measure break, the band plays a turnaround—a complicated bit of chromatic harmony designed to connect one section with the next.
0:42	Repeat of the opening melody.
0:54	The horns play a series of chords, then stop. The drummer plays several strokes on the cymbal, muting the vibration with his free hand.

Chorus 2

0:58	Over a major-mode blues progression, Miley takes a solo. For the first four bars, he restricts himself to a high, tightly muted note.

| 1:06 | Miley plays expressive bluesy phrases, constantly changing the position of his plunger mute over the pixie mute to produce new sounds that seem eerily vocal (wa-wa). |

Chorus 3

1:23	Miley begins with a pair of phrases reaching upward to an expressive blue note.
1:25	The cymbal responds, as if in sympathy.
1:26	In the next phrase, Miley thickens the timbre by growling into his horn.

Chorus 4

1:47	The band drops out while Ellington plays a cleverly arranged stride piano solo.
1:51	The left hand plays in broken octaves: the lower note of each octave anticipates the beat.
1:58	Ellington plays a striking harmonic substitution.

Chorus 5

2:11	Nanton begins his solo on tightly muted trombone.
2:15	He loosens the plunger mute, increasing the volume and heightening the intensity of the unusual timbre.
2:27	Nanton precedes his last phrase with a bizarre gesture, sounding somewhere between insane laughter and a donkey's whinny.

Chorus 6

| 2:36 | Miley returns for an explosive bluesy statement, featuring quick repeated notes. Each phrase is answered by a sharp accent from the rhythm section. |
| 2:50 | As the harmony changes, the band enters, reinforcing Miley's moan. |

Coda

| 2:57 | With Miley in the lead, the band ends by quoting Chopin's "Funeral March"—returning the piece to the minor mode. |

To appreciate the amazing progress jazz made in the 1920s, you could do worse than listen to "Black and Tan Fantasy" back-to-back with Jelly Roll Morton's "Dead Man Blues," which also involves a satiric fantasy that invokes death and was recorded the previous year. The differences between them exceed questions of musical technique—Morton's polyphony and Ellington's alternating themes. Far more significant is the difference in perspective. Morton's piece looked back, celebrating the traditions from which he sprang. Ellington's looked at the present in a provocative way that promised a vital future.

In the music of Ellington and others who achieved success in the jazz world of Prohibition New York, we hear little deference to jazz's Southern roots. Their music, channeling the city's cosmopolitanism, is smart, urban, fast moving, glittery, independent, and motivated. In liberating jazz from its roots, the Ellington generation is ready to take on everything the entertainment business and the world can throw at it. This sense of a second youth, of a new start, became a motive in the development of jazz, as each subsequent generation strove to remake it in its own image.

6 CHAPTER

Louis Armstrong and the First Great Soloists

Louis Armstrong (1901–1971)

Louis Armstrong is the single most important figure in the development of jazz. His ascension in the 1920s transformed the social music of New Orleans into an art that, in the words of composer Gunther Schuller, "had the potential capacity to compete with the highest order of previously known musical expression," one in which musicians of every geographical and racial background could find their own voice. He remains the only major figure in Western music to influence the music of his era equally as an instrumentalist and a singer.

◀ Louis Armstrong, described by Bing Crosby as "the beginning and the end of music in America," radiated an energy that amplified his artistry. Paris, 1960.

Within a decade, he codified the artistic standards of jazz, and his influence did not stop there. It penetrated every arena of Western music: symphonic trumpet players worked to adapt his bright vibrato, and popular and country performers adapted his phrasing, spontaneity, and natural sound.

Armstrong was also one of the most beloved musicians of the twentieth century—the man who, more than anyone else, conveyed the feeling and pleasure of jazz to audiences throughout the world. The matter of his popularity is important, because it had cultural and political ramifications beyond music. Though raised in unimaginable poverty and racial segregation, he was able to present his music in a generous way that exhilarated and welcomed new listeners. At a time when jazz was denounced from political and religious pulpits as primitive, unskilled, immoral, and even degenerate, Armstrong used his outsize personality to soothe fears and neutralize dissent. America had never experienced anything like him. He seemed to combine nineteenth-century minstrel humor and a nearly obsequious desire to please with an art so thunderously personal and powerful that audiences of every stripe were drawn to him. By the 1950s, he was widely accepted as a national "ambassador of good will" and of America's most admirable qualities. For Duke Ellington, he was "the epitome of the kind of American who goes beyond the rules, a truly good and original man."

Before Armstrong, jazz was generally perceived as an urban folk music that had more in common with ragtime and military bands than with the driving rhythms we now associate with jazz or swing. It was ensemble music, tailored for social functions ranging from dances to funerals, employing a fixed repertory and a communal aesthetic. Without Armstrong, it would surely have developed great soloists (it had already produced at least one in Sidney Bechet), but its progress as a distinctive art—a way of playing music grounded in improvisation—would have been slower and less decisive. His influence may be measured, in large part, by his innovations in five areas.

Blues: Armstrong emphatically established the blues scale and blues feeling as jazz's harmonic foundation at a time when significant jazz figures, especially those on the Eastern Seaboard, thought the blues might be a mere fashion, like ragtime. In 1924, when he first worked in New York, many jazz composers were under the sway of the arrangers who scored Broadway shows and commercial dance bands. The emotional power of Armstrong's music countered that trend like an overpowering tonic.

Improvisation: Armstrong established jazz as music that prizes individual expression. His creative spirit proved too mighty for the strictures of the traditional New Orleans ensemble. His records showed that an improvised music could have the weight and durability of written music. But his increasing technical finesse always remained bound to his emotional honesty. To compete on Armstrong's level, a musician had to do more than master an instrument; he had to make the instrument an extension of his self.

Singing: As a boy, Armstrong mastered scat-singing—using nonsense syllables instead of words, with the same improvisational brio and expressive candor as an instrumentalist. Until 1926, however, when he recorded "Heebie Jeebies," few people had heard a scat vocal. That recording delighted musicians, who imitated him shamelessly. In effect, he had introduced a true jazz vocal style, dependent on mastery of pitch and time as well as fast reflexes and imagination. He soon proved as agile with written lyrics as with scat phrases. Almost instantly, Armstrong's influence was heard in the work of singers as diverse as Bing Crosby and Billie Holiday.

Repertory: In the 1930s, New Orleans "purists" argued that jazz musicians should confine themselves to original New Orleans jazz themes, and avoid popular tunes as lacking in authenticity. Yet many traditional jazz pieces had themselves been adapted from pop tunes, hymns, blues, and classical works heard in the South. Armstrong resolved the debate by creating masterworks based on Tin Pan Alley songs. He showed that pop music could broaden jazz's potential both musically and commercially. His ability to recompose melodies was later summed up in the title of Jimmie Lunceford's Swing Era hit: "'Tain't What You Do (It's the Way That You Do It)."

Rhythm: Perhaps Armstrong's greatest contribution was to teach the world to swing. He introduced a new rhythmic energy that would eventually become second nature to people everywhere. As the most celebrated Negro artist in Western music history to that point, born just two generations after slavery, he incarnated the promise of a new age in which American music would rival that of Europe and Russia. And he did so in a peculiarly American way, defying conventional notions of art, artistry, and artists: his approach to rhythm exemplified the contagiously joyous, bawdy, accessible, human nature of his music.

Not the least miraculous aspect of Armstrong's achievement is that it was forged from such bleak beginnings. Unlike his predecessors in the Great Migration, Armstrong, the first major jazz figure born in the twentieth century, did not peak during the Jazz Age (1920s) and then fade away. He helped to spearhead the Swing Era of the 1930s; and although, like most of his generation, he was disconcerted by modern jazz (bebop) and the jazz-blues synthesis (rhythm and blues) that followed, he persevered beyond those developments with many successes, rebounding with a No. 1 hit record ("Hello, Dolly!") at the height of the Beatles frenzy in the 1960s.

Armstrong was born, on August 4, 1901, to an unwed teenager (no older than sixteen) and a laborer who abandoned them, in an area of New Orleans so devastated by violence, crime, and prostitution that its residents called it "the Battlefield." Mayann, as he called his mother, was physically fragile but strong-minded, and she instilled in her son a sense of worthiness and stoic pride. Armstrong, a prolific writer all his life, wrote of her in his distinguished autobiography *Satchmo: My Life in New Orleans*: "She never envied no one, or anything they may have. I guess I inherited that part of life from Mayann."

At age seven, Louis was already working, delivering coal to prostitutes by night and helping with a rag-and-bone cart by day, blowing a tinhorn to announce the cart's arrival. He organized a quartet to sing for pennies on street corners (the Singing Fools), and received his first cornet from the immigrant Jewish family that owned the rag-and-bone business; the first tune he learned to play, he recalled, was "Home, Sweet Home." In the early hours of New Year's Day, 1913, Louis was apprehended for shooting blanks in the air and was sent to the New Orleans Colored Waif's Home for Boys for eighteen months. There, he received rudimentary musical instruction from the home's bandmaster, Peter Davis, who initially refused to work with a boy of Louis's rough background. During his incarceration, as Davis's position softened, Louis progressed from tambourine to bugle to cornet. Ultimately, Davis made him leader of the institution's band. After his discharge, Louis apprenticed with his idol, Joe Oliver, running errands in return for lessons.

Things began to move quickly for Armstrong in 1918, when he married a violently possessive prostitute (the first of his four wives); adopted the son of a young cousin who had been raped by a white man; and worked saloons and parades, often leading his own trio (with bass and drums) in mostly blues numbers. His career began in earnest that same year with two jobs. When Oliver left for Chicago, he suggested that Louis replace him in the band he had co-led with trombonist Kid Ory. A short time later, Louis was recruited to play on Mississippi riverboat excursions. In order to prove himself eighteen and thus legally responsible, he applied for a draft card, backdating his birth to 1900—July 4, 1900, a patriotic date that became famously associated with him, and the only birthday he ever acknowledged.

Armstrong spent three years on riverboats operated by the Streckfus Steamboat Line, working under the leadership of Fate Marable, a stern taskmaster known for his vigorous playing of the calliope—a difficult instrument consisting of organ pipes powered by steam from the ship's boiler. Audible from a great distance, the calliope announced a steamboat coming to port. This was a decisive engagement for Louis on several counts: he greatly improved his ability to read a music score; he learned to adapt the earthy music of New Orleans to written arrangements; he absorbed a variety of songs beyond the New Orleans repertory; he saw another part of the world and experienced a different kind of audience (exclusively white, except for the one night a week reserved for black customers); and he grew accustomed to the rigors of traveling from one engagement to another, establishing a lifelong pattern.

One restriction, though, galled him: Marable's refusal to let him sing. Partly for that reason, Armstrong quit in September 1921, and returned to Ory's band. During this period, his reputation spread throughout the region. The celebrated New York singer and actress Ethel Waters toured New Orleans with her then little-known pianist, Fletcher Henderson, and attempted to lure him to New York. But Armstrong resolved not to leave his hometown unless Joe Oliver himself sent for him. That summons arrived in August 1922, in the form of a wire inviting him to become a member of Oliver's Creole Jazz Band at Lincoln Gardens, on Chicago's Southside.

In Oliver's band, Armstrong usually played second trumpet, though he occasionally played lead, as on "Dippermouth Blues." If the trumpet breaks he harmonized with Oliver astonished musicians, the brilliance of his timbre was overwhelming—evident on the Creole Jazz Band recordings of "Chimes Blues" and "Froggie Moore." In Oliver's pianist, Armstrong found his second wife. The well-educated Memphis-born Lil Hardin encouraged Louis to leave Oliver and establish himself as a leader. He resisted at first, but in 1924, when Fletcher Henderson, now leading a much-admired orchestra in New York, offered him a seat in the band, he accepted.

Armstrong spent little more than a year in New York, which turned out to be a crucial period for him and for jazz. In a time of strict segregation, Henderson's dance band hired the best black musicians of the day—much as his counterpart and friend Paul Whiteman did with white musicians. Henderson's men—citified, well dressed, self-assured—initially viewed Armstrong as a rube, a newcomer from the country who had made a modest name for himself in Chicago playing in a style that was already deemed old-fashioned. The mockery ceased when they heard his trumpet. Armstrong's authority and originality, his profound feeling for blues, and his irresistible, heart-pounding rhythmic drive converted them all.

Armstrong also became a favorite of record producers. Blues divas had become immensely popular after Mamie Smith's "Crazy Blues" in 1920, and Armstrong was their accompanist of choice. In addition to Bessie Smith ("Everything I did with her, I like," he recalled), he recorded with Ma Rainey, Sippie Wallace, Bertha Hill, and others. In that same year (1924), he and Sidney Bechet participated in Clarence Williams's Blue Five sessions, which combined the breezy entertainment of Southern vaudeville with the sweeping exuberance of a lean New Orleans–style ensemble.

During his fourteen months with Henderson, Armstrong recorded more than three dozen numbers with the band (including "Sugar Foot Strut," the orchestration of Oliver's "Dippermouth Blues"). With Armstrong on board, Henderson's men played with a more prominent beat, while embracing the blues and longer solos. Each of the band's fine musicians sought in his own way to reproduce something of Armstrong's clarion attack, exciting rhythms, and diverse emotions. Every bandleader wanted to hire a soloist in Armstrong's mold, from Paul Whiteman to Duke Ellington.

Armstrong's association with Henderson ended, in part, because of disagreement (again) over one of his talents. Like Louis's boss on the Mississippi riverboat, Henderson would not let him sing—beyond a brief scat break on one record ("Everybody Loves My Baby"). Louis, confident of a vocal ability that everyone else denounced because of his gravelly timbre, angrily returned to Chicago in late 1925.

The Hot Fives and Sevens

Back in Chicago, Armstrong earned his living playing in a pit orchestra that accompanied silent movies, offering overtures and quasi-jazz numbers during intermission. But before the year 1925 was out, OKeh Records, under the supervision of Richard M. Jones, who had been King Oliver's pianist back in New Orleans, invited him to make his first records as a leader. Armstrong agreed with the proviso that he would choose the music and musicians; it is likely that he also notified the company of his intention to sing and speak on the recordings. Other than his wife Lil, he surrounded himself with New Orleanians, three musicians he had already worked with: clarinetist Johnny Dodds and banjoist Johnny St. Cyr in Oliver's band, and trombonist Kid Ory in New Orleans. Louis called his band the Hot Five, and unlike Oliver's group, it existed only to record.

It would be difficult to overstate the impact of the discs made by the Hot Five and Hot Seven (the same instrumentation plus tuba and drums) between 1925 and 1928—sixty-five titles in all, not including similar sessions in which Armstrong appeared as a sideman in support of vocalists or other bandleaders. Here at last we witness jazz's rapid evolution from a group concept dominated by polyphony to a showcase for soloists and individual expression. The modest embellishments heard in Oliver and Morton performances give way here to daring improvisations; two- and four-bar breaks are extended to solos of a full chorus or more; and the multiple strains of ragtime are winnowed down to the single-theme choruses of popular song and blues. Each of these elements can be found in other recordings of the day, but the force of Armstrong's creativity and instrumental control—the vitality and spirit—impart the sensation of a great art coming into flower.

"HOTTER THAN THAT"

This 1927 performance is an illuminating example of how Armstrong revolutionized the New Orleans tradition. The thirty-two-bar chorus is based on the chords of the main strain of "Tiger Rag," a New Orleans jazz tune, popularized in 1918 by the Original Dixieland Jazz Band, though no one knows who wrote it. An unusual aspect of this recording is the addition of a guest to the usual Hot Five. The pioneer guitarist Lonnie Johnson, a native of New Orleans, apprenticed on riverboats and went on to enjoy two dramatically different careers: as one of the first jazz guitar soloists in the 1920s and, from the 1940s through the 1960s, as a popular blues singer-guitarist. His presence reminds us that long after New Orleans generated jazz, the city also provided sustenance for rhythm and blues and rock and roll.

The group's banjoist, Johnny St. Cyr, doesn't play on "Hotter Than That," allowing the dialogue between Armstrong and Johnson the emphasis it deserves. Armstrong plays the first chorus, which is entirely improvised: there is no written theme to set up the improvisations, only the harmonic underpinning borrowed from "Tiger Rag." The third chorus features one of his most memorable scat-singing vocals, especially the episode that follows the mid-chorus break, where Armstrong sings counterrhythms of insistent complexity. Try counting four beats to a measure here, and you may find yourself losing your moorings, because his phrases are in opposition to the ground beat—a technique that later became standard in jazz.

HOTTER THAN THAT

Louis Armstrong and His Hot Five

Louis Armstrong, trumpet; Kid Ory, trombone; Johnny Dodds, clarinet; Lil Hardin Armstrong, piano; Lonnie Johnson, guitar

LABEL: OKeh 8535; *Louis Armstrong: The Complete Hot Five & Hot Seven Recordings,* vol. 3 (Columbia/Legacy CK 87011)
DATE: 1927
STYLE: New Orleans Jazz
FORM: 32-bar popular song (**ABAC**)

Introduction

0:00   The band begins with collective improvisation, with Armstrong's trumpet clearly in front. The remaining instruments provide support: the trombone plays simple single-note figures, while the clarinet is distantly in the background. The harmonies are those of the last eight bars of the chorus.

Chorus 1

0:09   **A**   Armstrong begins his improvisation. Many of his notes are ghosted—played so lightly that they're almost inaudible.

0:18   **B**

0:25   Trumpet break.

0:27   **A**   Coming out of the break, Armstrong places accents on the backbeat, before finishing with a quick triplet figure.

0:36   **C**   Armstrong emphasizes a high note with a shake—an extra vibrato at the end.

0:43   During a two-measure break, Dodds begins his clarinet solo.

Chorus 2

0:45   **A**   Dodds plays his solo in the clarinet's upper register. Beneath him, Hardin plays rhythmic piano fills.

0:54   **B**

1:02   Dodds's clarinet break ends on a blue note.

1:03   **A**

1:12   **C**

1:19   A scat-singing break introduces the next solo, by Armstrong.

Chorus 3

1:21   **A**   Armstrong begins his solo by singing on-the-beat quarter notes, backed by the guitar's improvised lines. The timbre of his voice is rough but pleasant.

1:30   **B**   As his melodic ideas take flight, he stretches the beat in unpredictable ways.

1:36		Scat-singing break.
1:39	A	Armstrong ingeniously uses melody, rhythm, and scat syllables to create a strong sense of polyrhythm.
1:47	C	

Interlude

| 1:55 | | In a loose extension of the previous chorus, Armstrong exchanges intimate, bluesy moans with Johnson's guitar. |
| 2:13 | | Hardin on piano calls the band together with four bars of octaves. |

Chorus 4

2:17	A	Ory takes a sharply accented trombone solo, which echoes the beginning of Armstrong's scat solo.
2:26	B	
2:33		Trumpet break: Armstrong interrupts Ory's solo with a rocket-like string of quick notes, ending with a high B♭.
2:35	A	Collective improvisation, with Armstrong hitting his high note again and again in a short, syncopated riff.
2:43	C	The last eight bars are in stop-time: Armstrong generates tension by playing unpredictable short lines.

Coda

| 2:50 | | Johnson and Armstrong exchange brief solos. |
| 2:56 | | Johnson's line ends on a dissonant diminished-seventh chord, which leaves the harmony suspended. |

ENTER Earl Hines (1903–1983)

In 1926, Armstrong was hired as featured soloist with the Carroll Dickerson Orchestra, at the Sunset Café in Chicago. For the first time, his name was up in lights, as "the world's greatest trumpet player." White musicians, including Bing Crosby, Bix Beiderbecke, and the very young Benny Goodman, flocked to hear him. Throughout that year and the next, Armstrong studio units produced such benchmark recordings as "Potato Head Blues," "Wild Man Blues," "Willie the Weeper" (famous for its climax propelled by the drums of Baby Dodds), and "Struttin' with Some Barbecue." But something just as special was developing at the Sunset. While on tour, Dickerson had recruited a young pianist from Pittsburgh, Earl Hines, an utterly original stylist who subverted the techniques on which other jazz pianists relied.

Hines was content neither to play on-the-beat background chords, in the manner of Lil Armstrong, nor to confine himself to the propulsive rhythms of stride or boogie-woogie (a Midwestern phenomenon in which the pianist's left hand plays eight beats to every bar). He preferred to combine those approaches, with the result that his idiosyncratic style seemed to play games with the rhythm. Above all, he was determined to use the piano much as Armstrong used the trumpet, as a solo instrument improvising single-note melodies. To make them audible, he developed an ability to improvise in tremolos (the speedy alternation of two or more notes, creating a pianistic version of the brass man's vibrato) and octaves or tenths: instead of hitting one note at a time with his right hand, he hit two and with vibrantly percussive force—his reach was so large that jealous competitors spread the ludicrous rumor that he had had the webbing between his fingers surgically removed.

Hines and Armstrong hit it off immediately. As Hines recalled, "I was amazed to find a trumpeter like Louis who was playing everything that I was trying to do on the piano. So, there were the two of us expressing the same spirit." For the 1928 Hot Five recordings, Armstrong changed the personnel to employ Hines and the younger musicians he worked with in Dickerson's band at the Sunset Café and New York's Savoy Ballroom. (The Savoy posters had advertised: "Special attraction. The great Louis Armstrong in person!" To capitalize on his success in New York, many of the 1928 records made in Chicago were released as Louis Armstrong and His Savoy Ballroom Five.) On occasion, he recruited guests—notably Fletcher Henderson's aide de camp Don Redman.

The new recordings, representing a marked advance on their sensational predecessors, included the seminal "West End Blues," "Basin Street Blues," "Muggles," "St. James Infirmary" (Armstrong put this old song on the map with a breakthrough vocal, proving he was just as compelling with lyrics as he was scat), and the tour de force "Tight Like That," in which Armstrong develops three thematic choruses of architectural grandeur. With these records, the polyphonic New Orleans ensemble all but disappeared, replaced by the mixture of solos and homophonic section work that continues to dominate jazz today. The best example of the interplay between Armstrong and Hines came about at the end of a session, when the ensemble had finished for the day. The two men improvised a duet on an old Armstrong rag they had played in concert, "Weather Bird." Worried that fans of the Hot Five would object, the record company did not release it until 1930.

"WEATHER BIRD"

"Weather Bird" has a dizzying stop-and-go momentum, punched up with humor, competitive daring, and an evolving beauty. Armstrong wrote "Weather Bird" for King Oliver and recorded it with him in 1923. Unlike his other compositions, it uses the traditional ragtime structure of three sixteen-bar strains. On Oliver's record, the piece is played as a ragtime march, with a stop-time section and brief breaks (including one by the twin trumpets); there is no sustained improvisation.

Armstrong and Hines follow the same format, but turn the piece into a friendly battle, packed with broken rhythms, shifty jabs and feints, until the grand finale: a sixteen-bar coda, during which they exchange phrases with a mocking "where-are-we-going-with-this" wariness, concluded by Armstrong's exquisitely timed ascending scale, cradled by Hines's final chords.

WEATHER BIRD

Louis Armstrong and Earl Hines

Louis Armstrong, trumpet; Earl Hines, piano

LABEL: OKeh 41454; *Louis Armstrong: The Complete Hot Five & Hot Seven Recordings,* vol. 3 (Columbia/Legacy CK 87011)
DATE: 1928
STYLE: early jazz
FORM: march/ragtime

Introduction

0:00	Armstrong plays the opening melody on trumpet, discreetly backed by Hines's piano.

Strain A

0:04	Armstrong displays his command of dynamics. Some notes are played at full volume; others (ghosted) are so soft that they virtually disappear. Underneath him, Hines plays surprising syncopations, undermining the steady rhythm: he has no intention of playing the well-behaved accompanist. His style is not ragtime or stride, but a more idiosyncratic mixture.
0:13	The strain comes to rest on a half cadence.
0:18	The harmonies begin a drive to a full cadence. (We will call this passage, already heard in the introduction, the *cadence figure.*)

Strain B

0:23	A new strain, marked by a striking melodic phrase. Armstrong primarily sticks to the original tune, leaving room for Hines to improvise.

0:28	Armstrong plays a static ragtime polyrhythm, against which Hines adds his own melodies and rhythms.
0:33	At times, they seem to read each other's minds: Armstrong plays a short phrase that Hines instantly echoes; a few seconds later, when Armstrong briefly rests, Hines pounces in with a dramatic flourish.
0:39	Armstrong ends his line with the last few notes of the *cadence figure*.

Strain B

0:41	Hines begins to solo in stride piano style.
0:49	At the place where a break would normally occur in early jazz, he suddenly shifts to a new pianistic texture. For the next several measures, his playing is highly polyrhythmic and unpredictable.
0:56	As the strain ends, he returns to a more normal texture, clearly playing the *cadence figure*.

Strain A

1:00	Armstrong repeats the melody for strain **A**, embellishing it, and then abandoning it for outright improvisation.
1:07	He begins a phrase with a vivid high note and a flurry of eighth notes.
1:14	He returns to the *cadence figure*.

Interlude

| 1:18 | A transitional passage: Armstrong and Hines begin with simple syncopated figures, but rapidly increase the rhythmic intensity to unnerving levels. |

Strain C (trio)

1:23	Unusually, the trio doesn't modulate: it's in the same key as the first two strains. Hines plays a piano solo.
1:32	Hines pushes his improvisation so far that it outraces even his own abilities: we can occasionally hear mistakes.
1:37	At the end of the strain, he dissolves tension by returning to a variation of the *cadence figure*.

Strain C

1:41	The strain begins with a break for Armstrong.
1:44	The two men test each other's mettle, phrasing both on and off the beat, in a kind of call-and-response match.
1:51	During a break, Armstrong ascends to a new high note.
1:58	He returns to the *cadence figure*.

Strain C

| 2:00 | The call-and-response roles are reversed: Hines begins with a break, Armstrong responding. |
| 2:10 | During an oddly impromptu break, Hines plays a disorienting rhythm ending on an aggressively dissonant note, resolved—at the last second—with a consonance. |

| 2:14 | Armstrong plays the *cadence figure* with an interesting rhythmic twist. |

Coda

2:18	Once again, Armstrong begins with a break.
2:20	Hines responds with dissonant harmonies, suggesting that he wishes to end the piece.
2:22	Armstrong answers, matching the dissonance in his melodic line.
2:25	Hines moves toward a final cadence. The exchanges become shorter, as the two musicians try to figure out where to go.
2:32	Suddenly, Armstrong begins a new phrase, ascending slowly but with steady acceleration, virtually eliminating all previous sense of meter.
2:36	In response to Armstrong's high note, Hines adds the concluding harmonies.

Before Armstrong came along, most jazz groups reflected the concepts of their leaders (Jelly Roll Morton and King Oliver) or took an ensemble approach (Original Dixieland Jazz Band). Armstrong's brilliance as a soloist blew the old polyphonic ensemble apart, inspiring countless young musicians to study jazz as a new kind of musical expression that allowed a relatively unfettered improvisational freedom.

Armstrong seemed to be offering jazz as a gift to anyone who could feel and master it, of any region or race. By the end of the 1920s, the fad of naming jazz bands after New Orleans had virtually disappeared. And the arrival, in those same years, of gifted and original white musicians underscored the reality that jazz had the potential to become an idiom of universal acceptance. Armstrong put it this way: "Jazz is only what you are." By 1929, dozens of forceful musical personalities, some of them older and more experienced than Armstrong, were following suit. They forged a music in which the soloist emerged as prince of the realm, in which the best composers and arrangers were those who made the most creative use of their soloists. Among the most original of those soloists were Bix Beiderbecke and Coleman Hawkins.

Bix Beiderbecke (1903–1931)

Leon Beiderbecke, known throughout his life as Bix (a corruption of his middle name, Bismark), was born in Davenport, Iowa. His mother played church organ and encouraged her son to pick out melodies on the family piano. Bix took a few lessons but relied chiefly on his exceptional musical ear. The piano influenced his harmonic thinking as he started on cornet

(here, he was entirely self-taught), and he never abandoned it: he auditioned for the musicians' union as a pianist and composed his most ambitious music for piano, specifically four short pieces ("In a Mist" is the most
accomplished) that have been much adapted and orchestrated.

Beiderbecke belonged to the first generation of musicians who learned
about jazz from recordings. This kind of introduction had an immediate
threefold influence. First, young people were exposed to jazz without having to live in a particular area or sneak into off-limits places (saloons) where
it was performed. Second, owning records encouraged, through repeated
plays, study and memorization. Third, records freed the imagination of
young listeners to interpret jazz as they pleased, without the constricting
influence of tradition. In the era before network radio, recordings could
bring a New Orleans jazz ensemble, and the faraway world it represented,
into non-Southern towns like the stolid German-American community of
Davenport.

Bix was fourteen when the Original Dixieland Jazz Band issued its first
records, and they affected him deeply—much to the vexation of his parents, whose abhorrence of jazz and Beiderbecke's association with it never
abated. He taught himself cornet by mimicking and harmonizing with
recorded performances. Live jazz played by Southern black musicians also
came his way, thanks to the Streckfus steamers that regularly docked at
Davenport, one of the northernmost ports on the Mississippi River. Without knowing it, he may have heard the teenage Armstrong at a riverboat
musicians' serenade, though there is no evidence to support that romantic
image.

While Bix was haunting jazz clubs, he neglected his schoolwork and
even suffered a humiliating run-in with the police. As a result, in 1921
his parents sent him to Lake Forrest Academy in Illinois, a move that Bix
experienced with anguish as an exile from his family, but one that put him
within train-hopping distance of Chicago. Soon he was making regular vis-
its to Lincoln Gardens and other Chicago nightclubs, soaking up the music
of King Oliver, Louis Armstrong, the New Orleans Rhythm Kings, and
other bands that passed through town. More truancies led to his expulsion
from Lake Forrest, and in 1923 he joined the Wolverines—the first band
of Northern whites formed in imitation of the New Orleans style. A year
later, they recorded for Gennett; their thirteen numbers, often awkwardly
played, would be forgotten today except for the clarity and supple drive of
Beiderbecke's cornet, which suggests a highly individual, almost detached
temper, like none other in that period.

Late in 1924, Beiderbecke also recorded with the Sioux City Six, alongside C-melody saxophonist Frank Trumbauer (1901–1956)—the beginning of a lifelong association. The C-melody saxophone enjoyed popularity in the early years of the twentieth century for its strong limber sound— suggesting a cross between an alto and a tenor—and because it's in the key of C, the same as the piano. It never made much headway in jazz; Trumbauer was its only important exponent. He presided over the most admired white small-group jazz records of the 1920s, and his sweet-without-being-corny timbre, lyricism, phrasing, and songlike use of smears and glides (or portamentos) introduced a delicacy to saxophone playing that made an indelible impression on several major black saxophonists, notably Lester Young and Benny Carter.

Beiderbecke and Trumbauer became the figureheads for a generation of white jazz musicians (almost all born between 1904 and 1909) often referred to as the Austin High Gang, after those who had attended Chicago's Austin High School: pianist Joe Sullivan, drummer Dave Tough, tenor saxophonist Bud Freeman, cornetist Jimmy McPartland, and clarinetist Frank Teschemacher. Their associates, white musicians who had either grown up in Chicago or, like Beiderbecke, gravitated there from other points in the Midwest, included clarinetists Benny Goodman, Pee Wee Russell, and Don Murray, guitarist Eddie Condon, bass saxophonist Adrian Rollini, and drummer Gene Krupa. Collectively, they created the Chicago style, which began by imitating New Orleans bands and evolved into a more slapdash, aggressively rhythmic school that combined expansive solos with polyphonic theme statements. Their music represented both homage to black jazz and a rebellion against the gentility of the white middle class.

While some black musicians came from homes where the saxophone was considered "the devil's instrument" and the blues decried as vulgar, the majority were committed professionals, devoted to perfecting their art and honing their careers. The neighborhoods in which they flourished (New Orleans, Chicago's Southside, and New York's Harlem) gave them little reason to think of themselves as youthful rebels. But for white musicians of Bix's generation to align themselves with African Americans and their music was a daring act, a gauntlet thrown down to their disapproving parents. As Eddie Condon, the most verbal and obstinate proponent of the Chicago school (sometimes referred to as Condon-style jazz) boasted, they were out to rile "the Republicans." He proudly recalled of an early performance: "One of the ladies told me it was just like having the Indians in town again."

Beiderbecke's flamelike career, cut short at twenty-eight, chiefly from alcoholism, strengthened their rebellious conviction, despite the financial security Bix had achieved in his last years as featured soloist in Paul Whiteman's orchestra. Largely unknown to the public during his life, his gentle genius accrued in death the lineaments of martyrdom. Bix recorded between 1924 and 1930, and the high-water mark of his legacy is the series of sessions made in 1927 with Trumbauer (they were initially released as Frankie Trumbauer & His Orchestra) and the influential and serenely capable guitarist Eddie Lang. "Singin' the Blues," one of the most imitated of all recordings, is generally considered their masterpiece, but it's only one of several imperishable gems.

"SINGIN' THE BLUES"

Three things to keep in mind while listening to this recording: (1) the source material is a popular song, introduced in 1920; (2) the song is never actually played as written except in the eight-bar ensemble passage following the cornet solo; (3) the tempo and feeling of the performance are indicative of a ballad. These aspects were considered novel in 1927, when jazz musicians rarely drew on Tin Pan Alley songs, when improvisers embellished the written melody instead of displacing it with original variations, and when contemplative tempos were usually reserved for the blues.

This performance is dominated by full-chorus solos by Trumbauer and Beiderbecke, accompanied by Lang, whose firm second- and fourth-beat accents and fluid, responsive arpeggios give it much of its propulsion and charm. Trumbauer's virtues are beautifully displayed in this, his most famous solo. Beiderbecke's endlessly celebrated solo conveys instantly the qualities that so startled his contemporaries. Jazz is a music of individuality and, therefore, of sensibility. Beiderbecke introduced a new sensibility, quite different from the extroverted Armstrong. There is a shy politeness to Bix's playing, as he rings each note with the precision of a percussionist hitting chimes. He plots his variations with great care—as Lang does his accompaniment, playing with greater harmonic daring to match Bix's melodies.

The two long solos on "Singin' the Blues" quickly entered the lexicon of jazz, and have since been incessantly studied and imitated. Fletcher Henderson recorded a version in which his reed section played the Trumbauer solo and cornetist Rex Stewart played Bix's improvisation, as though they were composed pieces of music, which in this instance they were (by virtue of being played from a written score). These solos are also believed to be the first to which lyrics were written (a process that came to be known as "vocalese" when it blossomed in the 1950s). In 1935, Marion Harris made a very fine recording singing the Beiderbecke and Trumbauer solos.

SINGIN' THE BLUES

Frankie Trumbauer and His Orchestra

Frankie Trumbauer, C-melody saxophone; Bix Beiderbecke, cornet; Bill Rank, trombone; Jimmy Dorsey, clarinet; Doc Ryker, alto saxophone; Paul Mertz, piano; Eddie Lang, guitar; Chauncey Morehouse, drums

LABEL: OKeh 40772; *Bix Beiderbecke,* vol. 1: *Singin' the Blues* (Sony/BMG 723808)
DATE: 1927
STYLE: Chicago-style jazz
FORM: 32-bar popular song (**ABA′C**)

Introduction

| 0:00 | | In a passage arranged by Bill Challis, the horns enter in block-chord texture, accompanied by fills on the cymbals. |

Chorus 1

0:07	A	Trumbauer begins his solo on C-melody saxophone, swooping up to his first note, accompanied by Lang on guitar (with the pianist distantly in the background).
0:16		Lang's accompaniment occasionally provides improvised countermelodies.
0:21	B	Trumbauer's high note is preceded by a lengthy scooped entrance.
0:31		A two-measure break features Trumbauer's subtle phrases. The break ends with guitar chords and a cymbal crash.
0:35	A′	
0:41		A passage by Trumbauer in rapid triplets is neatly extended by Lang's guitar.
0:49	C	
0:59		Trumbauer's concluding break is fast and unpredictable.

Chorus 2

1:03	A	Beiderbecke enters on cornet. He plays with a cool, introverted feeling, pulling back in volume at the end of each phrase.
1:17	B	His melody features the hint of a blue note.
1:28		On his break, Beiderbecke improvises a fast passage that ends with delicately played repeated notes.
1:31	A′	He suddenly erupts into a dramatic upward rip. This heated emotion quickly subsides, as if he were letting off a bit of steam.
1:46	C	

1:52   To bring his solo to a close, he adds touches of the blues.

Chorus 3

2:00 **A** The band states the original melody of the song, disguised by a mild version of New Orleans polyphony. The drummer adds accents on the cymbals.

2:15 **B** Dorsey's clarinet solo loosely suggests Beiderbecke's restrained style.

2:26   Dorsey's break ends almost in a whisper.

2:29 **A'** The band returns with collective improvisation, with Beiderbecke's cornet on top.

2:44 **C**

2:46   A one-measure break features Lang playing a rapid upward arpeggio on guitar.

2:51   Beiderbecke begins his last line with another aggressive rip, followed by short riffs on a repeated note.

2:58   A cymbal stroke brings the piece to a close.

Coleman Hawkins (1904–1969)

In contrast with Beiderbecke's meteoric career, Coleman Hawkins's spanned five decades of jazz history, at the end of which he had become one of its universally admired patriarchs. His great period came in the 1930s and 1940s, but it was in the 1920s that he created an almost universally imitated template for playing tenor saxophone.

Hawkins, born in St. Joseph, Missouri, began learning piano at age five from his mother, a teacher and organist. He also studied cello, and added the C-melody saxophone at nine; as a teenager, he played both instruments professionally at Kansas City dances. In 1922, Hawkins joined with Mamie Smith and Her Jazzhounds; that summer he took up the tenor saxophone. Touring with Smith, he traveled from Kansas City to Chicago and eventually to both coasts, electing to stay in New York to freelance with top musicians, including ragtime clarinetist Wilbur Sweatman. When Fletcher Henderson heard Hawkins with Sweatman's band, he engaged him for a record session and then for a spot in his new orchestra. Hawkins stayed with Henderson for eleven years, establishing himself as the leading figure on his instrument.

From the beginning, he demonstrated tremendous authority, bringing to the saxophone qualities more often associated with the cello: wide vibrato, dynamics, and a huge sound. What he lacked in swing, blues sensibility, and emotional clarity became clear to him when Henderson hired

Louis Armstrong in 1924. Like everyone else in the band, Hawkins was stunned by the strength of Armstrong's music. During the next few years, he strove to adapt Armstrong's style to the tenor saxophone. An early indication of his increasing maturity was an explosive solo on Henderson's 1926 record "Stampede," a great success among musicians and often cited by the next generation of tenor saxophonists as a decisive influence on their education.

Hawkins's 1939 masterpiece "Body and Soul" has been called the greatest of all jazz solos, but it was a decade in the making, and the 1929 "One Hour" was a benchmark in that process. Up to this point, Hawkins's playing had conspicuously lacked a legato, or smooth, attack. His phrasing had consisted of clearly articulated notes, even at very fast tempos. An essential component of swing was missing: relaxation. Nor was there any romance in his music. Playing legato meant learning how to soften the gruff edges of his timbre and to move from one note to another with a fluid, more gracefully commanding manner. In "One Hour," Hawkins unveiled a radically new approach to the tenor saxophone—one that transcended the smooth melodicism of Trumbauer with nearly rapturous power.

"ONE HOUR"

"One Hour" was recorded at an integrated session—a circumstance that in 1929 was very infrequent in recordings and unheard-of in live performance. Hawkins and bassist Pops Foster are the black musicians in a white band led by Red McKenzie, who created studio groups under the rubric Mound City Blue Blowers. Except for trombonist-arranger Glenn Miller, all the white musicians were closely identified with the Chicago style, though you wouldn't know it from this performance.

The piece consists of a series of improvised variations on the song "If I Could Be with You One Hour Tonight," composed by James P. Johnson with lyrics by Henry Creamer. The song was published in 1926, but did not become a hit until 1930, when Louis Armstrong, cabaret singer Ruth Etting, and McKinney's Cotton Pickers (a big band arranged by Don Redman) each recorded it—the latter achieving a No. 1 hit. In other words, when "One Hour" was made, few people had ever heard the actual melody on which it was based.

The structure is that of a sixteen-bar song, following the ABAC format; each segment is four bars rather than the usual eight. Unlike the original song, however, this version adds two measures to each C section, in what amounts to a soloist's coda, extending each chorus to eighteen measures. The first chorus, by leader Red McKenzie, has a dated, pleading quality, very much of its time, emphasized by the raspy sound of his signature instrument—a pocket comb wrapped in tissue to simulate a kazoo.

But the spotlight belongs to Coleman Hawkins, who plays with a romantic ardor new to jazz. Hawkins's style is strongly influenced by Louis Armstrong: we can easily imagine the trumpeter playing many of Hawkins's phrases, though not with his amorous attack. The most telling aspect of his improvisation is the calm sureness with which it is played. He has everything under control: a richly virile timbre; superb intonation; rhythmic, melodic, and harmonic variety underscored by his use of long, expressive phrases. Hawkins carries the listener along with his force, logic, and character.

Pee Wee Russell, a highly original clarinetist who strenuously resisted being stereotyped as a Chicago-style musician, follows with a gripping solo. The Armstrong influence is especially clear in Russell's clipped percussive notes at the beginning of his solo, each clearly articulated and colored while providing affecting contrast to Hawkins's lavish melodies. Glenn Miller's comparatively conventional and restrained closing solo on trombone offers, in turn, a sharp contrast to Hawkins's romanticism and Russell's idiosyncrasies.

ONE HOUR

Mound City Blue Blowers (with Coleman Hawkins)
Red McKenzie, pocket comb; Coleman Hawkins, tenor saxophone; Glenn Miller, trombone; Pee Wee Russell, clarinet; Eddie Condon, banjo; Jack Bland, guitar; Pops Foster, bass; Gene Krupa, drums

LABEL: Victor V-38100; *Coleman Hawkins* (Verve 314549085-2)
DATE: 1929
STYLE: early jazz
FORM: 18-bar popular song (**ABAC**, with two bars added to the **C** section)

Introduction (6 bars)

0:00   Hawkins begins on his own, the band quickly entering to support him. His playing is rhapsodic and rhythmically unpredictable.

Chorus 1

0:17   **A**   McKenzie enters playing the pocket comb. His melodies feature sweeping bluesy phrases with variable intonation, a wide vibrato, and throaty timbre. Behind him, the horns play simple chords, outlining the song's harmonic progression.

0:22		The bass enters, adding a firmer rhythmic foundation. McKenzie plays a kind of melodic paraphrase, coming close to the original tune without quite stating it.
0:28	B	
0:39	A	
0:50	C	
1:04		Hawkins enters a bar early, on a repeated note.

Chorus 2

1:06	A	Hawkins begins with a pair of gently matched phrases, fitting the original melody's mood but with notes of his own.
1:16	B	Hawkins imitates Armstrong's style by hardening his tone to play more vigorous double-time figures.
1:27	A	
1:32		He returns to a more rhapsodic rhythmic style.
1:37	C	Once again, he hardens his tone, aiming for a climax on his highest note.

Chorus 3

1:53	A	Russell begins his clarinet solo. His first phrase is slow and tentative, but gains intensity when it reaches a blue note.
2:03	B	
2:13	A	
2:16		He colors certain notes with a distinctive growl.
2:24	C	
2:29		Russell's solo concludes with a series of blue notes.

Chorus 4

2:40	A	Miller takes a trombone solo. His playing is simple, building on the mood of Russell's solo but gradually becoming more lyrical.
2:50	B	
3:01	A	
3:11	C	As the piece nears the end, all the musicians enter in collective improvisation.

SATCHMO'S WORLD

Louis Armstrong's Hot Fives and Sevens emancipated jazz from the conventions of an inherited, ritualized tradition, and paved the way for a new music. They sold well by the standards of "race" labels, distributed to targeted urban communities, but they caused barely a ripple in the mainstream compared with popular white musicians of the day, like Paul Whiteman and singers Al Jolson and Gene Austin. Musicians, however, eagerly awaited every new Armstrong release, and his reputation in jazz circles grew accordingly. This equation was reversed in the late 1930s. By the time the mainstream audience discovered him, establishing Armstrong as one of the world's most successful recording artists, musicians looked to younger players for new directions.

After the last of the 1928 Hot Five sessions, Armstrong went on the road with Carroll Dickerson, performing in Detroit and at Harlem's Savoy Ballroom. His next record date, in March 1929, was a double milestone. It included the first integrated jazz ensemble that was generally acknowledged as such: the band released only one track—an impromptu blues, "Knockin' a Jug"—but its personnel (three blacks, three whites) symbolized the fact that jazz had crossed the racial divide and had produced a new crop of musicians who had the technical and creative abilities to function as soloists. The three white participants—Eddie Lang, trombonist Jack Teagarden, and pianist Joe Sullivan—all became prominent jazz figures.

At the same session, Armstrong fronted a completely different, integrated, ten-piece orchestra, under the musical direction of Luis Russell, a Panamanian-born pianist, arranger, and bandleader who as a teenager had won a $3,000 lottery and used the prize to move to New Orleans. This band not only mingled black and white, but also encompassed a broad geographical sweep, with musicians from South America, New Orleans, Georgia, Alabama, Indiana, and Boston. They were not chosen for that reason, nor were their diverse backgrounds widely known. But for those paying attention, the lesson was clear: jazz had a global, pan-racial future. The orchestra recorded two numbers that day: a traditional New Orleans anthem, "Mahogany Hall Stomp," on which Armstrong improvised a very untraditional three-chorus blues solo; and "I Can't Give You Anything but Love," a New York show tune by the team of Jimmy McHugh and Dorothy Fields. This was the record that proved how effective a singer Armstrong could be with standard pop fare and how completely he could reinvent it as jazz.

There was no stopping him now. Weeks later, in July 1929, he achieved a major hit with Fats Waller's song "Ain't Misbehavin'," which he performed that summer on Broadway in more than 200 performances of the revue *Hot Chocolates*. Also that July, he recorded another Waller song, "(What Did I Do to Be So) Black and Blue," altering it in his interpretation from a torch song, about a dark-skinned woman who loses her man to a lighter-skinned rival, to a statement of social protest. During the next few years (1930–33), Armstrong recorded every kind of song, from "St. Louis Blues" and "Tiger Rag" to "Star Dust" and "Song of the Islands." New York celebrities feted him with a banquet, while younger musicians and fans, black and white, imitated everything he did. The clarinetist Mezz Mezzrow recalled people copying his trademark white handkerchiefs, his slouch, his slang, his growl, and his fondness for marijuana: "All the raggedy kids, especially those who became vipers [pot smokers], were so inspired with self-respect after digging how neat and natty Louis was, they started to dress up real good."

There were bumps along the way: he was arrested in Los Angeles for smoking pot, and was then obliged to work for the mobbed-up agent who got him sprung. After long engagements in Los Angeles, New York, and Chicago and tours that took in most of the Midwest and Northeast, Armstrong sailed for Europe in 1932, triumphing in London and Paris. The reviewers were ecstatic. One British journalist mispronounced one of Louis's nicknames (Satchelmouth) as "Satchmo," and the name stuck for good. He returned to Europe to even greater acclaim in 1933 and 1934—thousands greeted him at the train station in Copenhagen. By this time, he had begun to star in short films, which invariably employed demeaning stereotypes. Yet Armstrong transcended them, seemingly winking at the audience, which venerated him as a great artist who subverted the clichés of racial condescension.

The years 1935 and 1936 found Armstrong taking the steps that allowed him to conquer the American mainstream audience. The Swing Era had been launched, and the whole country wanted to dance to big-band jazz. Armstrong signed a long-term contract to front Luis Russell's Orchestra, in effect making it his own. He took on a powerful manager, Joe Glaser, whose control of Louis's career began with a lucrative Decca Records contract that lasted nearly twenty years. Armstrong published his first (heavily ghostwritten) autobiography, *Swing That Music*, and received star billing for a cameo appearance in a Bing Crosby movie, *Pennies from Heaven*. He released dozens of hit records, appeared in other movies, and became the first black performer to host a nationally sponsored radio show.

In this period (the mid-1930s), Armstrong's voice developed into a surprisingly mellow tenor, and he was widely acclaimed as one of the great singers in jazz or popular music. His trumpet playing achieved an astonishing brilliance, famous for intricate high-note flourishes and melody statements that imparted unsuspected depths to familiar songs. Among his great big-band recordings are a glittering remake of "Struttin' with Some Barbecue," "Swing That Music," "Jubilee," "Love Walked In," "Ev'ntide," "I Double Dare You," and "Skeleton in the Closet." There was no place to go but down.

Things began to sour during the Second World War, as tastes changed and some of his own musicians complained that his orchestra had lost its spark—that he was bored and simply going through the motions. The younger audience had discovered rhythm and blues, and many forward-looking musicians were entranced by new jazz styles, later known as bebop or cool jazz, and shunned the good-natured, old-fashioned show business presentation Armstrong had come to represent. His career was in a slump when, in 1946, he appeared in a Hollywood travesty, *New Orleans* (he later observed, "The things those Hollywood people make us do are always a sham"), which had the beneficial result of encouraging him to return to a small-band format for the first time in seventeen years. Subsequent triumphs at New York's Carnegie Hall and Town Hall in 1947 led to the formation of an integrated sextet billed as Louis Armstrong and His All Stars, the unit he would lead for the rest of his life.

In its early years, the All Stars really *were* stars, including his old friend trombonist Jack Teagarden, clarinetist Barney Bigard (formerly of Duke Ellington's Orchestra), drummer Sid Catlett (an audience favorite who had played in the big bands of Fletcher Henderson and Benny Goodman), and his early partner Earl Hines, who had himself become a major bandleader during the Swing Era. Armstrong continued to make movies and hit records throughout the 1950s, regularly appearing on television, traveling constantly, and earning his reputation as America's ambassador of good will. In the latter part of that decade, however, he found himself at the center of a political storm.

In 1956, CBS News arranged for Armstrong to visit Africa as part of a documentary film it was preparing about him. When he arrived in Accra, in Ghana, thousands stormed the tarmac to see him. After lunching one day with Prime Minister Kwame Nkrumah, a longtime fan, he was escorted to the stadium, where he performed for an audience of 100,000; CBS cameras captured Nkrumah in tears as Armstrong sang "(What Did I Do to Be So) Black and Blue." The experience was no less emotional for Armstrong, who remarked, "After all, my ancestors came from here and I still have African blood in me." Inspired by Ghana's independence, he faced a quandary on his return home: how to deal with the fight for civil rights in his own country. Armstrong insisted on touring the South with an integrated band or not at all, even when the audiences were segregated (with blacks in the balcony). Early in 1957, at one such concert in Knoxville, Tennessee, a stick of dynamite was hurled at the theater. Armstrong managed to avert panic by reassuring the audience, "That's all right folks, it's just the phone."

His humor failed him that September, though, when Arkansas governor Orval Faubus ordered the National Guard to block the admission of black students to Little Rock's Central High School. "The way they are treating my people in the South, the government can go to hell," he told a reporter. Meanwhile, the U.S. government, determined to capitalize on Armstrong's African success, planned to send him to the Soviet Union as part of the 1950s cultural exchange program. Armstrong balked: "The people over there ask me what's wrong with my country, what am I supposed to say?" When President Eisenhower finally sent federal troops to Arkansas, Armstrong sent him a supportive telegram. Yet the FBI investigated him, a conservative columnist asked for a boycott of his concerts and records, and a few black entertainers criticized him for speaking out.

At the same time, others characterized him as an Uncle Tom, confusing his persona as an entertainer with minstrel attitudes. His demeanor ("aggressively happy," in writer Truman Capote's words) made them uncomfortable. He was now a confusing figure: irresistible as an entertainer and artist, even to many of his detractors, but an embarrassing vestige of the era when black performers grinned and shuffled. By the mid-1960s, the controversy had passed, especially when young cutting-edge jazz musicians rediscovered him and lauded his genius. The totally surprising success of "Hello, Dolly!" in 1964 triggered one of the great reassessments in entertainment history: although Armstrong had never stopped touring, recording, and broadcasting, he was once again beloved by all. In his last years, he devoted much of his energy to writing an unfinished memoir, detailing the grueling hardships of his youth in New Orleans. His death, on July 6, 1971, was mourned worldwide. Incredibly, seventeen years later, Satchmo had the best-selling record in the country, with the rediscovery (thanks to a film score) of the previously ignored "What a Wonderful World."

7

CHAPTER

Swing Bands

FROM JAZZ TO SWING

t took ten years for jazz to develop from an often disdained urban phenomenon, played mostly by young male musicians for black audiences, into a national obsession that crossed geographical, generational, gender, and racial borders. Louis Armstrong inaugurated his Hot Five recordings in November 1925; Benny Goodman inadvertently launched the Swing Era in August 1935. In the decade that followed, *jazz* was used almost exclusively to describe traditional New Orleans music. The new word was *swing*, which encompassed "hot" orchestras, like those of Duke

◀ Ella Fitzgerald, "the first lady of song," brought the stars out, including Swedish clarinetist Stan Hasselgård (behind Ellington), Duke Ellington, Benny Goodman, and music publisher Jack Robbins. New York, 1949.

Ellington and Count Basie, and "sweet" bands, like those of Sammy Kaye and Hal Kemp, which had little or nothing to do with jazz. Many bands played both hot and sweet in attempting to create stylish dance music that combined elements of jazz with lush instrumentation and pop songs.

The swing bands revived a music industry considered moribund in the dark days of the Depression, and lifted the country's spirits during the darker days of World War II. Even the Nazis, who spurned jazz as a symptom of American degeneracy, were forced to issue imitation swing records to attract listeners to their broadcasts in occupied countries. In the United States, swing created new styles in slang, dress, and especially dance—an energetic, athletic "jitterbugging" that kept ballrooms jumping from coast to coast. Millions of fans debated the merits of bands and knew the names of key soloists: in that era, jazz and pop were largely inseparable.

Yet there was more to swing than big bands and riotous dancing. A new virtuosity had taken hold—a technical bravura that advanced the harmonic and rhythmic underpinnings of jazz, spurring innovations that would last long after the Swing Era had faded. Jazz singing came into its own, the guitar found a new voice through electronic amplification, and orchestrating became an art in its own right. If jazz of the 1920s, created in times of plenty, illuminated a defiant individualism, the Swing Era responded to years of hardship and war with a collective spirit that expressed a carefree, even blissful optimism.

Even so, swing retained the basic elements of jazz: polyrhythm, blues phrasing, timbre variation. And though it relied on written music more than had previous forms of jazz, swing continued to balance composition against improvisation. The size of the bands transformed dance music into an orchestral music, thereby realizing some of the aspirations of symphonic jazz; but the style was not demanding. Swing offered a smooth, readily digestible sound, displacing the knotty polyphony of New Orleans jazz with clear homophonic textures, easy blues-laden riffs, strong dance grooves, and well-defined melodies. It was a thoroughly commercial phenomenon. Like film, radio, and popular song, swing was central to a nationwide system of mass entertainment.

The Swing Era was bounded by two of the century's crucial events, the Great Depression and the Second World War. The former, a consequence of the October 1929 stock market crash, ruined the banking system, cast millions into unemployment, and shifted America's political landscape. African Americans played a significant role in the new coalition—with organized labor, Southern whites, Catholics, and the dispossessed poor—that swept the Democratic candidate, Franklin Roosevelt, to the presidency in 1932. Roosevelt swiftly launched the New Deal, a blizzard of programs that stretched the nation's political and economic resources to help the unemployed and hurting. His actions, though not always successful, demonstrated a concerned and involved leadership after years of bromides and inaction, and he was reelected an unparalleled three times. But for all his efforts, recovery was slow and laborious. Not until the end of the decade, when the shadow of war jolted America into industrial overdrive, did the Depression finally lift.

Swing came of age during the hardest of times, yet it hardly caught the era's deep anxiety. Like most movies, it countered reality as an upbeat, slickly packaged commodity to distract people from their daily cares—and produced many great artists. While movies fed its audience fantasies in dark, enclosed spaces, swing inspired involvement. It was a young people's music, loud and brash, the first in the nation's history, demanding an exuberant response on the dance floor. Swing's improvisatory flair and buoyant energy encouraged America to recover from an emotional malaise; no less than the ingenuity of the New Deal, swing made average citizens feel alive, alert, and engaged. It also gave a tremendous economic boost to the entertainment industry.

If prosperity now seemed within hailing distance, the war changed everything once again, substituting patriotism for complaint and transforming America into a global powerhouse, defended by armed forces made up chiefly of citizens who put their lives on hold for two and three years. After the bombing of Pearl Harbor, the fight against fascism required the involvement of all the country's industries, resources, and manpower—not least the world of entertainment.

For four long years, while the country was on edge, shifting unsteadily from steely grimness to giddy recklessness, swing drew eager and anxious patrons to ballrooms and theaters. Its rhythms permeated the lives of millions, inspiring workers in defense factories while giving soldiers a taste of home. For many people, swing exemplified what Americans were fighting for: compared with Nazi or Japanese authoritarianism, the casual, participatory nature of swing, yoking together people from different backgrounds, was a rousing statement of democracy. Yet the war also helped to end the Swing Era, as hundreds of thousands of servicemen returned home to their families and jobs, shutting down the hyperactive dancing culture that had formed the basis for countless orchestras, national and local. The end of one era signified, with the introduction of atomic warfare, the beginning of a new one.

The Depression nearly destroyed the record companies. At a time when people could barely afford food and rent, the price of a record (one dollar, sometimes two) was too much to bear. Besides, why spend money on records when music was available over the radio for free? Sales of records plunged—from over 100 million in 1929 to 4 million in 1933. Familiar jazz labels like Gennett, OKeh, and the once-dominant Columbia went bankrupt or were bought up by speculators. The only major label that survived the early 1930s was Victor, because it had been amalgamated with the RCA radio network.

Things began to look up a few years later, thanks to the invention of the jukebox, the garish record-selecting machine that filled restaurants or bars with music for a nickel a side. By the late 1930s, the business had begun to turn around, and people who had declared records a thing of the past wanted into the business. CBS radio, locked in a constant unfriendly rivalry with RCA, bought Columbia Records out of receivership and signed up every swing band it could, stealing a few from RCA when their contracts came up for renewal. A few years earlier, in 1934, the height of the Depression, a third label, Decca, had muscled in, financed chiefly by British interests; recognizing that records were too expensive, Decca slashed the price in half, eventually offering three discs for a dollar. Columbia and Victor had no choice but to lower their prices. By 1942, the record business looked so attractive that a fourth company, Capitol, was launched, specializing in a jazzy brand of pop. These four labels, "the majors," as they were known, produced about 90 percent of the recordings Americans listened to.

Similar patterns of concentration could be found in other media. Millions of families listened to the weekly or daily radio broadcasts of comedians, singers, classical concerts, soap operas, serials, movie and literary adaptations, quiz shows, and anything else that the market would bear—all on just three national networks, two of them owned by NBC (until the government forced it to sell one, thereby creating the American Broadcasting Company). The Hollywood studios produced an endless stream of films for thousands of movie theaters, most of them owned by the studios (until the government forced them to sell their theatrical chains). In 1939, two-thirds of the public went to the movies at least once a week. Popular songs were at their peak: Tin Pan Alley companies published countless new tunes and competed to get singers and orchestras to perform them. All the entertainment branches intersected, however distrustful they had been of each other. At one point, the movie studios barred their stars from appearing on the hated rival, radio, until they realized that a radio plug could sell more movie tickets than any billboard. Songwriters similarly fought against having their songs played on the air, until a strike by the American Society of Composers, Authors, and Publishers (ASCAP: the union founded in 1914 to license music and protect copyrights) created a royalty system—along with a rival songwriters' union, Broadcast Music Incorporated (BMI).

Swing was a key part of this web of entertainment. A tune might be blasted over a restaurant's jukebox or on a late-night radio broadcast; it might be sung in the soundtrack of a movie or performed live in a nightclub or theater. For some, this sameness was a loss; they compared it to fascism, the fervor of the swing "jitterbugs" resembling "the abandon of a crowd of Storm Troopers demanding their Fuehrer." Today we're less likely to invoke Hitler than to complain that swing was swamped by commercialism. Many of the hard-core swing outfits were enormously successful in their day and retain our interest, but back then they competed with sweet or Mickey Mouse bands that might occasionally play a hot dance number but primarily focused on pop or novelty songs, funny hats, and old-fashioned dance music.

Nevertheless, the commercial buzz made jazz-as-popular-music possible. Musicians poured into the field from all over, and as competition for the best jobs increased, musical standards rose precipitously. A sideman was now expected to play his instrument flawlessly, sight-read efficiently, and improvise convincingly. Dance bands offered steady work at a respectable salary, making music one of the few skilled crafts open to African Americans. Swing was situated on the fault line of race. Its dance steps were worked out on the floor of black ballrooms, and its orchestral arrangements mimicked the call and response of black churches. The extraordinary success of swing boosted the careers of hundreds of musicians, not least dozens of black bandleaders, instrumentalists, singers, and dancers who attainted the realm of stardom or near-stardom. Yet most of the money went into white pockets, and many black musicians felt that their music had been "stolen"—a feeling that would later help to fuel the postwar musical revolution known as bebop.

Much of white America was dancing to an African American beat. But swing did not dissolve racial barriers. Though whites loved the music, they were not especially interested in its origins. How many knew that "Stompin' at the Savoy" referred to a Harlem dance palace, or that Duke Ellington coined the word "swing" three years before Benny Goodman made it an

American byword, or that much of Goodman's music was crafted for him by Fletcher Henderson and Edgar Sampson (the composer-arranger for Chick Webb's Harlem-based band), or that much of their after-school "jive" talk was black slang? Whites accepted and expected segregated bands because that's the way things were done; in the South, they expected audiences also to be segregated. Little was said of the way segregation worked to the financial advantage of white bands, yet no one could fail to notice that the best jobs—major hotel ballrooms, network radio broadcasts—were restricted to whites. Blacks and whites could play together in jam sessions, but racially mixed bands were no more tolerated than integrated army units. Swing would help to change that.

SWING AND DANCE

At the core of swing is its groove: a steady, unaccented four-beats-to-the-bar foundation, perfect for dancing. This was not in itself new. We hear the same groove in records by Louis Armstrong; we even hear it emerging in passages by Jelly Roll Morton's Red Hot Peppers. But in the early 1930s—when Ellington issued his dictum "It Don't Mean a Thing (If It Ain't Got That Swing)"—the four-beat groove became firmly established as the standard for hot dance music.

The swing dance style emerged from New York's Savoy Ballroom, which opened for business in 1926. The Savoy was an enormous space, filling an entire block in Harlem. Like other new dance halls, it offered a luxurious environment for a modest fee. Entering by the marble staircase, dancers saw "fancy wall decorations all over, thick patterned carpets on the floor, soft benches for sitting, round tables for drinking, and a heavy brass railing all around the long, polished dance floor." Two bands were hired on a given night, alternating sets on opposite sides of the hall. Harlem was proud of the Savoy, and opened its doors to white visitors from downtown and around the world; but unlike the Cotton Club, its primary constituency was the black neighborhood surrounding it.

In the Savoy, social dancing was an intense, communal activity. Thousands of dancers packed the hall. In the Cat's Corner, a special place next to the bandstand, the best dancers would execute their steps: the Charleston, the black bottom, or the fox-trot. Since the most ambitious often rehearsed their steps in the afternoon while the band was practicing, musicians and dancers could communicate closely on issues of tempo and groove. "For the dancer, you know what will please him," remembered trombonist Dicky Wells. "It has got to be something that will fit around him and with his step. When you see a dancer take his girl, and then drop her hands and walk off, something isn't right. Most likely the rhythm's wrong. But when you get that beat he's right in there saying: 'Play that again!'"

The Savoy dance style came to be known as the Lindy Hop—after Charles Lindbergh, whose 1927 flight across the Atlantic signified, among other things, a thrilling triumph for youth and ambition in the Jazz Age. The steady four-four beat opened up new possibilities. A good dancer, one professional recounted, "takes the unvarying accent, and dances *against* it." The new dance was more "African": lower to the ground, demanding flexibility in the knee and hip joints. There was also greater room for improvisation. While the fox-trot or waltz insisted that couples remain linked arm-in-arm, the Lindy Hop featured "breakaways" where the partners could separate at arm's length to execute their own steps. The best dancers began adding new acrobatic variations, including "air steps," in which the female was thrown heedlessly (but always with grace) over her partner's shoulders. White observers were amazed. Author Carl Van Vechten, who watched safely from the side, described its movements as "epileptic," but added that "to observe the Lindy Hop being performed at first induces gooseflesh, and second, intense excitement, akin to religious mania."

To help bands adjust to the new groove, major changes were made in the rhythm section. While the bass drum continued to play a rock-solid four-beat pulse, the tuba, commonly used in large dance bands of the 1920s, was replaced by the string bass. During the early years of recording, the tuba was able to project a clear, huffing sound. But the string bass had always been a specialty of New Orleans, and many players, including Wellman Braud in Duke Ellington's band, showed that the instrument had a special percussive flavor when the strings were given a pizzicato "slap." Change came gradually in the late 1920s, once word got around about how well the string bass worked. Tuba players realized that they'd better switch instruments if they wanted to keep working in dance bands.

The banjo, with its loud and raucous tone, was replaced with the guitar, which provided a more subtle, secure pulsation (*chunk-chunk*) in the foundation rhythm. As the saying went, the guitar was more *felt* than heard. Listeners experienced the combined sound of bass, guitar, and drums as a sonic force that rippled through and beyond cavernous dance halls. "If you were on the first floor, and the dance hall was upstairs," Count Basie remembered, "that was what you would hear, that steady *rump, rump, rump, rump* in that medium tempo."

To fit the new groove, dance-band arranging became more inventive.

To some extent, this was a belated influence of Louis Armstrong, whose rhythms continued to be absorbed by soloists and arrangers through the 1930s. Arrangers learned to write elaborate lines for an entire section, harmonized in block chords, called *soli*. They were conversant with chromatic (complex) harmony and knew how to make the most of their flexible orchestra. Arrangements could also arise spontaneously out of oral practice. This approach was especially popular in Kansas City, but even in New York, where bands prided themselves on their musical literacy, musicians could take improvised riffs and harmonize them on the spot. The result, known as a head arrangement, was an unwritten arrangement created by the entire band. One musician compared it to child's play—"a lot of kids playing in the mud, having a big time."

Both kinds of arrangements, written and unwritten, could be heard in the hundreds of 1930s records by Fletcher Henderson. For flashy pieces, Henderson relied on experienced arrangers, chiefly his brother Horace, Don Redman, and Benny Carter. But his biggest hits emerged from the bandstand or were adapted from earlier recordings, most successfully "King Porter Stomp," which became an exemplary anthem for the entire era, yet derived from one strain of a piano piece by Jelly Roll Morton—now shorn of its original two-beat rhythm and march/ragtime form.

Many of these pieces were ultimately written down by Henderson, who took over from Redman as his band's main arranger. His gift for rhythmic swing and melodic simplicity was so infectious that his music became the standard for numerous swing arrangers. Henderson was fond of short, memorable riffs—little more than blues fragments—in call-and-response patterns: say, saxophones responding to trumpets. In some passages, he distorted the melody into ingenious new rhythmic shapes, often in staccato (detached) bursts that opened up space for the rhythm section. Henderson was shrewd and efficient. He wrote only a few choice choruses, leaving the remainder of the arrangement open for solos accompanied by discreet, long-held chords or short riffs. As the piece headed toward its climax, the band erupted in an ecstatic wail.

"BLUE LOU"

The early Henderson band was dramatically effective in person: "We used to rock the walls," remembered Coleman Hawkins. But it was notoriously imperfect in the studio. Some of the best-known records from the early 1930s sounded, according to Hawkins, "like cats and dogs fighting." By

1936, the band had perfected its public presentation, and is in particularly splendid form on "Blue Lou."

The piece was composed by Edgar Sampson, a saxophonist and arranger with the Chick Webb band who also wrote for Henderson and later for Benny Goodman (his tunes include "Stompin' at the Savoy," "Don't Be That Way," and "If Dreams Come True"). It was arranged in the Henderson style by his brother Horace, who oriented it toward the band's chief soloists: the incendiary trumpeter Roy Eldridge and one of Coleman Hawkins's most impressive followers on tenor saxophone, Chu Berry.

Like many swing tunes, "Blue Lou" is built around an uncomplicated but effective idea. The tune is in major, but the opening riff (a descending two-note figure) introduces a flatted note from the minor mode. That peculiarity gives the piece its tension, and gives musically astute soloists an idea to use in their harmonic improvisation—as Berry does at the beginning of his solo, mimicking the opening riff, and as Eldridge does in the last eight bars of his solo, where the dissonant flatted note is blasted at the top of his range.

Although "Blue Lou" begins with a relaxed two-beat feeling, the four-four dance groove gradually takes over. The first chorus introduces the original tune (the tune is expanded in the second A section into an elaborate *soli*), while the fourth (and last) chorus deforms it through ecstatic starts and stops. But the piece doesn't end there: with half a minute to go, there is a sudden modulation to the unusual key of A major (notoriously difficult for brass instruments). The new sixteen-bar section doesn't last long, but its presence suggests that this arrangement may have been adjustable. Perhaps the drum stroke that precedes the modulation was a cue in case the band wanted to keep dancers on the floor. Eldridge's solo at the end sounds as though it could have gone on forever.

BLUE LOU

Fletcher Henderson and His Orchestra

Dick Vance, Joe Thomas, Roy Eldridge, trumpets; Fernando Arbello, Ed Cuffee, trombones; Buster Bailey, Scoops Carey, alto saxophones; Elmer Williams, Chu Berry, tenor saxophones; Horace Henderson, piano; Bob Lessey, guitar; John Kirby, bass; Sidney Catlett, drums

LABEL: Vocalion/OKeh 3211; *Fletcher Henderson: 1924–1936* (Giants of Jazz 634479088476)
DATE: 1936
STYLE: big-band swing
FORM: 32-bar popular song (**AABA**)

Chorus 1

0:00	A	The tune begins immediately with the saxophones playing a simple yet dissonant two-note riff, colored with a note borrowed from the minor mode.
0:01		The saxophone section is immediately answered by the brass, with short chords.
0:05		The saxophones continue with a *soli*—a simple syncopated melody.
0:09	A	The chord progression is repeated, but the saxophones now play a complicated *soli* in the style of an improvisation.
0:19	B	On the bridge, the tune modulates to a new key. The saxophone section plays another simple riff, answered by brief chords from the brass.
0:29	A	Return of the opening two-note riff.

Chorus 2

0:38	A	Eldridge takes a dominating trumpet solo, jumping quickly from his lower to his highest register. Behind him, the saxophone section plays jumpy background riffs or sustained chords.
0:48	A	
0:57	B	On muted trombone, Cuffee plays a melodic paraphrase of chorus 1's bridge.
1:06	A	Searching for a dramatic reentry, Eldridge begins in his highest register, playing the first few dissonant notes slightly out of tune.

Chorus 3

1:16	A	Berry, on tenor saxophone, begins his solo with the opening two-note riff. Underneath him, the brass section swells in volume on background harmonies.
1:25	A	
1:35	B	As Berry increases in intensity, the bass finally begins playing a walking-bass line.
1:44	A	

Chorus 4

1:53	A	The brass section plays a simpler *soli*, with short staccato notes, opening up a lot of space.
2:03	A	
2:12	B	Berry returns to take an eight-bar solo, accompanied only by the rhythm section.
2:22	A	As if interrupting, the trumpets reenter on a new variation (of the original two-note riff).

Chorus 5 (new tune: 16-bar AA)

| 2:31 | A | Signaled by a drum shot, the tune suddenly modulates to a new key, A major, offering a new melody over a new harmonic progression. The bass returns to a (mostly) two-beat feel. |

2:41   **A**

Coda

2:50	The band repeats a short, four-measure harmonic figure.
2:54	As the figure is taken up by the saxophones, Eldridge takes a muted solo.
3:03	Eldridge's solo is cut short by a brief cadence figure, ending the piece.

Benny Goodman (1909–1986)

As white musicians became increasingly drawn to jazz in the late 1920s and early 1930s, they had to confront the fact that much of their best music would be played for fun, at after-hours jam sessions. The bands that paid them their weekly salaries preferred a more soothing music, built on what songwriter Johnny Mercer once called "typewriter" rhythms—clickety-clack, steady and staid, and a far cry from the kind of thing Chick Webb was doing at the Savoy. Future swing bandleaders like Artie Shaw, Glenn Miller, and Tommy and Jimmy Dorsey gravitated toward jazz, mastered it, and added their own innovations, but most of their jobs found them playing long nights of demanding, uninspiring arrangements in genteel dance bands and radio orchestras while dreaming of getting away to play some real jazz. That changed with the astonishing breakthrough of the Benny Goodman orchestra.

Goodman grew up in the slums of Chicago, where his father, a recent immigrant from Warsaw, worked in the stockyards. The boy showed a prodigious talent on the clarinet, which gave him a way out of menial labor. He was accepted into the band at Hull House, founded by Jane Addams to provide educational and cultural opportunities to the city's poor, and acquired a solid training from Franz Schoepp, a clarinetist with the Chicago Symphony. At the same time, he heard the jazz buzzing around him and modeled his improvisations on those of its clarinetists, white (Leon Rappolo) and black (Jimmie Noone). By the 1920s, he was an elegant soloist with a decided penchant for the blues, distinguishing himself in bands and on records with musicians inclined toward jazz, from bandleader and drummer Ben Pollack to vaudeville showman and corny clarinetist Ted Lewis. His virtuosity was such that a music-publishing company issued a volume of transcribed Goodman exercises long before he was famous.

Goodman moved to New York, where his tastes led him to create a band that would bridge the gap between the jazz he loved and the commercial realities he had to heed. Taking his cue from vocalist Mildred Bailey, who advised him to "get a Harlem book" of arrangements, he hired some of the best underemployed black arrangers in the business: Benny Carter, Edgar Sampson, and Fletcher Henderson, who was struggling to hold his own band together and eager for the extra cash.

In 1935, Goodman's band was featured as the "hot" orchestra on a national radio program, *Let's Dance!*—one of three bands that played consecutive sets before a live audience. Benny's band went on last, when most New Yorkers were asleep. Still, he was booked on a national tour that would end in California and then bring him back by way of his hometown, Chicago. Despite his reluctant willingness to play his blandest charts, the band's reception seemed to get worse with each city, reaching a nadir in Salt Lake City and Denver, at which point his management suggested that they cancel the rest of the tour. But Benny persevered and, in August, arrived at the Palomar Ballroom in Los Angeles. When he opened with one of the mild pieces that the dance hall owners had been insisting on, the audience of young people looked puzzled. Goodman decided if he was going to die, he would die playing the music he cared about—he called for one of the Henderson arrangements, and before the band had played four bars, the place went crazy.

No one had taken into account the fact that those late-night broadcasts, when he was allowed to play jazz because few people were listening, were airing in prime time on the West Coast. He had inadvertently created a fan base, and when they heard him go into "King Porter Stomp," the kids cheered in recognition. Goodman's swing repertory suddenly found its audience. Through their vigorous, almost violent enthusiasm for this new Harlem-based sound, white teenagers awakened the music industry and launched the Swing Era. Goodman was held over at the Palomar and headed for Chicago, where he broke house records. By the time he returned to New York, he was the hottest commodity in show business.

Goodman's success electrified the country. White fans celebrated him as a hero, much as they would Elvis Presley two decades later. They unknowingly adapted black dancing and slang, driving their parents and even some musicians over the edge. Outside theaters, fans eager to see Goodman clogged traffic in lines that stretched for blocks; inside, they danced in the aisles. It was enough to make some people feel that the walls of civilization had begun to crack, though the bleak news from Europe ought to have given everyone a more level-headed perspective.

In the end, America accepted his music gracefully. Goodman's band blended his swing rhythms with up-to-date arrangements of current pop songs. The first chorus would be recognizable enough to satisfy Tin Pan Alley, even as the rest transported its listeners into jazz. As historian James Maher remembered: "These were our songs. They were part of the daily ordinary. And this I think is what took Benny Goodman over the gap, out of jazz into the American parlor. He arrived with 'Blue Skies.' . . . I mean, everybody knew Irving Berlin! So we were home free." Goodman managed to both satisfy the jitterbugs and make swing acceptable to the cultured middle classes. One of his most memorable achievements was to bring jazz and the jazz audience to New York's Carnegie Hall, a citadel of musical respectability, in January 1938. The musicians may have felt out of place (like a "whore in church," as trumpeter Harry James described it), but the band's rousing success cemented jazz's place in contemporary American culture.

Goodman also pioneered the return of small groups, including a trio with the same instrumentation (clarinet, piano, drums) that Jelly Roll Morton had once used, recasting them as a kind of swing chamber music—relaxed and spontaneous, yet highly polished and refined. The most remarkable thing about Goodman's trio, beyond the music, was that it was integrated—not a big deal on records, but a landmark in concert. Goodman had bonded musically with a dazzling young pianist, Teddy Wilson, and after the Palomar, he had the clout to include black musicians as a regular part of his shows. Most other bandleaders took a wait-and-see attitude before following his lead. Yet for Goodman, this was not about making a social statement. He was simply, by all accounts, determined to play with musicians who stimulated him.

Goodman first heard Teddy Wilson on returning to Chicago from California in 1935. The son of an English professor at Tuskegee Institute, Teddy grew up studying piano and violin. His role model was Earl Hines, whom he admired for his superb asymmetric stride technique. But where Hines was breathtakingly daring in his improvisation, Wilson's style was smooth and polished, cool and controlled even at high speed. When Goodman jammed with Wilson at a private party, he was thrilled by the pianist's panache, but dismayed by the risk of launching a mixed-race trio with his drummer, Gene Krupa. Fortunately, the trio recordings sold well, and Goodman found a compromise with contemporary mores by presenting Wilson not as a full member of the band, but as a "special guest," playing only with the Benny Goodman Trio. Within a few years, Goodman's "band-within-the-band" had been widely imitated in the industry by Cab Calloway (the Cab Jivers), Artie Shaw (the Gramercy Five), Tommy Dorsey (the Clambake Seven), Woody Herman (the Woodchoppers), and others.

The trio expanded to a quartet when Goodman added Lionel Hampton in 1936. Hampton was originally a drummer who had played with Louis Armstrong's big band in the early 1930s. At a recording session, Armstrong rolled a vibraphone out of the shadows and asked Hampton to play it. A new instrument at the time, the vibraphone uses rotating discs and amplification to enhance the sound of a metal xylophone. Within a few years, Hampton shifted to the vibes as his main instrument. Unlike Wilson, a shy man who rarely changed his facial expression while playing, Hampton was a tireless entertainer who used his whole body to communicate with audiences. "I have always been Mr. Showmanship," he later wrote. "There was a long, honorable tradition of clowning in black performing that I wanted to carry on." His extroverted energy, combined with the sweaty glamour of Gene Krupa, was a crucial part of the quartet's popular appeal. After leaving Goodman in the early 1940s to form his own band, Hampton carried his reckless energy into rhythm and blues, ultimately linking jazz with rock and roll.

"DINAH"

"Dinah," a thirty-two-bar AABA pop song composed in 1925, first became popular in Goodman's teenage years, and might have had a short shelf life like most tunes, lasting no more than six months. But jazz musicians were attracted to its harmonic structure, which was similar to that of "I Got Rhythm": an opening section firmly in the tonic, followed by a bridge with more elaborate harmonic movement. "Dinah" became an evergreen and a permanent addition to the jazz repertory.

In the Goodman Quartet's 1936 recording, the mood is exuberant and playful, even bewildering: during Lionel Hampton's introduction, it's virtually impossible to hear where the downbeat is. The four musicians play in an informal jam-session spirit, exercising their freedom to listen and interact spontaneously. In the first A section, Goodman plays the melody with delicacy and circumspection; but in the bridge, he obliterates it in a lengthy string of fast notes. When Hampton plays in the second chorus, he shifts between simple riff figures and complicated harmonic substitutions of his own devising.

The performance heats up steadily, as it might in an impromptu jam session. Krupa begins with a steady two-beat foundation, but soon barges in with his snare drum and tom-tom accents. Goodman's later improvisations have little to do with the original melody. In his brief solo spot, Wilson shows the kind of delicate filigree he could weave around the harmonies of the bridge. At the end, the three soloists coincide in a kind of ecstatic polyphony. It's not chaotic, however, and the ending is tightly controlled.

DINAH

Benny Goodman Quartet

Benny Goodman, clarinet; Lionel Hampton, vibraphone; Teddy Wilson, piano; Gene Krupa, drums

LABEL: Victor 25398; *The Legendary Small Groups* (RCA/Bluebird 090266-39942-0)
DATE: 1936
STYLE: small combo swing
FORM: 32-bar popular song (**AABA**)

Introduction

0:00		Hampton begins at a brisk tempo, playing a short introductory passage on the vibes.
0:02		Krupa enters, accompanying Hampton on the drums.

Chorus 1

0:04	A	The rest of the band enters. Goodman takes the lead on the clarinet, delicately paraphrasing the original melody. Behind him, Krupa thumps a two-beat pattern on the bass drum.
0:12	A	Wilson quietly plays a contrasting accompaniment.
0:20	B	As Goodman begins to improvise, Wilson plays a simpler stride accompaniment.
0:28	A	Goodman returns to the original melody.

Chorus 2

0:36	A	Reacting to Hampton's solo on the vibes, Krupa plays polyrhythms on the tom-tom drums.
0:43	A	As Hampton warms up, his line becomes a long, continuous string of even eighth notes, occasionally punctuated by Krupa's quick drum strokes.
0:51	B	
0:59	A	

Chorus 3

1:07	A	Hampton divides a cross-rhythm between his two hands.

1:13		Krupa plays a disorienting snare-drum accent just before his bass drum stroke.
1:15	**A**	
1:22	**B**	
1:30	**A**	To conclude his solo, Hampton plays a few simple notes polyrhythmically.
1:36		Goodman sneaks in at the end of Hampton's solo with a scooped blue note.

Chorus 4

1:37	**A**	
1:40		Goodman follows his opening bluesy phrase with another line that continues, unbroken, until halfway through the next **A** section.
1:45	**A**	
1:50		The next phrase begins with another piercing, descending blue note.
1:53	**B**	Wilson plays a discreet solo over the bridge.
1:58		At the end of the bridge, Wilson embellishes the chord progression with a harmonic substitution.
2:00	**A**	With a strikingly high entrance, Goodman concludes his solo.

Chorus 5

2:08	**A**	The three soloists play together: Wilson's riffs are responded to by Goodman, who paraphrases parts of "Dinah" before abandoning the melody in improvisation.
2:16	**A**	
2:23	**B**	Break: Hampton plays an unaccompanied solo, interrupted every two beats by a brief chord from Wilson.
2:29		Krupa reenters, followed by Goodman.
2:31	**A**	The entire band plays an untrammeled polyphonic conclusion.
2:38		The piece ends discreetly with a bass drum thump.

JOHN HAMMOND AND OTHER FANS

The interracial Goodman Quartet was encouraged by John Hammond (1910–1987), the most influential jazz entrepreneur and activist of the period. A list of artists whose careers he helped would include Bessie Smith, Fletcher Henderson, Goodman, Billie Holiday, Count Basie, and Charlie Christian—and in a later generation, Bob Dylan, Aretha Franklin, George Benson, and Bruce Springsteen. Hammond was no musician (although he was an amateur violinist for a while), but his intense commitment and political convictions made him a significant figure in jazz history.

Born into a wealthy New York family (his mother was connected to the Vanderbilts), Hammond grew up in an atmosphere of privilege on the Upper East Side. As a youth, he turned his back on the sweet sounds of popular music. Instead, he used his weekly violin lesson as an excuse to explore the music that excited him in Harlem's theaters and nightclubs. He attended Yale, but dropped out and, supported by a generous trust fund, plunged into the world of music. He became a jazz reporter, a producer of recordings, and the music's insistent political voice.

Hammond developed two passions. The first was a love of black jazz and folk music, which to him seemed infinitely superior to any other kind. "There was no white pianist to compare with Fats Waller," he said, "no white band as good as Fletcher Henderson's, no blues singer like Bessie Smith." The second was a hatred of racial injustice. Although raised on prejudice typical of his time (his mother once explained to him that black people were "different" because "their skulls harden when they are twelve"), he became outraged by inequality. His battles to fight racial injustice aligned him with the left, though he never joined the Communist Party. He did, however, become an active member of the NAACP and made a name for himself reporting on the 1931 Scottsboro Boys case: nine blacks, as young as twelve and thirteen, were falsely accused of raping two women on a freight train; eight were sentenced to death and all were found guilty by white Alabama juries in a series of trials, despite the recantation of one alleged victim and the prosecution's admitted doubts about the veracity of the other.

Hammond used a long-running association with Columbia Records to champion the music he admired. He became a ubiquitous figure in nightclubs, standing out with his conservative crewcut and uninhibited enthusiasm. "Hammond in action is the embodiment of the popular conception of the jitterbug," the *New Yorker* reported. "When the music jumps, he begins to move his head, his feet, and sometimes his whole body. His eyebrows go up, his mouth opens wide and reveals a set of even, gleaming teeth, and a long-drawn-out 'Yeah' slides out of his throat." He was responsible for hundreds of recording dates, having shepherded his latest discoveries into the studio. Some black musicians did not relish his overbearing personality—he was criticized for his patriarchal attitude. Duke Ellington broke publicly with him after Hammond complained in 1935 that Ellington's longer pieces were "vapid and without the slightest semblance of guts." But few nonmusicians rivaled Hammond in shaping the course of jazz.

Hammond was the most conspicuous and connected member of a new generation of ardent fans. The Swing Era saw the emergence of jazz record collectors—young men of privileged backgrounds who combed through discarded vinyl at flea markets and junk shops looking for forgotten old recordings. To distinguish one recording from another, they duly noted all the pertinent information: personnel, dates, matrix numbers (the codes inscribed on the disc that identify a particular master), release numbers. This data formed the beginnings of record classification, and was eventually collated and published as discographies—an indispensable source for researchers.

"Hot Clubs" were formed in towns throughout the country, bringing together fans and sponsoring public jam sessions. To suit their reading tastes, new mass-market magazines like *Down Beat* and *Metronome* and smaller fan-based journals like *Jazz Information* emerged. From their pages came the first American jazz critics (among them Leonard Feather, George T. Simon, and Hammond himself, who despite obvious conflicts of interest had been writing for the British music magazine *Melody Maker*). While jazz enthusiasts were gratified to see their music achieve popular success, their attitude toward swing was mixed. Many were uneasy about the commercial tainting of jazz, the loss in authenticity. Some argued that real jazz was beyond most people's ken. Joining their ranks was like joining a cult. "Sooner or later, you became acquainted with other zealots who I call 'jazzniks,'" said one observer. "And they of course are instantly telling you that all the people you like and admire, they all stink. They don't play jazz." Ironically, it was the commercial success of swing that fostered the idea that jazz proper was an "anticommercial" music.

A FEW MAJOR SWING BANDS (AMONG MANY)

As the dance business boomed, the number of new bands exploded. By 1940, there were hundreds of bands—some leaning toward conventional dance music, others specializing in hard-driving swing, and still others who worked both sides of the divide. Tommy Dorsey, a limited improviser but skilled trombonist (he pioneered the upper register, changing the way later trombonists approached the instrument) and hard-line bandleader with an infallible ear for talent, was especially good at this. Benny Goodman's own band was a seedbed for bandleaders: they emerged from his trumpet section (Bunny Berigan and Harry James), saxophone section (Vido Musso and Toots Mondello), and quartet (Wilson, Krupa, and Hampton). A few major figures like Fats Waller and Art Tatum continued to pilot small groups, but as most of the established figures, including Louis Armstrong and Earl Hines, switched to big bands, the wave of orchestral might rolled over the music industry—for a few years, it was easier for a booking agency to tour a big band than a small one.

Occasionally, an agent would convince a singer or emcee with an agreeable personality to front an orchestra, even if he had no musical ability. The real leader would remain behind the scenes, while the nominal leader would flash his matinee idol grin, handle introductions, and maybe sing. One of the most distinctive bands of the era functioned that way. Bob Crosby was hired to front a band created by bassist-arranger Bob Haggart and saxophonist Gil Rodin. Crosby had been recruited because he had an amiable bearing and was the younger brother of Bing—the agency figured that kids would pay to see Bing's kid brother. The band was a commercial and musical success (Ellington declared it one of his favorites), unique for combining swing orchestrations with Dixieland polyphony, and packed with first-rate soloists. But when Crosby took his role of "leader" seriously and attempted to count off a tempo, Haggart warned him, "You do the introduction, we'll take care of the tempo."

Most bandleaders, however, were authoritarian figures who had worked hard and long to pull a band together, and had a precise concept of the kind of music they wanted to play. One of the most gifted and eccentric figures in jazz history was Goodman's bête noir, Artie Shaw (1910–2004), a rival as leader and clarinetist. Like Goodman, Shaw was a child of the ghetto. Born to recent Jewish immigrants, Arthur Arshawsky was raised on the Lower East Side of Manhattan and quickly discovered that his prodigious skill on saxophone and clarinet was a ticket into the world of studio bands and dance orchestras. By 1930, he was studying with pianist Willie "the Lion" Smith in Harlem (he later wrote a short story based on those years, called "Snow White in Harlem, 1930") and listening to Armstrong, Hines, and the influential Chicago-based clarinetist Jimmie Noone, who had made a much-admired series of small-group recordings with Hines. Shaw recalled Chicago as "one of the foremost jazz conservatories in the world." Browsing in record stores, he became fascinated with music by Igor Stravinsky, Claude Debussy, and other "guys with screwy-sounding names" who were creating dissonant modern classical music.

During the early 1930s, Shaw lived a double life, working studio gigs like the CBS radio orchestra, playing for what he disdained as "soap and cereal programs," and jamming in Harlem with the Lion and others. "I was actually living the life of a Negro musician," he recalled, "adopting

Negro values and attitudes, and accepting the Negro out-group point of view not only about music but life in general." Shaw fancied himself an intellectual. An autodidact who read extensively and stored everything in his steel-trap memory, he hoped to earn a few thousand dollars in music so that he could quit and write a book. To his purported surprise, he became astronomically successful after the band he formed in 1938 sold millions of copies of "Begin the Beguine." He claimed to hate the fame, but celebrity had its privileges: he married eight times, a matrimonial parade that included movie queens Lana Turner, Ava Gardner, and Evelyn Keyes. His personal life, musical success, and dark good looks kept him on the pages of Hollywood magazines.

Yet he exploded with resentment against the jitterbugging fans who screamed with wild enthusiasm and demanded to hear his hits again and again, played exactly like the record: "They won't even let me play without interrupting me!" he once complained. He railed against the promoters and other hangers-on, eager for a share of his $30,000 weekly earnings. Shaw also protested against the mute acceptance of segregation, and fought it by hiring black arrangers, singers (including Billie Holiday), and musicians, including Roy Eldridge, who had already made social history by becoming the first black musician to sit in a white trumpet section (not as a "special guest") when he joined Gene Krupa's band. Eldridge ruefully remembered both associations:

♦ ♦ ♦

We arrived in one town and the rest of the band checks in. I can't get into their hotel, so I keep my bags and start riding around looking for another place, where someone's supposed to have made a reservation for us . . . then the clerk, when he sees that I'm the Mr. Eldridge the reservation was made for, suddenly discovers that one of their regular tenants just arrived and took the last available room. . . . One night the tension got so bad I flipped. I could feel it right up to my neck while I was playing "Rockin' Chair"; I started trembling, ran off the stand, and threw up. They carried me to the doctor's. I had a hundred-and-five fever; my nerves were shot. . . . Later on, when I was with Artie Shaw, I went to a place where we were supposed to play a dance, and they wouldn't even let me in the place. "This is a white dance," they said, and there was my name right outside, Roy "Little Jazz" Eldridge. . . . Man, when you're on the stage, you're great, but as soon as you come off, you're nothing. It's not worth the glory, not worth the money, not worth anything. Never again!

♦ ♦ ♦

Periodically, Shaw walked away from his band and show business—always a front-page story—to brood in silence, only to return to even greater acclaim. Finally, in 1954, after completing a superb series of small-group recordings (integrated racially and musically with modern jazz musicians), he retired from playing altogether. He published a memoir, novellas, and short stories, and worked on an as-yet-unpublished thousand-page fictionalized autobiography. He also spent much time trying to explain to bewildered fans how a man could abandon such an extraordinary talent.

"STAR DUST"

Shaw's various bands reflected his restless temperament. At times he wanted to satisfy his fans' desire for "the loudest band in the whole goddamn world." Other bands attempted to bridge the gap between jazz and classical music. His first claim to fame came in 1936 when he wrote, for the musicians' community, a piece for clarinet, string quartet (two violins, viola, cello), and rhythm. In 1940, now a celebrity, he enriched his swing band with a nine-piece string section, intelligently used by arranger Lennie Hayton.

"Star Dust," which dates from this period, is a restrained and lyrical performance, focusing on the haunting melody written by Hoagy Carmichael in 1927. The soloists treat the tune with love and ingenuity. In the opening chorus, trumpeter Billy Butterfield uses a rich vibrato and lyrical sense of embellishment to paraphrase the famous melody. Subsequent soloists explore the tune's mood of romantic sentiment in their own creations. Jack Jenney's brief but melting trombone solo is a highlight, notable for his expressive leap up an octave into the trombone's upper register. So is Shaw's. He was a brilliant technician on clarinet, and a fluid and supple improviser. This solo is finely sculpted, suggesting the reach of a great violinist when it climaxes in the stratosphere on a high A.

STAR DUST

Artie Shaw and His Orchestra

Artie Shaw, clarinet; George Wendt, J. Cathcart, Billy Butterfield, trumpets; Jack Jenney, Vernon Brown, trombones; Bud Bassey, Neely Plumb, alto saxophones; Les Robinson, Jerry Jerome, tenor saxophones; Johnny Guarnieri, piano; Al Hendrickson, guitar; Jud DeNaut, bass; Nick Fatool, drums; T. Boardman, T. Klages, B. Bower, Bob Morrow, Al Beller, E. Lamas, violins; A. Harshman, K. Collins, violas; F. Goerner, cello

LABEL: Victor 27230; *Artie Shaw: Greatest Hits* (RCA 68494)
DATE: 1940
STYLE: big-band swing
FORM: 32-bar popular song (**ABAC**)

Introduction

0:00		Tentatively holding out each note, an unaccompanied trumpet soloist (Butterfield) plays the first few notes of the tune.

Chorus 1

0:05	**A**	With a gentle slide, he signals the band to enter. Underneath, the saxophone section plays long-held chords in a slow, measured tempo.
0:14		Immediately after a dramatic chord change, the string section emerges from the background.
0:27	**B**	
0:49	**A**	The string section plays an elaborate variation on the main melody.
1:10	**C**	The trumpet returns on a high note, while the accompaniment returns a few seconds later (1:14).
1:21		For the final statement of the tune, the entire band enters.

Interlude

1:29		The band modulates for the next chorus.

Chorus 2

1:40	**A**	Shaw enters for his clarinet solo, with a highly decorated version of the melody that moves into double-time.
2:02	**B**	As Shaw begins exploring the chords through harmonic improvisation, his line becomes a string of eighth notes.
2:13		Shaw's line climaxes on a dramatic high note.
2:25	**A**	Jenney enters on trombone, playing a beautiful solo with subtle ornaments.
2:47	**C**	With the strings hovering in the background, the band takes over the melody. The drummer underscores the excitement with cymbals.
2:57		The last phrase is signaled by a sharp, syncopated accent.
3:01		Break: the band drops out, leaving Shaw to conclude the melody unaccompanied.

Coda

3:04		Shaw continues his line, improvising harmonically.
3:07		On a rising series of chords, the band reenters.
3:13		The string section emerges with its own dissonant harmonic progression, which finally resolves (by 3:18) to the tonic chord.
3:19		Final cadence.
3:23		Over a held chord, the strings have the last word, adding a decorative skein of dissonant chords.

Jimmie Lunceford (1902–1947) fit few swing stereotypes—like Paul Whiteman, with whose father he had studied as a high school student in Denver, he appeared onstage as a baton-waving conductor, not as a star instrumentalist. As a youth, he studied saxophone as well as guitar and trombone, but in his maturity he never played his favorite instrument, the alto saxophone, with his band. He was, however, a stern taskmaster and disciplinarian who brought an air of the school classroom with him onto the bandstand.

Lunceford had had an extensive education. After taking courses at City College in New York, he graduated from Fisk University in Nashville in 1926 and took a job as a music instructor at a Memphis high school. He saw music as a tremendous engine for social and economic uplift, and turned his students into a dance band, the Chickasaw Syncopators. From this initial group came his longtime drummer, Jimmy Crawford. The Syncopators soon became a professional orchestra, augmented by friends from Fisk such as alto saxophonist Willie Smith (the band's main soloist) and pianist Ed Wilcox. The band got its break in 1934 when invited to play at the Cotton Club in New York, one of the few places where a black band could broadcast in prime time. With his music pouring over the airwaves, Lunceford became a mainstay of the Swing Era, recording a succession of hits for Decca and Columbia and constantly going on tour.

A light-skinned, athletic man, Lunceford felt at ease in positions of authority. Nicknamed "the Professor," he drilled his band like a martinet, insisting on impeccable appearance ("he checked their socks," one bandleader remembered) and exacting musicianship through endless rehearsals. He refused to accept sloppy behavior, demanding that his musicians adhere to the three P's: punctuality, precision, and presentation. The result was a band that embodied the best in black middle-class dignity, with Lunceford at its center. "Until I met Jimmie, I'd never met anybody of whom I felt any intellectual fear," his arranger Sy Oliver recalled. "The musicians don't all realize it, but that man raised them. He changed their lives." Oliver was largely responsible for the band's signature style, which involved a two-beat feel and across-the-board harmonizing of instruments, rather than the usual call-and-response sectional divisions.

With the gradual decline of vaudeville, dance bands were often thrust onto the stage to pick up the slack, and the Lunceford band was always eager to put on a show. Audiences were treated not only to excellent swing music, but also humorous novelties ("I'm Nuts about Screwy Music," "The Merry-Go-Round Broke Down"), unusual repertory ("Organ Grinder's

Swing," "Annie Laurie") and deftly handled physical antics. Trombonist
Eddie Durham described a show at the Apollo Theater:

◆ ◆ ◆

> They would come out and play a dance routine. The Shim Sham Shimmy
> was popular then and six of the guys would come down and dance to it—
> like a tap dance, crossing their feet and sliding. Then Willie Smith would
> put his bonnet on and sing a sort of nursery rhyme. [Trumpeter] Eddie
> Tompkins hit the high notes and did a Louis Armstrong deal. Then they had
> a Guy Lombardo bit and a Paul Whiteman bit—see, they imitated bands.
> The lights would go down next and they'd all lay down their horns and come
> out to sing as a glee club. . . . The next number, they'd be throwing their
> horns and hats up to the ceiling. That was all novelty, and I liked it.

◆ ◆ ◆

The Lunceford band's downfall can be traced to the leader's penurious
salaries, which cost him the loyalty of Oliver and several of his most noted
sidemen, and his overeager work schedule. He kept his band on the road—
a grueling, continuous tour in worn-out buses. The sheer volume of touring was unbelievable: to give one example, the band played in Providence,
Rhode Island, on one night; in Martinsburg, West Virginia, the next; and
the following night in Clemson, South Carolina. Lunceford died at forty-
five, of a heart attack while signing autographs.

"'TAIN'T WHAT YOU DO (IT'S THE WAY THAT YOU DO IT)"

Melvin "Sy" Oliver, a trumpet player from Ohio, was already an experienced arranger by the time he first encountered the fledgling Lunceford
band in 1933. He was ready to quit music to return to school, but the
band's flawless sight-reading of his arrangements made him change his
mind. Until he was hired away in 1939 by Tommy Dorsey's more affluent orchestra, Oliver wrote dozens of witty, inventive charts that were a
mainstay of Lunceford's repertory, turning unlikely tunes like "The Organ
Grinder's Swing," "Annie Laurie," and "Put on Your Old Grey Bonnet"
into swing masterpieces.

On "'Tain't What You Do (It's the Way That You Do It)," Oliver's co-
composer was James "Trummy" Young, a skillful trombone soloist who
occasionally sang for the group. Like Ellington's "It Don't Mean a Thing (if
It Ain't Got That Swing)," this song offers a witting observation from the
African American perspective. As James Weldon Johnson noted in 1912,
a black preacher's eloquence "consists more in the manner of saying than

in what is said." "'Tain't What You Do" put this idea into the musical vernacular, and became a jazz axiom. Young's hip, understated delivery, with its subtle swoops and sideway slips into speech, matches the intent of the words. Set against him is the unvarnished sound of band members intoning the opening phrase. The rest of Oliver's arrangement uses improvised solos by alto saxophonist Willie Smith and elemental yet cleverly arranged riffs to suggest that the Lunceford band has been abiding by this bit of family wisdom all along.

'TAIN'T WHAT YOU DO (IT'S THE WAY THAT YOU DO IT)

Jimmie Lunceford

Eddie Tomkins, Paul Webster, trumpets; Sy Oliver, trumpet and arranger; Elmer Crumbley, Russell Bowles, trombones; Trummy Young, trombone and vocal; Willie Smith, Earl Carruthers, Dan Grisson, alto saxophones; Joe Thomas, tenor saxophone; Edwin Wilcox, piano; Al Norris, guitar; Moses Allen, bass; Jimmy Crawford, drums

LABEL: Vocalion/OKeh 4582; *Lunceford Special* (Columbia 65647)
DATE: 1939
STYLE: swing
FORM: 32-bar popular song (**AABA**)

Chorus 1

0:00	**A**	After a short drum upbeat, the tune begins in the saxophones, accompanied by the hollow sound of bass drum strokes alternating with tom-tom strokes. The melody is simple, beginning with a syncopated repetition of a single note.
0:07		The saxophones gradually increase in volume.
0:09		On one note, the saxophones briefly erupt into block-chord harmony.
0:11		The saxophone melody is answered by the brass.
0:13	**A**	The same melody is now heard with a more conventional accompaniment: a swing drum beat, a walking-bass line that moves down the major scale, and detached syncopated chords in the brass.
0:24	**B**	The brass take over, starting the melody from a new note and descending through a bluesy dissonance.
0:28		The melody is extended by Smith's alto saxophone improvisation.
0:32		Smith interrupts again with a falling blue note.
0:37	**A**	The melody is divided between saxophones and brass, alternating with their own *soli* in call and response.
0:46		To emphasize the last bluesy phrase, all the horns combine on a single line.

Interlude

0:48	The band plays a series of chords headed toward the dominant, ultimately ending on a half cadence.

0:59   A drum roll introduces the vocal.

Verse

1:00   Young steps forward to sing the tune. His wispy, understated vocal line
            is unaccompanied, punctuated occasionally by short chords in the bass
            and piano.
            "When I was a kid, about half-past three, my daddy said,
            'Son, come here to me.' Says, 'Things may come, things may go,
            but this is one thing you ought to know.'"

Chorus 2

1:13   **A**   The piece modulates upward to a new key. The melody is sung by the
            band, with Young answering in call and response, his voice dropping off
            to a speech tone by the end of the phrase. Underneath, the rhythm sec-
            tion provides steady rhythmic and harmonic accompaniment while the
            piano comps and adds fills.
            "'Tain't what you do, it's the way 't-cha you do it. [repeats two times]
            That's what gets results! Mama, mama!"

1:24   **A**   *"'Tain't what you do, it's the time that 'cha do it. [repeats two times]*
            That's what gets results! Oh. . . ."

1:36   **B**   Over the bridge, the band sings the entire line, leaving Young with
            humorous responses.
            "You can try hard, don't mean a thing! Don't mean a thing!
            Take it easy. . . . Greasssy! Then your jive will swing! Oh, it . . ."

1:48   **A**   *"'Tain't what you do, it's the place that 'cha do it. [repeats two times]*
            That's what gets results!"

1:58   As Smith enters a bar early on a blue note, the tune modulates upward
            yet again.

Chorus 3 (extended)

2:00   **A**   Smith takes a solo while the trumpet section plays a riff, using plungers
            to alter their timbre.

2:11   **A**   The trombones slide from one chord to another, answered by the saxo-
            phones with a paraphrase of the main melody. The trumpets continue
            their riff, making it denser and more syncopated.

2:23   **A**   The band builds intensity by repeating the **A** section one more time.

2:35   **B**   Over this extended bridge, Crawford takes a drum solo, playing primar-
            ily on his tom-toms. Barely audible underneath, the guitar and bass
            continue to provide the harmony.

2:40   Crawford complicates the groove with sharp syncopated accents on the
            bass drum and cymbals.

2:45   As Crawford finishes his solo, the band enters on a dominant chord,
            holding it for two additional measures.

2:49   **A**   Chord in the trombones is followed by a high-pitched chord in the
            trumpets and a unison line for the saxophones.

2:59   As the tune ends, the trumpets finish on the tonic chord.

Coda

....

| 3:01 | Crawford follows a pair of cymbal strokes with a bass drum stroke. |

As America entered the war, its most popular bandleader was Glenn Miller (1904–1944), an owl-eyed trombonist who brought swing firmly into mainstream entertainment. It was decidedly not Miller's intention to join the jazz canon. "I haven't [got] a great jazz band," he explained to an interviewer, "and I don't want one." Instead, the unmistakable sound of his arrangements, with their lush blend of clarinet and saxophones, aimed straight for the white mainstream audience, who heard his music as the embodiment of the Swing Era and of modern pop music.

Miller grew up in a Midwestern household where he absorbed his parents' habits of discipline and self-control. As a teenager, he developed a taste for jazzy dance music, prompting him to drop out of college to become a musician. Throughout the 1920s, he was an ambitious young sideman, sharpening his skills as a soloist and arranger in some of the same dance bands as his colleague Benny Goodman. Yet by the time Goodman became a celebrity in 1935, Miller was still working behind the scenes, coaching lesser-known bands toward the big time.

When he started his own dance band in 1938, Miller refused the path laid out by Goodman. He knew what his audiences wanted: unfiltered melodies, a smooth, danceable rhythm, and above all, a distinctive sound. To achieve the latter, he topped his saxophone section with a wide, pulsating clarinet (played by Willie Schwartz), creating a warm, mellifluous timbre that became his calling card. The sound can be heard on Miller's theme song, the lushly romantic "Moonlight Serenade," as well as on numerous other hit records ("A String of Pearls," "In the Mood") that dominated the charts in the early 1940s. Indeed, Miller's tunes were so popular that early in 1942, when shellac was limited by Japanese advances in the Pacific, RCA-Victor scaled back production of all other records so that it could press millions of copies of "Chattanooga Choo Choo."

That same year, Miller became the best-known bandleader to offer his services to the armed forces. The enormous Glenn Miller Army Air Force Band featured forty-two musicians and combined strings and brass. Like Paul Whiteman before him, Miller included jazz as part of an eclectic mixture that offered something for everybody. Miller's disappearance in December 1944, when his plane flew over the English Channel and never landed, was mourned as a national tragedy. Decades later, it was discovered that he may have been killed by a U.S. bomber, dropping its unexploded munitions on Miller's unseen plane.

Cab Calloway (1907–1994) was a curiously ambivalent icon of black culture during the Swing Era. To whites, he offered an entrée into the black ghetto: through his singing, with its suggestive use of slang, they could catch a glimpse of an alluring world of illicit drugs and sex. To blacks, he represented hope: he showed how a man with talent and ambition could rise to the top of the music business. He wowed the cats in New York's Harlem with his stylish, zoot-suited flair and straight hair, which invariably ended up falling over his forehead. Sammy Davis Jr. included himself among the thousands of black kids who, he said, jumped up and down before a mirror trying to get their hair to do that. The black establishment was more impressed with his flaunted material success.

Calloway grew up in Baltimore in the black middle class. He studied classical singing and diligently polished his enunciation. But in the evenings, unsuspected by his teacher (or his mother, who wanted her son to become a lawyer like his father), he discovered the joys of singing jazz. For a time he worked as a professional basketball player, but he gave that up for the world of entertainment, where he put his athletic ability to use in exuberant dancing. One musician remembers him winning over his audience by leaping over chairs and turning somersaults—while continuing to sing.

In the late 1920s, Calloway formed his own band, the Alabamians, which he took to New York's Savoy Ballroom; but the corny music they played was washed away by a young band from Kansas City, the Missourians. In 1930, when the Missourians were looking for a singer and leader, Calloway accepted their offer, changing their name to Cab Calloway and His Orchestra. He was ready to debut with the band at a new Harlem nightspot called the Plantation Club, only to find it destroyed just before opening night by hoodlums from the Cotton Club who were not eager for competition. His luck turned once again when the Cotton Club asked him to replace Duke Ellington as the house band.

The Cotton Club's staff songwriter Harold Arlen and lyricist Ted Koehler crafted new songs to match Calloway's exuberant personality with fantastic scenes meant to evoke Harlem's exotic underground. In "Kickin' the Gong Around" (a reference to opium and cocaine), Smokey Joe searches for his drug-addict girlfriend, Minnie. Calloway took that scenario a step further in "Minnie the Moocher," enriching the moody, minor-mode song with rhyming slang to turn Minnie into a powerful central character (the "toughest frail" with "a heart as big as a whale"). His performances of "Minnie" famously climaxed with a scat-singing call and response—as Cab's plangent wails of "hi-de-ho" were echoed by the band and audience.

Calloway was a fine singer, his voice ranging from a deep baritone to a high tenor. He was also a shrewd businessman who continually improved his band with the best musicians money could buy. He was unafraid to take his black band down South, where their New York hipness often attracted the hostile attention of racists ("We were not docile Negroes," he said). Calloway knew what it took to survive. "The only difference between a black and a white entertainer," he proclaimed, "is that my ass has been kicked a little more and a lot harder because it's black." His band traveled in style, in its own Pullman car, with Calloway's lime-green Lincoln stashed in its cargo. "Cab was like a breath of fresh air," his bassist Milt Hinton remembered. "He said, 'I feel obligated to try to show these people that there's a better way of life—that entertainment is higher than this.'"

By the late 1930s, Calloway was deeply immersed in jazz. He hired the best upcoming soloists, including tenor saxophonist Chu Berry, drummer Cozy Cole, and the young trumpet wizard Dizzy Gillespie, who tormented Calloway with his modernist playing and zany antics. After Calloway's band folded in the late 1940s, he developed a solo act in nightclubs, and worked as an actor in movies and on Broadway. His most celebrated role was Sportin' Life in a 1950 production of *Porgy and Bess*—a fitting twist, as Gershwin is said to have devised the part after watching Calloway at the Cotton Club. As late as 1980, at seventy-three in the movie *The Blues Brothers*, his every step radiated class and style.

CHAPTER 8

Count Basie and Duke Ellington

THE SOUTHWEST

One measure of the preeminence of the Duke Ellington and Count Basie orchestras is that even now, people who know little if anything about jazz have heard of them. They and, to a somewhat lesser degree, Woody Herman's orchestra transcend the Swing Era, in part because they remained on the road so much longer than the others and because their music is intrinsic to the development of jazz in ways that go beyond the jazz-pop-dance hall aesthetic that characterized their rivals. Yet without the Swing Era, Basie might never

◄ Count Basie accomplished the most with the least effort. Here we see his good humor in action, at the Newport Jazz Festival, 1955.

have come into his own, and Ellington almost certainly would not have enjoyed the commercial and artistic clout that generated his astonishing outpouring of masterpieces in the early 1940s. Ellington remained an abiding source of inspiration from the time he triumphed at the Cotton Club in 1927 to long after his death, in 1974, thanks to a head-spinning trove of posthumous releases. Basie, on the other hand, was past thirty when he rose from obscurity, groomed by two deceptively conflicting forces: his early years in the stronghold of Harlem stride and his more formative education in the wild and woolly precincts of the Southwest.

Although swing was a national music, disseminated by recordings and radio across the country, one region was strong enough to pull that national sound in a new direction. In jazz parlance, the Southwest was not, as we would have it today, the desert regions north of Mexico, but rather the area south and west of the Mississippi, including Missouri, Oklahoma, and Texas, with its urban headquarters in Kansas City. African Americans had known about the Southwest since the end of the Civil War, when, seeking economic opportunity and social freedom, they began heading toward what they called "the territory." Some founded all-black towns, such as Nicodemus, Kansas, and Boley, Oklahoma. Others sought jobs requiring unskilled manual labor. Working on the river or the railroad, in turpentine factories or mines, wasn't easy, but it beat the stifling agricultural labor of Mississippi, Arkansas, and Georgia.

The impact of the Southwest on the nation's musical taste is apparent in the rise of the blues piano style known as boogie-woogie. The provenance of boogie-woogie is uncertain, but one early nickname—"fast Western"—suggests the Southwest, while other bits of oral evidence point to east Texas and Louisiana. The style spread rapidly during the 1920s, following the urbanizing trend of the Great Migration, and secured a home in the Midwest, especially in Kansas City and Chicago. As with ragtime, boogie-woogie was built on a firm rhythmic foundation in the left hand. But unlike ragtime, or stride, which turned the four-beat measure into a two-beat feeling by alternating bass notes and chords, boogie-woogie doubled the pace with fierce, rhythmic ostinatos. Known as chains for their repetitive quality, these patterns divide each beat in two, so that the four-beat measure now has an eight-beat pulse. Heavily percussive, the torrent of sound in the pianist's left hand is the unfailing signature of this music. Against it, the right hand is free to improvise in percussive cross-rhythms.

Boogie-woogie was a social music—tumultuous and inexpensive, perfect for dancing and blues singing. In the countryside, it emerged from logging and turpentine camps where men listened to music in rough out-buildings known as barrelhouses. In cities, boogie-woogie was played in speakeasies where hard-working pianists played through the night for a few dollars plus tips. Much as stride served as an ideal accompaniment at New York rent parties, boogie-woogie provided the preferred rhythmic punch in the Midwest. Like its later progeny, rock and roll, its thunderous sound cut through the tumult, spurring dancers onto the floor.

Boogie-woogie found its way onto recordings in the 1920s. "Honky Tonk Train Blues" (1927), by Meade Lux Lewis, imitated the bustle of railroad travel through consistently overlapping ostinato patterns. The 1928 "Pine Top's Boogie Woogie," by Clarence "Pine Top" Smith, featured the pianist shouting as if to control an imaginary Saturday night crowd. The style probably got its name from the dance that Smith introduces at one point: "When I say 'hold yourself,' I want all of you to get ready to stop! And when I say 'stop,' don't move! And when I say 'get it,' I want all of you to do a boogie-woogie!"

The best place to hear boogie-woogie in Kansas City was the Sunset Café at 18th Street and Highland, where the star attractions were the singer Big Joe Turner (1911–1985) and the pianist Pete Johnson (1904–1967). Johnson had worked as a manual laborer (shining shoes, working in a slaughterhouse) before he found he could make a better living with his facility on the piano. He met Turner at a speakeasy, the Backbiter's Club, where he earned three dollars (plus tips) working literally all night. Johnson was a versatile pianist, playing ragtime and pop songs, but he became famous for hard-driving, percussive blues that seemed never to end. Turner, a young man with an intensely powerful voice, worked across the room as bartender, serving beer for fifteen cents in tin cans. Turner would sing from behind the bar, and occasionally step outside to the sidewalk to sing down the street—a method of luring customers he referred to as "calling the children home," much as Buddy Bolden and King Oliver had done in New Orleans.

Once the music started, it was hard to stop. John Hammond, who visited Kansas City for the first time in 1936, recalled slow tunes that would last for more than half an hour. Faster tunes were shorter (*only* twenty minutes), but they generated a palpable intensity. One overheated reporter wrote that "the colored patrons got excited and threw themselves on the floor, completely hysterical by the rhythm and atmosphere." Similar energy would resurface in the teenage hysteria of rock and roll: Turner himself emerged as one of the few performers of his generation to chart high in rock's early years (with his 1954 hit "Shake, Rattle, and Roll"), a connection about which he commented drily: "We was doin' rock and roll before anyone ever heard of it."

In the early 1930s, boogie-woogie struggled to survive. It was too rhythmically complicated to transfer to the printed page, and record companies were cutting back sharply on black dance music. Individual performers drifted by the wayside. Pine Top Smith was killed in 1929 by a stray bullet in a Chicago nightclub. Jimmy Yancey, a former vaudevillian who became one of the most successful boogie-woogie players, worked as a White Sox groundskeeper at Comiskey Park. Two leading pianists, Meade Lux Lewis and Albert Ammons, worked as cab drivers.

Yet just a few years later, boogie-woogie made a sudden turnaround and became a craze with the white mainstream audience. This startling comeback can be credited to a revival of vernacular music, which began as a self-conscious attempt to publicize black folk traditions; its central figure, once again, was John Hammond. Having seen black dance music marketed successfully as swing, Hammond decided to go further: why not show the world how swing was based on neglected traditions, such as blues and gospel? He scoured the countryside looking for performers and brought them together for a concert, "From Spirituals to Swing," held at Carnegie Hall in 1938, the same year as Benny Goodman's coup. For the first time, an audience heard the now-familiar sounds of swing juxtaposed with the Southern harmonica playing of blind Sonny Terry, the Chicago-style country blues (with a shrewd political edge) of Big Bill Broonzy, and gospel by the Golden Gate Quartet and Sister Rosetta Tharpe. To represent boogie-woogie, Hammond hired Lewis and Ammons from Chicago, and Pete Johnson to accompany Big Joe Turner. The concert program encouraged the audience to "forget you are in Carnegie Hall" and relax into the spirit of Kansas City.

Soon boogie-woogie became au courant, as pianists everywhere were expected to learn its thumping rhythmic patterns. The classical pianist José Iturbi, a frequent performer in Hollywood musicals, invariably had to show what a regular guy he was by playing boogie. The Andrews Sisters, the most popular female vocal group of the war years, sold so many records of "Beat Me, Daddy, Eight to the Bar" in 1941, that they immediately followed it with two sequels, "Scrub Me, Mama, With a Boogie Beat," and the ineffable "Boogie Woogie Bugle Boy," about a Chicago trumpet player who is drafted and finds he can't play in his favorite "eight to the bar" groove until the army provides him with a bass and guitar. "He makes the company jump when he plays reveille," the sisters sang: "He's the boogie-woogie bugle boy of Company B." The underground music of black Kansas City and Chicago had become part of the all-American soundtrack.

"IT'S ALL RIGHT, BABY"

Turner and Johnson were not new to New York: Hammond had brought them east in 1936, hoping to drum up excitement for their music. But at the "From Spirituals to Swing" concert, they had to compress their loose, casual backroom flavor into a tight three minutes—as at a record session. Fortunately, they had done precisely that two years earlier with a recording of "Roll 'Em Pete," a number roughly recast as "It's All Right, Baby" at Carnegie. Turner seems right at home from the outset. After a long, languorous introductory phrase ("Well, it's all . . . right . . . then!"), he barks encouragement to Johnson and keeps lively time with his feet while singing the three-line blues stanzas. After several choruses of Johnson's percussive playing, Turner's words melt down to throaty shouts, serving as calls to Johnson's inventive responses. Not for nothing were Turner and singers like him often called blues shouters. This exhilarating performance captures, like few others, the illusory ambience of Sunset Café craziness—until the business-like, abrupt ending makes it clear that the professionals were fully in charge all along.

IT'S ALL RIGHT, BABY

Big Joe Turner and Pete Johnson
Big Joe Turner, vocal; Pete Johnson, piano

LABEL: *From Spirituals to Swing: 1938 & 1939 Carnegie Hall Concerts* (Vanguard 169-171-2)
DATE: 1938
STYLE: boogie-woogie
FORM: 12-bar blues

Chorus 1

0:00	Johnson opens with a dramatic series of repeated chords on the piano.
0:05	(sung) *"Well, it's all . . . right . . . then!"*
	As the harmony shifts to IV, Johnson begins a boogie-woogie ostinato. Turner enters with a broad, sweeping phrase.

0:09	(spoken) *"Yeah, papa."*
	While commenting on Johnson's solid groove, Turner adds an additional rhythmic layer by tapping his feet.

Chorus 2

0:14	*"That's all right, baby, that's all right for you.*
	[Unintelligible] for you, babe, that's the way you do."
	Turner sings his first full chorus, full of subtle variations in rhythm. His first line begins on the offbeat, then shifts to the downbeat. Johnson's left hand continues the ostinato, while the right hand retreats to simple lower-register chords.
0:27	Johnson responds to Turner's melodies with a low melodic riff.

Chorus 3

0:29	*"Well, you're so beautiful, but you've got to die someday.*
	All I want [is] a little lovin' just before you pass away."
	At the end of his first line, Turner escapes into an expressive blue note.

Chorus 4

0:44	*"Baby, what's the matter now? Tryin' to quit me, babe, where you don't know how."* Behind Turner's vocal, Johnson begins playing short riffs.

Chorus 5

0:59	*"Roll 'em, boy . . . let 'em jump for joy. Yeah, man, happy as a baby boy.*
	Well, just got another brand-new choo-choo toy."
	Turner jumps in ahead of the bar line. In response, Johnson plays a familiar boogie-woogie riff.
1:12	(spoken) *"Ah, pick it, papa!"*

Chorus 6

1:14	Spurred by Turner's foot stomp and hand clap on the backbeat, Johnson begins his two-chorus solo.
1:16	(spoken) *"Yeah, yeah!"*
1:24	(spoken) *"Way down, way down!"*

Chorus 7

1:28	Johnson suddenly plays a high-pitched series of repeated notes at the top of the keyboard.
1:35	As Johnson returns to the middle register, Turner chuckles appreciatively.
1:39	(spoken) *"Solid, pops, solid!"*

Chorus 8

1:43	*"Yes, yes! Yes, I know!"* Turner's simple phrase becomes a call, prompting a response from Johnson's piano.

| 1:45 | Each time Turner repeats his phrase, he varies it in pitch and rhythm. |

Chorus 9

| 1:57 | *"Well, all right, then!"* Without taking a breath, Turner launches into a new phrase, again answered by Johnson. |

Chorus 10

| 2:12 | *"Bye . . . bye!"* Turner transforms his two-syllable phrase into a lengthy, expressive arc that spans several measures. |

Coda

| 2:24 | *"Bye-bye, baby, bye-bye!"* Johnson suddenly cuts off the boogie-woogie ostinato. With a few simple gestures, Johnson and Turner dismantle the rhythmic momentum and bring the performance to a close. Thunderous applause follows. |

TERRITORY BANDS: Andy Kirk (1898–1992) AND Mary Lou Williams (1910–1981)

During the 1920s and early 1930s, thousands of dance bands crisscrossed the United States. Known as territory bands, they worked a geographic area no more than a day's drive from their headquarters. Some "territories" were close to the center of the music business in New York, while others ranged from the Southeast to the upper Midwest (where the polkas of Lawrence Welk held sway) to Northern California. Some were white, others were black. Some specialized in "hot" swing, while others purveyed a more genteel music. A surprising number, including the Melodears, the Prairie View Co-Eds, and the International Sweethearts of Rhythm, were all-female. A few were even religious, like the mysteriously bearded and gentile House of David band, sponsored by a commune in Michigan. Bands often sported names that had little contact with reality: Art Bronson's Bostonians were based in Salinas, Kansas. Only a few territory bands ever set foot in a recording studio.

One that did and became a national favorite began as the Twelve Clouds of Joy, led by tuba player Andy Kirk. The group lived a typical life for a territory band during the Depression—constant touring under the abiding threat of financial failure. Unlike others, however, its unusual repertory of ballads and dance tunes found favor with the director of Brunswick Records, Jack Kapp, who began recording the band in 1929. Still, the

Swing Era was several years down the road, and during the early 1930s, when future star saxophonists Ben Webster, Lester Young, and Buddy Tate passed through the band, the Twelve Clouds of Joy endured night after night in small Southwestern and Midwestern towns, sometimes paid off in fried chicken. On at least one occasion, they stole corn and roasted the kernels.

Kirk caught his break in 1936, when Kapp signed them to his own, recently launched label, Decca Records. Decca expected its black bands to specialize in blues and up-tempo swing, but Kirk convinced Kapp to record a ballad—a feature for his tenor vocalist Pha Terrell—that had been popular in the Kansas City clubs. Several bands played it, including that of Harriet Calloway (no relation to Cab), who called it "The Slave Song," after the lyric "I'd slave for you." Kirk recalled the song as originating with three young ukulele-playing kids who hustled from club to club singing it. In fact, those kids, a professional cabaret trio called the Three Chocolate Drops, had spun their version from a song, "Till the Real Thing Comes Along," that Mann Holiner and Alberta Nichols wrote for Ethel Waters, in the 1931 revue *Rhapsody in Black*.

Meanwhile, Kapp had hired two young white songwriters, Sammy Cahn (subsequently one of the most prolific lyricists of all time) and Saul Chaplin (later a leading Hollywood musical director at Universal, Columbia, and MGM) to write material for his black bands; they had scored their first hit in 1935, with Jimmie Lunceford's "Rhythm Is Our Business." Now they revised the lyrics and structure of "The Slave Song," turning it into "Until the Real Thing Comes Along." Kapp was still reluctant to release it, feeling that Kirk should first prove his swing bona fides with an exciting version of "Christopher Columbus," a big hit that put the band on its feet. Three months after the success of "Christopher Columbus," Kapp released "Until the Real Thing Comes Along," which roared to No. 1 on the pop charts, became Kirk's theme song, and popularized a black crooning style (a high-pitched male voice) that was new to the public and spawned many imitators, most successfully a vocal group called the Ink Spots.

It wasn't crooning, however, that made Kirk's band important, especially to other musicians. The musical genius of the group was the pianist and arranger Mary Lou Williams, whose approach to big-band writing caught the ear of everyone from Duke Ellington and Benny Goodman (they both commissioned work from her) to an unknown teenager named Thelonious Monk. She had grown up in Pittsburgh, where she learned to play piano by listening to the local master Earl Hines and records by Jelly Roll Morton and James P. Johnson. Her talent was evident by age fourteen, when she left home to join a vaudeville show; a few years later, she married John Williams, who joined the Kirk band as a saxophonist. She remained backstage, occasionally earning money by driving the bus and styling hair, until 1929, when one day the band's pianist didn't show up for a recording session. Williams volunteered to sit in, having already learned the band's repertory by ear (she had perfect pitch and an uncanny memory). She was hired on the spot, and even began to record as a sideman, usually as Mary Leo Burley.

At first, unable to read music, Williams relied on her exceptional ear to negotiate difficult musical situations. For her first orchestrations, she sang the various section parts to Kirk, who put them into musical notation. But she soon mastered music theory. "She'd be sitting up at the foot of the bed, legs crossed like an Indian," Kirk recounts, "just writing and writing." Her writing became more individualistic and opulent, employing a wider range of keys. Some of her arrangements are so rigorously conceived they can't be "opened"—that is, loosened up to permit longer or more plentiful solos, as is the case with riff-based arrangements that can be stretched as long as the rhythmic groove holds. As an accompanist and band soloist, Williams was a powerful force. "I listened to how a pianist pushed, like Count Basie," she said, "and *I* pushed."

Yet the prejudice against mixed-gender bands was almost as great as that against mix-race bands. A few years later, during the war, when Rosie the Riveter—arms flexed in determination—symbolized the readiness of women to work on factory floors for their nation's defense, opportunities for women opened across the board. But even then, the entertainment business maintained certain prejudices. While some instruments were accepted as "female"—piano, harp, flute—most wind instruments were regarded as the exclusive province of men. It was one thing to travel in an all-women ensemble (the International Sweethearts of Rhythm, the Harlem Playgirls, and other outfits that were among the hardest-swinging territory bands of the day), but the majority of women associated with male outfits functioned as dancers and singers, showing off their bodies in luxurious or skimpy clothing.

The best of them had to tough it out. While touring with the Count Basie band, Billie Holiday ruined her stockings by playing craps on the floor of the bus. Anita O'Day, touring with Gene Krupa's band, tired of the expense of maintaining evening gowns and insisted on wearing the same band jacket that the men wore. This prompted accusations of lesbianism, leading O'Day to ask, "What does a jacket or shirt have to do with anyone's sex life?" Few women made names for themselves as instrumentalists in male bands: trumpeters Billie Rodgers and Norma Carson, vibraphonist Marjorie Hymans, trombonist Melba Liston. Ultimately, the pressures of the road proved too much for most women, whose careers were cut short by family duties, marriage, or social convention. Still, the war years had shown that swing was not gender-specific and that there was nothing unfeminine about playing jazz.

That was by no means as clear a decade earlier. According to Mary Lou Williams, though she had recorded with the band in 1929, in Kansas City, Kirk dithered about bringing her to Chicago the following year, until an irate Kapp insisted that the band "didn't sound the same" without her. She traveled alone, arriving at the studio in April after a hellish journey, having been raped on the train. While the band warmed up, Kapp asked her to play a couple of numbers. "I have always done my best composing while playing," Williams told the Smithsonian Institute's Jazz Oral History Project regarding that session: "I was almost scared to death, but got going, remembering the night life of K. C." The two solo piano pieces, "Night Life" and "Drag 'Em," the first sides released under her own name, are luminous improvisations suggesting a feverish tenacity, interweaving tricky cross-rhythms, hesitations, tremolos, and a stomp. She never falters, while showing how much piano she had soaked up from Eubie Blake, James P. Johnson, Fats Waller, and Earl Hines in the development of an obstinately self-sufficient pianistic personality. Those solos were little noted at the time, but she returned with the Kirk band in the new era of 1936. Her forcefulness established her as the most prominent female instrumentalist in jazz or swing. As one of her arrangements put it, she was "the lady who swings the band." She once proudly claimed that she played "heavy, like a man"—an assessment that says more about her social upbringing than her playing. She strenuously avoided cheesecake shots, an obligation most women musicians and singers fulfilled to generate publicity. Insiders accepted her as someone in the know, someone to learn from.

"WALKIN' AND SWINGIN'"

"Walkin' and Swingin'" was written by Mary Lou Williams in 1936, shortly after the agent Joe Glaser had taken control of the Twelve Clouds of Joy's bookings and vetted their contract with Decca Records. Although Williams's arrangement earned her only a few dollars—a small bonus to her salary as pianist—she was satisfied that the piece furthered her reputation as a performer and arranger, and helped pave the way for her to eventually lead her own smaller bands. Though not a big hit (practically all of Kirk's charted hits feature Pha Terrell's ballad singing), "Walkin' and Swingin'" is the piece most often used by today's jazz repertory ensembles to capture the quality of the band and of Williams's early writing style.

Like Fletcher Henderson's "Blue Lou," it begins with a dissonance from the minor mode that resolves to the major. Yet the arrangements are distinctly different—partly because of individual style, but also because Kirk's band was slightly smaller. While most arrangers depended on four or five saxophones to fill out their harmonies, Kirk's band had three. Williams's solution was ingenious: she asked one of the trumpet players to "talk into a hat"—to use a metal derby mute—to help it blend with the saxophones. The mood is sly and conversational, as if the collective voice of the band had continually new things to say. One of Williams's most memorable melodic ideas appears near the end of the second chorus (1:12)—her friend Thelonious Monk combined it with a lick from Ellington's "Ducky Wucky" to create his own tune, "Rhythm-a-ning," first recorded in 1957. Others, less friendly, also took from her. Her composition "What's Your Story, Morning Glory?" was lifted whole and turned into the standard pop tune "Black Coffee."

WALKIN' AND SWINGIN'

Andy Kirk and His Twelve Clouds of Joy

Harry "Big Jim" Lawson, Paul King, Earl Thompson, trumpets; Ted Donnelly, Henry Wells, trombones; John Williams, John Harrington, alto saxophones; Dick Wilson, tenor saxophone; Mary Lou Williams, piano; Ted Robinson, guitar; Booker Collins, bass; Ben Thigpen, drums

LABEL: Decca 809; *Andy Kirk & The 12 Clouds of Joy* (ASV/Living Era 5108)
DATE: 1936
STYLE: big-band swing
FORM: 32-bar popular song (**AABA**)

Chorus 1

0:00	**A**	The saxophones begin a long, swooping melody, supported by a see-sawing riff in the brass. The bass plays a two-beat pattern (although we still feel the overall four-beat framework).
0:08		After the saxophone melody finishes, the brass section emerges with a brief figure on the offbeats.

0:10 **A**

0:20 **B**   The piece modulates to a new key. The brass take the lead, with the saxophones quietly in the background.

0:30 **A**   The tune modulates back to the original key.

Interlude

0:38   The saxophones, topped by a solo trumpet, extend the seesawing riff to a full cadence.

Chorus 2

0:43 **A**   The piece modulates again, this time to yet a different key. The saxophone/trumpet combination plays a chorus-long passage in block-chord texture (*soli*). By subtly changing dynamics and rhythm, the band suggests an improvising soloist.

0:52 **A**   As it passes over the same chord progression, the band plays shorter, more propulsive figures.

1:02 **B**   Again the tune modulates, with the written-out *soli* line rising and falling over the chords.

1:12 **A**   The *soli* settles into a simple, on-the-beat riff.

Chorus 3

1:21 **A**   Williams begins her piano solo, interspersing punchy percussive phrases with delicate, intricate runs.

1:31 **A**   She simulates a blue note by crushing two notes together.

1:41 **B**   Wilson plays a tenor saxophone solo, accompanied by background riffs.

1:50 **A**   Williams returns to continue her solo.

1:56   She plays a riff that sounds like an improvisation. But when the band immediately repeats it (in a two-bar break), we realize that the entire passage is part of Williams's arrangement.

Chorus 4 (abbreviated)

2:00 **A**   In a climactic chorus, the saxophones return to their seesawing riff while the bass switches to a four-beat pattern. Above them, the brass punctuate strongly on the offbeat.

2:08 **A**   In the next section (which arrives two bars early), a simple brass riff is answered by the saxophones.

2:17 **B**   As the arrangement reaches its climax, saxophones scurry beneath a brass high note.

2:28 **A**   The brass play a new two-note riff, answered by the saxophones.

2:35   The two-note riff falls to a final cadence.

Andy Kirk's career ended in the late 1940s, though he occasionally fronted pickup groups over the next dozen or so years. Mary Lou Williams accomplished some of her finest work long after the Swing Era, notwithstanding a few self-imposed sabbaticals. In 1942, tiring of continuous band travel, she left Kirk's band and took a spot at Barney Josephson's Café Society in New York, the country's first completely integrated nightclub. She also became more active as a composer, recording elaborate pieces such as *Zodiac Suite* (1945). Her interest in complex chromatic harmonies (she called them "zombie chords") pulled her into the bebop revolution of the 1940s, where she assumed a position of leadership. Her apartment on Hamilton Terrace in Harlem became a gathering place for such musicians as Dizzy Gillespie, Kenny Clarke, Bud Powell, and especially Monk, whom she took on as a protégé. Gillespie credited her with helping them to rethink the formation of chords.

In the 1950s, Williams underwent a conversion to Roman Catholicism, and renounced music in favor of charitable work. But Gillespie convinced her to participate with his big band at the 1957 Newport Jazz Festival, and in the 1960s she became a devoted teacher of jazz history. After another slow period, in the early 1970s, she talked Barney Josephson into leasing a piano for his successful Greenwich Village restaurant, The Cookery. As word got around that Mary Lou Williams was playing there, lines began to form, and during the next several years The Cookery became a major music venue, launching the comebacks of singers Helen Humes and Alberta Hunter and harmonica virtuoso Larry Adler.

Williams was now busier than ever (Fr. Peter F. O'Brien, a Jesuit priest, took over her management), organizing bands of different sizes, composing religious oratorios, recording and concertizing (she persuaded the avant-garde pianist Cecil Taylor, who used to listen to her at The Cookery, to play and record an evening of duets with her at Carnegie Hall), writing and dictating memoirs, and taking a position as professor in the Music Department at Duke University. She instilled in her students a vision of jazz as a continuous tradition and illustrated her points at the piano. Her concerts similarly featured lengthy pieces designed to show the evolution of jazz, from ragtime to modal. She remained a fearless champion of jazz in all its forms.

Count Basie (1904–1984)

Most of the major figures in Kansas City jazz were not raised in Kansas City, but they did hail from the South and Southwest. Not William

"Count" Basie, by far the most famous Kansas City bandleader of them all: he grew up Red Bank, on the New Jersey shore, not far from New York City. His father worked as a coachman, until cars replaced horses, and then as a groundskeeper for private families; his mother took in laundry and put a quarter aside to pay for Bill's piano lessons. After dropping out of junior high school, he took odd jobs at the local Palace Theater to see the shows, determined to become a musician—"playing music has never really been work," he once said. His first apprenticeship was accompanying silent movies. He learned his trade in New York, in the mid-1920s, studying the work of the stride masters (Fats Waller gave him lessons on pipe organ) while trying to avoid direct competition with pianists like James P. Johnson, who were far above him in ability. When the chance came to leave town as the accompanist for a touring TOBA vaudeville show, he grabbed it.

In 1927, he found himself stranded in Kansas City, recovering from spinal meningitis. Within a year, he was freelancing with bands and singers, accompanying silent movies, and going out on short tours. He also changed his name, printing business cards that read "Count Basie – Beware the Count is Here." One morning, from his hotel window at the Red Wing Hotel in Tulsa, he heard a new type of jazz played by a territory band from Oklahoma City, the Blue Devils, who were using the back of a truck as a bandstand. "I had never heard anything like that band in my life," he remembered. "Everybody seemed to be having so much fun just being up there playing together. . . . There was such a team spirit among those guys, and it came out in the music, and as you stood there looking and listening you just couldn't help wishing that you were a part of it."

Basie became an irregular member of the Blue Devils, which was nominally led by the bassist Walter Page. Like many other groups of the time, it was a "commonwealth" band, distributing its funds evenly among its members and relying on group consensus for decisions. This informality ultimately spelled disaster. As one band member remembered, "Whenever we wanted to do something, accept a job, we have to sit down and have a discussion. . . . Seven would vote for it and six would vote against it." The band finally dissolved in 1933 when funds ran out altogether in Bluefield, West Virginia.

By this time, Basie and Page had already been scooped up by the most prosperous band in the Kansas City region, led by Benny Moten (1894–1935). Moten was a skilled ragtime pianist but an even more successful businessman. In Kansas City, he dealt shrewdly with the powerful city organization led by Tom Pendergast, whose *laissez-faire* attitude toward illegal activities guaranteed a boisterous night life. According to trumpet player Oran "Hot Lips" Page, Moten's proposition to his musicians was simple: "If we would provide the music, he would provide the jobs." Having Pendergast on your side was money in the bank—his grip on Kansas City was as clenched as Al Capone's on Chicago. Technically, he was only a city alderman, but behind the scenes his political machine turned the city into a haven for gambling and alcohol. In Tom's Town, as it was known throughout the Southwest, violators of Prohibition were rarely convicted and saloons stayed open all night. A self-styled populist, championing "the poor, the black, the Italian, the immigrant," he ultimately went the way of Capone, convicted in 1939 for income tax evasion. Yet out of his regime came Harry S. Truman and Kansas City jazz. Black musicians didn't escape racism in Kansas City (it "might as well have been Gulfport, Mississippi," one performer remembered), but they could always find work. The corner of Twelfth Street and Vine was not chic, but it was the hippest place to be on a Saturday night.

In 1935, Benny Moten's career came to an abrupt end when he entered a hospital for a tonsillectomy and bled to death from a severed artery. Moten's demise, while devastating for many musicians, inadvertently helped to launch Basie. He retreated to the Reno Club, one of the less prepossessing clubs in Kansas City, where he gathered together several of Moten's musicians in the course of creating his own band. This tiny, L-shaped saloon was so small that Walter Page often had to sit on a stool outside and lean in the window. Basie's band was also small, with only nine pieces—three trumpets, three saxophones, and three in the rhythm section—and managed to create music without written arrangements. "I don't think we had over four or five sheets of music up there," Basie recalled. "We had our own thing, and we could always play some more blues and call it something."

The unwritten music created by Basie's band was based on head arrangements, so called because the music, created collectively, was stored in the heads of the musicians who played it. Head arrangements typified the casual but intensely creative and often competitive atmosphere of the jam session in Kansas City. A club like the Sunset Café would typically hire only a pianist and drummer, expecting the rest of the music to be created by musicians who dropped by in the course of an evening. Tunes lasted as long as the musicians wanted. "It wasn't unusual for one number to go on about an hour or an hour and a half," the drummer Jo Jones recalled.

"Nobody got tired. They didn't tell me at that time they used to change drummers, so I just sat there and played the whole time for pure joy."

Although only one soloist played at a time, the mood of the jam session was collective, with horn players waiting their turn to join in. If one musician played a riff, others nearby would harmonize it, searching for notes to fit the riff in block-chord texture. According to bassist Gene Ramey, this skill derived from black folk traditions. It reminded him of "revival meetings, where the preacher and the people are singing, and there's happenings all around." The more musicians, the more notes were needed: a saxophonist might add extra extended notes to standard chords (sixths, ninths) to avoid "stepping on" someone else's "line," or chord tone. At the same time, since this spontaneous music was created by professionals, it had a slick, orchestral polish. All that was needed to transfer it to the dance band was a group of musicians capable of remembering what they had played.

For dance bands, head arrangements offered special flexibility. Some became fixed arrangements, written down to preserve the order of riffs. But in the heat of performance, musicians could extend the tune to extraordinary lengths. New riffs could be created to match the dancers' ingenuity. Basie was particularly skilled at creating head arrangements from the piano, by cuing the saxophones with one keyboard riff and the brasses with another. "When you play a battle of music, it's the head arrangements that you could play for about ten minutes and get the dancers going," remembered Teddy Wilson, whose music-reading dance band could not keep up with Kansas City–style spontaneity. Once the Basie band began playing "One O'Clock Jump," the contest was over: "That was the end of the dance!"

"ONE O'CLOCK JUMP"

"One O'Clock Jump" was a fluid, twelve-bar blues arrangement that had evolved gradually for more than a decade before finding its final form; only after it was recorded was it notated so that the copyright could be reserved. Many of its riffs were collected over time by Basie long-timers like saxophonist Buster Smith, trumpeter Hot Lips Page, and trombonist Eddie Durham. The main theme (not played until the ninth chorus) can be heard in the 1920s Don Redman arrangement "Six or Seven Times." Originality was hardly the issue: like the blues itself, these riffs were assumed to be public property. Once again, it wasn't what you did, but how you did it.

There is little else holding the piece together. The band knew it as

"Blue Balls," an admittedly indecent title they never expected to make public. When the tune was finally performed on the radio, community standards ("You can't call it *that!*") forced a change. "One O'Clock Jump" presumably commemorates the hour of the morning it was first broadcast. Stark and even elemental, it was tremendously effective and became Basie's first hit.

Basie begins with a piano solo that locks the rhythm section into its groove. He often insisted on starting off on his own, playing several choruses until the tempo felt right—"just like you were mixing mash and yeast to make whiskey," his trumpet player Harry "Sweets" Edison once said, "and you keep tasting it." A sudden modulation switches from Basie's favorite key (F major) to the distant key the horn players preferred (D-flat major). The arrangement is primarily a string of solos, featuring the best of the Basie band with riff accompaniment. Then comes what might be called a "rhythm section solo" (chorus 7): Basie is the main voice, but his minimal jabs divert our attention to the light, clear sound of what was widely thought of as the best rhythm section of the Swing Era.

The last three choruses consist of interlocking riffs. The famous version is the commercial recording, a 78-rpm disc limited by technology to three minutes. Some radio broadcasts extended the piece for several minutes; musicians have said it could go on for half an hour. The maximum length, one supposes, depended on the fortitude of the musicians. Like African music, it could be extended to suit any occasion.

ONE O'CLOCK JUMP

Count Basie and His Orchestra

Count Basie, piano; Buck Clayton, Ed Lewis, Bobby Moore, trumpets; George Hunt, Dan Minor, trombones; Earl Warren, alto saxophone; Jack Washington, baritone saxophone; Herschel Evans, Lester Young, tenor saxophones; Freddie Green, guitar; Walter Page, bass; Jo Jones, drums

LABEL: Decca 1363; *The Complete Decca Recordings* (GRP 36112)
DATE: 1937
STYLE: Kansas City swing
FORM: 12-bar blues

Introduction

0:00   Basie begins with a vamp—a short, repeated figure in the left hand. Other members of the rhythm section enter gingerly, as if feeling Basie's tempo and groove.

Chorus 1

0:11   With the rhythm section now in full gear, Basie begins his solo with a clear melodic statement. His left hand, playing a spare and tentative stride accompaniment, blends in with the consistent on-beat attacks of the guitar, bass, and drums.

Chorus 2

0:28   Basie suddenly attacks the piano in octaves, ending his phrases with a tremolo (a rapid shaking of the notes in a chord).

0:43   Closing off the introduction, Basie quickly modulates to a new key.

Chorus 3

0:45   On the tenor saxophone, Evans plays a stately chorus with full vibrato. Behind him, the muted trumpets play a simple, two-note harmonized riff.

Chorus 4

1:02   Hunt (trombone) takes over smoothly for the next chorus, accompanied by a background riff by the saxophones. The drummer moves the pulse to the high-hat cymbal.

1:15   The trombonist uses his slide to create blue notes.

Chorus 5

1:19   Young (tenor saxophone) begins his chorus with false fingerings—playing the same note with different fingerings to create new timbres.

1:21   To match Young's sound, the drummer adjusts his pattern to an accent on the bass drum every other measure.

1:32   At the end of the chorus, the drummer plays the backbeat.

Chorus 6

1:36   On trumpet, Clayton starts his solo with a simple riff (resembling the beginning of "When the Saints Go Marching In"). Behind him, the saxophones play a long descending riff. The drummer returns to playing the high-hat cymbal with occasional snare drum accents.

Chorus 7

1:53   Basie plays sparely, accompanied only by the rhythm section. Each of his chords has a distinctive sound: high-pitched, spanning slightly over an octave. The bass, drums, and guitar play unflaggingly.

2:02   For a few measures, the bass plays slightly sharp (above pitch).

Chorus 8

2:10   The band reenters with overlapping riffs: a simple melody, played by the saxophones, is interwoven with three trumpet chords. Both are answered by a trombone chord.

Chorus 9

....

| 2:27 | The riffs remain the same except for the saxophonists', who play the melody usually recognized as the theme to "One O'Clock Jump." |

Chorus 10

....

| 2:43 | The saxophones change to a simple, unharmonized riff. The drummer reinforces the trombone chord with a sharp accent on the snare drum. |
| 2:57 | With a short series of chords, the saxophones signal the end. |

In Kansas City, Basie's world was limited to the ten-block black neighborhood in which he lived and worked (at the Reno Club). As critic Gerald Early noted, he "did not aspire to live in an integrated world." Then one night in 1936, John Hammond happened to hear the band on the shortwave radio built into his car, broadcasting from the peripatetic local radio station W9XBY. He began writing short pieces about the band for music magazines, and soon traveled to Kansas City to hear the band for himself. Entranced with its loose, easy swing, Hammond—who hit it off with Basie from the start—was determined to bring the band into the commercial mainstream. Unfortunately, he was slow in producing a contract. A representative of Decca, who may have been alerted to Basie by Hammond's writings, swooped in and, letting Basie think that he was somehow involved with Hammond, signed him to a shamelessly exploitative indenture. There was nothing Hammond could do, except wait for Basie to fulfill his recording obligations to Decca before signing him to Columbia Records. But he did two things anyway: he embarrassed Decca into revising the contract to ensure royalty payments, and he grabbed Basie, his vocalist Jimmy Rushing, and four of his key musicians to secretly make their first records for Columbia under the pseudonym Jones-Smith Incorporated.

For Basie's musicians, moving from the Reno Club was not easy. Some of their instruments were held together with rubber bands and string. Some members left, while others were added to raise their number from nine to thirteen, and later to the industry standard of fifteen. On the road to New York, when asked to play conventional dance music ("I don't think I even knew what a goddamn tango was," Basie remembered), the band floundered. "By the time you read this," a Chicago newspaper reported, "they will be on their way back to Kansas City." But over the long road trip, Basie worked out the musical kinks. In 1937, having made it to New York, the band began practicing in earnest in the basement of Harlem's Woodside Hotel, developing their own repertory. As Basie later remembered:

✦ ✦ ✦

It was like the Blue Devils. We always had somebody in those sections who was a leader, who could start something and get those ensembles going. I mean while somebody would be soloing in the reed section, the brasses would have something going in the background, and the reed section would have something to go with that. And while the brass section had something going, somebody in the reed section might be playing a solo. . . .

That's where we were at. That's the way it went down. Those guys knew just where to come in and they came in. And the thing about it that was so fantastic was this: *Once those guys played something, they could damn near play it exactly the same the next night.* . . . And a lot of times the heads that we made down there in that basement were a lot better than things that were written out.

✦ ✦ ✦

Basie was no arranger, but he worked closely with trombonist Eddie Durham to cast these collectively created charts into permanent form. He also edited many an elaborate chart down to a clean, uncluttered piece, in accordance with the maxim "less is more." The result was not technically dazzling—few Kansas City arrangements are swing landmarks—but Basie made history by insisting on simplicity and establishing and sustaining the most irresistible rhythmic pulse of the day. His name became synonymous with "time." If Benny Goodman was King of the Swing Era, everyone knew that Basie was the King of Swing; you could not listen to him without dancing or at least tapping a foot. His own piano technique, though still grounded in the techniques of stride, melted away as he remade himself as the most laconic pianist ever. Yet every note he played contributed to the band's electrifying yet paradoxically easygoing swing. "The Count don't do much," one band member explained, "but he does it better than anyone else."

The most crucial characteristic of Kansas City jazz was its distinctive groove of four beats to the bar, and at its core was Walter Page, a large man nicknamed "Big 'Un" who made dancers happy by evening out the beat. The drummer, Jo Jones—like Page, a veteran of the Blue Devils—played with extraordinary lightness and a keen sense of ensemble. Guitarist Freddie Green was added in 1937, recommended by John Hammond, who had spotted him at a Greenwich Village club. "He had unusually long fingers, a steady stroke, and unobtrusively held the whole rhythm section together," Hammond remembered. "He was the antithesis of the sort of stiff, chugging guitarist Benny Goodman liked." The propulsive lightness of what became known as the "All-American Rhythm Section" was perhaps the band's most far-reaching innovation. "When you listened to that Basie section," bassist Gene Ramey remembered, "the drums didn't sound any louder than the guitar, the piano—it was all balanced. . . . It showed the rhythm section was 'teaming.'"

Basie's soloists initially included Blue Devils veteran Hot Lips Page, but in 1936 Page decided to strike out on his own as a solo trumpet player and singer. His replacement was the debonair trumpeter Buck Clayton, a handsome man who brought years of versatility and experience, including a stint in Shanghai in the 1920s. A year later, Clayton was joined by Harry Edison, nicknamed "Sweets" in ironic tribute to his caustic tone and witty, low-register solos, often distorted with the derby mute. The trombone section included Eddie Durham, who was also one of the earliest electric guitarists; and Dickie Wells, whose solos are often identifiable by tone alone.

One reason the Basie band became famous was its dueling tenor saxophonists. The elusive Lester Young, the band's most celebrated and influential soloist, played with a swift, blissful grace, combining hardy riffs and oblique harmonies. In stirring contrast, Herschel Evans, a powerful saxophonist from Denton, Texas, embodied a full-bodied approach to the tenor known as "Texas style." Basie typically featured Evans in slow blues tunes and ballads like his own "Blue and Sentimental," recorded months before Evans died from a heart condition at age twenty-nine. Evans and Young could not have presented greater dissimilarity. Although their personal relationship was reportedly warm, they sat on opposite sides of the saxophone section and played as though they were in open competition, with crowds cheering each soloist. This two-tenor rivalry (with Buddy Tate taking Evans's place in 1939) was widely imitated by other swing bandleaders.

Another ace in the hole that helped put Basie over was his vocalist, Jimmy Rushing—Big Joe Turner's only major rival among Kansas City blues shouters, yet a very different kind of singer. Rushing, popularly nicknamed "Mr. Five by Five" in honor of his rotund girth, had a penetrating tenor that later fell into the baritone range, but remained capable of surprising high notes. He had an uncannily serene way of singing blues lyrics and of making standards, good ("Exactly Like You") and not so good ("Georgiana"), sound, if not quite like blues, then certainly like vehicles expressly conceived for him. Where Turner was rough-hewn, Rushing was urbane, yet both had outsize voices. Rushing enhanced many of Basie's recordings without in the least bit stifling its soloists or the ensemble's power; at his best ("I Left My Baby"), he could bring to the blues a meditative poetry verging on hard-won wisdom.

Basie's incalculably influential Swing Era period lasted from his recording debut in 1936 to the late 1940s. Like other bandleaders, Basie struggled after World War II and finally broke up the band, reducing his group to an octet in 1948. Several years later, when he decided to revive his big band, only Freddie Green was left from the original crew. The rest of the musicians were drawn from the large number of excellent studio musicians and from soloists who had come of age with bebop, like saxophonists Frank Foster and Ernie Wilkins and trumpeter Thad Jones, all of whom also served as important arrangers. This group, known as the "New Testament" Basie band in theological deference to its predecessor, was a decidedly different outfit. The head arrangements were gone, replaced by sturdy written scores. The new musicians were equally at home with "mainstream" swing and modern jazz, and were accustomed to a written repertory. Basie often joked about his musical turnabout. "You know, don't you," he once said, "that if the lights go out on this band, the music will stop!"

Fortunately, the written arrangements were excellent. In addition to the incredible team of writers sitting in the band, Basie hired some of the best arrangers in the business, including Benny Carter, Quincy Jones, and Neal Hefti. On the 1957 *Atomic Mr. Basie* (featuring a memorable cover photograph of an atomic explosion), the band shows its versatility in switching from up-tempo swing charts to Hefti's "Lil Darlin'," a number that must be played at an exquisitely slow tempo or it will fall apart. Basie's new singer Joe Williams helped bring the band to the pop charts with his rendition of "Every Day I Have the Blues," outfitted in an elaborate two-sided arrangement by Ernie Wilkins. Basie came to exemplify the swing sound in the 1950s and after; he was the ideal choice for singers such as Frank Sinatra, Sarah Vaughan, Tony Bennett, and Billy Eckstine, who wanted to spark their mainstream pop with the drive of an orchestra that had lost none of its strength or wit. For thirty years, Basie toured the world as a roving ambassador of swing. At the end, he sat in a wheelchair, supervising his band and continuing to play spare piano—the twilight of a splendid career.

THE INCOMPARABLE Ellington

We last saw Duke Ellington at Harlem's swank Cotton Club in the late 1920s. From that point until the middle 1930s, Ellington displaced

Fletcher Henderson as the most prominent black bandleader in the world. With the advent of the Swing Era, however, it became almost irrelevant and even ludicrous to talk about Ellington primarily in terms of race, despite his astute focus on race as thematic material. He was America's great composer, America's great bandleader—acknowledged as such by nearly everyone, including the public. In 1940 and 1941, his record sales (he enjoyed complete control of his work at RCA-Victor) had few rivals, and in 1943 the jazz, pop, and classical worlds met in a moment of rare solidarity to acknowledge his debut at Carnegie Hall, and the premiere of his most ambitious work to date, *Black, Brown, and Beige*. His renown was international, his influence pandemic. He was of swing and beyond swing.

Ellington's orchestra lasted until his death. When swing bands began to disappear after the war, Ellington kept his musicians together by subsidizing them with his own money. He spent the rest of his life as a self-described "itinerant song and dance man," shuttling between sumptuous concert halls and international festivals on the one hand and county fairs and 4-H clubs on the other. Yet we define him today, as we do classical composers, by the scope of his written music, which constitutes one of the peak accomplishments in the American arts.

Ellington refuted the designation "jazz composer." For one thing, he disliked the word "jazz," which he sensed tended to marginalize the creativity of black musicians. Sometimes he claimed that he wrote "Negro folk music." He described Ella Fitzgerald and other artists for whom he had the greatest esteem as "beyond category," a term that applies—as he knew very well—equally to himself. In what category do you place a pianist, bandleader, composer, and arranger who created an ensemble unlike any other and wrote practically every kind of Western music other than grand opera—from ragtime to rock and roll, from blues to ballet, from stage and film scores to tone poems, oratorios, and sacred concerts, not to mention works for instrumental combinations from piano-bass duets to symphony orchestra. A proudly black artist, whose subject matter never departed for long from African American history and life, he also wrote about the full breadth of America and much of the world.

European classical music has taught us to think of composers as working in isolation, scribbling music on manuscript paper for others to perform. Ellington *could* work this way. Whenever he traveled, he carried a pad of paper and a pencil. And when caught without the paper, he was known to write bars of music on his shirt cuffs or cocktail napkins. At odd moments throughout the day, and in the unlikeliest places (often on the train or in hotel rooms loud with partying), he jotted down ideas as they came to him.

But the real business of composition—turning his musical ideas into actual pieces—was social. Ellington preferred to collaborate with his musicians. Rather than present them with a score, he would invite the band to work with him: explaining the mental picture that inspired it, playing parts, and assigning the musicians their roles. Writer Richard Boyer, who traveled with the band in 1944, described such moments as a "creative free-for-all" that sounded "like a political convention" or "a zoo at feeding time": "Perhaps a musician will get up and say, 'No, Duke! It just can't be that way!' and demonstrate on his instrument his conception of the phrase or bar under consideration. Often, too, this idea may outrage a colleague, who replies on *his* instrument with *his* conception, and the two players argue back and forth not with words but with blasts from trumpet or trombone."

Ellington's muse was inspired by this ongoing ruckus, which made his orchestral parts a copyist's nightmare. Dizzy Gillespie, who joined the band briefly in the 1940s, recalled the complicated jumble of his trumpet parts. "I'm supposed to remember that you jump from 'A' to the first three bars of 'Z,' and then jump back to 'Q,' play eight bars of that, then jump over to the next part, and then play the solo." Another musician, the bassist Jeff Castleman, found his entire part for a piece (four bars) scrawled on a cocktail napkin. No permanent record survives for Ellington's music, which was reconceived as new soloists entered the band. The Smithsonian Institution holds a set of scores derived from recordings and manuscripts that combine carefully notated Ellington harmonies with vague verbal directions ("Tricky ad lib" meant for Tricky Sam Nanton to take a solo). The scores were presented to Ellington on his sixtieth birthday; the composer thanked everyone, but forgot to take them home. He knew his music could not be contained by notation.

It's not surprising that Ellington's stature as composer has been frequently misunderstood. The most notorious case came in 1965 when the music committee for the Pulitzer Prize unanimously recommended him for an award to honor the entire body of his achievement, but was overruled by the Pulitzer board, which chose to give no award that year. The sixty-six-year-old composer responded: "Fate is being kind to me. Fate doesn't want me to be too famous too young." The Pulitzer board later defended itself by arguing that it did not give lifetime achievement awards, but on the occasion of Ellington's centenary, a quarter-century after his death, it did precisely that. By 1999, even the Pulitzer could no longer pretend that Ellington was a minor or passing figure.

Fortunately, Ellington's legacy has been comprehensively preserved on recordings, thousands of them, many produced by Ellington and stockpiled for posthumous release. Unlike swing bands that sounded much better live than on record, Ellington was "at the height of his creative powers" in a recording studio. For the first half of his career, he squeezed hundreds of recordings into the three-minute limit dictated by the 78-rpm format. His first attempts at longer pieces were spread out awkwardly over several discs, but eventually technology caught up with him. By the 1950s, the LP made it easy for him to conceive his music in broader terms. He was among the first composers to write specifically for microgroove. Ellington's recordings continue to enchant us today. The compositions have a life of their own, open to interpretation by any orchestra that chooses to take them on. But the records are irreplaceable—the truest representation of his genius.

In his autobiography, *Music Is My Mistress*, Ellington identified his co-creators as "dramatis fedilae"—the "cats" in the band. His music was inseparable from the musicians who performed and helped him create it. Most swing bands organized musicians by sections—saxophones, trombones, trumpets, and rhythm—and arrangers treated the individual musicians somewhat interchangeably. Basie's New Testament band, for example, was based on the principle that it would not be beholden to spectacularly individual soloists like Lester Young, because, as Basie ruefully noted, if Young left, he would have to scramble for an equally compelling replacement. Similarly, when Benny Goodman lost one trumpet soloist, he found another, and neither the arrangement nor the audience's expectations greatly suffered. In other words, these bands followed the template of classical music: musicians playing a written score.

Ellington was the grand exception to this rule. In the Cotton Club, where musical effects resonated with scenery and imagery, he had learned how to use orchestral sounds creatively. Moreover, he knew that "sound" in jazz was individual. His music proved inimitable because the sonorities he relied on derived from musicians he worked with year in and year out. "You can't write music right," he once said, "unless you know how the man that'll play it plays poker." Among Ellington's most remarkable achievements was his ability to command the loyalties of outstanding musicians for decades—in some instances, for the entire duration of their professional lives.

By 1935, Ellington had already gathered an ensemble easily recognized by the musical (and personal) quirks that stimulated his imagination: brass players who specialized in muted effects and vocalized timbres, saxophonists with a noble or blustery or heartbreakingly romantic attack, and radically different trombonists (understated and overstated) who nonetheless blended together like pigments of color. For each of these voices, Ellington created pieces that set them off as a fine jeweler sets off his prized stones. Some of his most valued associates joined him in the early years. The baritone saxophonist Harry Carney was barely seventeen when he signed up with Ellington in 1927, earning the nickname Youth, which clung to him through the forty-seven years he remained with the band. (Carney died four months after Ellington, some said of bereavement.) His deep, rich sonority was an integral part of Ellington's sound, floating to wherever it was needed but generally anchoring the band. Most saxophone sections assigned the lead voice to the alto saxophone. Ellington's music was made instantly recognizable by his voice-leading baritone. Miles Davis once said of Carney, "If he wasn't in the band, the band wouldn't be Duke."

Other musicians lasted far less long, but exerted a powerful influence. Bubber Miley in some ways epitomized Ellington's musical values—his motto was "If it ain't got swing, it ain't worth playin'"—but his behavior was impossible. After drinking too much, he would crawl under the piano to sleep it off. Ellington let him go in 1929, hiring Cootie Williams in his place. True to form, Ellington did not tell Williams what to do. He simply let the new musician listen carefully and realize, after playing in the trumpet section for a while, that something was missing—and that it was up to him to provide it. Williams laughed when he first heard Tricky Sam Nanton's yowling trombone, but soon took on the esoteric art of mutes to create his own idiosyncratic sounds. Ellington described his growling solos as having "a sort of majestic folk quality." But Williams continued to play open horn as well. "Those were my two ways of being," he once said. "Both expressed the truth."

Sometimes musicians were drawn in for their musical style. Playing with Sidney Bechet in the mid-1920s gave Ellington a taste for the elegance and earthy quality of the New Orleans clarinet. His love of that "all wood" sound led him to lure Barney Bigard, a sometime tenor saxophonist, back to his original instrument. Bigard had learned to play the clarinet in New Orleans through an old-fashioned system of fingering that was harder to play but was thought to offer a richer, more open timbre. With his admirable facility and soulful sound, Bigard would probably not have wanted for work (after fifteen years with Ellington, he became a member of the Louis Armstrong All-Stars), but like so many of Ellington's top musicians, he lacked the leadership qualities and stylistic individuality to establish an important career on his own. With Ellington maximizing his particular talents in empathic settings, Bigard became an indispensable part of his musical palette—an Ellingtonian.

"MOOD INDIGO"

According to Ellington, his 1930 tune "Mood Indigo" was inspired by a plaintive scene. While having his back rubbed between shows, he described it to a newspaper reporter:

◆ ◆ ◆

"It's just a little story about a little girl and a little boy. They're about eight and the little girl loves the little boy. They never speak of it, of course, but she just likes the way he wears his hat. Every day he comes by her house at a certain time and she sits in her window and waits." Duke's voice dropped solemnly. The masseur, sensing the climax, eased up, and Duke said evenly, "Then one day he doesn't come." There was silence until Duke added: "'Mood Indigo' just tells how she feels."

◆ ◆ ◆

That was the explanation given to casual observers, and an instance of Ellington's quick-witted verbal dexterity. He invented things like that all the time. In fact, the melody for "Mood Indigo" came to Ellington from Barney Bigard (who had probably acquired it from his New Orleans teacher, Lorenzo Tio). But Ellington made it his own by adding a memorable bridge and casting the whole thing in a daringly original arrangement. The instrumentation at the beginning suggests, superficially, New Orleans jazz—clarinet, trumpet, and trombone—but the sound is as different as night from day. The brass players (Nanton and trumpeter Arthur Whetsol) are distant and deliberately muted, holding their sound in check and playing in the high range, while the clarinet, instead of being the highest instrument, is plunged into its deep and rich lower register.

According to Ellington, this unusual combination represented, at least in part, an adjustment to technology. In the recording studio, a faulty microphone reacted strangely to the sound of his horns, producing an illusory pitch that ruined several takes. Eventually, Ellington decided to work with what he had, and adjusted the horns so that the microphone's errant tone became "centralized" in the overall sound. However it was achieved, the opening bars of "Mood Indigo" are unearthly and mystifying—the source of conductor-pianist André Previn's famous comment: "Duke merely lifts a finger, three horns make a sound, and I don't know what it is!"

MOOD INDIGO

Duke Ellington and His Cotton Club Orchestra

Duke Ellington, piano; Arthur Whetsol, Freddy Jenkins, Cootie Williams, trumpets; Joe "Tricky Sam" Nanton, Juan Tizol, trombones; Johnny Hodges, alto saxophone and clarinet; Harry Carney, baritone saxophone and clarinet; Barney Bigard, clarinet; Fred Guy, banjo; Wellman Braud, bass; Sonny Greer, drums

LABEL: Victor 22587-A; *The Best of Duke Ellington* (RCA/Legacy 886972136523)
DATE: 1930
STYLE: early big band
FORM: 16-bar popular song

Chorus 1 (16 bars)

0:00	Whetsol, Nanton, and Bigard play their three horns (trumpet, trombone, and clarinet) in block-chord texture, but the trumpet and trombone are on top, heavily muted, while the clarinet is in its lowest register. Guy plays a steady, thrumming beat on the banjo.
0:15	To connect from one harmony to another, Ellington plays a chromatic scale on the piano.
0:22	Nanton's trombone, producing unearthly sounds from a combination of straight pixie mute, plunger mute, and throat growls, can be briefly heard on its own.

Interlude

0:43	On piano, Ellington provides breathing space between the first two choruses.

Chorus 2

0:54	Whetsol (trumpet) continues reharmonizing the theme, this time supported by a clarinet trio (with Hodges and Carney joining Bigard on clarinet).
1:15	Whetsol ascends to a long-sustained top note, leaving room for the clarinets to take the lead.
1:36	A brief flourish by the brass signals the next chorus.

Chorus 3

1:37	Bigard plays a new melody on clarinet, over a background of sustained brass chords. While the banjo continues its steady thrumming, the bass often doubles its pace to eight beats to the bar.

| 2:04 | For several bars, Bigard chooses pitches that clash with Ellington's elusive harmony. |

Chorus 4

| 2:20 | The final chorus reprises the unusual instrumentation of the opening chorus. |
| 3:01 | The banjo finally comes to a rest on a tremolo chord, punctuated by a single piano note. |

No Ellington voice was more important than that of the alto saxophonist Johnny Hodges (1906–1970), who joined the group in 1928 and remained, excepting one five-year sabbatical, for nearly five decades. Ellington had been searching for a saxophonist with the visceral punch and stylish majesty of Sidney Bechet, and in Hodges he found someone who had already taken Bechet as his model. He immediately became one of Ellington's main soloists, his notes slicing the air with unassailable authority, sometimes projecting a spirited blues-wise toughness, at other times a gentle lyricism that could turn on a dime to dark, passionate romanticism. As the years went on, the romantic aspect flourished. He used agonizingly slow glissandos created from his embouchure (a technique known as "lipping up"), and a full sound that reminded Charlie Parker of the soprano Lily Pons. But he could also swing like a sledge, with a deceptively casual minimum of notes. Much as Coleman Hawkins established the tenor saxophone as a serious jazz instrument, Hodges, along with Benny Carter (whose style was more prolix, evenly dynamic, and harmonically adventurous), established the alto.

Ellington's trombonists, in addition to Tricky Sam Nanton, were an interesting pair. Lawrence Brown was a dignified man from a minister's family in Kansas who joined the band in California in 1932. He originally wanted to be a doctor, which made his quietly steady presence in the livelier setting of a swing band surprising. He brought a lithe middle-register grace to the trombone, occasionally enriched by the more orchestral characteristics associated with a cello. It was Brown's lyricism and straightforward virtuosity (nothing like Tricky Sam Nanton's *wa-wa* growling) that spurred John Hammond's lingering feud with Ellington, after he wrote that Brown sounded too "white" for a black band. Brown stayed with Ellington for nineteen years, took a sabbatical (along with Hodges) in 1951, returned to Ellington in 1960 for another ten years, and then quit playing altogether.

Alongside him was the Puerto Rican valve trombonist Juan Tizol, who joined the band in 1929 (an extremely early instance of integration, though not one that was widely noted beyond musical circles), carving out a niche for himself as the band's "legitimate" (or classical) trombone player, incapable of improvising but perfect for realizing a written part with a beautiful, polished tone. He was also one of the few people Ellington trusted to copy out parts for the rest of the band. Among the signature Ellington tunes that Tizol either wrote outright or contributed ideas to were the rhythmically exotic confections "Caravan," "Perdido," and "Conga Brava," through which Ellington updated the Cotton Club's "jungle" sound to more modern circumstances.

For all his personal charisma and charm (he was a ladies' man of legendary accomplishment), Ellington had to learn how to function as a celebrity. In 1933, he took his band to England and France, where knowledgeable critics and adulatory fans who compared his music to Shakespeare made him realize how much larger his ambitions could be. Back home, he divided his time between theaters and dance halls. "It's a primitive instinct, this dancing business," he told an interviewer, "but it also signifies happiness, and I like to see happy people." From dancing came the maxim that he turned into a song in 1932: "It don't mean a thing if it ain't got that swing." In truth, Ellington learned much about tempos by accompanying dancers and paying close attention to how they moved and what got them to move, though by the late 1930s even dedicated dancers began standing around the bandstand, all ears, for fear of missing something.

Ellington continued to develop the persona he had introduced at the Cotton Club in 1927, becoming familiar to millions the world over for his flashy, natty suits, the wide, welcoming smile, the extravagant style of speaking that made him an aristocrat of the swing world. In the film *Symphony in Black* (1935), Ellington plays himself: an urban sophisticate writing and conducting a score about black manual labor and rural worship (illustrated in the film with graphic, if highly stylized images). Backstage, a more private Ellington was so relaxed and at ease that band members nicknamed him Dumpy. His lassitude in the midst of the day-by-day hustle of running a dance band caused his road manager to complain, "This band has no boss."

Boss or not, Ellington sensed the responsibilities that came with being a black celebrity. He became a "race man," a spokesperson for black America, and whenever possible reminded his audiences about race consciousness. In 1941, he insisted that the black man was the country's "creative voice": "It was a happy day in America when the first unhappy slave was landed on its shores. There, in our tortured induction into this 'land of liberty,' we built its most graceful civilization. Its wealth, its flowering fields and handsome homes; its pretty traditions; its guarded leisure and its music, were all our creations." Black audiences everywhere understood this message. When his band toured the country, passing through cities and small towns with their splendid uniforms and evocative sounds, they were "news from the great wide world." Author Ralph Ellison, who heard him in Oklahoma, asked: "Where in the white community, in any white community, could there have been found images, examples such as these? Who were so worldly, who so elegant, and who so mockingly creative?"

Ellington's passion for racial justice led him to create a musical revue, *Jump for Joy*, which opened in Los Angeles in 1941 (Orson Welles, in an enthusiastic and uncredited act of admiration, helped to stage it). The show was designed to "take Uncle Tom out of the theater, eliminate the stereotyped image that had been exploited by Hollywood and Broadway, and say things that would make the audience think." Among its tunes—one, in fact, so provocative that it was excised from performance—was "I've Got a Passport from Georgia (and I'm Going to the U.S.A.)."

Jump for Joy never reached Broadway, but with *Black, Brown, and Beige*, Ellington made an orchestral statement that was just as persuasive. This forty-eight-minute piece, premiered at his 1943 Carnegie Hall concert, conveyed in tones the history of the American Negro. Unfortunately for Ellington, the piece did not have the effect he had hoped. Jazz fans initially found his symphonic rhetoric pretentious, while classical critics declined to hear it as a serious work. "I guess *serious* is a confusing word," Ellington mused. "We take our American music seriously." One movement, however, became an enduring standard, the hymn "Come Sunday" (lyrics were added shortly after the premiere), and over time the entire work, which Ellington revised from time to time, attracted increased respect. *Black, Brown, and Beige* turned out to be the capstone to Ellington's most remarkable period, 1939 to 1943, when the addition of arranger Billy Strayhorn, bassist Jimmy Blanton, trumpeter-violinist-singer Ray Nance, and Ben Webster, the gruff hard-blowing tenor saxophonist he had been trying to recruit for years, combined to stimulate him to a creative peak.

"CONGA BRAVA"

By 1940, the Cotton Club was safely stored in Ellington's past. But the habits of mind that had been formed there—"exotic" evocations of distant lands, unusual timbres—continued to shape new compositions, as exemplified by "Conga Brava." It was probably a successor to an earlier piece,

"Caravan," co-written with Juan Tizol. The opening melody—Tizol's contribution—is admirably suited to his trombone, played here with unfailing classical excellence evocative of Romantic opera. ("I don't feel the pop tunes," Tizol once said, "but I feel 'La Gioconda' and 'La Bohème.' I like pure romantic flavor.") This opening mood, however, is complicated seconds later by Barney Bigard's elaborate improvised curlicues and snarling commentary by Cootie Williams, Rex Stewart, and Joe Nanton. Ellington covers a staggering amount of territory in his customary three minutes, from a Kansas City–style blowing session for Ben Webster to a stunning virtuosic *soli* for the brass. Playing by ear, Webster adds new notes to the chords, extending them into more dissonant territory and enriching Ellington's harmonic palette. Ultimately, though, all these moments are folded back into the mood of the opening. It's as though Ellington has taken us on a short but eventful trip, eventually escorting us gently home.

CONGA BRAVA

Duke Ellington and His Famous Orchestra

Duke Ellington, piano; Wallace Jones, Rex Stewart, Cootie Williams, trumpets; Joe "Tricky Sam" Nanton, Lawrence Brown, Juan Tizol, trombones; Johnny Hodges, Otto Hardwick, alto saxophones; Ben Webster, tenor saxophone; Harry Carney, baritone saxophone; Barney Bigard, clarinet; Fred Guy, banjo; Jimmy Blanton, bass; Sonny Greer, drums

LABEL: Victor 26577; *Never No Lament: The Blanton-Webster Band* (Bluebird 50857)
DATE: 1940
STYLE: big-band jazz
FORM: extended popular song (**AABA**)

Introduction

0:00		The rhythm section establishes a Latin groove, contrasting a syncopated bass line with an ostinato pattern by Ellington on piano. Greer (drums) plays a disorienting accent on the fourth beat of the measure.

Chorus 1

0:04	**A**	(20 bars) Tizol enters with a long, lingering melody on the valve trombone. Ellington continues his ostinato, adjusting it up and down to suit the harmonies.
0:21		Tizol holds out the last note of his melody. Underneath, Bigard enters with a clarinet countermelody.
0:24	**A**	(20 bars) Tizol repeats his long melody. In place of Ellington's ostinato, a trio of muted brass (Williams, Nanton, Stewart) accompanies him with snarling, syncopated chords.

0:41   Bigard reenters underneath Tizol's last note; the brass chords continue.

0:44   **B**   (8 bars) The groove shifts from Latin to straightforward swing. Over a new harmonic progression, Bigard's low-register solo competes for our attention with the brass chords.

0:52   **A'**   (6 bars) The band as a whole enters in a brief passage in block-chord texture, ending on the dominant chord.

Chorus 2

0:59   **A**   (20 bars) Firmly within the swing groove, Webster enters on tenor saxophone for a "blowing chorus" accompanied by the rhythm section. The harmonic progression is the same as in chorus 1.

1:13   In bars 15 and 16, Ellington marks the closing of the first section with two simple chords.

1:17   The bass drops down to the lower octave.

1:19   **A**   (20 bars) Webster continues his solo.

1:33   Ellington again plays his two simple chords.

1:36   In his last phrase, Webster increases the volume and intensity of his playing.

1:39   **B**   (8 bars) The muted brass trio returns in block-chord texture.

1:47   **A**   (20 bars) The saxophones enter in rich harmonies, reestablishing the opening melody. The drums stay within the swing groove, but recall the Latin opening by again accenting the fourth beat of the measure.

1:51   Against the melody, Stewart (trumpet) improvises a countermelody.

2:05   Ellington briefly reprises his ostinato figure.

Interlude (based on A)

2:07   The brass enters with a rhythmically brilliant *soli*. Greer (drums) answers each of the first two phrases with an accent on the fourth beat.

2:17   A repeat of the *soli*.

2:22   Halfway through, the harmony heads toward a cadence, ending with a dominant chord.

Introduction

2:28   A sudden drop in volume signals the return of the Latin groove.

Chorus 3 (abbreviated)

2:32   **A**   Tizol (trombone) plays the opening melody, once again accompanied only by the rhythm section.

Coda

2:52   Over the opening vamp, the band fades out.

After a long period on top, Ellington was due for a fall. It came with the decline of the Swing Era in the middle 1940s and, despite some fine work along the way (including "The Clothed Woman" and "The Tattooed Bride"), continued for nearly a decade. The strain of continuous touring over twenty years had exhausted his musicians; one trumpet player claimed that he slept for nearly a year after leaving the band. More tellingly, Ellington suffered his first on-the-job death when Tricky Sam Nanton was felled by a stroke in 1946. Other musicians left to cash in on their growing reputations. The first and most famous defection occurred when Cootie Williams accepted an offer from Benny Goodman. (He had Ellington's blessing, though Ellington drew the line when Goodman also tried to lure Johnny Hodges.) The composer and bandleader Raymond Scott commemorated the event with a piece, "When Cootie Left the Duke." Ellington's laconic response was, "He'll be back"—and he was, in 1962, staying until Ellington's death in 1974. In the mid-1940s, Ellington had to scramble to replace Webster, Tizol, and Stewart. In 1951, the loss was even greater when Johnny Hodges and Lawrence Brown departed, partly out of irritation with Ellington's habit of appropriating musical ideas—during a tune he felt was actually his own, Hodges would mimic counting out money onstage.

The business landscape was changing as well. Scores of theaters were demolished or renovated. Radio no longer aired live music, and only the sweet and soggy white show bands (Lawrence Welk, Guy Lombardo, Sammy Kaye) got much traction on television. With the rise of modern jazz, Ellington's music no longer seemed central. He stubbornly kept his band together by pouring in his own royalties—fittingly enough, considering the band's contributions to several of his most lucrative songs. He had changed labels from RCA to Columbia to Capitol Records, where he recorded one last hit song, Strayhorn's "Satin Doll." Yet he seemed to be having doubts about the value of his own achievement, judging from the radical and often misguided renovations he made on several of his classic works. He played for ice skaters, wrote mambos and rhythm and blues, and waited.

The turnaround came, spectacularly, in 1956. Johnny Hodges had returned to the band, giving Ellington a psychic jolt. He had recruited several gifted musicians, who had yet to really prove themselves to the public, including the swaggering drummer Sam Woodyard, and tenor saxophonist, Paul Gonsalves (born in Brockton, Massachusetts, but nicknamed Mex). A sweet-tempered but indefatigably swinging musician with a smooth, insinuating timbre, Gonsalves reflected the influences of Ben Webster and the harmonic advances of the bop generation—he had worked with Dizzy Gillespie and Count Basie before joining Ellington in 1950. The band was in prime form when it was invited to the third Newport Jazz Festival, one of the first of the new summer extravaganzas that helped to transform the way jazz was heard and promoted.

Ellington came on late at night, after waiting for what seemed an eternity ("What are we—the animal act, acrobats?" he complained). Members of the audience began to head for the parking lot, but when the band broke into a two-part piece from 1937, "Diminuendo and Crescendo in Blue," the exodus came to a halt. In between the orchestral movements, there was an open-ended blues solo, assigned to Gonsalves, who instantly created a contagious and growing musical energy. As the tension mounted, Ellington kept the solo going. A blonde woman in the crowd began dancing, and the audience went wild. Jo Jones helped to beat out time with a rolled newspaper on the stage apron. Gonsalves played a full twenty-seven blues choruses, earning him Ellington's nightly introduction for the next eighteen years as "the hero of the Newport Jazz Festival." The whole proceeding, preserved on tape but improved with some studio dubbing, was issued as *Ellington at Newport*, the best-selling album of Ellington's career. The Newport triumph put Ellington on the cover of *Time* magazine. A new era had begun.

In his last twenty years, Ellington took advantage of the space afforded by new LP recordings to write lengthy pieces. Most were suites—collections of characteristic Ellington miniatures loosely organized around a theme—written for a Shakespeare festival (*Such Sweet Thunder*), a State Department–sponsored tour (*The Far East Suite*), a television program (*A Drum Is a Woman*), a ballet (*The River*), three sacred concerts performed in churches, or a visit with the Queen of England (*The Queen's Suite*, pressed privately by Ellington as a gift for Her Majesty and released posthumously, at which time it was widely declared an Ellington masterwork). He also worked as a film composer (*Anatomy of a Murder, Paris Blues*), and joined forces with traditionalists, including Louis Armstrong, Count Basie, and Ella Fitzgerald, and modernists, including Dizzy Gillespie, John Coltrane, Charles Mingus, Max Roach, and Ray Brown.

Ellington's devoted partner in all this late activity was the ingeniously protean yet personally reserved Billy Strayhorn (1915–1967), a composer in his own right as well as Ellington's co-composer, rehearsal pianist, deputy conductor, and occasional lyricist. A diminutive, introverted, owlishlooking intellectual who declined the limelight, Strayhorn seemed to be Ellington's polar opposite at first glance. Yet he was Ellington's closest associate for twenty-eight years, the one man to whom any musical task could be reliably delegated. Born in Pittsburgh, Strayhorn was initially drawn to classical music. By the time he graduated from high school, he had already composed and performed a concerto for piano and percussion. But because black careers in classical music were limited, he moved into popular music, where his creativity could be given free rein. His first classic tune, "Lush Life" (a major hit for Nat "King" Cole, who slightly simplified the challenging harmonies), written as a teenager, reflected his love of densely chromatic music and his sense of isolation as a black man who refused to compromise his homosexuality. (Ellington said the song brought him to tears.) When Strayhorn encountered Ellington's music, he realized he had found a home where classical ambitions and American vernacular music were one and the same.

Strayhorn joined Ellington in 1938 after meeting him backstage in Pittsburgh and serenading him with different versions of "Sophisticated Lady"—one replicating Ellington's mannerisms, the other adding his own variations. Ellington, who was comfortable enough to recognize new talent without feeling threatened, invited him to join him in New York. Strayhorn's first tune with Ellington was based on the directions Ellington gave him to his apartment: when you get to Manhattan, take the A train (rather than the D train, which headed off to the Bronx) to reach Harlem. "Take the A Train" relied heavily on swing conventions, but its harmonic ingenuity and the sureness of its orchestral textures provided the band with a new classic. When the radio networks refused to accept ASCAP's demands for higher rates, restricting ASCAP members like Ellington from presenting new compositions on the air for most of 1941, Strayhorn's "Take the A Train" became the band's new theme and a hit record—featuring a glorious cornet improvisation by Ray Nance that became so renowned it was adopted as a de facto part of the score.

Nicknamed "Swee' Pea" (after the baby in "Popeye"), Strayhorn steadily rose in stature through the 1950s and 1960s. The two composers worked so closely, sharing insights and completing one another's phrases, that it is often impossible to separate their work. Most of the major works, including the larger suites from the 1950s, carry both their names as composers. A significant number of pieces were the work of Strayhorn alone: "Satin Doll" (Ellington's last pop hit), "Chelsea Bridge," "A Flower Is a Lovesome

Thing," "Day Dream," "Rain Check," "Something to Live For," "Lotus Blossom," and the haunting "Blood Count," among many others

"BLOOD COUNT"

As Billy Strayhorn turned fifty, he developed cancer of the esophagus. Two years later, his health had declined so severely that he was in around-the-clock treatment in a New York hospital, where he continued to compose. One of the tunes was originally entitled "Blue Cloud"; but as Strayhorn became mesmerized by his declining vital signs, it was reconceived as "Blood Count," his last composition. "That was the last thing he had to say," a close friend remembered. "And it wasn't 'Good-bye' or 'Thank you' or anything phony like that. It was 'This is how I feel . . . like it or leave it.'" Before Strayhorn died, Ellington performed an effective but preliminary arrangement of it in concert, allowing the composer to hear it on tape. Shortly afterward, Strayhorn slipped into oblivion. The band recorded the piece three months later, as part of an emotional tribute to Strayhorn— one of Ellington's most magnificent achievements—in the album entitled *". . . and his mother called him Bill."*

The tune begins with more harmonic ambiguity than was usual for Strayhorn. We don't know where we are or where we're heading. In this bleak territory, Johnny Hodges, Strayhorn's favorite soloist (he wrote several pieces for him, including "Day Dream" and "Chelsea Bridge"), plays the lead melody with his characteristic knife-edged timbre, controlled vibrato, and unnerving glissandos. The piece proceeds with quiet resignation, first through D minor, then D major, until the second bridge (in chorus 2), when it erupts in a violent *crescendo*. It's as if the normally serene Hodges, overwhelmed by the resentment and impatience Strayhorn had encoded in the chromatic harmonies, explodes into an outpouring of grief, pressing against the physical limitations of his alto saxophone.

The moment subsides, and as the piece draws to a close, we can hear one of Strayhorn's dramatic farewell gestures. Over a coursing pedal point, the harmonies drop chromatically, one by one, toward the tonic. It's a bittersweet climax to a bittersweet tribute. The original LP recording ends with an almost unbearably private moment: while the band files out of the recording studio, Ellington sits at the piano playing "Lotus Blossom" over and over, hushing the departing musicians through his devotion. In the album's notes, Ellington offered this eulogy:

✦ ✦ ✦

His greatest virtue, I think, was his honesty—not only to others but to himself. . . . He demanded freedom of expression and lived in what we consider
the most important of moral freedoms: freedom from hate, unconditionally;
freedom from all self-pity (even throughout all the pain and bad news); freedom from fear of possibly doing something that might help another more
than it might help himself; and freedom from the kind of pride that could
make a man feel he was better than his brother or neighbor.

✦ ✦ ✦

BLOOD COUNT

Duke Ellington and His Orchestra

Duke Ellington, piano; Cat Anderson, Mercer Ellington, Herbie Jones, Cootie Williams, trumpets; Lawrence Brown, Buster Cooper, trombones; Chuck Connors, bass
trombone; Johnny Hodges, Russell Procope, Jimmy Hamilton, alto saxophones; Paul
Gonsalves, tenor saxophone; Harry Carney, baritone saxophone; Aaron Bell, bass;
Steve Little, drums

LABEL: RCA LSP-3906; *". . . and his mother called him Bill"* (Bluebird/RCA 63744)
DATE: 1967
STYLE: big band
FORM: 32-bar popular song (**AA′BA′**)

Chorus 1 (32 bars)

0:00	**A**		Hodges (alto saxophone) begins playing melodic fragments over ambiguous harmonies. The band accompanies with slow, sustained har-monies and occasional chromatic lines. The bass plays two beats to the bar. The drums add color with the cymbals, with occasional accents on the tom-toms.
0:17			The harmony settles into a new key area in the minor mode, with the bass holding a pedal point. The saxophones increase tension with a gradually rising chromatic line. Hodges repeats a short, quick motive.
0:34	**A′**		A return to the opening melody.
0:50			The harmony is now in the major mode.
1:08	**B**		The new melodic phrase starts on a high pitch, descending sharply to a blue note.
1:16			By manipulating his embouchure, Hodges slides up to the high note.
1:33			The harmony rises chromatically.
1:41	**A′**		Hodges returns to the opening melody, expressing his emotions through swelling dynamics.
1:58			As the harmony settles into the major mode, the mood is hushed and expectant.
2:12			Driven by a drum roll, the band rises suddenly in a dramatic crescendo.

Chorus 2 (abbreviated)

2:15	B	The band has the melody. Hodges improvises furiously in response.
2:31		As the intensity of his line increases, Hodges's tone thickens. Some of his individual notes are almost forced out, like barks.
2:39		Over a chromatic rise in harmony, he plays a violent two-note rising motive.
2:45		At the end of the phrase, the dynamics begin to abate.
2:48	A′	In a return to the opening, Hodges now sounds resigned, reflective.

Coda

3:20	The music continues quietly in the same vein.
3:37	The harmony has reached the dominant, preparing for the final cadence. Over a pedal point, the harmony falls chromatically. Hodges plays simple, mournful figures with a quiet, bluesy feeling.
3:45	The bass finally reaches the tonic, but the baritone saxophone continues to hold its note until the end.
3:47	The brass section, tightly muted, continues the chromatic falling chords.
3:52	Hodges uses variable intonation to color his melodies.
4:01	In his last phrase, Hodges plays a phrase from the opening of the tune, leaving us feeling unsettled.

As if to prove he could survive without Strayhorn, Ellington immersed himself in work during his last six years, accepting commissions that ranged from ballets to public occasions (a tone poem for the 150th anniversary of Jacksonville, Florida). He reserved his finest efforts for suites reflecting his travels, among them the *Latin American Suite* and *The Afro-Eurasion Eclipse*. His death was mourned as the end of an era and of a career that could never be duplicated—no other composer would ever manage to have his own orchestra at his beck and call for half a century.

CHAPTER 9

A World of Soloists

JAMMIN' THE BLUES

During the Swing Era, the leading bands were almost as well known for their star performers as for their overall styles. These soloists, like actors in a play, were assigned specific parts, which rarely allotted them as much as a full chorus and often no more than eight measures. As a result, they developed styles so distinct that fans tuning in to radio broadcasts could quickly identify them by their timbres, melodic phrases, and rhythmic attacks.

◀ Billie Holiday, the quintessential jazz vocalist, has an angel over her shoulder, partly obscured by smoke at this 1949 recording session.

When these performers stood up to play in a ballroom, dancers crowded the bandstand to listen and cheer.

Still, soloists were merely components in a larger unit, shining only as bright as the leader permitted. They might quit or be lured away, traded (like athletes) or fired, but the band went on. For obvious reasons, soloists were dissatisfied by the restrictions imposed on them. One way they worked off their frustrations was in jam sessions, usually played after hours. In the 1940s, when the wartime draft depleted the ranks of virtually all major orchestras, staged jam sessions became popular with the public. Soloists also found relief in small-group bands, which many successful orchestra leaders—Goodman, Ellington, and Herman—formed as supplementary units.

The smaller groups had a social as well as musical impact on jazz and popular entertainment. Although, in a sense, the big bands had been integrated early on when white leaders hired black arrangers and composers, it was a radical step to offer a racially mixed group onstage. Goodman used his trio and quartet as a wedge to integrate his concerts and recording sessions, and others followed suit—but in carefully concertized situations. Smaller units also favored musical experimentation. Ellington crafted some of his most challenging pieces for seven-piece bands that recorded under the nominal leadership of whichever soloist was featured. Artie Shaw used a harpsichord for his Gramercy Five records. Some bandleaders gave their secondary bands distinct names: Woody Herman had his Woodchoppers and Bob Crosby his Bobcats—each an occasion to bring soloists to the fore. John Hammond assembled all-star groups for recording sessions (most famously those built around singer Billie Holiday) by combining key members of various orchestras. These makeshift studio groups achieved an unceremonious, spontaneous flavor recalling the free spirit of 1920s recordings by Louis Armstrong and Bix Beiderbecke.

The increasing popularity of soloists portended a new respect for jazz musicians. As free agents, they enjoyed diverse professional opportunities—working on records, in pit bands, and even in movie and radio studios, though most of those well-paid positions were reserved for white musicians. Beginning in the 1930s, fans voted for their favorite bands, soloists, and singers in magazine polls. The friendly and not-so-friendly rivalries helped to spur a rapid development in musical technique. Compare, say, Armstrong's 1928 "West End Blues" and Benny Carter's 1938 "I'm Coming, Virginia," and you cannot fail to hear daunting developments in harmony, rhythm, and technical agility. Armstrong established free reign for the individual soloist; within a few years of "West End Blues," jazz was inundated by gifted musicians, each attempting to forge a personal approach to his or her instrument and to jazz itself.

In 1944, as the Swing Era ground to a standstill, Norman Granz, a producer of staged jam sessions, hired photographer Gjon Mili to direct the classic ten-minute film *Jammin' the Blues*, which featured soloists who had become famous for their work with Count Basie, Lionel Hampton, and other bandleaders. Fastidiously directed, photographed, and edited, this film captured the idea of what its narrator calls "a midnight symphony," an informal letting-go by musicians in an environment free of written scores and other constraints. It foreshadowed the turnaround in jazz that took place in the postwar years, as small groups and extended improvisations replaced the checks and balances of big bands.

THE Coleman Hawkins SCHOOL

No one exemplifies the rise of the independent soloist better than Coleman Hawkins. We have already seen how he adapted Armstrong's ideas during his years with Fletcher Henderson, eventually producing a legato style that, in performances like "One Hour," refined the jazz ballad. But Hawkins's overall impact went way beyond that performance and era. The jazz singer Jon Hendricks once introduced him to a concert audience as "the man for whom Adolphe Sax invented the horn," an engaging way of saying that beyond dominating the instrument for many years, Hawkins established its legitimacy in contemporary music.

In his later years, Hawkins modestly claimed, "People always say I invented the jazz tenor—it isn't true. . . . Why, gangs of tenors would be coming into New York all the time from bands on the road." The saxophone had been around for sixty years before Hawkins's birth, occasionally used in symphonic music by Hector Berlioz, Georges Bizet, and Maurice Ravel, among others. But when Hawkins began playing, it was best known as a starchy novelty instrument. Its most famous proponent was vaudevillian Rudy Wiedoeft, whose tongue would snap against the reed to articulate each note, producing a brisk, staccato, comical music; this way of playing was considered technically "correct." The titles of his compositions— "Saxophobia," "Sax-O-Phun"—indicate the limits of his ambition.

The first important saxophonists in jazz focused on soprano (Sidney Bechet) and C-melody (Frank Trumbauer), but those instruments disappeared or declined in popularity as Hawkins established the tenor as the embodiment of jazz—much as the guitar came to signify rock and roll. Imbuing the instrument with individuality, passion, dignity, and romance, Hawkins expunged its association with comic antics. He made the goosenecked horn look cool, virile, and even dangerous. Thanks to Hawkins, the tenor rivaled and ultimately usurped the trumpet as jazz's most iconographic instrument.

Musicians called him Hawk or Bean (as in "He's got a lot on the bean"). During his eleven years with the Henderson band (1923–34), Hawkins had few rivals and no peers. His style was now considered the "correct" one, characterized by heavy vibrato, powerful timbre, emotional zeal, and a harmonic ingenuity that fascinated musicians. His great musical innovation, beyond remaking the tenor saxophone in his own image, was to change the emphasis in jazz improvisation from embellishing the melody to creating variations based on the song's harmonies.

Hawkins mastered chords and the way they relate to each other by developing a style based on arpeggios. In an arpeggio, a chord's notes are played successively, one at a time. They can be played in any order: a C7 chord may be arpeggiated as C, E, G, B-flat or in reverse or in another sequence entirely. Hawkins found myriad ways to maneuver through chords by breaking them down into these component notes, which he shaped into powerfully rhythmic melodies. This was a major breakthrough, prefiguring the modern jazz movement (or bebop) of the middle and late 1940s. In the course of breaking down chords, Hawkins frequently added harmonic substitutions—chords richer and more intricate than those the composer had provided. These interpolated chords increased the variety of his inventions and spurred his melodic imagination. The broken chords of arpeggios don't mean much unless they form melodies that enchant the listener.

Hawkins's mastery of chords steadily deepened during his years with Henderson. One example is his composition "Queer Notions," recorded by Henderson's band in 1933, which employs augmented chords (in which an interval has been made larger by a half step) and the whole-tone scale. During this same period, Hawkins recorded many sessions as a sideman and, in 1933, organized his own recording unit, with New Orleans trumpeter Henry "Red" Allen, who similarly gravitated toward sophisticated harmonic ideas—a good example is their "Heartbreak Blues."

In 1934, Hawkins signed with British bandleader Jack Hylton to tour England. He set sail expecting to stay for six months, but, bowled over by the size and enthusiasm of crowds that greeted him at every stop, ended up living in Europe for the next five years. During this time, he performed and recorded in London, Paris, the Hague, Zurich, and elsewhere, establishing an international paradigm for the tenor saxophone and jazz. While he was gone, a serious rival appeared in Lester Young, who offered an almost diametrically opposed approach that attracted many adherents. Hawkins kept up with the American scene and the newer crop of tenor saxophonists through recordings; he expressed particular admiration for Ben Webster.

In July 1939, weeks before Germany invaded Poland, Hawkins had no choice but to return to the United States, where observers wondered if he could retain his standing as the No. 1 tenor saxophonist. In September, he appeared on a Lionel Hampton session alongside two tenors who had been influenced by him, Webster and Chu Berry (who had recently enjoyed success with a recording he and Roy Eldridge made of "Body and Soul"), as well as an unknown trumpet player, Dizzy Gillespie. This session was a warm-up for Hawkins.

"BODY AND SOUL"

A month later, Hawkins conducted his own session, which unexpectedly turned out to be one of jazz's seismic events. The idea was to showcase the nine-piece band he commanded at a New York nightclub, Kelly's Stables. The band spent most of the session nailing down the three difficult arrangements Hawkins had prepared; but the record label needed a fourth side in order to release two discs. The producer cajoled him into playing an ad-lib rendition of a song he had performed at the nightclub, "Body and Soul." Hawkins wasn't happy about it, but he agreed to play it just once, without rehearsal.

Hawkins's "Body and Soul" is a pinnacle in jazz improvisation. Recorded entirely off the cuff, it has the weight and logic of formal composition and the tension and energy of spontaneous invention. John Green had composed the thirty-two-bar AABA melody for a Broadway revue (*Three's a Crowd*) in 1930, and it quickly became a favorite among "torch singers"—women who specialized in heart-on-sleeve laments. Louis Armstrong adapted the tune as a jazz piece, and memorable renditions followed by Benny Goodman, guitarist Django Reinhardt, and Berry-Eldridge. Hawkins's version confirmed it as a jazz and pop standard, and made it an everlasting challenge to other tenor saxophonists.

After the piano introduction by Gene Rodgers, the performance is all Hawkins for two choruses and a coda. He begins briskly, his tone smooth as worn felt. Then, after two measures, something unusual happens: "Body and Soul" disappears. More dramatically than on "One Hour," Hawkins heads into new territory, extending his initial phrase into an original melodic arc. His spiraling phrases, representing a zenith of the arpeggio style, advance with assurance and deliberation, building tension. Hawkins later described the climactic passages as a kind of sexual release. This record proved to be a critical milestone and a tremendous commercial success.

BODY AND SOUL

Coleman Hawkins

Tommy Lindsay, Joe Guy, trumpets; Earl Hardy, trombone; Jackie Fields, Eustis Moore, alto saxophones; Coleman Hawkins, tenor saxophone; Gene Rodgers, piano; William Oscar Smith, bass; Arthur Herbert, drums

LABEL: Bluebird B-10253; *Coleman Hawkins* (Verve 314549085-2)
DATE: 1939
STYLE: small group swing
FORM: 32-bar popular song (**AABA**)

Introduction

| 0:00 | | Rodgers (piano) plays a four-bar introduction in D♭ major. |
| 0:09 | | Hawkins begins his solo with three introductory notes. |

Chorus 1

0:10	**A**	Hawkins plays a decorated version of the original melody of "Body and Soul"—the opening phrases (in the lower register) with a breathy tone and somewhat behind the beat. Behind him, the piano keeps time by playing on every beat, with the bass tending to play every other beat.
0:15		The drums' cymbals enter, lightly emphasizing the backbeat.
0:31	**A**	Hawkins's phrases curve upward as they begin to escape the gravity of the original melody.
0:51	**B**	A modulation leads to the bridge, in the distant key of D major.
1:08		Through a chromatic chord sequence, the tune modulates back to D♭ major.
1:11	**A**	Hawkins's improvisation is now securely in double-time, moving in 16th notes, twice as fast as the accompaniment.

Chorus 2

1:32	**A**	The horns enter, playing a solid chordal background behind Hawkins's solo.
1:35		Hawkins begins adding even faster figures (32nd notes).
1:47		The improvised line uses sequences: short melodic patterns repeated on different pitches.

1:52	**A**	
2:00		An intense, piercing entry in the upper register (over a diminished-seventh chord).
2:13	**B**	During the second bridge, the horns drop out, leaving Hawkins accompanied only by the rhythm section.
2:33	**A**	The horns reenter; with a series of ascending leaps, Hawkins's solo suddenly reaches its climax.
2:39		His highest note of the solo.

Coda

2:48	During the last two bars of the second chorus, Hawkins allows both the horn and rhythm sections to dissipate. He continues to play with no accompaniment, his line dropping in register and volume.
2:56	He holds his final note, signaling the end to the rest of the band, which enters (somewhat untidily) on the tonic chord.

Hawkins's recording of "Body and Soul" scored on the pop charts for six weeks in the beginning of 1940—audiences demanded he play it at virtually every appearance. Significantly, they clamored not for the original song, but for his recorded improvisation. In later years, he performed the 1939 solo as if it were the written theme, following it with additional variations. In 1948, Hawkins adapted the song's harmonic framework for a piece he called "Picasso," the first jazz work conceived entirely for unaccompanied tenor saxophone. In the 1960s, the singer Eddie Jefferson put lyrics to the 1939 solo, and Benny Carter transcribed and orchestrated it for a band. Just about every important tenor saxophonist in jazz eventually took a shot at "Body and Soul," from Lester Young and Ben Webster to Sonny Rollins and John Coltrane to David Murray and Joshua Redman. Charlie Parker memorized the solo, quoting from it on his first radio broadcasts.

The idea of improvising on the harmonic foundation of songs advanced the development of modern jazz, as it emerged after the war. Adventurous musicians like Parker, Dizzy Gillespie, and Bud Powell were encouraged to forge their own paths. Hawkins himself, however, continued to work in the swing style with which he felt most comfortable, though he often played with young modernists—and, in fact, hired Thelonious Monk when others kept their distance.

Hawkins's impact on jazz was not unlike that of Louis Armstrong. His solos on Fletcher Henderson's records so mesmerized musicians around the country that many who had taken up the C-melody saxophone after hearing Trumbauer switched to the tenor. Hawkins's combustible riff-laden solo on Henderson's "The Stampede" (1926) was especially influential: for the first time, the tenor leaped from the band, punching and feinting with the dynamism of a trumpet. During the next decade, Hawkins's primacy was nearly absolute, except in Kansas City and the Southwest, where an indigenous tenor saxophone style took root, exemplified by Lester Young. Yet even Young acknowledged the preeminence of Hawkins, who, after all, had also apprenticed in the Southwest before traveling to New York in 1922. That fact led the critic Martin Williams to wonder whether the "so-called Southwest tenor style" was, in fact, first "expounded by Coleman Hawkins in a New York recording studio." One highly individual proponent of Hawkins's model was Bud Freeman, a member of the Austin High Gang in Chicago who, spurred by Hawkins's tonal projection, fashioned a smoother timbre and an idiosyncratic improvisational style. Others developed even more dramatic extensions.

Born in Kansas City, Ben Webster (1909–1973) studied violin and piano before taking up the tenor. His mentors included Budd Johnson, who later emerged as a tenor star and arranger with Earl Hines's big band, and Lester Young, whose father gave Ben his first important band job. It's a measure of Hawkins's power that Webster chose him as his muse—knowing his music only from 78-rpm records—over Young, with whom he traveled. Webster arrived in New York in 1932 as a member of Benny Moten's orchestra, and worked with several key bandleaders—including Andy Kirk, Fletcher Henderson, Cab Calloway, and Teddy Wilson—before Duke Ellington recruited him; with Ellington, he made his name.

In later years, Webster frequently accompanied singers and achieved distinction as a ballad player. This surprised those who remembered him as the tempestuous soloist of Ellington's "Cotton Tail." (Musicians nicknamed him the Brute for his rambunctious playing and capricious temper.) Trumpeter and memoirist Rex Stewart, who worked alongside Webster in both the Henderson and Ellington bands, wrote of him, "During his early period, he blew with unrestrained savagery, buzzing and growling through chord changes like a prehistoric monster challenging a foe. With the passage of time, this fire has given way to tender, introspective declamations of maturing and reflective beauty." Webster's gruff yet empathic style established him as one of the three great pillars of prewar tenor saxophone, along with Hawkins and Young. Of the three, Webster ripened the most in later years; his playing in the 1950s and 1960s is arguably more distinctive and satisfying than the innovative triumphs of his youth. Ironically, the 1960s enshrined the kind of musical volatility Webster had left behind. His mature, mellow style—marked by an idiosyncratic embouchure technique involving audibly heavy breathing—fell out of favor. In search of work, Webster moved to Europe, where he spent his last nine years.

Leon "Chu" Berry (1908–1941), born in West Virginia and educated at West Virginia State University, began on alto saxophone and switched to tenor in 1929. A year later, he traveled with a band to New York and soon became a musical mainstay, working and recording with such important musicians as Benny Carter and Charlie Johnson (a little-remembered band-leader who led a popular group at Small's Paradise in Harlem). As Hawkins toured Europe, Berry took his spot as Henderson's tenor soloist from 1935 to 1937. His work on "Blue Lou" is characteristic of his rhythmic drive and weighty timbre; his second bridge (in the fourth chorus, at 2:12) is an especially good example of his ability to remain melodically relaxed at a speedy tempo—an aspect of his playing that impressed the young Charlie Parker. Berry achieved his greatest success in 1937 when he joined the Cab Calloway band, a tenure tragically cut short by his death in an automobile accident, at thirty-three.

Roy Eldridge (1911–1989), who plays the exciting first solo and climax on "Blue Lou," was an outstanding high-speed, high-note, harmonically daring, bravura trumpet player. He inherited Armstrong's mantle as the most original and influential brass man of the Swing Era, and set the stage for the ascension of Dizzy Gillespie (who called him "the messiah of our generation"). Born in Pittsburgh, Eldridge joined a carnival at sixteen: "I got that job," he recalled, "because I could play Coleman Hawkins's chorus on 'Stampede' on the trumpet, which was unheard of then." He created his singular style in part by looking to tenor saxophonists, not trumpet players, for inspiration.

After working throughout the Midwest, Eldridge moved to New York in 1930. Within two years, his competitive spirit and short size earned him the nickname Little Jazz; among musicians, he was known simply as Jazz. He closely studied Armstrong, but his primary stimulation continued to come from saxophonists. One admirer was Hawkins. "He told me he liked my playing from some records he heard in Europe," Eldridge said. "He was saying, 'Man, this cat ain't playing harsh like the rest of them cats. He's kind of playing more or less like a saxophone, lot of legato things, playing changes.' But he didn't realize that I was playing some of his stuff, and Pres's [Lester Young's] and Chu's."

Eldridge joined Henderson in 1935, and left a year later to form his own eight-piece group. That band's few recordings, like "Heckler's Hop" and "Wabash Stomp," raised the bar on jazz trumpet and on jazz's emotional resources. A fierce battler at jam sessions, Eldridge possessed an extraordinary dramatic talent and an ear for the unusual notes in a chord that stimulated musicians of every generation. He avoided cliché, and his penchant for raising the roof with stratospheric climaxes thrilled jazz fans. His timbre was unmistakably personal, bright yet coated with grit, as effective on ballads as on showstoppers—making him a natural for backing singers, including Ella Fitzgerald and Billie Holiday.

In the 1940s, Eldridge became a focal point in the battle for integration in the entertainment world, as the first black musician to sit in a white orchestra, but his stay with Gene Krupa's band (1941–43) was of primary importance for his breakthroughs as an artist. His sexy vocal duet with Anita O'Day, "Let Me Off Uptown," was a racial breakthrough in its own right, and his classic trumpet solos, including what many consider his masterpiece, "Rockin' Chair," remain benchmark performances, as are his solos with Artie Shaw's band in 1944 and his participation in after-hours Harlem sessions that contributed to the birth of bebop. Eldridge moved to Paris in 1950 for a year, where he was revered and briefly importuned to write a newspaper column. In later years, back in the United States, he performed with musicians of both the swing and bop eras (sessions with the pianist Oscar Peterson were especially rewarding, producing a noted solo on "The Man I Love"), ending his career only when his doctor warned him he was putting too much stress on his heart. He continued to show up at informal sessions, singing.

Lester Young (1909–1959) AND THE LESTORIAN MODE

Lester Young's tenor saxophone style was initially considered so radical that he was hooted out of the Henderson band. Born in Mississippi, Young grew up in New Orleans, where his father, W. H. Young, trained him and his siblings to play a variety of instruments, with the intention of forming the Young Family Band. This band, in which Lester played violin, drums, trumpet, and several kinds of saxophone, toured tent shows in the summer and wintered in Minneapolis. An ardent admirer of Frank Trumbauer, whose records he carried everywhere, Lester sought to reproduce Trumbauer's lighter, vibratoless sound on tenor (creating an approach sometimes compared with that of Bud Freeman). According to Ben Webster, Lester developed a distinctive tenor saxophone timbre as early as 1929.

After leaving the family band in 1927, Young traveled the Midwest, performing with King Oliver, Benny Moten, the Blue Devils, and others. In 1933, he settled in Kansas City, where he was quickly accepted. When Fletcher Henderson's band came to town in December of that year, Young and Hawkins squared off at a legendary jam session involving several tenor saxophonists including Webster, lasting all night and into the morning. By all accounts (and there are several), Young emerged the victor.

When Hawkins departed for Europe in 1934, Henderson convinced Young to come to New York. He didn't last long there, however: the other musicians in Henderson's band ridiculed his light sound and introverted personal style, and Henderson's wife made him listen to Hawkins's records, insisting he learn to play like the older man. Henderson reluctantly let him go, after lecturing his musicians that Lester played better than any of them, and Young worked his way back to Kansas City as a member of Andy Kirk's band. Safe at home, he returned to Count Basie, with whom he had previously played. Basie's sizzling, rangy swing was an ideal platform for Young; unlike Henderson's detailed arrangements, Basie's were streamlined and blues-driven. His soloists were encouraged to improvise at length, accompanied by the rhythm section and the ad-libbed head riffs. In that atmosphere, Young created a free-floating style, wheeling and diving like a gull, banking with low, funky riffs that pleased dancers and listeners alike. Stan Getz, one of countless young musicians who began by imitating Young, called his style of playing the Lestorian Mode—a fount of ideas expressing a new freedom in jazz.

Young's way of improvising on a song differed from Hawkins's in almost every particular. Where Hawkins arpeggiated each chord in a harmonic progression, Young created melodic phrases that touched down on some chords and ignored others. Given, for example, an eight-measure passage with a dozen or so chords, Young would improvise a melody that fit the overall harmonic framework without detailing every harmony. He also had a more liberal attitude toward dissonance and rhythm. One of his favorite gambits was to repeat a note while slightly altering its pitch (often by changing the fingering), making it a bit flat. And while Hawkins's phrases were tied to the beat, Young's sometimes disregarded the beat, creating an uninhibited counterrhythm.

When Basie brought his band to Chicago and New York, in 1936, the world was ready for Lester, though he would always remain something of an outsider. More than any other musician, Young introduced the idea of "cool," in musical style and personal affect. Shy and diffident, he stood aloof from most conventions. "I'm looking for something soft," he said. "I can't stand that loud noise. It's got to be sweetness, you dig? Sweetness can be funky, filthy or anything." He famously wore a broad-brimmed porkpie hat—a kind of Western fedora with a flat top—and narrow knit ties. When he played, he held the saxophone aloft and at a horizontal angle, almost like a flute. He spoke a colorful, obscure slang of his own invention, some of which became a part of jazz diction, including his nicknames for musicians. He called Billie Holiday Lady Day, a sobriquet that stuck. She returned the favor by nicknaming him Pres (as in president of all saxophonists), an honorific that also stuck.

Many of the musicians who went on to pioneer modern jazz worshipped Young, learning his solos and imitating his look. White saxophonists (like Stan Getz, Zoot Sims, and Al Cohn) tended to focus on his lyricism and feathery timbre in the upper register. Black saxophonists (like Dexter Gordon, Wardell Gray, and Illinois Jacquet) preferred his blues riffs and darker timbre in the middle and lower registers. Young's style was so stirring and varied that it spurred the Swing Era, bebop, *and* rhythm and blues. The tenor saxophone choruses on dozens of 1950s rock and roll records have their pedigree in his style.

"OH! LADY BE GOOD"

In "Oh! Lady Be Good," you can hear the youthful zest of Lester Young's style at its peak—indeed, this two-chorus solo is often cited as his finest work on records. All the attributes he brought to jazz are apparent, from the initial entrance, followed by a rest and a long rolling phrase, to the slurred (connected) notes, polyrhythms, staccato single notes, pitch variation, and unfailing swing that make this improvisation a riveting experience. The song, by George and Ira Gershwin, originated in their score for the 1924 Broadway musical *Lady Be Good*. Count Basie plays the melody; Young leaves it behind, inventing melodies that float over the song's chords.

"Jones-Smith Incorporated" was the pseudonym created by John Ham-

mond when he determined to be the first to record Basie, despite the contract with Decca. The session was held early one morning in Chicago, after
the band had played through the night. To release the records, Hammond
took the names of trumpeter Carl "Tatti" Smith and drummer Jo Jones,
pretending it was a new group—fooling no one who had ever heard Basie
or Young.

OH! LADY BE GOOD

Jones-Smith Incorporated

Carl Smith, trumpet; Lester Young, tenor saxophone; Count Basie, piano; Walter
Page, bass; Jo Jones, drums

LABEL: Vocalion 3459; *Lester Young* (Verve 549082)
DATE: 1936
STYLE: Kansas City swing
FORM: 32-bar popular song (**AABA**)

Chorus 1

0:00	**A**	Basie begins by stating the melody to the song with his right hand. Behind him, Jones on drums plays quietly on the high-hat cymbal.
0:10	**A**	At times, Basie begins to show traces of a stride foundation in his left hand.
0:20	**B**	
0:29		The drums begin to build intensity by playing a backbeat.
0:30	**A**	

Chorus 2

0:40	**A**	Young enters with a three-note statement, accompanied by a drum accent. His phrases are inflected with notes from the blues. Behind him, Basie plays chords on the beat.
0:51	**A**	
0:59		In one of the phrases, Young bends one of his pitches.
1:01	**B**	He begins to build intensity by starting phrases with accented, scooped notes.
1:11	**A**	He creates polyrhythms out of a single note.
1:16		Another striking use of variable intonation.

Chorus 3

1:21	**A**	Young's second chorus begins higher in pitch and adds faster rhythmic values.
1:24		On bass, Page relaxes from four beats to two beats to the measure.
1:32	**A**	Beginning with a scooped note, Young creates polyrhythms from a short phrase. Page returns to four beats to the measure.

1:42	B	At the bridge, Young plays a descending phrase that becomes poly-rhythmic through off-center repetition; the drummer responds with a drum roll.
1:48		Young reaches the high point of his solo.
1:52	A	He starts the last section with a dramatic syncopation, followed by another off-center repetition.
2:00		Young's last phrase bids us a bluesy farewell.

Chorus 4

2:03	A	Smith begins his trumpet solo. Behind him, Young starts playing a back-ground riff figure.
2:13	A	
2:23	B	Smith's solo and Young's syncopated riff tangle in a complex polyrhyth-mic interaction.
2:34	A	

Chorus 5 (abbreviated)

| 2:44 | B | While the drums drop out, the bass line quietly rises to a higher register. Basie plays a simple piano solo. |
| 2:54 | A | With a sudden increase in volume, the two horns and the drums reenter for a climactic final chorus. |

As an artist, Young represented a blend of tenderness and exuberant non-conformity. Yet his personal story suggests the cautionary tale of an artist too fragile for life's hard knocks. Young remained with Basie until 1940, during which time he also appeared on a series of records with Billie Holiday. Feeling hampered by Basie's increasingly intricate arrangements, however, he decided to set out on his own. He led his own small groups, toured army camps with the Al Sears band, and briefly reunited with Basie. Then his life changed irrevocably when he was drafted, in October 1944—he was starring in *Jammin' the Blues* when he received the summons.

After admitting to officers that he smoked marijuana, and additionally nettling them with his perplexing lingo, Young was subjected to a ninety-five-minute trial and sentenced to a year of hard labor at a debilitation barracks (D. B.) in Georgia. Although he announced his return to civilian life nine months later with a triumphant 1945 recording, "D. B. Blues," he never completely recovered from the incarceration and soon surrendered to alcoholism. His playing in later years was often spirited and inventive, but the spark had dimmed: his timbre became drier, his interpretations eccentric, his youthful radiance replaced by a candid, vulnerable lyricism.

Charles Mingus's tribute "Goodbye Pork Pie Hat" expresses the feeling of loss that accompanied Young's death, at forty-nine.

OVER THERE: Django Reinhardt (1910–1953)

Having spread out from New Orleans and the South to Chicago, New York, Kansas City, California, and other parts of the United States, jazz leaped the oceans as quickly as recordings could carry it. Adherents listened to and learned to play jazz in Europe, Asia, South America, Australia, and Africa, as it returned to the nations whose emigrants had first transported the musical ingredients that Americans fused into a unique New World music.

Two contrary factors stimulated jazz's growth abroad. First, it was recognized as a serious, exhilarating new art—"a new reason for living," in the words of French critic Boris Vian. When Armstrong, Ellington, Fats Waller, and Hawkins appeared in France, England, Holland, and Denmark, they received the kind of respect due major artists, and many black musicians, singers, and dancers followed their lead. Racism continued to rear its head, but it was not supported by laws that defined its victims as second-class citizens. In France, Negro entertainers were considered chic: some stereotypes, involving jungle exoticism, actually redounded in their favor.

The second factor tried to quash the first. In the Soviet Union and Germany, jazz was illegal, and thus came to represent rebellion and liberty. Music that prized personal expression as its highest aesthetic goal could not help but exemplify the lure of freedom and democracy. In these societies, jazz flourished underground. (This remained true into the 1980s, when Czechoslovakia banned the Prague Jazz Section and jazz musicians in East Berlin performed in hiding.) In the 1930s, Soviet jazz fans nursed their devotion at the risk of imprisonment. When Benny Goodman toured Moscow in the 1950s, he was amazed to discover that he had thousands of Russian fans who referred to his records by catalog numbers—a practice once intended to fool spies.

The Nazis banned jazz as decadent, the product of barbaric blacks and Jews. Then as the world moved toward war, German leaders were obliged to face the fact that in the countries they occupied, citizens were far more likely to listen to the local radio stations, which played jazz constantly, than to German broadcasts. Instead of combating the jazz craze, they tried to join it, as German musicians recorded (unintentionally hilarious) imitations of American swing hits. After the war, liberated cities like Paris, Copenhagen, and Amsterdam treated jazz musicians as heroes. A ballad by French guitarist Django Reinhardt, "Nuages," had become an anthem of the resistance. Conversely, jazz temporarily lost its popularity in those same cities, in part because many people associated it with the horrific days of the occupation.

Wherever jazz landed, it developed a bond with local musical practices. Argentina's tango, Brazil's samba, and Cuba's clave influenced jazz and were influenced by it in turn. Jazz similarly mixed with the music of Africa, Japan, Finland, and Hawaii, generating new compounds. American jazz musicians remained stars in all these places, but local musicians also achieved fame. In 1971, Duke Ellington introduced *The Afro-Eurasian Eclipse* by pointing out that as various cultures lose their provincial identities, "it's most improbable that anyone will ever know exactly who is enjoying the shadow of whom."

Only one European jazz artist was universally conceded a seat at the table of prime movers—those figures who decisively changed the way jazz is played. Django Reinhardt was born in a Gypsy caravan passing through Belgium. He and his two younger siblings (his brother Joseph also became a guitarist) grew up in a settlement near Paris. Their father, an itinerant entertainer, abandoned the family when Django was five, and their mother supported them by weaving baskets and making bracelets from artillery shells found in World War I battlefields.

Django learned violin and banjo from relatives before taking up guitar, which he began playing professionally at twelve. A habitué of music halls, where he usually worked as an accompanist, he mastered waltzes and traditional themes as well as pop tunes. Then in 1928, shortly before he turned nineteen, Reinhardt was struck by a tragedy that would have ended the ambitions of most musicians: his caravan caught fire and he was trapped inside. His left hand, which held tight the blanket that saved him, suffered severe burns and mutilation—the fourth and fifth fingers were paralyzed, folded inward like a claw. Determined to continue with the guitar despite this setback, he developed a way of playing single notes and chords with only two fingers and his thumb; at the same time, he had to learn to arch his hand so that the paralyzed fingers did not get in the way.

Within a few years, Reinhardt created new fingerings to play chords while perfecting rapid-fire single-note improvisations that ranged over the entire length of the fret board. His right hand picked the strings with such percussive strength that, long before the introduction of the electric guitar, his sound had a vital, piercing tone. With the help of a microphone, he had no trouble being heard. Reinhardt's love of music was transformed by the first jazz records to reach Paris. When he heard duets by guitarist Eddie Lang and violinist Joe Venuti, he recognized an immediate kinship with jazz improvisation and rhythm. At a time when most American guitarists played little more than rhythm and chords, Reinhardt emerged as a soloist of stunning originality and a deeply personal romanticism.

The turning point for European jazz came in 1934, the year Coleman Hawkins embarked on his five-year visit. A couple of years earlier, a few French fans, including critics Hugues Panassié and Charles Delaunay, had formed the Hot Club de France, an influential organization for enthusiasts and musicians. Then in 1934, Panassié published *Le jazz hot*, the first serious critical book on jazz in any language—and the first to suggest the preeminent role of African Americans. That same year, he and Delaunay prepared to launch a magazine, *Jazz Hot* (still in existence today), and a band to represent the club's musical point of view: Quintette du Hot Club de France.

The Quintette, which arose out of informal jam sessions, included two powerful and like-minded soloists: Reinhardt and violinist Stephane Grappelli, a largely self-taught musician who had played both piano and accordion, accompanying silent movies from the age of fourteen before gravitating toward dance bands and jazz. Working from the model created in the 1920s by Lang and Venuti, Reinhardt and Grappelli developed a hard-swinging and playful interaction. The setting in which they worked, however, was like no other in jazz. Instead of a piano and drums, the Quintette's rhythm section included two rhythm guitars (Roger Chaput and Joseph Reinhardt) and bass (Louis Vola).

Recordings by the Quintette drew avid praise in Europe, and were eagerly sought in the United States. If Bix Beiderbecke had shown that whites could master jazz with individuality, the Quintette du Hot Club demonstrated that Europeans could do the same. It confirmed the idea that jazz, though American in origin, was a musical art of universal potential. Grappelli was regarded on a par with Venuti and the preeminent black violinist of the Swing Era, Stuff Smith. Django was in a class by himself: after Lang's premature death in 1933, jazz guitar had receded in prominence, but Django brought it back with a vengeance.

Given Reinhardt's immediate acceptance by Americans (after the war,

Ellington would sponsor his only visit to the United States), Delaunay began recording him with visiting Americans: Hawkins, Benny Carter, violinist Eddie South, trumpeter Bill Coleman, clarinetist Barney Bigard, and others. Hawkins was the most prominent of the guest soloists, but Carter was perhaps the most significant: in addition to playing superb alto saxophone and trumpet, he wrote arrangements that epitomized international jazz.

King Carter (1907–2003)

Press agents and pundits could call who they liked king, but musicians privately reserved the royal epithet for a hero of the Swing Era who received little popular acclaim: the modest, soft-spoken jack-of-all-musical-trades Benny Carter. Born in New York City, Carter learned piano from his mother, but was largely self-taught as an instrumentalist, composer, and arranger. He began touring professionally at seventeen, and soon attracted attention with his playing and writing for Fletcher Henderson, Charlie Johnson, and McKinney's Cotton Pickers, which he took over in 1931. In addition to alto saxophone and trumpet, Carter tried his hand at clarinet (playing a renowned solo on his 1930 "Dee Blues"), tenor saxophone, soprano saxophone, trombone, and piano. He even sang once, imitating Bing Crosby. He formed his own orchestra in 1932.

Carter's importance to jazz has four components: instrumentalist, composer-arranger, bandleader, and social activist. Along with Johnny Hodges, Carter established the alto saxophone as a major jazz instrument, paralleling Hawkins's impact on tenor. He played with an unruffled, melodic flair, underscored by compositional logic. His improvisations flowed with timeless elegance—indeed, his style changed little between the 1930s and 1990s. He also developed a personal approach on trumpet, which he played less frequently. An excellent example is his 1939 recording of "More Than You Know." Hugues Panassié declared it "one of the most beautiful, inventive trumpet solos ever waxed."

As a composer, Carter emerged in the 1930s as one of the most accomplished tunesmiths in jazz; a few of his melodies became popular standards, including "When Lights Are Low" and "Blues in My Heart." His writing for big bands was acclaimed for its melodic ingenuity and streamlined rhythms. He was the first important jazz arranger to cut away the complex ornamentation of most dance bands, setting a standard for swing that would soon be echoed in the writing of Fletcher Henderson and Count

Basie. The most imitated trademark in Carter's orchestrations was his writing for the reed section, which could swing with the impulsiveness of an improvised solo: the highlight of many of his works is a chorus by unified saxophones (*soli*). Carter's early recordings ("Lonesome Nights," "Symphony of Riffs") shimmer with ageless originality, and his most acclaimed album, *Further Definitions*, appeared as late as 1961 on a label (Impulse!) associated with jazz's avant-garde. A favorite of singers, he wrote arrangements for Ella Fitzgerald, Ray Charles, Sarah Vaughan, and Peggy Lee, among others.

As a bandleader, Carter enjoyed little commercial success; at a time when most bands courted dancers, he concentrated on musical refinement. Even the ballad singers that he featured in the hope of getting a hit were framed in unusually understated settings. One of those singers, the obscure Roy Felton, who sings on "More Than You Know," had an influence way out of proportion to his small oeuvre. A baritone of impeccable diction who sang in his lowest register with a throaty vibrato, Felton was later tagged as "the first black Bing," by which it was meant that he created a highly original take on the overall Crosby style. A year later, another black Bing, Herb Jeffries, helped Duke Ellington to a major hit by singing the chorus on a 1940 recording of "Flamingo," for which Ellington specifically asked him to "stay on Bing." By far, the most famous of Felton's brood was the hugely popular ballad singer Billy Eckstine. But then, practically everything Carter did was studied assiduously by other musicians; numbers like "Scandal in A Flat" or his breezily swinging adaptation of the old standard "Sleep" were textbook examples of creative, classy swing writing. Carter was so much admired by fellow musicians that he had his pick of players. Musicians who worked in his bands in the swing years include Ben Webster, Chu Berry, Teddy Wilson, Dizzy Gillespie, trombonists Vic Dickenson and J. J. Johnson, drummer Max Roach, and Miles Davis.

As an activist, Carter steadfastly fought racism by opening doors closed to African Americans. In 1937, two years after arriving in Europe, he organized, at a Dutch resort, the first integrated and international orchestra in jazz history. Determined to create similar opportunities at home, he worked his way into the Hollywood studio system, one of the last bastions of segregation in the entertainment world. There, his temperament (mild-mannered but very tough: legend has it that he once cold-cocked the intemperate Ben Webster so politely that when Webster came to, he thanked him), business savvy, and uncommon versatility allowed him to crack the "color bar." As a result, he enjoyed a rare level of financial security in jazz, living in Beverly Hills and driving a Rolls Royce. He worked on dramatic and musical films, from *Thousands Cheer* (1942) to *Buck and the Preacher* (1972), and more than two dozen television programs, beginning with the l950s police series *M Squad*. In 1978, Carter was inducted into the Black Filmmakers Hall of Fame. It was at that point that he revived his career as a soloist, achieving his greatest success as a touring jazz musician in his seventies and eighties, while also writing and conducting expansive new pieces, notably *Central City Sketches*.

"I'M COMING, VIRGINIA"

Many of Carter's stylistic strengths are apparent in his 1938 treatment of the 1926 standard "I'm Coming, Virginia," by black songwriters Will Marion Cook (the man who brought Sidney Bechet to Europe in 1919) and Donald Heywood. Carter leads an integrated and pan-national ensemble (it was recorded in Paris) in an arrangement that offers his own exceptional alto saxophone solo, a chorus by Django Reinhardt, and a signature climax featuring a four-part voicing of the saxophones. By the middle and late twentieth century, the world outside the United States produced countless accomplished jazz musicians, some of them achieving international renown and exercising an influence that would be absorbed by American players abroad and at home. For Europe, the spark that ignited that jazz fever was fanned in the short period before the war when travelers like Carter and Hawkins made common cause, inviting the world's musicians to join in. They wanted to spread jazz, not keep it to themselves.

I'M COMING, VIRGINIA

Benny Carter and His Orchestra

Benny Carter, Fletcher Allen, alto saxophones; Bertie King, Alix Combelle, tenor saxophones; Yorke de Souza, piano; Django Reinhardt, guitar; Len Harrison, bass; Robert Montmarché, drums

LABEL: Swing (F)20; *Django: With His American Friends* (DRG 8493)
DATE: 1938
STYLE: big-band swing
FORM: 24-bar popular song (**AA′B**)

Introduction

| 0:00 | The piano plays a four-bar introduction, lightly accompanied by the drums. |

Chorus 1

0:05	A	The four saxophones enter with a *soli* in block-chord harmony. This arrangement by Carter is based on the original tune, but varies it through new rhythmic patterns reminiscent of speech.
0:16	A'	
0:28	B	

Interlude

| 0:39 | | The saxophones continue their block-chord texture, accompanied only by a faint pulse on the bass drum. |

Chorus 2

0:44	A	The Belgian tenor saxophonist Combelle takes a solo. Behind him, Reinhardt on guitar plays a heavy eight-beats-to-the bar pattern.
0:55	A'	
0:58		Reinhardt relaxes into a more normal texture, playing chords on the backbeat.
1:06	B	

Chorus 3

1:18	A	Reinhardt enters with a dissonant harmonic arpeggio on guitar. Underneath him, the piano plays a stiff accompaniment.
1:22		Reinhardt plays a blue note, which tails off at the end of a phrase.
1:29	A'	
1:40	B	

Chorus 4

1:51	A	Carter takes a solo. The other saxophones support him with simple chords in the background.
2:02	A'	
2:14	B	

Interlude

| 2:22 | | The tenor saxophones interrupt with a syncopated phrase. The full band then plays a series of chords that modulate to a new key. |

Chorus 5

2:28	A	The saxophone section reenters, this time with a much freer and rhythmically varied *soli*. It begins with a new riff in bare octaves, followed by a tumultuous plunge in block-chord harmonies.
2:37		Reinhardt interjects a brief phrase in octaves.
2:39	A'	

2:41		For dramatic relief, Carter reduces the sound of the ensemble to an octave.
2:50	**B**	
2:56		A familiar chord progression leads to the final cadence.

SINGERS: Lady Day (1915–1959) AND THE First Lady of Song (1917–1996)

Singers have a peculiar relationship to jazz. Instrumentalists model them-selves on the flexibility and expressiveness of the voice, while singers aim for the rhythmic freedom of instrumentalists. But there is a crucial differ-ence: singers for the most part concentrate on melody, leaving the abstrac-tions of ad-lib variations to instrumentalists. They occupy a middle ground between jazz and commercial entertainment, with a far greater chance of acceptance by the mainstream. Louis Armstrong reached more people sing-ing than playing trumpet.

Most successful American pop singers who came along in the 1930s and 1940s were influenced by jazz. Few of them were true jazz singers, but the best were accepted as tasteful, creative interpreters of the same pop songs that fueled instrumental jazz. At the same time, they were resented for achieving a level of financial security not available to jazz instrumentalists—especially if they were hired as much for their looks as their voices. Singers were expected to charm audiences and give the musicians a breather. By the late 1940s, however, big-band jazz struggled to support itself, while the ex-band singers were reborn as recording and television stars.

In the early days of the dance bands, instrumentalists who could carry a tune "doubled" as vocalists. If an audience could hear lyrics, it was more likely to enjoy and remember the melody. That's how hits were made: peo-ple left theaters and ballrooms humming melodies and seeking them out in sheet music and on records. Inevitably, dedicated singers were added to the payroll. When Paul Whiteman recruited the first full-time singers in a dance band—Bing Crosby in 1926 and Mildred Bailey in 1929—he introduced a new and frequently rivalrous relationship between instrumen-talists and singers. By the time Bailey entered the Whiteman fold, Crosby was on his way toward becoming the most listened-to singer in history. He created a template for the jazz-influenced pop singer who garners ever-greater popularity by singing every kind of song, usually with diminished or nonexistent jazz content, and then translates that success into movie and broadcast stardom. Bailey created a different template and a demand for singers who could provide a feminine touch in the otherwise masculine world of the big bands.

Many women singers, however talented, doubled as sexual adornments and were obliged to pose flirtatiously for *Down Beat* and *Metronome*, the leading swing journals. They were routinely referred to with bird synonyms: a female band singer was a thrush, a canary, a sparrow, a chick or chickadee. Such images were far removed from those associated with 1920s blues divas like Bessie Smith and Ma Rainey, who were depicted as tough and independent. Bailey, with her light timbre and gentle embellishments, represented a stylistic extension of the more adaptable Ethel Waters, who roamed the blues and Tin Pan Alley with imperious self-assurance. Neither woman was physically cut out to be a sex symbol, but they brought an erotic edge to risqué blues and romantic ballads.

Yet those who followed Waters and Bailey, white or black, were confronted with songs that helped to typecast women as weaker vessels. Where blues singers used double entendres to celebrate sex, these younger performers tended to either pine for their men or offer cheerful courtship fantasies. Great vocal artists emerged, even so, including two particularly ingenious singers who incarnated contrary views of life. Billie Holiday and Ella Fitzgerald, each in her way, exemplify a degree of cultural resilience beyond the scope of all but a few instrumentalists.

The life of Billie Holiday is shrouded in myths. Born in Philadelphia and raised (as Eleanora Fagan) in Baltimore, she was the illegitimate daughter of a teenage guitarist, Clarence Holiday, who declined to acknowledge his paternity until she became famous. Her young mother moved to New York soon after Billie's birth, leaving her in the care of abusive relatives. At ten, Holiday was remanded to a school for delinquent girls. In 1929, she joined her mother in New York, where she worked at menial labor and was arrested for prostitution. She began singing a year later, and by 1933 was ensconced at a Harlem club, where John Hammond heard her and invited her to record with Benny Goodman's still-unknown band. A year later, she wowed the notoriously demanding audience at the Apollo Theater.

Now a professional musician, Holiday renamed herself by combining the names of her father and the silent screen star Billie Dove—though she was also apparently nicknamed Bill in childhood. In 1935, Hammond built a series of recording sessions around her, directed by Teddy Wilson and involving top musicians of the day, including Artie Shaw, Goodman,

Roy Eldridge, Johnny Hodges, and several members of the Basie band, most significantly Lester Young, with whom she shared one of the most musically fertile partnerships in jazz.

Holiday briefly worked with big bands—first Basie and then Shaw—until racial injunctions forced Shaw to let her go. Mostly she sang in night-clubs, including, in 1939, New York's new and defiantly integrated Café Society. Her records, which were made with the growing jukebox market in mind, sold well, and her recording of "Strange Fruit" (1939), the vivid depiction of a Southern lynching, enhanced her standing with the New York intelligentsia. "Strange Fruit" was considered too controversial for Columbia Records to release, so she made it for Commodore Records, a small independent operated by another influential producer, Milt Gabler. This important association eventually took her to Decca, where Gabler recorded her with strings, which she felt enhanced her stature and moved her toward the commercial mainstream. Her growing fame included a fling in Hollywood: she was cast as a singing maid in the film *New Orleans*, but walked off the set before it was finished.

The singer suffered a long, public downfall that was caused by her dependency on narcotics and a thug who married her, encouraged her addiction, and betrayed her to the police to save himself. After a sensationalized drawn-out trial in 1947, she was jailed for eight months and deprived of her cabaret card—the permit (abolished in 1960) necessary for working in New York nightclubs. In the 1950s, Holiday continued to command a loyal following, recording with large ensembles and all-star small bands, though her voice weakened. She began to focus on ballads, developing a more mannered, expressive style. As her voice declined, she experienced a few musical reprieves, including a triumphant 1957 appearance on a television broadcast, *The Sound of Jazz*, in which she was supported by an astonishing band that included Young, Hawkins, Webster, Eldridge, and the postbop baritone saxophonist Gerry Mulligan. At the time she died, at forty-four, her voice was little more than a whisper, yet through good times and bad, she was always Lady Day, the enchantress with the white carnation in her hair, a hot-tempered yet sweetly generous truth-teller who didn't know how to fake a performance.

Holiday initially drew inspiration from Ethel Waters (her supple middle register and wry approach to blues), Bessie Smith, and Louis Armstrong. The Armstrong influence proved decisive: from him, she learned to swing, paraphrase and embellish a melody, and impart a blues feeling to everything she sang. When Hammond introduced her to Teddy Wilson, the pianist initially expressed disappointment. He preferred Ella Fitzgerald and thought Holiday was a gimmick—a woman who sang like Armstrong. But he quickly changed his mind and helped her to mature into the riveting artist whose voice expressed so much of the human condition.

Holiday does not fit the cliché of the jazz singer: scat-singing held no interest for her, and she rarely sang true twelve-bar blues. Her range was limited to about an octave and a half, and her voice had a thin, edgy timbre. None of this mattered, because she had a gift for altering a melody in such a way as to make it extremely personal. She managed to imbue even the most insufferably trite numbers with such profound import that some of them—"What a Little Moonlight Can Do," "Miss Brown to You," "A Sunbonnet Blue"—became her signature songs. After her death, Frank Sinatra, born in the same year as Holiday, called her "unquestionably the most important influence on American popular singing in the last twenty years."

Jazz musicians adored her phrasing, which is at once guileless and clever and always rhythmically assured. They considered her one of them—a jazz artist of the first rank. She revised melodies to suit her voice and interpreted lyrics in a way that made them seem vital. Her musical romance with Young is unequaled, suggesting an intimate solidarity in performances like "A Sailboat in the Moonlight," which begins as singer-and-accompaniment and becomes a true collaboration between two comparable personalities riding out the night.

"A SAILBOAT IN THE MOONLIGHT"

"A Sailboat in the Moonlight" is Holiday alchemy. The Carmen Lombardo melody was a No. 1 hit for his brother, Guy Lombardo and His Royal Canadians (a band that specialized in sugary music with no jazz content). Its sentimental cadences emphasize a thoroughly banal lyric. Yet Holiday, abetted by Young and Count Basie's rhythm section as led by a good Teddy Wilson imitator (Jimmy Sherman), is rhythmically inspired and genuinely touching. How does she do it? The transformation begins immediately as she replaces the song's corny ascending melody with a repeated pitch, each of three notes ("A-sail-boat") articulated for rhythmic effect—not unlike the way Young begins many of his solos. From then on, she alters this note and that, stretches one at the expense of another, never obscuring the appealing qualities of the song (which has the saving grace of pretty harmonies). She makes the fantasy of sailing away with her lover to a remote rendezvous a dream worth cherishing.

A SAILBOAT IN THE MOONLIGHT

Billie Holiday

Billie Holiday, vocal; Buck Clayton, trumpet; Edmond Hall, clarinet; Lester Young, tenor saxophone; James Sherman, piano; Freddy Green, guitar; Walter Page, bass; Jo Jones, drums

LABEL: Vocalion/OKeh 3605; *The Best of Billie Holiday* (Legacy 886972136127)
DATE: 1937
STYLE: swing
FORM: 32-bar popular song (**AABA**)

Introduction

0:00		Clayton on trumpet plays a matched set of phrases, each ending on a half cadence (on the dominant). Jones accompanies on the high-hat cymbal.

Chorus 1

0:08	A	*"A sailboat in the moonlight and you.* *Wouldn't that be heaven, a heaven just for two?"* As Holiday sings the song, she paraphrases the melody and swings hard against the beat. Young on tenor saxophone plays both underneath the solo (countermelody) and in answer to it (call and response). In the background, the clarinet plays sustained notes. The bass (Page) plays a simple accompaniment of two beats to the bar.
0:21		Over the turnaround, Young responds to Holiday by raising his volume and playing a phrase that lags noticeably behind the beat.
0:24	A	*"A soft breeze on a June night and you.* *What a perfect setting for letting dreams come true!"* Holiday continues to add rhythmic variations, while Young improvises a new line.
0:36		Young's response to the vocal line is bluesy.
0:40	B	*"A chance to sail away to Sweetheart Bay beneath the stars that shine,* *A chance to drift, for you to lift your tender lips to mine!"* The bridge provides contrast by moving to unexpected new harmonies.
0:52		The harmony moves to a half cadence.
0:57	A	*"The things, dear, that I long for are few:* *Just give me a sailboat in the moonlight and you!"* Holiday falls farther behind the beat.
1:03		She emphasizes the tune's title by singing the last phrase with a sharper timbre.

Chorus 2

1:12	A	Sherman plays a light, spare piano solo. Behind him, Jones switches to a dry, staccato accompaniment on the cymbals. Page on bass occasionally fills in the texture by adding extra notes.
1:28	A	
1:44	B	Clayton (trumpet) enters. Jones returns to a splashier high-hat sound, responding to the trumpet's phrases with sharp snare-drum accents.
1:53		In the background, someone shouts "Yeah!"
2:00	A	Young plays an eight-bar solo in a smooth, relaxed style.
2:09		The last phrase of the solo wraps things up by descending through a bluesy phrase to the tonic.

Chorus 3 (abbreviated)

2:16	B	*"A chance to sail away to Sweetheart Bay beneath the stars that shine. A chance to drift, for you to lift your tender lips to mine!"* Holiday returns, her notes falling unpredictably within the measure. Young retreats to accompaniment, joining Hall (clarinet), who plays sustained notes deep in the background.
2:24		Holiday suddenly sings firmly on the beat, with the rhythm section instead of against it, helping to intensify the sense of groove.
2:32	A	*"The things, dear, that I long for are few: Just give me a sailboat in the moonlight and you!"* As if responding to Holiday, Page switches to a steady walking bass (four beats to the bar).
2:38		Holiday marks her last phrase by repeatedly hitting her highest pitch.

Coda

2:44		At the end of the vocal, the accompanying instruments (piano, tenor saxophone, and clarinet) combine in a brief polyphonic clamor.

If Billie Holiday is a singer associated with emotional pain—a wounded sparrow, in songbird parlance—Ella Fitzgerald is the irrepressible spirit of musical joy. Like Holiday, she rarely sang the blues, but where Billie had an unmistakable feeling for them, Ella saw blues as just another song form, useful for up-tempo scat improvisations. Her vocal equipment was also the opposite of Holiday's: she had four octaves at her disposal, and was not averse to adding falsetto (higher than her normal range) cries and low growls. In her peak years, her timbre had a luscious, ripe quality. She was an accomplished, peerless scat-singer, one of very few who could improvise on chords as imaginatively as the best instrumentalists. Benny Carter once orchestrated her solo on "Oh! Lady Be Good" as evidence of her compositional prowess. Shy and demure in her personal style and extremely private, she came vivaciously, aggressively to life in scat vocals, reaching emotional zeniths verging on euphoria, delighting audiences and mesmerizing musicians.

Fitzgerald was born in Virginia and raised in Yonkers, New York, where she sang in church and taught herself to dance. When her mother died, she was sent to live with an aunt in Harlem, and treated as an orphan. By 1934, she had dropped out of school and was living off her wits on the streets. That November, she entered the Apollo Theater's amateur night as a dancer, but at the last minute chose to sing. Fitzgerald, who lacked Holiday's great physical beauty, was hooted when she walked onstage—a big, clunky girl, awkward in manner and badly dressed—until she broke into song. Her enchantingly girlish voice and dynamic rhythm triumphed, and she won the competition.

Because of her looks, however, bandleaders refused to hire her until Carter recommended her to Chick Webb, who was instantly hooked. He became her legal guardian, bought her clothes, and restructured his band to feature a voice he predicted would be heard for decades. From the summer of 1935, she was present on most of his record sessions, and instantly attracted an enthusiastic following. Webb's best-selling 1938 recording of "A-Tisket, a-Tasket," based on an old nursery rhyme she set to a catchy melody during a hospital stay (and cleverly arranged for her by Van Alexander), made her famous. Within months she was billed as the "First Lady of Swing"—in later years the "First Lady of Song."

After Webb's death, Fitzgerald recorded dozens of ballads, swingers (sometimes with killer tempos), and novelties, effortlessly making the transition to bebop (her "Air Mail Special" is a bop version of a swing classic). Norman Granz recruited her for his Jazz at the Philharmonic concert tours (he also signed Holiday), and became her personal manager, building a new record label, Verve, around her. Fitzgerald's innovative songbook albums, each devoted to one songwriter, garnered tremendous acclaim in the 1950s and 1960s. She was regarded universally as the gold standard for both jazz and pop singing.

"BLUE SKIES"

"Blue Skies," a pop standard frequently adapted by jazz musicians, was recorded for the album *Ella Fitzgerald Sings the Irving Berlin Songbook*. But her rendition is so adventurous (it's more Ella than Berlin), it was initially dropped from that album and included on another, *Get Happy!*—an emblematic Fitzgerald title (a typical Holiday title, by contrast, is *Songs for Distingué Lovers*). She begins with a scat intro, employing cantorial phrases that suggest Jewish liturgical music. She sings the lyric at a medium clip, accompanied by Harry "Sweets" Edison's trumpet obbligato, mildly embellishing the melody, yet making every phrase swing. Then she takes off on a three-chorus scat improvisation, singing variations with the imagination of an instrumentalist. With typical high-flying insouciance, she quotes from Richard Wagner's "Wedding March" in chorus 2, and a few bars of Gershwin's *Rhapsody in Blue* in the last chorus before reprising the lyric for the final bridge. She never runs out of steam or breath, carrying the rhythm like an ocean current.

BLUE SKIES

Ella Fitzgerald

Ella Fitzgerald, vocal, with Paul Weston Orchestra: John Best, Pete Candoli, Harry Edison, Don Fagerquist, Manny Klein, trumpets; Ed Kusby, Dick Noel, William Schaefer, trombones; Juan Tizol, valve trombone; Gene Cipriano, Chuck Gentry, Leonard Hartman, Matty Matlock, Ted Nash, Babe Russin, Fred Stulce, woodwinds; Paul Smith, piano; Barney Kessel, guitar; Joe Mondragon, bass; Alvin Stoller, drums

LABEL: *Ella Fitzgerald Sings the Irving Berlin Songbook* (Verve 830-2); *Gold* (Verve 602517414549)
DATE: 1958
STYLE: big-band swing
FORM: 32-bar popular song (**AABA**)

Introduction

0:00   Over sustained orchestra chords, Fitzgerald begins to scat-sing, using open, resonant nonsense syllables ("da," "la") instead of words. The vocal line lazily moves through arpeggios: notes drawn from the underlying chords.

0:17   As the accompanying instruments come to rest on a dominant chord, the vocal line falls to its lowest note.

Chorus 1

0:22 **A**   *"Blue skies smiling at me, nothing but blue skies do I see."*
Fitzgerald sings the melody to "Blue Skies" with its original text. In each **A** section, the melody gradually falls from the minor into the major mode (at "nothing but *blue* skies"). Behind her, the rhythm section plays a steady, even pulse, with countermelodies from muted trumpet (Edison) and piano.

0:34   **A**   *"Bluebirds singing a song, nothing but bluebirds all day long."*
Fitzgerald adds slight decorative touches to individual notes, and alters the melody at phrase's end (0:43).

0:46   **B**   *"Never saw the sun shining so bright, never saw things going so right. Noticing the days hurrying by, when you're in love, my, how they fly."*
As the melody moves into the major mode and a higher register, the saxophones counter with a restrained lower accompanying line.

0:58   **A**   *"Blue days, all of them gone, nothing but blue skies from now on."*

1:08   The saxophones begin playing a riff.

Chorus 2

1:11   **A**   Picking up on the rhythm and melody of the saxophone riff, Fitzgerald begins scatting.

1:17   For a few measures, she sings slightly behind the beat, adding rhythmic tension.

1:23   **A**   Using variable intonation (blue note), she gradually pulls the first note upward.

1:29   Using her head voice (higher register), she sings a series of relaxed triplets.

1:32   Unexpectedly, she quotes the beginning of Wagner's "Wedding March."

1:35   **B**   As the saxophones play gruff chords, Fitzgerald hints at singing in double-time.

1:42   She sings a phrase, then repeats it at a higher pitch level as the song returns to its original minor key.

1:47   **A**   Starting on a dramatic high note, she launches into a loose, bluesy phrase.

1:53   She sings a three-note motive; repeating it, she turns it into a polyrhythmic motive.

Chorus 3

1:59   **A**   As the accompaniment intensifies, Fitzgerald digs into the beat, turning her line into a riff figure and using more percussive syllables ("bop," "dee-yowwww").

2:05   Searching for more consonants, she begins a new phrase with a misplaced (but arresting) "sssssssss" sound.

2:11   **A**   Fitzgerald marks the arrival at the next **A** section with a startling dissonance. She repeats it several more times to make it clear to the casual listener that it's not a mistake.

2:23   **B**   Picking up on a phrase she's just sung, she bounces back and forth between two notes in the major scale.

2:29   A lengthy phrase finally ends on the downbeat of the next **A** section.

2:35   **A**   More complicated rhythmic figures suddenly precede an extended passage in her upper register.

Chorus 4

2:47	A	As the background orchestra reaches the peak of its intensity, Fitzgerald retreats to a simple riff figure.
2:54		She quotes a famous theme from Gershwin's *Rhapsody in Blue*.
3:00	A	She begins each phrase by leaning on the tonic, sometimes decorating it unexpectedly with triplets.
3:06		As the harmony moves to the major mode, her lines strongly evoke the blues.
3:12	B	*"I never saw the sun shining so bright, never saw things going so right. Noticing the days hurrying by, when you're in love, my how they fly."* The band retreats to a simpler texture. Fitzgerald returns to the song's lyrics and, at times, its original melody.
3:24	A	*"Blue days, all of them gone, nothing but blue skies from now on."* The last lines are distorted into soaring arpeggios.

Coda

| 3:34 | | As Fitzgerald hits her high note, the band plays two sharp dominant chords, then drops out to let her add a bit more scat-singing. |
| 3:37 | | The band ends with a caterwauling of chords, piano phrases, and drumming. |

10 CHAPTER

Rhythm in Transition

RHYTHM IS OUR BUSINESS

I n May 1935, the No. 1 record in the country was Jimmie Lunceford's "Rhythm Is Our Business." Released a few months before Benny Goodman triggered the national craze for all things swing, the song offered a foretaste of the coming deluge. "Rhythm is our business / Rhythm is what we sell," Lunceford's singer declared: "Rhythm is our business / Business sure is swell." If rhythm defined the swing bands, its foundation lay in the rhythm section, which was undergoing a thorough overhaul. In bands big and small, the pianists, guitarists, bass-

◄ Jo Jones, the Count Basie drummer who was said to play like the wind, changed the feeling of swing with his brisk attack on the high-hat cymbal. New York, 1950.

ists, and drummers fused into a unified rhythmic front, supplying the beat and marking the harmonies. Each of the leading bands presented a distinct, well-designed rhythmic attack that complemented its particular style. The rhythm sections of Ellington, Basie, and Lunceford, for example, sounded nothing alike. Yet just as the soloists were champing at the bit of big-band constraints, rhythm players were developing techniques and ideas that demanded more attention than they usually received. In the 1930s and early 1940s, rhythm instruments made dramatic advances toward the foreground of jazz. In the process, they helped set the stage for postwar modern jazz.

PIANO:
Fats Waller (1904-1943) AND Art Tatum (1909-1956)

Bands led by pianists (Ellington, Basie, Hines) allowed for plenty of piano solos, but the pianist-bandleaders tended to limit themselves to introductions, solo choruses, and an occasional mini-concerto. Long before jazz, however, the piano had enjoyed a history of self-sufficiency, from Bach to ragtime, which was maintained in the styles of stride and boogie-woogie. Keyboard technique continued to develop and prosper during the swing years, but the main advances took place in more intimate settings—for example, Teddy Wilson's precision lyricism in the small Goodman groups. Two of the most remarkable pianists in jazz history found their fortes in unusual settings: Fats Waller in the womb of a studio group bent on comedy, and Art Tatum as a radio recitalist.

Thomas "Fats" Waller achieved, during a brief but incredibly prolific career, a matchless standing in jazz and pop, straddling the dividing line with his humor and instrumental technique. A radiant pianist, canny vocalist, musical satirist, and important songwriter, he made more than 500 records (most within a span of eight years), and succeeded as a composer on Broadway and as an entertainer in movies.

Waller was born in New York City, the son of a Baptist lay preacher. His mother taught him piano and organ, instilling in him a lasting love for J. S. Bach. She died when Fats was in his mid-teens, at which time he came under the spell of James P. Johnson. He began playing professionally at fifteen, on call to accompany silent movies. Three years later (1922), he recorded two pieces for solo piano, both stylistically indebted to Johnson. Like other stride pianists, Waller found additional work at rent parties, and also participated in cutting contests—largely amiable, usually respectful, but deadly serious keyboard competitions—winning admirers with his flawless keyboard touch and outgoing, ebullient personality. If he lacked Johnson's imaginative bass lines and breakneck speed, he was a more expressive interpreter of blues and ballads, exhibiting greater subtlety and a fluent rhythmic feeling that perfectly meshed with swing. By the late 1920s, Waller had become a prominent figure in jazz and theater, thanks chiefly to the widely performed songs he wrote for theatrical revues. He was known as someone who could write the score for a show over a week-end and still have time to consume copious quantities of food and alcohol. Louis Armstrong established several of his songs as standards—including "Ain't Misbehavin'," "(What Did I Do to Be So) Black and Blue," and "Honeysuckle Rose." (After Ellington, Waller remains jazz's most success-ful pop songwriter.) Yet as he approached his thirtieth birthday, Waller was unknown to the general public.

In 1934, RCA-Victor signed up Fats Waller and His Rhythm, a six-piece band. The first tune he recorded, "A Porter's Love Song to a Chamber-maid," written for him by James P. Johnson and Andy Razaf, introduced a new Fats—a larger-than-life comic personality and irresistible vocalist who could kid a song and make it swing at the same time. The second song he recorded at that same session, "I Wish I Were Twins," became a best seller. During the next five years, Waller was rarely absent from the pop charts.

Adapting the guise of a Harlem dandy—in a derby, vest, and tailored pinstripes—Waller burlesqued the worst of Tin Pan Alley, creating satiri-cal gems with painfully sentimental material like "The Curse of an Aching Heart." At the same time, he could be touchingly sincere with good songs, like "I'm Gonna Sit Right Down and Write Myself a Letter." He possessed a mildly strident voice of surprising suppleness, using different registers for different effects: middle octave for straightforward singing, low notes for rude asides, high ones for feminine mockery. Humor enabled Waller to sweep up the musical debris of the day, inflecting it with his own spirit. At the same time, he created several impeccable solo piano works—usually of his own invention though some were based on standards—that suggested an artistic potential far beyond his studio repertory. His rare recordings on pipe organ suggested an additional unfulfilled promise. Fats's immense suc-cess had put him in a bind. RCA wanted nothing but hits, and jazz lovers failed to appreciate the artistry of his clowning. Significantly, at the time of his death (from pneumonia, at thirty-nine), Waller the recording artist had yet to record some of the finest songs by Waller the composer.

"CHRISTOPHER COLUMBUS"

"Christopher Columbus" represents Waller in a typically uproarious mood, very funny and very musical. The melody, by Chu Berry, who adapted the chords to "I Got Rhythm" for the bridge, generated several hits in 1936, though Waller's version (subtitled "A Rhythm Cocktail") was not among them. Fletcher Henderson, Benny Goodman, Andy Kirk, and Teddy Wilson all scored with it, but the tune didn't become a jazz hallmark until 1938, when Goodman interpolated it as the secondary theme in his version of "Sing, Sing, Sing." Andy Razaf, Waller's friend and favorite lyricist, wrote the harebrained words, which Waller mocks, drawing on each of his vocal registers.

This performance shows Waller integrating stride piano into small-group swing, emphasizing rhythmic power—especially the cross-rhythms in his dashing solo chorus. His band remained fairly stable during the RCA years, with two prominent supporting roles taken by saxophonist and clarinetist Gene Sedric and trumpet player Herman Autrey. Accomplished musicians, Sedric and Autrey were nonetheless second-string players who reflect the dominating influences of the period: Sedric shows the inspiration of Hawkins and Chu Berry, while Autrey blends the sound and temperament of Armstrong and Roy Eldridge. The rhythm section has its hands full keeping up with Waller.

CHRISTOPHER COLUMBUS (A RHYTHM COCKTAIL)

Fats Waller and His Rhythm
Herman Autrey, trumpet; Gene Sedric, tenor saxophone; Fats Waller, piano and vocal; Albert Casey, guitar; Charles Turner, bass; Arnold Boling, drums

LABEL: Victor 25295; *If You Got to Ask, You Ain't Got It! Fats Waller and His Rhythm* (Bluebird/Legacy 81124)
DATE: 1936
STYLE: small-group swing
FORM: 32-bar popular song (**AABA**)

Introduction

0:00	Waller plays the simple opening riff in octaves.
0:04	When the riff is repeated, it quickly subsides into a stride accompaniment.

Chorus 1 (extended)

0:07   **A**   As the rest of the rhythm section enters in the first two sections of a 32-bar form, Waller begins to sing.

"Mister Christopher Columbus sailed the sea without a compass.
When his men began a rumpus,
[spoken gruffly] *Up spoke Christopher Columbus, yes!"*

He changes the timbre of his voice for comic effect.

0:22   **A**   *"There's land somewhere, until we get there,*
We will not go wrong if we sing, swing a song.
Since the world is round-o, we'll be safe and sound-o.
Till our goal is found-o, we'll just keep rhythm bound-o."

The band continues with another 16-bar **AA** section. Columbus is parodied in a high-pitched sing-song that gradually falls to Waller's normal speaking voice.

0:36   **B**   (sung) *"Since the crew was makin' merry—*
[spoken] *Mary got up and went home!*
There came a yell for Isabel, and they brought the rum and Isabel."

This section, which serves as the bridge to the broader 32-bar **AABA** form, borrows its chord progression from "I Got Rhythm."

0:43   **A**   *"No more mutiny, no! What a time at sea!*
With diplomacy, Christory made history! Yes!"

A return to the **A** section.

Chorus 2 (abbreviated)

0:50   **A**   (sung) *"Mister Christopher Columbus! Uh-huh!*
He used rhythm as a compass! Yes, yes! Music ended all the rumpus! Yes!
Wise old Christopher Columbus! [spoken] *Latch on, Christy! Yeah!"*

Waller reduces the melody line to a simple riff. Each line of text is answered by a short exclamation, as if Waller were in call and response with himself.

Chorus 3

1:04   **A**   Sedric takes a tenor saxophone solo, spurred on by Waller's enthusiastic replies ("yes, yes!").

1:11   **A**

1:18   **B**   Waller signals the bridge by playing a two-note background line.

1:25   **A**

Chorus 4

1:33   **A**   Waller plays the opening melody in exuberant stride style, emphasizing the offbeats.

1:40   **A**

1:47   **B**   Over the bridge, he plays a complicated cross-rhythmic pattern.

1:52   He signals the end of the bridge with a descending octave pattern.

1:54   **A**

| 2:00 | | At the end of the chorus, Waller interjects an excited "Yes!" |

Chorus 5

2:01	**A**	Autrey (trumpet) enters with an excited single-note pattern. Behind him, Sedric (tenor saxophone) plays a bluesy riff.
2:08	**A**	
2:15	**B**	During the bridge, the riff temporarily disappears (it will reappear during the last **A** section).
2:22	**A**	

Coda

| 2:30 | (spoken) *"Well, look-a there! Christy's grabbed the Santa Maria, And he's going back! Yeah! Ahhhh, look-a there!"* The band moves suddenly to a quieter volume, with Waller playing the opening riff. In response, Autrey plays his own trumpet riff while Waller improvises some concluding remarks. |
| 2:43 | *"Uh-huh. . . . In the year 1492, Columbus sailed the ocean bluuuuue!* [quickly] *What'd I say?"* The band drops out entirely, leaving Waller the last word. |

The peculiar nature of Art Tatum's genius is epitomized by the fact that twenty-first century listeners respond to his records much as 1930s listeners did—with gawking amazement. Whatever we may think of his music, there is no getting around its spectacular dexterity. The fact that Tatum was legally blind magnifies his legend. The son of amateur musicians, Tatum was born in Toledo, Ohio, with cataracts on both eyes. Minor gains made through operations were undone when he was mugged as a teenager and lost all sight in his left eye, retaining a sliver of light in the right.

Tatum began picking out melodies at three, attended the Cousino School for the Blind and the Toledo School of Music (where he studied violin and guitar as well as piano), led his own bands at seventeen, and signed a two-year radio contract before he was twenty. His reputation spread quickly. While passing though Ohio, Duke Ellington sought him out and encouraged him to head for New York, where the competition would raise his sights and sharpen his wits. After singer Adelaide Hall hired Tatum in 1932, the New York stride pianists instantly acknowledged his superiority, a capitulation made easier by his friendly, unassuming demeanor. A couple of years later, George Gershwin threw a party at his home to introduce him to the classical elite.

The word "virtuoso" is used to identify an artist of masterly technique and skill. Most accomplished artists in any field have achieved a measure of virtuosity; still, when it comes to Tatum, there is a temptation to call him a virtuoso and then retire the word. No other jazz player is so closely associated with dazzling, superhuman nimbleness. That's because his style is fundamentally inseparable from his technique. Tatum was championed by some of the great classical pianists of his time, including Sergei Rachmaninoff and Vladimir Horowitz. Jazz pianists universally regarded him as peerless. Waller, whom Tatum often named as his inspiration (you can hear the influence in Tatum's use of stride), once interrupted a number when Tatum entered a club where he was performing, and announced, "Ladies and gentlemen, I play piano, but God is in the house tonight!" Pianist Hank Jones has said that when he first heard Tatum's records, he felt certain they were "tricks" achieved through overdubbing.

Tatum was indefatigable. He worked in top nightclubs and then dropped by dives and after-hours joints, where he would play till dawn. If a particular piano was out of tune or worse, he would play a two-handed run to test the keyboard and then avoid the bad or missing keys for the rest of the night. But though he was a frequent guest on radio broadcasts, he was never embraced by the mainstream. He appeared in few concert halls and recorded mostly for independent labels. Did his very brilliance put people off? Virtuosity is often regarded as a pitfall; an artist is expected to use it as the means to an end, not as the end itself. Tatum used his skill to create a thoroughly original approach to piano music, one that offers pleasure as much from his flashing runs and change-ups as his underlying harmonic and rhythmic ingenuity: means *and* ends.

Tatum was primarily a solo pianist. His orchestral style depended on his freedom to change harmonies and rhythms at will. As an accompanist, he created backgrounds that were sometimes overly busy, threatening to obscure the soloist. There were exceptions (his album with Ben Webster, recorded shortly before Tatum succumbed to kidney failure, is a classic of mutual empathy), and, unexpectedly, he found his greatest popular success leading a trio with guitar (Tiny Grimes) and bass (Slam Stewart). Audiences enjoyed watching the three instrumentalists challenge each other with oddball quotations from songs other than the ones they were playing. Alone, however, Tatum, was a fount of surprises. He developed set routines on many of his favorite songs, but no matter how often he played them, he was able to astound the listener with harmonic substitutions of unbelievable complexity. His ability to interject and superimpose additional harmonies influenced established musicians, like Coleman Hawkins,

and helped inspire the young modernists coming up—Charlie Parker and
Charles Mingus named him as a primary influence.

"OVER THE RAINBOW"

Tatum's 1939 "Over the Rainbow"—the first of his five surviving versions,
recorded over a sixteen-year span—was made when the song was new to
the public. It was written by Harold Arlen and E. Y. Harburg for *The Wizard of Oz*, a movie that debuted only days before Tatum made this recording to be broadcast on radio. The fact that he brings so much feeling and
control to a song new to his repertory is impressive; that he understands the
mechanics of the song well enough to rewire its harmonies and deconstruct
its melody is extraordinary.

 This was one of many performances made by Tatum and other musicians
for a company called Standard Transcriptions, which produced recordings exclusively for radio stations. Transcriptions, as the discs were called,
could not be sold in stores. Broadcasters preferred creating their own music
libraries to paying licensing fees to air commercial recordings. Eventually,
the networks cut a deal with the labels, and transcription discs disappeared.
In some ways, however, transcriptions were superior to records: fidelity was
enhanced because the discs were larger (sixteen inches instead of the usual
ten), and the artists had more latitude in terms of length. This performance
is a minute longer than a record would have allowed. Even so, Tatum has
to hurry to squeeze in his ending.

OVER THE RAINBOW

Art Tatum, piano
LABEL: Black Lion (E)BLP30194; *Art Tatum: The Standard Sessions, 1935–1943 Broad-
cast Transcriptions* (CD-919(2))
DATE: 1939
STYLE: stride piano
FORM: 32-bar popular song (**AABA**)

Introduction

| 0:00 | | Tatum begins with an intensely dissonant dominant chord, rolled up from the bottom. It's answered by a pair of octaves in the right hand. |

Chorus 1

| 0:07 | A | Tatum plays the melody harmonized by chords, without the stride accompaniment. He plays rubato, adjusting the tempo for expressive |

		purposes (sometimes accelerating slightly, at other times slowing down dramatically).
0:12		The first of many descending runs into the bass register.
0:14		Throughout the performance, Tatum plays the melody with faithful accuracy, but alters the chord progression with harmonic substitutions.
0:19		He decorates the end of the first **A** section with new chords and a dramatic upward-sweeping run.
0:23	**A**	For the second **A** section, he repeats the melody, in more or less the same sequence he had used earlier.
0:36	**B**	Tatum plays the bridge simply, accompanied only by sparse chords in the left hand.
0:40		Where the original tune is harmonically static, he adds a new series of chords.
0:52		He marks the end of the bridge with several runs.
0:57	**A**	Return of the original melody, now beginning in the bass register.
1:01		Another intensely dissonant chord.
1:08		He begins to move into a steady tempo.

Chorus 2

1:17	**A**	In a moderate, relaxed tempo, Tatum uses a stride accompaniment in his left hand.
1:31		At the cadence, he throws in melodic lines that suggest a bluesy feeling.
1:36	**A**	
1:38		He moves from the original melody into a complicated, dissonant 16th-note line, featuring harmonic substitutions.
1:44		The intensity of this passage is "erased" by a descending fast run.
1:55	**B**	Once again, Tatum plays the melody to the bridge accompanied by simple left-hand chords.
2:01		As the phrase ends, the harmonies suddenly move into unexpected chromatic territory.
2:13		As Tatum nears the end of the bridge, his melodic line becomes increasingly fast and dissonant; it resolves directly on the downbeat of the new **A** section.
2:15	**A**	
2:20		As he settles into his groove, the harmonies take on more of a bluesy tinge.

Chorus 3

2:36	**A**	
2:51		Over the last two measures of the **A** section, Tatum's improvisation drifts out of the main key and accelerates as it heads for a resolution on the downbeat of the next section.
2:56	**A**	
3:02		Over a few simple chords, he plays a blindingly fast passage.

3:11		Another bluesy cadence.
3:16	**B**	The bridge, which had been a point of relaxation, suddenly becomes more intense: over steady eighth-note chords in the left hand, the harmonization departs radically from the original.
3:26		Finally, Tatum resolves to the tonic harmony.
3:31		Suddenly, as if under extreme time pressure, he speeds up the performance and races through the rest of the tune in record time.
3:33	**A**	

PLUGGING IN: Charlie Christian (1916–1942)

As the guitar replaced the banjo in jazz bands (except those that played in the traditional New Orleans vein), its role grew increasingly subtle. On occasion when a bandleader hired a singer but wanted him to sit in the ensemble, he would have the vocalist pretend to play guitar, strumming on rubber or loosened strings and smiling. Without a mike, no one could hear him anyway. The great rhythm guitarists were indispensable in filling out the sound of the section, but they did little more than strum a steady four-to-the-bar *chunk-chunk-chunk-chunk*, reinforcing the roles of the drummer and bassist. The guitar had lost the prominence it had earned as a solo instrument in the 1920s, when Eddie Lang and Lonnie Johnson appeared on records with Beiderbecke, Joe Venuti, Armstrong, and Ellington. Lang (who was white) and Johnson (who was black) had even recorded together, with Lang using a pseudonym (Blind Willie Dunn) to disguise the integrated nature of the session. Lang also recorded duets with Carl Kress, a pioneer of rhythm guitar. The short-term fate of the guitar may be measured by the fate of those three men: Lang died in 1933 (at thirty, of a botched tonsillectomy); Kress left jazz for mainstream studio work and to run a nightclub; and Johnson left jazz to reinvent himself as a blues (and, briefly, rhythm and blues) star.

Even rhythm guitar lost ground. While Freddie Green (who never recorded a single solo in a career of half a century) became a mainstay of the Count Basie band, adding immeasurably to the unique sound and style of the Basie rhythm section, other guitarists found their services no longer in demand. Many bandleaders, including Ellington, saw the instrument as an unnecessary accoutrement. They wanted freer rhythms and felt that the guitar stood in the way.

The problem with the acoustic guitar was volume. Whether the band was large or small, the guitar lacked the dynamic presence of other instruments. Various attempts were made to amplify it, using resonators, external microphones, and pick-ups (magnets coiled with wire that transmit an electrical impulse from the strings to an amplifier). Meanwhile, recordings by Django Reinhardt showed that the guitar was a jazz instrument of barely explored potential.

In the early 1930s, the Gibson Company began building prototypes for an electric guitar, achieving a breakthrough in 1936. The new instrument was taken up by a few musicians, notably Floyd Smith of Andy Kirk's band, Eddie Durham of Count Basie's Kansas City Six, and Western swing musicians like Bob Dunn and Leon McAuliffe, who combined the traditions of Hawaiian steel guitar and jazz with the new technology to create a signature sound in country music: electric steel guitar. In the late 1940s, Gibson introduced the solid body electric guitar, and within a decade it was the representative instrument of rock and roll, urban blues, and country music. Those early technological advances meant little, however, until one remarkable musician demonstrated the artistry possible on electric guitar. Charlie Christian showed that it was more than a loud acoustic guitar: it was a separate instrument with a timbre and personality of its own.

In a career of tragic brevity (only twenty-three months in the public spotlight), Christian transformed the guitar and provided yet another channel of momentum to the younger musicians who would soon introduce bebop. In his hands, the guitar acquired the same rhythmic independence and dynamic confidence associated with the saxophone and trumpet. His warm, radiant sound had a suitably electrifying effect.

Charlie Christian was born in Texas and grew up in a poor section of Oklahoma City, where, according to his neighbor, novelist Ralph Ellison, he was a wonder in grade school, playing guitars made from cigar boxes and taking up trumpet, piano, and bass. His father and brothers were musicians as well, and Charlie began touring with Southwestern bands in his teens, soaking up the swing and blues echoing from Kansas City and Western swing bands. In 1938, Christian hooked up an electric pick-up to his acoustic guitar, and word of his prodigious gifts spread. Mary Lou Williams raved about him to John Hammond, who in 1939 arranged for him to audition for Benny Goodman. At first reluctant to hire a guitarist, Goodman changed his mind when he heard Christian's limber phrases soaring over the rhythm section.

Goodman signed Christian to his sextet, which made weekly radio broadcasts, and featured him on records with the big band in concerto-like arrangements. Extremely laconic, Christian usually let his music do the talking, yet three months after he joined with Goodman, he lent his name to a Chicago newspaper article (presumably ghostwritten) whose headline read "Guitarmen, Wake Up and Pluck! Wire for Sound; Let 'Em Hear You Play." The article argued that a guitarist is "more than just a robot plunking on a gadget to keep the rhythm going." It promised that "electrical amplification has given guitarists a new lease on life."

Christian made his case on record after record, mostly with Goodman. Seemingly overnight, a flood of guitarists plugged in, determined to capture the spare clarity of Christian's solos—every phrase enunciated, logical, and decisive. Recording with some of the finest musicians of the era, Christian always stood out with his ricocheting riffs, inspired melodies, and deep blues feeling. One of his most successful acolytes, Barney Kessel, later compared his importance to that of Thomas Edison. That may seem like an exaggeration, yet by the time Christian succumbed to tuberculosis at twenty-five, few would have argued the point. He had given the electric guitar a permanent lease on life.

"SWING TO BOP" ("TOPSY")

This performance, one of Christian's best, exists by accident. In 1941, an engineer named Jerry Newman took his wire recorder (a predecessor to tape recorders) to Harlem after-hours clubs to document jam sessions. The sessions at Minton's Playhouse proved especially illuminating, because the rhythm section included two men who later figured as key bebop innovators, drummer Kenny Clarke and pianist Thelonious Monk. Among the soloists who dropped by to jam were adventurous swing stars like Christian, Roy Eldridge, saxophonist Don Byas, and fledgling modernist Dizzy Gillespie.

When, years later, Newman's wire recordings were released commercially, they were greeted as a revelation, capturing the first steps in what proved to be the transformation from swing to bebop. Newman in fact released this track as "Swing to Bop," a title that couldn't have existed in 1941 because the word "bop" had not yet been coined. The tune is actually "Topsy," a swing hit by Eddie Durham and Edgar Battle, though the melody isn't played: Newman began recording this number as Christian was completing his first chorus. (This excerpt consists only of his six-chorus solo.) "Topsy" is the only swing tune that returned to the charts two decades later: when jazz drummer Cozy Cole recorded it in 1958, at the height of Elvismania, it unaccountably became the No. 1 rhythm and blues and No. 3 pop hit in the country. Christian is inspired by the song's harmonies, consistently varying his riffs and rhythmic accents, building on motives and playing with a relaxed lucidity—notice, too, how the harmonies of the bridge, especially, *always* liberate his melodic imagination.

SWING TO BOP (TOPSY)

Charlie Christian •

Charlie Christian, electric guitar; Kenny Clarke, drums; unknown piano, bass

LABEL: *Live Sessions at Minton's* (Everest FS-219); *Live Sessions at Minton's Playhouse: New York, May 1941* (Jazz Anthology 550012)
DATE: 1941
STYLE: small-group swing
FORM: 32-bar popular song (**AA′ BA**)

Chorus 1

0:00	**A**	The recording fades in during the middle of Christian's six-chorus solo on electric guitar. He's just completing the first **A** section of the tune.
0:03	**A′**	For the **A′** section, the harmony changes to IV for four bars. In the background, the pianist loudly plays a stride accompaniment.
0:12	**B**	As the piano retreats to comping, the walking bass gradually takes over as the rhythmic foundation.
0:21	**A**	Christian's tone hardens. He begins playing a simple three-note figure, shifting it in different rhythmic positions in the measure.

Chorus 2

0:29	**A**	The three-note motive now becomes the beginning of a longer, more involved phrase.
0:32		Christian throws in a triplet.
0:38	**A′**	
0:47	**B**	As he enters the more complex chord changes of the bridge, Christian uses harmonic improvisation in long, flowing lines. Clarke occasionally interrupts with bass drum accents.
0:56	**A**	The harmony returns to the tonic, and Christian turns the three-note motive into short repeated riffs.
1:02		Christian's riffs speed up; Clarke adds counterrhythms.

Chorus 3

1:05	**A**	The next chorus begins with a new riff, loosely based on the three-note motive.

1:13	A′	
1:19		A final bluesy phrase rounds out the **A′** section. It's followed by silence.
1:22	B	Christian begins the bridge on a high note. The drums strongly accent the backbeat.
1:31	A	Christian's line becomes detached, falling firmly on the offbeat.

Chorus 4

1:40	A	Christian repeats a simple riff.
1:46		When he extends it with a syncopated beginning, Clarke coincides with accents on the snare drum.
1:48	A′	The line suddenly rises to match the harmony.
1:57	B	A sudden return to straight eighth-note patterns, arpeggiating the underlying chords.
2:06	A	
2:11		The line ends with a single note, decorated with tremolos and repeated in a cross-rhythmic pattern.

Chorus 5

2:15	A	The fifth chorus begins with a riff that uses the tremolo pattern to create a new polyrhythm (three beats against four).
2:17		In the distant background, another instrument can be heard tuning up.
2:23	A′	The line concentrates on a single note, played rhythmically on the beat and building intensity through repetition.
2:30		The first two **A** sections finish with a sharp, direct, and bluesy phrase.
2:32	B	Christian begins two beats early with a driving, descending chromatic pattern.
2:35		The pattern gets "turned around"—shifting slightly to an eighth note earlier, creating cross-rhythmic intensity.
2:41	A	The line again falls strongly on the offbeat.
2:49		Christian and Clarke coincide on strong offbeat accents.

Chorus 6

2:50	A	Christian plays a new riff, starting with the flat fifth degree.
2:58	A′	He plays a pattern with strong rhythmic contrast, prompting Clarke to match it with drum accents.
3:04		Christian plays a phrase that accents the weakest notes in the measure (one-*and*-two-and, three-and-four-*and*).
3:07	B	Once again, he launches himself into the tune's chord pattern.
3:16	A	After the climactic final phrase, Christian retreats, allowing another instrument (trumpet) to continue the jam session.

THE BASS AND Jimmy Blanton (1918–1942)

Of all the instruments in the jazz ensemble, the bass was the slowest in reaching maturity. One reason is that since the bass traditionally served to bind the rhythm section, firming the tempo and outlining the harmonic progression, bassists had little incentive to expand their technical abilities. But as with rhythm guitar, the function was of more significance to the musicians who relied on its steady support than to listeners, who hardly noticed the bass unless it was featured in a solo. Until the late 1930s, the average bass solo was a predictable four-to-the-bar walk. Technique was so lacking that poor intonation was commonplace even in some of the top bands.

There were a few exceptions. Walter Page codified the walking bass. Born in Missouri, he developed his style in the middle 1920s, while leading the Blue Devils in Oklahoma. An important figure in Kansas City, he worked for Benny Moten's orchestra before joining with Count Basie, who built his rhythm section on the metronomic reliability of Page's walking bass: pizzicato notes in stable, stepwise patterns, usually four evenly stated pitches per measure. This style, ideal for Basie, was a dead end for others. Few bassists in the 1930s expanded on its potential.

Most prominent among those who did was Milt Hinton, a much-loved musician whose robust swing and excellent intonation reflected his genial personality. Hinton possessed an instinctive harmonic erudition that enabled him to make the leap from swing to bop. He expanded the bass walk by using more advanced harmonies and syncopating his rhythmic support with inventive, melodic figures. Initially known for his long stay with Cab Calloway and a shorter one with Louis Armstrong, he became the most in-demand and frequently recorded bassist of his generation, appearing on hundreds of jazz, pop, and rock and roll sessions, shifting effortlessly from Bing Crosby and Billie Holiday to Aretha Franklin and Bobby Darin—just to mention a few of the singers he backed. At jam sessions with Dizzy Gillespie and other young modernists, he showed he could master the latest chord changes. Yet as a soloist, he remained committed to swing. Hinton also won respect as an important jazz photographer, whose candid shots document the life of musicians touring the South as no one else's ever did.

Another remarkable bassist was the prodigy Israel Crosby, who became famous in the 1950s and 1960s for his virtuoso turns with the Ahmad

Jamal Trio. He began recording at sixteen, with pianists Jess Stacey, Albert Ammons, and Teddy Wilson (Crosby created a powerful ostinato for Wilson's "Blues in C Sharp Minor") and drummer Gene Krupa. He also spent three years with Fletcher Henderson's orchestra (1936–39). In each situation, he was encouraged to play solos that demonstrated a melodic and rhythmic confidence rare in those years.

By contrast, the best-known bassist of the Swing Era, John Kirby, was famous not because of his playing, which was conventional and flawed, but because he led the most popular small jazz band of its day (1937–42), an unusually minimalist sextet that prefigured the cool style of the 1950s. The band featured Kirby's wife, the enchanting vocalist Maxine Sullivan, and performed jazz adaptations of classical themes. Slam Stewart also won fame in this period, as part of the duo Slim and Slam, with singer-guitarist-humorist Slim Gaillard, and later as a member of the Art Tatum Trio. A gifted musician with rock-steady time and perfect pitch, Stewart was known for his ability to simultaneously scat-sing and improvise bass lines played with a bow.

Oddly enough, the man who did the most to advance the cause of the bass didn't play it. Duke Ellington was partial to the lower end of the musical spectrum—as noted, he often assigned the lead saxophone part to the baritone rather than the alto. In the 1920s, he wrote arrangements that required the elaborate participation of his Louisiana-born bassist, Wellman Braud, whose large sound and solid beat had been heard in New Orleans as early as 1910. With Ellington, Braud helped to develop the walking bass and popularized the bowing technique, heard in tandem with the wind instruments. As Ellington's music grew beyond the skills of Braud, he added a second bassist (Billy Taylor) to play with him.

Ellington's greatest contribution to jazz bass, however, came with his discovery of Jimmy Blanton, the man who revolutionized the instrument. Blanton became such a central figure in the edition of the Ellington band that also introduced Ben Webster that the band was later referred to by fans as "the Blanton-Webster band." Blanton's brief life and career parallels that of Charlie Christian (they succumbed to the same illness), and his transformation of jazz bass was every bit as complete as Christian's remaking of the guitar. In little more than two years—the same period in which Christian emerged (1939–41)—Blanton changed the way the bass was played and, by extension, the nature of the rhythm section. He expanded the walking bass into a fully involved musicianship that, while continuing to provide the harmonies and keep the tempo, added melodic, harmonic, and rhythmic nuances.

Jimmy Blanton started out on violin and switched to bass while attending Tennessee State College. He began working professionally on summer riverboat excursions (led by Fate Marable, who had helped launch Louis Armstrong a generation earlier), and soon dropped out of college to work with a band in St. Louis. In 1939, Ellington heard him and invited him to join the band, then began writing pieces that made the most of Blanton's unparalleled authority. The bassist's attributes included a Tatumesque grounding in harmony that allowed him to add substitute chords; a distinctly attractive and personal timbre; and an authoritative rhythmic pulse. Blanton recorded the first bass solos that departed from the walking-bass style in favor of a freely melodic conception. In his hands, the bass, no longer a cumbersome instrument, could maneuver with speed and flexibility. Blanton's work buoyed Ellington's music with a metrical panache in such works as "Jack the Bear," "Ko-Ko," and "Concerto for Cootie." Ellington also recorded piano-bass duets with him, though by then Blanton was already suffering from the effects of tuberculosis, which took his life at twenty-three.

DRUMMERS STEP OUT

Unlike the bass, the drums quickly reached a high plateau of accomplishment in the Swing Era. Because drums played a loud, dominant, visibly important role in the jazz band, they focused the attention of the audience. As a result, they became a selling point and drummers became showmen: they tossed their sticks in the air and surrounded themselves with exotic accoutrements, designing and even illuminating the heads of their bass drums. They often soloed with more physical exertion than was strictly necessary. At the same time, a genuine musical virtuosity emerged, as drummers competed to create distinct and imaginative ways to keep time, shape arrangements, and inspire soloists. The nature of drumming would change radically after the war, promoting a different kind of involvement in the ensemble, but it already achieved a level of perfection in the 1930s, equal to that of the best pianists and wind players.

William Henry Webb (1909–1939), nicknamed Chick for his small size, was the first great swing drummer and the first to lead his own orchestra, a fiercely competitive outfit that ruled New York's Savoy Ballroom in the early 1930s. He didn't look the part of a powerful drummer and commanding bandleader: mangled by spinal tuberculosis, Webb was a dwarfed hunchback who lived most of his short life in pain. Drums of reduced size were built to accommodate him. Even so, his drumming had a titanic power, and even by contemporary standards his short solos and rattling breaks impart a jolt: each stroke has the articulation of a gunshot. He spurred his soloists with flashing cymbals or emphatic shuffle rhythms derived from boogie-woogie. Those who learned from him include most of the major Swing Era drummers, among them Gene Krupa, Sid Catlett, Jo Jones, Dave Tough, Buddy Rich, and Cozy Cole. Gene Krupa said of Webb, "When he really let go, you had a feeling that the entire atmosphere in the place was being charged. When he felt like it, he could down any of us."

Born in Baltimore, Webb began teaching himself drums at three and bought his first set of traps at eleven. He came to New York in 1924, where two years later Duke Ellington arranged an engagement for him that led to his forming a stable band. He struggled until 1931, when he was booked into the Savoy. When Louis Armstrong came to New York that year, Webb's band was selected to accompany him. Soon Webb was recording with Armstrong and, as the leader of his own band, introducing new work by Benny Carter and Edgar Sampson that would become indispensable to the Swing Era—especially the Sampson pieces (including "Don't Be That Way," "Stomping at the Savoy," and "Blue Lou") that were successfully covered by Benny Goodman. A generous nurturer of talent—Ellington turned to him to find young musicians—and the first bandleader to feature flute, he hit the big time when he found Ella Fitzgerald.

Webb's rim shots and explosive breaks gave his music a unique kick. In 1937, he enjoyed the satisfaction of engaging in a "battle of the bands" at the Savoy with Goodman and trouncing him. The victory was particularly sweet because Goodman's drummer was the nationally publicized Krupa, who at the end faced Webb and bowed down in respect. But Webb didn't have long to savor his success; he died at thirty, of tuberculosis and pleurisy.

Gene Krupa (1909–1973), one of the white Chicagoans who congregated around Bix Beiderbecke and the Austin High guys, was the first drummer to achieve the status of a matinee idol. During four years with Goodman's band (1934–38), he created a sensation with his histrionic solos, characterized by facial contortions, broad arm movements, and hair falling over his brow. A solid musician, Krupa wasn't one of the era's best drummers, but he knew how to stir a crowd. His trademark was a dramatic figure played on the tom-toms ("Sing, Sing, Sing"). In 1938, given his growing fan base, Krupa was encouraged to leave Goodman to start his own band, which proved adventurous and tasteful, and made social and musical history by hiring Roy Eldridge. In 1943, Krupa's career was derailed by a trumped-up arrest for possession of marijuana. He won the case on appeal, but by then the Swing Era was in remission, although he regrouped with an exceptional postwar orchestra that employed several of the young Turks who were fermenting bop, including trumpet player Red Rodney and arranger Gerry Mulligan. Krupa spent most of his later years leading small groups and teaching—he and Cozy Cole founded a school for drummers.

No less mesmerizing and more musically accomplished was Jo Jones (1911–1985), born in Chicago and raised in Alabama, where he toured in tent shows as a tap dancer; gradually he transferred his fastidious dancing skills to the drums, creating the fleet four-four drive that made Count Basie's rhythm section a swing touchstone. It was said that "he played like the wind." His great innovation was to transfer rhythmic emphasis from the snare and bass drums to the high-hat cymbal: this created a tremendous fluidity, replacing *thump-thump-thump* with a sibilant *ching-a-ching-ching*. Jones created some of the most exciting moments of the era, announcing pieces on the high-hat, as in "Clap Hands, Here Comes Charlie," or spurring the soloists with razor-sharp stick work (note his accompaniment to Lester Young and Buck Clayton on "One O'Clock Jump"). In later years, he was reverently known as Papa Jo; on some nights, he would walk through the clubs he worked and drum on every surface.

Sidney Catlett (1910–1951) was a masterly, flashy musician who played intricate cross-rhythms with a delicacy and precision that made them seem elemental. Born in Indiana, he played with several bands in Chicago before moving to New York, where he worked with Benny Carter, Don Redman, Fletcher Henderson, Louis Armstrong, and Benny Goodman, among others. The remarkable thing about Big Sid (he stood well over six feet), besides his infallible technique, was his willingness to play every kind of jazz with grace and commitment. He was as comfortable with Jelly Roll Morton and Sidney Bechet as with Charlie Parker and Dizzy Gillespie. He was one of the first drummers to work out a coherent, logical approach to solos. He created dynamics and contrasts with an array of cymbals, rim shots, bass drum rumbles, and unexpected rests—a good example is his work on Louis Armstrong's "Steak Face." Catlett died of a heart attack backstage at a concert, at forty-one.

Many drummers distinguished themselves before and during the war. Dave Tough, a leader of the Austin High Gang, is widely considered the first white drummer to master African American percussion. The swing bands he worked with include those of Goodman (he replaced Krupa), Tommy Dorsey, and Woody Herman, with whom he tailored discrete accompaniments for each soloist. Jimmy Crawford was a crucial member of the Jimmie Lunceford band, perfecting a relaxed two-beat feeling while framing the ensemble's every phrase with scrupulous punctuations. Crawford later became a favorite of singers, including Billie Holiday, Frank Sinatra, and Ella Fitzgerald. Buddy Rich was regarded by other drummers as the instrument's foremost virtuoso for his unrivaled adroitness and speed. His show business career began in vaudeville before his second birthday; within a few years, he was touring theaters as "Traps, the Drum Wonder." After working with several important bands in the 1930s, Rich made his name with Tommy Dorsey's orchestra. He later played with Benny Carter and Basie before forming his own successful bands, large and small.

For Swing Era audiences, the music of the big bands seemed like a preview of paradise. It defined and unified American culture as no other style of music ever had or would—in contrast, even the 1960s era of the Beatles, which evoked the optimism and broad reach of swing, exposed a "generation gap." Swing was innovated by men and women in their thirties, and if their initial audiences were young, their music almost immediately suspended all gaps. Swing was bigger than jazz. Country music performers like Bob Wills organized Western swing bands; comic personalities like Kay Kyser fronted novelty swing bands. Some liked it hot, others sweet; some liked it highbrow, others lowdown.

No matter how it was played, swing was an improbably luxurious music, chiefly the work of big bands with at least a dozen musicians plus singers, crisscrossing the country to play in ballrooms, up close to their fans, several sets each evening. Of course, it couldn't last. The irony of swing is that it flourished during the Depression, when luxury was in short supply except in popular culture; this was also the era of cinematic spectaculars like *Gone with the Wind* and *The Wizard of Oz*, of Fred Astaire / Ginger Rogers musicals and Cary Grant / Irene Dunne comedies, when actors played characters who wore tuxedos and gowns and hobnobbed with the very rich in laughably glamorous settings.

That fantasy crashed in the aftermath of the war, when the recovering economy was offset by the abruptly disclosed barbarism of the death camps, a new fear of nuclear devastation, and the reentry into civilian life of thousands of troops, attempting to pick up where they had left off. The music that dominated the next decade of American life emanated directly from swing bands—not from its stars, but rather from its mavericks, musicians considered tangential to or insignificant in the world of swing. They would lay the groundwork for rhythm and blues, salsa, star vocalists, and a way of playing jazz that was more intellectual and demanding than its predecessors. True to form, the mainstream press tagged it with a silly onomatopoetic name that it could never discard: bebop.

11 CHAPTER

Modern Jazz: Bebop

BEBOP AND JAM SESSIONS

In the mid-1940s, jazz stood at a crossroads, along with the country. The war transformed the economy, speeded the pace of life, and spurred the demand for civil rights. Segregated black troops who fought to liberate foreign lands from tyranny were determined to liberate themselves from a second-class citizenship. Many young musicians, black and white, found a bond and a social message in the jazz represented by the incendiary brilliance of a new generation of musicians who had apprenticed in the big bands but developed contrary ideas

◄ While Kenny Clarke devised his new techniques as a swing drummer in the 1930s, he came alive in after-hours jam sessions. As a member of the house band at Minton's Playhouse, he was central to the birth of modern jazz.

of their own. Those ideas reflected the changing times in ways that went beyond race. The relief and triumph that attended the Allied victory led almost instantly to disillusionment and paranoia, as the fear of nuclear devastation and Communist infiltration and demands for equality generated social discord. Television responded with a homogenized view of American life, emphasizing middle-class satisfactions. Jazz, contrarily, no longer served as an optimistic booster. If it now alienated much of the audience that had rallied around swing, it attracted younger fans who admired its irreverence and subtlety—fans often characterized as beatniks, hedonists, and intellectuals.

The swing jazz that had risen from its New Orleans origins to become an extroverted popular music, inseparable from mainstream American culture, turned a sharp corner with the sounds known as bebop, or bop. Jazz was suddenly an isolated music, appearing in tiny cramped nightclubs rather than brightly lit dance halls. Its music—small-combo tunes with peculiar names such as "Salt Peanuts" and "Ornithology"—was complex, dense, and difficult to grasp. It traded in a mass audience for a jazz cult that revered musicians known by terse, elliptical names, real or bestowed: Bird (Charlie Parker), Diz (Dizzy Gillespie), Klook (Kenny Clarke), Monk (Thelonious Monk), Bud (Bud Powell), Dex (Dexter Gordon). Like swing, bebop was still a music that prized virtuosity; if anything, its standards were higher. But most people saw it as an outsider's music, especially after it developed fault lines associated with drug abuse and racial hostility.

Jazz historians, taking a cue from musicians and fans, initially described bebop as a revolution, emphatically breaking with the past. In 1949, the incalculably influential alto saxophonist Charlie Parker insisted that bebop was a new music, something "entirely separate and apart" from the jazz that had preceded it. This view suggests the existence of powerful cultural forces that pushed musicians out of conventional career paths into an unknown, risk-filled style. Historians today, however, tend to treat bebop as an evolution from swing, placing it firmly in the center of the jazz tradition while acknowledging that its status was altered to that of self-conscious art music. The evolutionary view links bop to a particular backstage phenomenon of the Swing Era: the jam session.

The swing musician's day began in the evening, as people drifted toward theaters and ballrooms for their after-work entertainment. By the time those audiences went home to bed, musicians in large cities, especially

Manhattan, were gearing up for more work. "The average musician hated to go home in those days," remembered Sonny Greer, Duke Ellington's drummer. "He was always seeking some place where someone was playing something he ought to hear." The jam session offered relaxation at the end of a hard day. Free of the constraints of the bandstand, musicians could come and go as they pleased. A version of "I Got Rhythm" could stretch out for half an hour. But jam sessions were also an extension of the work-place. Cutting contests—pitting trombonists, drummers, or saxophonists against each other—offered significant competition; if you lost and were any good at all, your defeat was merely another stage in your jazz educa-tion. "Everybody would get up there and take [their] shots," one musi-cian remembered. "Some of them we could handle and some of them we couldn't. But every time you do that you're sharpening your knife, see."

To keep people from wandering in who didn't belong, jam sessions offered a series of musical obstacles. The simplest way to make an inex-perienced interloper feel unwelcome was to count off a tune at a ridicu-lously fast tempo or play it in an unfamiliar key. Sometimes tunes would modulate up a half step with every chorus, challenging everyone's ability to transpose. Favorite tunes like "I Got Rhythm" would be recast with blisteringly difficult harmonic substitutions. Those who could take the heat were welcome; those who couldn't went home to practice. In this way, the musicians who would become the bebop generation had their musi-cal skills continually tested. The more ambitious of them embraced this atmosphere, relishing the advanced harmonies and daunting tempos that generally made their peers and even their mentors feel slightly uncomfort-able. When Ben Webster first heard Parker play, he asked, "Man, is that cat crazy?" and reportedly grabbed the horn away, exclaiming, "That horn ain't supposed to sound that fast."

Charlie Parker and other young Turks could be heard regularly at Minton's Playhouse, on 118th Street in Harlem, which hosted some of the most celebrated jam sessions in Manhattan. Many of the innovations that took place there reflected its professional clientele's hunger for musi-cal challenge. Consider, for example, how bebop changed drumming. As Kenny Clarke once explained it, his technical breakthrough came when he was playing for a swing band led by Teddy Hill in the late 1930s. During an exceptionally fast arrangement of "Ol' Man River," he found it nearly impossible to keep time in the usual fashion by striking his bass drum for each beat. Suddenly it occurred to him to shift the pulse to the ride cymbal. This innovation gave him two new tactics: a shimmering cymbal that became the lighter, more flexible foundation for all of modern jazz, and the powerful bass drum, now available to fill in the holes in the band's arrangements with its thunderous booms.

Clarke's style was not popular with musicians who had become used to the heavy swing beat. "He breaks up the time too much," one musician complained. Reluctantly, Hill let Clarke go in 1940. But in an ironic twist, when Hill's own band collapsed shortly thereafter, his next employer was Minton's owner, who was looking for someone to stimulate the sessions at his new Playhouse. Realizing that the drum techniques that had irritated and bewildered musicians in a dance hall might delight them in a jam session, Hill brought Clarke into the Minton's Playhouse rhythm section, where he soon earned the nickname "Klook" because his combined snare drum and bass drum hits evoked a "klook-mop" sound. Given the startup of the war and especially the recently endured Battle of Britain, Clarke's style of unexpected bass drum explosions was referred to as "dropping bombs." Young, hip musicians fell in love with Clarke's simmering poly-rhythms. Drummers like Max Roach and Art Blakey found in his playing the methods they needed for a more modern style.

Over this new accompaniment, the rhythms played by soloists (inspired by Lester Young's and Charlie Christian's fluid, discontinuous approach) were disorienting and unpredictable. Listeners were startled by the spurts of fast notes, ending abruptly with a two-note gesture that inspired the scat syllables "be-bop" or "re-bop." Older musicians were not amused. While jamming at Minton's, Fats Waller supposedly yelled out, "Stop that crazy boppin' and a-stoppin' and play that jive like the rest of us guys!"

Pianists who came of age with the stripped-down playing of Count Basie dropped stride patterns in favor of comping—the rhythmically unpredict-able skein of accompanying chords that complemented the drummer's strokes and added yet another layer to the rhythmic mix. The acoustic gui-tar's insistent chording that once thickened the sound of a swing rhythm section was superfluous in the context of bebop's ride cymbal and walk-ing-bass line. Guitarists either steered clear of bebop or, following Charlie Christian's lead, switched to electric amplification, which allowed them to take a more active, syncopated role in the rhythm section or step into the limelight as soloist.

The bassists' role didn't change—they remained timekeepers at the bot-tom of the texture—yet thanks to the jam session, as well as the instantly influential Jimmy Blanton, who had begun to undergird the Ellington band in the years directly preceding Minton's, a new generation of bass players raised the level of virtuosity. One of the most impressive musicians to expand on Blanton's innovations was Oscar Pettiford, a young black musician of Choctaw and Cherokee ancestry who handled the bass with rhythmic assurance and athletic swiftness. In jam sessions, even the bassists were prodded into taking solos—a challenge that Pettiford embraced with glee. On a 1943 Coleman Hawkins recording of "The Man I Love," Pettiford plays a wonderfully melodic solo made intensely rhythmic by his gasps of breath between each phrase.

"Nobody Plays Those Changes"

Bebop was famous—and sometimes reviled—for its complex, dissonant harmonies. To be sure, these sounds had been part of the jazz vocabulary for years. Art Tatum turned popular songs into harmonic minefields through the complexity of his chord substitutions, leaving other musicians—including a nineteen-year-old Charlie Parker, who worked as a dishwasher in a restaurant that featured Tatum—to shake their heads in wonder. Arrangers listened closely to Duke Ellington's instrumentation, trying to decipher how he voiced his astringent chords. Improvisers took their cue from Coleman Hawkins, who showed in "Body and Soul" how to use dense chromatic harmonies in popular song.

The challenge for the bebop generation came in translating these dissonant harmonies into a vocabulary all musicians could share. Soloists and members of the rhythm section had to learn to coordinate. This could be done deliberately, as when Dizzy Gillespie and bassist Milt Hinton got together on the roof of the Cotton Club and planned substitute harmonies for that evening's jam sessions. At other times, harmony was emboldened by the shock of discovery. When Charlie Parker first heard pianist Tadd Dameron's unusual chord voicings, he was so pleased he kissed him on the cheek. "That's what I've been hearing all my life," he said, "but nobody plays those changes."

The new harmonies fastened onto dissonances like the tritone—the chromatic interval known to the Middle Ages as the "devil in music" and to the beboppers as the flatted fifth. (The unimpressed Eddie Condon, a rebel turned traditionalist, commented, "The boppers flat their fifths. We drink ours.") The tritone could be found in the chords used by pianists like Dameron and in the spiky solos musicians like Gillespie devised in response to them. Other extended notes (sixths, flat ninths) were added to the palette, making the job of harmonic improvisation that much more difficult. Keeping track of such harmonic nuances was a demanding task, turning a physical, emotional music into the realm of the intellectual. "With bop, you had to *know*," trumpet player Howard McGhee stated firmly. "Not feel; you had to *know* what you were doing."

At the same time, nonmusical forces—racial and economic—were driving musicians out of swing into the unknown future, and these forces formed the basis for the notion that bop was revolutionary. During the Swing Era, black bands were barred from two kinds of jobs. The first was a sponsored prime-time radio show (such as *The Camel Cavalcade*, subsidized by Camel cigarettes). The second was a lengthy engagement at a major hotel ballroom or dance hall in New York City. These jobs offered free late-night broadcasts, invaluable for publicity, as well as a chance to rest from the rigors of travel. For several months of the year, the musicians in top white bands could unpack their bags, rehearse new tunes, and live with their families.

The top black bands were obliged to stay on the road. A few, like Ellington's and Calloway's, could afford the comforts of a private railroad car, but the rest toured the country in rattletrap buses. Continuous travel was enough to exhaust even the hardiest musicians, especially when it took them into the heart of the Jim Crow South. As highly visible African American celebrities headquartered in New York, jazz musicians aroused the ire of white Southerners, from the man on the street to uniformed police. Musicians from the Deep South understood this, but their Northern colleagues had to learn the hard way how to stay out of trouble. They had to eat at "colored" restaurants, sit in the Jim Crow car of a railroad, and avoid eye contact with white women—or risk violence. Milt Hinton, touring with Calloway, shot photographs of musicians pissing on whites-only signs or shaking their heads in disbelief. Few musicians were actually harmed, but the specter of public lynching (still active in some states: at least twenty lynchings have been documented between 1940 and 1945) made it clear how far things could go.

Under these circumstances, musicians became bitter—especially younger ones, impatient with the hypocrisy that protected racist conventions while allowing the country to boast of its crusade against totalitarian bigotry and injustice. The most talented quit the swing bands, sometimes out of exhaustion, sometimes disgust. Increasingly, they turned toward the jam sessions, hoping to find some way to carry on their music outside the system. Bebop absorbed their energy: it was subversive, "uppity," daring, and hell-bent on social change. "There was a message to our music," proclaimed Kenny Clarke. "Whatever you go into, go into it *intelligently*. . . . The idea was to wake up, look around you, there's something to do." By the early 1940s, a new approach to jazz, based on progressive chromatic harmonies and supported by an interactive rhythm section, was in place. The final piece in the puzzle was a new kind of virtuoso soloist, taking standards of improvisational excellence to unforeseen levels.

Bird (1920–1955) AND Diz (1917–1993)

One of the most gifted instrumentalists in musical history, Charlie Parker earned an imperishable nickname early in his apprenticeship, while touring with a Kansas City–based territory band led by the pianist Jay McShann (a boogie-woogie specialist). On a short trip, for which the band traveled in a small caravan of cars, Parker's ride ran over a chicken. He yelled at the driver to stop and, to everyone's amusement, rushed to the dying bird and carried it back to the car. When the band arrived that night at a boarding house, he proudly presented the freshly killed chicken as the main ingredient for his meal. His bandmates teasingly called him Yardbird, but as the name got shortened over time to Bird, the joking aspect disappeared, to be replaced by an unmistakable reverence. Within five years, young musicians would no longer take the name Bird in vain. It signified melodious beauty, mastery of the air, and quickness of flight.

Parker, who was born in Kansas and grew up in Missouri's Kansas City, didn't seem at first to have any special gift for music. He played baritone horn in his high school marching band, pecking out notes in the accompaniment. Eventually, he picked up the alto saxophone, teaching himself to play by ear standard jazz fare like Fats Waller's "Honeysuckle Rose." When he tried to sit in on jam sessions, though, he met only humiliation. According to a well-traveled legend, after he sat in on "Body and Soul" and flailed around in the wrong key, the drummer Jo Jones gonged him out by tossing his ride cymbal on the floor. "Bird couldn't play much in those days," recalled one musician, "and he was mad about it, too." That kind of experience spurred him into a furious regimen of practicing. During one summer in the Ozarks, he learned how to play fluently in *every* key—an uncommon achievement even for established players.

He listened to famous alto saxophonists of the day, from the luscious Johnny Hodges to the flashy Jimmy Dorsey to the forward-thinking and little-recorded local hero Buster Smith, a gifted blues player who gave him pointers and influenced his timbre. Yet Parker paid most attention to tenor saxophonists; he played his favorite records by Chu Berry, Coleman Hawkins, and Lester Young repeatedly—he memorized Young's 1936 solo on "Oh! Lady Be Good." (Parker's own improvisation on that song, recorded exactly ten years later at a Jazz at the Philharmonic jam session involving Young, became one of *his* most imitated solos, and remains a textbook example of how to transform a pop tune with deep blues feeling.) By the time he returned to Kansas City in late 1937, his rhythm had become supercharged: one musician conveyed the impression of Parker's attack by playing a Young record twice as fast.

He was consumed with music. Musicians and friends remembered him spending hours in movie theaters, studying the scores, and rifling through sheet music shops, memorizing the changes. Now an expert soloist, Parker quickly earned a position in the McShann orchestra, a top band in Kansas City after Count Basie left for the big time. But he also began using alcohol and pills; a car accident that killed one of his best friends and seriously injured Parker required a long recovery for which he was prescribed morphine. Still in his teens, he soon found his way to heroin, a substance that eventually controlled much of his life.

Parker's playing struck people at first as modern, but still classically blues-driven. For his solo on McShann's "Hootie Blues" (1941), he upgraded the twelve-bar blues with new chromatic chord progressions and enlivened it with rapid flurries of notes. He also proved that he could be a model citizen in a swing band, blending beautifully in the saxophone section and devising endlessly varied riffs behind soloists during head arrangements. His heroin addiction forced a break with McShann, but not before the band played the Savoy Ballroom in New York, giving Parker a different view of life and inciting his ambition. Members of the jazz elite began talking about him—both his phenomenal playing and his dependency on drugs. Some had seen him rise from a stupor, practically nodding out on the bandstand, to play a magnificent solo. But McShann and other bandleaders found it too taxing to keep him. Instead, Parker settled into a precarious New York existence where narcotics were available and jam sessions offered a place to musically stretch out. He became a magnet for a network of musicians similarly attuned to what he once called the "real advanced New York style."

The musician most attuned to Parker's achievement, and the intellectual force behind the music that would be called bebop, was an extravagantly talented trumpet player, John Birks "Dizzy" Gillespie. His astounding solos, crackling in the upper register and accelerating to speeds not thought possible, matched Parker's note for note, but seemed to many listeners even more dramatic—especially when ripping into the trumpet's upper register. The excitement he generated combined with a razor-sharp wit, organizational savvy, and steady hand brought him a larger audience than Parker, and a renowned and graceful career that lasted more than fifty years. If Parker was bebop's inspiration, the Pied Piper of modern jazz, Gillespie pulled the style into shape like a master craftsman. But if Gillespie was the showman who knew how to sell the new music to skeptics, Parker accrued the saintly aura of a martyr whose every solo demanded preservation and analysis, whose improvisations suggested an emotional density that best captured the agitated temper of the times.

Like Parker, Gillespie came to New York from the provinces. He grew up in Cheraw, South Carolina, where his father labored as a bricklayer. Gillespie taught himself trumpet so unconventionally that he damaged his neck muscles, causing his cheeks to protrude, frog-like, when he played. (Doctors have now named this condition "Gillespie pouches.") He earned a scholarship to the Laurinburg Institute, across the border in North Carolina, where he studied trumpet and piano. After hearing broadcasts of great jazz players, especially Roy Eldridge, whom he later called "the messiah of our generation," he headed north—first to Philadelphia, joining local bands, and later to New York. By the time he was eighteen, his brash solos, excellent sight-reading, and growing ability to compose and arrange had made him a valuable addition to Swing Era orchestras.

By 1939, Gillespie had reached the inner circle. For the next several years, he was employed by the Cab Calloway Orchestra, perhaps the most lucrative black band in existence—in any case, the only one vying with Ellington for the prime spot. He thrived in this atmosphere, flying high in the trumpet section and creating such tunes as "Pickin' the Cabbage," a 1940 Calloway recording that combines a hip harmonic bite with a Latin groove. Still, he couldn't help feeling dissatisfaction with the status quo: "I worked hard while I played with Cab, and practiced constantly. I could seldom get much encouragement from the guys in Cab's band. Mostly they talked about real estate or something, never talked about music. That atmosphere kept me acting wiggy and getting into a lot of mischief."

Gillespie had earned his nickname back in Philadelphia for his fiery temperament and wicked sense of humor. He brought this unpredictable behavior onto the Calloway bandstand, devising practical jokes and irritating the bandleader with his wildly experimental solos. One night in 1941, a spitball flew directly into Calloway's spotlight. Gillespie was innocent of the crime (a fellow musician had thrown it), but it was the kind of thing Dizzy did and Calloway assumed he was the culprit. After a brief backstage confrontation erupted into violence, Gillespie was fired—a stroke of fortune in that it spurred him into action. He now worked as a freelance musician and composer (Woody Herman bought and recorded one of his early pieces), earning a living through whatever means possible, including the jam-session performances that led to the establishment of bebop—a phenomenon that ultimately caused Calloway and his musicians more grief than all the spitballs in creation.

Gillespie became the nerve center for the new music. In Miles Davis's words, he was bebop's "head and hands," the "one who kept it all together." His apartment on 7th Avenue in Harlem was a gathering place for adventurous musicians eager to share information. Gillespie was quick to grasp the music's novelties and was generous enough to spread them as far as possible. In jam sessions, he showed pianists how to play the appropriate chords, and sat on the drum stool to demonstrate to drummers the more flexible, interactive style. He absorbed the creativity of others as well, noting chords created by Mary Lou Williams or Thelonious Monk and working them into new tunes and arrangements as well as his solos. Thanks to his piano skills, Gillespie was fully aware of the harmonic possibilities of bebop. He loved the edge that dissonant chords gave his melodies, among them "Salt Peanuts," a bracingly fast reworking of "I Got Rhythm": its title was sung to a riff based on a bebop drum lick (the quick alternation of snare and bass drum). "Salt Peanuts" introduced a humorous side to the new music, with verbal inanity covering the avant-garde complexity. "A Night in Tunisia" offered a more exotic groove. Completed in 1942 as the Allied troops invaded North Africa, "Tunisia" adapted modern chord changes to a Latin bass line, deepening Gillespie's fascination with Caribbean music—he even became a respectable conga player.

On 52nd Street

Gillespie and Parker first crossed paths in the early 1940s. Parker reveled in Gillespie's radiant sound and his deep knowledge of harmony. Gillespie focused on the fluidity of Parker's phrases: "Charlie Parker brought the

Ma Rainey, the "Mother of the Blues," in 1924, with blues musician "Georgia Tom," also known as Thomas Dorsey. By 1932, Dorsey had composed "Precious Lord" and turned his back on secular music, becoming the father of gospel music.

James P. Johnson, the most influential of the pioneering stride pianists and a Broadway composer whose songs include the 1920s anthem "Charleston," at a 1930s jam session.

Bix Beiderbecke, seen here in 1923, was the first major white jazz star and the first to acquire a mythological aura after his early death.

Mary Lou Williams, "the lady who swings the band," was the chief arranger and pianist for Andy Kirk's Clouds of Joy. Cleveland, 1937.

The quartet led by Benny Goodman brought racial integration to the public and invaluable opportunities to its members. Within a few years, each musician—pianist Teddy Wilson, vibraphonist Lionel Hampton, and drummer Gene Krupa—had become a bandleader. New York's Paramount Theater, 1937.

Duke Ellington used his wiles to convince his musicians to do exactly what he wanted, but he treated Billy Strayhorn (right), a brilliant composer who was an essential figure in the post-1930s Ellington band, with unwavering friendship and respect. This picture dates from 1960, when they were in Paris to score the film *Paris Blues*.

Coleman Hawkins, nicknamed Bean (as in "He's got a lot on the bean"), performed with characteristic passion at the second annual Newport Jazz Festival, 1955.

Lester Young, nicknamed Pres (as in president of all saxophonists) by Billie Holiday, epitomized cool in his music, his lingo, and even the angle at which he held the tenor saxophone. A New York club, 1948.

Banjoist Elmer Snowden, the original leader of what became the Duke Ellington band, stands beside two incomparable pianists in a Greenwich Village nightclub, 1942: Art Tatum (right), who claimed Fats Waller as his primary influence, and Waller (center), who introduced Tatum to a nightclub audience by saying, "I play piano, but God is in the house tonight!"

Dizzy Gillespie once called Charlie Parker "the other half of my heartbeat." They posed playfully for the camera at the peak of bop, in 1949.

Charles Mingus wrote grand tone poems, suites, jazz standards, parodies, and threnodies while leading his cutting-edge Jazz Workshop and maintaining his stature as one of the greatest bass players of all time. From the 1960s.

Arranger Gil Evans and Miles Davis take a break during the momentous Columbia Records sessions that produced *Porgy and Bess*, 1958.

Bill Evans (center) created an ideal trio with bassist Scott LaFaro (left) and drummer Paul Motian, pictured here in 1961 at the Village Vanguard, where they made their most memorable recordings.

John Coltrane forged an expressionistic way of improvising that helped to instigate the avant-garde movement and led a classic quartet in the 1960s.

Ornette Coleman generated controversy with just about everything he did in the late 1950s, not least playing a white plastic alto saxophone that underscored his raw timbre.

Stan Getz was a major jazz star known for his gorgeous timbre long before he discovered the bossa nova. Here he performs with bassist Ray Brown in Paris, 1960.

Cecil Taylor was a controversial newcomer at the Newport Jazz Festival, 1957.

Composer Bill Russo (arm raised) rehearses his Choir Ensemble with such notables as cellist-educator David Baker (third from left), Ornette Coleman (center, seated), and pianist Steve Kuhn (fourth from left) at the Lenox School, 1959.

Anthony Braxton wrote music for every conceivable ensemble and played every conceivable saxophone, including the giant contrabass. At the Kitchen, New York, 1977.

rhythm," he said. "The *way* he played those notes." The two worked side by side in 1942, when Earl Hines hired them for his big band (with Parker switching to tenor saxophone). None of Hines's recordings feature them, but a private recording in a hotel room captured their skills offstage. Two years later, they again joined forces when Hines's vocalist, Billy Eckstine, started his own band. With Gillespie serving as music director, Eckstine's was the first big band to fully embrace bop, recruiting young players who would become major jazz stars (among them Sarah Vaughan, Gene Ammons, Art Blakey, Dexter Gordon, Sonny Stitt, Fats Navarro, and Kenny Dorham) and astonishing audiences everywhere it played—including a concert in St. Louis, where a teenage Miles Davis sat in, becoming a member of the band when it traveled to Chicago.

Tunes like "Salt Peanuts" and "A Night in Tunisia," with their tricky interludes, elaborate breaks, and sudden shifts in texture, now seem naturally adaptable to the big-band environment. Yet the new music remained unnerving to many, including record company executives who would only record Eckstine as a blues singer and romantic ballad crooner, keeping the musicians in the background. The nascent style of modern jazz never found its way to a mass audience, and by the end of 1944 Dizzy and Bird had quit the Eckstine band, turning instead to small groups as the best way to present their music. With the draft depleting the ranks of big bands and a cabaret tax inclining venues to put tables and chairs where once there were dance floors, the advent of small bands was inevitable. But the kind of group Parker and Gillespie had in mind was nothing like the winnowed ensembles that the big bands had offered for contrast. It would have to embody the daring and impetuousness of a jam session, but rehearsed and charged—it would have to pin your ears back.

By the time Gillespie brought a quintet to 52nd Street, the emergent style was known as bebop (less frequently as rebop), though serious types preferred Modern Jazz. In tightening up the flamboyant go-for-broke music heard at Minton's, it added a new and decisively challenging wrinkle: at the beginning of a tune, where one might expect to hear a familiar harmonized melody, the horns played a bare, sinuous theme in disjointed rhythms, confusing those not already familiar with the Harlem jam sessions and offering no clue of what was to come. In this way, the jam-session style, already shielded from the public, became a way of transmuting blues and standards into a new repertory. The white swing drummer Dave Tough, who heard the 1944 band, remembered its uncanny impact: "As we walked in, see, these cats snatched up their horns and blew crazy stuff. One would stop all of a sudden and another would start for no reason at all. We never could tell when a solo was supposed to begin or end. Then they all quit at once and walked off the stand. It scared us."

If they had listened closely to tunes with such watch-your-step titles as "Ornithology," "Anthropology," "Bebop," "Groovin' High," and "Now's the Time," they would have recognized familiar structures and harmonic progressions. But they weren't supposed to recognize them; these tunes were contrived to announce a brave new world. They were also designed to play hide and seek with the copyright laws. In the United States, the melody of a tune can be protected, but not its chord progression, encouraging jazz musicians to create "original" tunes by superimposing a new melody over the changes of a copyrighted pop song. Tunes like "I Got Rhythm," "How High the Moon," "Honeysuckle Rose," and "Indiana" were frequently recast as harmonic grids for bop originals, relieving the record companies of the irritating obligation to pay royalties and leveling the playing field for musicians whose improvisations were not covered by copyright.

BIRD ON RECORD

The first true bebop records date from early 1945, a chaotic period just before the end of the war that saw the emergence of small, independent record labels—Savoy, Apollo, Dial—with a view toward a low-cost way of entering the business: no arrangements, occasional vocals, plenty of blues, but mostly just let the musicians do their thing. The delay in getting bop recorded was largely caused by two recording bans that lasted almost three years, instituted by the despotic boss of the musicians' union, James Petrillo (his name shows up in a few songs, notably Dinah Washington's "Record Ban Blues"). As a result, most people had never heard of bop and certainly didn't have the chance to follow its development during those crucial three years. In 1942, they were listening to Ellington or Crosby or Tommy Dorsey (who had the hottest new singer around, Frank Sinatra); three years later, they got the Dizzy Gillespie Sextet (with Parker) playing the supersonic "Dizzy Atmosphere" and the teasing "Groovin' High," based on the chords of "Whispering," an old Paul Whiteman hit (not that anyone but insiders could figure that out), and Sarah Vaughan (backed by Dizzy and Bird) singing the sensous "What More Can a Woman Do?" But the real shock came with Parker's first session under his own name, recorded late in 1945 and released early the following year.

"KO KO"

"Cherokee," written by the British bandleader Ray Noble in 1938 and turned into a popular hit the following year by Charlie Barnet, was an alleged tribute to Native Americans, with lyrics to match ("Sweet Indian maiden / Since I first met you / I can't forget you / Cherokee sweetheart"). Musicians were intrigued by its sixty-four-bar form, twice the length of the standard AABA. Soloists shied away from the bridge, though, which jumped precipitously to a distant key and wound its way back home through continuous modulation. When Count Basie recorded this tune in 1939 (on two sides of a 78-rpm disc), the bridge appeared only during the head. The rest of the time, the soloists stayed with the simpler harmonies of the A section.

Parker practiced this tune assiduously as a kid in Kansas City and later in New York, reveling in its difficult harmonic progression. He once recalled that it was while working through its changes with a New York guitarist named Biddy Fleet that he had the epiphany that changed his music—the realization that any note, no matter how dissonant, could be made to resolve in a chord. The song soon became his favorite showpiece. To accommodate him, McShann's band concocted a loose head arrangement. When they finally made it to the Savoy Ballroom, Parker celebrated his New York debut by letting loose a "Cherokee" solo that seemed never to end, with the band spontaneously supplying riffs behind him. Like many others who heard that performance via radio, the trumpet player Howard McGhee was struck dumb with amazement: "I had never heard anything like that in my *life*," he remembered. "Here's a guy who's playing every-thing that he wants to play . . . and *playing* it, you know. I never heard nobody play a horn like that—that *complete*."

"Cherokee" was transformed into "Ko Ko" in 1945, when Parker brought a new quintet to the studio of Savoy Records. Originally a radio-parts store in Newark, New Jersey, Savoy expanded into a recording opera-tion despite the relentless miserliness of its owner, Herman Lubinsky. Like other small record company owners, Lubinsky tried to avoid copyrighted tunes. So it's no surprise that on the first take, after Parker and Gillespie follow an abstract introduction with the melody to "Cherokee," someone shouts, "Hold it!" This was probably Parker, who, royalties aside, must have realized that a full chorus of the melody would limit his solo time. In any case, a subsequent take left the "Cherokee" melody out altogether. The name "Ko Ko" may have been borrowed unconsciously from the 1940 Ellington recording of the same name. "Naming-day at Savoy," one critic has said, "must have been an exhilarating, if random experience."

The recording session was comically misassembled. Bud Powell was supposed to be the pianist, but in his absence Argonne Thornton (later known as Sadik Hakim) was hastily recruited. Gillespie, who showed up primarily for moral support, substituted on piano on some tunes. Miles Davis, a new member (at nineteen) of Parker's band, played trumpet on most of the session, but was not up the blazing eight-bar exchanges at the beginning and end of "Ko Ko," so Gillespie took up the trumpet for those elaborate passages. Gillespie sounds like the pianist on the released (master) take; but Thornton must be the pianist on the false start, when Gillespie is clearly on trumpet. Somehow, out of this chaos came a bellwether jazz masterpiece—bop's equivalent of Louis Armstrong's "West End Blues." Parker's two white-hot choruses (only on repeated listening does it become evident that, for all his speed and seeming volatility, Parker plays melodies and riffs), preceded by the boldly disorienting introduction and followed by a lightning-fast Max Roach drum solo, was a music so startlingly different that it demanded a new name: *bebop*, at once an insider's term and a trivialization of the music, stuck to it like crazy glue.

KO KO

Charlie Parker's Re-Boppers
Charlie Parker, alto saxophone; Dizzy Gillespie, trumpet; Curley Russell, bass; Argonne "Dense" Thornton, piano; Max Roach, drums

LABEL: Take 1 (fragment)—Savoy MG-12079; master take—Savoy 597; *Savoy and Dial Master Takes* (Savoy 17149)
DATE: 1945
STYLE: bebop
FORM: 64-bar popular song (**AABA**; each section lasts 16 bars)

Take 1 (fragment)

Introduction
....
0:00   In an elusive introduction, Gillespie and Parker play a single composed
              line in bare octaves. There is no harmonic accompaniment; the only

rhythmic backdrop is the snare drum, played lightly by Roach with brushes.

0:05	The phrase ends suddenly with an octave drop, reinforced by sharp accents on the drums.
0:06	Gillespie plays a trumpet solo that implies a harmonic background through skillful improvisation. Many of the notes are ghosted—played so quietly that they are suggested rather than stated.
0:12	Parker enters, overlapping slightly with the trumpet. His improvised line is fluid, with a brief interruption by silence at 0:13. The drums add cross-rhythms.
0:18	A loud "thump" on the bass drum pulls the two instruments back together. The composed line is now harmonized.
0:21	Gillespie plays a high note, followed immediately by a note an octave lower from Parker. Roach responds with a "thump."
0:22	The two instruments play briefly without any accompaniment. During the brief silence, Roach exchanges his brushes for drum sticks.

Chorus 1

0:24	A	The two horns begin playing the melody to "Cherokee," with Parker adding a harmonized line. The piano comps in the background.
0:29		As the melody nears the end of a phrase, Parker improvises a rapid bebop-style countermelody.
0:33		Someone—probably Parker, who has stopped playing—shouts, "Hey, hey! Hold it!" and whistles and claps his hands loudly. The tape suddenly ends.

Master take

Introduction

0:00	The opening is identical to the previous take: the two horns enter with a precomposed melody in octaves.
0:06	Gillespie's solo is nearly identical to the previous take, suggesting that he had carefully prepared his line.
0:12	Parker's solo is strikingly different, underscoring the unpredictability of his improvisations.

Chorus 1 (abbreviated)

0:25	A	Parker begins improvising in a steady stream to the chord progression to "Cherokee." Roach marks time through a shadowy halo on the ride cymbal. The bass is walking, and the piano comps.
0:27		Parker's line ends with a sudden dissonant pair of notes—a rhythm that was undoubtedly one source for the term "be-bop."
0:28		On the downbeat, Roach plays an unexpected accent on his bass drum—the first of many examples of dropping bombs.
0:35		Parker's improvisation is a continuous string of fast notes. The rhythms are disorienting, not simply because the tempo is extraordinarily fast,

but because the accents are constantly shifting: sometimes on the beat, sometimes off.

0:37 **A** Parker's line continues through this **A** section, in a phrase that recalls the opening of the solo. The drummer's improvisation is more intense and interactive.

0:44 After the first few notes of this phrase, an entire string of notes is ghosted until Parker suddenly returns to playing in full volume.

0:50 **B** The bridge to "Cherokee" begins with a sudden shift away from the home key to more distant harmonies. Parker marks it by a relatively simple melodic phrase that ends with piercing, bluesy notes.

0:57 As the bridge begins to modulate back to the original key, Parker plays a long, involved phrase that continues through the beginning of the next **A** section.

1:03 **A**

1:05 Two sharp drum accents signal the start of another Parker phrase.

1:13 Parker prepares for his next chorus by resting on a single note, echoed by the piano and accents from the bass drum.

Chorus 2

1:16 **A** Parker suddenly demonstrates his encyclopedic knowledge of jazz's history by quoting the famous piccolo obbligato from the New Orleans march "High Society."

1:29 **A**

1:41 **B** The piano marks the harmonic progression through simple chords. Parker disorients the listener with a series of phrases, alternately accenting the strong and weak beats of the measure.

1:48 As the harmony continues to move toward the tonic, Parker accelerates into particularly fast passages.

1:54 **A** A line that started toward the end of the bridge continues through the beginning of this **A** section, ending on the disruptive two-note "be-bop" rhythm.

2:01 Parker's improvised line is interrupted by a squeak from his notoriously unreliable reed.

2:04 The two-chorus solo ends with a bluesy gesture.

Chorus 3 (abbreviated)

2:07 **A** Roach begins his chorus-long solo with a simple alternating of the bass and snare drums, followed by a lengthy passage on the snare drum.

2:10 He repeats the opening pattern.

2:12 The snare drum pattern continues, occasionally punctuated by accents from the bass drum.

2:18 **A** Roach doesn't articulate the beginning of the second **A** section.

2:21 He plays a pattern of accents on the downbeat of each measure.

2:23 The drum accents turn into a cross-rhythm.

2:28	With a sudden two-note figure (*ch-bop!*), Roach ends his solo.

Coda

2:30	In a repetition of the introduction, Gillespie and Parker play the opening passage.
2:36	Gillespie improvises harmonically, while Roach quietly plays the backbeat behind him.
2:42	Parker fluently improvises on a harmonic progression that circles wildly through many key centers.
2:52	The back-and-forth octave exchange, which had previously served to introduce the first chorus, now returns as the piece's sudden and inconclusive end.

"EMBRACEABLE YOU"

Parker had an extraordinary musical memory. Through brief snippets quoted in his solos (such as the piccolo line from "High Society" in "Ko Ko" or a snippet of Armstrong's "West End Blues" cadenza played during a concert version of the same piece), we can get a sense of how much music he processed and stored. He also loved classical composers, especially Stravinsky, whose early modernist pieces (*Petrushka*, *The Firebird*) deeply impressed him, as well as hundreds of popular songs. His companion of several years, Chan Parker, recalled him walking around the house bellowing Mario Lanza's hit "Be My Love," and referring to "All the Things You Are" as "YATAG," an acronym of his favorite line from the lyric, "you are the angel glow."

"Embraceable You," recorded in 1947, is the best known of his several interpretations of the chord changes to George Gershwin's celebrated ballad; on none of them, however, does he play the actual tune—in fact, he usually gave his recorded interpretations new titles, like "Meandering" and "Quasimodo." Yet here he uses Gershwin's title, sacrificing his potential royalties, perhaps because he knew he had achieved something especially fine and wanted people to know how inventive it was. Instead of beginning with the melody, Parker introduces a two-bar phrase from a relatively obscure song, "A Table in the Corner," composed by Dana Suesse (who in her earlier years had been promoted as "the girl Gershwin") and recorded by Artie Shaw, in 1939. We can't know how he happened to think of it while playing this take—he doesn't use it on the other take recorded at the same session—but he makes this fragment fit into the harmonic progression of "Embraceable You" hand in glove, developing and modulating the phrase as though he had been working on it for years.

The remainder is a dazzling rhythmic swirl. Parker plays with a softness and earnestness that beautifully captures the song's romantic essence. Yet he barely touches down on Gershwin's melody, floating instead on rapid and constantly shifting phrases, playing a stream of thirty-second notes at a paradoxically very slow tempo. As is typical for a bebop recording, Parker's solo comes first, leaving Miles Davis the unenviable job of following him. Davis may have felt like Howard McGhee, who also followed Parker on recordings in the 1940s. "I used to hate to go to work," McGhee remembered, "knowing he would put a heavy whipping on me. And yet I couldn't wait to get there, because I knew what I was going to hear when I got there. And damn, he didn't never let me down."

EMBRACEABLE YOU

Charlie Parker

Charlie Parker, alto saxophone; Miles Davis, trumpet; Duke Jordan, piano; Tommy Potter, bass; Max Roach, drums

LABEL: Dial 1024; *Yardbird Suite: The Ultimate Collection* (Rhino/WEA 72260)
DATE: 1947
STYLE: bebop
FORM: 32-bar popular song (**ABAC**)

Introduction

| 0:00 | Pianist Jordan builds a lovely introduction around a questioning four-note motive. |

Chorus 1

0:13	**A**	Parker quotes the melody to "A Table in a Corner." The accompaniment is simple: a slow walking-bass line, quiet piano chords, and the drums played almost inaudibly with brushes.
0:27		Having taken his quotation as far as it will go over the chord progression to "Embraceable You," Parker moves to bebop-style improvisation.
0:31		Over the next two measures, he plays a phrase that lags slightly behind the beat.
0:41	**B**	The high accented notes in his line derive from the melody to "Embraceable You" ("*Just* one look at *you* brings out the *gyp*-sy in me").
0:51		As Parker focuses his line onto one note, his tone becomes rougher and more intimate.

0:54		His rhythmic feeling begins to fall into double time.
1:00		Shifting suddenly to a more staccato articulation, Parker plays a line that's rhythmically unpredictable.
1:07		The next double-time lick is one of Parker's favorites.
1:10	A	
1:17		Parker plays a lick, then transposes by sequence, starting on a different pitch.
1:26		An impassioned entry results in a blown note.
1:29		The next phrase begins on a high note.
1:33		Parker plays another motive in sequence, moving it higher and higher.
1:38		Over a dominant chord, he raises the tension level by playing bebop dissonances.
1:40	C	After a silence, Parker continues in double time.
1:50		He begins his last phrase with a different rhythmic groove and more staccato articulation. His line emphasizes high notes on the downbeat, falling from there.

Chorus 2 (abbreviated)

2:09	B	Davis begins quietly playing a lyrical line on muted trumpet. His line is restrained and simple, lacking Parker's dramatic rhythmic changes.
2:38		To signal the return to the A section, Roach adds a discreet roll with his brushes.
2:40	A	As Davis continues his solo, Parker plays hushed countermelodies behind him.
3:03		Roach suggests a double-time groove, but Davis declines to follow.
3:10	C	
3:19		Davis's improvisation, which is primarily stepwise (moving to adjacent notes), is interrupted by an octave lick; he repeats the lick a few seconds later.
3:26		The two horns together play the conclusion of "Embraceable You."

Coda

3:34	Underneath the horns' held-out note, the bass continues to walk while Roach plays a final roll.

"NOW'S THE TIME"

Parker once described bebop as the collision of New York's progressive intensity with the Midwestern blues. While some working-class blacks were alienated by bebop's intellectual complexity, he knew they would respond to what he called "red beans and rice music." There were many kinds of blues in the 1940s. As African Americans adjusted to the demands of the industrial North, the blues reflected time and place. In addition to the swing bands, there were the harsh reinventions of Southern blues in Muddy Waters's electrified, Chicago-based take on the Mississippi Delta and in the guitar virtuosity of the Texan T-Bone Walker. Parker added to the mix by melding blues vocal nuances to chromatic harmonies while perfecting a sweepingly fluid sense of rhythm. He showed how the blues could be made modern, and many of the more traditional blues musicians showed they understood this by adopting his harmonies and rhythms.

"Now's the Time" is one of Parker's most direct statements, built on a single riff, repeated and varied throughout the twelve bars. One of his early compositions, it was first recorded at the same 1945 session as "Ko Ko." Four years later, Savoy's proprietors conveniently ignored Parker's authorship and retooled it as "The Huckle-Buck" for a rhythm and blues saxophonist, Paul Williams. "The one was jazz, the other was rock and roll, and we were hungry," explained go-between producer Teddy Reig. "And Lubinsky owned everything anyway." Linked in the public mind with a slow, erotic dance, "The Huckle-Buck" became a huge hit. It was soon covered by musicians ranging from Lucky Millinder to Frank Sinatra to Louis Armstrong. Even rock and roll singer Chubby Checker had a top-ten hit with it in 1961. Parker earned nothing from this—much as Duke Ellington and Mary Lou Williams earned nothing when his "Happy-Go-Lucky Local" was turned into the pop hit "Night Train," and her "What's Your Story, Morning Glory?" was appropriated as "Black Coffee."

This quartet version of "Now's the Time" was made toward the end of Parker's short life, at an inspired 1953 session (one of Parker's finest compositions, "Confirmation," was recorded at the same date). Backing Parker was the elegant pianist Al Haig, who combined the light touch of swing players like Teddy Wilson with the fleet and harmonically dauntless vision of the preeminent bop pianist, Bud Powell. By this point, Parker was recording for one of Norman Granz's class labels (Clef, which later became Verve), and the fidelity is excellent. Rhythm section nuances, dimly audible in 1940s recordings, now take sonic precedence. As a result, we can fully appreciate Max Roach's drumming, particularly his masterly interaction with Parker—a superb example of heightened musical reflexes.

NOW'S THE TIME

Charlie Parker Quartet

Charlie Parker, alto saxophone; Al Haig, piano; Percy Heath, bass; Max Roach, drums

LABEL: Clef EPC208; *Bird's Best Bop* (Verve 731452745224)
DATE: 1953
STYLE: bebop
FORM: 12-bar blues

Introduction

0:00	Haig (piano) plays a four-bar introduction, accompanied by Roach's high-hat cymbal.

Chorus 1 (head)

0:05	Parker plays the opening riff. Roach answers in call and response.
0:10	As the harmony moves to IV, Parker ends his riff with a syncopated accent, doubled by the drums.

Chorus 2 (head)

0:20	In repeating the previous twelve bars, Parker leaves slight room for improvisation (notice the ad lib interpolation at 0:22).

Chorus 3

0:35	Parker begins his five-chorus solo.
0:40	Over the "bluesiest" part of the progression (where the harmony moves to IV), Parker plays slightly behind the beat.
0:46	He plays a rapid lick (identical to the one at 1:08 in "Embraceable You").

Chorus 4

0:49	Beginning of chorus.
0:53	Parker adds to his bluesy sound with a brief stuttering figure.

Chorus 5

1:03	As he warms up, his rhythm imitates the looser, conversational quality of speech.

Chorus 6

1:18	He takes a simple phrase and turns it into a complex polyrhythm.

Chorus 7

1:32	Beginning of chorus.
1:44	Parker's last line signals the end of his solo, but still leaves us hanging.

Chorus 8

1:46   After a brief pause, Haig begins his piano solo.

Chorus 9

2:00   Haig's chorus begins with simple phrases, moves to fast, complicated
            phrases, and then returns to the style of the opening.

Chorus 10

2:14   Heath (bass) takes a solo, accompanied by a tightly muffled cymbal and
            brief piano chords.

Chorus 11

2:28   Roach takes a solo, alternating between the snare drum and bass drum.

Chorus 12 (head)

2:42   A repetition of the opening, but with more intense response from the
            rhythm section.

Coda

2:54   With a slight ritard (slowing down), Parker brings the piece to its end.

The collaboration between Charlie Parker and Dizzy Gillespie lasted only a few years. It foundered in early 1946, weeks after they took their band to Los Angeles in hopes of publicizing their radical new music on the West Coast. California proved indifferent, even hostile. Disappointed, Gillespie took the band back to New York. Parker, still in thrall to drugs that were suddenly in short supply, cashed in his airplane ticket to pay his connection. He remained in Southern California for a year, sinking deeper into heroin addiction in a place where suppliers were few and ruthless. He not only titled a tune after a drug dealer ("Moose the Mooche"), but signed away his royalties for the record in the hope of keeping his supplies intact. When the heroin ran out, Parker began mixing alcohol and barbiturates.

The end of his California stay was unpleasant and public. In July 1947, Parker had a recording session for Dial, the tiny outfit that had been recording him since he arrived in Los Angeles. This time he was unprepared and the result is captured on agonizing recordings that he unsuccessfully tried to keep off the market. On "Lover Man," as he drifts in and out of the microphone's range, jagged fragments of bebop-style technique intermingle with a harrowing statement of the melody. Parker lasted only a few tunes before collapsing. Later that night, he strolled through his hotel lobby wearing only his socks, and was arrested after accidentally setting fire to his bed. Convinced he was a schizophrenic, the police chained him to a cot and committed him to the state hospital at Camarillo. There he would remain for another six months.

For a brief time, Parker was free of his drug addiction. Rested, restored, and physically fit, he announced his return to New York with a fiendishly clever blues called "Relaxin' at Camarillo." But there was no escape from heroin. "They can get it out of your blood," he once said, "but they can't get it out of your mind." For the remainder of his life, his genius was steadily undercut by physical and professional decline. Miles Davis, who played with him on and off for several years, finally left in disgust in 1949, fed up with his "childish, stupid" behavior. "All we wanted to do was to play great music, and Bird was acting like a fool, some kind of . . . clown."

Parker's last years played out on two levels simultaneously. In his more ambitious mode, he found a trace of commercial success through Norman Granz, who supported and recorded him, attempting at one point to make a short film with Parker and Coleman Hawkins, a kind of sequel to *Jammin' the Blues*, though it was never completed and the footage remained hidden for more than half a century. Granz found new contexts for Parker, including a Latin rhythm section, vocal choirs, and all-star jams (Parker's solo on "Funky Blues" is a highlight, with Johnny Hodges and Benny Carter sharing the performance). When Parker expressed his longing to record with strings, Granz commissioned an album's worth of arrangements in which his alto saxophone was cushioned in much the same way vocal stars were featured in the bosom of violins, cellos, and even a harp. One of the strings records, "Just Friends" (1949), received a fair amount of radio play and achieved the status of a near hit. Parker himself commissioned more venturesome strings pieces by friends as varied as swing composer Jimmy Mundy and the up-and-coming star of 1950s cool jazz, Gerry Mulligan, but did not get to record them in the studio (superior concert versions do exist). In the early 1950s, he enjoyed two triumphant tours of Europe, where he was greeted as a major artist and charmed everyone. Driving in the countryside with Swedish musicians, he was told that farmers played music to soothe cows; Parker asked the driver to stop, bounded over a fence with his horn, and played in a field, serenading a cow. He also continued to perform straight-ahead bebop and made some of his finest recordings in 1953, including a stirring version of the song that symbolized his calamity in Los Angeles, "Lover Man."

But Parker's addiction to alcohol proved even more ruinous than drugs.

As he became increasingly unreliable, he was barred from the nightclub named in his honor, Birdland, and occasionally turned up playing with amateurs in storefronts. Bloated and sluggish, his intonation slackened. Jazz itself was beginning to move beyond him. Even so, he might have bounced back as he had done before, but when his two-year-old daughter Pree died of pneumonia, he crumpled and never fully recovered—there was a 1954 suicide attempt followed by a voluntary commitment in the psychiatric facility at Bellevue Hospital. He was thirty-four at the time of his death in 1955, but the coroner estimated the age of his enervated body as fifty-three. His passing received little notice in the press, most of it sensationalistic since he had died in the hotel apartment of a famous jazz patron, Baroness Pannonica de Königswarter, a Rothschild heiress. For musicians, his passing was a dark turning point. As soon as the news got out, someone began scrawling "Bird Lives!" on Greenwich Village walls, a phrase that morphed into an ongoing obituary.

Dizzy Gillespie offered a different model. Unlike Parker, he disdained hard drugs, claiming that his wife Lorraine wouldn't stand for it. He relaxed with pot and, in later years, imported a brand of near-beer to his home in New Jersey. His career demonstrated how bebop could be the musical and professional foundation for working jazz musicians. On returning from California in 1946, Gillespie sensed that the larger public was ready for his music in a more conventional framework. Even so, he continued to innovate. He formed a big band, adapting his bebop arrangements to the full resources of a swing dance orchestra, but added touches that would ultimately have as large an influence on modern jazz as bop itself.

In commissioning compositions from a young ex-drummer named George Russell, Gillespie introduced modality into big-band jazz, anticipating aspects of the 1950s and 1960s avant-garde before the public had made peace with bop. At the same time, he almost single-handedly spurred the Afro-Cuban jazz movement: he hired the great Cuban percussionist and composer Chano Pozo and teamed up with several major Latin jazz figures, including Mario Bauzá, Machito, and Chico O'Farrill, setting the stage for salsa and other rhythmic cross-cultural fusions. (In that regard, it would be hard to overestimate the impact of his 1947 collaboration with Pozo, "Manteca." We'll get to it in a discussion of the postbop era.) He encouraged other young and untested writers as well, including Gil Fuller and John Lewis, whose work in Gillespie's rhythm section led directly to the formation of the Modern Jazz Quartet.

Yet leading a dance band was not comfortable for Gillespie at first. When he was not playing his trumpet, he had trouble knowing how to act. Eventually, he borrowed from an unlikely source: his former showboating employer, Cab Calloway. He soon created a matchless stage persona appropriate for his time: like Louis Armstrong, he balanced his artistry against his wit and penchant for genial silliness. Gillespie brought his bebop-flavored big-band entertainment to cheering crowds well into the 1950s, and occasionally fronted large bands for the rest of his life. Audiences not ready for bebop could still enjoy his mordant sense of humor, his hip-twisting dancing, and his elaborate scat-singing translations of bebop riffs on tunes like "Oop-Bop-Sh'Bam" and "Ool-Ya-Koo." A signature ploy was to say that he would now introduce the musicians and then turn and introduce them to each other. This may not sound like much, but it always got a big laugh, erasing the intimidation factor at a time when jazz was remaking itself as a listener's rather than a dancer's music. Through it all, Dizzy's exhilarating bebop lines soared, the trumpet section performing dazzling block-chord-textured phrases that sounded as close to his as possible.

As bebop declined in popularity through the 1950s, Gillespie remained clean-living, gregarious, and generous to a fault. While some of his colleagues converted to the more militant forms of black Islam, Gillespie became devoted to Baha'i, a gentle religion committed to ideals of unity and peace. Never without a band, big or small, he nurtured the careers of such musicians as Lewis, Ray Brown, Milt Jackson, John Coltrane, Yusef Lateef, Jimmy Heath, Paul Gonsalves, Percy Heath, Quincy Jones, Lee Morgan, Melba Liston, Wynton Kelly, and on and on. In the 1950s, when the State Department began to realize that jazz could be used as an overseas weapon of propaganda, Gillespie took his band on official tours, carefully balancing his patriotism against his insistence on speaking openly about the state of American race relations.

Over time, Gillespie's eccentricities melted into the stuff of celebrity. His goatee, his beret, his specially raised trumpet (designed to compensate for a lifetime habit of playing with the bell pointed down), and especially his distended cheeks made him instantly recognizable. In later years, as his chops gradually declined, Gillespie played less and joked more. Yet his musical inquisitiveness never let him down. In the 1960s, he took a leadership role in introducing bossa nova and organized one of the great quintets of his career, with his former big-band sideman and now-established saxophone and flute star James Moody and the prodigious young pianist Kenny Barron. In the 1970s, he groomed a virtuoso teenage trumpet player, Jon

Faddis, as his protégé, testing his own mettle against that of the younger man. In the 1980s, he created his United Nations Orchestra, introducing such outstanding musicians as the Panamanian pianist Danilo Perez and the Puerto Rican saxophonist David Sanchez. Nor did he cease to maintain his standing as a resolute master of the jam session, recording impromptu encounters with players of every generation, from Mary Lou Williams, Bobby Hackett, Benny Carter, Count Basie, and the idol of his youth, Roy Eldridge, to Sonny Rollins, Stan Getz, Freddie Hubbard, and the avant-garde saxophonist Sam Rivers, who became a member of his last small band. As jazz continued to build on its increasing sense of history and tradition, Gillespie remained a central figure until his death in 1993, which, unlike that of Charlie Parker, was front page news everywhere.

THE BEBOP GENERATION

Parker and Gillespie were only the most visible part of the bebop generation. In the 1940s, hundreds of young musicians, mostly but not exclusively black, were swept up into the new jazz, pulled by a modernist sensibility to previously unseen social and musical realities. They felt in bebop a personal, generational aesthetics and derived from it a renewed sense of purpose, as did the fans—as captured in the recollections of the poet, dramatist, and jazz critic Amiri Baraka:

✦ ✦ ✦

I listened to bebop after school, over and over. At first it was strange and the strangeness itself was strangely alluring. Bebop! I listened and listened. And began learning the names of musicians and times and places and events. Bird, Diz, Max, Klook, Monk, Miles, Getz, and eventually secondary jive like Downbeat, Metronome . . . And I wasn't even sure what the music was. Bebop! A new language a new tongue and vision for a generally more advanced group in our generation. Bebop was a staging area for a new sensibility growing to maturity. And the beboppers themselves were blowing the sound to attract the growing, the developing, the about-to-see. . . .

My father had asked me one day, "Why do you want to be a bopper?" Who knows what I said. I couldn't have explained it then. Bebop suggested another mode of being. Another way of living. Another way of perceiving reality—connected to the one I'd had—blue/black and brown but also pushing past that to something else. Strangeness. Weirdness. The unknown!

✦ ✦ ✦

The path was not easy. Some musicians, watching Charlie Parker, concluded that his musical achievements were somehow associated with drugs and became hooked on heroin. Theodore Navarro, one of Gillespie's most brilliant followers on trumpet, made just a few dozen recordings before succumbing to addiction. Nicknamed "Fats" or "Fat Girl" because of his stocky weight, he died emaciated from tuberculosis—just "skin and bones," as Miles Davis remembered him. Others, like Red Rodney, who for nearly a year played trumpet alongside Parker, found their careers interrupted by incarceration for drug use before finally kicking heroin once and for all. (Rodney enjoyed a return to glory in the 1970s and 1980s.)

The technical achievements of this generation were remarkable. Who would have imagined, on first hearing Parker play in the early 1940s, that anyone could equal him in speed and fury? Yet hard on his heels came the alto saxophonist Sonny Stitt, whose style so closely resembled Parker's that for a time he switched to tenor, hoping to avoid the unflattering comparison ("Don't call me Bird!" he once begged a journalist). As for the tenor saxophone, Parker's influence was filtered through Coleman Hawkins's harmonic mastery and Lester Young's cool idiom, resulting in the syntheses pioneered by Lucky Thompson, Don Byas, and Illinois Jacquet, until it was unleashed in the thoroughly renovated yet varied styles of players like Dexter Gordon, Stan Getz, Zoot Sims, Gene Ammons, and Wardell Gray. The trombonist J. J. Johnson kept pace with his peers by jettisoning his instrument's limited rips and smears for a cool, angular, and unbelievably swift sound. Bebop spread to the baritone saxophone (Serge Chaloff, Gerry Mulligan, Leo Parker), the vibraphone (Milt Jackson), the harmonica (Toots Thielemans), and every other instrument playing jazz.

Bud Powell (1924-1966)

Bud Powell, the finest pianist of the bebop generation, and arguably the most influential keyboard player of the past seventy years, came by his talent naturally. His father was a New York stride pianist, his older brother played trumpet and hired young Bud for his first gigs, and his younger brother Richie also became a bop pianist, though of considerably less skill. Powell was drilled in classical music technique, studying Bach and Chopin, while becoming fascinated by jazz. As a teenager, he frequented Minton's Playhouse, where Thelonious Monk spotted his talents: "I was the only one who dug him," Monk once said. "Nobody understood what he was play-ing." He may have initially intuited that the brilliant pianist was best suited to interpret his own challenging compositions. In return, Powell showed a stubborn loyalty to Monk's music, featuring the knotty "Off Minor" on his first recording session in 1947, and returning to his compositions throughout his life.

Powell's career initially shot upward. He dropped out of high school to join the swing band of Cootie Williams, then on leave from Duke Elling-ton. (To assuage Powell's parents, Williams served as his legal guardian.) Powell fit in beautifully with the music's elite, as broadcast recordings show. But while he was touring with the band in Philadelphia, he was unjustly apprehended by the police and brutally beaten, leaving him with crippling headaches—the beginning of a long nightmare that may have been com-plicated by a form of epilepsy. For a full third of his adult life, Powell was subjected to "psychiatric supervision" that was often hostile and punitive, including dousing with ammoniated water, hardly unique for blacks in that period. He was incarcerated and medicated, and underwent electroshock treatments so severe that they affected his memory. Alto saxophonist Jackie McLean remembered conversations about the day's events that ended in befuddlement. "He had to stop and think and ask me, 'Who?' and 'Tell me about it. . . . or 'What did I do?'" Combine this confusion with a weak-ness for alcohol so profound that a single drink might leave him slumped against a wall, and it's hard to believe that he was able to function at all, let alone forge a career as a radiant stylist, virtually reinventing jazz piano and codifying the modern piano trio.

It would be hard to overstate Powell's impact. His ingenious technique and originality as an improviser and composer established the foundation for all pianists to follow. Long after bop had faded, Powell remained a source of inspiration for pianists as varied as the harmonically engrossed Bill Evans and the rhythmically unfettered Cecil Taylor. In other words, there is jazz piano Before Powell and After Powell. While his left hand played a neutral backdrop of chords, his right hand would explode into a blindingly intricate improvisatory cascade, rivaling (and even surpassing) Parker and Gillespie in rhythmic imagination. Watching Powell play was almost frighteningly intense. The jazz critic Ira Gitler, who observed him at close quarters, described him as "one with the music itself": "Right leg digging into the floor at an odd angle, pants leg up to almost the top of the shin, shoulders hunched, upper lip tight against the teeth, mouth emitting an accompanying guttural song to what the steel fingers were playing, vein in temple throbbing violently as perspiration popped out all over his scalp and ran down his face and neck." Yet for all his virtuosity—and this is perhaps the central achievement of his art—Powell was always emotionally candid and decisive. He never played a flourish just to play a flourish. Comfortable at the most expeditious tempos, he also favored tempos so slow that the rests became fraught with suspense.

Sometimes Powell used block chords: combining his two hands to play a melody supported by fat chords, like a big-band *soli*. On other occasions, he played stride piano, borrowing from the overshadowing presence of Art Tatum: his version of "Over the Rainbow," for example, is stride scattered with Tatum-like runs. He could be as lighthearted and robust in his music as he could be dark and bracingly aggressive. Although he appeared as a sideman with Parker and Gillespie and led a celebrated quintet session (with Navarro and introducing Sonny Rollins and Roy Haynes), Powell usually recorded with bass and drums. Indeed, he did far more than any other pianist to pioneer this now-standard piano trio format, replacing the rhythm guitar favored by Tatum with the rhythmic power of drummers like Haynes, Art Blakey, and Max Roach.

By the end of the 1950s, Powell had moved to France, where adoring crowds watched him gradually disintegrate. There were times when he returned to his youthful self, performing at the peak of his ability. On other occasions he would play haltingly or stop, staring blankly at the wall with what Miles Davis once described as a "secret, faraway smile." In the mid-1960s, he returned to New York, where he died of tuberculosis. His funeral cortege steadily swelled as it moved through Harlem. Like Charlie Parker, Powell was a visionary whose legacy lay in what he might have done as well as in what he actually did.

"TEMPUS FUGUE-IT"

Early 1949 was a good time for Bud Powell. He had just emerged from Creedmore Sanitorium, where he had been incarcerated for several months, and was raring to make a record for Clef. It was a brief window, as he soon returned to Creedmore for more treatment. Difficult as it may be to imagine musical creativity taking place under these conditions, Powell seemed untouchably inspired, ready to display not only his pianistic fancy but also his talent as a composer. He was a remarkable tunesmith whose work ranged from the pure delight of "Bouncing with Bud" to the forbiddingly haunted "Glass Enclosure" to the bop march "Dance of the Infidels," which begins with a harmonized bugle call. Drawing on his knowledge of Baroque counterpoint and his command of modern jazz harmony, he couched his tunes and many of his arrangements of pop songs in intricate structures. In light of his mental instability, it's telling that some of his best-known tunes have painfully self-reflective titles, like "Hallucinations" and "Un Poco Loco." The latter is an insistently aggressive, utterly original Latin tune, pitting Powell's frenetic energy against Max Roach's clanging cowbell and polyrhythmic accompaniment.

On the 1949 sessions, accompanied by Ray Brown and Roach, he turned out a number of masterpieces. A dazzlingly fast and boldly reharmonized "Cherokee" visited and challenged territory previously claimed by Charlie Parker, while the easygoing "Celia" (dedicated to his infant daughter) explored the gentle side of bop, combining relaxed triplets and his canny use of syncopated rests. The darkly colored "Tempus Fugue-It" is a tempestuous performance that nonetheless suggests Powell's witting familiarity with Baroque polyphony and the Latin proverb *Tempus fugit*. The form is standard thirty-two-bar AABA, with the A section barely moving from the tonic. Harmonic variety is pushed to the bridge, which moves rapidly from chord to chord. "Tempus Fugue-It" shows Powell pushing his technique to the limit. There are undoubtedly a few miscalculations that later record producers, armed with tape and digital technology, would have edited out—but they would have robbed this performance of its blunt intensity.

TEMPUS FUGUE-IT

Bud Powell

Bud Powell, piano; Ray Brown, bass; Max Roach, drums

LABEL: Clef 11045; *The Complete Bud Powell on Verve* (Verve 731452166920)
DATE: 1949
STYLE: bebop
FORM: 32-bar popular song (**AABA**)

Introduction

0:00   Powell jumps in unaccompanied, playing a line in octaves. Its last few notes are accented by the drums.

| 0:04 | | He juxtaposes a dissonant note in the right hand with syncopated chords in the left. |

Chorus 1 (head)

0:07	**A**	The opening melody is a sinuous bebop line with stops and starts. Each empty beat is filled in by a subtle brush hit on the drums.
0:14	**A**	
0:20	**B**	The melody is nearly overshadowed by a powerful bass line played in octaves by the left hand.
0:25		Dissonant chords are decorated with fast grace notes (ornamental, quickly played notes).
0:27	**A**	

Interlude

| 0:34 | | Disjointed chords enter in unexpected rhythms, doubled by the bass and drums. |
| 0:37 | | During a two-measure break, Powell begins his solo. |

Chorus 2

0:39	**A**	Powell plays a fast, elaborate melody in the right hand. When the melody pauses, we can hear his left hand alternating neutral, open harmonies with a sharp dissonance (the flatted fifth) deep in the bass.
0:45	**A**	He fills the next eight bars with a continuous phrase.
0:51	**B**	As the harmonies change, he improvises a line that matches the notes of each chord.
0:58	**A**	The drums interact with the line, adding sharp accents with the brushes.
1:01		Powell ends the chorus with simple octaves. (We'll see the same technique in Monk's "Thelonious" in Chapter 13.) The left hand maintains tension by lingering on the dissonant interval.

Chorus 3

1:04	**A**	Powell plays a short fragment over and over that clashes polyrhythmically with the meter.
1:10	**A**	The same polyrhythmic effect is created by a new melodic fragment.
1:17	**B**	Over the rapidly moving harmony, Powell begins a line that disappears a few measures later, as if his concentration were temporarily thrown off.
1:20		After a few beats, he begins a new line that continues well into the next **A** section.
1:23	**A**	

Chorus 4

| 1:29 | **A** | Powell repeats the fragment from the previous chorus, with less precision. |

1:35	**A**	In an apparent miscalculation, he begins playing the chords to the bridge. After a bar or two, he realizes his mistake and seamlessly corrects himself.
1:41	**B**	Now he plays the correct chords with exactitude.
1:45		For a few beats, he's suddenly disrupted from the groove, playing a few notes out of rhythm.
1:47	**A**	Within a few seconds, he returns to his brilliantly quick improvised line.

Chorus 5 (head)

1:53	**A**	Powell plays the head an octave higher, matching pitch to the heat of performance.
1:59	**A**	
2:06	**B**	
2:12	**A**	

Coda

| 2:18 | | As a signal for the ending, Powell repeats the last phrase. |
| 2:19 | | He holds out the last chord, a dissonantly voiced tonic, with a tremolo. |

JAZZ IN LOS ANGELES: CENTRAL AVENUE

Bebop was born in Harlem and nurtured on New York's 52nd Street, but despite a confused initial reception, it also resonated three thousand miles away on the West Coast. Though geographically remote, Southern California had rivaled New York as the center of the national entertainment industry since the birth of film. And jazz had been a part of California life ever since vaudeville brought the music west early in the century. Restless New Orleans musicians used California as a convenient second home, easily reachable by railroad lines running direct from the Crescent City. It was in Los Angeles, in 1922, that the first recording by a black jazz band (led by trombonist Kid Ory) was made—a year before King Oliver's band.

The Los Angeles jazz scene spread along Central Avenue, which ran southward from downtown toward the black suburb of Watts. Los Angeles absorbed thousands of black workers through the Great Migration, but treated them with Southern disdain: musicians who worked there referred to it as "Mississippi with palm trees." Central Avenue was the core of a narrow, all-black neighborhood, thirty blocks long and only a few blocks wide. ("Housing covenants" in other neighborhoods prevented white residents from selling their property to people of other races.) The avenue was crowded and lively, and became even more so during the war. With its extensive shipbuilding industry, California took a disproportionate share of defense contracts, pulling unemployed workers to its factories. Los Angeles's black population more than doubled during the war years, from 64,000 in 1940 to 175,000 in 1945.

Central Avenue was a Mecca for entertainment, offering its share of blues, comedy, dance, and early rhythm and blues. In 1945, that scene began to include modern jazz, with Coleman Hawkins's quintet, bop groups led by trumpet player Howard McGhee, and the star-crossed visitation by Dizzy Gillespie and Charlie Parker's quintet. Musicians adopted the new language as quickly as possible. Soon there was a bevy of California bebop practitioners, led by the charismatic tenor saxophonist Dexter Gordon.

Gordon (1923–1990) was a product of the black middle class. His father, a jazz-loving doctor, counted Lionel Hampton and Duke Ellington among his celebrity patients and took his young son to hear the big swing bands that came regularly to the Coast. At the integrated Jefferson High School, Dexter studied clarinet with Sam Browne, the school's first black teacher, who demanded excellence from all his students. He soon switched from clarinet to saxophone, with Browne keeping him after school to practice his scales. In the evenings, Gordon studied with swing veteran Lloyd Reese, who drilled local students (including Eric Dolphy and Charles Mingus) in the intricacies of chromatic harmony and ran a rehearsal band.

Like many aspiring tenor players, Gordon initially saw Coleman Hawkins as the model for harmonic improvisation. "Hawk was the master of the horn," he later said, "a musician who did everything possible with it, the right way." But his creative inspiration was Lester Young, whom he first heard when the Basie band came to Los Angeles in 1939. Young's "bittersweet approach" to melody and rhythm mesmerized Gordon. "When Pres appeared, we all started listening to him alone. Pres had an entirely new sound, one we seemed to be waiting for." The next phase of Gordon's education began when he joined the Lionel Hampton band at age seventeen. In the saxophone section, he sat next to Illinois Jacquet, a hard-blowing tenor saxophonist whose exuberant improvisation on Hampton's hit "Flying Home" foreshadowed the rhythm and blues era. From Jacquet, Gordon learned how to construct an extroverted solo, one that told a story—bold, spare, and forthright. He gained additional professional experience working with other bands, including those of Fletcher Henderson and Louis Armstrong. He was introduced to bebop in New York, where he studied music theory with Dizzy Gillespie. His first encounter with Charlie Parker's penetrating authority left him speechless. Under Parker's influence, he headed into the bop orbit, adding a new level of rhythmic intensity to his music while picking up a debilitating addiction to heroin.

Of the new bebop saxophonists, Gordon was the most flamboyant. On the street, he cut a fine figure, dressing in the latest style with wide-shouldered suits accentuating his lanky frame and topped by a wide-brimmed hat that made him seem "about seven feet tall." He had a dimpled smile and a chesty baritone speaking voice, and was so good-looking that some thought he should be an actor. That ambition was later fulfilled, though his first role was as an uncredited inmate (he had been busted for possession and sentenced to two years) in the 1955 movie *Unchained*, about the minimum security prison in Chino; for a jam-session scene in which Gordon is seen playing, the studio dubbed a solo by swing saxophonist Georgie Auld to replace Gordon's. In 1960, he played a musician-addict in the West Coast production of Jack Gelber's New York hit *The Connection*. A quarter-century later, he surprised everyone by winning a well-deserved Oscar nomination for his lead role (inspired by the lives of Lester Young and Bud Powell) in Bertrand Tavernier's 1986 film *'Round Midnight*.

But it was his musical style that turned people's heads. Gordon combined the looseness of Young, playing slightly behind the beat, with Parker's rhythmic volatility. He was also quirky and humorous, with a charming habit of interpolating into his solos fragments of popular songs, suggesting that just beneath the language of bebop lay a world made up of beautiful Tin Pan Alley melodies. Before performing a ballad, he would often quote the tune's lyrics, as if inviting his listeners to take part in the deeper world of the song. Gordon's improvisational style was forged in after-hours jam sessions, where he could be ruthlessly efficient, using his quick-witted command of phrases and his broad, implacable timbre to leave his competitors helpless. One of his partners was Wardell Gray, a fellow saxophonist from Oklahoma City who sparred with Gordon at Jack's Basket on Central Avenue, a fried-chicken joint where musicians gathered for late-night sessions. "There'd be a lot of cats on the stand," Gordon remembered, "but by the end of the session, it would wind up with Wardell and myself." A memento of these occasions was "The Chase" (1947), a frenzied tenor saxophone battle spread out over two sides of a 78-rpm recording for Dial. Featuring

Gordon and Gray trading eight-, four-, and finally two-bar segments, it was one of the longest jazz improvisations on record.

"LONG TALL DEXTER"

In January 1946, Gordon recorded a youthful, emergized group for Savoy Records. The rhythm section included Bud Powell (twenty-one), Max Roach (twenty-two), and veteran bassist Curley Russell (at twenty-eight the oldest musician present). The trumpet player was Leonard Hawkins, a high-school friend of Roach's from Brooklyn who was making his recording debut. But the focus was on Gordon, as the titles from that day's work made clear: "Dexter Rides Again," "Dexter Digs In," and a blues that took a nickname inspired by Gordon's six-foot-five-inch frame, "Long Tall Dexter." The tune is built on a riff as elemental and effective as the one in Parker's "Now's the Time," and like it strategically introduces an unexpected bit of dissonance (0:13).

Gordon's five-chorus solo on "Long Tall Dexter" is, from its dramatic beginning, a perfectly paced tour de force, a condensation of what he might use to triumph in a jam session. After he and Hawkins play a send-off riff (a composed segment that takes up the first four bars of a chorus), Gordon enters on a dramatic note, held for a long time before dissolving into a dissonance. The remainder of this chorus is spare and restrained, setting up what is to come. In chorus 4, he expands the range of his solo, sending his line into a number of sharp dissonances (e.g., at 0:51). But it's with chorus 5 that he begins ratcheting up the intensity. Restricting himself to a single note, he punches out riffs with rhythms so unpredictable that Powell and Roach are virtually pulled into the conversation. From here the riffs keep piling on, until at the beginning of chorus 7 he mounts a climax of virtuosic display. Early on, Gordon drops to a honking low note—the sort of gesture that would soon be a staple of nearly all rhythm and blues saxophonists. And in the solo's last few measures, he cools down the temperature with false fingerings, a delicate and inventive way of emphasizing a closing nod to the blues.

LONG TALL DEXTER

Dexter Gordon Quintet

Dexter Gordon, tenor saxophone; Leonard Hawkins, trumpet; Bud Powell, piano; Curley Russell, bass; Max Roach, drums

LABEL: Dial 603; *Dexter Digs In* (Savoy Jazz 17546)
DATE: 1946
STYLE: bebop
FORM: 12-bar blues

Introduction

0:00	Over a shimmer of cymbals, Roach creates a complex polyrhythm on the drums, alternating strokes on the snare and bass drum.

Chorus 1 (head)

0:04	Gordon (tenor saxophone) and Hawkins (trumpet) play the simple riff-based melody in octaves. Underneath, Powell comps with dense, dissonant chords on piano.
0:07	Hawkins adds a slight but noticeable rhythmic decoration to the head.
0:08	Roach punctuates the end of the phrase with a sharp snare drum accent.
0:09	As the harmony changes from I to IV, the riff figure adjusts by flatting one of the notes.
0:13	The horns play a simple ascending scale. When the harmony changes to V, they move it up a half step, creating an intense dissonance.

Chorus 2 (head)

0:18	As is typical for bebop blues, the head is repeated.
0:31	Gordon lets his last note tail off.

Chorus 3

0:32	The two horns play a send-off riff—a composed four-bar melody designed to lead directly to the next soloist. This riff is built on a harmonic substitution, beginning with a remote harmony that modulates quickly back home to the tonic.
0:34	At its conclusion, the send-off riff becomes stridently dissonant, featuring flatted fifths against the prevailing harmony.
0:37	As the harmony shifts to IV, Gordon enters with a long-held note that finally descends to yet another dissonance, the chord's flatted fifth.
0:45	Roach punctuates the chorus's end with a few loud fills.

Chorus 4

0:46	Gordon plays even strings of notes that climb into his highest register.
0:51	He plays a prominently dissonant note over the IV chord.

Chorus 5

1:00	Gordon plays punchy, short riffs in continually changing rhythms. The drummer and pianist respond by filling in the spaces.
1:09	After reaching its melodic peak, the phrase winds down.

Chorus 6

1:15	Gordon starts a new riff, maintaining a simple rhythm (long, short-short) while shifting the pitch in sequence.
1:20	Over the IV chord, he drops down to a sonorous low note. When he repeats the figure, the note moves up a half step to a sharp dissonance.
1:25	As the chorus ends, he plays a rhythmically intricate riff.

Chorus 7

1:29	Gordon compresses the riff into a long, complex phrase that finally ends in a repeated note.
1:39	Using false fingering, he creates a note with a hollow timbre. Because it's slightly less than a half step higher and falls on the third degree of the scale, it has a distinctly bluesy tone.

Chorus 8

1:43	Slightly off-microphone, Hawkins enters with the send-off riff. Gordon enters after a moment's hesitation.
1:48	Hawkins's solo begins with a simple two-note phrase. Immediately afterward, the drums stop playing for a several beats, creating an unexpected sense of space.
1:52	Hawkins plays the rest of his solo with a broad, open tone, ghosted notes, and occasional rapid bebop-style decorations.
1:57	Roach responds with rapid fills.

Chorus 9

1:58	As Hawkins digs into a short riff, his timbre becomes coarser.
2:03	For a brief moment, he makes an apparent mistake: he hits a note that contradicts the IV harmony underneath.

Chorus 10

2:12	Powell enters in octaves, emphasizing the first note with a "crushed" grace note. In the background, you can hear his rough singing.
2:16	He accompanies his intricate right-hand melodies with simple lines and two-note "shells" of chords in the left.

Chorus 11

2:27	Powell suggests a faster, double-time feeling.

Chorus 12

2:41	Instead of reprising the head, the two horns play a different (if equally simple) riff-based tune.
2:46	As the harmony shifts, the riff's top-most note is flatted.

Coda
....

2:54	A final new melodic phrase closes out the piece.
2:56	At the piece's end, Roach continues playing.
2:58	Powell has the last word with a dissonant lick that ends a tritone away from the tonic.

For Gordon, the 1950s were a mess. His career was twice interrupted by jail sentences for heroin use, culminating with a stint in California's Folsom Prison. But in the next decade, he firmly reestablished his reputation as one of the finest saxophonists of his generation, recording masterful albums for Blue Note, including *Go!* (1962: with the gifted Powell acolyte Sonny Clarke and one of the best of the younger drummers, Billy Higgins) and *Our Man in Paris* (1963: a reunion with Powell and Kenny Clarke). Gordon spent fourteen years in Europe, where black musicians could take refuge from racial prejudice; most of the time, he lived in an apartment in Copenhagen, where he mastered Danish, played locally, and toured the Continent. "Since I've been over here," he told an interviewer, "I've felt that I could breathe, and just be more or less a human being, without being white or black." When he returned home to New York and opened at the Village Vanguard in 1976, he received a rousing welcome. In his last years, Gordon occupied a role he was never to relinquish—the gracious elder statesman of acoustic jazz. Shrewd promotion by Columbia helped his new albums succeed, and films gave him fame way beyond bebop.

AFTERMATH: BEBOP AND POP

For a brief time in the late 1940s, bebop was aggressively marketed as popular music. As the swing bands began to fade, the music industry turned nervously to the new jazz style, offering it to the marketplace as both edgy modern music and comic novelty. Its public face was Dizzy Gillespie, whose goatee, glasses, and beret gave cartoonists a convenient shorthand for jazz modernism. Jazz slang was parodied (endless repetitions of "cool," "daddy-o") and ultimately became 1950s beatnik clichés. Bing Crosby and Patti Andrews (of the Andrews Sisters) recorded a parody lyric called "Bebop Spoken Here," which left their usually reliable fans nonplussed. Gillespie contributed to the confusion when he appeared in *Life* magazine in 1948, exchanging a "bebop handshake" with Benny Carter, their high fives supposedly representing the flatted fifth. "There was no such thing in real life," Gillespie later protested. "It was just a bunch of horseplay that we went through so they could pretend we were something weird. . . . We were helping to make bebop seem like just another fad, which it wasn't."

Bandleaders like Woody Herman and Benny Goodman enjoyed several modest hits with bebop-flavored arrangements, but their popularity faded. Audiences became aware of bebop's dark underside through the highly publicized arrests of heroin addicts. The media began to treat the style as a vaguely degenerate idea whose time had passed. Leonard Feather published a landmark overview of the music's origins, *Inside Be-Bop,* in 1949; when it was later reprinted, he dropped the arcane word in favor of the more neutral title *Inside Jazz.* Still, at the same time that bebop failed as popular music, it steadily gained strength among musicians. As professionals, they saw it less as a fashion than a musical system to be mastered. To be a jazz musician meant learning to play like Charlie Parker and Dizzy Gillespie. That part remains true today—more than six decades later, jazz novices learn to improvise by studiously practicing transcriptions of classic bop solos. But if bop became the foundation for contemporary jazz and a symbol of professional identity for its musicians, it posed the challenge of finding a commercial niche. The solution lay in going back to the origin of bop, the jam session, and making it public—this time mounted on a stage as a rowdy spectacle, held in large auditoriums across the country. Nobody was more central to this transformation than Norman Granz.

The son of Ukrainian immigrants, Granz (1918–2001) grew up in Los Angeles, where he supported himself in college by working part time as a film editor. He was also a record collector and habitué of local jazz clubs. Like John Hammond, Granz approached jazz as a musical and political phenomenon. He found the musicians endlessly fascinating and was repelled by the racial discrimination that determined their lives. His first concerts, held toward the end of the war (1944), were aggressively interracial, designed both to promote jazz and to attack long-held habits of segregation.

One of his early venues was Los Angeles's classical music center, the venerable Philharmonic Hall. By featuring his favorite musicians there, both white and black, in jam-session-style groups, Granz attracted a large, jazz-loving audience. Such subversive behavior was not long tolerated. In 1946, his concerts at the Philharmonic were banned, allegedly because of the management's fear of violence from unruly audiences. (Granz himself insisted that the managers were horrified by the sight of mixed-race couples in the crowd.) By this time, Granz was ready to take his concerts on the road. He had his revenge by naming his touring show Jazz at the Philharmonic, soon referred to by knowing fans as Jazz at the Phil and then as JATP.

Jazz at the Philharmonic did not distinguish between styles. At its core were a handful of stars from the Swing Era: Coleman Hawkins, Roy Eldridge, Buck Clayton, Nat "King" Cole, and Lester Young were eager for lucrative employment in the waning days of the big bands. But Granz also admired the innovations of bebop and included both Dizzy Gillespie and Charlie Parker in his early concerts, as well as soloists whose frenetic posturing evoked the nascent world of rhythm and blues. The result was a "nervous jazz," heavy on improvisation—hovering, in the assessment of jazz critic Whitney Balliett, "somewhere between small-band swing and bebop."

Granz made the jam-session format accessible to the casual fan by underscoring its competitive nature. The tenor saxophonists Illinois Jacquet and Flip Phillips engaged in notorious dustups, squawking and squealing to the delight of blissed-out fans and the chagrin of critics who considered the entire display vulgar and incoherent. Trumpets screeched their highest notes and drummers engaged in marathon solos. "I like my musicians to be friends offstage," Granz once said. "But when they're on stage, I want blood." Audiences responded with gusto no matter how staid the concert hall, matching the visceral enthusiasm of what they saw onstage with ear-splitting whistles and cheers. The "heated teenage faces," Balliett noted, resembled jitterbuggers who danced in the aisles at Benny Goodman's theater gigs in the 1930s but were "more warlike": "They rarely move from their seats, yet they manage to give off through a series of screams (the word 'go' repeated like the successive slams of the cars on a fast freight), blood-stopping whistles, and stamping feet a mass intensity that would have made Benny Goodman pale."

Granz profited handsomely from this madness, becoming in effect the first man to make a million from jazz and a major figure in postwar music. Well before the civil rights movement, he insisted that his troupes of black and white musicians perform before integrated audiences; if promoters balked, he was ready to withdraw the entire show. He took a special interest in the careers of Ella Fitzgerald and pianist Oscar Peterson, becoming their personal manager and making both international stars, encouraging them to bridge the worlds of jazz and pop.

In retrospect, the Granz circuses seem like a transitional mode between bop and rock and roll, at least on the scale of organized musical hysteria. The irony of bebop is that its era didn't last long; the key years of pure bop were 1945–49, after which it began to turn cool or hard or modal or Latin or avant-garde or something else. Yet bebop endures as the lingua franca on which all those variations were built. As the first vernacular music with attitude, hastening social change and demanding cultural respect, bebop changed the conversation about jazz, renewing its role in the culture. Bebop is still the ground on which jazz builds its many and varied mansions.

CHAPTER

The 1950s:
Cool Jazz and Hard Bop

NEW SCHOOLS AND INTERPRETATIONS

Not surprisingly, bebop created a kind of Rubicon that many fans, critics, and musicians could not cross. They had come to jazz in the years of swing, when it functioned as dance music with an unembarrassed emphasis on entertainment, and they dismissed the new way of playing as a fad; when it failed to fade, they lost interest in jazz. Far from fading, bop became so much the language of jazz that its influence proved retroactive: even young musicians who played in swing or traditional styles adapted elements of the new

◄ Dave Brubeck pioneered unusual time signatures and became emblematic of jazz as a hip, sophisticated, modern music for the age of affluence. Los Angeles, 1953.

harmonies, rhythms, and melodies. Still, the very intricacy of bebop made it a more introverted listening experience. Jazz had evolved, and no single musician—not Louis Armstrong or Duke Ellington or Charlie Parker— could be depicted as a defining figure for its entire canvas. It now had a convoluted history: from New Orleans traditionalism to the styles developed in Northern and Midwestern cities to swing to bop. In the 1950s, additional styles grew out of bebop—cool jazz, hard bop, funk, avantgarde, and others—leading jazz historians to speak in terms of schools, as if it had splintered off into discrete realms.

It's important to remember that bebop did not cause the first schism in jazz. Conservative music lovers always prefer what they know. Hidebound critics in the 1920s attacked Armstrong and Ellington for sacrificing "authenticity"—Armstrong because he interpreted popular songs, Ellington because he orchestrated his music. Those critics shunned swing, just as some swing critics, in turn, shunned bebop; the French critic Hugues Panassié, so passionate an advocate of jazz in the 1930s, wrote that Parker and Gillespie "gave up jazz in favor of bop." Later, some of the most ardent proponents of bebop would similarly shun the avant-garde. The word *jazz* achieved its present-day meaning only in the aftermath of bop, when the multiplicity of schools necessitated a unifying term. During the Swing Era, *swing* was used to distinguish a generation's popular dance music from the New Orleans jazz style that preceded it. Now, with so many new schools competing for attention, *jazz* became an essential umbrella-term to cover them all.

Jazz had been recognized, in some rarified circles, as art music from almost the beginning—recall Ernest Ansermet's remarks in 1919 about Sidney Bechet. After bop, as the association between jazz and dance diminished, the jazz world grew increasingly self-conscious of its status. Musicians sought respect as serious artists. They performed in major concert halls, collaborated with symphony orchestras and chamber groups, created ballets and theatrical scores. They expanded the parameters of improvisation and found new ways to combine it with composition. As jazz won acceptance as art music, it ceded its role as dance and entertainment music to new styles in pop, which peaked with the worldwide embrace of rock and roll. This development has been interpreted in various ways, reflecting either acceptance or resistance.

Modernists accept bebop and its successors as the natural outcome of a musical evolution that progresses from simplicity to complexity; in this narrative, jazz, like painting, literature, and classical music, is subject to inevitable change. Those who advocate a fusion narrative see the severance of jazz from pop music as a tactical error; they argue that jazz ought to take its cue from the public rather than from its most audacious artists. In the ethnic interpretation, jazz should look only to the African American elements that give the music its power, and shun experimentation and borrowings from contemporary Europe and other cultures—including black ones like Motown and hip-hop—that dilute the essentials of swing and improvisation. Finally, the cyclical view sees bebop as part of a normal pattern of modernism and elaboration. In the 1920s, for example, jazz was established as innovative new music, and the 1930s made those innovations more accessible via swing; this cycle is repeated in the 1940s (bebop) and 1950s (cool jazz, hard bop, funk); and again in the 1960s (avant-garde) and 1970s (assimilation). In jazz's post-cyclical history, all its styles compete for attention with its now classical past.

COOL JAZZ

The omnipresence of the word *cool* in present-day American speech derives in large measure from its association with the lingo of modern jazz. By the early 1950s, *cool* was used to describe a particular school of jazz born out of bebop that had a light, laid-back, reticent quality. As cool jazz grew in popularity, it was usually associated with white musicians who relocated from the East Coast to California, where the (largely segregated) film studios offered them financial security with musical day jobs. Their collective styles became known as West Coast jazz. There is much racial irony here, because the notion of coolness has deep roots in African American culture. Ralph Ellison recalled: "One countered racial provocation by cloaking one's feelings in that psychologically inadequate equivalent of a plaster cast—or bulletproof vest—known as 'cool.' . . . Coolness helped to keep our values warm, and racial hostility stoked our fires of inspiration."

Cool has a long pedigree in jazz as the antithesis of hot, which emphasized aggressive rhythms and improvisations, heavy timbre and vibrato, evocative blues scales, and overt expressiveness. Musicians like Bix Beiderbecke and Lester Young dissented from the hot approach with music that was relatively unflappable—played with limited vibrato, restrained timbre, stable dynamics, melodic calm, and sophisticated harmonies that tempered the blues idiom. During the Swing Era, coolness was exemplified by such musicians as Teddy Wilson, Benny Carter, vibraphonist Red Norvo, bassist John Kirby (who adapted classical melodies for his small ensemble), and arranger Eddie Sauter, among others. At the height of bebop, Charlie Parker advanced the cool style with such compositions as "Yardbird Suite" and "Cool Blues," while his young sideman Miles Davis created a blues, "Sippin' at Bells," with so many elaborate chord changes that the feeling of blues was deliberately obscured. A radical link between bop and the distinctive style that would soon be known as cool jazz is heard in the music of two stylistically dissimilar pianist-composers, Lennie Tristano and Tadd Dameron.

Lennie Tristano (1919–1978) was a radical bopper, determined to carve out his own musical niche. He admired Charlie Parker, but his approach to jazz reflected his schooling in the European classics. Blind since childhood, Tristano began to play piano professionally at twelve, and studied at the American Conservatory in Chicago. He soon enticed a circle of bright young musicians who functioned as collaborators and even disciples. These included guitarist Billy Bauer and an ingenious fifteen-year-old alto saxophonist, Lee Konitz. In 1946, Tristano moved to New York, where he played with Parker and Gillespie and built a small but fervent following with his own groups, which included Bauer, Konitz, and Warne Marsh, a tenor saxophonist from Los Angeles stationed in New York for military service. Tristano followed the usual bop practice of adapting the chord changes of popular songs, but went further, superimposing convoluted, spacey melodies (he telegraphed his intentions with such titles as "Supersonic" and "On a Planet"). These pieces sounded experimental and emotionally aloof, and showed off an almost profligate virtuosity. One of his most memorable recordings is the justly titled "Wow," with whirling, meticulous, dual-saxophone phrasing. As a pianist, he created lengthy, winding phrases that employ counterpoint and two or more simultaneous meters.

By 1949, Tristano was conducting "free" sessions, which were entirely improvised. A few years later, he took a contrary approach, seeking increased control by replacing his drummer with taped percussion tracks. (This practice, though never accepted in jazz, prefigured the electronic dance mixes of the 1980s.) Tristano's music drew only a cult following, and by the early 1950s he was devoting most of his time to teaching. Yet his influence proved lasting, especially through the music of the incredibly prolific Konitz, the one alto saxophonist of the bop era with a sound and attack utterly unlike that of Charlie Parker. The aspect of Tristano's teachings that Konitz enshrined and perfected was the refusal to play familiar licks, riffs, and other auto-pilot clichés.

Unlike Tristano, Tadd Dameron (1917–1965) had limited keyboard technique and rarely improvised solos; he played what musicians call arranger's piano, consisting of crafty accompanying chords. Dameron was one of the few major bop composer-arranger-bandleaders who initially made their mark in swing. Born in Cleveland, he studied pre-med at Oberlin College before dropping out to compose full time for various entertainers and orchestras, mainly the Kansas City big band Harlan Leonard and His Rockets, for which he wrote such signature pieces as "Dameron Stomp" and "Rock and Ride." During that time, he became friendly with the young and unknown Parker.

While Tristano's classical training predisposed him to a strenuous, intellectualized version of bop, Dameron's swing background inclined him to a gentler approach, defined by lyrical melodies and breezy rhythms, sometimes with a Latin feeling. Dameron wrote the most successful bop ballad, "If You Could See Me Now," and the fast instrumental anthem "Hot House," which combines intricate harmonies (adapted from the pop song "What Is This Thing Called Love") with a cool melody. His other pieces include the jazz standards "Good Bait" and "Our Delight." In 1948, Dameron was hired to organize a small band at the Royal Roost, a Broadway restaurant that had previously offered swing bands. There he put together an outstanding ensemble with trumpet player Fats Navarro and two tenor saxophonists, Wardell Gray and Allen Eager, who represented divergent approaches to Lester Young—respectively, earthy and ethereal. Dameron's spare melodies and plush voicings with this band and others ("Lady Bird," "Jahbero") prefigured the cool-school breakthrough of the following year.

THE BIRTH OF THE COOL

Every artistic movement sows the seeds of its undoing, as experimentalism always leads to more experimentalism. In 1945, when Miles Davis played trumpet on Charlie Parker's first Savoy session, it was apparent then that while he lacked the bravura technique of Dizzy Gillespie (who consequently had to replace him on the explosive "Ko Ko"), he offered a more lyrical approach to improvisation (as, for example, in his solo on the original "Now's the Time" or the later "Embraceable You"), with an emphasis on personal timbre, longer tones, and suggestive silences. Four years later, Davis emerged as the leader of a group of adventurous musicians who idolized Parker and Gillespie yet sought to explore ideas that would slow down the feverish pace of bebop in favor of supple melodies and plush harmonies. Above all, they aimed for a more balanced relationship between composition and improvisation. Instead of a performance that began with a written theme, followed by improvised choruses and a reprise of the theme, they challenged themselves to write music where the composer's hand was always apparent—where the improviser interrelated with the ensemble.

These precepts had already been explored by the big bands, especially in the work of Duke Ellington. But the young modernists, liberated from the jazz past by bop, also looked to classical music for chamber-like sonorities that favored the introspective middle range over rousing high notes. Temperamentally inclined toward emotional reserve, they filled out the instrumental palette with tuba and French horn, and preferred insinuating rhythms to the thumping beats that spurred dancers. After two years with Parker's band, Davis in particular had grown disenchanted with steeplechase harmonies and hurtling melodies. In his autobiography, he explained:

◆ ◆ ◆

Diz and Bird played a lot of real fast notes and chord changes because that's the way they heard everything; that's the way their voices were: fast, up in the upper register. Their concept of music was *more* rather than *less*. I personally wanted to cut the notes down, because I've always felt that most musicians play way too much for too long. . . . I didn't hear music like that. I heard it in the middle and lower registers. . . . We had to do something suited for what we did best, for our own voices.

◆ ◆ ◆

In 1949, Davis at twenty-three was one of the youngest participants in the cool group and one of the least accomplished as a composer-arranger. He had made an immediate splash in jazz circles as Parker's trumpet player, but had yet to establish himself as a prominent stylist or bandleader. As an energetic and determined organizer, however, he assumed the pivotal role in a circle of second-generation bop musicians. He encouraged frequent discussions, organized rehearsals, promoted new compositions, and landed a record contract for which he coordinated a nine-piece ensemble called the Miles Davis Nonet. The ensemble's size suggested a middle road between a big band and a small combo, and its unusual brass-heavy instrumentation underscored links to classical chamber music. Several members of the nonet would become leading jazz figures for decades to come.

Gil Evans, at thirty-seven the oldest and most experienced member, did not play an instrument (in later years, he taught himself to play arranger's piano) but was known as a resourceful orchestrator whose dramatic adaptations turned familiar melodies into virtually new compositions. Born in Canada in 1912 and self-taught, Evans led bands in California as early as 1933, but he achieved his signature style in his postwar work for the open-minded Claude Thornhill, who relished Evans's elaborately textured harmonies (prominently using two French horns, tuba, flute, and bass clarinet in addition to the usual jazz band instruments), including lengthy whole-note chords that seem to hang in the air like cloudbanks. Given a free hand with Thornhill's orchestra, Evans adapted jazz, pop, and classical themes—from Charlie Parker's "Donna Lee" to Modest Mussorgsky's "The Troubadour."

Evans lived in a cellar apartment on New York's West 55th Street, conveniently located beneath a laundry and within blocks of the 52nd Street jazz clubs and rehearsal studios. Originally a storage room, Gil's pad (as it was known) became a meeting place for musicians who dropped by for conversation, a drink, or a nap. As Evans left the door unlocked, his place attracted a broad coterie of instrumentalists, composers, and singers eager to explore the wide-open terrain of modern jazz. Among the regulars were two men who worked with him in the Thornhill band as well as Davis's nonet: Lee Konitz and Gerry Mulligan. Evans featured Konitz's fluid, unusually light alto saxophone on several Thornhill pieces. The lanky, multitalented Mulligan was then known primarily as an arranger; within a few years, he would win lasting fame as the most popular baritone saxophonist in jazz history. Mulligan did most of the writing for the nonet. Another key nonet participant was John Lewis, a distinctive piano stylist who worked with Parker and Gillespie and would soon create the Modern Jazz Quartet and write many jazz classics. When Davis lined up a two-week engagement for the nine-piece group at the Royal Roost (the only live engagement it ever played), he insisted that a sign be posted at the club entrance: "Arrangements by Gerry Mulligan, Gil Evans, and John Lewis." Never before had jazz arrangers received such prominent credit.

The Miles Davis Nonet created a new coalition that was interracial, pangenerational, and culturally diverse. Of the key musicians, Davis, Lewis, drummers Kenny Clarke and Max Roach, and trombonist J. J. Johnson were black, while Evans, Mulligan, Konitz, and trombonist Kai Winding were white. Most of these musicians had apprenticed with swing bands; a few rode the first wave of bop (Davis, Lewis, and Roach had worked with Charlie Parker); several had trained in classical music. The "birth of the cool" band (as the nonet was later marketed) was a collaborative experiment on every level. The improvisations were woven into an ensemble texture that favored the middle range, whether the instruments were high (trumpet, alto saxophone, French horn) or low (trombone, tuba, baritone saxophone), as well as medium dynamics, economical phrasing, and plenty of rests.

As influential as it proved to be, the nonet initially garnered little interest from public or press. At three sessions in 1949 and 1950, involving more than twenty alternating musicians and composers, it recorded twelve numbers; eight were issued on four records—one every four months or so. These sporadic releases failed to build long-term interest in the band. Not until 1954, when this handful of pieces was collected on an album called *Birth of the Cool,* were they acknowledged as innovative achievements and the genesis for the cool jazz school that had, in the intervening years, become a national sensation.

"MOON DREAMS"

"Moon Dreams," one of two arrangements written by Gil Evans for the group, is a radical example of the nonet's ambitions. The melody, composed by pianist Chummy MacGregor of the Glenn Miller band, is a conventional 1940s romantic ballad, though the forty-bar form indicates structural complexity. Johnny Mercer wrote lyrics in the hope of creating a pop hit for Miller, but although Miller recorded a vocal version with his Army Air Force Band, the song won favor with neither the public nor musicians. Evans's affection for it seemed peculiar, to say the least. His version represented something new in modern jazz, in that it has no sustained improvised solos. Instead, there are brief interludes by alto saxophone, baritone saxophone, and trumpet, which serve as transitional episodes in an orchestration that constantly calls attention to its subtly shifting harmonies, instrumental voices, and contrapuntal phrases. The most surprising element is the two-part structure: Evans orchestrates the forty-bar chorus only once, bringing it to a close with all instruments landing on F-sharp at 2:07. The rest of the performance is a new composition, built with minute and often dissonant instrumental details, suggesting an ominous breaking down of a pop melody as each instrument struggles to hold its place amid the chromatic chords.

MOON DREAMS

Miles Davis Nonet

Miles Davis, trumpet; J. J. Johnson, trombone; Lee Konitz, alto saxophone; Gerry Mulligan, baritone saxophone; Gunther Schuller, French horn; Bill Barber, tuba; John Lewis, piano; Al McKibbon, bass; Max Roach, drums

LABEL: Capitol T762; *Birth of the Cool* (Capitol 724353011727)
STYLE: cool jazz
FORM: 40-bar popular song (**ABA'CC'**)

Chorus 1

0:00	**A**	The band begins a slow ballad. Davis (trumpet) has the melody, the other horns play intricate harmonies in block-chord texture underneath. The sound is dominated by the lower instruments: tuba, baritone saxophone, French horn.
0:08		As the melody note is held, the horns swell in volume.
0:25	**B**	Konitz (alto saxophone) takes the lead, while the horns underneath create their own rhythmically independent line.
0:36		A return to block-chord texture, with the bass adding a line beneath.
0:51	**A'**	The band returns to the melody and harmony of the opening.
0:55		Schuller (French horn) leads from the middle of the texture.
1:12		Barber (tuba) plays a surprisingly fast and intricate countermelody.
1:17	**C**	Konitz retakes the lead.
1:24		His solo blends in with a faster, bebop-flavored line. The bass begins to ascend, step by step.
1:30		As the trumpet sustains a long held note, the background horns continue the faster rhythmic feeling.
1:43	**C'**	Mulligan (baritone saxophone) takes the melody.
1:57		Davis returns for the block-chord conclusion of the melody.
2:03		He hits the final note. Abandoning their tonic harmony, the other parts begin climbing up to reach that note.

Coda

2:07	Finally, all voices coincide on a single pitch (with the alto getting there last).
2:10	Konitz on alto is left holding the note; behind him, Roach accompanies quietly on cymbal.
2:13	The high note is suddenly accompanied by a new chord. As each line moves chromatically, the harmony becomes dissonant and unstable, held together by the unchanging alto note. Any sense of meter evaporates.
2:26	Konitz plays a quick ornament, continuing to hold the note.
2:34	As the harmonies continue to shift, the alto note finally fades out.
2:37	Konitz plays a fragment from the original melody, sounding plaintive in this unsettled harmonic atmosphere.
2:39	On horn, Schuller plays a new motive: a stuttering single note, ending with an upward turn.
2:48	Various horns trade back and forth fragments that resemble either Konitz's melodic fragment or Schuller's stuttering motive.
3:03	The tuba and baritone begin a descending scale.
3:07	The final chord is almost there, needing only the melody to fall into place.
3:11	As the chord resolves, the light cymbal pulse finally stops. The band sustains its chord, in a key different from the beginning one.

Gerry Mulligan (1927–1996) AND WEST COAST JAZZ

As individual members of Miles Davis's circle carried each other's ideas over to their own bands, the influence of the nonet exceeded popular awareness of its recordings. A turning point came in 1952 with two events, one on each coast: in New York, John Lewis assembled what would become known as the Modern Jazz Quartet; in Los Angeles, Gerry Mulligan organized what would become known as his "piano-less" quartet.

If one group more than any other symbolized West Coast jazz, it was the Gerry Mulligan Quartet of 1952. Born in New York, Mulligan began writing big-band arrangements as a teenager for Philadelphia radio bands. Soon he was touring with bands, writing, and playing saxophones and clarinet. In 1948, as a member of the Claude Thornhill band, he became a confidante of Gil Evans, who brought him into the nonet, for which he wrote seven of the twelve arrangements. Shortly afterward, in 1951, Mulligan hitchhiked to Los Angeles, seeking a job with Stan Kenton, the self-anointed king of progressive jazz.

Kenton and his hugely popular orchestra were often belittled for pomposity: he gave his pieces titles like "Artistry in Rhythm" and "Concerto to End All Concertos." Still, his canny ability to combine big-band jazz, pop vocals, and experimental modernism (his 1951 recording of Bob Graettinger's "City of Glass" was an avant-garde assault on conventional jazz) made him a force to be reckoned with. In the 1940s and 1950s, Kenton hired dozens of important musicians and arrangers, many of whom looked to European classicism as a model of distinction and cutting-edge complexity. Almost all of them were white, encouraging simplistic characterizations of West Coast jazz as a white, intellectual, even pretentious kind of jazz. Kenton was not especially responsive to Mulligan, and declined to hire him as a player, a decision he surely regretted once Mulligan's popularity on baritone saxophone soared. He did, however, record a few Mulligan compositions ("Young Blood," "Limelight," "Walking Shoes") that combined polyphony and simultaneous meters in ways that built on the achievements of the nonet. These arrangements influenced a generation of jazz composers, especially those—including the outstanding Bill Holman, a Kenton mainstay until he went out on his own—living in California.

Mulligan returned briefly to New York to lead and record his own ten-piece band, but in 1952 he returned to Los Angeles and accepted a Mondays-only job at a small restaurant called the Haig, distinguished by its white picket fence and location: across the street from the Hollywood nightclub the Cocoanut Grove. There he formed a quartet consisting of baritone saxophone, trumpet, bass, and drums. According to legend, the Haig's bandstand was too small to accommodate a grand piano. The absence of a piano or chordal instrument was widely noted. An article in *Time* magazine drew attention to the "piano-less" group and its balmy music, which was thought to personify the laid-back temperament of Southern California. As crowds descended on the Haig, the quartet recorded a version of the Rodgers and Hart ballad "My Funny Valentine" that sold unusually well. The breezily swinging lyricism of cool jazz had found its star.

Without a piano to fill out the harmony, Mulligan and his young Oklahoma-born trumpet player, Chet Baker, expanded the contours of their music with contrapuntal interplay. Sometimes they achieved genuine two-part polyphony; at other times, one simply supported the other by playing whole notes to signify the song's chord sequence. Baker, an intuitive improviser, played almost exclusively in the middle register in a style that superficially resembled that of Miles Davis, but with lighter timbre and less dramatic force; he also won admirers as a soft-voiced ballad singer. The quartet's drummer, Chico Hamilton, known for the quiet rolling rhythms he created with mallets, later became an important bandleader in his own right. As an African American, Hamilton automatically symbolized postwar integration in jazz and the society at large.

The Gerry Mulligan Quartet lasted little more than a year before each man went his own way, yet its popularity was so lasting that the three key figures were taken up by Hollywood during the next several years: Mulligan and Hamilton appeared in movies, while actors playing jazz musicians mimicked Baker's baby-face looks and surly attitude. In later years, Mulligan divided his time between small groups and big bands, writing several jazz standards ("Rocker," "Line for Lyons," "Festive Minor") and winning polls as best baritone saxophonist for twenty years. A capable pianist, he came to dislike piano-less small groups and refused to lead them except for occasional reunions with Baker. Yet when he created his splendid Concert Jazz Band, in 1960, an audacious attempt to divorce big-band jazz from its associations with dance, and a workshop for the most creative arrangers of the day, he dropped piano from the rhythm section—either playing it himself or assigning it to his valve trombonist and chief composer Bob Brookmeyer when necessary. Baker's career was blighted by drug addiction, though he maintained a loyal following. Hamilton led bands for six decades, introducing such influential musicians as guitarist Jim Hall, bassist Ron Carter, and saxophonists Eric Dolphy, Charles Lloyd, and Arthur Blythe, among others.

John Lewis (1920–2001)
AND THE Modern Jazz Quartet

The Modern Jazz Quartet (MJQ) emerged, in some ways, as a reverse image of the Gerry Mulligan Quartet. It was an African American East Coast band that lasted more than four decades with only one change in personnel. As such, it was called the longest-running chamber group in or out of jazz. Created by pianist John Lewis, who had written two of the nonet pieces, it was a genuine cooperative, with each member assigned specific extra-musical duties such as travel arrangements, finances, and public relations. Lewis was in charge of the music; his arrangements reflected a lifelong fascination with polyphony and counterpoint, and the conviction that J. S. Bach and blues were compatible.

Lewis was raised in Albuquerque, where he attended the University of New Mexico and saw the Duke Ellington band—a formative experience. While stationed in France during the war, he performed with drummer Kenny Clarke, who helped him to join Dizzy Gillespie's big band in 1946. In the next few years, Lewis resumed his studies at the Manhattan School of Music while working with Gillespie and participating in recording sessions with Charlie Parker (his blues playing on "Parker's Mood" was much admired) and other modernists. He immediately demonstrated a unique piano style: spare, light, melodic yet rhythmically firm and persistently inflected with the blues. Gillespie encouraged him to compose for the band and to work up separate pieces that featured only the rhythm section, which consisted of Lewis, Clarke, vibraphonist Milt Jackson, and bassist Ray Brown—the nucleus of the MJQ.

By 1952, Lewis believed he had found the right musicians and the right concept. Milt Jackson, a native of Detroit, was the first major vibraphone player in a decade, since Lionel Hampton and Red Norvo in the 1930s. The vibes perfectly complemented the chimes-like sound Lewis coaxed from the piano, as well as offering a dramatic contrast: Jackson played with teeming energy, less subtle than Lewis and drenched in soulful gospel-like figures he had learned in the church. Clarke, the most established member of the group, played with rambunctious, interactive enthusiasm yet also created an unmistakably debonair, tasteful brand of timekeeping with brushes or sticks. The least experienced member was bassist Percy Heath, a replacement for Ray Brown, who had left to tour with his wife, singer Ella Fitzgerald. Heath, the eldest brother in a celebrated family of Philadelphia musicians, had been playing bass for only a few years, having first taken it up after his discharge from the air force in 1946.

Lewis was determined to undo popular misconceptions about jazz, not only in the manner of his music but in its presentation. He had ideas about the way the quartet should dress (in identical tuxedos or suits, in the tradition of the swing bands), enter and exit the stage, and introduce pieces. Every performance was to be regarded as a concert, whether they were actually playing a concert hall or a jazz club. This attitude puzzled many. As Percy Heath recalled:

♦ ♦ ♦

We had a hard time getting people to quiet down and listen. At that time in nightclubs, people were talking about hanging out. In order to break that down, instead of trying to play over the conversation, we'd use reverse psychology and play softer. Suddenly, they knew we were up there and realized the conversation was louder than the music. Of course, if it got too loud, we'd come off—just stop playing and walk off. It didn't take long for them to realize they were wasting their time, because we weren't going to entertain them in that sense. We didn't have funny acts, we didn't have any costumes. We were conservatively dressed, we played conservative music, and if you didn't listen you didn't get it. We were four instruments going along horizontally, contrapuntally. There was no back-up and soloist, the concept was changing.

♦ ♦ ♦

Only after the MJQ was lauded in Europe did the American critics get on board. By the late 1950s, the MJQ ranked as one of the world's most successful jazz ensembles. In appearance and manner, it seemed genteel and cerebral. But its music was, in fact, profoundly rhythmic and emotionally intense—in other words, cool on the surface, hot at the core.

"ALL THE THINGS YOU ARE"

At its first recording session, in December 1952, the MJQ recorded four pieces: two pop standards and two Lewis compositions, each of them arranged by Lewis to employ aspects of Baroque counterpoint (à la Bach) in a jazz setting. "All the Things You Are" is an important song in jazz history. Written for an unsuccessful 1939 Broadway musical by Jerome Kern and Oscar Hammerstein II, it was salvaged by Tommy Dorsey, whose recording of it topped the charts in early 1940. A few years later, it emerged as a personal favorite of the boppers. They admired the harmonic progression, which stimulates improvisation, and the poetic lyrics (which inspired Parker's "YATAG" acronym). At the beginning, Lewis's arrangement isolates each individual layer in the ensemble. The rapidly running bass line and the sporadic drumming fit strangely against the unison theme played by vibes and piano. Gradually, this framework is displaced by a more conventional, bebop-oriented one; but at no point do we feel that we are hearing a lone soloist accompanied by a rhythm section. The quartet always sounds like a quartet, with the primary melodic voice shifting between vibes and piano. Note the careful integration of the closing bass solo. Although rhythm and texture are always in play, the performance flows with seeming effortlessness.

ALL THE THINGS YOU ARE

Modern Jazz Quartet

Milt Jackson, vibraphone; John Lewis, piano; Percy Heath, bass; Kenny Clarke, drums

LABEL: Prestige LP7059; *The Complete Modern Jazz Quartet Prestige and Pablo Recordings* (Prestige 4PRCD-4438-2)
DATE: 1952
STYLE: cool jazz
FORM: 36-bar popular song (**AA'BA"**; **A"** has 12 bars)

Introduction

0:00		In a moody introduction, Heath plays a double-time walking-bass line on a Dorian scale. On drums, Clarke enters with his own ostinato pattern: three quick accents, followed by a bass drum stroke and a mallet stroke on a cymbal.
0:08		Jackson (vibraphone) and Lewis (piano) play the melody in bare octaves. The bass ostinato undercuts the harmonies implied by the melody.
0:26		The melody line suddenly drops to a dissonant note, where it hangs unresolved.

Chorus 1

0:29	**A**	With a sudden dramatic change in the rhythm section, the head begins. Jackson and Lewis play a varied version of the melody, harmonized by the piano's block chords.
0:38		The phrase ends with a rapid Latin figure. The break that follows is filled by the drummer.
0:41	**A'**	Jackson improvises over the pianist's simple line.
0:53	**B**	Lewis takes over for a delicate eight-measure solo.
1:04	**A"**	Jackson and Lewis return to a composed part of the arrangement, with chromatic harmonies and unexpected rhythms.
1:16		At the chorus's end, the melody collapses into a single unharmonized line.

Interlude

1:22	A series of syncopated chords sets up Jackson's solo, which opens with a two-bar break.

Chorus 2

1:27	A	Jackson plays a bebop-style solo, with dissonant passages and varied rhythms. Clarke plays a neutral accompaniment.
1:39	A'	In the background, Lewis comps quietly on the offbeat.
1:50	B	
1:57		Jackson reaches his highest point.
2:02	A"	Lewis's comping is often reduced to a single contrapuntal line.
2:12		As Jackson nears the end of his solo, his phrases become more bluesy.

Chorus 3 (abbreviated)

2:19	B	Switching suddenly to the bridge, Lewis improvises briefly in the high register.
2:31	A	Heath takes a short solo, beginning with a phrase that recalls his opening ostinato. Behind him, Jackson and Lewis play a line that quietly lingers on dissonant notes.

Coda

2:48	Jackson and Lewis return to a composed part that reprises the final eight bars of chorus 1.
2:57	Without transition, we return to the introduction. Jackson and Lewis play one phrase, then stop.
3:09	Clarke ends with a cymbal explosion, followed by chords from Jackson and Lewis.

Lewis, like Ellington, benefited from the loyalties of his musicians. The MJQ survived forty-two years, forty of them with the same musicians: drummer Kenny Clarke left the group in late 1954, unwilling to commit to a long-term endeavor that placed as much emphasis on composition as on improvisation. He was replaced by Connie Kay, a model of precision and nuance, who stayed until his death. (Kay also exerted an influence on early rock and roll as the leading session drummer for Atlantic Records.) During those forty years, Lewis merged the MJQ with symphony orchestras, chamber groups, big bands, singers, and individual guest soloists. He wrote many benchmark works, including "Django," "England's Carol," "Afternoon in Paris," "Two Degrees East, Three Degrees West," "Little David's Fugue," the film scores *Odds Against Tomorrow* and *No Sun in Venice*, the ballet *The Comedy*, and the suite *A Day in Dubrovnik*. Lewis also functioned as an educator and jazz activist, directing the Lenox (Massachusetts) School of Jazz between 1957 and 1960 and the Monterey (California) Jazz Festival between 1958 and 1982. And as an early proponent of performing jazz classics with the respect given classical repertory, he co-founded and conducted Orchestra U.S.A. (1962) and the American Jazz Orchestra (1986–92).

The most controversial of Lewis's alliances gave birth to a short-lived idiom that composer, conductor, and musicologist Gunther Schuller called the Third Stream. Schuller played French horn in the Miles Davis Nonet and worked with Lewis at the Lenox School and in Orchestra U.S.A. In a 1957 lecture, he predicted that a musical Third Stream would emerge, synthesizing elements in "Western art music" with "ethnic or vernacular" music. Collaborating with Lewis on the 1960 album *Jazz Abstractions*, Schuller introduced his own Third Stream example, "Variants on a Theme of Thelonious Monk." For several years, composers from both worlds self-consciously contributed to this movement. Their music was not cool per se, but it had been stimulated in an environment nurtured by cool's architects. Although classical techniques would continue to figure in jazz as sources of creative inspiration (as they had, occasionally, in prewar jazz as well), the movement soon faded and the term "Third Stream" fell into disuse.

HEATING THE COOL AND CHANGING THE TIME

For some important musicians, Third Stream acted as a buffer between cool jazz and countermovements, including hard bop and avant-garde. Their experiments in blending jazz and classical music served as an apprenticeship for careers that assumed genuine significance in the late 1950s, when their music returned to an emphasis on hard jazz. The composer-bassist Charles Mingus exemplified the way many musicians navigated from one stream to another. In 1953, he joined the Jazz Composers' Workshop, which consisted chiefly of white composers adapting their classical training to modern jazz. There he created several Third Stream works before developing a mature style that was more aggressive, jazz-rooted, and blues-driven.

Earlier, in 1950–51, Mingus played bass with the Red Norvo Trio. Norvo had started on xylophone in the 1920s, creating a stir in 1933 with his "Dance of the Octopus," a whimsical piece combining xylophone and bass clarinet; Schuller cited it as a precursor of the Third Stream. Norvo then led an audacious Swing Era orchestra, featuring vocalist Mildred Bailey (his wife). By the early 1950s, he had recorded with Charlie Parker and formed a trio made up of vibraphone, guitar (the influential Tal Farlow), and bass (Mingus). Its texture was delicate, but its swing and improvisational zest were hot. The pianist George Shearing developed a similar cool-bop sound with a quintet that included vibraphone and Latin percussion, yet stayed light on its feet and achieved enormous popularity.

Lightness was a significant aspect of cool jazz. Lester Young's influence on a generation of tenor saxophonists produced two approaches that tended to break down along racial lines. Black tenors (like Dexter Gordon, Wardell Gray, Illinois Jacquet, and Gene Ammons) modified Young's legato (smooth) phrasing into a more forthright attack, emphasizing the expressive robustness of his style. White tenors (like Stan Getz, Zoot Sims, Al Cohn, and Allen Eager) focused instead on Young's airy lyricism. As Dexter Gordon said, "We used to jam together—Zoot, Al Cohn, Allen Eager. Zoot and I worked in a club in Hollywood. He was playing Lester and I was playing Lester, but there was always a difference." The most accomplished "white Lesters" worked together in the Woody Herman Orchestra. After Herman recorded Jimmy Giuffre's "Four Brothers," a fast bop piece that featured the reed section, the title phrase was used to characterize that reed section and any tenor who approximated that style ("the Lestorian mode," in Getz's phrase). These saxophonists perfected timbres that avoided vibrato while aiming for a high, transparent sound. Gerry Mulligan made the baritone saxophone sound almost like a tenor; Giuffre made the tenor sound almost like an alto; and Paul Desmond made the alto sound almost like a flute.

Paul Desmond made his name with the Dave Brubeck Quartet, the most popular jazz group of the 1950s. Brubeck (b. 1920) grew up in Concord, California, in a musical family; his first instructor was his mother, a classical pianist. He later studied with composer Darius Milhaud, whose 1923 ballet *La Création du monde* was one of the first orchestral works to employ blues harmonies. In the late 1940s, Brubeck organized an octet along lines similar to those of Davis's nonet, but with reversed priorities. More classical than jazz, it produced a ponderous, academic music, lacking rhythmic power. Then in 1951, Brubeck hooked up with Desmond and organized his first quartet (piano, alto saxophone, bass, drums). Success was almost immediate. He was pictured on the cover of *Time* in 1954, a rare acknowledgment for a jazz musician, and won acclaim from younger listeners by playing and recording on college campuses.

The Brubeck Quartet blew both hot and cool, in the contrast between Desmond's ethereal saxophone and Brubeck's heavy-handed piano. Both musicians excelled at unusual chord substitutions, but where Desmond improvised appealing melodies, Brubeck built his solos in a pattern that began with single-note phrases and climaxed with repetitive blocks of chords, generating either excitement or tedium, depending on the listener's taste. Brubeck's primary trademark was an innovative use of irregular meters such as 5/4 and 9/4. After decades of jazz played almost exclusively in 4/4 (even waltzes were rare), his approach to time was exotic, charming, and frequently catchy. Brubeck's 1959 album *Time Out* became a national sensation, especially his "Blue Rondo à la Turk" (in 9/4) and Desmond's "Take Five" (in 5/4), which was released as a hit single. These meters were so unusual that musicians often mastered them by mentally subdividing the beats. A composition in 5/4 might be counted as 2 plus 3 or the reverse: "Blue Rondo à la Turk" breaks down to 1-2, 1-2, 1-2, 1-2-3. By the end of the twentieth century, unusual time signatures, some borrowed from Eastern music, were commonplace.

HARD BOP AND MICROGROOVE

The most profound counterstatement to cool jazz was essentially a revival of bop but with a harder edge. By the middle 1950s, the umbrella term *hard bop* was adopted by critics to describe a populous East Coast school of jazz that placed itself in direct opposition to the more arid precincts of cool. Ironically, Miles Davis helped pilot the turn. Put off by underfed, overintellectualized music that claimed to be derived from his nonet, he switched directions in 1954, with recordings ("Walkin'," "Blue and Boogie") that restored jazz's earthy directness. Even his subsequent collaborations with Gil Evans emphasized powerful emotions and vigorous rhythms. As Davis, never one to languish in a movement, moved forward according to his own lights (as did Mulligan, the Modern Jazz Quartet, Brubeck, Mingus, and other major stylists of the 1950s), hard bop came to embody a general attitude (tough, urban, straightforward) and a new mainstream in jazz—one that made a point of resisting overt experimentation.

Born largely of musicians who came to New York from the nation's inner cities, especially Detroit and Philadelphia, hard bop was said to reflect the intensity and hustling tempo of city life. To these musicians, the cool school represented a more tranquil, stress-free environment. This idea paints a superficial gloss on the relationship between art and geography; obviously, West Coast musicians were as stressed as anyone else. Still, it seems fair to suggest that the West Coast school's expression of life's irritations was relatively introverted, while the East Coast's was decidedly extroverted.

One instantly apparent difference concerned timbre. If cool jazz aimed for a light timbre, hard bop preferred a sound that was heavy, dark, impassioned. The tenor replaced the alto as the saxophone of choice, and drummers worked in an assertive style that drove the soloists. Some hard bop bands winnowed bop's harmonic complexity in favor of elemental chords reminiscent of the sanctified church or rhythm and blues, creating a subset of hard bop called soul jazz. A subset of soul jazz popularized an instrument that had previously been little used in jazz (like the cool school's French horn): the electric organ, a mainstay of church music. In effect, the soul musicians were attempting to reconnect modern jazz to popular music. Ultimately, the contrast between cool and hard bop, though unmistakable, was not radical enough to suggest a schism like the one that divided swing and bop. For the most part, cool and hard bop represented the natural development of bop in a changing world. Part of the change was technological.

In 1948, Columbia Records patented a recording process called microgroove, or long-playing records (LPs): twelve-inch platters that turned at 33 1/3 revolutions per minute and accommodated about twenty minutes of music per side with excellent fidelity. They were manufactured from a flexible plastic (or vinyl) that was promoted as unbreakable. By contrast, the three-minute 78-rpm platter that had dominated the industry for half a century was extremely brittle and easily shattered. As Columbia announced its breakthrough, its competitor RCA-Victor introduced a similar system, also using microgrooves and improved vinyl, but smaller and with less playing time, a speed of 45 rpm, and a large donut-hole in its center. The industry quickly accepted both technologies, reserving the LP for serious or extended works and the 45 for pop songs no longer than those heard on 78s. The LP had an immediate impact on jazz, particularly the new generation of hard bop musicians. Like every kind of recorded music, bebop had accommodated itself to the 78's time limit. While musicians could play longer pieces with extensive soloing in concert or at jam sessions, most performances were kept short to please audiences who expected to hear music familiar from records.

In 1944, when Norman Granz recorded his Jazz at the Philharmonic concerts, live recordings of jazz were virtually unheard of. They could only be done on disc-recorders with one microphone (tape had not yet been invented), so audio control was narrow and sound-mixing impossible. To release these numbers, Granz created his first record labels (Clef, Norgran) and divided the performances into sections, on several three-minute 78-rpm records—not unlike symphonies and operas. When the LP arrived soon thereafter (almost simultaneously with the introduction of audio tape), it not only opened the door to extensive live recording, but also influenced the way music was played in the studio. Duke Ellington was one of the first to take advantage of the liberty it afforded him, composing extended works specifically for the new medium. Record producers encouraged musicians to play marathon solos to test the reaction of the fans. An early instance involved a session by Zoot Sims, a Four Brothers saxophonist known for his smooth timbre, volatile swing, and fertile imagination. Backed by drummer Art Blakey, Sims was about to finish "East of the Sun" when the producer waved him on for an interpretation that ultimately ran eleven minutes.

Partly because of the LP, hard bop bands were especially inclined toward longer solos. Shunning counterpoint and complicated ensemble arrangements, they relied on the yeoman display of extended improvisations. The average performance consisted of a theme, solos by some or all the band members, and a reprise of the theme. As the lengthy improvisations threatened to alienate audiences accustomed to more succinct solos, major labels like Columbia and RCA were disinclined to pursue hard bop. But new, independent labels were delighted to take up the slack, among them Blue Note, Prestige, Contemporary, and Riverside. They realized that a large segment of the audience was eager for a style of jazz that was at once expansive and closer to its roots. One way the bands maintained the interest of a mainstream audience was to fortify the beat with a pronounced backbeat. A powerful accent on the second and fourth beats of each measure stimulates a physical response in the listener. In the 1950s, jazz fans congregated in nightclubs where physical reactions like foot-tapping, finger-snapping, and head-wagging amounted to a kind of dancing while seated. The independent record companies liked the longer tracks for another reason: the fewer tunes on an album, the less they had to pay in songwriter royalties.

Art Blakey (1919–1990) AND Horace Silver (B. 1928)

Art Blakey was the primary figurehead of hard bop. Raised amid the Pittsburgh steel mills, he was a tough, muscular leader who insisted that his sidemen put aside everything in their private lives when they mounted a bandstand and give their all to the music, as he did. He began on piano, switched to drums, and made his way to New York in 1942 to work with Mary Lou Williams. Two years later, Dizzy Gillespie recruited him for the Billy Eckstine band, positioning him to become one of the most influential percussionists of the bop era. Blakey had an earthier approach than Kenny Clarke and Max Roach, and was their equal in finding precisely the right rhythmic figures or colorations to complement and inspire a soloist. He became famous for his press-roll: an intense rumbling on the snare drum, usually at a turnaround, which had the effect of boosting a soloist into the air for a few seconds and then setting him down in the next chorus, as the swinging pulse continued. Blakey's attentiveness made him an ideal drummer for Thelonious Monk, with whom he had a long association—even though Monk's own music was quirky and convoluted while Blakey's was brash and straightforward.

In 1953, Blakey and pianist-composer Horace Silver formed a quintet (trumpet, tenor saxophone, piano, bass, and drums) called the Jazz Messengers. They made a few live recordings (including *A Night in Birdland*, with trumpet player Clifford Brown), and within two years had codified hard bop as quintet music that combined bebop complexity (in the harmonic improvisations) with blunt simplicity (in bluesy or gospel-inspired themes and backbeat rhythms). In 1956, after Silver left to organize his own quintet, Blakey formally assumed leadership, and the band became Art Blakey and His Jazz Messengers.

The number of important musicians who either began or matured in Blakey's groups is remarkable. Among many others, they include trumpet players Kenny Dorham, Lee Morgan, Freddie Hubbard, Woody Shaw, and Wynton Marsalis; saxophonists Hank Mobley, Jackie McLean, Benny Golson, Wayne Shorter, and Branford Marsalis; and pianists Cedar Walton, John Hicks, Keith Jarrett, Joanne Brackeen, and Mulgrew Miller. Blakey telegraphed the consistent attitude of his music in classic album titles: *Moanin', Drum Suite, The Freedom Rider, The Big Beat, Indestructible, Hard Bop, Straight Ahead*.

In the three years he worked with Blakey, Horace Silver composed several of the tunes that incarnated the hard bop aesthetic. Born and raised in Connecticut, Silver soaked up a far-ranging assortment of musical influences. He learned Cape Verdean folk music from his father, an immigrant of Portuguese ancestry, and studied tenor saxophone with a church organist. He listened to blues singers, boogie-woogie pianists, swing (he idolized Jimmie Lunceford), and especially bebop. At twenty-one, Silver was discovered in Hartford by Stan Getz, who took him on tour and into recording studios. During the next few years, he worked with major musicians, including Coleman Hawkins, Lester Young, and Charlie Parker; he appeared with Miles Davis on the 1954 sessions that helped turn the tide from cool to hard. Beyond his ability to filter bop through gospel, rhythm and blues, and folk song structures, Silver brought to his music an uncanny ability to create catchy melodies that sounded familiar and new at the same time. One of his earliest pieces, "Opus de Funk" (1953), a play on Stan Getz's "Opus de Bop" (1946), popularized a word for Silver's brand of soulful jazz: funky. Partly derived from nineteenth-century slang for spoiled tobacco, *funky* also has a long history in African American usage to describe any kind of foul odor. (Jelly Roll Morton uses it in his version of "I Thought I Heard Buddy Bolden Say.") Thanks to Silver, the term was reborn to signify basic back-to-roots musical values. Many of his tunes became jazz standards; several attracted lyricists and vocalists. Significantly, a few were covered by pop or soul artists, including "Doodlin'," "Señor Blues," "Peace," and "Song for My Father."

"THE PREACHER"

One of Silver's best-known and most recorded tunes, "The Preacher" instigated what Silver later described as his only argument with the founders of Blue Note Records, Alfred Lion and Francis Wolf. They implored him not to record the song because it sounded too much like Dixieland. They were wrong but prophetic: over the next several years, "The Preacher" emerged as one of the few postwar jazz tunes to enter Dixieland repertory. Silver considered withdrawing it, but Blakey pulled him aside and encouraged him to hold his ground. It was at the "Preacher" session that the Jazz Messengers was born.

With its sixteen-bar structure, undemanding harmonies, and memorable melody, "The Preacher" suggests a distant past when American folk melodies, church music, and blues seemed to share the same terrain. Note the melodic similarities to "I've Been Working on the Railroad" or "Show Me the Way to Go Home," along with the blues-like chord structure (little harmonic movement in the first half of each eight-bar section, and a climactic use of the dominant chord in the second half). The lighthearted melody is echoed throughout the improvisations and emphasized by the piano chords. In allowing the slightly muddled playing of the background riffs to stand (instead of calling for another take), Silver adds to the church-like mood established by such deliberate techniques as tremolos, false fingerings, two-beat and backbeat rhythms, and blues phrasing.

THE PREACHER

Horace Silver Quintet

Kenny Dorham, trumpet; Hank Mobley, tenor saxophone; Horace Silver, piano; Doug Watkins, bass; Art Blakey, drums

LABEL: Blue Note BLP5062; *Horace Silver and the Jazz Messengers* (UPC 724386447821)
DATE: 1955
STYLE: hard bop
FORM: 16-bar popular song (**AA'**)

Chorus 1 (head)

0:00		A drum beat kicks off an introductory break, Mobley (tenor saxophone) and Dorham (trumpet) entering on the upbeat.
0:01	**A**	The two horns play in close harmony, as if mimicking the sound of gospel singing. The bass plays two firm beats to the bar, answered by the piano's bluesy background riff.
0:11		The first eight-bar section ends on a half cadence.
0:12	**A'**	
0:15		The second eight-bar phrase moves in a new harmonic direction, heading for a full cadence.

Chorus 2 (head)

0:23	**A**	
0:34	**A'**	
0:43		As Blakey plays a fill (press-roll) on drums, Dorham (trumpet) begins to improvise.

Chorus 3

0:45	**A**	Dorham's opening lingers over a long held note before descending with a bluesy phrase. The bass begins to walk.
0:55	**A'**	Dorham's improvisation begins to resemble straightforward bebop, with long strings of eighth notes.

Chorus 4

1:06	**A**	The next chorus rises to the top of the trumpet's register before falling into a more comfortable range.
1:17	**A'**	

Chorus 5

1:27   **A**   Mobley (tenor saxophone) enters with a sharp, bluesy dissonance.

1:38   **A'**   Holding out a note, he decorates it with short flutters.

1:43   During a bluesy lick, the melodic line rises as if aiming for a particular note, but never quite reaching it.

Chorus 6

1:48   **A**   As with Dorham, Mobley's rhythm moves closer to a bebop string of eighth notes.

1:59   **A'**

2:04   To vary his timbre, Mobley uses false fingerings.

Chorus 7

2:09   **A**   Silver (piano) enters with a simple riff, stressing the flatted third of the blues scale. Blakey reduces his drumming to a simple accompaniment, making it easier to hear the improvised bass line.

2:20   **A'**   He hits a chord and plays it tremolo (with a small shake).

Chorus 8

2:30   **A**   Silver's second chorus begins with a descending riff. The notes are straightforward, but the rhythm is subtle and complicated.

2:40   **A'**   He continues playing the same descending riff.

2:43   As the harmonies begin to change, Silver introduces a new motive.

Chorus 9

2:50   **A**   Dorham and Mobley play a riff in octaves. Against this pattern, Silver improvises phrases in call and response.

3:01   **A'**

3:04   Dorham and Mobley play different notes, as if they disagreed about where the riff should go. The saxophone drops out for a measure, yielding to the trumpet.

Chorus 10

3:11   **A**   The horn players continue playing their riff. Behind it, Silver plays chords in tremolo.

3:21   **A'**

3:25   Mobley follows Dorham's example, playing the figure clumsily, as if still learning it.

3:31   With the bass still walking, the two horns return to the opening melody.

Chorus 11 (head)

3:32   **A**   The opening tune returns with a cymbal crash. The rhythm section reestablishes its initial two-beat gospel groove.

3:42   **A'**

Chorus 12 (head)

3:53   A

4:03   A′

Coda

4:13   A short drum figure leads to the final chord—a sustained bluesy disso-
         nance on the piano, punctuated by a resounding cymbal.

By the 1960s, few observers could doubt that the unofficial rivalry between cool and hot had been decided in favor of hot. The stars of cool jazz retained their popularity, but most—including Stan Getz, Zoot Sims, and Al Cohn—had begun to play in an unmistakably harder style, reflecting the East Coast movement's impact. Moreover, the whole direction of jazz had developed an increasingly aggressive and brazen attitude, which would culminate in the raucous howls of the avant-garde. The tenor saxophone had long since supplanted the trumpet as the most vital instrument in jazz, and many of the tenors who pushed 1960s jazz into exploring the middle ground between bebop and radical avant-gardism had learned their trade playing hard bop—among them John Coltrane in Miles Davis's band, Wayne Shorter in Art Blakey's band, and Joe Henderson in Horace Silver's band. Coltrane ultimately repudiated the structures and harmonies of bop in favor of avant-garde jazz, while others remained faithful to bop, adapting it to the freer environment of the 1960s. Three major soloists who found their own paths amid the competing jazz schools were Clifford Brown, Sonny Rollins, and Wes Montgomery.

Clifford Brown (1930-1956)

The career of Clifford Brown lasted barely four years, but in that time he became one of the most admired and beloved musicians of his day. His death in an automobile accident at age twenty-five was mourned as a catastrophe for jazz. Born in Wilmington, Delaware, the son of an amateur musician, he took up trumpet at thirteen and attracted attention for his remarkable facility while studying at Maryland State College. After playing in Philadelphia and touring with a rhythm and blues band, word quickly spread that "he had it all"—gorgeous tone, virtuoso technique, infallible time, and a bottomless well of creative ideas. Nor was his importance exclusively musical. At a time when the jazz ranks were devastated by heroin addiction, Brown embodied an entirely different attitude. Here was an immensely likable young man whose musical ability rivaled that of Charlie Parker, but who had none of Parker's bad habits. He didn't smoke or drink, let alone take drugs, and his example inspired other musicians to change the way they lived.

Brown received encouragement from Dizzy Gillespie, Red Rodney, and especially Fats Navarro, with whom he shared a particular stylistic bond: each man was noted for his unusually plush timbre. After Navarro's tragic death, Brown was acknowledged as his heir—especially after he stepped into Navarro's shoes for a 1953 Tadd Dameron recording session. Weeks later, Brown joined Lionel Hampton's big band, which brought him to Europe. Upon returning, he participated in several recordings as leader and sideman, but it was an Art Blakey engagement at Birdland in early 1954 that made him the talk of the jazz elite: the two albums recorded at Birdland helped to clinch his growing reputation.

In the summer of 1954, Max Roach brought Brown to Los Angeles to make a concert recording. That event resulted in the formation of the Clifford Brown–Max Roach Quintet, with which Brown was associated for the remainder of his short life. Often cited as the last great bebop ensemble, the quintet influenced the emerging hard bop bands with its exciting vitality and canny arrangements, including a few unlikely pieces ("Delilah," from the score of the film *Samson and Delilah*) and originals by Brown ("Joy Spring," "Daahoud," and "The Blues Walk" became jazz standards). Brown conquered Los Angeles as easily as he had New York, recording with the new quintet as well as with Zoot Sims and singer Dinah Washington. The latter association generated other requests from singers; on returning to New York, he made landmark albums with Sarah Vaughan and Helen Merrill, as well as the most successful jazz album with strings since Charlie Parker. In November 1955, the Brown-Roach quintet's talented tenor saxophonist, Harold Land (who seemed to expand on the style of Wardell Gray, another victim of narcotics, much as Brown expanded on Navarro's), left and was replaced by Sonny Rollins, creating an even more potent ensemble.

Brown's work as a trumpet player penetrated every aspect of jazz on both coasts but especially in the East, where a succession of hard bop trumpeters modeled themselves after him, determined to replicate his lyricism, gorgeous sound, and infectious enthusiasm. He offered an alternate approach to the meditative calculations of Miles Davis, and remained for decades a paradigm for upcoming trumpet players, including all those who succeeded him in Art Blakey's Jazz Messengers.

"A NIGHT IN TUNISIA"

Clifford Brown's "A Night in Tunisia" is a posthumous recording, one of many that have turned up since the introduction of portable recording devices. A few weeks before he died, in 1956, Brown sat in with the local band at a small jazz club in Philadelphia. Three numbers were taped, though the tape didn't surface until the early 1970s, when it was released to tremendous acclaim by Columbia Records. His five-chorus solo on this Gillespie classic is an inspired romp that, because of its length and the relaxed ambience, allows us a glimpse into the way Brown thinks in the heat of action, using various gambits, pivotal notes, and motives; and altering speed, range, and meter as he produces a stream of stimulating musical ideas. This performance is also interesting for showing a great musician accompanied by a journeyman group—the jazz equivalent of a garage band—working hard to keep up (the drummer, who owned the jazz club, is especially alert) and not always succeeding, while an eager audience adds percussion-like fills with its shouts and hollers. Brown's solo achieved theatrical renown in 1999, when it was heard in Warren Leight's play *Side Man*: one character plays the recently discovered tape for a couple of friends, who marvel and gasp in response.

A NIGHT IN TUNISIA (EXCERPT)

Clifford Brown

Clifford Brown, trumpet; Mel "Ziggy" Vines, Billy Root, tenor saxophones; Sam Dockery, piano; Ace Tesone, bass; Ellis Tollin, drums

LABEL: Columbia KC32284; *The Beginning and the End* (Columbia/Legacy 66491)
DATE: 1956
STYLE: hard bop
FORM: 32-bar popular song (**AABA**), with an interlude

Introduction

0:00	The rhythm section plays a vamp: an open-ended, two-measure figure in a Latin groove, with an asymmetric, syncopated bass line. Conversation can be heard in the background.
0:12	A saxophone enters, playing a background riff.

Chorus 1 (head)

0:17   **A**   Brown enters, playing the tune on the trumpet over the two-chord progression of the vamp. Every time he reaches for the high note, it falls slightly behind the beat.

0:25   As the phrase reaches a cadence, Brown's line is doubled by the other horns.

0:28   **A**   Brown repeats the **A** section, adding a melodic variation at 0:32.

0:37   The drummer marks the end of the eight-bar section with a drum fill.

0:39   **B**   For the bridge, the accompanying horns drop out, leaving Brown alone on the melody. The rhythm section leaves the Latin groove behind for a straight bebop-style four-four, with walking bass.

0:49   **A**   The band returns to the Latin groove of the opening.

Interlude (16 bars)

0:59   The band plays a complicated interlude, designed to connect the head with the solos. The horns play a short riff with a constant rhythm; the melody changes slightly with each chord. Not everyone in the band knows this passage: the bass drops out entirely, while the pianist does his best to approximate the chords.

1:15   The interlude ends with a four-measure break. Brown plays a string of clean, even eighth notes that reach a peak at 1:17.

Chorus 2

1:20   **A**   Brown's descending line connects smoothly with his solo, drawing applause from the crowd. The piano enters on the downbeat, the drums following a beat later.

1:31   **A**   Brown's playing remains relaxed and relatively simple.

1:37   A sudden burst of faster notes serves as a harbinger of rhythmic complexity to come.

1:42   **B**   At the bridge, Brown plays a descending line that interrupts the smooth rhythmic flow with unexpected polyrhythmic accents.

1:52   **A**

Chorus 3

2:03   **A**   The new chorus begins with a four-note motive, played in a simple descending pattern.

2:08   The next phrase is a mirror image of the first: another four-bar pattern, this time ascending.

2:12   The phrase ends with a bar left in the **A** section—enough space for an excited fan to yell, "Hey, Brownie!"

2:13   **A**   Brown plays a fanfare-like statement on a high-pitched note—A, the fifth degree of the home key of D minor.

2:24   **B**   Playing in the upper register of his trumpet, he starts a line that will continue throughout the bridge.

| 2:32 | | The lengthy phrase is finally rounded off with a quick two-note figure, prompting cries of "Oh, yeah!" from the excited crowd. |
| 2:34 | A | Brown now plays with the two-note figure, placing it in different parts of the measure; the drummer responds by playing unexpected bass drum accents (dropping bombs). |

Chorus 4

2:45	A	Brown returns to a high A, playing a series of triplets that encourage the drummer to follow his rhythm.
2:51		Aiming for a climax, he hits and holds a sharply dissonant note.
2:55	A	Again returning to a high A, Brown plays a sharp, detached cross-rhythm that is instantly reinforced by syncopated bass-drum accents.
3:02		Having played for several measures at the top of his horn, he starts a phrase too difficult to finish; he subsequently descends to a more comfortable register.
3:06	B	
3:14		Brown suddenly breaks into a quick, upward run.
3:17	A	Seizing on the run as a compositional idea, he folds it into a series of repeated phrases, each ascending higher than the last.
3:21		In response, he plays a rapid descending sequence based on a four-note motive.

Chorus 5

3:27	A	Once again, Brown begins by blasting out a high A, but quickly shifts to a series of triplets. The accent for the triplet falls on the normally unaccented last note of each group.
3:38	A	Brown plays a pair of phrases, each beginning with insistent triplets.
3:48	B	The bridge begins with a fast barrage of notes.
3:51		In the midst of this fast passage, Brown turns a simple five-note scale into a complex polyrhythm.
3:57		The drummer marks the end of the bridge with an intense fill.
3:58	A	Brown's fast solo passage begins to disintegrate into shorter fragments.

Chorus 6

4:09	A	Brown begins again on a high A, playing a line strikingly similar to the line heard at 2:13.
4:15		Playing at the very top of his register, he squeaks out a line that is slightly out of tune until it descends into normal range.
4:19	A	For the last time, he begins on a high A before quickly descending.
4:22		He finds a new pattern and turns it into an ascending sequence.
4:30	B	
4:40	A	During his last melodic pattern, Brown plays dissonant intervals within a rhythm drawn from the "Night in Tunisia" theme.
4:51		His solo ends. As the excerpt fades out, a tenor saxophone solo begins.

Sonny Rollins (B. 1930)

One of the most influential and admired tenor saxophonists in jazz history, Sonny Rollins initially played a role in jazz similar to that of Clifford Brown. In the 1950s, countless young saxophonists and some older ones tried to assimilate his creative energy, brawny timbre, and rhythmic authority. He projected a measure of individuality and power—in the tradition of Louis Armstrong and Rollins's idol, Coleman Hawkins—that could not be contained in a conventional band. Unlike Brown, however, Rollins enjoyed a long, vigorous career, performing for sixty years, snatching a few rest periods along the way to refuel but always challenging himself to change, even to the point of taking on different musical identities. At times, when he seemed to have reached an artistic peak, he would turn a sharp corner, altering his sound, repertory, and instrumentation. Unpredictability and playfulness rank high among his abiding and controversial attributes. Rollins represents continuity with the jazz past (through his use of pop tunes and swinging rhythms), while pointing the way to a promising future.

Born and raised in Harlem, Rollins studied piano and alto saxophone before taking up the tenor at sixteen. Two years later, Thelonious Monk invited him to participate in a program of rehearsals that went on for months, boosting his confidence and ambition. One of Monk's guiding principles, thoroughly adopted by Rollins, was that improvisation should elaborate the melodic as well as the harmonic content of a song. Why play a tune if you're going to discard it after the theme chorus? At nineteen, Rollins recorded as a sideman with Bud Powell and J. J. Johnson, among others, combining the gruff heaviness of Hawkins's sound with the quicksilver facility of Charlie Parker. Recording with Miles Davis a few years later, he revealed an unusual capacity for writing jazz pieces that other musicians jumped at the chance to perform ("Airegin," "Oleo"); with the Clifford Brown–Max Roach Quintet, he introduced the first widely noted bebop waltz, "Valse Hot."

In 1955, Rollins achieved an impressive stylistic breakthrough with the quartet album *Worktime*, following it a year later with *Saxophone Colossus*, one of the most lauded albums of the era. Rollins's music reflects a love of sentimental popular tunes that he heard on radio and in movies. He often astonishes audiences by dredging up and rigorously renovating such unlikely material as "There's No Business Like Show Business," "Toot Toot Tootsie," "Sweet Leilani," "I'm an Old Cowhand," "To a Wild Rose," and

"Autumn Nocturne." In 1959, depleted by a decade of work and puzzled by the new stylistic currents, Rollins put his career on hold for more than two years, which he devoted to intense practicing. It was the first of three sabbaticals, each a restorative that inclined him toward further experimentation, ultimately leading him into the heart of the avant-garde—a journey from which he returned to his patented method, but with more technical skills than ever.

Rollins's music possesses great wit and concentration, evident in the frequent musical allusions within his solos. Although he has remained faithful to the precepts of bop, he has taken its harmonic complexity, vigorous swing, and melodic invention into diverse areas. These include calypso ("St. Thomas" was the first of many highly rhythmic jazz calypsos), avant-garde (he pioneered the saxophone-bass-drums trio to maximize his improvisational freedom), and rock (he has recorded with the Rolling Stones and written pieces that show rapprochement with post-1960s pop music).

In addition to humor, Rollins's solos are characterized by his idiosyncratic approaches to timbre, motives, cadenzas, and—a nonmusical word—ebullience. Rollins's timbre is something of a paradox in that it has changed several times, yet is always recognizably his. In the early 1950s, his tone was harsh and splintered, almost grating. A few years later, in what is generally considered his first great period, 1955–59, he produced an enormously attractive timbre: commanding, virile, and smooth as oak. He continued to experiment with his tone, occasionally sounding hollow or blustery, and eventually producing, in the late 1970s, a capacious, bigger-than-life timbre remarkable in its sumptuous expressiveness. Regarding motivic improvisation, Rollins broke with bebop's tendency to favor improvised melodies grounded on a song's harmonies at the expense of the song itself. Instead of discarding the melody after the theme chorus, he reprises key phrases during the course of an improvisation as touchstones, reminding the listener that he is elaborating on a particular melody and not just its harmonic underpinnings.

The cadenza is an integral part of jazz, not unrelated to the breaks that characterized early New Orleans jazz; Louis Armstrong's "West End Blues" cadenza signaled jazz's independence and maturity as a serious art form. But no one has done as much with cadenzas as Rollins, who makes them an anticipated part of live and recorded performances. His sometimes go on longer than the ensemble sections, and almost always generate audience excitement. They tend to function as an extension of his emotional generosity, which he expresses with an uninhibited ebullience. The emotional meaning of a musical performance is entirely subjective: what thrills one listener may bore another. Still, Armstrong introduced a feeling of elation that has since remained a part of the jazz experience, whether achieved through high notes, big-band riffs, virtuosic runs, or other means. Rollins, perhaps more than any other soloist of his generation, consciously aims for transcendence. Sometimes he achieves it through obstinacy in prolonging a solo or revving up the rhythm until he reaches a satisfying climax.

This last aspect of Rollins's music works best in concert, particularly in the outdoor and stadium settings he has favored since the 1980s, where audiences are primed to follow him in search of ecstatic release. It doesn't work in studio recordings, where expansive repetition quickly palls. As a result, Rollins has split his music into two modes: the concert mode, which aims for a spiritual intensity, and the studio mode, which is systematic and frequently pithy. The two modes come together in his best live recordings.

"AUTUMN NOCTURNE"

Rollins's signature traits are fully displayed in his 1978 concert performance of "Autumn Nocturne," a fairly obscure 1940s song by the little-remembered team of Kim Gannon and Joseph Myrow. Rollins recalled the tune from a staid 1941 record by Claude Thornhill's band, which featured little improvisation. Rollins's version is anything but staid. For the first two-thirds of the performance, he improvises a cadenza that hints at the melody with allusive fragments; these are instantly overrun as he ranges through several keys, shaping and distorting his timbre, and priming the audience for a dynamic transition into the ensemble chorus. Rollins plays only that one chorus of the tune, but he configures it to extend the emotional intensity established in the cadenza. He continues to toy with timbre, using astounding virtuoso passagework and dissonances to depart from the melody without really leaving it. At no point during the chorus are we in doubt that he is playing "Autumn Nocturne," yet the notes he actually plays consistently skirt the song's cloying melody. The response of the audience says a lot about the complexity of the experience Rollins offers, involving suspense and laughter, tension and release, irreverence and romance.

AUTUMN NOCTURNE

Sonny Rollins

Sonny Rollins, tenor saxophone; Mark Soskin, piano; Aurell Ray, electric guitar; Jerome Harris, electric bass; Tony Williams, drums

LABEL: Milestone M55055; *Silver City* (Milestone 2MCD-2501)
DATE: 1978
STYLE: hard bop
FORM: 32-bar popular song (**AABA**), with lengthy solo introduction

Introduction

0:00	Rollins begins improvising at top speed, ending with a descending run. In the abrupt silence that follows, we can hear murmurs of audience conversation.
0:07	Still warming up, Rollins plays fragments, some short, others lengthy.
0:18	He plays the opening melody of "Autumn Nocturne" in its home key of B-flat major.
0:27	The melody begins to lose rhythmic momentum in softer, disjointed passagework, finally running down to a loud, squawky note.
0:29	Rollins begins a new phrase with a bold, upward statement, then shifts it to a new key. As he reaches for upper notes, his tone is deliberately thin and strained.
0:39	A new phrase modulates to a different key.
0:48	A descending chromatic scale lands on a new note, suggesting yet another modulation.
0:52	Rollins rapidly repeats a short melodic pattern.
0:59	In the spirit of the original melody, Rollins plays in an earnest, romantic style.
1:09	Suddenly returning to B-flat major, he once again plays the opening melody to "Autumn Nocturne."
1:21	Rollins plays with a triad (three-note chord), moving it up and down experimentally. Sensing that the introduction is now going into overdrive, the audience begins to applaud and cheer.
1:28	The harmony becomes more "outside," with a descending melodic sequence built on the interval of a fourth.
1:41	Rollins moves into uncertain harmonic territory before returning to B-flat.
1:58	He suddenly shifts to a simple riff, played with greater volume and timbre intensity. He repeats the riff until the audience shouts its approval.
2:08	He fastens onto a two-note motive, moving rapidly between keys.
2:22	He quotes a phrase from "Today" by Randy Sparks ("I'll be a dandy and I'll be a rover").
2:29	Rollins holds a note and distorts it before moving to much faster material.

2:49		Settling in a major key, he plays more bluesy material.
2:59		A much faster passage moves through unsettled harmonies.
3:05		Rollins plays with a motive, dropping the last note a half step with each repetition.
3:25		He again holds and distorts a note.
3:31		Settling into F major, he ironically quotes "Home Sweet Home."
3:39		After playing a single note, he awkwardly answers it with a verbal squawk. He repeats the gesture, drawing yet more cheers from the crowd.
3:41		Once again, Rollins moves into a bluesy mode.
3:58		He begins to move down the chromatic scale. The notes become increasingly detached and accelerate in speed.
4:05		As the timbre of the notes becomes more distorted, the line reaches bottom and turns back upward.
4:11		Rollins settles into a slow, deliberate tempo, which becomes a cue for the band to enter.

Chorus 1

4:18	A	As the audience roars its approval, Rollins plays the melody of "Autumn Nocturne" with fiercely distorted timbre. By sounding the beat clearly, the rhythm section makes it easier to hear the subtleties of Rollins's rhythmic gestures.
4:36		Off to the side, the electric guitar adds chords.
4:40		As the harmonic progression reaches the turnaround, Rollins launches into an extremely fast, dissonant, and heavily distorted passage.
4:46	A	Rollins returns to playing the melody.
4:54		He focuses his line on a single note, decorating it with neighbor notes (adjacent notes).
5:07		The last phrase becomes lost in an ecstatic, dissonant passage.
5:13	B	The bridge begins in a new key, with Rollins returning to the melody.
5:17		For several measures, the bass suggests a double-time rhythmic feeling.
5:27		The tune modulates to a new key. Rollins's improvisation becomes more earnest and impassioned.
5:35		As the tune begins to modulate back to the original key, Rollins plays another impossibly fast and distorted passage.
5:40		Williams signals the return with a drum roll.
5:42	A	
5:45		Rollins's melody descends instead of rising.
5:50		His line soars upward, reaching a brief climax.
5:54		As the tune nears its last few bars, Williams begins playing the cymbals more intently.
5:59		He plays a strong polyrhythm, augmenting it in the next measure by adding bass drum strokes.
6:07		A three-note rhythm ends the tune. All the musicians play their instruments simultaneously.

| 6:19 | Seeming to have a few more notes in mind, Rollins tries to squeeze them out. |
| 6:21 | Finally, over a long saxophone tremolo, the tune ends to applause. |

Wes Montgomery (1923–1968)

The arrival of Charlie Christian in the late 1930s opened the floodgates to electric guitarists who played in a linear style, adapting the single-note phrasing of horn players. Several combined linear solos with chords, voicing them in ways unique to the six-string configuration of the guitar. Those who achieved prominence in the 1950s include Barney Kessel, Tal Farlow, Johnny Smith, Billy Bauer, Jim Hall, and Kenny Burrell—each took Christian's example and developed a distinctive style of his own. None, however, had the impact of Wes Montgomery, who radically altered the instrument's sound with his innovative approach to chordal harmonies.

Born in Indianapolis, Montgomery was the second of three jazz musician siblings. His older brother, Monk, gave him a four-string guitar when he was twelve, but he showed little interest in it until he heard Christian's recordings several years later. Montgomery was twenty and married when he bought an electric guitar and amplifier, and began spending hours at night after work teaching himself to play. When his wife complained that the amplifier was too loud, he dispensed with the pick and used his thumb, achieving unparalleled mastery with this technique as well as a remarkably mellow tone. Montgomery elaborated on that dulcet sound by playing in octaves. From octaves, he moved on to full and intricate chords, manipulating them with the same speed and dexterity of his single-note improvisations, continuing to pluck and strum with his thumb. Soon he developed a signature approach to soloing: after a theme statement, he would play choruses of single-note phrases, followed by choruses of more rhythmically intense octaves, climaxing with riff-laden chords. In 1948, he went on tour with Lionel Hampton's big band.

Bored with travel and one-night stands, Montgomery returned to Indianapolis and formed a group with his brothers, Monk on bass and Buddy on piano and vibes. Montgomery was thirty-four and virtually unknown when alto saxophonist Cannonball Adderley heard him and alerted his record label to this major undiscovered talent. From the moment he arrived in New York, the critical reception was highly favorable; guitarists gawked at his impossibly fast thumb, and he came to be regarded as a musician's musician.

Then in the early 1960s, the guitar moved to the center of America's musical consciousness, and Montgomery's alluring octaves were seen as having great commercial potential. As he switched affiliations from a jazz label to a pop label, in 1967, he emerged as a mainstream recording star, performing with large studio ensembles in easy-listening arrangements of pop songs that featured his octaves and minimized improvisation. Those records failed to reflect the stimulating jazz he continued to play in live performance, but firmly established him as one of the best-selling musicians of his time.

"TWISTED BLUES"

Montgomery's harmonic and rhythmic ingenuity led him to compose pieces that admiring musicians described as "tricky." "Twisted Blues" is a good example; as the title implies, it seems to start out as a blues but goes off in a different direction, ending up as a thirty-two-bar structure built on a *near* sixteen-bar blues played twice. Montgomery initially recorded it with a small group in 1961, and made it an almost nightly part of his sets. By the time he rerecorded it in 1965, with a big band deftly arranged by Oliver Nelson, the piece was practically second nature to him. Although this version was made just as he was beginning to make the transition to pop, it is far more effective than the original. The tempo is taken way up, yet Montgomery plays with ease, phrasing on and against the beat, combining bebop harmonies with blues cadences, alternating chromatic riffs and melodic sequences. Toward the close of the third chorus, he introduces a rhythmic series of two-note chords (1:39). In the choruses that follow, he turns on the heat with his trademark octaves and chords. Also impressive is his interaction with the orchestra, which paces and inspires him, and the attentive playing by Grady Tate, Montgomery's preferred drummer.

TWISTED BLUES

Wes Montgomery

Ernie Royal, Joe Newman, Donald Byrd, trumpets; Wayne Andre, Jimmy Cleveland, Quentin Jackson, Danny Moore, trombones; Tony Studd, bass trombone; Phil Woods, Jerry Dodgion, alto saxophones; Romeo Penque, Bob Ashton, tenor saxophones; Danny Bank, baritone saxophone; Herbie Hancock or Roger Kellaway, piano; Wes Montgomery, electric guitar; George Duvivier, bass; Grady Tate, drums; Candido Camero, congas; Oliver Nelson, conductor and arranger

LABEL: Verve MGV8642; *Goin' out of My Head* (Verve 000940202)
DATE: 1965
STYLE: hard bop
FORM: 32-bar popular song (**AA'**)

Introduction

0:00		The full band enters with loud chords on the offbeat, played in the upper range of the trumpet's register.
0:02		Beneath the shrieking trumpets, the saxophones hold a dissonant chord.
0:04		The instrumentation now quiets down, with the trombones in the lead.

Chorus 1 (head)

0:08	**A**	Montgomery, introduced by two loud trumpet chords, plays a bluesy melody. The harmony behind it is *not* the tonic, but a IV chord—which we would normally find in the fifth bar of a blues.
0:11		The saxophone section responds to the guitar's melody with short, crisp chords, doubled by the guitar.
0:13		The first phrase is repeated.
0:17		Montgomery plays a short motive, leading the band to play a long chain of descending chromatic chords.
0:25	**A'**	Montgomery repeats his bluesy opening melody, answered by a corresponding melody in the saxophones.
0:38		The full band plays the descending chromatic chords, with trumpets shrieking in their extreme highest register.

Chorus 2

0:42	**A**	Montgomery begins improvising in a bebop style over the rhythm section.
0:54		Over the gradually descending chromatic chords, he takes a melodic idea and repeats it (a sequence), starting each time on a different pitch to match the movement of the chords.
0:59	**A'**	
1:03		Montgomery plays a short three-note motive, drifting it up and down to match the harmony. The drums react to its polyrhythm.

Chorus 3

1:16	**A**	Montgomery trims his line to simple, short phrases.
1:19		He hits a bluesy chord, followed by a bluesy phrase.
1:29		As the chords descend chromatically, Montgomery plays another motive in sequence.
1:32	**A'**	
1:39		Playing on two strings at once, Montgomery creates another polyrhythmic riff.

| 1:43 | | The change in harmony suddenly jolts him away from the blues lick into a more complex line. |

Chorus 4

1:48	A	Moving from single-note lines to chords and octaves, Montgomery plays short, choppy phrases, creating a call and response with a two-note riff in the upper register.
1:59		Playing in octaves, he creates another sequence—this time with a distinctive syncopated rhythm.
2:04	A'	Montgomery ends this part of his solo with a simple arranged riff, its opening rhythm doubled by the drums and piano.

Chorus 5

2:20	A	For the next two choruses, the band enters with riffs (here, trombones) that accompany Montgomery for eight bars, leaving him free to improvise over the more complex chord changes of the next eight bars.
2:29		The trombones exit while Montgomery continues to play with a two-note motive that stretches into the upper register before tumbling back down.
2:37	A'	The saxophones enter with a new riff, and Montgomery continues to improvise over it.

Chorus 6

2:53	A	The trombones play a two-note riff, which Montgomery uses as the backdrop for an extended cross-rhythm.
3:06		His syncopation finally collapses into a simple rhythmic line that falls directly on the beat.
3:10	A'	With the return of the two-note riff, Montgomery moves back to a syncopated pattern.
3:15		The trumpets join the trombones on the riff.
3:18		Montgomery fastens onto a two-note motive, played to a steady rhythm.

Interlude

| 3:26 | | The drums play an eight-bar solo. |

Chorus 7

| 3:34 | A | Two loud chords in the trumpets signal a return to the head. |
| 3:50 | A' | |

Coda

| 4:05 | | The saxophones play a series of descending chords that land on the tonic. |
| 4:06 | | The trumpets play a final sharp dissonance, holding the chord for a long time until the drums cut them off. |

Sadly, Montgomery did not have long to enjoy his skyrocketing success. The 1965 album that included "Twisted Blues" (*Goin' out of My Head*) received a Grammy Award, and his more commercial debut on the pop label A&M, *A Day in the Life*, was cited as the best-selling jazz album of 1967. From that point on, his record producers demanded he hew to the proven formula: familiar tunes played with octaves, backed by a large, easy-listening ensemble, with little improvisation to confuse the target audience. In 1968, he died suddenly of a heart attack, at forty-three. Montgomery's career was interpreted by many as a jazz parable, with the moral being: for every album an artist does for the company, he ought to insist on doing one for himself. In concert, Montgomery continued to perform brilliantly, rarely playing the pop tunes that made him famous and never touring with large ensembles. Yet none of that work was formally documented after 1965. Indeed, the impact of his popular success was so pervasive that after his death, Verve released tracks by his quartet with an overdubbed string ensemble to simulate the pop recordings. Decades later, those magnificent tracks were released as Montgomery (and a first-class rhythm section including pianist Wynton Kelly) performed them at a New York club, the Half Note, to much acclaim. By then, virtually every jazz guitarist had studied and many had mastered his octaves and harmonies.

13

CHAPTER

Jazz Composition in the 1950s

DEFINITIONS: NEW AND OLD

Composition is not easily defined in music driven by improvisation. Before the advent of records, composers may have improvised in concert (Beethoven was celebrated for his extemporizations), but formal composition was something committed to a written score. From the twentieth century on, records often supplanted or eliminated the need for scores, making the idea of improvisation-as-lasting-music possible. Coleman Hawkins's "Body and Soul" has been published as a score, but the truest representation of the

◀ Thelonious Monk, a powerful force at the jam sessions that fed the birth of modern jazz, works on a score at Minton's Playhouse in Harlem, 1948

work must be his recording, which alone documents such essential components as his timbre and rhythmic pulse.

Simply by calling it Coleman Hawkins's "Body and Soul," we contest the traditional attribution of composition, since the performance is based on a published melody written by John Green. Indeed, international copyright laws fail to acknowledge the improviser's contribution: all "mechanical" (or composer) royalties that accrue from sales of Hawkins's record are divided between the song's composer, lyricist, and publisher. Hawkins does not participate in the profits, although Green's chord progression (which Hawkins does adhere to) is not copyrightable, while virtually every melodic phrase Hawkins plays after the first two bars is his own invention.

At what point does improvisation end and composition begin? If Hawkins had written his "Body and Soul" variations at a desk and published them as "Variations on a Theme by John Green," no one would question his function as a composer or his right to reap financial reward. Yet as a jazz musician, Hawkins was trained to do something classical composers don't do: compose durable music spontaneously. His solo on "Body and Soul" became so renowned that it was subsequently transcribed and arranged for ensembles to perform. But that is one of several exceptions that prove the rule, which may be stated as follows: A composition is a musical work that may be played by any number of musicians and bands while remaining basically unchanged; an improvisation, though it may prove as durable and adaptable as a composition, exists first and foremost as a particular performance.

In the postbop era of the 1950s, the nature of jazz composition changed, and not simply because the influence of classical music on bop and postbop musicians augured a Third Stream. The major currents in 1950s composition derived less from classical borrowings than from reinvestigations of the jazz past: the most influential composers combined modern jazz with such traditional techniques as polyphony, stride piano, short breaks, and cadenzas, as well as standard jazz and pop themes. In this period, jazz began to produce full-time composers who did not necessarily work as instrumentalists.

The four composers examined here represent four approaches to expanding the jazz canvas. Thelonious Monk worked almost exclusively with blues and song forms, rarely composing themes longer than thirty-two bars. Charles Mingus also worked with conventional forms, adding effects from gospel, ragtime, bop, classical music, and other sources, and expanding those forms into longer works. Gil Evans focused on the music of other composers, radically altering it into imaginative new pieces. George Russell introduced modalism into jazz, which spurred fresh ways of approaching harmony and the connection between improvisation and composition.

Thelonious Monk (1917–1982)

After Duke Ellington, Thelonious Monk is the most widely performed of all jazz composers. This is remarkable when you consider the differences in their output: Ellington wrote between 1,500 and 2,000 pieces, while Monk wrote around 70. Ellington composed, in addition to big-band, chamber, symphonic, and vocal works, dozens of popular songs, including major hits. Monk composed no hits and only one song ("'Round Midnight") that achieved a marginal mainstream acceptance. Yet every jazz player knows at least a few Monk pieces: they have been adapted for swing band, Dixieland, cool jazz, hard bop, avant-garde, and classical music settings. With the addition of lyrics, they have found increasing favor with singers. Although in his early years Monk was regarded as an eccentric, difficult, and not very talented pianist, his music—including his singular and immensely skillful piano style—is beloved today, even among people who have no interest in or feeling for jazz. Grade school teachers have found that very young children respond enthusiastically to his melodies.

Born in North Carolina, Monk was four when his family moved to New York. In grade school, he began listening to his older sister's piano lessons and teaching himself. As a teenager, he added a middle name, Sphere—Thelonious Sphere Monk—and quit high school to tour with an evangelist, accompanying her on organ. He heard the leading stride pianist–composers, including Duke Ellington, James P. Johnson, and Mary Lou Williams, and began writing distinctive tunes that were melodically angular and harmonically dissonant. In 1939, he briefly studied music, and a year or so later was recruited by Kenny Clarke to play in the house band at Minton's Playhouse.

Monk's involvement in Minton's after-hours jam sessions and cutting contests, where he accompanied Charlie Christian, Dizzy Gillespie, and other advanced musicians, placed him at the center of bebop's development. The dazzling Bud Powell, whom Monk mentored, admired his quirky rhythmic attack and progressive harmonies. Yet that very quirkiness mandated that Monk would flourish, if at all, as a leader of his own groups and not as a sideman. Before that happened, several of his compositions were enthusiastically taken up by swing and bop musicians, including "Epistrophy" (written by Monk and Clarke), "Hackensack" (introduced by Coleman Hawkins as "Rifftide"), and "52nd Street Theme," a nearly universal bebop anthem that Monk never recorded.

The most important of Monk's early compositions was the ballad "'Round Midnight," which trumpet player Cootie Williams recorded in a big-band version in 1944, with Powell on piano. Williams made it his theme song, and after lyrics were added (by Bernie Hanighen), singers began to perform it. Dizzy Gillespie recorded an important version in 1946, adding an introductory passage that became part of the song, and Monk recorded the first of his many versions in 1947. By 1956, when Miles Davis made Monk's ballad the centerpiece of his album 'Round About Midnight, it was fast becoming one of the most frequently performed songs in jazz. Monk's other ballads, each a distinctively poignant work, include "Ruby, My Dear," "Coming on the Hudson," "Reflections," "Ask Me Now," "Pannonica," and "Crepuscule with Nellie."

In 1944, Hawkins hired Monk for the quartet he was leading, taking him on tour and recording with him. As word of Monk's unusual music spread, he found an important admirer in Alfred Lion, whose record company, Blue Note, signed him in 1947 and documented much of his most important work over the next five years. Monk was often regarded as a figure apart from the bop movement, and his percussive piano style was mocked by many critics and fans.

In the years since Monk's death, medical observers have speculated that he may have had a neurobiological disorder called Asperger's syndrome, a nondebilitating form of autism, first described in 1944 and frequently associated with genius: others thought to have been similarly afflicted include Sir Isaac Newton, Albert Einstein, Ludwig Wittgenstein, Glenn Gould, and Stanley Kubrick. Among the symptoms are a heightened ability to recognize and analyze patterns, exceptional talent in a particular area, undeveloped social and verbal skills, physical awkwardness, and compulsive behavior. It can also lead to mood disorders and depression. Monk was known for his long silences (in speech and in music), onstage dancing (he would twitchingly whirl in a circle as the other musicians soloed), peculiar hats and sunglasses, and obsessive concentration on a few compositions. Monk was further isolated in 1951, when he was imprisoned for two months on a trumped-up narcotics charge; by all reports he was innocent, but he riled authorities by refusing to testify against others. As a result, he lost his cabaret card, which functioned as a license (subsequently found to be unconstitutional) to perform in New York venues where liquor was sold. He spent the next six years composing and recording and occasionally performing in concert halls or in other cities.

In 1955, Monk signed with a new independent label, Riverside, and reluctantly agreed to begin his contract by recording well-known themes by Ellington and other popular songwriters. The idea was to disarm skeptical listeners by demonstrating that he could play in a conventional jazz setting, before focusing on original music. The plan worked. Monk's third Riverside album, *Brilliant Corners*, which featured Sonny Rollins and Max Roach, was hailed as a major jazz event in 1956, though the title piece proved so difficult to play that the final version had to be spliced together from three takes. Listeners around the world had no trouble humming the tune's irresistible, ominous, march-like cadences.

Monk's cabaret card was finally restored in 1957, an event that inaugurated his historic six-month residency at the Five Spot, leading a quartet that included tenor saxophonist John Coltrane. For contractual reasons (Coltrane was signed to another label, Prestige), little of this music was recorded, but it attracted the attention of dozens of New York artists: jazz and classical musicians, painters, actors, and poets. Monk was taken up as a hero of the beats and of a generation of self-defined outlaw artists. His work with Coltrane had lasting influence on both men, who spent most of their careers leading quartets that built on Monk's precepts. A magnificent example of their collaboration was recorded at a Carnegie Hall concert for overseas broadcast by the Voice of America; it remained unknown here until 2005, when the tape was discovered in the Library of Congress and released on Blue Note.

Monk's fame steadily grew. In 1962, he was signed by Columbia Records, the country's premiere record label, and two years later *Time* ran a cover story about him that clinched his standing as one of jazz's most admired musicians. Monk's quartet, with his longtime saxophonist Charlie Rouse, toured the world, finally reaping the rewards of his refusal to compromise. As he once witheringly remarked, "I say play your own way. Don't play what the public wants—you play what you want and let the public pick up on what you are doing—even if it does take them 15, 20 years."

Having achieved acceptance, Monk began to withdraw personally and professionally. His composing slowed to a standstill, though he seemed to open up emotionally with his joyous devotion to solo piano, perfecting a style that combined modern harmonies with stride rhythms, often inspired by old, forgotten, and unlikely tunes ("I love You Sweetheart of All My

Dreams," a forgotten 1928 ditty, is reborn as a delightful meditation on memory and sentiment in Monk's 1964 treatment). Monk made his last records in 1971, and appeared in concert only a few times after that. By the middle 1970s, he had slipped into seclusion; soon he stopped speaking to anyone but his wife and a few friends. He spent his last years in the home of his longtime friend and supporter Baroness Pannonica de Königswarter, and died of a stroke in 1982. In 2006, he received an absurdly belated Pulitzer Prize in music.

Monk's compositions are abstractions of the song forms that had always predominated in jazz and popular music: AABA tunes and blues. In some instances, he altered standard harmonic progressions with whole-tone and chromatic scales, so that "Just You, Just Me" became "Evidence," "Blue Skies" became "In Walked Bud," and "Sweet Georgia Brown" became "Bright Mississippi." A worklist of the seventy-one compositions attributed to Monk (some were written in collaboration with other musicians or had lyrics subsequently added) suggests the gearing up, development, pinnacle years, and slowing down of his genius. The individual dates denote the earliest recorded versions by Monk, not necessarily the year of composition; where a decade is given, Monk never recorded the tune.

◆ ◆ ◆

1940s: "52nd Street Theme" (aka "The Theme"), "Harlem Is Awful Messy"
1946: "Introspection"
1947: "Humph," "In Walked Bud," "Off Minor," "'Round Midnight," "Ruby, My Dear," "Thelonious," "Well, You Needn't," "Who Knows?"
1948: "Epistrophy," " Evidence," "I Mean You," "Misterioso"
1950s: "Two Timer" (aka "Five Will Get You Ten")
1951: "Ask Me Now," "Criss Cross," "Eronel," "Four in One," "Straight, No Chaser"
1952: "Bemsha Swing," "Bye-Ya," "Hornin' In," "Let's Cool One," "Little Rootie Tootie," "Monk's Dream," "Monk's Mood," "Reflections," "Sixteen," "Skippy," "Trinkle Tinkle"
1953: "Friday the 13th," "Let's Call This," "Think of One"
1954: "Blue Monk," "Hackensack," "Locomotive," "Nutty," "We See," "Work"
1955: "Brake's Sake," "Gallop's Gallop," "Shuffle Boil"
1956: "Ba-lue Bolivar Ba-lues-are," "Brilliant Corners," "Pannonica"
1957: "Crepuscule with Nellie," "Functional," "Light Blue," "Rhythm-a-ning"
1958: "Blues Five Spot," "Coming on the Hudson"

1959: "Bluehawk," "Jackie-ing," "Played Twice," "Round Lights"
1960: "San Francisco Holiday"
1961: "Bright Mississippi"
1963: "Oska T"
1964: "Monk's Point," "North of the Sunset," "Stuffy Turkey," "Teo"
1966: "Green Chimneys"
1967: "Boo Boo's Birthday," "Ugly Beauty"
1968: "Raise Four"
1971: "Blue Sphere," "Something in Blue"
1972: "A Merrier Christmas"

◆ ◆ ◆

Each new composition had its own unmistakable integrity. The particular dissonances Monk favored—including minor ninths, flatted fifths (tritones), and minor seconds (semitones)—had been widely regarded as mistakes until he established them as essential components in jazz harmony. Monk played minor seconds, for example (two adjacent notes on the piano), as though his finger had accidentally hit the crack between the keys, making them both ring and forcing the listener to accept that jarring sound as a routine part of his musical language. Nellie Monk, his wife, described an incident in their home life that suggests a parallel with the way Monk altered the way we hear jazz: "I used to have a phobia about pictures or anything on a wall hanging just a little bit crooked. Thelonious cured me. He nailed a clock to the wall at a very slight angle, just enough to make me furious. We argued about it for two hours, but he wouldn't let me change it. Finally, I got used to it. Now anything can hang at any angle, and it doesn't bother me at all."

This doesn't mean that Monk advocated a kind of free jazz in which any note was acceptable, or that he didn't make mistakes. In "Thelonious," which is chock-a-block with dissonances, there is a revealing moment (at 1:52) where he concludes an arpeggio by landing on the wrong note. He then plays the right one, and combines them so as to resolve the error, making it a viable part of the performance. (Musicians call this a "save.") A fastidious composer-improviser, Monk paid scrupulous attention to details and demanded the same level of attention from his musicians. He believed that a meaningful improvisation should flow from and develop the composed theme. Unsurprisingly, his compositions sound like his improvisations, and his improvisations often sound like his compositions—even when he didn't write the theme. For example, classical pianists have transcribed his solo interpretations of pop songs like "I Should Care" or "April in Paris," performing them as if they were Monk originals. His music has altered our perception of harmony, space, swing, and melody, all while remaining tied to the traditions from which it sprang.

"THELONIOUS"

A product of Monk's first session as a leader, "Thelonious" is considered his first masterpiece, a work that shuns the usual theme-and-variations format of bop and shows off his compositional ingenuity and fierce independence. In 1947, a *Billboard* reviewer called it a "controversial jazz disking worked out on a one note riff." But that repeated note, a B-flat (sometimes doubled as a B-flat octave), is a deceptively simple front for the descending chromatic chords that shadow this thirty-six-bar variant on the AABA song. The A sections are eight bars, the bridge is ten, and the last A section includes a two-bar coda. This pattern demands heightened attention from musicians, who, as a matter of habit, tend to think in terms of four eight-bar sections. As John Coltrane observed, "I always had to be alert with Monk, because if you didn't keep aware all the time of what was going on, you'd suddenly feel as if you'd stepped into an empty elevator shaft." In "Thelonious," the three wind instruments are used to voice the chords, and the only soloists are piano and, briefly, drums. The result is a kind of piano concerto, incorporating various elements of jazz history from stride to bop.

THELONIOUS

Thelonious Monk

Idrees Sulieman, trumpet; Danny Quebec West, alto saxophone; Billy Smith, tenor saxophone; Thelonious Monk, piano; Gene Ramey, bass; Art Blakey, drums

LABEL: BLP 1510; *Genius of Modern Music,* vol. 1 (RVG 781510)
DATE: 1947
STYLE: bebop, Monk-style
FORM: 36-bar popular song (**AABA**; the bridge and the last **A** section are 10 rather than 8 bars long)

Introduction

0:00	Unaccompanied, Monk plays the main theme of the piece: a syncopated figure on the first note of the scale (the tonic). Pianistically, it is simple, built comfortably around an octave.
0:02	As Monk continues, he is joined by Blakey on cymbals. The theme ends on a blue third, which Monk holds out.

0:04   Blakey plays a brief solo, alternating snare drum with bass drum. In the
           background, we can hear Monk's voice counting off time.

Chorus 1 (head)

0:08   **A**   The entire band plays the theme: Monk's insistent, repetitive octave,
               supported by descending chromatic chords in the horns. The bass line
               for the **A** section remains consistent throughout the performance.

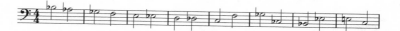

0:18   **A**

0:27   **B**   The bridge begins with a *cadence figure*, deriving its rhythm from the **A**
               section and promising a conclusion to its chromatic harmonies. But the
               harmony is *not* resolved: instead, the melody blends into a slower line
               that floats above ambiguous harmonies.

0:31   When the melody reaches the tonic, it is supported not by conventional
           harmony but by the whole-tone scale, which distorts our sense of
           tonality.

0:32   The melody slowly descends by half step.

0:37   As the melody reaches a half cadence, Monk connects the bridge to the
           concluding **A** section with a whole-tone scale.

0:38   **A**

0:47   The chorus ends with the cadence figure heard at the opening of the
           bridge, this time resolving to the tonic in the second bar.

Chorus 2

0:49   **A**   Monk begins his solo with simple melodic fragments, all derived from
               his opening octave.

0:58   **A**   Suddenly, responding to the harmonies implied by the chromatic bass
               line, he shifts to a bebop-style improvised line.

1:07   **B**   Monk begins the bridge by paraphrasing its melody.

1:12   With a few dissonant notes and unexpected silences, he complicates his
           connection to the underlying harmony.

1:17   He finally returns to the tonic octave—a full bar early.

1:19   **A**   Monk plays a syncopated pattern with the tonic octave in the highest
               register of the piano, accompanied by only the bass and drums.

1:28   At the end of the chorus, he returns to the middle of the piano to play
           the cadence figure.

Chorus 3

1:30   **A**   Sounding uncannily like a ragtime piano player, Monk begins playing in
               stride style, firmly doubling the bass line.

1:39   **A**   With his left hand shifting restlessly between chromatic chords, his right
               hand remains firmly rooted in the tonic.

1:48	**B**	Monk starts the bridge by once again paraphrasing its melody.
1:52		He "misses" a note by a half step, corrects it, and returns to a literal statement of the melody.
2:00	**A**	
2:02		A new three-note motive borrows its rhythm from the bebop standard "Salt Peanuts."
2:09		Monk plays the cadence figure, connecting it seamlessly to the beginning of the next chorus.

Chorus 4

2:11	**A**	Once again, the chorus begins with an unaccompanied statement of the main theme.
2:16		Fastening onto a short chromatic triplet, Monk pulls it down the length of the piano.
2:20	**A**	He plays a long, involved melodic line based on the chromatic harmony.
2:29	**B**	The bridge begins in the upper octave; Monk plays it delicately.
2:41	**A**	The band returns with a full statement of the theme.

Coda

2:50		The band plays the cadence figure, stopping on the next-to-last chord. While the horns hold out the unresolved harmony, Monk plays a lengthy descending whole-tone scale.
2:56		He ends his improvisation with a striking high note.
2:58		A three-note stroke from the drummer closes the performance.

"RHYTHM-A-NING"

One of Monk's best-known pieces, "Rhythm-a-ning" has a long history, which testifies to his gift for collating bits of music and renewing them in his own way. The AABA tune is based on the chord changes of "I Got Rhythm," but the primary eight-bar melody draws on two big-band recordings of the 1930s: Duke Ellington's "Ducky Wucky" (1932) for two measures, and Mary Lou Williams's "Walkin' and Swingin'" for four. Williams's lick was later picked up by Charlie Christian and other musicians, but only Monk turned it into a postbop classic, in part by connecting it seamlessly to the Ellington figure and adding a bridge of modern harmonies.

Although he wrote the piece much earlier, Monk did not record "Rhythm-a-ning" until 1957, at which point it became a regular part of his repertory. An especially fine version dates from five years later, the period when he first signed with Columbia Records. Tenor saxophonist Charlie

Rouse was Monk's most consistent partner; he joined the quartet in 1959 and stayed for eleven years. His soft, sandy sound suggests an uncanny affinity with Monk's piano, and his quick-witted responses provide countless moments of give and take with Monk's comping. This performance is taken at a medium up-tempo, flowing smoothly through the introduction, theme, two choruses by Rouse, two choruses by Monk, theme, and coda. But close listening discloses how much each musician relies on Monk's cues and the demands of the piece. The drummer states the rhythm but also responds to rhythmic ideas introduced on piano. Rouse improvises variations on the theme, but also echoes melodic suggestions played by Monk. The bassist enables the others with his rock-solid harmonic and rhythmic foundation.

RHYTHM-A-NING

Thelonious Monk

Charlie Rouse, tenor saxophone; Thelonious Monk, piano; John Ore, bass; Frankie Dunlop, drums

LABEL: Columbia CL2038; *Criss-Cross* (Legacy 074646353721)
DATE: 1962
STYLE: bebop, Monk-style
FORM: 32-bar popular song (**AABA**)

Introduction

0:00	Monk plays the opening riff on solo piano.
0:02	At various points, he plays several adjacent keys (minor seconds) simultaneously—sometimes deliberately (as in the underlying harmony), but other times apparently from "sloppy" technique.
0:05	The second part of the tune is a repeated three-note riff, its last note falling in unexpected places and given extra weight by Monk, who doubles it in his left hand.
0:08	Dunlop on drums adds a response.

Chorus 1 (head)

0:09	A	With a cymbal crash, the entire band enters. Rouse (tenor saxophone) and Ore (bass) join the piano on the melody, with the drums reinforcing its syncopations.
0:14		Underneath the three-note riff, the bass begins to walk.
0:19	A	
0:28	B	Over the chord progression to "I Got Rhythm," Monk continues the rhythm of the three-note riff, accenting the last note of each phrase.
0:36		A rising scale ends with a startling, splatted dissonance.
0:37	A	

Chorus 2

0:47	**A**	The first solo, by Rouse, is introduced by Monk's comping. Monk plays a dissonant chord that lands squarely on the opening beat of the chorus, then falls silent. Rouse paraphrases the theme's melody, accompanied by a crisp backbeat in the drums.
0:51		Monk plays the same chord, again falling on the downbeat. This pattern (a chord on the downbeat, followed by four measures of silence) continues throughout the **A** sections of this chorus.
0:56	**A**	Rouse moves away from the melody toward bebop-style lines. The drums similarly drift from the backbeat into more interactive rhythms.
1:05	**B**	
1:10		Monk's chords become more frequent, falling every other beat.
1:15	**A**	Monk returns to his spare comping.

Chorus 3

1:24	**A**	Monk signals a new chorus, still Rouse's, by placidly repeating a single chord.
1:29		For the next twelve measures, Monk stops playing altogether.
1:33	**A**	Rouse plays a phrase derived from the theme, then clashes with the bass line by repeating it a half step higher.
1:39		As Rouse returns to the tonic through a long descending line, the drums play complex patterns, accenting different offbeats in the measure.
1:43	**B**	Monk begins a new pattern of accompaniment, and Rouse improvises in response.
1:52	**A**	Monk returns to his favorite chord.
1:54		Rouse improvises another line that pulls a half step away from the tonic.

Chorus 4

2:01	**A**	Monk begins his solo by borrowing a common harmonic pattern from bebop. He shifts to a distant chord and returns by a series of substitute chords to the tonic four bars later. (Since the bass immediately responds to Monk's chords, we can assume that this substitution was planned.)
2:10	**A**	Monk repeats his harmonic substitution, improvising a more dissonant line.
2:19	**B**	On the bridge, Monk plays dissonant whole-tone fragments in his right hand against loud single notes in his left hand. The drums disorient us by playing consistently on the offbeat.
2:29	**A**	Monk returns to the theme, occasionally altered by dissonant half-step splats and left-hand notes.
2:34		The last phrase reaches for a dissonant high note—the tritone, or flatted fifth.

Chorus 5

2:38	**A**	Playing entirely in the upper register of the piano, Monk builds a line that consistently accents the dissonant flatted fifth.

2:47	A	Monk turns the flatted-fifth pattern into an ostinato in the right hand. The only accompaniment is the drum's accents and an occasional open fifth in the left hand.
2:53		The flatted-fifth pattern descends precipitously into the bass.
2:56	B	Infusing his harmonies with the whole-tone scale, Monk transforms the "I Got Rhythm" progression into a series of unsettling sounds.
3:05	A	Monk turns the opening theme into a descending scale that interacts with the improvised drum part.
3:09		To close out his solo, Monk turns the tonic chord into a peculiar ostinato.

Chorus 6 (head)

3:14	A	The band returns to repeat the head.
3:21		Monk responds to the theme with a dissonant chord cluster (with closely spaced notes), emphasizing the flatted fifth.
3:23	A	
3:27		Monk accents the end of the three-note riff with loud bass notes.
3:31	B	The bridge begins an octave lower than in the beginning.
3:40	A	

Coda

3:48		Over the last sustained piano chord, Monk repeats a jarringly dissonant minor ninth.
3:50		Dunlop plays a short drum fill, but Monk's dissonance holds out just slightly longer.

Charles Mingus (1922-1979)

Charles Mingus was a bigger-than-life figure who made an indelible mark in many areas of jazz. As a bassist, he was among the most accomplished virtuosos of his time. As a composer, he expanded the variety and scope of American music, assimilating influences as far ranging as the sanctified church, New Orleans polyphony, swing, bop, Romantic classical music, and modern classical music. As a spokesman, he made jazz relevant to the civil rights era. As a memoirist, he brought new insights into the tribulations of African American artists trying to surmount the constrictions of prejudice.

Mingus was extremely sensitive to Negro stereotypes, which he exploited to poke fun at racist attitudes. He bristled at being called Charlie, which he thought disrespectful, and resented critical semantics that used the word "jazz" as a means of ghettoizing his art. About "Meditations on Integration" (1964), he wrote: "You'll say that it sounds almost classical. It *is* classical. You see, black faces aren't expected to play classical. But they do. We, too, went to school. We, too, studied music." He was also sensitive about his light skin, claiming a racially mixed background, including Chinese (he posed as a Chinese mandarin for the cover of his album *Mingus Dynasty*). A few days after the debut of "Meditations on Integration," he was the subject of a television portrait made in Toronto. Asked to describe himself, he said:

◆ ◆ ◆

I am Charles Mingus, a famed jazz musician but not famed enough to make a living in society, that is, in America, my home. I cannot even support my family, honestly that is, from the fame that I gain to the right of being a Negro musician. I am a human being born in Indian Territory, conquered by white skins, or invisible skins, transparent skins, people who killed and robbed to inherit the earth for themselves and for their children. Charles Mingus is a musician, a mongrel musician who plays beautiful, who plays ugly, who plays lovely, who plays masculine, who plays feminine, who plays music, who plays all sounds, loud, soft, unheard sounds, sounds, sounds, sounds, solid sounds, sounds, sounds. A musician just loves to play with sound.

◆ ◆ ◆

Born in Nogales, Arizona, Mingus was only three months old when his family moved to Watts, an area of Los Angeles with a large population of blacks and Mexican Americans. The family belonged to the African Methodist Episcopal Church, where Charles heard the gospel music that had a lasting influence on him. He played piano, trombone, and cello before taking up the bass in high school, studying with the excellent jazz bassist Red Callender and with Callender's teacher, Herman Rheinschagen, formerly of the New York Philharmonic. In later years, Mingus recalled being advised to switch from cello to bass because as a black man he could not succeed in classical music and would find work only if he learned to "slap that bass, Charlie!"

Mingus soon began playing dances and parties, and composing elaborate works that reflected his classical training, most notably "Half-Mast Inhibition" (a characteristically telling Mingus title), completed in his teens and reflecting his admiration for Richard Strauss. He worked in diverse ensembles, including a Dixieland band with Kid Ory, Louis Armstrong's big band, and studio sessions with singer Dinah Washington. In the late 1940s, he organized recording sessions for fly-by-night Los Angeles labels that were poorly distributed and little heard. The range of these recordings is fantastic: rhythm and blues, big-band swing, pop crooning, classicism, and original works that, slightly revised, prefigure the style of his mature music.

At the same time, he toured with Lionel Hampton, who debuted his first important recorded work, "Mingus Fingers." Not until 1950, however, when he came to New York with the Red Norvo Trio, did he receive national attention. Mingus's virtuosity made him a mainstay of the city's best musicians, resulting in important engagements with Charlie Parker, Bud Powell, Stan Getz, Miles Davis, and the Duke Ellington Orchestra, among others. In 1952, Mingus and drummer Max Roach organized their own record label, Debut, which lasted five years and documented Mingus's flirtation with cool jazz. Its most successful recording was of the Canadian Massey Hall concert of 1953, a bebop pinnacle featuring Parker, Gillespie, Powell, Mingus, and Roach. A year later, Mingus took a job with Art Tatum, whose harmonic ingenuity dazzled him as much as it had Charlie Parker a decade earlier.

In 1953, Mingus began contributing music to the pioneering cooperative called the Jazz Composers' Workshop. Other than Mingus, all the participants were white and their music is little heard today, though one member, Teo Macero, would have a lasting impact as a Columbia Records producer who supervised recordings by Mingus, Monk, and Miles Davis. The music that emerged from this workshop tended to fuse cool jazz and classical techniques, prefiguring the Third Stream, which Mingus quickly recognized as an inadequate forum for the emotions he wished to express.

In 1956, Mingus signed with Atlantic Records and created his breakthrough album, wittily titled *Pithecanthropus Erectus*, which demonstrated how explosive yet lyrical his music could be. The following year, he was invited to contribute a work to Brandeis University's Festival of the Arts ("Reflections"), a benchmark event for the Third Stream movement. He also completed his more significant second Atlantic album, *The Clown*, which introduced two musicians who would remain longtime members of his circle—the trombonist Jimmy Knepper and the drummer Dannie Richmond—and placed Mingus in the forefront of advanced jazz thinkers. This album, played by a quintet he called the Charles Mingus Jazz Workshop, combined rousing passions with an almost nostalgic serenity, and demonstrated to anyone in doubt that Mingus might be the finest bass player alive, in or out of jazz. It also proved that he could produce a compelling work with little more than a fragment of composed music. The lead-off selection, "Haitian Fight Song," opens with a thunderous bass cadenza—"bass slapping" taken to a new and stirring level. The written material consists of two riffs amounting to eight bars, plus a twelve-bar blues grid for the solos.

Mingus became increasingly notorious for outspoken comments on and off the bandstand. One piece, "Gunslinging Bird" (also known as "If Charlie Parker Was a Gunslinger, There'd Be a Whole Lot of Dead Copycats"), expressed his loathing for musicians who played clichés or failed to find original, personal ways of measuring up to his music. During public performances, he would occasionally stop a piece to berate a musician and then begin again. Mingus's comments turned political after 1957, when President Eisenhower reluctantly sent federal troops to force Arkansas governor Orville Faubus to integrate Little Rock's Central High School. In 1959, Mingus recorded "Fables of Faubus," a piece that satirizes Faubus with its melodically whimsical theme. Columbia Records, however, refused to let him sing his lyric, which he recorded for a smaller label (Candid) the following year, proclaiming Faubus "ridiculous" and "a fool." As the civil rights era heated up, other jazz musicians followed Mingus's example of speaking out through their music. Mingus inevitably heaped equal scorn on the "jazz industry," which deprived musicians of control over their own work.

For all his insistence on originality, Mingus remained respectful of jazz traditions. He never tired of citing as his core inspirations Ellington, Tatum, Parker, and the church, though his music took in far more than that. During the bop years, modernism had been embraced as a kind of religion by younger musicians, who belittled earlier styles of jazz. Mingus was the first composer of his generation to pay indelible tributes to great figures of the past, including Lester Young, the subject of his famous threnody (perhaps the best known of his tunes) "Goodbye Pork Pie Hat," and Jelly Roll Morton, in the affectionate parody "Jelly Roll."

At times, his versatility verged on split-personality: one day, the fastidiously arranged "Far Wells Mill Valley," written for a friend on the West Coast and thus in the style of cool jazz (the instrumentation includes flute and vibes), and the next, the raucous and self-descriptive "Wednesday Night Prayer Meeting." As the Jazz Workshop developed, Mingus retreated from writing out his ideas in favor of a more flexible form of collaboration with his musicians. This policy worked for shorter pieces, but caused problems as he continued to write exceedingly long orchestral works that required an organizational discipline he often lacked. In a famous 1962 debacle, he held a concert at New York's Town Hall for which he was so unprepared that the musicians were seen correcting their scores as the curtains parted. Mingus began hiring arrangers (notably Sy Johnson) to help organize his pieces; however many hands were involved, though, the end product always sounded like unadulterated Mingus. At the same time, he began revealing more of his personal life, encouraging documentary filmmakers to follow him around, writing unusually candid liner notes (in 1971 he published his memoir, *Beneath the Underdog*), inviting his psychiatrist to publicly analyze his music, and speaking at length on the bandstand.

Mingus's most successful and ambitious longer works include *The Black Saint and the Sinner Lady*, *Let My Children Hear Music*, *The Shoes of the Fisherman's Wife Are Some Jive Ass Slippers*, *Cumbia and Jazz Fusion*, and *Epitaph*—the work he presented in part at the 1962 Town Hall concert, completed posthumously by Gunther Schuller. Mingus's large body of work (some 300 compositions) spans cool jazz and hard bop while combining daunting experimentalism with visceral pleasure. Some of his music, with its heady, polyphonic textures, gloomy dissonances, and intimations of outright terror, is as difficult for musicians to master as it is for listeners to understand. Mingus died in 1979 at fifty-six, from the effects of amyotrophic lateral sclerosis (Lou Gehrig's disease). He composed and conducted his final works from a wheelchair.

"BOOGIE STOP SHUFFLE"

Mingus generates express-train momentum with "Boogie Stop Shuffle," a twelve-bar blues that builds vibrantly on the eight-to-the-bar rhythms of boogie-woogie. Although he has only seven instruments at his disposal, he employs multiple textures and variations on the theme. The soloists express themselves freely, yet the main impression is of a tightly organized work in which the improvisations serve to elaborate on the composer's vision. The theme alone requires the first five choruses, with its ostinato, staccato chords, unison moaning, three-note riff, and bop variation punctuated first by cymbals (fourth chorus) and then by piano (fifth chorus). The expeditious tempo means that each of the eighteen choruses is played in about eleven seconds.

All the musicians heard here were important figures in the Jazz Workshop, especially Dannie Richmond, formerly a rhythm and blues tenor saxophonist who switched to drums under Mingus's tutelage and became his second in command. Pianist Horace Parlan developed a powerful left-hand style to compensate for the fact that his right hand was partly paralyzed by polio. The key soloist here, Booker Ervin, was one of the most instantly recognizable tenor saxophonists of his generation, known for his huge sound and relentless energy. This is the original recording of "Boogie Stop Shuffle" as edited by Mingus for the Columbia album *Mingus Ah Um*. After his death, Columbia reissued the album with the cuts restored. In some cases, such restorations are welcome. In this instance, Mingus knew what he was doing: increasing the excitement of the performance by excising inessential passages and enabling the tenor saxophones to make especially dramatic entrances. Incidentally, fans of the Spider-Man movies may experience déjà vu: the theme song is suspiciously similar to "Boogie Stop Shuffle."

BOOGIE STOP SHUFFLE (EDITED VERSION)

Charles Mingus

Willie Dennis, trombone; John Handy, alto saxophone; Shafi Hadi, Booker Ervin, tenor saxophones; Horace Parlan, piano; Charles Mingus, bass; Dannie Richmond, drums

LABEL: Columbia CL1370; *Mingus Ah-Um* (Sony/BMG Jazz 88697127572)
DATE: 1959
STYLE: experimental hard bop
FORM: 12-bar blues

Chorus 1

0:00	The piece opens with an ostinato riff played by the tenor saxophones, piano, and bass, in a rhythm reminiscent of a boogie-woogie left hand.
0:04	As the harmony changes to IV in the 12-bar blues progression, the riff moves in sequence, starting four steps higher.
0:06	When the harmony falls back to I, the motive returns to its original pitch.
0:08	As the harmony falls from V to IV to I, the band plays a new, continuous phrase.

Chorus 2

0:11	Parlan (piano) and Mingus (bass) continue the ostinato. Above it, the horns (three saxophones and trombone) mark the end of the ostinato's phrases with sharp, dissonant chords. These chords are extended, containing major triads that clash with the prevailing minor tonality.
0:19	By controlling their volume and bending pitches, the saxophones manage to match their sound to that of the trombone with a plunger mute.

Chorus 3

0:22   The phrase played by the horns spills over into the next chorus. Each line now begins with a crisp, three-note riff on the same chords.

Chorus 4

0:34   Suddenly the horns switch to a bebop-style line, played in unison. The bass ostinato continues underneath.

0:43   At the end of the last phrase, the line suddenly expands into a complex dissonant chord.

Chorus 5

0:45   As the horns repeat the same line, the groove changes to a more standard bebop feeling: Mingus switches to a more conventional walking-bass line, while Parlan begins to comp.

Chorus 6

0:55   A barely audible shift marks the spot where Mingus edited out the first two choruses of Ervin's tenor saxophone solo. What was originally his third chorus begins with a dramatic series of upward rips, supported by block-chord riffs by the saxophones and trombone.

Chorus 7

1:07   Ervin uses false fingering while the background horns continue their riffs.

1:14   For a split second, he hits a high note before returning to a more comfortable register to round off his solo.

Chorus 8

1:18   The horns and the bass return to the riff. Above them, Parlan oscillates between three piano chords.

Chorus 9

1:29   In the upper register, Parlan plays a short, bluesy phrase, its endless repetitions forming a cross-rhythm against the background riff.

Chorus 10

1:40   The groove switches once again, with the bass moving to a walking pattern. Parlan begins to improvise.

1:48   Toward the end of the chorus, Parlan lands on a harsh, bluesy dissonance.

Chorus 11

1:52   Parlan continues on the same chord, effectively blurring the boundary between the two choruses.

Chorus 12

2:03   Another bit of editing eliminates five choruses from the original. The ostinato returns in the bass, accompanied by a slow, mournful counter-melody by the alto saxophone. Richmond on drums, preparing for a solo, plays more aggressively.

Chorus 13

2:14   Richmond takes a solo. The first phrase fits neatly over the first four bars of blues form.

Chorus 14

2:25   His second chorus begins with a short three-stroke motive.

2:28   Richmond plays a phrase that alternates between the snare drum and the tom-toms.

Chorus 15

2:35   The ostinato bass line returns, supported by the horn chords from chorus 2.

Chorus 16

2:47   A repeat of chorus 3.

Chorus 17

2:58   A repeat of chorus 4.

Chorus 18

3:09   A repeat of chorus 5.

Coda

3:18   As the horns sustain their last chord, the rhythm comes to a halt. The sound of the chord pulsates as individual horns change their volume.

3:21   The alto saxophone adds an anguished squeal.

3:24   The other horns join in, creating polyphonic chaos.

3:28   Inspired by the moment, Richmond begins an impromptu free-rhythm drum solo.

3:36   With a final cymbal crash, the tune comes to an end.

Gil Evans (1912–1988)

The name Gil Evans, as Gerry Mulligan was the first to notice, is an anagram of Svengali, and although no one could be less like the malevolent musical hypnotist of nineteenth-century fiction than the easygoing, often selfless Evans, he did have the power to make musicians and singers rise above themselves. Evans occupies a unique place in jazz: he composed several memorable pieces ("La Nevada," "Flute Song," "Proclamation," and "General Assembly" among them), but he was primarily an arranger who, in Gunther Schuller's words, "elevated arranging virtually to the art of composition."

The Canadian-born dance band and studio arranger came to New York, after a spell of radio work in Los Angeles, to write for Claude Thornhill in 1941; after leaving Thornhill seven years later, he became one of the prime movers of cool jazz. In those years, he did not play an instrument or lead his own ensemble. With the decline of the big bands, he struggled as a work-for-hire orchestrator—although greatly admired by other musicians, he was considered too daring for the kinds of projects that kept other arrangers busy. Evans took on random assignments, writing for Charlie Parker, Gerry Mulligan, swing trumpeter Billy Butterfield, and vocalist Helen Merrill, as well as a few anomalous projects, including the first album by ballad singer Johnny Mathis. He was forty-five when he achieved national recognition. Reuniting with Miles Davis for the groundbreaking 1957 album *Miles Ahead*, he crafted a series of trumpet concertos that emphasized the power and expressiveness of Davis's playing. He also wrote transitional interludes between selections, replacing the usual silences between tracks—a technique that remained unexplored until the Beatles did the same thing a decade later in *Sgt. Pepper's Lonely Hearts Club Band*.

Miles Ahead led to further collaborations with Davis and invitations to write for others. More important, it established Evans as a recording artist in his own right, piloting his own albums with hand-picked ensembles. His choice of material ranged widely, as it had during his Thornhill years—from operetta (Kurt Weill's "Bilbao Song") to folk-blues (Lead Belly's "Ella Speed") to mainstream pop (Irving Berlin's "Remember")—but the majority of tunes were drawn directly from jazz. Evans's reinventions of classic jazz pieces stimulated a revival of interest in jazz history. Like Monk and Mingus, Evans did not subscribe to the idea that modernism had trumped all that preceded it. His music was characterized by a generous use of counterpoint, sonorous slow-moving chords, and a sound palette that combined very low instruments with very high ones. For Evans, a melody was a skeleton to be dressed from the ground up in his own harmonies, countermelodies, timbres, and rhythms. The same might be said of most good arrangers, but few performed this task with his imagination or matched his ability to phrase passages so that they simulated the spontaneity of a good improvisation. As for his transformations of contemporary music, John Lewis spoke for many when he said that Evans's version of "Django" taught him things about his own composition he had not previously realized.

Evans is best known for his use of the concerto form. In addition to Miles Davis, he built works around soprano saxophonist Steve Lacy, mellophonist Don Elliott, trumpeter Johnny Coles, and guitarist Kenny Burrell, among others. In 1958, Evans adapted classic jazz themes for an album, *New Bottle, Old Wine*, featuring alto saxophonist Cannonball Adderley. The instrumentation is pure Evans, favoring nine brasses (trumpets, trombones, bass trombone, French horn, and tuba). Other than Adderley, he uses only two woodwind players, and assigns them atypical jazz instruments: flute, piccolo, and bass clarinet.

Julian "Cannonball" Adderley (1928–1975), a former schoolteacher from Tampa, Florida, achieved instant recognition when he moved to New York in 1955, shortly after Charlie Parker's death: he was quickly acclaimed as "the new Bird." In 1958, he joined the Miles Davis Sextet, but within a year (after appearing on Davis's *Kind of Blue*), he would form his own quintet with his brother, trumpet player Nat Adderley, and enjoy a series of hit records that placed him at the forefront of the soul-jazz wing of hard bop—leaping high onto the pop charts in 1966 with "Mercy, Mercy, Mercy." Adderley combined bebop proficiency with funky backbeats, and his extrovert personality suited Evans as a contrast to Miles's introvert nature.

"KING PORTER STOMP"

Other than W. C. Handy's "St. Louis Blues," Jelly Roll Morton's 1923 piano piece "King Porter Stomp" was the oldest work on *New Bottle, Old Wine*. (In fact, it may have been older than Handy's tune, if we can believe Morton's claim that he composed it as a teenager.) In 1958, the title would still have been familiar to jazz fans because of the Fletcher Henderson arrangement that Benny Goodman turned into a 1935 hit. But while Henderson's arrangement employed only one strain of Morton's piece, Evans returned to the 1923 original and adapted all four strains, including Morton's tricky upbeat syncopations in the A strain, which did not readily fit in with the Swing Era. Evans makes it swing harder than ever even as he transforms Morton's piece with dissonant harmonies and slashing bop-influenced phrases. The interaction between Adderley's improvisations and the written ensemble passages recalls the give-and-take perfected by

Ellington in pieces like "In a Mellotone." Whether the ensemble initiates or responds in its exchanges with Adderley, it engenders the illusion of unstoppable energy.

KING PORTER STOMP

Gil Evans

John Coles, Louis Mucci, Ernie Royal, trumpets; Joe Bennett, Frank Rehak, Tom Mitchell, trombones; Julius Watkins, French horn; Harvey Philips, tuba; Cannonball Adderley, alto saxophone; Jerry Sanfino, reeds; Gil Evans, piano; Chuck Wayne, guitar; Paul Chambers, bass; Art Blakey, drums

LABEL: World Pacific WP1246; *The Complete Pacific Jazz Recordings* (Blue Note 583002)
DATE: 1958
STYLE: modernist big band
FORM: march/ragtime

Introduction

0:00	Blakey (drums) plays a vigorous roll on the tom-toms, keeping the backbeat on the high-hat cymbal.
0:06	By pressing on the heads, he produces a subtle descent in pitch.
0:07	The horns enter unaccompanied on sustained chords. Over this background, Adderley (on alto saxophone) improvises.

Strain A

0:15	Adderley begins to solo over the rhythm section, while the low brass (trombones, tuba, horn) play short chords on the fourth beat of each measure.
0:26	All the horns join in on an extended soli, each horn occupying its own melody part, ending in a tritone-colored cadence.

Strain A

0:30	Adderley's solo continues, accompanied by lower brass chords.
0:35	The solo is interrupted by a line played by the trumpet and trombones.
0:39	Adderley reenters, accompanied only by the bass and drums.

Strain B

0:45	The new strain, starting in the minor mode, is marked by an arpeggiated theme scored delicately for guitar, piano, and clarinet.
0:49	The theme is answered by a sassy melody for the trumpets.
0:53	The arpeggiated theme is played again, this time in a higher register.
0:56	Once again, it's answered by the band.

Strain B

1:01	The arpeggiated theme is heard again, this time scored for trombone, alto saxophone, and clarinet. Underneath it, the lower brass reinforce the bass line.
1:05	The theme is followed by quiet trills from the reeds over a descending bass line.
1:09	The theme makes one more appearance.
1:12	The band responds with loud brass *soli*.
1:15	During a break, Adderley begins a solo.

Transition

1:17	The composed line, modulating from the key of the first two strains to the key of the trio, is bolstered by rich *soli* scoring.

Strain C

1:21	In a new key, Adderley plays over just the drums and the bass.
1:29	He accidentally makes a distorted honking sound on a low note. Emboldened, he returns to this sound again and again—essentially turning a mistake into a motive.

Strain C

1:37	Under Adderley's solo, a low-pitched line for the trombones and the tuba descends, then ascends, through the chromatic scale. The guitar begins playing the chords to the tune very softly.

Strain D

1:53	The band now plays the piece's main theme, recognizably the same as it was originally written by Jelly Roll Morton.
1:57	As it continues, the theme is paraphrased—its harmonies and melodies changed.
2:01	Halfway through, when the melody is repeated, the rhythms are distorted.
2:08	During a one-bar break, the brass instruments (with Adderley on top) play a *soli*.

Strain D

2:09	Borrowing again from Jelly Roll Morton, the brass instruments play a riff made up of restrained and delicate chords, most of them falling securely on the beat.

Strain D

2:25	The brass chords turn into a background for an Adderley solo.

Strain D

| 2:42 | The band plays a *soli* with familiar Swing Era rhythms, but its harmonies are unusually dissonant. |
| 2:50 | Adderley improvises a response. |

Strain D

| 2:58 | The *soli* becomes rhythmically sparse and its harmonies increasingly dissonant. |
| 3:03 | The band suddenly switches to a riff taken straight from the 1930s arrangement by Fletcher Henderson. |

Coda

| 3:10 | The coda—once again borrowed from Henderson—begins with a short riff fragment played over and over, creating a cross-rhythm against the underlying meter. |
| 3:13 | The drums stop: the horns ascend with a richly voiced *soli* to the final tonic chord. |

The first appearance of strain B on "King Porter Stomp" represents a rare, early instance where Evans's piano comes to the fore. By the 1960s, however, he had decided to forsake freelance work in favor of leading his own orchestra. Seated at the piano (often electric), he used chords to pump up the energy level of the ensemble and its soloists. Evans's orchestra never achieved commercial success, but it was so admired by musicians—especially players who worked for him, sometimes turning down far more lucrative engagements to do so—that he managed to sustain it for more than twenty years. During much of that time, his band held down Monday night spots at New York jazz clubs, and toured Europe and Japan, where it was warmly received.

By 1970, Evans had begun to jettison the music that had made him famous, and, like Miles Davis, with whom he maintained a close friendship, added percussion instruments to his rhythm section and embraced a free-spirited fusion of jazz and rock. His 1969 album *Gil Evans*, though little noted at the time, was a major statement in that direction, preceding Davis's heralded *Bitches Brew*. A planned collaboration with Jimi Hendrix was halted by Hendrix's death; instead, Evans recorded orchestral versions of the rock guitarist's music—"Up from the Skies" is a superior example. Evans also began devoting much of his performance energy to head arrangements. In 1961, he recorded a gripping version of his piece "La

Nevada," actually shaping it (even handing out a last-minute riff scribbled on a matchbook) while the recording was in progress. By the 1970s and 1980s, having created an orchestra as steadfast as Ellington's, he routinely extended and revised pieces on the bandstand with physical gestures, piano chords, and vocal commands. Until his death in 1988, Evans continued to lead his band while also writing film scores (*Absolute Beginners*), mentoring young composers (Maria Schneider), and working with rock stars (Sting). His band continued into the 1990s under the direction of his son, Miles Evans, and thereafter in occasional reunions.

George Russell (1923–2009), VOCALESE, AND MODALISM

Among the major jazz figures in the bop and postbop eras, George Russell is singular on two counts. First, he worked exclusively as a composer-bandleader, not as an instrumentalist; second, he devoted much of his life to formulating an intricate musical theory, published in 1953 and revised in 2001 as *George Russell's Lydian Chromatic Concept of Tonal Organization, Volume One: The Art and Science of Tonal Gravity*. (The planned second volume has not yet appeared.) As a result of his thesis and challenging music, Russell is generally perceived as an archetypal jazz intellectual—too difficult for the general public.

This is hardly fair. While some of his music was considered ahead of its time and presents challenges even today, a great deal is richly entertaining in a peculiarly pop-oriented way: his 1957 masterpiece "All About Rosie," for example, is based on a universal playground tune and never fails to charm audiences on those rare occasions when it is performed. His 1959 suite *New York, N.Y.*, which combines three original pieces with three adaptations of popular songs that celebrate Manhattan, was recorded with a rhyming rhythmic narration by singer Jon Hendricks that prefigures rap. This in itself furthered another compositional movement that gained popularity in the 1950s, involving a kind of libretto writing—not song lyrics per se, which are conceived in tandem with a composer, but rather a kind of narrative tale fit to improvised jazz solos. It was a verbal and performance process known as vocalese.

A lyricist might get assigned a jazz composition, like Ellington's "Sophisticated Lady" or Monk's "Round Midnight," and write a conventional romantic lyric to it. But the masters of vocalese, working with multiple-chorus improvisations taken from recordings, needed more of a story to sustain the flow of words. The first major hit in the idiom came about when a singer named King Pleasure recorded the words that Eddie Jefferson had written to James Moody's 1949 improvisation on "I'm in the Mood for Love." Released in 1952 as "Moody's Mood for Love," the recording caused a mild sensation, as other singers began doing what jazz fans had always done—memorized their favorite solos—but with a difference. Instead of just scatting them, these wordsmiths turned the solos into genuine songs in their own right. Some of the adapted solos, like Coleman Hawkins's "Body and Soul," which Jefferson turned into an extended homage to Hawkins, were already classics, but most became famous only after the vocalese versions were released, including two benchmark tenor saxophone solos by Wardell Gray: "Twisted," a medium-tempo blues that singer Annie Ross made a hallucinogenic romp about a child who was told to sleep tight ("That's why I drank a fifth of vodka one night"), and his steamingly fast, extended solo on Count Basie's record of "Little Pony," which Jon Hendricks turned into a stream-of-consciousness tour de force about a horse race, ending with the ensemble (actually singers Annie Ross and Dave Lambert) riffing, "Don't be quittin' just when you're hittin' the peak," and Gray (actually Hendricks) responding, "Get a record that will play a week."

"Little Pony" was a highlight from one of the most remarkable recordings of the 1950s, *Sing a Song of Basie* (1957) by Lambert, Hendricks & Ross. The trio did not yet exist as a regular group in the year it took to conceive and execute its unique debut, a triumph of multitracking in which three singers become the entire Count Basie Orchestra (aside from the rhythm section) and capture more of its dynamics and swing than anyone had thought possible. With Annie Ross hitting the trumpet tuttis, Dave Lambert covering the trombone range, and Jon Hendricks wailing the saxophone solos and—in one of the most prodigious verbal feats in jazz history—writing all the lyrics, they replicated the band while infusing it with an exhilaration that only the voice can impart. The singing is so precisely articulated that all the words, some of them delivered in high-speed torrents, are easily understood. With that album's success, the trio signed with Columbia Records and took to the road, triumphing at several festivals and touring until 1962, at which time Yolanda Bavan replaced Ross; Lambert, Hendricks & Bavan continued for another two years. From the 1970s on, Hendricks spearheaded vocalese revivals, which achieved mainstream acceptance in the recordings of Manhattan Transfer.

George Russell used words only sporadically, but almost all of his music since the 1970s incorporates funk and even disco rhythms. Paradoxically, the *Lydian Chromatic Concept* is so dense that few people have actually read it, and fewer still can understand it, yet its influence is everywhere. Russell is the de facto father of modal jazz, the harmonic approach that produced such classics as Miles Davis's *Kind of Blue*, John Coltrane's *Giant Steps*, and Herbie Hancock's *Maiden Voyage*, as well as countless offshoots and imitations.

Born out of wedlock to a racially mixed couple, Russell was adopted and raised by a black family in Cincinnati. In high school, he took up drums and received a scholarship from Wilberforce University to play in the college band. He left after two years and volunteered for the draft in 1941, only to learn at the recruitment center that he had tuberculosis. He was placed in a TB ward, but released prematurely. In 1944, Benny Carter hired him, and then fired him in favor of Max Roach. Russell described the experience of hearing the extraordinary Roach as marking the end of his ambition to play drums and the beginning of his determination to compose. A year later, he was stricken full-force by a tubercular attack, and spent fifteen months in a hospital. During this long recuperation, he began to formulate his Lydian concept.

Russell's theory was inspired in part by a conversation with Miles Davis, who wanted Russell to help him understand how chords relate to each other. Russell began to analyze chords in terms of related scales, which ultimately led him to the conclusion that using fewer chords, and focusing on their underlying scales or modes, would incline the improviser to think more melodically. Ultimately, it would even lead to the undoing of song and blues form. This was the basis for modalism as an improvisational method. As Davis realized: "It's not like when you base stuff on chords, and you know at the end of 32 bars that the chords have run out and there's nothing to do but repeat what you've done with variations. I was moving away from that and into more melodic ways of doing things. And in the modal way I saw all kind of possibilities." The "modal way" would come to dominate jazz in the 1960s, particularly in the realm of jazz-rock fusion.

Russell believed that in every culture the human ear detects the "greatest unity and finality" in the C Lydian scale: on a piano, the white keys from C to C but with an F-sharp (a tritone) instead of F at the very center of the scale. In building his theory, Russell set out to show how other scales relate to the C Lydian and to each other. He rejected the idea of major and minor keys and the harmonic rules contingent on them; instead, he advocated superimposing different scales, so as to eliminate a tonal center. Charlie Parker showed that any note could be made to fit harmonically within a chord. Russell believed that any chord could be made to fit within a scale.

All this sounds complicated, and it is. Yet the net effect for other musicians was quite simple. Instead of improvising against a scrim of two or more chords in each measure, they could replace all the chords in, say, an eight-bar passage with one scale. The harmonic progression would no longer guide the direction of the piece. Instead, as Davis realized, "The challenge here, when you work in the modal way, is to see how inventive you can be melodically." Russell's ideas—which were communicated more in conversation or through musical examples (*Kind of Blue*) than through his obscure text—liberated musicians from bebop's harmonic grids. But although Russell felt vindicated by Davis's success, his own music was ignored, and he rankled at the new clichés that became ubiquitous in the 1960s and 1970s:

♦ ♦ ♦

I thought that *Kind of Blue* was beautiful music, of course. But I also thought that a lot of modal jazz that came out of it was a little simplistic. Too many jazzmen played simple modal tunes like "So What" and played long, long solos based on just a couple of modes. It could get very monotonous listening to that. . . . That kind of thing was only a part of what I intended with the theory. It should have opened up all kinds of new possibilities to musicians, not produced monotony.

♦ ♦ ♦

Some of the best examples of what Russell intended may be found in his own work, beginning with "Cubana Be / Cubana Bop," a two-part arrangement he wrote for Dizzy Gillespie in 1947 that fused jazz and Afro-Cuban music and introduced modal orchestral writing. Russell's immersion in classical music, involving close study of Stravinsky, Stefan Wolpe, and others, produced a work for clarinetist Buddy DeFranco called "A Bird in Igor's Yard" (1949). Not until 1956 did he record under his own name: the result, *Jazz Workshop*, by the George Russell Smalltet, is among his finest achievements.

"CONCERTO FOR BILLY THE KID"

Russell was held in great esteem by the most advanced jazz musicians of the 1950s, and he surrounded himself with many of them, including John Coltrane and Max Roach. But he also had a good ear for raw talent. His most influential discovery was the pianist Bill Evans, whom he eventually introduced to Davis. Evans had appeared on a few record sessions yet was virtually unknown when Russell recruited him for *Jazz Workshop*. To showcase his immense talent, Russell conceived "Concerto for Billy the Kid." Evans's rigorous solo, coming to a head in his whirling stop-time cadenza, is far removed from the more meditative approach that later became his signature, but it remains one of his most compelling performances.

Working with only six musicians in this piece, Russell creates tremendous harmonic density. His clashing scales give the performance a dramatically modernistic edge, though he also uses a standard chord progression (from the 1942 Raye-DePaul standard "I'll Remember April," an enduring favorite among jazz musicians) for the Evans sequence. In creating a capacious harmonic landscape that obliterates the usual tonal centers, Russell makes his sextet sound like a much larger ensemble. For all the dissonances, rhythmic change-ups, and fragmented melodies, the piece swings with a pure-jazz élan. The inventiveness of the composer and his soloists never wavers. After more than half a century, "Concerto for Billy the Kid" sounds not only fresh but avant-garde, in the truest sense of the term. It would sound modern if it were written and recorded today.

CONCERTO FOR BILLY THE KID

George Russell

Art Farmer, trumpet; Hal McKusick, alto saxophone; Bill Evans, piano; Barry Galbraith, electric guitar; Milt Hinton, bass; Paul Motian, drums

LABEL: Victor LPM1372; *The Complete Bluebird Recordings* (Lone Hill Jazz LHJ10177)
DATE: 1956
STYLE: modernist small-group composition
FORM: original, including 32-bar **AA'** and 48-bar **ABA**

Introduction

0:00	The drums begin by playing a Latin groove: a syncopated rhythm on the cymbals alternates with the bass drum on the main beats and the snare drum on the backbeat.
0:05	Above the groove, two horns (muted trumpet and alto saxophone) play two independent lines in dissonant counterpoint. The rhythms are disjointed and unpredictable.
0:09	The horns become stuck on a dissonant interval—the major second, or whole step. They move this interval up and down.
0:11	Hinton enters on bass, doubled by piano, repeating two notes a half step apart. (This bass line will remain in place for most of the introduction.)

0:15	The horns play a descending riff that ends, once again, on a major second. This riff repeats at unpredictable intervals.
0:18	The texture is thickened by a new line, played by the electric guitar.
0:24	The horns switch to a new key and begin a new ostinato that clashes, polyrhythmically, with the meter. Evans (piano) and Galbraith (guitar) improvise countermelodies.
0:34	The horns begin a new ostinato in call and response with the guitar.
0:44	The ostinato changes slightly, fitting more securely into the measure. Evans adds complicated responses.
0:58	Farmer (trumpet) removes his mute. The ostinato becomes a more engaging Latin riff, forming a four-bar pattern. Underneath it, Hinton plays a syncopated bass line.
1:11	In a dramatic cadence, the harmony finally reaches the tonic.
1:13	The drums improvise during a short two-bar break.

Chorus 1 (32 bars, AA')

1:15	**A**	The rhythm section sets up a new Latin groove, with an unexpected syncopation on one beat. Evans plays a peculiar twisting line in octaves on piano, moving dissonantly through the chord structure.
1:22		Over one chord, the piano line is more strikingly dissonant.
1:28	**A'**	As the chord progression begins over again, Evans's melody continues to dance above the harmonies.

Chorus 2

1:42	**A**	The horns repeat Evans's line note for note. Underneath, Evans plays a *montuno*—a syncopated chordal pattern typically found in Latin accompaniments, locking into the asymmetrical bass line.
1:56	**A'**	

Transition

2:11	The walking-bass line rises and falls chromatically, while melodic themes are tossed between the instruments.
2:21	The band returns to the Latin groove and the melodic ideas previously heard in the introduction.

Chorus 3 (48-bar ABA, each section 16 bars)

2:28	**A**	This new chord progression—based on "I'll Remember April"—begins with an extended passage of stop-time. Evans improvises for four bars in a single melodic line.
2:31		The band signals the next chord with a single sharp gesture while Evans continues to improvise.
2:35		The band enters every two bars, with Hinton filling in on bass.
2:42	**B**	The band's chords are irregular, often syncopated.
2:56	**A**	Evans's improvisations are so rhythmically slippery that the band misplays its next stop-time entrance.

| 3:08 | | A walking bass reestablishes a more conventional groove. |

Chorus 4

3:09	**A**	Evans plays a full chorus solo, featuring his right hand only.
3:23	**B**	He distorts the meter by relentlessly repeating a polyrhythmic triplet figure.
3:37	**A**	He switches to a series of bluesy gestures.

Interruption

| 3:50 | | The chorus is interrupted when the bass (doubled by piano) suddenly establishes a new triple meter. Against this, the horns play a dissonant line, harmonized in fourths (quartal chords). |

Chorus 5

3:55	**A**	We return to the piano solo, a full five bars into this chorus.
3:58		Evans joins with the drummer in playing sharp accents (or "kicks") on harshly dissonant chords.
4:05	**B**	Farmer takes a trumpet solo.
4:12		Underneath, McCusick (alto saxophone) adds a background line, harmonizing with the guitar's chords.
4:19	**A**	McCusick plays a melody previously heard in the introduction (at 0:34).
4:26		The trumpet suddenly joins the saxophone in quartal harmonies, fitting obliquely over the harmonic progression.

Coda

4:31		As the bass drops out, the instruments revisit ideas from the beginning of the introduction.
4:36		The guitar begins a final upward flurry.
4:39		Evans plays the final gesture on piano.

The *Jazz Workshop* album received glowing reviews. Critic Leonard Feather wrote of Russell, "Such men must be guarded with care and watched with great expectations." As a result, and despite poor sales, it provoked enough interest to enable Russell to sign with other labels and to tour with a small group. He initiated an especially productive collaboration with the saxophonist Eric Dolphy, who played an important role in the burgeoning avant-garde of the 1960s. One of Russell's earlier compositions, "Ezz-thetic," an ingenious variation on the Cole Porter song "Love for Sale," became a jazz standard, recorded by Miles Davis, Lee Konitz, and others.

After the critical success of "All About Rosie" and *New York, N.Y,* Russell was determined to maintain a band, but he found it increasingly difficult to find work in the United States. In 1963, he moved to Scandinavia, accepting a teaching post at the University of Sweden, touring with his sextet (which included many of the most admired young improvisers in Europe), and writing longer and more challenging pieces, including *Othello Ballet Suite* (1967) and *Electronic Sonata for Souls Loved by Nature* (1969), a major work that fused jazz, rock, and prerecorded tapes. In 1969, Russell returned to the United States to teach at the New England Conservatory, where he spent more than twenty-five years. He reunited with Bill Evans to record his album-length concerto *Living Time*, and adapted that name for his orchestra, which made occasional appearances in New York and Europe. His later works include *Vertical Form 6* (1977) and *The African Game* (1983). *The London Concert* (1989) documents the bravura spirit, rhythmic ebullience, and uncanny beauty Russell could produce onstage; the album includes his arrangement of Davis's "So What," built not on the theme but rather on Davis's 1959 improvisation. Russell remained a controversial figure: the Jazz at Lincoln Center program in New York infamously refused to book him on the grounds that his orchestra used electric bass.

CHAPTER

Modality: Miles Davis and John Coltrane

THE SORCERER: Miles Davis (1926–1991)

No one looms larger than Miles Davis in postwar jazz, because no one had a greater capacity for change. Yet Davis was no chameleon, adapting himself to the latest trends. His innovations, signaling what he called "new directions," altered the musical landscape at least five times in the two decades of his greatest impact. In 1949–50, his nonet helped focus the attention of a generation of musicians looking beyond bebop and launched cool jazz. In 1954, his "Walkin'" session acted as an antidote to the cool

◀ At twenty-three, Miles Davis had served a rigorous apprenticeship with Charlie Parker and was now (1949) about to launch the cool jazz movement with his nonet.

school's increasing refinement and reliance on classical music, providing an impetus for hard bop. From 1957 to 1960, Davis's three major collaborations with Gil Evans enlarged the scope of jazz composition, big-band music, and recordings, projecting a deep, meditative mood new in jazz. In 1959, *Kind of Blue*, the culmination of Davis's experiments with modal improvisation, transformed jazz performance and replaced bebop's harmonic complexity with a scalar approach that favored melody and nuance. In 1969, *Bitches Brew* initiated an era of jazz-rock fusion, shifting the emphasis from melody to rhythm.

Davis's work involved a continuous rethinking of the four primary elements that define jazz and most other kinds of music: harmony, melody, rhythm, and instrumentation. Yet despite all the contextual changes that his music underwent, his approach to the trumpet remained ardently personal and relatively consistent. In the 1950s especially, his power as a performer had the effect of resolving musical opposites while leading jazz to a multi-faceted future that broadened its audience. By the 1970s, he had achieved the rare distinction of remaining on the edge of jazz innovation while borrowing montage techniques from avant-garde classical music (producer Teo Macero would be a big help here) and signaling a rapprochement with the latest currents in both black and white pop music.

Davis's importance supersedes his musical questing. His personality—often belligerent, always independent, and given to periods of reclusiveness—mesmerized musicians and the public. He became an inescapable symbol of his time, and a magnet for artists in and out of music. Handsome and charismatic, Davis emerged as the archetypal modern jazz musician (distant, unflappable, romantic) and the civil-rights-era black man (self-reliant, outspoken, confident). Imitated for his personal and musical attributes, including his dress and candor, Davis generated a series of epithets: he was the man who walked on eggshells, the Prince of Darkness, the Sorcerer. His record sales dropped precipitously in the 1960s, and critics lambasted him for pandering to pop fashions in the 1970s, yet he retained an aura of mystery and respect. Amiri Baraka described Davis as "my ultimate culture hero: artist, cool man, bad dude, hipster, clear as daylight and funky as revelation."

Miles Dewey Davis III was born in Alton, Illinois, to a wealthy black family who moved to East St. Louis when he was a year old. His grandfather was an Arkansas landowner and his father a prominent dental surgeon and pillar of their St. Louis community. Davis's comfortable background instilled in him unshakable self-possession, spurred by his father's education and prosperity and his equally strong-willed mother's fashion-conscious beauty. He studied trumpet in school and received private lessons from a member of the St. Louis Symphony. He listened avidly to trumpet players, including the local phenomenon Clark Terry, who befriended Davis and would soon be renowned for his work with Count Basie and Duke Ellington. When Billy Eckstine's orchestra visited St. Louis in 1944, Davis sat in alongside Dizzy Gillespie (who advised him to learn piano and harmony) and Charlie Parker. Davis soon persuaded his father to send him to New York to study at the Juilliard School. He attended classes for a year and took piano lessons, before dropping out to pursue his real goal: learning from and working with Parker.

In 1945, Parker hired the nineteen-year-old Miles for his quintet and first recording date. Davis soloed with affecting resolve on "Now's the Time" and "Billie's Bounce," but as we have seen lacked sufficient technique to play on the pièce de résistance, "Ko Ko." Although Davis worked with Parker's band on and off for the next three years, until December 1948, the "Ko Ko" session characterized his dilemma during that period. He was attempting to forge a trumpet style in the shadow of Gillespie's (and Parker's) blazing virtuosity—an ambition that virtually doomed him to failure. In addition to Parker, Davis toured with the big bands of Benny Carter and Gillespie, among others, and his relatively introverted style and improving technique earned him admirers. Some listeners, however, thought of him as a second-drawer bebop trumpet player who lacked the technique not only of Gillespie but also of rivals in his own generation, including Fats Navarro, Red Rodney, and Kenny Dorham. In Parker's quintet, Davis had to solo after the leader in almost every piece, and the contrast did not favor him.

Davis's approach was different. He preferred the middle register to the more exciting high register, and focused on timbre and melody, playing fewer and longer notes. He found a temperamentally sympathetic model in Freddie Webster, a rather obscure swing band player who made a couple of notable bop sessions before his death at thirty; Gillespie said that Webster had the most beautiful trumpet sound he had ever heard, but only Miles seems to have consciously assimilated his approach. For a short time, Davis attempted to compensate for his perceived limitations by writing excessively intricate tunes—such as "Sippin' at Bells," a blues with so many chord changes that the blues feeling is nullified. Parker, switching to tenor saxophone, played as a sideman on Davis's first session as a leader and commented, sarcastically, that some of those changes were too complicated for a "country boy" like him.

In early 1949, having just broken with Parker, Davis began to experiment with the musicians and composers who would form the historic nonet. That same year, he visited Paris to play the first Festival International de Jazz, an important presentation of old and young musicians, which gave him a more positive perspective, given the respect that jazz and his own music enjoyed in Europe. He was now increasingly recognized for the emotional and rhythmic restraint of his solos. At twenty-three, he projected a lonely resilience that attracted many imitators. The sound of Miles Davis had become unmistakable, though it would achieve greater distinction in the next few years.

If his acceptance in Europe buoyed Davis's spirits, it also added to his bitterness and disillusionment about the realities of race in America. He had resisted the lure of narcotics during his years with Parker, but now descended into heroin addiction, which took him through circles of hell utterly foreign to his privileged upbringing, forcing him to occasionally steal and pimp. Heroin hooked him for four years, during which time he completed *Birth of the Cool*, recorded as an accompanist to Sarah Vaughan, reunited with Parker, and freelanced as a leader of record dates that, despite the contributions of excellent musicians, often proved to be merely adequate.

A turning point came in 1954, when, after suffering withdrawal from heroin and recuperating at his father's farm, he returned to jazz with renewed energy and ambition. He now faced the double challenge of reestablishing himself as a serious force in jazz and as a reliable professional, no longer in thrall to drugs. Under contract to Prestige Records, he presided over five remarkable 1954 sessions with many of the best musicians of the day, and an exemplary rhythm section—the first of several in his career—consisting of Horace Silver, Percy Heath, and Kenny Clarke. These performances revealed Davis to be a toughened, street-wise musician, thoroughly in charge of his timbre and playing with steely conviction. His evenly phrased solos, combined with his dark good looks and quietly pugnacious stance, introduced a new kind of black masculinity in American entertainment, at once tender and invincible. His coiled power came fully to the fore in "Walkin'," an extended, endlessly inventive performance that turned the jazz tide back to forthright, blues-driven improvisations. Combining a twelve-bar blues with an eight-bar preamble, "Walkin'" has the dramatic grandeur of a march; while all the solos are accomplished (it was a good day for trombonist J. J. Johnson, tenor saxophonist Lucky Thompson, and pianist Horace Silver), Davis's has the spellbinding logic of a fable, with meaningful silences and none of the high-note or speed-demon pyrotechnics associated with bop trumpet.

Two months after "Walkin'," at a session with Sonny Rollins, he debuted three Rollins compositions that became instant jazz standards ("Airegin," "Oleo," "Doxy") and demonstrated a little-known muting device that would become emblematic of Davis's style. The Harmon mute, introduced in the 1860s, was ignored during the 1920s jazz vogue for mutes generated by King Oliver and the Ellington brass men. Unlike other metal mutes, it is held in place by a cork ring, forcing the musician's entire air column into the appliance to produce a thin, vulnerable humming sound. The Harmon mute augmented the brooding intensity of Davis's music. By December, when he recorded another sustained blues benchmark, "Bag' Groove," with its composer Milt Jackson and Thelonious Monk, Davis had not only clinched his comeback in jazz but seemed poised for a larger role in American music.

In the summer of 1955, Davis made a brief but much-acclaimed appearance at the Newport (Rhode Island) Jazz Festival, creating a stir with his version of Monk's "'Round Midnight." It was the first time most critics and fans had ever seen a Harmon mute. On the basis of this performance, Davis signed a contract with Columbia Records—a major career leap beyond independent jazz labels like Prestige that he had doggedly pursued. Davis, however, still owed Prestige three years under his existing contract, which he fulfilled by recording five albums of music at two marathon sessions. The proliferation of Davis albums in the late 1950s from both labels (the Prestiges were memorably titled with descriptive gerunds: *Relaxin'*, *Steamin'*, *Cookin'*, *Workin'*) boosted his celebrity.

For the cover of his debut Columbia album, *'Round About Midnight* (1955), Davis was photographed through a red lens, wearing dark glasses, embracing his trumpet, unsmiling—an iconic image. That album also introduced his first great quintet, one of the most admired small bands in history, with tenor saxophonist John Coltrane, pianist Red Garland, bassist Paul Chambers, and drummer Philly Joe Jones. Miles's old friend

Gil Evans crafted the arrangement of "'Round Midnight," adding a tempo change and making the quintet sound fuller than on the other selections. Davis revealed an unmistakably kinetic edginess on this album, even when revisiting his past, as in a ferocious version of Charlie Parker's contrapuntal "Ah-Leu-Cha," which he had recorded with Parker in 1948.

Three aspects of this quintet were particularly noticeable. The contrast between Davis's sparing, poignant solos and Coltrane's more demonstrative virtuosity reversed a similar disparity between Parker and Davis, this time favoring Davis; the rhythm section boasted an assertive independence, thanks to Jones's insistent attack and Chambers's authoritative pulse and harmonic skill; and the diverse repertory combined original pieces with pop songs dating back to the 1920s or borrowed from current or recent Broadway shows. Garland, a living thesaurus of pop music, suggested many of the tunes that Davis recharged. In this regard, Davis was also influenced by Frank Sinatra, who was revitalizing his own career at the same time, often with old songs that were considered too dated or corny for modern jazz. By adapting such unlikely songs as "Bye Bye Blackbird" (from a 1926 revue), "Diane" (from the 1927 silent movie *Seventh Heaven*), "The Surrey with the Fringe on Top" (from the 1943 show *Oklahoma!*), and "If I Were a Bell" (from the 1950 show *Guys and Dolls*), Davis opened up jazz repertory and affirmed the old saw "'Taint What You Do."

After the success of *'Round About Midnight* and mindful that Prestige would soon be issuing annual albums by the quintet, Davis's shrewd producer, George Avakian (who proved equally at home piloting sessions by Louis Armstrong, Benny Goodman, Sonny Rollins, and Keith Jarrett), wanted to do something entirely different for Davis's second Columbia release, in 1957. He suggested an orchestral album and mentioned a few possible arrangers. Without hesitation, Davis chose Gil Evans. After several discussions, Miles and Gil settled on a nineteen-piece ensemble, extending the sonorities of the nonet's French horns and tuba to include flutes, piccolos, and harp. Davis would be the only soloist. The result, *Miles Ahead*, was a hit with the critics and public and a benchmark in recording history. Evans composed links between the selections, something never done before, to create the illusion of a tone poem without breaks. New post-production techniques (splicing and overdubbing) compensated for inadequate rehearsal and recording time, and allowed Davis to perfect his solos.

Meanwhile, Davis had disbanded his quintet, partly in disgust because a few of his musicians had been derailed by drugs. At a loss for what to do next, he agreed to a tour of Europe, where he would perform with local musicians. Upon arriving, he learned that several engagements had been canceled, but he was offered something more intriguing: the chance to compose a film score for a French police thriller starring Jeanne Moreau and directed by Louis Malle. Gambling on Davis's ingenuity, Malle asked him to improvise the score at one late-night session, creating music cues as he watched the picture, *Ascenseur pour l'echafaud* (*Elevator to the Gallows*). In devising themes for the film, Davis improvised on scales instead of chords, simplifying the music harmonically and maximizing emotional content with slow, drawn-out phrases—often based on nothing more than a D minor scale. The international success of *Ascenseur* inspired a vogue for movies with scores by or featuring jazz stars, but for Davis it was a personal "eureka moment," and he returned home eager to elaborate on this new way of improvising.

His first problem was to reorganize his band. One musician he wanted to work with was alto saxophonist Cannonball Adderley, whom he recruited in 1958 after agreeing to appear as a sideman on Adderley's Blue Note album. Davis had fired Coltrane because of his dependency on stimulants, but Coltrane had by now experienced what he later described as a rebirth, inspirational and (after working a year with Thelonious Monk) musical. Davis's new band—a sextet made up of trumpet, two saxophones, and his old rhythm section (Garland, Chambers, and Jones)—recorded *Milestones* (1958), his most mature work to date, exploring devices he had used in the film.

Three weeks later, Davis returned to the studio for an ambitious project with Gil Evans, a reconceived version of George Gershwin's 1935 opera *Porgy and Bess*. Unlike the aggressively free-spirited music he made with his sextet, Davis's work with Evans on *Porgy* and other records possessed a sensuous luster that appealed to people who lacked the patience for long jazz improvisations. To everyone's surprise, these records, which redefined concerto form in jazz and exemplified Davis's soul-baring anxiety, doubled as make-out albums. This was particularly true of their third epic, the 1960 *Sketches of Spain*: a fusion of jazz with Spanish classical and folk music (including a gloriously revived adaptation of the second movement of Joaquin Rodrigo's guitar concerto *Concierto de Aranjuez*), where the orchestrations frame Davis's chilling laments—the jazz musician as confessional poet.

Kind of Blue

In the year between *Porgy and Bess* and *Sketches of Spain*, Davis regrouped his sextet to record a few unrehearsed musical ideas that he had been toying with and soon released as *Kind of Blue*. This album represented the fruition of the modal approach he had been working on since the film scoring in Paris, and would alter the playing habits of countless musicians. Here, in contrast to the strenuous orchestral projects with Evans, Davis kept the compositional demands minimal. Determined to stimulate each of his musicians, he did not show them the pieces until they arrived at the recording sessions. His goal was nothing less than to banish the clichés of modern jazz.

By 1959, jazz had been fixated for fifteen years on chromatic harmony and the technical challenge of improvising smoothly and efficiently within it. The liberating innovations of Charlie Parker now loomed as an unavoidable and endlessly imitated model. His followers often made chord progressions more concentrated and difficult; soloing became a task rather like running hurdles, clearing a new obstacle every few yards. In his early years, Davis had tried to prove himself precisely in that manner. But modal jazz sent him in the opposite direction: fewer chords and less concentrated harmonies—or rather, scales that override harmonies, clearing away the hurdles. Modal improvisation was not new to jazz. It is, in essence, an abiding idea found in early jazz in the use of the blues scale and in melodic paraphrase. In the 1950s, though, modalism emerged as a specific technique in reaction to the busyness of bop harmony. It offered a solution to the problem of revitalizing the relationship between improvised melodies and the harmonic foundations on which those melodies are based.

As we've seen, Davis was not alone in trying to move jazz beyond the dominion of chord changes. Charles Mingus, who publicly excoriated musicians for "copying Bird," wrote pieces with minimal harmonies to provoke fresh approaches, Dave Brubeck sought to inspire musicians with novel meters, and George Russell created his Lydian concept as a theoretical justification for modal jazz. For that matter, an as-yet-unknown avant-garde was approaching over the horizon, more than willing to run roughshod over all of jazz's ground rules. Yet the dark, flowing introspection of *Kind of Blue*, probably the best-selling jazz album ever, caught the spirit of the times like no other recording. The modal arrangements and modified tempos underscored Davis's strengths and not his weaknesses, encouraging his predilection for the middle range, his measured lyricism, his reserved disposition. It also provided an ideal middle ground between his laid-back ("walking on eggshells") style and the exuberance of the saxophonists, especially Coltrane, who even in the absence of multiple chord changes filled every scale and space with an almost garrulous intensity.

In order to realize this project, Davis made a couple of changes in the rhythm section. He hired drummer Jimmy Cobb, a musician steeped in hard bop, as a replacement for Philly Joe Jones. Cobb had been a member of Adderley's group before both of them joined with Davis, and had also worked with singers Dinah Washington and Sarah Vaughan. He tempered Jones's forcefulness with moderation, suggesting the vigilant restraint of Kenny Clarke. On one track only, "Freddie Freeloader," a relatively conventional twelve-bar blues, Davis used his group's recently hired pianist, Jamaican-born Wynton Kelly, a veteran of hard bop known for his infectious blues playing; Kelly would remain with Davis's band through 1962. For the remaining four selections, Davis recruited Bill Evans, who had been his pianist in 1958. Evans's return to the fold for the two days it took to record *Kind of Blue* proved to be a crucial component in the album's success and that of his own career.

Bill Evans (1929–1980)

One of the most influential musicians of his generation, Bill Evans was on the verge of achieving recognition when George Russell introduced him to Davis. He had attracted attention with his dazzling virtuosity, but his linear cadenza on Russell's "Concerto for Billy the Kid" did not typify his approach to the piano, which inclined toward an improvisational style no less introverted and meditative than Davis's. Like Davis, too, he possessed an instantly identifiable sound on his instrument.

Born in Plainfield, New Jersey, Evans began classical piano and violin studies at six, and worked in dance bands as a teenager. Despite occasional jazz gigs, he did not seriously devote himself to jazz until after he graduated from Southeastern Louisiana College and served a stint in the army. Returning to New York, he freelanced with several groups. After wowing critics with his work for Russell, he was invited to record with his own trio in 1956. His debut album, earnestly titled (by his devoted producer Orrin Keepnews) *New Jazz Conceptions*, introduced "Waltz for Debby," a classic jazz ballad that marked him as a composer of promise. A perfectionist, Evans did not feel his "conceptions" were fully formed, and refused to record for the next two years except as a sideman. During that interim, in addition to Miles Davis, he recorded with Mingus, Adderley, Gunther Schuller, Chet Baker, and others, finally returning to the studio under his own steam in 1958 with an album called *Everybody Digs Bill Evans*, festooned with admiring quotations from other musicians. A highlight of this session was his spontaneous "Peace Piece," improvised freely over a simple alternation of tonic and dominant chords.

In 1959, Evans made a significant leap, first with his work on *Kind of Blue*, and later that year with his third album, *Portrait in Jazz*. Drawing on his classical background and modal jazz, he developed an original approach to voicing harmonies that made his chords sound fresh and open-ended. The practice of voicing is practically as old as jazz itself. On the most basic level, instead of advancing from a definite C chord (C-E-G) to a definite F chord (F-A-C), a pianist might place the E or G rather than the root note on the bottom of the C chord, and A or C at the bottom of the F chord; by dropping the root notes altogether and adding, say, the interval of a ninth to each chord—D for the C chord and G for the F chord—the original harmonies have been dramatically altered but not obliterated. The possibilities for voicing chords are vast, and Evans had a genius for realizing those possibilities. By thinking of chords as loosely connected to their roots, he found ingenious ways to modulate from one chord to another, adding harmonic extensions and substitute chords to alter standard progressions. His melodic and harmonic resourcefulness was especially apparent in his adaptations of standards, some of them unusual for jazz (like the sentimental movie ballad "My Foolish Heart" and the theme from the Disney movie *Alice in Wonderland*). But even great tunes that had been done numberless times—"Night and Day," "In a Sentimental Mood," "But Beautiful," "My Man's Gone Now"—revealed unexpected facets in Evans's hands.

Portrait in Jazz also premiered a new approach to the piano trio, in which each member was a fully active participant. In the usual bebop piano trio as perfected by Bud Powell, the pianist was almost always the central figure, with the bassist and drummer serving as accompanists. Powell liked interacting with a vigorous drummer, but his bassists typically marked the harmonies and followed his lead. Evans favored the bassist, who was free to respond with strong melodic ideas of his own. He found ideal allies in the soft and deftly responsive punctuations of drummer Paul Motian and the superb intonation, smooth timbre, and melodic fancies of bassist Scott LaFaro. The early death of LaFaro in a car accident shortly after the group reached its peak (*The Complete Village Vanguard Recordings, 1961*) disrupted Evans's progress for a few years, but he rebounded with a series of interdependent trios, and continued to compose challenging, introspective tunes, among them, "Peri's Scope," "Turn Out the Stars," "Very Early," and "Remembering the Rain."

Evans's best-known composition (and one of Davis's most moving recordings) is "Blue in Green," first performed on *Kind of Blue*. It's a ten-measure circular sequence of chords that, as Evans configured them, has no obvious beginning or ending. Its hypnotic quality continues to challenge instrumentalists and singers today. Elsewhere, Evans's quartal harmonies (built on fourths rather than thirds) help to invigorate the modal achievement of *Kind of Blue*. On "Flamenco Sketches," the soloists are required to improvise on a sequence of scales, usually modulating every four or eight bars, though the soloist can extend his use of a scale if he desires. Evans's chords support the scales without linking them to a specific harmonic progression. Still, the piece that really popularized modal jazz is the album's opening selection, "So What."

"SO WHAT"

"So What" presents modal jazz in the context of a thirty-two-bar AABA tune, which makes the piece's only harmonic change stand out like a red tuxedo. The A sections are based on the D Dorian mode (on a piano keyboard, the white keys from D to D) and the bridge, a half step higher, shifts to the E-flat Dorian mode (same scale, same intervals, starting on E-flat). In practice, this means that musicians improvise mostly on a D minor triad. A great deal of Davis's lyrical solo, particularly in the opening measures, employs just the triad's three notes (D-F-A). Yet he found the experience melodically liberating, and his variations—lucid, moving, and memorable—don't sound the least bit constricted or forced. This beautifully executed solo has been much studied and imitated: the singer Eddie Jefferson put lyrics to it, and George Russell orchestrated it for his band.

The opening episode by the rhythm section creates a fascinating prelude, thought to be sketched by Gil Evans. Paul Chambers's bass prompts a three-note piano phrase, leading to a bass-like figure played in tandem by bass and piano, followed by the pianist's enigmatic, Spanish-style chords and the bassist's introduction of a swing beat and the theme. Note Evans's surprisingly dissonant piano clusters toward the end. Davis continued to play the piece for years, at ever-faster tempos. By the middle 1960s, modal jazz was everywhere, as young musicians rose to the test of improvising without the supportive guideposts of chord changes.

SO WHAT

Miles Davis

Miles Davis, trumpet; John Coltrane, tenor saxophone; Cannonball Adderley, alto saxophone; Bill Evans, piano; Paul Chambers, bass; Jimmy Cobb, drums

LABEL: *Kind of Blue,* Columbia CL1355; *Kind of Blue* (Columbia/Legacy CL5173303)
DATE: 1959
STYLE: modal jazz
FORM: 32-bar popular song (**AABA**)

Introduction

0:00		Chambers quietly plays a rising bass line, evoking a two-note response from Evans on the piano: this prefigures, in slow tempo, the main head. The chords drift ambivalently, fitting no particular key area.
0:13		In a slightly faster tempo, Chambers and Evans combine on a precom-posed melody.
0:20		The bass drops a step. Evans drifts elusively between chords.
0:30		After a pause, Chambers rumbles incoherently in the bass's lowest register.

Chorus 1 (head)

0:34	**A**	Suddenly striking up a steady tempo, Chambers plays a repetitive riff, answered by Evans with the famous two-note "So What" chord in quartal harmony (voiced in fourths). Cobb quietly supports on drums.
0:49	**A**	The response is now voiced by the three wind instruments. Cobb ratchets up the intensity by adding a backbeat on the high-hat cymbal.
1:03	**B**	In a subtle change, Chambers moves a half step higher. The horns play the riff in the new key.
1:17	**A**	All the instruments drop back to the original key.
1:30		Over drum fills, Davis begins his two-chorus solo.

Chorus 2

1:31	**A**	Davis plays a few short phrases, answered by Evans with the riff.
1:37		Davis continues with a longer phrase. As it reaches its melodic peak, he pulls slightly behind the beat.
1:45	**A**	He plays short, concise phrases, leaving ample space for the rhythm section.

1:59	**B**	Evans moves a densely voiced chord cluster (with closely spaced notes) up a half step to signal the bridge. Davis plays over the harmonic cluster.
2:07		Evans returns to the "So What" motive.
2:14	**A**	The shift downward is signaled by a sharp drum accent.

Chorus 3

2:28	**A**	Davis plays a hauntingly lyrical, sustained passage over a rhythmically active but harmonically static bass ostinato.
2:42	**A**	Chambers returns to a walking bass.
2:56	**B**	With a surprising dissonance, Davis signals modulation one beat early.
3:10	**A**	A drum crash leads the return back to the original key. Davis reprises his lyrical passage.
3:19		Davis's last phrase has a bluesy tinge.

Chorus 4

3:24	**A**	While Cobb plays strong accents at the end of Davis's solo, Coltrane begins his two-chorus tenor saxophone solo with the same restrained mood.
3:38	**A**	Suddenly he switches to a more intense style of improvising, with flurries of fast notes. Evans responds with a peculiar comping pattern: holding a few notes, releasing others.
3:52	**B**	Cobb plays interactively on the snare drum, prodding Coltrane to greater intensity.
4:02		As Coltrane reaches the upper limits of his phrase, his timbre coarsens.
4:06	**A**	He plays a phrase in his lower register, repeating and extending it.
4:18		Cobb adds a Latin polyrhythm.

Chorus 5

4:20	**A**	As in chorus 3, Chambers moves to a bass ostinato. Coltrane's line aims toward a melodic peak.
4:33	**A**	The bass returns to a walking-bass pattern.
4:41		Coltrane plays a motive, then repeats it in sequence (starting on a different pitch).
4:47	**B**	His improvisation lingers around a single note.
5:01	**A**	His last phrase begins in his highest register.

Chorus 6

5:15	**A**	The rhythm section quiets down to allow Adderley (alto saxophone) to enter, mimicking Coltrane's extensive double-time lines.
5:29	**A**	For a moment Adderley digs into the groove, but soon returns to his double-time improvisation.
5:41		He suddenly moves up a half step, clashing against the background. Evans responds with the appropriate chord several seconds later.
5:42	**B**	

| 5:56 | A | Adderley returns to the tonic by repeating, on varied tones, a two-note motive. |

Chorus 7

6:10	A	Adderley plays a pair of phrases in the same rhythm.
6:17		In the midst of his double-time improvisation, he inserts a trill.
6:24	A	He begins a simple rhythmic phrase with blues inflections, but once again moves back to faster passages.
6:38	B	A high-pitched phrase elicits a delayed chord from Evans.
6:50		Adderley's return comes a beat early, adding a touch of dissonance to the drummer's roll.
6:51	A	
7:00		His last phrase is distinctly blues-linked.

Chorus 8

7:05	A	The horns enter with the "So What" riff, shifting their role from the response to the call. Evans plays dense, dissonant chords.
7:19	A	Evans plays slow, single-note lines, recalling Davis's lyrical phrases.
7:33	B	On the bridge, he returns to short, dissonant chord clusters.
7:47	A	Back in the home key, he plays thinner chords: two notes a mere step apart.

Chorus 9

8:02	A	Evans shifts the "So What" riff back to its original position. The bass continues to walk.
8:16	A	Chambers plays the call, with the horns joining Evans in responding with the "So What" chords.
8:30	B	
8:44	A	

Coda

| 8:58 | | Evans continues to respond to the bass, while the other instruments drop out. The music fades to silence. |

John Coltrane (1926–1967)

No one motivated a larger circle of major jazz figures than Miles Davis. Unlike most of the great players who populated the Ellington band or Art Blakey's Jazz Messengers, the musicians who passed through Davis's groups would extend his influence beyond his own music, creating their own waves and ripples. Even in this fast company, however, John Coltrane holds an exclusive place. His musical and personal impact eventually equaled—some would argue, surpassed—that of Davis. Coltrane became the most intrepid explorer of modal jazz and a cultural-ethical leader of avant-garde jazz in the 1960s. Yet his career was short-lived, barely a dozen years, and his later music alienated most of his early admirers, producing a windstorm of controversy that has not yet completely settled.

Although he was the same age as Davis (younger by four months), Coltrane made no significant recordings until 1955, as a member of Davis's quintet, a decade after Davis had recorded with Charlie Parker. He made dozens of records during the next few years—many under his own name, establishing himself as Sonny Rollins's main rival among the era's leading tenor saxophonists—and finally organized his own working band in 1959, the year of *Kind of Blue*. Despite the immense success of that album, it led to a falling off for Davis, as he cast about to organize his next ensemble. Consequently, Coltrane's belated and meteoric rise, at age thirty-five, had the effect of filling a leadership role vacated by Davis.

Davis continued to perform with creative authority in the early 1960s, but Coltrane now seemed to personify jazz's future. When, in late 1964, Davis presented his second great quintet, Coltrane released *A Love Supreme*, the first envelope-pushing small-band work since *Kind of Blue* to receive near-unanimous acclaim from critics and fans. Still, it soon became apparent that Coltrane and Davis were dissatisfied with the music they were creating, as they headed down very different paths, each in its way a departure from the central orthodoxies of jazz. For Davis, this meant examining rock, a fusion that he fully embraced a couple of years after Coltrane's death. For Coltrane, it meant embracing the expressionistic chaos of the avant-garde. Both roads were paved with modality.

Born in Hamlet, North Carolina, John William Coltrane grew up in a racist, hardscrabble community, where his family's precarious situation was devastated by the death of his father when John was twelve. The loss distracted him from his studies while strengthening his growing obsession with music. At fifteen, he switched from clarinet to alto saxophone; when he wasn't practicing, he took odd jobs, like shining shoes, to help support his family. After graduating from high school, he moved to Philadelphia, where his musical training began in earnest. He enrolled at the Ornstein School of Music and took an intensive course in theory at Granoff Studios, where he developed a fascination with scales, tenaciously playing them for hours at a time. He occasionally worked with local bands, usually in rhythm and blues joints, where he was sometimes reduced to "walking the bar"—grandstanding for tips. After service in the navy, he joined a big band led by a friend, the much-admired saxophonist and composer Jimmy Heath, the younger brother of Dizzy Gillespie's bassist, Percy Heath.

Together, Coltrane and Heath listened to classical music and bebop and worked at exploring the higher reaches of the saxophone, extending its range upward. In 1949, Gillespie brought both men to New York. Soon, Coltrane switched to tenor saxophone, working in various bands, some well known (Earl Bostic, Johnny Hodges), others buried in music's lower depths. In this period, he discovered Nicolas Slonimsky's *Thesaurus of Scales and Melodic Patterns* (1947), a manual that redoubled his obsession with scales. Where Coleman Hawkins had emphasized every chord in a harmonic sequence, Coltrane experimented with a rapid-fire attack in an attempt to play every note in every chord, unleashing what critic Ira Gitler described as "sheets of sound." By the time Miles Davis hired him in 1955, Coltrane's attack was distinctive if not fully formed, but his career was hobbled by narcotics and drink. Within six months of his joining Davis, Coltrane was invited by Sonny Rollins to record with him ("Tenor Madness"), a prescient tribute when you consider that Coltrane's first important session with Davis had yet to be released. But critics were ambivalent: Coltrane was attacked for his harsh tone and lengthy solos. When Davis asked him why he played so long, he said, "It took that long to get it all in."

Coltrane's dependency on drugs forced Davis to fire him twice. After the second time, in 1957, Coltrane turned his life around. Claiming to have undergone a profound religious experience (the subject of *A Love Supreme*), he renounced all stimulants, devoting himself entirely to music. He spent most of the year working with Thelonious Monk, an education in itself, exhibiting a glowing timbre and emotional perseverance. His freelance work showed his talent as a composer ("Blue Trane," "Moment's Notice") as well as his facility with supersonic tempos and slow romantic ballads. In 1959, Coltrane signed with Atlantic Records, assuming his first important leadership role with impressive self-confidence—though it would take him a couple of years to recruit his ideal band.

Early in 1959, Coltrane recorded *Kind of Blue* and albums with Adderley and Milt Jackson. Then, in May, he recorded his own landmark album,

Giant Steps, backed by leading bebop pianist Tommy Flanagan; Davis's bassist, Paul Chambers; and hard bop drummer Art Taylor. Coltrane composed all the selections, of which three became jazz standards—"Giant Steps," "Naima," and "Mr. P. C." (a tribute to Chambers). Most of *Giant Steps* other than the title tune signifies an extension of *Kind of Blue*, with its investigation of scales and chords, and Coltrane's subsequent work demonstrated a deepening interest in the liberating implications of modal jazz. The melodic arc of his measured and poignant ballad "Naima" is based on two scales. "Impressions," released on the album of that name, is a direct spin-off of "So What" (Coltrane even called it that the first time he played it), employing the AABA format with a release built on a phrase from Maurice Ravel's "Pavane pour une infante défunte." As Coltrane explored the relationships between chords and scales, "stacking" chords on top of a scale to see how many note combinations and phrase permutations he could develop, he also composed more complicated harmonic sequences.

"GIANT STEPS"

"Giant Steps" has been called Coltrane's farewell to bebop, because the chord structure is so busy and difficult to play, especially at the roaring tempo he demanded. One of his most influential pieces (it became a test pattern for music students attempting to master fast-moving harmonies), it may be seen as a rejoinder to the scalar concepts of *Kind of Blue*. "Giant Steps" is a sixteen-bar composition in which almost every note of the melody is signaled by a new chord—playing the chord changes is practically the same thing as playing the melody. The harmony extends the chord progression between equally distant tonal centers (the giant steps of the title). One goal of this harmonic sequence was to stimulate fresh ideas. Taking a page from Davis, Coltrane decided not to show the piece to the musicians until the day of the recording session, which in this instance turned out to be a disservice to them.

The piece's difficulty is especially evident in the piano solo. The chords alone would not have presented a problem for a pianist as harmonically sophisticated as Tommy Flanagan. The tune consists mostly of half notes, which means a chord change every two beats—no big deal if the tempo is leisurely or medium-fast. But the point of "Giant Steps" lay partly in playing it extremely fast, to trigger a sheets-of-sound jolt. Even for Coltrane, who had been working on these changes for years, the challenge was thorny, and his solo contains many repeated patterns. For Flanagan, the situation was virtually impossible. His solo begins with uncharacteristically jumpy phrases before retreating into a sequence of chords. (Flanagan, a perfectionist, later mastered the piece for his superb 1982 Coltrane tribute album, also called *Giant Steps*.) Coltrane's solo aims for a quite different effect from bebop; unlike most of the improvisations we've heard, including Coltrane's on "So What," the import of his eleven-chorus solo here resides less in details than in the aggregate attack—the overall whooshing energy.

GIANT STEPS

John Coltrane

John Coltrane, tenor saxophone; Tommy Flanagan, piano; Paul Chambers, bass; Art Taylor, drums

LABEL: *Giant Steps,* Atlantic LP311; *Giant Steps* (Atlantic/WEA 1311-2)
DATE: 1959
STYLE: hard bop
FORM: 32-bar popular song

Chorus 1 (head)

0:00   Coltrane begins with a rhythmically simple melody disguising the dauntingly difficult chord progression voiced by Flanagan on piano. The tune changes keys 10 times in 13 seconds.

Chorus 2 (head)

0:13   Beginning of chorus.

0:26   The last two chords serve as the beginning of Coltrane's 11-chorus solo.

Chorus 3

0:27   Coltrane launches into his solo with a pattern he'll return to again and again. The drummer changes from the open cymbal to a more tightly restrained sound.

Chorus 4

0:40   Coltrane's intensity increases on a high, held-out note—a melodic peak that he reaches again two seconds later, over a different chord.

Chorus 5

0:53   Coltrane repeats the opening of chorus 3 before shifting into a new direction.

0:59   A return to the melodic peak of chorus 4, again repeated over two different chords.

Chorus 6

1:06   Coltrane takes a short break before continuing his solo.

1:11   Another short break may reflect a momentary lapse of attention at such fast speed.

1:18   At the end of the chorus, he reaches a new high note (a half step higher than before).

Chorus 7

1:20   Coltrane's solo remains in the upper register, reaching the highest note at 1:22 and 1:24.

1:29   The end of the chorus settles into a familiar pattern, with one high note being replaced by the next.

Chorus 8

1:33   Beginning of chorus.

1:40   Coltrane erupts into a rapid ascending E-flat major scale.

1:43   He seems to return to his high-note pattern. But instead of completing it, he dips back down to return to the customary opening for the next chorus.

Chorus 9

1:46   Beginning of chorus.

Chorus 10

2:00   His phrasing is choppier and more discontinuous.

Chorus 11

2:13   The standard opening is interrupted by faster rhythmic gestures.

2:19   As Coltrane looks for ways to intensify his improvisation, the melodic line features ghosted notes and half-formed pitches.

Chorus 12

2:26   Coltrane interrupts his usual chorus opening with a high-note flurry, continually circling his line back toward its melodic goals.

Chorus 13

2:39   Coltrane's last chorus is built primarily around ever-higher notes, with a throaty timbre.

2:49   He finally tires and brings his line down.

| 2:52 | A series of hard knocks on the side of the drum head signals the end of the solo, which spills over slightly into the next chorus. |

Chorus 14

2:53	Beginning of chorus.
2:55	Announced by a big cymbal crash, Flanagan (piano) starts his solo.
2:57	Early on, it becomes obvious that he can't remember all the chords; when he reaches an unfamiliar spot, his line stops.

Chorus 15

| 3:05 | Flanagan begins with a major scale that quickly becomes out of sync with the changing chords. |

Chorus 16

| 3:18 | He halts his line to reestablish himself with the correct chord. |
| 3:22 | The gaps between lines become uncomfortably long. |

Chorus 17

| 3:31 | Flanagan stops trying to create a single-note line, and simply plays chords. |

Chorus 18

| 3:44 | Coltrane returns to solo, taking up his improvisation where he left off. |
| 3:51 | Long-held notes add expression to his line. |

Chorus 19

| 3:57 | Coltrane's final chorus begins with a short break before plunging in for another continuous string of notes. |

Chorus 20 (head)

| 4:10 | He returns to the simple melody of the head. |

Chorus 21 (head)

| 4:23 | Beginning of chorus. |

Coda

| 4:35 | As the band holds out the final chord, Coltrane plays a skittering run that descends into his lower register. His last note is drowned out by a snare-drum roll. |

Incredibly, Coltrane followed *Giant Steps* in 1960 with the one thing no one could have anticipated: a hit record—perhaps the most improbable jazz hit in the twenty years since Coleman Hawkins's "Body and Soul." His adaptation of "My Favorite Things," a cheerful waltz from Rodgers and Hammerstein's current Broadway blockbuster *The Sound of Music*, was a rarity in every way. With its fifteen-minute running time, it was a particularly unlikely candidate for frequent radio play. Yet it *was* broadcast, making Coltrane a major jazz star while popularizing the use of modes in a more dramatic yet no less accessible manner than "So What." Coltrane's arrangement transformed the piece by accenting the waltz meter with an insistently percussive vamp, and reducing the song's chords to two scales, one major and one minor. This gave the familiar theme an incantatory quality, underscored by deliberately repetitive improvisations and a surf-like rhythm. He accentuated the Eastern feeling by performing the piece on soprano saxophone, which, in addition to its higher range, has a keening timbre that suggests music from the Third World. The soprano had rarely been used in jazz since the days of Sidney Bechet; after "My Favorite Things," it was everywhere.

"My Favorite Things" was also the first recording to document the classic Coltrane quartet, with pianist McCoy Tyner and drummer Elvin Jones. (The quartet reached peak strength a year later with the addition of bassist Jimmy Garrison.) Tyner begins the piece with one of the best-known introductory passages in jazz. Like the 5/4 vamp of Dave Brubeck's "Take Five," it alerts audiences to what's coming—a combination of modal harmony and polyrhythm—in two measures. Throughout the performance, Tyner's ambiguous and persistent quartal chords create a constantly shifting background. If his harmonies recall Bill Evans, however, his touch is entirely different: weighty, forceful, tense. "My Favorite Things" suggested a procedure for interpreting all kinds of songs, which Coltrane applied to sundry pieces, including the sixteenth-century English folksong "Greensleeves," Sigmund Romberg's "Softly, as in a Morning Sunrise," "Body and Soul," and "Chim-Chim-Cheree" from the movie *Mary Poppins*.

A Love Supreme

McCoy Tyner, born in Philadelphia, attended the Granoff Studios and met Coltrane while still in his teens. Initially modeling himself after Bud Powell, Richie Powell (Bud's younger brother), Art Tatum, and Thelonious Monk, Tyner went on to create a highly individual style. Coltrane had worked with first-rate bop pianists, including Flanagan and Wynton Kelly, but not until Tyner did he find a true soul mate, with a heavy, harmonically advanced attack, a partiality for vamps, a gift for economy, and a rhythmic strength inseparable from his dramatic purpose. Coltrane said of him:

◆ ◆ ◆

He gets a very personal sound from his instrument and because of the clusters he uses and the way he voices them, his sound is brighter than what would normally be expected from most of the chord patterns he plays. In addition, McCoy has an exceptionally well-developed sense of form both as a soloist and an accompanist. Invariably in our group, he will take a tune and build his own structure for it.

◆ ◆ ◆

Tyner's intensity was matched by that of drummer Elvin Jones, the youngest of three gifted brothers (pianist Hank and trumpet player–composer Thad) who grew up in Pontiac, Michigan. In the 1950s, he worked with key musicians in New York, including Davis, Mingus, Rollins, and J. J. Johnson, without earning recognition as an innovator in his own right. With Coltrane, Jones suddenly burst loose of all restraints, taking the dynamic style of Philly Joe Jones (no relation) to a new level. He quickly became known as a drummer's drummer, a master of polyrhythms. Jones used two related approaches to polyrhythms: playing two rhythms simultaneously himself (for example, a three-beat rhythm and a four-beat rhythm) and playing a different rhythm from the rest of the band (for example, a three-beat waltz rhythm in contrast to the quartet's four-beat rhythm). His superimpositions of waltz meters gave Coltrane's band a rhythmic freedom—propulsive yet, in its way, as open-ended as the modal harmonies. He and Coltrane developed a mutual volatility that led them to long improvisational duels; at the height of some of these bombardments, Tyner would desist from playing altogether. The cumulative fervor of their performances was liberating and spiritual, especially after Coltrane discovered bassist Jimmy Garrison. Raised in Philadelphia, Garrison came to New York as a protégé of Philly Joe Jones and landed a job with the free-jazz quartet of Ornette Coleman. One evening Coltrane sat in with Coleman's band and was so impressed by Garrison that he hired him on the spot. Elvin Jones called Garrison "the turning point" for the quartet: "His aggressiveness, his attitude toward the instrument gave us all a lift."

In 1961, Coltrane signed a lucrative contract with the fledgling label

Impulse!, which began to advertise itself as "The New Wave in Jazz." Recording live at the Village Vanguard, he performed a ferocious sixteen-minute blues, "Chasin' the Trane," so antithetical to "My Favorite Things" that it split his audience in two. Critics who once championed him went on the attack. *Down Beat* magazine accused him of playing "musical nonsense" and "anti-jazz." Others found the performance invigorating and defended him as the new hope of jazz. The oratory almost drowned out the music—was he a misdirected zealot or the hero of a new black consciousness? "Chasin' the Trane" couldn't fail to cause a furor. Occupying one whole side of an LP, it is as relentless as it is long and played at tremendous velocity. Coltrane wails some eighty choruses, using multiphonics (chords played on an instrument designed to play one note at a time), split tones (cracked notes played that way on purpose), cries, and squeals. He asked Tyner not to play on it, so that the primary drama is between Coltrane and Jones. Though the piece is a twelve-bar blues, there are instances when Coltrane seems determined to knock down the bar lines and play with complete freedom; Jones and Garrison forcefully pull him back to the blues structure by signaling the end of each chorus—a significant feat of concentration given the electrifying energy of the performance.

Here was jazz as an existential squawk, a taunting rush of unbridled release. In a sense, "Chasin' the Trane" logically expands on Coltrane's earlier work: it combines the vigorous attack of "Giant Steps" with the harmonic simplicity of the modal pieces. But it requires a new way of listening; without melodic phrases, toe-tapping rhythms, or anything remotely suggesting relaxation, the listener either enters the experience of musical exultation or is left in the cold. "Chasin' the Trane" doesn't really end, it stops; it doesn't really begin, it starts. The performance is all middle.

For the next six years, until his death, Coltrane's audience would be constantly "chasin' the Trane," as he took ever larger steps beyond the rudiments of conventional jazz, challenging the validity of everything he had mastered—ultimately alienating even Tyner and Jones. But first, he made another surprise detour. In 1962 and 1963, he participated in a series of romantic recordings in which improvisation takes a back seat to individualized statements of pure melody. He recorded albums with Duke Ellington and vocalist Johnny Hartman, and one called *Ballads*—eight songs associated with pop crooners he had grown up with (Bing Crosby, Frank Sinatra, Dick Haymes, Nat "King" Cole). *Ballads* was a disarming, exquisitely played showcase for his quartet at its most settled. The pinnacle was to follow, a personal outpouring like none other in jazz. This time the audience and critics were on the same page.

In December 1964, Coltrane recorded the autobiographical four-part suite and canticle *A Love Supreme*, to almost universally enthusiastic reviews. His influence was at this point pervasive. An expanding coterie of musicians looked to him as a leader (he used his clout at Impulse! to get several of them recording contracts), and a generation of listeners trusted him to map the no-man's-land of the new music. *A Love Supreme* solemnizes Coltrane's 1957 devotional conversion, and his liberation from addiction, in four movements: "Acknowledgement," "Pursuance," "Resolution," and "Psalm." Though the arc of the piece moves from harmonic stability to chromatic freedom, *A Love Supreme* represented a type of avant-garde jazz that the public found approachable and satisfying; his old and new admirers closed ranks behind it. In retrospect, the album was a spectacular lull before the storm.

"ACKNOWLEDGEMENT"

Coltrane's liner notes for *A Love Supreme* describe his religious experience and include a psalm that inspired the fourth movement, which is improvised entirely from the psalm's syllabic content. Unlike the usual canticle, this one is "sung" on the tenor saxophone. The first movement, "Acknowledgement," like the whole work, is a culmination of Coltrane's music thus far, involving scales, pedal points, multiphonics, free improvisation, and shifting rhythms. Toward the end of the movement, a vocal chant signals a harmonic change from one key to another.

Coltrane's sound instantly demands attention, with its heraldic phrases based on the pentatonic scale. It has the feeling of an invocation. Many listeners think the four-note vocal figure is the movement's theme, but in fact it is one of four; the others are motives that spur his improvisation. If the movement opens and closes with incantations, the central section suggests spiritual wrestling as Coltrane works his way through those nagging motives to triumphant tonic chords, shadowed by the ever-alert rhythm section. Some critics were put off by the religious aspect of the piece, arguing that Coltrane abandoned musical coherence for the aesthetics of faith. This view (which drew posthumous support from the 1971 founding of the Church of Saint John Coltrane, in San Francisco) is no more valid or helpful in understanding his music than it is in analyzing Bach's *B Minor*

Mass. "Acknowledgement," including its freest passages, is strictly ordered by musical logic.

ACKNOWLEDGEMENT

John Coltrane Quartet

John Coltrane, tenor saxophone, voice; McCoy Tyner, piano; Jimmy Garrison, bass; Elvin Jones, drums

LABEL: *A Love Supreme,* Impulse! A(S)77; *A Love Supreme* (Impulse! 314 589 945-2)
DATE: 1964
STYLE: late Coltrane
FORM: open-ended

Introduction

0:00	The sound of a gong, combined with a piano chord, opens the piece. The music unfolds in free rhythm. Coltrane plays with a few notes from a pentatonic scale in the key of E, while the pianist scatters clusters up and down the keyboard.
0:03	The drums enter with a quiet shimmering in the cymbals.
0:15	The saxophone gently fades out.
0:20	The pianist settles on one chord, playing it with a fast tremolo.
0:29	As the bass and drums drop out, the drummer continues tapping on the cymbals.

Improvisation

0:32	Garrison (bass) begins a four-note syncopated ostinato, which we'll call motive A.

0:40	Jones plays a Latin-style groove, with bass drum and tom-tom accents coinciding with accents in the ostinato.
0:48	Tyner (piano) enters, playing quartal harmonies.
1:00	The drums switch to a more intense, double-time feeling.
1:04	Coltrane enters with a three-note motive, repeated sequentially on a higher pitch: motive B.

He plays this motive three times, each time with more variation. The bass moves away from the ostinato, improvising within the pentatonic scale.

1:11   Tyner's chords begin to drift, pulling the harmony toward a more dissonant and chromatic sound.

1:16   Coltrane plays an ascending pentatonic scale: motive C.

1:21   He returns to motive B.

1:32   Reaching a climax, he ascends to a cadence figure, played with a roughened tone: motive D.

1:35   Coltrane descends with fast passagework, drawn from the pentatonic scale.

2:00   He begins playing with motive C.

2:11   He moves motive C in sequence, shifting the music out of the pentatonic scale. Tyner adjusts his harmonies accordingly. The drums become still more polyrhythmic.

2:31   Coltrane reaches an anguished high note; he descends in pentatonic spirals.

2:44   Again he returns to motive C, quickly sending it into other keys.

2:51   As the dissonance intensifies, the bass drifts away from the home key.

3:06   Coltrane modulates through all possible keys.

3:15   The band finds its way back to the home key.

3:26   For a moment, the intensity and volume begin to fade.

3:37   Coltrane begins again with motive C.

3:47   He begins modulating to new keys.

3:52   He finally reaches motive D, playing it repeatedly with an increasingly torturous sound.

4:13   Coltrane's improvisation renews itself with motive C. His modulations ascend in a chromatic swirl. On bass, Garrison follows him into the topmost register.

4:22   Coltrane reaches the tonic and falls downward through the pentatonic scale.

4:33   The improvisation gradually subsides.

4:55	He plays motive A, moving it restlessly through all possible keys. The bass and piano follow.
5:50	Finally all instruments come to rest on the tonic. As the mood dies down, Coltrane repeats motive A endlessly.
5:54	Garrison plays a close variant of motive A.
6:05	The saxophone disappears; in its place, Coltrane's overdubbed voice sings "a love supreme." Its incessant repetition induces a trance-like sense of calm.
6:36	Suddenly the voices sink down a whole step, settling into a new key (which will be the key of the next movement).

Coda

6:44	The voices disappear, leaving Garrison playing his variant of motive A. The piano and drums occasionally add tension, but the bass is at the center.
7:09	The piano drops out.
7:23	The drums drop out. Garrison continues the motive's rhythms, but begins improvising its melody.
7:40	Garrison ends by quietly strumming two notes at once.

Within a year of *A Love Supreme*, Coltrane disbanded his quartet for an even more expressionistic group. He replaced Elvin Jones with Rashied Ali, another Philadelphian, but one tutored almost exclusively in the avant-garde; on occasion, Coltrane would use two or three drummers. His wife, Alice, a former student of Bud Powell with relatively workmanlike technique, replaced Tyner. After Coltrane's death, she would earn her own following as a composer of religious-themed music with internationalist echoes, elaborating on her husband's interest in the music of Africa, India, and the Middle East. (Their son, Ravi Coltrane, toured with her in 1987, and developed into a talented tenor saxophonist in his own right.) Jimmy Garrison continued to play with the group, which became a quintet with the addition of tenor saxophonist Pharoah Sanders.

Born in Little Rock, Arkansas, Sanders was regarded as one of the most intractable members of the avant-garde. His shrieking, guttural explosions of sound, often within a modal framework, were thought to pick up where Coltrane left off, taking jazz into a realm where the only rule was the inspiration of the moment. After Coltrane's death in 1967, Sanders's music grew increasingly restrained, backpedaling from modes to chords and melodic statements with minimal improvisation. Although the free music Coltrane embraced in his last years was undeniably a product of its time, reflecting the tragedies of the civil rights struggle (his "Alabama" remains an incomparable cri de coeur) and the slaughter in Vietnam, it exerted lasting influence on musicians who adapted free improvisation along with ghosted notes, broken notes, squawks, and growls as part of the musician's arsenal.

Coltrane's most extreme work is the 1965 album *Ascension*, a vexatious piece that takes the heady effusiveness of "Giant Steps" and "Chasin' the Trane" to the limit of musical reason. The piece, improvised by ten musicians, is based on a minor triad and a couple of ground chords for the ensemble passages; the format consists of free solos that alternate with free ensemble blowouts. Yet even *Ascension* develops a de facto logic. (Decades later, it was transcribed and performed as a "composed" piece.) Coltrane always claimed not to understand the fuss. "The main thing a musician would like to do," he said, "is to give a picture to the listener of the many wonderful things he knows of and senses in the universe."

MILES DAVIS'S SECOND QUINTET

After the back-to-back triumphs of *Kind of Blue* and *Sketches of Spain*, Miles Davis endured a slump of uncertainty. Coltrane, Adderley, and Evans had left to pursue their own careers, and Davis expressed contempt for the avant-garde. He continued to release effective records, including a reunion with Coltrane that produced a minor hit in "Some Day My Prince Will Come." But his music was caught in a bind, much of it devoted to faster and harder versions of his usual repertory, including "Walkin'" and "So What."

Then in 1963, once again, he produced magic. He turned to younger musicians who would surely have had important careers on their own but who, under Davis's tutelage, merged into a historic ensemble, greater than its very considerable parts. The rhythm section consisted of three prodigiously skillful musicians who valued diversity over an allegiance to one style of music: pianist Herbie Hancock, bassist Ron Carter, and seventeen-year-old drummer Tony Williams. Davis auditioned many saxophonists before temporarily settling on George Coleman, who played with facility and intelligence but lacked the drive and curiosity of the younger guys. In late 1964, Wayne Shorter, who had made his name as a saxophonist and composer with Art Blakey's Jazz Messengers, joined the band, a decision that changed his life and Davis's, and made this second great quintet a worthy follow-up to the 1955 group with Coltrane. This time, however, Davis took as much from his sidemen as he gave, drawing on their compositions (especially Shorter's) and sensibilities. These musicians were keenly interested in the avant-garde, and Davis adjusted his music to assimilate their tastes, as he struggled to make a separate peace in a confusing era.

Jazz was beset on one side by avant-garde experimentalism that estranged much of the audience, and on the other by rock, which had matured from a teenage marketing ploy to the dominant pop music. Davis would eventually inch his way to a fusion of jazz and rock, but first he adapted modal jazz to include elements of the avant-garde in a postbop style far more extreme than anything he had previously done. This approach, which also attracted other accomplished musicians caught between the conventions of modern jazz and the excitement born of the avant-garde, involved harmonic ambiguity, original compositions with new harmonic frameworks (rather than those built on standard songs), and a radical loosening of the rhythm section. Some of the tunes written by Davis's sidemen actually encouraged free improvisation (Ron Carter's "Eighty One" is a blues but also a minefield of open terrain). In the most advanced of these pieces, chord progressions were omitted while time and meter might evaporate and coalesce several times in the course of a performance.

Most first-rate rhythm sections work like the fingers in a fist. Coltrane's quartet, for example, achieved a fiercely unified front, devoted to supporting the leader. Davis's group was no less unified, but its parts interacted with more freedom, often rivaling the soloists. So much was going on between Hancock's unruffled block chords, Carter's slippery bass lines, and Williams's rhythmic brushfires that they all appeared to be soloing all the time. Davis gave them leave, enjoying the excitement they created, but he imposed a discipline that left space for the lyrical drama of his trumpet. Interestingly, on those few occasions when Davis failed to show up for a set in a jazz club, the other four musicians played in a more traditional, straight-ahead style. Free of chord changes, unapologetic about fluffs, and stimulated by his band's ceaseless energy, Davis became a more expansive trumpet player. He began to forage in the upper register at precipitous tempos, ideas spilling from his horn with spiraling confidence despite infrequent technical failings. He cut back on his signature ballads and began to jettison standard tunes and his classics. Between 1965 and 1968, he found his own way to be avant-garde.

"E.S.P."

The 1965 album *E.S.P.* was a critical event, but not a popular success. It represented the first studio recording by the new quintet, and the seven new compositions, all by members of the group, challenged listeners who expected to hear the tender, meditative Davis who incarnated jazz romanticism. This music is audacious, fast, and free. The title of the album (and first selection) emphasized the idea that extra-sensory perception is required to play this music. Shorter composed "E.S.P." as a thirty-two-bar tune, but its harmonic structure is far more complicated than that of "So What."

The melody is based on intervals of fourths (recalling the indefinite quartal harmonies of "So What" and "Acknowledgement"), and is married to a mixture of scales and chords in a way that offers direction to the improvisers without making many demands. The main part of the piece (A) hovers around an F major scale, while the B sections close with specific harmonic cadences that are handled easily and quickly—especially at this expeditious tempo. The soloists (Shorter for two choruses, Davis for six, Hancock for two) take wing over the rhythm, bending notes in and out of pitch, soaring beyond the usual rhythmic demarcations that denote swing. No less free is the multifaceted work of the rhythm section: the bass playing is startlingly autonomous, and the drummer's use of cymbals has its own narrative logic.

E.S.P.

Miles Davis Quintet

Miles Davis, trumpet; Wayne Shorter, tenor saxophone; Herbie Hancock, piano; Ron Carter, bass; Tony Williams, drums

LABEL: *E.S.P.* (Sony B00000DCH2)
DATE: 1965
STYLE: postbop
FORM: 32-bar popular song (**AA'**)

Chorus 1 (head)

0:00	**A**	The tenor saxophone and trumpet enter with the tune, which initially alternates between three notes. Because the notes harmonize equally well with two different chords, it's hard to determine the piece's key. Underneath, Carter (bass) plays two beats per bar, while Williams rattles busily on the cymbals.
0:07		The melody descends from a high note, while the bass rises chromatically. For several measures, the piano is silent.

0:13		The phrase ends with a dissonant bass note.
0:14	A'	The A section is repeated with a higher-pitched bass line.
0:21		The bass harmonizes underneath in tritones by playing two strings at once (double stops).
0:27		The tune ends in a major key that may be the tonic, but the sense of closure lasts less than a second.

Chorus 2

0:28	A	Shorter (tenor saxophone) begins a two-chorus solo with an upward-rising line that ends in a bent note. Carter (bass) begins to walk.
0:35		Shorter plays pitches that are out of time and slightly flat before blending them back in to a continuous line.
0:42	A'	He improvises an even stream of notes.
0:49		He plays a descending three-note motive twice before continuing his line.

Chorus 3

0:55	A	Shorter leaves spaces for Hancock (piano) to enter with chords.
1:02		With a sudden ascent, Shorter returns to the tune's melody. He ends a flurry of notes with a dismissive honk.
1:09	A'	Shorter plays with a motive that, in its alternation of two pitches, recalls the theme.
1:15		His melody is chromatic, matching the tension of Hancock's dissonant chords.

Chorus 4

1:22	A	Davis begins his six-chorus solo. He concentrates on a few mid-register notes.
1:29		As the harmonies become more tense, Davis rises to a dissonant note.
1:34		His notes begin to crack.
1:36	A'	
1:41		Davis suddenly rises into the upper register. He plays a few shrill notes before tumbling, somewhat untidily, back down.

Chorus 5

1:49	A	As Williams (drums) and Hancock play more aggressively, Davis's solo becomes more disjointed, breaking into short fragments.
2:02	A'	Davis begins a new phrase with a repeated-note fanfare, followed by a series of short phrases.

Chorus 6

2:15	A	The trumpet hits an accent that coincides spontaneously with a drum accent.

2:29   **A'**   Carter takes his walking-bass line into the upper register.

2:35   As the bass drops back down, Davis rises step by step.

2:40   Davis again makes a sudden swoop upward.

Chorus 7

2:42   **A**   Davis screeches out a descending four-note line in his upper range. Williams's drumming hits a new level of intensity with powerful drum strokes.

2:55   **A'**   The band retreats to a lower volume. Davis plays a continuous line of notes in his middle register.

Chorus 8

3:08   **A**   Davis's new motive has a bluesy tinge.

3:21   **A'**

3:31   Davis abruptly drops out; the space is filled by Hancock's comping.

Chorus 9

3:34   **A**   Davis plays a motive that rocks back and forth a half step, interrupting it with several swoops up to his highest register.

3:47   **A'**   He returns to a variant of the bluesy motive from chorus 8.

Chorus 10

4:00   **A**   Hancock starts his solo, imitating the rhythm of Davis's last motive.

4:06   Hancock introduces his own substitution in the harmonic progression.

4:13   **A'**   Playing a single-note line, he sounds like a saxophonist or trumpet player.

Chorus 11

4:27   **A**   Hancock plays a riff, then modifies it subtly to fit the chord progression.

4:40   **A'**   His improvised line interacts with his left-hand chords.

Chorus 12 (head)

4:53   **A**   As Davis and Shorter reenter with the tune's melody, Carter on bass returns to a slower pattern.

5:00   Carter plays tritone double stops, Williams adding a few cymbal colors.

5:07   **A'**   Williams reestablishes his drum pulse, but fades in and out for the rest of the tune.

Coda

5:20   When the tune ends, Carter is on an unexpected note. He resolves it downward to the opening chord.

The public reception accorded *E.S.P.* and succeeding albums by Davis's quintet (*Miles Smiles, Sorcerer, Nefertiti*) suggested the tremendous changes that had taken place in the cultural landscape in the few years since *Kind of Blue* and *Sketches of Spain.* They were received favorably and sometimes enthusiastically by musicians, critics, and young fans, but achieved nothing of the broader cachet enjoyed by his earlier work: there was nothing easy or soothing about these records. By 1965, rock and roll could no longer be dismissed by jazz artists as music for kids, and Davis was feeling the heat, not least from his disgruntled record company.

15 CHAPTER

The Avant-Garde

FORWARD MARCH

The term *avant-garde* originated in the French military to denote troops sent ahead of the regular army to scout unknown territory. In English, the word was adapted to describe innovative composers, writers, painters, and other artists whose work was so pioneering that it was believed to be in the vanguard of contemporary thinking. Avant-gardism represented a movement to liberate artists from the restraints of tradition, and often went hand-in-hand with progres-

◄ Sonny Rollins combined the harmonic progressions of bop with the freedom of the avant-garde and sustained an international following. He appeared with percussionist Victor See Yuen and trombonist Clifton Anderson at a stadium in Louisiana, 1995.

sive social ideas. Those who championed avant-garde art tended to applaud social change, while those who criticized it for rejecting prevailing standards couched their dismay in warnings against moral laxity or political anarchy. In the end, of course, avant-garde art, no less than the conventional kind, must stand on its merits, independent of historical considerations. The art that outrages one generation often becomes the tradition and homework assignments of the next: the paintings of Paul Cézanne and Pablo Picasso, music of Gustav Mahler and Claude Debussy, and writings of Marcel Proust and James Joyce are no longer considered avant-garde. Perhaps only in the twelve-tone musical bloc founded by Arnold Schoenberg (at around the same time jazz was leaving New Orleans) and in the extremes of postwar jazz has the avant-garde retained a free-standing status, divorced from cutting-edge futurism. If avant-garde jazz initially fulfilled all the requirements of irreverent innovation, it has long since come to define a particular style or movement. You may not think the music of Ornette Coleman and Cecil Taylor, after more than half a century, is avant-garde per se, but it continues to be defined as such in the same way that Benny Goodman is defined by swing and Charlie Parker by bebop.

Two especially prominent avant-garde movements gathered steam in the decades following the world wars, and jazz was vital to both. The 1920s avant-garde, which included such factions as surrealism, cubism, and imagism, as well as twelve-tone music, consciously sought to rupture artistic conventions. It was a response to the devastation of the First World War, the expansion of women's rights, and startling advances in technology—radio, talking pictures, transcontinental flight—that seemed to shrink the world while expanding its potential. This avant-garde was provocative and sometimes rude, but generally hopeful. Jazz fit in very well. It was a new musical fashion, socially daring and emblematic of freethinking young people. Although pilloried by some conservative tastemakers as low-born and vulgar, jazz was regarded by many members of the cultural elite as an inspirational resource and a powerful component of courageous modernism. Artists in diverse fields—painters Henri Matisse and Piet Mondrian, composers Igor Stravinsky and Kurt Weill, poets Hart Crane and Langston Hughes, photographer Man Ray, sculptor Alexander Calder, dancer Josephine Baker—found inspiration in jazz and its New World vitality.

Within the closed and frequently possessive precincts of jazz itself, as we have seen, practically every new style was considered avant-garde in a negative way—as inauthentic or compromised or incomprehensible. As early as the 1920s, the traditionalists complained that Armstrong, Ellington, and swing music muddied the alleged purity of New Orleans jazz. Those complaints, however, were few and relatively calm compared with the outrage generated by bebop. Unlike purists who disparaged swing for commercializing jazz, the opponents of bop blamed it for sacrificing jazz's connection to dance and mainstream popular culture. Instead of accommodating the dictates of the marketplace, bop proudly adapted an avant-garde agenda of self-consciously examining the relationship between jazz and society and between jazz and other kinds of music. Even so, jazz remained largely accessible. Bebop made jazz more intellectual but maintained the basic rules of musical coherence. The second avant-garde challenged even those rules.

The cultural wave of the late 1950s and 1960s reflected conditions similar to those of the 1920s, only more so. The rebuilding of Europe and Asia after the Second World War was countered by new colonial wars, occupations, and the Cold War, in which America and the Soviet Union employed technology to threaten annihilation and turned the conquest of space into an ideology-driven contest. As the struggle for racial equality in the United States led to the Civil Rights Act of 1964, which outlawed discrimination on grounds of race, color, religion, sex, and national origin, women unsurprisingly demanded professional, social, and sexual parity. Some of society's settled conventions, including the nuclear family (working dad, stay-at-home mom), unraveled.

The radical changes in racial and gender politics, as well as the threat of a push-button atomic war, created a reverse avant-garde from the one that glorified modernism as a citadel of healthy change. Instead of expressing faith in a liberating future, the avant-garde of the Cold War bared uncertainty and anguish while celebrating the plebeian, the ordinary, the absurd. Instead of abstraction or surrealism, painters looked to comic strips, visual trickery, and commercial design. A characteristic literary work was Samuel Beckett's *Waiting for Godot* (published in 1952), an intricately symbolic play that recycled as avant-garde stagecraft the most commonplace aspect of popular entertainment, vaudeville. By the early 1960s, existential themes—life is without meaning, the world is mad, mankind is abandoned ("to freedom condemned," as Jean-Paul Sartre put it)—permeated the arts.

Among the most potent avenues for the avant-garde in the 1960s were the two art forms born in the twentieth century, movies and jazz. A challenging new direction in cinema emanated from Europe, often described as the New Wave. These films examined prevailing themes of confusion and desperation, and pioneered techniques in narrative style. Jazz in this period also developed new techniques to express its disavowal of tradition. Despite the disarming, apparently unifying popularity of albums like *Kind of Blue*, jazz had split into so many schools that Duke Ellington spoke for most listeners when he said, "I don't know how such great extremes as now exist can be contained under the one heading." The label *avant-garde* eventually attached itself permanently to the most radical of those extremes.

WHAT'S IN A NAME?

The jazz school that came to be called avant-garde was first known by other names, few of them neutral. One critic coined the term "anti-jazz" to attack its apparent rejection of mainstream jazz. Another widespread designation echoed the title of an album by Ornette Coleman, *Free Jazz,* released in 1961 with a cover reproduction of a Jackson Pollock painting, as if to underscore its challenging modernity. Some called it Black Music, arguing that its ferocity expressed the particular frustration of African Americans during the civil rights years. Others called it new music, the New Thing, revolutionary music, and fire music. Ironically, the name that finally stuck had been indicated in the title of the first avant-garde album, Cecil Taylor's 1956 *Jazz Advance.*

As musicians in later decades enlarged the canvas of free jazz or new music, the inoffensive *avant-garde* emerged as an umbrella term to describe an inclusive, ongoing school of jazz that, despite connections to mainstream jazz, evolved as a separate entity, a tradition in its own right. By definition, *avant-garde* is now something of a misnomer: music that is four or five decades old can hardly be representative of today's vanguard, let alone tomorrow's. Yet the word continues to apply because it encompasses an approach to jazz that remains outside the practices that govern the usual musical performance. It continues to question principles that the mainstream takes for granted.

If postwar jazz innovators greatly enlarged the parameters of mainstream (or swing) jazz, the avant-garde stretched those parameters to the breaking point. Although the key figures of the avant-garde—most prominently Ornette Coleman, Cecil Taylor, and John Coltrane—approached music from very different angles, they collectively challenged the status quo. In refusing to be bound by rules of the past, they questioned and changed every facet of jazz's identity. Concerning rhythm, the avant-garde dispensed with the steady beat, preferring an ambiguous pulse or several pulses at once. Concerning harmony, the avant-garde did away with patterns based on chords or scales, creating a serendipitous harmony as the musicians instinctively felt their way through a performance. Concerning melody, the soloist might shoot for angelic lyricism or indulge in a fury of squeals and squawks—either way, melody no longer relied on harmonic patterns and resolutions. Concerning structure, the avant-garde frequently rejected blues and songs, and encouraged *free* improvisation, in which the sheer energy or emotionalism of a performance dictated its overall shape. Concerning instrumentation, the avant-garde favored the widest variety of instruments, from the hand drums and wood flutes of formerly colonized Third World countries to symphonic standbys like the cello and oboe. Concerning presentation, jazz could be witty, even funny, but it wasn't entertainment merely; it was a serious, challenging music, requiring the listener's full concentration—art for art's sake. Concerning politics, jazz became entrenched in the increasingly militant racial and antiwar struggles of the 1950s and 1960s; whether or not it referred to specific events, it adopted an assertive posture.

As the avant-garde developed beyond its initial stage, musicians embraced it as an arena in which anything could be tried. A spontaneous improvisation and a twelve-bar blues might follow one another in the same set, or in the same piece. The avant-garde refused to be pinned down to any one style or idiom. Two pioneers, Ornette Coleman and Cecil Taylor, burst onto the scene with an originality that divided the jazz world, inciting international controversy that found them acclaimed as geniuses and derided as charlatans. At the height of the furor, the soft-spoken Coleman said, "Musicians tell me, if what I'm doing is right, they should never have gone to school." Many musicians and critics considered these two a threat. Duke Ellington once observed, "Bebop is like playing Scrabble with all the vowels removed." As far as their detractors could tell, Coleman and Taylor had removed the consonants as well.

Ornette Coleman (B. 1930)

Ornette Coleman is now almost universally revered as one of American music's most original figures. Several of his compositions are jazz standards, and his influence is beyond calculation. In 2007, he received the Pulitzer

Prize—the first ever awarded for a recording (his album *Sound Grammar*). Yet when he first arrived in New York, he was the most disruptive figure in jazz. During a long 1959 engagement at the Five Spot, dozens of established musicians came to hear his music. Some, including classical composers Leonard Bernstein and Gunther Schuller, declared him a genius. Others, including Miles Davis and Charles Mingus, were skeptical and derisive. Mingus expressed a prevailing confusion about Coleman's music when he said, "It's like not having anything to do with what's around you, and being right in your own world."

Coleman, who grew up in Fort Worth, Texas, began playing alto saxophone at fourteen and proceeded to work in rhythm and blues and carnival bands. In the late 1940s, he became enamored of the innovations of Charlie Parker. But his attempts to play in a style of his own were invariably greeted with hostility. The situation came to a head at a dance when he was attacked and his saxophone destroyed. He moved to New Orleans in 1949, where he met the gifted drummer Ed Blackwell, the first in a cadre of disciples who encouraged Coleman to persevere. Later that year, Coleman traveled with a rhythm and blues band to Los Angeles, where he took a job operating an elevator and taught himself theory. He remained unnoticed for five years, during which he wrote some of his benchmark tunes.

In 1956, Coleman and Blackwell formed the American Jazz Quintet, and Coleman also began rehearsing with other forward-thinking musicians, including three major interpreters of his music with whom he formed his quartet: drummer Billy Higgins, bassist Charlie Haden, and Don Cherry, who played a compact cornet that looked more like a toy than a serious instrument (he called it a pocket trumpet). Two years later, Coleman was signed to record two albums for the Los Angeles–based label Contemporary. He was accompanied by Cherry, Higgins, and a few established bebop musicians suggested by the label.

Even without his own band, these albums proved Coleman to be a mature and inventive musician. The titles were deliberate provocations: *Something Else!!!!* and *Tomorrow Is the Question: The New Music of Ornette Coleman*. John Lewis of the Modern Jazz Quartet persuaded his label, Atlantic Records, to sign and record Coleman in Los Angeles and bring him to New York. Lewis also helped arrange for Coleman and Cherry to attend his Lenox School of Jazz in the Berkshires, and perform at the Five Spot in New York. The six Atlantic albums recorded between 1959 and

1961, all but one featuring his quartet, generated a cultural storm, not least for album titles that continued to lay emphasis on the group's challenging attitude, which—without once mentioning the civil rights struggle—seemed to incarnate the authority of the New Negro: *The Shape of Jazz to Come, Change of the Century, This Is Our Music,* and *Free Jazz.*

Two aspects of Coleman's music were evident from the very beginning. First, his compositions possessed strong melodic, emotional character. Some suggested the solemnity of dirges, others were deeply blues-based, and many were as quirkily memorable and disarmingly simple as those of Thelonious Monk. Even his early detractors, put off by what they perceived to be a chaotic improvisational style, expressed admiration for such captivating melodies as "Turnaround," "Ramblin'," "Una Muy Bonita," "Congeniality," "Tears Inside," "R.P.D.D.," and the much covered "Lonely Woman." Second, Coleman's sound on alto saxophone jarred listeners, even those who were favorably disposed to his music. His timbre had a rough-edged, elemental, vocal quality, a raw backwoods sound, as sharp and astringent as a field holler. That harshness was accentuated by his preferred instrument—a white plastic alto saxophone. The bop drummer Shelly Manne, who recorded with him, said that he sounded like a man crying or laughing through his horn. Coleman himself emphasized the value of "vocal" projection: "You can always reach into the human sound of a voice on your horn if you are actually hearing and trying to express the warmth of a human voice." Coleman and his compositions sounded at once avant-garde and strangely primitive.

On a more technical level, Coleman was said to play the alto saxophone with microtone pitches, which challenged the familiarity of the tempered scale. The classical composer Hale Smith, who wrote a few pieces for avant-garde jazz musicians, observed that Coleman's hearing was so acute that he played his in-between pitches in correct ratio to each other, so that if his E was slightly sharp, his F (and F-sharp, G, and so forth) was slightly sharp *to the same degree.* Coleman may have been at odds with the tempered scale, but he was in tune with himself. Coleman has argued that there is no such thing as an absolute pitch, and that the playing of a note ought to reflect its context: an F, for example, ought not to sound the same in a piece expressing sadness and a piece expressing joy. He explained in his characteristically elliptical manner: "Jazz is the only music in which the same note can be played night after night but differently each time. It's the hidden things, the subconscious that lies in the body and lets you know: You feel this, you play this."

Coleman's approach to pitch was a decisive component in his over-hauling of jazz, and his other innovations appeared to follow from it. He rejected preset harmony. On rare occasions when he played a standard song, he approached the piece solely through its melody, improvising on the song's melodic phrases rather than its chord changes. He offered an open-ended inspiration for musical creativity—both horizontally, in the linear development of solos, and vertically, in the chance harmonies that followed.

This approach inclined him to dispense with the piano, which inter-fered with his music on two counts: it emphasized the tempered scale and promoted chords. The stark texture Coleman preferred in his quartet underscored the startling newness of his music. The listener hears a strik-ing theme played by alto and trumpet, over a jolting rhythm that doesn't accent regular beats; the subsequent solos have no governing structure. The listener is challenged (assaulted, some would say) by the sharp pitch and the absence of a familiar frame of reference—there are no choruses, no harmonic resolutions, no steady meters. That doesn't mean that rhythm and harmony are absent, only that they are improvised along with melody. Cherry developed a sound on the pocket trumpet that merged with Cole-man's alto on the themes, sometimes harmonized in octaves. The chief source of harmony emanates from the bassist's response to the soloists. The drummer is free to spontaneously add to the musical whole. He produces plenty of rhythm, but not the toe-tapping, 4/4 meter kind. As Coleman explained, "Rhythm patterns should be more or less like natural breathing patterns."

"LONELY WOMAN"

Coleman wrote "Lonely Woman," his best-known and most frequently performed piece, in 1954, inspired by a painting he saw in a gallery. One reason it became popular is that most of his 1959 recording consists of statements of the melody, and Coleman's solo sounds almost like a transi-tional passage between melody statements, extending the feeling and char-acter of the piece.

The unhurried, yearning melody comes as a surprise after the intro-duction, which suggests opposing rhythmic possibilities as Charlie Haden plays measured two-note chords on the bass and Billy Higgins ignites a swift rhythm on the ride cymbal. The melody floats free of those specific cues, bluntly voiced by alto and trumpet. Throughout the piece, rhythm exerts a powerful presence. But try to count measures: there are no absolute downbeats or upbeats. Still, the piece undoubtedly swings in a jazz sense— especially during Coleman's solo (for example, at 2:01–2:21), where he holds his rhythmic authority in reserve, suggesting swing without emphasizing it. Although "Lonely Woman" has no preset chords, the performance is harmonically interesting, from the octaves played by alto and trumpet to the two sections of the tune, each indicating a different harmonic sphere. Of particular interest is the creative bass playing by Haden, who implies major and minor key changes, augmenting the overall drama as he lags behind, doubles, or anticipates Coleman's phrases. Toward the end of the final chorus (4:02), Cherry hits a clinker. Coleman once said that it wasn't until he made mistakes that he knew he was on the right track. Whenever two or more musicians perform together, harmony is created, which means that in almost any context some notes will fit and others won't.

LONELY WOMAN

Ornette Coleman

Ornette Coleman, alto saxophone; Don Cherry, cornet; Charlie Haden, bass; Billy Higgins, drums

LABEL: *The Shape of Jazz to Come,* Atlantic SD 1317; *The Shape of Jazz to Come* (Rhino UPC-075678133923)
DATE: 1959
STYLE: avant-garde
FORM: loose **AABA**

Introduction

0:00	The drummer (Higgins) begins quietly tapping out a short motive on cymbals. On bass, Haden joins in with a resonant double stop (playing two strings at the same time).
0:07	Higgins switches to a rapid accompaniment. As if in a slower rhythmic space, Haden simultaneously holds down a pedal tone with one string while soloing with the other.

Chorus 1 (head)

0:18	A	Coleman and Cherry enter, playing the melody in octaves. Like the bass line, the melody floats rhythmically above the drum accompaniment.
0:30		Coleman plays a short, plaintive reply. The bass falls to the dominant.

0:34		The two horns harmonize in parallel intervals.
0:36		On the upper string of the bass, Haden temporarily changes the harmony from minor to major. The mode changes back to minor when the horns reenter.
0:43	**A**	Coleman and Cherry repeat the melody.
0:55		As Coleman plays his plaintive reply, Haden doubles him on the bass.
1:03		On the last phrase, Coleman rises to a yearning wail.
1:08	**B**	Over a new harmony, Coleman repeats a riff-like phrase. Behind him, Cherry and Haden creep upward chromatically, their background line accentuated by drum strokes.
1:16		Underneath Coleman's last phrase, the drum plays with richer timbres while the bass shifts to the dominant.
1:20	**A**	A drum stroke signals the return to the tonic harmony and the free-floating melody.

Chorus 2

1:46	**A**	(indeterminate length) Coleman plays simple, bluesy phrases, unaffected by the rising chromatic line Haden suggests behind him.
2:01		As his emotional temperature begins to rise, Coleman's tone becomes rough and uneven.
2:08		He moves to a harder-swinging rhythmic feeling, evoking a cry of "whoo!" from one of the musicians.
2:21	**B**	The bridge is signaled by the return of the rising chromatic line in the trumpet, doubled erratically by the bass.
2:31		At the end of the bridge, the harmony and Coleman's line focus on the dominant.
2:33	**A**	With a dramatic return to the tonic, Coleman leads the group back to the **A** section. Haden, playing double stops, holds the bottom note in a pedal point while moving the upper voice up and down chromatically.
2:49		Rising in intensity, Coleman's line reaches its climax.

Chorus 3

2:54	**A**	The two horns return to the melody in octaves.
3:17	**A**	
3:41	**B**	
3:47		Cherry hits high notes, followed by quick descending blurs.
3:53	**A**	
4:02		At one point, Cherry hits the wrong pitch.

Coda

| 4:19 | | The two horns combine to play blues-like wails. |
| 4:25 | | Coleman holds out his last note; underneath, Cherry adds low, breathy comments. |

| 4:32 | The bass continues playing his double stops, rising chromatically until reaching the upper octave (at 4:42); he continues to play until the drums finally stop. |

Coleman worked on two important projects at the close of 1960. On December 19 and 20, he participated in Gunther Schuller's Third Stream album *Jazz Abstractions*, as a featured soloist on "Abstraction" and "Variants on a Theme of Thelonious Monk." These twelve-tone compositions by Schuller present Coleman's improvisations in the context of strict notation. He's backed by an ensemble of seven strings and a few other jazz musicians—notably the virtuoso Eric Dolphy on bass clarinet. On the 21st, Coleman returned to the same studio with what he called his Double Quartet, made up of his own group and some of the Schuller personnel, including Dolphy. This group recorded *Free Jazz*, an immensely influential work that offered, intentionally or not, a strong counterstatement to the concerto format represented by *Jazz Abstractions*. In *Free Jazz*, the entire ensemble was free to shape the thirty-seven-minute performance, although introductory sections were composed, and an order created for solos, duets, and broader collective improvisations. The composition comes to life in the give-and-take among the musicians, as they listen to each other and respond accordingly.

For all the fuss caused by *Free Jazz*, Coleman had by no means abandoned notation. Indeed, the rest of his career can be seen as an attempt to juggle the fastidious kind of composition represented by Schuller's work and the spontaneity of free improvisation. In working out a theory in which both approaches could coexist, Coleman coined a word, *harmolodic*—a contraction of harmony, movement, and melody, and a catch-phrase to characterize his take on ensemble music, written and improvised. One abiding aspect of harmolodic music is the idea that musicians may improvise register, even when their parts are notated. They may transpose written phrases to any key or octave while maintaining the music's melodic integrity.

In exploring the harmolodic landscape, Coleman composed music for string quartet, woodwind octet, symphony orchestra, rock bands, and other groups. He played trumpet and violin in addition to alto, deriving from them his own "unschooled" timbres. In 1972, he recorded his most elaborate piece, *Skies of America*, with the London Symphony Orchestra.

Although the piece was conceived to combine symphony orchestra and his own ensemble, Coleman was forced—by Columbia Records, concerned about the high cost of the project—to eliminate his band and appear instead as the only improvising soloist. In later concert performances, the piece emerged as intended. Thanks to the harmolodic idea of willful transposition and the freedom given Coleman's band, it can never be played the same way twice.

A few years after debuting *Skies of America*, Coleman put together an electric band, Prime Time, which also performed pieces that were mostly notated. This ensemble came as a jolting addition to the fusion movement, combining elements of jazz and rock; several of the sidemen, including guitarist James Blood Ulmer, electric bassist Jamaaladeen Tacuma, and drummer Ronald Shannon Jackson, created offshoot bands that extended the idea of fusing different musical idioms. Significantly, Prime Time played some of the same themes created for *Skies of America* and Coleman's acoustic band. Through all these varied settings, Coleman never compromised his unmistakable sound. His instantly recognizable alto is the one unvarying factor in his contextually varied musical world.

Cecil Taylor (B. 1929)

While the leaders of bop served parallel apprenticeships in big bands and developed styles that were sufficiently alike to allow them to perform and record together, the avant-garde's primary creators represent divergent backgrounds. Of the three main leaders, only John Coltrane served his apprenticeship in jazz. Ornette Coleman's background, as we have seen, included rhythm and blues. Cecil Taylor's involved classical music. Significantly, they never performed in the same group, although Coltrane recorded once with Taylor and once with Coleman's sidemen. Taylor and Coleman rehearsed together at least once—a tape is said to exist—but the experience did not encourage further collaboration.

Taylor was the first of the three to record as the leader of his own ensemble and the last to earn widespread recognition. He had his supporters, and his virtuoso keyboard facility was never much doubted; but detractors, weighing his music against the prevailing styles, questioned his ability to swing, play blues, and otherwise function in the conventional bop-derived jazz idiom. Like Coleman's, his approach was so startling that even when he recorded standard songs, he made them all but unrecognizable. Taylor's personal style also put listeners off. Like classical recitalists, he never speaks onstage, though he often begins his concerts by reciting his poetry (not always audibly) as a kind of prelude to the music. More alienating is the length of his performances: concerts of three and more hours were, at least in his early years, not uncommon. Uniquely, he never performs the same work twice. Notoriously obsessive about practicing, he once had his ensemble rehearse for a year in order to perform one concert and make one recording—after which, the pieces were retired.

Taylor has courted controversy throughout his career, arguing that since the musician prepares, the audience ought to prepare as well. This attitude has been criticized as arrogant, yet "preparation" is commonplace in attempting to understand other kinds of avant-garde art. Listeners with experience in modern classical music frequently find Taylor's music more accessible than jazz fans. This irks Taylor, who sees himself in the tradition of the jazz pianist-composers he admires, among them Duke Ellington, Bud Powell, Thelonious Monk, Lennie Tristano, Erroll Garner, and Horace Silver—each famous for his percussive style. Taylor takes that percussiveness to an unparalleled extreme. It has been said that he treats the piano as if it consisted of eighty-eight tuned drums.

Cecil Taylor grew up on Long Island, New York, the son of educated African Americans whose own mothers were full-blooded Indian (Kiowa and Cherokee). His mother, a pianist, encouraged him to take up the instrument at five, the same year she took him to see Chick Webb's swing band at the Apollo Theater, an intoxicating event. The pivotal moment of his childhood was her death, when Taylor was fourteen. He developed an ulcer that year and grew increasingly introverted and devoted to music, studying percussion in addition to piano. In 1951, he enrolled at the New England Conservatory, where he grew resentful at the lack of respect accorded African and African American culture, which he recognized as a resource for much avant-garde music in and out of jazz. During summers and vacations, Taylor occasionally found work in jazz bands (including one led by Johnny Hodges, then on sabbatical from the Ellington band), but those jobs were of short duration. One bandleader said he took pity on Taylor because he couldn't play the blues. Still, in 1956, shortly after graduating from the New England Conservatory, he convinced the Five Spot to hire his quartet—a six-week engagement that turned the neighborhood bar into a home for futuristic jazz and exposed Taylor's music to enthusiastic if often bewildered scrutiny.

———

Few jazz clubs have had as profound an impact on the development of a particular kind of jazz as the Five Spot, which allowed the avant-garde to develop much as Minton's Playhouse had allowed bop to develop. The main difference is that Minton's created a jam-session atmosphere in which individual players proved themselves, while the Five Spot became a showcase for major bands to perfect their music during open-ended engagements. Taylor, Coleman, and Coltrane all had career-changing engagements there, as did Charles Mingus and Eric Dolphy, among others. The Five Spot began as a family-operated bar on New York's Bowery. The owners, Iggy and Joe Termini, cared little about jazz, but in the middle 1950s a musician who held jam sessions in his loft offered to hold the sessions in their bar if the Terminis would buy a piano. In 1956, the Five Spot played host to two important engagements. Alto saxophonist Phil Woods organized an all-star tribute to Charlie Parker and recorded it—the first of many Live at the Five Spot albums. Then Cecil Taylor, utterly unknown in the jazz world, began the long residency that attracted a following of painters, writers, actors, and musicians.

The room was unprepossessing, small and dark, with a bar along one wall and the stage at the rear. Filled with smoke and the bohemian chatter of the regulars, it achieved national renown in 1957 when it presented a long engagement by Thelonious Monk's quartet, featuring John Coltrane—the first of several extended Monk appearances through 1962, averaging six to eight months a year. In 1959, the Five Spot became the focal point for the jazz world when it presented Ornette Coleman in his New York debut, for three months. Three years later, the club moved a few blocks from its original Cooper Square address to a larger space on Third Avenue and Seventh Street, where it continued to violate the usual practice of booking a different band each week by encouraging long residencies. By 1967, the neighborhood had changed: rock palaces opened nearby, and the jazz business languished. The Termini brothers darkened the stage and sold food from a street-side vestibule. Though a renewed interest in avant-garde jazz in the 1970s, a period later known as the Loft Era, encouraged them to reopen the club for a few years, it closed down for good in 1976.

Taylor's success at the club led directly to the recording *Jazz Advance*. His group consisted of Steve Lacy, the first important soprano saxophonist in jazz since Sidney Bechet, who until he hooked up with Taylor usually worked in Dixieland and swing bands (Lacy later became a world-traveling figure in the avant-garde); a classically trained bassist, Buell Neidlinger; and a self-taught drummer, Dennis Charles, whose inexperience pleased Taylor. Like Coleman, Taylor required malleable musicians who could follow him into new territory. For *Jazz Advance*, the band recorded intense versions of songs by Monk and Cole Porter, but the highlights were original compositions that suggested a free-form atonality and ferocious rhythmic attack (aspects of his mature style are heard in embryo in the album's most accomplished performance, "Rick Kick Shaw"). On the basis of that album, Taylor's quartet was invited to play at the 1957 Newport Jazz Festival, where he received respectful if hesitant notices largely concerned with physical descriptions of his ferociously rapid attack, creating pealing cascades of notes. Other records and engagements followed, but the public remained indifferent and Taylor took day jobs to survive. As of 1960, he was regarded as one of several forward-thinking musicians who played mostly in Greenwich Village, exploring the spacier precincts of modern jazz and by no means the leader of a movement.

A turning point came the next year, as he began to work with more accomplished musicians who hastened his break with the last vestiges of bebop principles. These included tenor saxophonist Archie Shepp, who later recorded with Coltrane and made an important series of politically blunt avant-garde recordings (Shepp's 1965 *Fire Music*, perhaps his masterpiece, is an indispensable album of that period), and two musicians who would go on to play critical roles in Taylor's music: alto saxophonist Jimmy Lyons, who remained with him for twenty-five years, and drummer Sonny Murray, who worked with him for only a few years but profoundly influenced his approach to rhythm.

Unit Structures

Rather than writing conventional scores, Taylor preferred an arcane system of sketches, fragments, codes, and arrows. He did not, however, provide his musicians with these scores. Instead, he played episodes on the piano, which the musicians picked up by ear and developed by way of improvisation. As he explained it:

♦ ♦ ♦

The eyes are really not to be used to translate symbols that are at best an approximation of sounds. It's a division of energy and another example of Western craziness. When you ask a man to read something, you ask him to take part of the energy of making music and put it somewhere else. Notation can be used as a point of reference, but the notation does not indicate music, it indicates a direction.

◆ ◆ ◆

Taylor coined the term *unit structures* (also the title of a celebrated 1966 album) as a means of describing his method. Rather than compose a single theme to spur improvised variations, he constructed his works out of modules, or units; the group worked through each unit in sequence. Because the separate units were flexible (the band could work through any of them quickly or expansively), the performance of a particular piece could run ten minutes or an hour.

Jimmy Lyons, with his quick ear and particular affinity for Taylor's method, became a kind of translator, interpreting Taylor's figures on alto saxophone and showing the other musicians how to phrase and develop them. Lyons brought to Taylor's music a vivid tie to the bebop past, through his timbre and phrasing. Sonny Murray, on the other hand, helped to trigger Taylor's most radical departure from the past: a way of playing rhythm based not on a preset meter, but on the energy level of the performance. In Ornette Coleman's music, the usual 4/4 patterns disappear, yet the rhythm section still plays a supportive role, maintaining a pulse that suggests swing. Working with Murray, Taylor intensified the level of interaction with the drums, so that rhythm followed from the force of the band's energy. The center of that force could be the piano or the drummer or another soloist.

Not surprisingly, Taylor performed duets with many drummers, from bebop's high prince Max Roach to John Coltrane's mainstay, Elvin Jones, to major avant-garde drummers around the world. After he and Murray parted, Taylor developed his second closest association (after Lyons) with the drummer Andrew Cyrille, who had played and studied every kind of jazz drumming; he worked with Taylor from 1964 to 1975, and then formed his own Taylor-influenced ensemble. Cyrille explained Taylor's process:

◆ ◆ ◆

We had a magical dialogue. This kind of improvising is a matter of very close listening and trading of information. It's like a game. We put forth sounds, ideas, rhythms, and melodic fragments that turn into much longer statements, and we surprise each other with replies and continue to evolve within the dialogue. It can be endless. And when we decide to resolve what's happening, it's as though we've finished a conversation. We have grown, matured, to some degree even mellowed.

✦ ✦ ✦

Taylor's rhythmic attack was an example of his fundamental differences with Coleman. Both musicians were emotional, but if Coleman wore his heart on his sleeve, Taylor was virtuosic and intellectual. Coleman avoided the piano, developed his theories outside the framework of the educated tradition, perfected a raw timbre descended from the roots of African American music, and eventually employed relatively conventional notation and a dance-beat fusion he called *Dancing in Your Head*. Taylor emphasized the piano's drum-like quality, studied modern classical theory and atonality, avoided any kind of conventional notation (even in his several big bands), and turned to dance in the tradition of ballet—he famously collaborated on a project with Mikhail Baryshnikov. Taylor's particular kind of emotional commitment is evident in his method as a performer, which has been captured in several films. His hands work so quickly they become a blur, as he produces great cataracts of sound. He pummels the keyboard with both hands, occasionally using the flat of his palm or his elbows. In the more meditative passages, he seems to pluck the keys, judging the particular sound of each one, producing delicate melodies that echo nineteenth-century Romanticism but with a constantly shifting tonal center.

"BULBS"

In 1961, under the aegis of Gil Evans, Taylor assembled a quintet to record "Bulbs," a summation of everything he had achieved in the first stage of his career. From the first notes, we hear how figures introduced on the piano are quickly echoed by the other instruments. The blend of two saxophones is characteristic of Taylor, especially at 0:54, where they are voiced in thirds to suggest the driving edge of a big-band reed section. Harmonically, the piece demonstrates a variety of approaches, from traditional triad harmonies to whole-tone and pentatonic scales to free passages. Taylor's melodic units are often subtle, yet their appearances and reappearances (there are no fewer than nine motives or thematic riffs, A–I) give the overall work an integral unity that may not be apparent at first blush. Taylor's piano solo introduces and develops particular figures, which he later reprises in accompanying the saxophonists. His percussive attack, clusters (closely spaced dissonant chords), and melodic/rhythmic patterns animate the entire performance.

Lyons's solo is startling and rather comforting in its wit and historical finesse. Despite Taylor's accompanying dissonances, Lyons's initial phrase has the fluid feeling and warm timbre associated with Charlie Parker. His responsiveness to Taylor produces a whimsical moment at 3:12, when he quotes a phrase from Franz von Suppé's *Poet and Peasant* Overture—a fragment known to moviegoers of his generation for its use in various Looney Tunes. In the last minute, motives seem to multiply in a burst of polyphony that suggests, however distantly, an avant-garde take on New Orleans traditionalism.

BULBS

Cecil Taylor Orchestra

Jimmy Lyons, alto saxophone; Archie Shepp, tenor saxophone; Cecil Taylor, piano; Henry Grimes, bass; Sonny Murray, drums

LABEL: *Into the Hot: The Gil Evans Orchestra,* Impulse! A(S)9, 12922; *Mixed* (GRP 270)
DATE: 1961
STYLE: avant-garde
FORM: Taylor's unit structures

Head

0:00	A short piano arpeggio by Taylor leads to a chromatic line played by the saxophones. Grimes bows a few dissonant notes on bass.
0:08	A two-note motive frames dense, dissonant piano chords, moving up and down the chromatic scale. We will label this motive A.
0:11	Taylor plays a chord with a distinct harmony, answered briefly by the saxophones.
0:15	After a slight pause, the band erupts into an arching phrase in the whole-tone scale. It's followed by dark chords over a rumbling oscillation in Taylor's left hand.
0:21	The whole-tone scale returns, only to be interrupted by a rising chromatic line that suggests a cadence (motive B).
0:27	Another whole-tone phrase is followed by more bass rumbling. Shepp briefly improvises on tenor saxophone.
0:42	Taylor plays a melodic fragment, then repeats it.
0:47	Shepp improvises over a dissonant chord.
0:54	The band is suddenly roused into a more rhythmic groove. Over a bass and piano ostinato, the saxophones harmonize in thirds.

1:05	Over a whole-tone riff, Taylor plays a Latin-based melody. When he repeats it, he shifts it upward.
1:19	In a faster tempo, the piano and saxophones play an intricate riff accompanied by a descending bass line.
1:26	The horns repeat the melody while Taylor improvises freely.
1:33	Chaos ensues, as each instrument goes in its own direction.
1:41	Taylor plays dissonant chord clusters up and down the keyboard.

Piano solo (Taylor)

1:45	The texture thins out; the bass begins to walk.
1:51	Taylor plays a back-and-forth pattern (motive C).
1:57	He switches to shorter patterns. Each new pattern tends to be repeated before being discarded for a new one.
2:01	Taylor plays two-note clusters, followed by an octave riff (motive D) by Shepp. He follows it with several more patterns.
2:18	One passage begins with the rhythm for motive C before dissolving into chromatic chaos.
2:22	Shepp distantly echoes Taylor's ideas.
2:29	Taylor reintroduces motive A.
2:32	Behind Taylor, Shepp enters with a riff figure (motive E).
2:42	Shepp enters with another riff figure (motive F), followed by a return of motive A.

Alto saxophone solo (Lyons)

2:51	Lyons improvises, accompanied by Taylor's aggressively dissonant piano chords.
3:00	In his comping, Taylor revisits motives A and C; these ideas penetrate Lyons's improvisation.
3:12	Lyons briefly quotes von Suppé's *Poet and Peasant* Overture.
3:19	As the harmony passes through the whole-tone scale, Shepp plays motive D.
3:25	After Taylor plays motive A, his comping becomes more dense and polyrhythmic, spurring Lyon to new levels of intensity.
3:37	Shepp reenters with motive E.
3:48	A return of motive A leads to a repetition of motive E.
3:59	A return to the whole-tone scale and motive D.
4:06	A final Shepp riff is based on motive B.

Tenor saxophone solo (Shepp)

4:10	Shepp begins his solo. His tone is warm, rich, and somewhat indistinct in pitch.
4:16	Taylor again includes motives A and C in his accompaniment.
4:36	Shepp's improvisation hints at motive F.

4:42	Taylor foregrounds motive C.
4:49	In response to Taylor's new harmony, Shepp plays motive F.
4:59	Taylor's accompaniment becomes sharper and more percussive, creating a call and response with Shepp's saxophone.
5:21	A return to motive A.
5:39	Taylor reintroduces motive B; as Shepp and (eventually) Grimes join in, the tempo grinds to a halt.

Head (abridged)

5:45	The band returns to the sequence first heard at 0:16, beginning with the arching whole-tone phrase and concluding with motive B.
5:58	After a brief pause, the band returns to the opening chromatic melody.

Coda

6:06	Taylor plays a questioning piano melody (motive G), rising to an unresolved dissonance. It's imitated with near exactitude first by the unaccompanied alto saxophone, then by the tenor.
6:13	The alto and tenor play a riff (motive H) accompanied by occasional sharp piano chords.
6:19	Entirely unaccompanied, the two horns play a final, concluding riff (motive I).
6:21	The two saxophones and piano overlap motives G, H, and I in an intricate polyphonic texture.
6:28	As the polyphony reaches its climax, Murray adds a brief roll on drums.
6:34	The polyphonic texture dies down, and the instruments briefly regather on motive I.
6:37	As the bowed bass and tenor saxophone hold out a note, Taylor and Lyons trade short, percussive patterns.

Taylor recorded "Bulbs" at a time when his professional fortunes were at ebb tide. His records did not sell, and audiences were put off by the non-stop fury of his live appearances. In 1962, he left for Copenhagen, where he performed with the young saxophonist Albert Ayler and recorded his trio, with Lyons and Murray. These performances represented his most forceful incursion into rhythmic freedom to date. Back in America, Taylor found little work and made no records for four years. In 1966, he recorded two of his most admired ensemble albums, *Unit Structures* and *Conquistador!* These were followed by another long silence, as he embarked on several years of teaching at colleges in the Midwest.

In 1973, he returned to New York and released a self-produced album,

Spring of Two Blue J's, a work (conceived half for solo piano and half for his quartet) that signaled a new maturity. The solo section in particular suggested an emotional coherence and generosity new to his music. Over the next several years, Taylor garnered awards, grants, critical renown, and a cult audience, especially in Europe; in 1988, a festival was devoted to him in Berlin, resulting in more than a dozen albums, including works for large orchestra. He now played the major jazz clubs and continued to perform internationally as a recitalist (for example, *Air Above Mountains, For Olim, Willisau Concert*), and as leader of bands of various sizes (*3 Phasis, Dark to Themselves, The Owner of the River Bank*), attracting a growing coterie of musicians and fans. He remains a symbol of the avant-garde innovator at his most unbowed and uncompromising.

WILLISAU CONCERT, "PART 3"

Taylor's piano recitals usually consist of a long work created for the event, followed by brief encores. His performance in Willisau, Switzerland, is one of his most impressive and lucid, showing off his theme-and-variations method as applied to the units that comprise the finished piece. The main piece, consisting of two movements totaling little more than an hour, is followed by three encores, averaging ninety seconds each. The first encore ("Part 3") is a capsule example of Taylor's vivacious keyboard style, exemplifying his virtuosity and organizational coherence. Taylor begins with a five-note motive and in a very brief time explores several tonal centers while ranging over the entire breadth of the keyboard. His use of space and contrast underscores the drama, setting off a characteristically explosive passage (at 0:42) when the notes surge down from the treble range at tremendous speed. He employs dissonance, but contrasts those episodes with consonant harmonies. The details are carefully articulated. Playfulness governs the temperament of this etude-like piece, which, despite its brevity, feels complete and satisfying.

WILLISAU CONCERT, PART 3

Cecil Taylor, piano

LABEL: *The Willisau Concert,* Intakt 072
DATE: 2000 (Willisau Jazz Festival, Switzerland)
STYLE: avant-garde
FORM: Taylor's unit structures

0:00	Taylor begins with a simple motive: five notes, spread out over several octaves.
0:05	He repeats the motive, with variations; when he pauses momentarily, you can hear him humming.
0:13	With sudden rhythmic movements, Taylor repeats a chord that sounds like the dominant.
0:22	He begins quietly exploring a new chord (which we will call the "Willisau chord"), combining dissonant notes over a minor triad. This chord is occasionally interrupted by dense chord clusters and bass rumblings.
0:29	Taylor moves the chord down chromatically.
0:31	After a brief pause, he begins spreading the chord out over the keyboard. Once again, he moves downward chromatically.
0:37	The harmony changes to a new chord, somewhat closer to the dominant sound of 0:14.
0:40	The left hand rises with an emphatic octave run.
0:42	Suddenly the texture changes. Beginning in the uppermost register, Taylor uses both hands to alternate chords in a dizzyingly fast array of complex chromatic chords, descending across the entire keyboard.
0:46	Having reached the bottom of the keyboard, he starts once again at the top. A few seconds later, he does so again.
0:50	The dissonant chords are replaced by the dominant chord, split between notes in the right hand and loud, percussive octaves in the left.
0:54	Suddenly we return to the Willisau chord. As at 0:32, it's spread across the keyboard and descends chromatically.
1:02	The bass continues to drop, revealing a new chord that offers a point of contrast.
1:09	Taylor moves rapidly back and forth between loud chord clusters in the bass and in the upper register.
1:12	Returning to the Willisau chord, he once again moves down chromatically.
1:21	A sudden loud percussive outburst in the bass shuts the piece down.

THE NEW THING:
Eric Dolphy (1928–1964) AND Albert Ayler (1936–1970)

Ornette Coleman and Cecil Taylor emerged as core figures in a much larger faction that divided the jazz world in half, generating strident brickbats on both sides. Many critics dismissed avant-garde jazz as political music, and indeed its musicians over the years did associate themselves with various causes, from civil rights and protests against the war in Vietnam to Black Power, Marxism, mysticism, feminism, and pacifism. Its proponents sometimes characterized the New Thing, as it was most often called in the middle 1960s, as "people's music," although it alienated far more people than it attracted. The most charismatic figure of the era was John Coltrane, who, as we've seen, commanded respect at the outset for having proved himself a master of the bop idiom. Unintentionally, Coltrane became an unofficial referee between certified jazz masters like himself, whose embrace of the avant-garde had to be taken seriously, and previously unknown provocateurs whose radical styles generated casual contempt. The contrast can be seen in the work of two dominant saxophonists, Eric Dolphy and Albert Ayler.

Dolphy, an exceptionally skillful alto saxophonist, flutist, and bass clarinetist, was born in Los Angeles, where he played in dance bands in the late 1940s and jammed with local and visiting musicians, including Charles Mingus. Dolphy attracted little attention until 1958, when he came to New York as a member of drummer Chico Hamilton's quintet, which also included a cellist. A year later, he began an on-and-off-again association with Mingus, lasting until shortly before Dolphy's death from heart failure and diabetes. In 1960, he appeared on Coleman's *Free Jazz*; in 1961, he toured Europe as a member of Coltrane's band, appearing on several of his albums, including *Africa/Brass* and *Live at the Village Vanguard*.

During his brief time in the sun, Dolphy made many records—often with another tragic figure of the period, trumpeter Booker Little, who died of uremia at twenty-three—including a series of discs taped during their engagement at the Five Spot. As noted earlier, Dolphy was also affiliated with the Third Stream. He performed works by classical composers (including Hale Smith and the already legendary Edgard Varèse, whose focus on timbre and the way it relates to rhythm proved hugely influential), and single-handedly made the bass clarinet a significant instrument in jazz. Dolphy built his style on bebop, but stretched its harmonies and his own timbre into areas of extreme dissonance. Although he played flute with a centered pitch, he favored a vocalized and strident sound on alto saxophone and bass clarinet, which gave his robust, chromatic phrases an electrifying immediacy. Dolphy's liberal approach to intonation reflects the influence of Coleman, but his evident control of intonation also made it more palatable to skeptics like Mingus. As an interpreter of Mingus's music, Dolphy helped to maneuver Mingus closer to the avant-garde fold. His key albums include *Live! At the Five Spot, Out There* (accompanied by drums, bass, and cello), *Out to Lunch*, and *Last Date*.

Albert Ayler exploded on the scene with a musical style so extreme that observers competed to find suitable metaphors. The poet Ted Joans likened Ayler's tenor saxophone sound to "screaming the word 'FUCK' in Saint Patrick's cathedral on a crowded Easter Sunday." Amiri Baraka described his disarmingly naive melodies as "coonish churchified chuckle tunes," and critic Dan Morgenstern compared his ensemble to "a Salvation Army band on LSD." The subject of these heated tributes was born in Cleveland, where he studied alto saxophone for over a decade, beginning at age seven. In his teens, he worked with rhythm and blues bands, then joined the army, at which time he switched to tenor saxophone (he later added soprano as well). While stationed in France, Ayler experimented with the tenor's so-called hidden register—the highest pitches, verging on caterwauling tempests that few saxophonists knew how to control. Although he continued to perform awkwardly in the bop idiom for a few years, he felt stifled by the harmonies and rhythms. Sitting in with Cecil Taylor in Copenhagen in 1962 helped to liberate his instincts.

Ayler soon returned to the United States with a trio (bass and drums), and in 1964 issued a trio album that, among other things, transformed a tiny label created to spread the international language of Esperanto, ESP-Disk, into a major source for avant-garde jazz. The album, *Spiritual Unity*, was both cheered and ridiculed, though almost everyone conceded that the completely interactive nature of the trio was impressive; the listener is always aware of every note that each of the three players—Ayler, bassist Gary Peacock, who would later find fame as a longtime member of Keith Jarrett's trio, and drummer Sonny Murray—contribute. Ayler's huge sound evoked lusty hysteria. His room-filling timbre, ripe with opulent overtones, sounds as if he is playing two or three notes at a time (multiphonics). His rejection of musical gestures that might link him to conventional jazz offended some and influenced others, including Coltrane, who insisted that he learned as much from Ayler as Ayler did from him, an important endorsement.

In a span of barely eight years, 1962 to 1970, Ayler went through several stylistic changes, at one point focusing on composition almost to the exclusion of improvisation; one of his groups included a front line of saxophone, violin, and trumpet (his brother Donald), and played waltzes and other works that suggested a fusion of jazz and classical music. In the end, he reluctantly tried to reach the rock audience with a far less imposing flower-power brand of fusion. Its failure exacerbated an already present despondency, and he died, a suicide, at thirty-four.

"GHOSTS"

"Ghosts" was Ayler's signature theme, recorded by him numerous times in different contexts—twice on *Spiritual Unity* alone, accounting for half of the album's four tracks. "Ghosts" combines three primary elements in Ayler's music: old-time religious fervor, marching, and simple melodies. In his early versions of the piece, the theme statement is followed by a free improvisation. By the time Ayler performed his brief 1966 version, on a German radio broadcast, he was leading a five-piece ensemble that aimed for total group music. There are no solos, although Ayler's powerful sound occasionally dominates the performance. Nor is the theme stated with unequivocal clarity. Rather, the musicians play around it, each contributing to the interpretation without really spelling it out. The result—as the instruments splinter away, after an authoritative opening—might be considered an example of musical *trompe l'oeil*, an illusion of melody. Looked at closely, the individual contributions and the performance itself seem incoherent, a jumble of scattered sounds that sporadically meet to convey the tune. But step back, as you would from a painting, and it is all perfectly logical. These musicians work together so closely that each one knows how to minimally fill out the canvas without overwhelming it.

The performance consists of three sections: an introduction, a collective interpretation of the theme, and a coda. Though "Ghosts" never swings in a traditional jazz sense, it never lacks for strong rhythms. In one passage (1:09–1:22), the performance suggests a kind of Scottish dance. Elsewhere, we hear the insistence of a march, accenting the first beat of each measure; the martial aspect is underscored by a bugle call in the coda. Most surprising is the nostalgic quality of the piece, especially as it concludes. The performance cuts against the grain of convention, but it leaves us with the conventional feelings generated by folk music—the vague recognition that we've heard this before.

GHOSTS

Albert Ayler Quintet

Albert Ayler, tenor saxophone; Don Ayler, trumpet; Michel Samson, violin; William Foxwell, bass; Beaver Harris, drums

LABEL: HatMUSICS 3500; *Lörrach, Paris, 1966* (hatOLOGY 573)
DATE: 1966
STYLE: avant-garde
FORM: idiosyncratic

Introduction

0:00	Ayler begins with a simple diatonic phrase, fluffing the highest note. His phrase, slow and with much rubato, is echoed by the trumpet and supported by the bowed bass.
0:04	Over repeated double stops in the violin, Ayler plays intense, distorted sounds in his upper register.
0:09	Ayler stops; the violinist gradually slows to a halt.
0:13	Ayler plays simple melodies in a major key, loosely doubled by the trumpet.
0:27	The violinist plays chords that are deliberately out of tune.
0:33	All the instruments join in a loose polyphonic texture.

The tune

0:41	Ayler and the trumpet suddenly shift to a brisk tempo, joined by the drum set. The melody they play is the opening phrase of "Ghosts" (A). Around it, the violinist and bassist add their own melodies and rhythms.
0:47	Ayler repeats the melody, occasionally adding counterpoint.
0:54	They begin a new phrase of the tune (B), setting a firm tempo that is not matched by any of the other instruments.
0:58	The trumpet continues the melody while Ayler harmonizes above it.
1:02	They repeat B.
1:09	On another repetition of B, Ayler again harmonizes above, the melodic content suggesting a Scottish dance.
1:22	The tune slows to a stop.
1:28	Ayler holds out a note, raising it through microtonal inflections before allowing it to sag down again.
1:33	Everything coalesces on a single note: the violinist saws back and forth on top of it.
1:38	Ayler returns to the mood of the introduction, adding rubato pentatonic phrases that are echoed by the other instruments.
1:49	He reinitiates the tempo, beginning a new melodic phrase (C) marked by a more chromatic opening. The bassist follows with a similar line, while the drummer plays on the cymbals.
1:57	As the trumpet moves to the next melody phrase (D), Ayler plays ecstatic squawks, alternating between his gruff middle register and the extreme upper reaches of his horn. His intensity is matched by the drummer's shift to the louder drums in his kit.
2:05	The trumpet returns to the beginning of the tune (A).
2:22	As Ayler and the trumpet harmonize loosely on the second melodic phrase (B), the drummer's strokes become still louder while the violinist rapidly plays scales.
2:30	The horns repeat B. The drums retreat, leaving the violin in the foreground.
2:35	The trumpet slows down the tempo, ending on a dramatically held-out note.

| 2:45 | The violinist returns to playing double stops, accelerating in tempo. |

Coda

2:50	Ayler reenters with his introductory phrases.
3:00	He ends with a phrase that sounds strikingly like a bugle call.
3:08	At the end, the trumpet continues to hold out his last note after all the other instruments have stopped; applause follows.

The avant-garde carried jazz to what musicians and other artists often refer to as the cutting edge—the last frontier of hip adventurousness. It ratcheted up the emotional expressiveness of music (unlike the classical avant-garde, which often preferred an extreme intellectualism, shorn of overt emotional content), but audiences reared in the swing and post-swing eras found it loud, disjointed, and unappealing. Their children had an easier time with rock and roll. Although the avant-garde eventually generated an international cult audience that supported the key figures, it was never going to be a commercially successful music. Cecil Taylor was nearly sixty years old when a MacArthur Foundation grant gave him his first taste of financial independence. Ornette Coleman (another MacArthur winner) supplemented his income with several nonmusical ventures. Others followed the classical avant-garde into the academy, where they found teaching positions and students eager to learn their music. The popular outlook for jazz looked bleak in the late 1960s, as rock achieved a level of sophistication and excitement—melodic, danceable, verbally relevant—that attracted people who a decade earlier might have been drawn to jazz.

Given the avant-garde's permanent outside status, it is worth contemplating three paradoxical aspects of its achievement: (1) for all the outrage it generated, the avant-garde engrossed and influenced many established and previously neglected musicians; (2) despite its insistence on the New Thing, the avant-garde turned out to be more inclusive than any previous jazz style; (3) although it failed to find popular or commercial acclaim, the avant-garde proved as durable as mainstream jazz.

THREE PARADOXES: THE FIRST PARADOX AND OLDER MUSICIANS

Several prominent musicians who had already attained popular acceptance working in established idioms found the lure of the cutting edge irresistible. Major jazz stars, including Sonny Rollins, Charles Mingus, Miles Davis, and John Coltrane, adjusted their performing styles to address techniques associated with the avant-garde, overcoming their own initial skepticism to explore the new musical freedoms. Consider Coltrane and Kenny Dorham, Charlie Parker's former trumpet player. In 1958, they and two other hard bop musicians appeared as sidemen on Cecil Taylor's album *Hard Driving Jazz*. Dorham was appalled at Taylor's procedures, but Coltrane was intrigued. In 1960, Coltrane co-led, with Ornette Coleman's trumpet player Don Cherry, an album eventually issued (after a long corporate delay) as *The Avant-Garde*. The following year, he hired Eric Dolphy and recorded *Live at the Village Vanguard*, the breakthrough album that included the fifteen-minute blues rant "Chasin' the Trane." And in 1965, he assembled eleven avant-garde musicians for the ultimate free-jazz blowout, *Ascension*. By that time, even the stubbornly faithful Dorham was recording hard bop classics (*Whistle Stop*, *Trumpeta Toccata*) that reflected, however subtly, the expansions in harmony and timbre that the avant-garde had put on the table.

Similarly, Sonny Rollins teamed with Don Cherry and Coleman drummer Billy Higgins in 1962 to record *Our Man in Jazz*, a surprisingly witty session combining extended improvisation with interactive group dynamics; the next year, he toured Europe with Cherry. Although Rollins ultimately returned to a bop-based music, his serious flirtation with the avant-garde left a lasting imprint—his timbre grew more expressive and his improvisational style more aggressive. His 1966 "East Broadway Run Down" is a classic example of his use of consecutive motives to shape his solos. His later work achieved a seamless rapprochement between the verities of bop and the expressive potential of the avant-garde.

At the same time, lesser-known veteran musicians found that the avant-garde created an environment suitable to their music. Working in the outer precincts of jazz, they had been ignored or derided as weird and lacking in seriousness. The avant-garde gave them validity; it shone a light on artists who created their own world yet remained invisible. For some, like the pianist and composer Herbie Nichols, the avant-garde came too late to earn them proper recognition; after his death, Nichols was honored as a prophet—a 1990s band called the Herbie Nichols Project devoted itself to his sly, thorny compositions. Others, like the ingeniously idiosyncratic pianist and composer Andrew Hill, were revitalized by the avant-garde; after a decade of obscurity, Hill went on to create a powerful body of work, from such 1960s benchmarks as *Point of Departure* and *Judgment* to such twenty-first-century triumphs as *Dusk* and *Time Lines*.

The most peculiar of these invisible men was a pianist, composer, and bandleader who called himself Sun Ra (1914–1993). Born Herman Blount in Birmingham, Alabama, Sun Ra came to Chicago in the 1930s, touring with a college band and then leading his own group as Sonny Blount. During the war, he was imprisoned for two months after declaring himself a conscientious objector. In 1946, he worked with a rhythm and blues band before hiring on for a year as pianist for Fletcher Henderson—an important association that grounded him in the big-band tradition.

After studying black nationalism and Egyptian history, Blount created a cosmology involving the planet Saturn, renamed himself Sun Ra, and organized a band he called the Arkestra. His 1950s recordings are like no others in that era and were heard by only a few people, basically his followers in Chicago. They combined familiar and experimental jazz textures with rhythm and blues (including doo-wop singing), unusual time signatures (7/4 was a favorite), and electric instruments (he was one of the first musicians to use electric piano and Moog synthesizer). Sun Ra and his acolytes, who included a broad mixture of accomplished and untried musicians, privately pressed and distributed their records, both albums and singles, some of them recorded in a garage.

In 1961, Sun Ra brought his followers to New York, and by the mid-1960s he had found regular work in jazz clubs, at festivals, and throughout Europe; his elaborate theatrical presentation included singers, dancers, stage props, and gaudy costumes. Despite the financial burden, he insisted on leading a big band, playing a repertory that acknowledged no boundaries between swing, avant-garde, pop (he played songs like "Hello, Dolly!"), classical music (he collaborated with composer John Cage), and jazz-rock fusion. Increasingly celebrated as a visionary maverick, Sun Ra continued to tour the world until his death. Highlights among his dozens of albums are *Jazz in Silhouette*, *The Heliocentric Worlds of Sun Ra*, *Atlantis*, and *When Angels Speak of Love*.

THE SECOND PARADOX AND THE AACM

Although critics routinely pilloried the avant-garde for rejecting jazz conventions, it ultimately proved to be the most inclusive form of jazz in history. The innovators of bop apprenticed in swing bands but played exclusively in their own modern styles as they became prominent; they never played Dixieland (except to belittle it) or attempted to create new versions of Jelly Roll Morton tunes. A later innovator, Miles Davis, constantly changed his perspective but always focused on the present, even when his source material included old pop tunes. Yet the avant-garde, which seemed to incarnate the very definition of futurism, welcomed every kind of musical influence and allusion. It brought instruments previously ignored or underemployed in jazz (bass clarinet, cello, tuba, wood flutes, soprano and bass saxophone, exotic rhythm instruments, the African kalimba, and the Australian didgeridoo, among others) into the thick of things. The avant-garde was impatient with clichés, but not with historical styles and achievements. Like Sun Ra, it refused to be limited to any one idiom, including avant-garde jazz.

The full canvas of avant-garde interests did not became apparent until a second generation of avant-garde musicians, most of them schooled in the Midwest, made names for themselves in the 1970s. For the first time since the early days in New Orleans, these musicians came together as members of collectives (not unlike the New Orleans fraternal societies), which helped to arrange rehearsals, secure work, and encourage the creation of new music—as opposed to new versions of old tunes. One such organization, BAG (Black Artists Group), arose in St. Louis. In Los Angeles, the composer and pianist Horace Tapscott organized the Underground Musicians' Association. Several New York musicians, including Rahsaan Roland Kirk, Cecil Taylor, Andrew Cyrille, and Archie Shepp, attempted to launch the Jazz and People's Movement. Each of these organizations eventually failed, but one that didn't was the immensely influential AACM—the Association for the Advancement of Creative Musicians, which has produced concerts for more than four decades.

The AACM originated in Chicago as the brainchild of the pianist, composer, and bandleader Richard Abrams (b. 1930). A member of several of Chicago's bop-based ensembles going back to the late 1940s, Abrams founded the Experimental Band in 1961, as a way of allowing musicians to write their own music and hear it performed. In 1965, he and other musicians from the Experimental Band launched the AACM, with Abrams as president, insisting that each member create original works. "We were not in the business of showcasing standards," Abrams explained. Noting that jazz musicians played new music in the early years, he argued that the AACM "was just hooking up with the real tradition. Besides, there was so much talent, so much originality, and we thought it should be encouraged."

Abrams, a reticent but charismatic and resolute man, also insisted on high personal standards of morality and behavior; his quiet integrity inspired younger musicians to adopt his values. The saxophonist Joseph Jarman recalled, "Until I had the first meeting with Richard Abrams, I was like all the rest of the 'hip' ghetto niggers; I was cool, I took dope, I smoked pot, etc. . . . In having the chance to work in the Experimental Band with Richard and the other musicians there, I found something with meaning/reason for doing." Jarman became a charter member of the most important band to emerge from the AACM, the Art Ensemble of Chicago (AEC), along with saxophonist Roscoe Mitchell, trumpeter Lester Bowie, bassist Malachi Favors Maghostut, and drummer Famoudou Don Moye. The AEC popularized the use of "little instruments"—an array of bells, whistles, and drums that originated at AACM concerts as a way of incorporating African instruments. Hundreds of these little instruments, enough to cover a concert stage, generated a uniquely tintinabulating suspense as the group focused on long meditative preludes of tinkling, shaking, and hand drumming before turning to the "big" instruments.

The AEC's theatricality also extended to startling facial makeup and Lester Bowie's white lab coat, which became his trademark—an indication of the wit that animated his music. Concerts unfolded in an unbroken stream-of-consciousness, climaxing with a hard-swinging number or blues. The AEC bannered its music with the motto "Great Black Music: From the Ancient to the Future," and invariably fused elements of free improvisation, notated compositions, and a variety of rhythms, from extreme rubato to modern dance beats. On his own, Bowie took the mix further with other bands, including Brass Fantasy and New York Organ Ensemble, creating a capacious American jukebox with a repertory that included pop songs, swing themes, early rock and roll, country music hits, and hip-hop. Ironically, the AACM dictum to write new music triggered a generous investigation of repertory outside the usual jazz curricula. The most prolific of AACM artists, Anthony Braxton, wrote literally hundreds of original pieces, some of them as long as Mahler symphonies, but also launched a series of *In the Tradition* projects that reinvestigated the compositions of Charlie Parker.

Though AACM musicians began recording in 1966 (for an adventurous Chicago jazz and blues label, Delmark), they were largely ignored outside of Chicago for several years. The AEC began to attract attention in Paris during a 1969 tour, but the real breakthrough came in 1976, when Abrams, who had adopted the name Muhal, and other AACM musicians moved to New York. Suddenly, Muhal Richard Abrams seemed to be everywhere, recording for several labels (representative albums, each quite different from the others, include *Young at Heart / Wise in Time, Lifea Blinec, The Hearinga Suite,* and *Blu Blu Blu*) and performing an immense variety of concerts, from solo piano to trio (even Abrams explored standard songs, though not when he recorded) to big band. Two other important AACM bands that took hold in New York were the Revolutionary Ensemble and Air. Violinist Leroy Jenkins (1932–2007) created the former with bassist Sirone (born Norris Jones) and percussionist Jerome Cooper. Jenkins developed a distinctive violin timbre and style, combining classical and jazz techniques, and encouraged collective rubato improvisations, as in *The People's Republic.* Left to their own devices, Sirone and Cooper performed solo bass and drum recitals, something unheard-of in jazz. After the Revolutionary Ensemble broke up in 1977, each member separately worked with Cecil Taylor.

Henry Threadgill (b. 1944) led the trio Air, with bassist Fred Hopkins and drummer Steve McCall, in the late 1970s and early 1980s. Threadgill, an alto, tenor, and baritone saxophonist and flutist, also built what he called the hubcapphone—two tiers of hubcaps played with mallets. In addition to Threadgill's rhythmically knotty originals, including a couple of tangos, Air played interpretations of Scott Joplin rags and Jelly Roll Morton piano pieces (*Air Lore*). Threadgill later inaugurated a series of bands notable for the unpredictability of his writing and unusual instrumentation. Among these were the Henry Threadgill Sextet (*Rag, Bush and All*), consisting of seven musicians (he counted the two percussionists as one component); Very Very Circus (*Spirit of Nuff...Nuff*), with trombone, French horn, two electric guitars, and two tubas; Make a Move (*Where's Your Cup?*), with guitar and accordion; and Zooid (*Up Popped the Two Lips*), with guitar, tuba, cello, and oud (a Middle Eastern type of lute).

THE THIRD PARADOX AND THE LOFT ERA

By 1980, it was clear that the avant-garde, which had been accused of annihilating the jazz audience, had no less staying power than swing or bop. Indeed, it had created its own tradition, with different schools in

Germany, Scandinavia, Russia, England, and just about everyplace else where improvising musicians congregated. It rescued American jazz from what many perceived to be popular compromises, but no longer circled its wagons around any particular approach. The idea of free jazz had come to mean the freedom to play anything musicians felt like playing. Ultimately, this approach would sway practically the entire jazz world. To pick one of a thousand examples, in 2008, two guitarists—the universally admired Jim Hall, who had been an individualistic force since the middle 1950s, and his former student Bill Frisell, who had proved just as influential combining jazz, rock, and country styles in the 1980s—recorded a series of duets (*Hemispheres*) that merged original pieces with classics by Billy Strayhorn, Rodgers and Hart, and Bob Dylan, as well as a fifteen-minute free improvisation involving tape loops. Only the high quality of the work turned anyone's head, yet the sheer eclecticism of the project would have been unthinkable before the arrival of the third avant-garde generation, contemporary with but younger than the AACM musicians.

The musicians who gave jazz this kind of freedom gathered in New York in the 1970s, in one of the largest migrations since the height of bebop. Among them were three prominent saxophonists from St. Louis's Black Artists Group: altos Julius Hemphill and Oliver Lake and baritone Hamiet Bluiett. They appeared in individual recitals, saxophone duets, and with groups of every size. From California came tenor saxophonist and bass clarinetist David Murray, alto saxophonist Arthur Blythe, flutist James Newton, bassist Mark Dresser, and composer-trumpeter Butch Morris. Blythe, typically, led simultaneous bands—a conventional saxophone and rhythm quartet, a trio with organ, larger ensembles with guitar, vibes, and other horns. This was quite a difference from just a few years earlier, when a jazz leader like Davis or Coltrane had one band at a time. Morris pioneered a form of big-band music he called "conductioning": through a system of conducting gestures, he was able to improvise orchestral pieces by spontaneously cuing the soloists and ensemble sections.

The influx of musicians spurred the need for new performing venues. Some important concerts took place in private apartments, recalling the old days of New York rent parties. And several full-time concert spaces were created in gentrified loft spaces in New York's largely abandoned warehouse district. Hence the Loft Era (1974–86) and loft jazz, which created fantastic excitement in New York's downtown. Loft jazz offered a kind of purist salvation at a time when jazz had been on the run from commercial interests and a general malaise had seen the demise of jazz clubs and labels (including Impulse!, ESP-Disk, and even, for a short time, the hallowed Blue Note). New record labels, some of them owned by musicians, documented the new music, and a mostly youngish audience heard it live in lofts, art galleries, churches, and other spaces not usually associated with jazz. The Loft Era ended, after a dozen years, as the established clubs and record labels began to accept these musicians as part of mainstream jazz culture.

One landmark event was the opening in 1987 of the Knitting Factory, a large downtown venue that replaced the lofts and encouraged musicians to cut across discrete idioms and reach broader audiences. In 1994, the club moved to a larger space, three stories tall, where several performing spaces could operate at the same time. The musicians who became Knitting Factory regulars had an immediate impact on jazz and the entire arts community. They drew on their individual backgrounds and interests to find musical avenues that had been previously unexplored. The saxophonist and composer John Zorn found ways to combine his training in the classical avant-garde with his love for the music of the Ornette Coleman Quartet and Jewish klezmer ensembles, while guitarist James Blood Ulmer's harmolodic bands meshed jazz with the sounds of Delta blues and country music. A critical byword of the Loft Era was *eclecticism*, used to signal an enlightened approach to all musical styles. These musicians fused jazz, pop, free improvisation, funk, sambas, Indian ragas, and anything else they found appealing. Drummer Beaver Harris, a baseball player in the Negro leagues before he turned to music, summed up the attitude with the name of his band, the 360 Degree Music Experience, and a recording, *From Ragtime to No Time*.

If one musician came to represent the synthesis between the avant-garde and the jazz tradition it was saxophonist David Murray (b. 1955). Born in Oakland, California, Murray came from a musical family that disdained jazz. The Murray Family Band—mother on piano and directing, father on guitar, and three sons on reeds and percussion—played four nights a week and all day Sunday at the Missionary Church of God in Christ. A teacher introduced David to jazz, but he was not allowed to play it at home until his mother died, when he was thirteen. He promptly joined a local soul band, playing alto saxophone. After falling under the spell of Sonny Rollins, he switched to tenor and proceeded to explore the entire history of the tenor, memorizing solos by Coleman Hawkins, Lester Young, Ben Webster, and a particular favorite of his, Paul Gonsalves, the Ellington band's star tenor in the 1950s and 1960s.

Murray came to New York in 1975 as a twenty-year-old college student to research a thesis on the tenor saxophone, but after getting a taste of performing (and receiving rapturous reviews), he dropped out of college and embarked on a remarkable career. He was initially hostile to the avant-garde, but eventually warmed to Archie Shepp and Albert Ayler—his best-known composition, "Flowers for Albert," is a requiem for Ayler. Murray's stylistic approach made it clear that he did not accept a barrier between the avant-garde and the jazz tradition. By the late 1970s, he was well on his way to becoming one of the most frequently recorded musicians in jazz history, and the leader of several bands at once, including a large orchestra. He played with musicians of every generation, perfecting an exuberant improvisational style at ease with and without preset harmonies. His timbre was gruff but his intonation was essentially correct, except when he worked the "hidden" register, usually to climax his solos. As a composer, he wrote several pieces with a blues or gospel mood ("Morning Song," "The Hill," "Blues for Savannah," "Shakhill's Warrior"), and recorded an album of spirituals, *Deep River*. He wrote deliriously complex pieces for his octet and big band, including orchestrations of improvisations by Gonsalves (his marathon blues solo from the 1956 Newport Jazz Festival) and Coltrane ("Giant Steps").

Murray co-founded the World Saxophone Quartet, the first successful jazz ensemble without a rhythm section, along with the three BAG saxophonists: Julius Hemphill, who wrote most of the group's repertory, Oliver Lake, and Hamiet Bluiett. After Hemphill's death, his place was taken by Arthur Blythe, whose uncannily ripe pear tones suggested an earlier approach to the saxophone. Murray also played in Clarinet Summit, focusing exclusively on bass clarinet, an instrument he did more to popularize than anyone since Eric Dolphy, and worked with musicians from other cultures, notably the Gwo-Ka Masters, a percussion ensemble from Guadeloupe.

"EL MATADOR"

As a newcomer to jazz, Murray enhanced his credibility by collaborating with several established artists, including the brilliant pianist Don Pullen, who had worked in many areas of jazz and pop (including Charles Mingus's group and his own quartet, co-led with saxophonist George Adams). Pullen could play bop or free, and was known for a technique that involved turning his hands upside down and playing great swashes of sounds with the backs of his fingers (his knuckles were thoroughly scraped and calloused). Switching to organ, he played a key role in Murray's acclaimed album *Shakhill's Warrior*. After Pullen's death in 1995, Murray recorded a tribute album, a quartet session called *The Long Goodbye*. On one track, "El Matador," written by Murray's frequent associate Butch Morris, he plays a duet with pianist D. D. Jackson—a Murray protégé and a Canadian of African American and Chinese parentage. Jackson's intense and flashy keyboard attack, combining conventional and avant-garde techniques, is not unlike Pullen's.

In "El Matador," Murray and Jackson explore Spanish scales and feelings dear to Pullen, as exemplified by his memorable 1988 trio recording "At the Café Centrale." Yet unlike Pullen's piece, which is raucously festive, "El Matador" is dark and ruminative, progressing from a solemnly heraldic theme (suggesting the matador entering the ring) to piercing climactic cries. It combines tender respect for the fallen hero—underscored by Murray's heavy use of vibrato in his opening phrases—with a candid expression of grief. During its two dramatic choruses, Murray is the lead voice, as Jackson creates a setting that sustains and, in a sense, fields the saxophonist's tonal variations. They converge in harmonic consonance, diverge in spiky dissonance, and exult together on attaining tonic chords.

EL MATADOR

David Murray

David Murray, tenor saxophone; D. D. Jackson, piano

LABEL: *The Long Goodbye: A Tribute to Don Pullen* (DIW 930)
FORM: ABA'B'(A'B' are one step lower than AB)
DATE: 1996
STYLE: loft jazz

Chorus 1
....

0:00   **A**   With a slow and stately tone, Murray begins with a fanfare motive in the key of D. The opening melodic gesture establishes a "Spanish" scale: a major scale with two flatted notes, the second and seventh degrees.

The rhythm is free and unmetered. Underneath, Jackson plays a simple but rich chordal accompaniment on piano.

0:08   Jackson echoes Murray's last melodic fragment, letting it fall several octaves.

0:15   A new chord, outside the scale, begins a movement away from the tonic—a modulation. The chords begin to rise.

0:20   The harmonic movement reaches an upper chord, then begins to fall by step.

0:26 **B** We arrive on a new tonic (G), having moved to it by a half-step cadence typical of the Spanish scale. As Murray repeats a simple figure,

the harmony shifts between the tonic and its surrounding chords, the flatted second and seventh degrees. The two musicians move back and forth at their own pace, with Murray often lagging behind.

0:49   The oscillations finally stop. Jackson allows the harmonies to subside.

0:54 **A′** Murray repeats the opening section, this time in a new key (C).

1:05   Again, the chords begin to move from the tonic.

1:17   We begin another Spanish-scale cadence.

1:20 **B′** We arrive, by half step, on F.

1:24   As the harmonies surround the tonic, Murray repeats the cadence melody.

1:49   Jackson plays the lower chord simply, using it to return to the opening tonic (D).

Chorus 2

1:51 **A** Murray now plays more expansively, letting his improvisation rise into the upper register; the Spanish scale takes on a more bluesy tone. Jackson uses the sustain pedal on the piano to blur his harmonies, creating a fuller sound.

2:05   While Murray plays loose, expansive melodic figures, Jackson pushes the modulation forward.

2:16		As the modulation nears its goal, the two musicians join forces, Murray harmonizing Jackson's melody in thirds.
2:23	**B**	We arrive on the new tonic (G). Murray lets loose with a long, rhythmically intricate run.
2:29		Over the oscillating chords, Murray hits a long, agonized high note. His descent is mildly dissonant against the harmony.
2:38		The volume of his playing increases.
2:44		As his lines reach higher and higher, Murray's tone begins to disintegrate.
2:50		He reaches a climax with an extraordinarily high note, barely supported by his breathing.
2:53		Jackson signals the new section by forcefully descending the bass line toward the new tonic.
2:55	**A'**	Murray celebrates the new key with a major scale.
3:03		Descending into his lower register, Murray's sound becomes harshly distorted.
3:05		His gestures take on an ecstatic rhythm, barely touching on actual pitches.
3:14		As Jackson moves forward with the modulation, his playing is similarly rough: octaves are played with crushed grace notes.
3:20	**B'**	As Jackson plays his chords with abandon, Murray responds with lines that sometimes support the harmonies, but more often clash with them. The timbre often is enriched with multiphonics.
3:42		Murray's playing becomes more detached; he rises steeply in register, reaching a high, wailing note.
3:51		Jackson momentarily lightens the sound of his piano playing to highlight the climax. Echoing the piece's opening fanfare, Murray moves to a high note, sustaining a tone several octaves above the saxophone's normal range.
3:55		As Jackson triumphantly plays his F major chord, Murray gradually descends in a disruptive flurry of notes.
4:02		The harmony changes once again.
4:05		Murray's line restarts in the lower register, finally reaching a note sustained through false fingerings.
4:12		After a brief pause, the chords descend back to the opening key, D. Murray fades out with a trill.
4:27		At the end, all you can hear is the faint sound of Murray's breath.

By 2009, the avant-garde had continued to develop for half a century, influencing every kind of jazz with its approach to timbre, instrumentation, and repertory. Yet it struggled to survive even in the few American and European cities where it attracted a significant audience. In New York, avant-garde musicians continued to create their own venues and record labels. Among the key activists were John Zorn, who established a performance space (Tonic) and a record label (Tzadik, Hebrew for "righteous one"), and bassist William Parker, who worked with dozens of cutting-edge musicians, including a decade with Cecil Taylor. In the 1970s, Parker and his wife, dancer and choreographer Patricia Nicholson-Parker, helped to start various multicultural arts organizations. In 1996, they introduced the ongoing Vision Festival, combining jazz, dance, and poetry. Vision Festival eventually developed into a major nonprofit arts producer, presenting concerts year-round. It also promoted political activism, in trying to get the city of New York to support the study of what it calls *avantjazz*. In a mission statement, Vision Festival emphasized the international and multimedia aspects of art that "exhibits a disciplined disregard for traditional boundaries," and incarnates "the freedom to choose any tradition or vocabulary." Still, avant-garde jazz is all but unknown outside of a few cities, an educated taste for a small, eager audience.

16 CHAPTER

Fusion I: R&B, Singers, and Latin Jazz

NEW IDIOMS

I n the late 1960s, as jazz musicians began to employ the instrumentation, rhythms, and repertory of rock in an effort to reposition jazz in the sphere of popular music, the word *fusion* was coined to denote this new synthesis, also known as jazz-rock. Yet fusions of one sort or another have always played a role in jazz history. Jazz, after all, emerged as an American phenomenon through the melding of traditions from Africa, Europe, and Latin America, and from an amalgamation of such sources as blues, ragtime, and Tin Pan Alley.

◄ Sarah Vaughan was called the Divine One in praise of her peerless voice and musicianship, which won over the boppers and the general public. At Birdland, 1949.

No musical form grows in a cultural vacuum. Europe's classical composers worked with popular airs and folk styles, and jazz has similarly borrowed from other forms. In the words of saxophonist Dexter Gordon, "Jazz is an octopus"—it will take whatever it needs or can use. The Third Stream merged the techniques of jazz and classical music, but most of jazz's syntheses resulted from its ongoing relationship with mainstream or vernacular music, especially in the afterglow of the Swing Era, and *fusion* is a perfectly good word to describe all such music situated on the bounding line between jazz and pop. Some fusions are natural, while others are more deliberate, whether motivated by genuine creativity or meretricious pandering. The most successful fusions tend to create new idioms in their own right, among them: organ trios, jazz-pop vocals, salsa, and bossa nova.

Any discussion of fusion must, however, depart from the usual narrative of jazz as a series of chronological creative leaps, in which each generation of musicians expands on the styles and accomplishments of the preceding generation while reflecting modern times. In that telling, jazz develops in a fairly straight line, from the relatively insular community of New Orleans to the international popularity of swing to the modernist reformation of bop to the art-for-art's sake credo of the avant-garde. In looking at jazz from a fusion perspective, the narrative tacks back and forth between jazz and parallel changes in popular culture. It focuses on the stylistic developments and fashions beyond the parameters of jazz, including new dance grooves and advances in musical technology that have altered jazz itself.

In the early years of the twentieth century, New Orleans musicians played to please audiences and employers, tailoring their music to a specific situation: advertising wagons, street parades, funerals, dancing in saloons or at pavilions. As jazz moved around the country, finding new opportunities in nightclubs and vaudeville shows, it continued to mind the needs of the audience, frequently incorporating comedy routines and double-entendre song lyrics. In Chicago, New York, and elsewhere, jazz encouraged dancing, but a gap quickly widened between musicians who played jazz for the sake of playing jazz and those who organized ensembles to suit the prevailing tastes of the public. By the middle 1920s, the split was inescapable: jazz musicians groused as society band leaders inhibited their rhythms and reduced their improvisations to occasional breaks in otherwise gummy-sweet ballroom arrangements. Attempts to enliven those dance bands with jazzy condiments indicated an early, forced, and frequently awkward fusion of jazz and pop.

With the coming of the Swing Era in the middle 1930s, jazz was thoroughly integrated into the popular entertainment industry. The art vs. commerce chasm continued to divide hot swing bands from sweet ones, yet each borrowed elements from the other—sweet bands ventured cautiously into jazz, and hot bands promoted pop singers, ballads, and novelty songs. Huge audiences clamored for both kinds of music, and there was relative peace in the kingdom, until the bands began to fade in popularity, at which point it became evident that bebop would not be their only successor. In fracturing the connection between jazz and pop, bebop opened the door to more easily accessible interpretations of songs and dance rhythms. Specifically, three listener-friendly alternatives emerged to take up the slack, all involving artists grounded in the Swing Era: rhythm and blues (R&B), mainstream pop vocals, and Latin jazz. Until the arrival of rock and roll, they would simultaneously dominate American popular music in the postwar era.

THE R&B CONNECTION

During the 1940s, an offshoot of swing called jump music was popularized by bandleader Louis Jordan and other former big-band musicians. This kind of "race music," which countered the experimental trends of modern jazz, eventually became known as rhythm and blues, largely because the trade magazine *Billboard* was casting about for a less onerous designation than Race Records to track the sales of recordings that appealed chiefly to black audiences. A staff writer, Jerry Wexler, came up with the phrase Rhythm and Blues, which was quickly adopted to signify a new school in American music. As an executive at Atlantic Records in the 1950s and 1960s, Wexler become a key R&B producer. One of the few veteran artists he signed was the 1930s shouter Big Joe Turner, whose grounding in the heavy-beat, eight-to-the-bar style of boogie-woogie piano found acceptance in jazz, R&B, and early rock.

As Turner's career illustrated, it was only a matter of time before the appeal of R&B reached the white mainstream, with boogie-woogie as one of its primary ingredients. But as his career also demonstrated, there wasn't—at first—much of a gap between jazz and the elements of black pop that would become codified as rhythm and blues. The jump style usually focused on blues played at a fast tempo and featured brash vocals backed with ensemble riffs. Lyrics might be risqué, satirical, serious, or socially relevant, but they were almost always marked by a humorous attitude. Several black bandleaders of the 1930s and 1940s—including Lionel

Hampton, Cab Calloway, Lucky Millinder, and Buddy Johnson—made jump blues a part of their repertory, and produced some of R&B's leading lights. Millinder, for example, hired Dizzy Gillespie and Thelonious Monk, among other jazz innovators, but also featured future R&B stars like Sister Rosetta Tharpe, Wynonie Harris, and Bullmoose Jackson. The same Jay McShann band that introduced Charlie Parker featured the smooth R&B-style vocals of Walter Brown; two of the earliest small-group sessions that Parker made in New York spotlighted the R&B-influenced vocals of Tiny Grimes and Rubberlegs Williams. But the gap steadily widened until R&B assumed prominence as a black popular music in its own right and modern jazz went in another direction entirely. The breakthrough for R&B was chiefly engineered by Louis Jordan.

Jordan (1908–1975), a saxophonist, singer, and songwriter as well as an influential bandleader, was an unlikely phenomenon in American entertainment history. He recorded nearly sixty charted hits between 1942 and 1951; many of them reached the No. 1 and No. 2 positions on the R&B charts and crossed over to the predominantly white pop charts. He was born in Arkansas, and began playing saxophone in his father's touring group, the Rabbit Foot Minstrels. He worked in other bands in the South and Midwest before arriving in New York in 1936, to join the Chick Webb Orchestra. During his two years with Webb, Jordan achieved only marginal recognition as a musician—primarily on alto saxophone, though he sometimes doubled on tenor and baritone—and occasional novelty singer. It was enough to encourage him to start his own group.

In 1938, he organized the band that he eventually named Louis Jordan and His Tympani Five (his drummer, Walter Martin, used tympani in his traps set), consisting of two saxophonists, one trumpet player, and a three-man rhythm section. Jordan was a martinet, yet for all his endless rehearsing, the ensemble retained a loose-limbed joy, playing with such zest that it seemed to have the power of a big band. At the height of the Swing Era, he proved that a small group could achieve great commercial success. Widely imitated in the 1940s, he set the direction that the music industry followed after the war, as small bands took over in jazz and pop. Jordan's music derived much of its appeal and humor from the everyday life and current trends of Southern black culture, which—good, bad, and ridiculous—he often skewed and always celebrated. His songs are about sexual and marital mores, Saturday night parties, the draft, and the church; in emphasizing good times, they explore personal peccadilloes rather than hardship and injustice. Jordan reminded people that African Americans had a life, not just a grievance. If he generally ignored modes of contemplation, he also rejected mean-spiritedness, dejection, and self-pity.

In the 1940s, Jordan's popularity was such that he recorded successful duets with Bing Crosby, Louis Armstrong, and Ella Fitzgerald, and appeared in several movies. His tunes blended elements of jazz, boogie-woogie, and Latin rhythms like the rumba, and he put them over with the kind of showmanship he had learned working on the minstrel and vaudeville circuits—complete with funny hats and comical sketches. No one, however, doubted his craftsmanship. As Sonny Rollins, who called Jordan "my first idol," observed, "He really was a great musician" with "the heart and soul of rhythm and blues." Several of Jordan's songs have endured as all-time standards, including "Is You Is or Is You Ain't My Baby," "Caldonia," "Let the Good Times Roll," "Don't Let the Sun Catch You Crying," and "I'm Gonna Move to the Outskirts of Town." Jordan helped to pioneer the electric guitar in pop music, with Carl Hogan on "Reet Petite and Gone," and the use of the Hammond organ, as he encouraged his pianists Wild Bill Davis and Bill Doggett, to master it. Although his career slowed down in 1951 because of illness, his influence carried on in the music of Chuck Berry, T-Bone Walker, Bill Haley, B. B. King, and Ray Charles.

Rhythm and blues was not only a forerunner of rock; it was also a lateral influence on jazz. Several musicians of Jordan's generation managed to succeed on both sides of the R&B–jazz divide, as the need for a party music increased in direct proportion to the sophisticated challenges proffered by modern jazz. Consider these tangled examples:

The alto saxophonist Earl Bostic studied harmony and theory before he took jobs playing and writing arrangements for big bands, including those of Don Redman, Cab Calloway, Louis Prima, Artie Shaw, and Lionel Hampton. He received little popular recognition until 1951, when he recorded a rhythm and blues version of a song made famous a decade earlier by Duke Ellington, "Flamingo"; the record established him as the No. 1 instrumentalist of the year. His small band became, in turn, a training ground for such future jazz luminaries as John Coltrane and pianist Jaki Byard.

When Johnny Hodges took his five-year sabbatical from the Ellington orchestra to lead his own small group, he had a hit straightaway, in 1951, with the R&B tune "Castle Rock"; it did so well that even Frank Sinatra recorded a version. Significantly, Hodges himself did not solo on his own recording. In a way, he was slumming to attract a mainstream audience. He had come of age in the 1920s; musicians who came up with Jordan in the 1940s recognized that the template for commercial success had changed. The younger audience now wanted brazen, brassy music with a strong backbeat. A musician like Hodges, known for the dynamic elegance of his playing, would have to meet that audience on its terms, not his.

The most influential of Jordan's sidemen proved to be the keyboard player and arranger Wild Bill Davis. Born in Missouri, Davis studied music at Tuskegee Institute and Wiley College, where he developed a piano style influenced by Fats Waller and Art Tatum. After freelancing with big bands in Chicago, he was hired by Jordan in 1945, and served as his pianist and chief arranger for four years. Upon leaving Jordan in 1949, he began to focus on the organ, an instrument he had played intermittently ever since hearing a recording of Fats Waller on the pipe organ in the 1930s. Davis's work on organ attracted the attention of musicians, but found little commercial success; he is best remembered for adapting his organ arrangement of the song "April in Paris" for the Count Basie Orchestra—No. 8 on the R&B charts in 1956.

Davis's replacement in Jordan's band, from 1949 to 1951, was the more experienced jazz pianist and arranger Bill Doggett, who had worked with several big bands; he had arranged Thelonious Monk's "'Round Midnight" for the Cootie Williams Orchestra. After hearing Davis play the Hammond electric organ, Doggett followed suit, and in 1956 scored the No. 1 record in the country with his rock and roll organ opus "Honky Tonk (Parts 1 & 2)." The success of that record reflected a period when rock and roll, as yet undefined, sought inspiration from R&B and technical know-how from jazz. In his later years, Doggett returned to the jazz-pop mainstream, writing arrangements for Ella Fitzgerald, Louis Armstrong, and the Ink Spots.

One musician single-handedly represented a fusion between swing, bop, R&B, gospel, and rock: the blind singer and pianist Ray Charles (1930–2004), whose influence was so pervasive that no one contested Frank Sinatra's nickname for him (adopted by his record label), "the Genius." Initially, though, Charles was a divisive figure among churchgoing blacks, who resented his pioneering use of gospel techniques to intensify his vocals and rhythms. African American church music had always found a way into jazz (e.g., the call-and-response method used by big bands), and complaints had long been raised about mixing religious music with "the devil's music"—Louis Armstrong was criticized in 1938 for his recording of "When the Saints Go Marching In." Charles went much farther than anyone else, merging pop and gospel to an unparalleled degree. Observers said that he was no different than a Baptist church singer, except that he sang "baby" instead of "Jesus." He additionally emphasized the church connection by playing the kind of basic, blues-drenched piano chords associated with gospel music, and hiring a backup choir of women singers, called the Raelettes.

Charles struggled as a musician for several years before he turned to his gospel roots. Born to an impoverished family in Georgia, he was raised in Greenville, Florida, by his mother, who took him to the Shiloh Baptist Church on Sundays. At seven, Charles was blinded by glaucoma, and at fourteen he was orphaned. He left school and tried to earn a living in jazz and hillbilly bands. In 1948, he moved to Seattle, where he found acceptance in the black musical district and made his first records. Over the next several years, he led a trio in shameless imitation of Nat "King" Cole; by emulating Cole's cool, jazzy style, Charles placed a few hits on the R&B charts.

Meanwhile, on road tours, Charles perfected an original style that combined the blues, progressive bebop harmonies, and the testifying shouts and backbeat rhythms of gospel. In 1952, he signed with Atlantic Records; his recording of "I Got a Woman" reached the No. 1 slot on the 1954 R&B hit parade. In 1958, he brought a band to the Newport Jazz Festival, a septet modeled after the hard bop groups of Art Blakey and Horace Silver but with two saxophonists, two trumpeters, and backup singers. The diversity of his music, which ranged from bop themes by Max Roach and Milt Jackson to original, gospel-inspired rock and roll tunes like "I Got a Woman" and "A Fool for You," astonished the audience and the other musicians on the bill.

During the next few years, Charles triumphed in every area of international show business. On his 1959 two-part hit "What I Say," a rock and roll landmark that firmly secured for him the white audience, Charles and the Raelettes used gospel-style call and response to mimic the sounds of lovemaking. That year, he signed with a better-financed label, ABC-Paramount, insisting on the right to use big bands and string orchestras and to choose his own material. His hugely popular version of "Georgia on My Mind," a 1930 tune by Hoagy Carmichael arranged by Woody Herman alum Ralph Burns, proved that he could sing anything, a point he drove home with albums of country and western songs, many of them adapted—by an arranging staff that included Benny Carter, Gerald Wilson (formerly of Jimmie Lunceford's band), and Gil Fuller (formerly of Dizzy Gillespie's band)—to the style of the classic jazz orchestras.

Ray Charles and other vocalists reached a larger audience than any jazz musician could. They flourished not as singers with big bands, as in the Swing Era, but instead as solo attractions leading their own groups, usually trios. For jazz musicians who wanted to reach the mainstream audience, the most successful avenue was a hard bop subsidiary called soul jazz. An obvious offshoot of music innovated by Art Blakey, Horace Silver, and Cannonball Adderley, this style employed a similarly strong backbeat, aggressive urban sound, and gospel-type chords, but it simplified the result—preferring basic harmonies, short solos, and clearly defined dance rhythms. Soul jazz paid particular attention to ethnic orientation, sometimes through slang or colloquial spelling, as in such titles as Silver's "Doodlin'" and pianist Bobby Timmons's "Moanin'" (written for Blakey) and "Dis Here" (written for Adderley). Other song titles celebrated the aspects of black life that characterized Louis Jordan's music: soul food, churchgoing, Saturday night parties.

In the 1960s, the exemplary modern jazz label Blue Note enjoyed a series of unlikely hits as successful hard bop records were assimilated into the mainstream: these included Herbie Hancock's "Watermelon Man" (adapted to a Latin style by bandleader Mongo Santamaria), Lee Morgan's "The Sidewinder" (used for a series of razor ads), and Silver's "Song for My Father" (covered by soul singer James Brown). The leaders of soul jazz attempted to cut out the middle man: rather than make records that generated pop versions, they made three-minute singles suitable for pop radio. In 1965, pianist Ramsey Lewis topped the charts with a ditty called "The 'In' Crowd"; in 1967, Adderley did as well with an abbreviated version (from which his solo was cut) of "Mercy, Mercy, Mercy"—the uncut version appeared only on an album.

Jimmy Smith (1925-2005)

The enormous popularity and influence of organist Jimmy Smith was a direct expression of the fusion between jazz and R&B, and helped to sustain a strong popular audience for jazz in black communities of the 1950s and 1960s. Like "the Genius" Ray Charles, Smith picked up his own nickname, "the Incredible Jimmy Smith"—and his imitators and rivals were legion.

He launched a new kind of trio centered on the Hammond B3 organ, supported by drums and either guitar or tenor saxophone. The music was brash, bluesy, lean, and rocking, and it became ubiquitous in urban bars around the country, whether it was live or on jukeboxes.

Smith was born in Norristown, Pennsylvania, and studied piano with his parents, occasionally getting pointers from a young pianist in nearby Willow Grove, Bud Powell, whose influence on him proved as lasting as it was on every other major postwar keyboard player. At nine, Smith won an amateur contest on Philadelphia radio, playing boogie-woogie. He began touring with his father, honing a song and dance act in nightclubs. Thus far, he had been schooled largely in blues and gospel music. After serving in the navy during the Second World War, he returned to Philadelphia to study theory, harmony, piano, and string bass. For several years, Smith played piano with local R&B bands. In 1953, while traveling with one such group, he heard Wild Bill Davis play organ and was smitten. He later recalled hearing Davis as early as the 1930s, but in those years the organ was mostly associated with the enormous pipe instruments in theaters and churches. Count Basie and Fats Waller occasionally recorded organ solos, but they were regarded as diversions, indicative of the influence of church or classical music. During the war, however, small organs were routinely used in military chapels, and returning servicemen like Smith were more receptive to it as a jazz instrument.

Smith's fascination with the organ coincided with an important technological advance. The inventor Laurens Hammond had introduced the first Hammond organ (model A) in 1935. His goal was to replicate the opulent sound of a pipe organ through purely electronic means, creating a relatively compact, portable alternative. Model A never caught on with the public or musicians: it was expensive, bulky, and complicated, involving two keyboards, foot pedals, and a system of drawbars (similar to stops) to control volume and timbre. In 1955, Hammond presented the model B3, an altogether tidier version that caught Smith's attention—so much so that he went into semi-seclusion for three months to study it. Wild Bill Davis warned him that it might take him a decade just to learn the bass pedals, but Smith wasn't discouraged:

♦ ♦ ♦

When finally I got enough money for a down payment on my own organ I put it in a warehouse and I took a big sheet of paper and drew a floor plan of the pedals. Anytime I wanted to gauge the spaces and where to drop my foot down on which pedal, I'd look at the chart. Sometimes I would stay there four hours or maybe all day long if I'd luck up on something and get some new ideas using different stops.

✦ ✦ ✦

Smith's mastery of the foot pedals combined with his earlier study of the bass allowed him to play complete bass lines with his feet, setting a powerful precedent for subsequent jazz organists. He also realized that the B3's keyboard, called a "waterfall keyboard" for its light construction, rounded edge, and absence of an overhanging lip, encouraged rapid melody lines and glissandos played with the palm of the hand. His tremendous technique enabled him to develop an attack that combined R&B rhythms and gospel feeling with daunting bebop virtuosity.

Smith introduced his trio in Atlantic City in September 1955. The following January, he scored a much touted New York debut at Harlem's Small's Paradise. Blue Note signed him and promptly released his album *A New Star—A New Sound: Jimmy Smith at the Organ*. The timing could not have been better: 1956 was the year Bill Doggett released "Honky Tonk," establishing the organ as a trendy new sound. But Smith showed how much more could be done with the instrument. At first, jazz critics were predictably ambivalent. Smith played a torrent of notes with the right hand, supplementary chords or drones with the left, and bass walks with his feet, often sparking his solos with glissandos that varied in speed (some were sensuously slow-moving) and texture—a consequence of his peerless ability to combine keyboards, drawbars, and pedals. He recorded prolifically, using album titles that echoed the same categories Louis Jordan had popularized: leisure time (*House Party*, 1957), church (*The Sermon*, 1958), and food (*Back at the Chicken Shack*, 1960). In 1962, he signed with a larger label, Verve, and achieved even greater success, often with big bands or in collaboration with Wes Montgomery. At a time when the avant-garde was splintering the "serious" jazz audience, Smith maintained a fervent popular following.

"THE ORGAN GRINDER'S SWING"

"The Organ Grinder's Swing" is the leadoff track of an album (*Organ Grinder Swing*) that captures Smith at his peak. At the time of its release (1965), it was regarded as a welcome return to the trio format after he had made several big-band albums. By then, most critics agreed that Smith was a musician to be reckoned with. The album included blues and ballads in addition to "The Organ Grinder's Swing," a 1936 Swing Era novelty recorded by, among others, Will Hudson (its composer), Chick Webb (vocal by Ella Fitzgerald), Benny Goodman, and, most memorably, Jimmie Lunceford. Smith's version is only a bit longer than two minutes, yet it demonstrates his rigorous personality, wit, and technical mastery.

The session teamed Smith with the versatile studio drummer and occasional ballad singer Grady Tate and reunited him with his frequent and perhaps finest partner, the Detroit-born guitarist Kenny Burrell, who performed with everyone from Ray Charles to John Coltrane to Gil Evans. Smith and Burrell are superb blues players, yet their approaches are different and they seem to temper each other. Burrell, with his cool sound, economy, and harmonic subtlety, brings out the lyricism in Smith, while Smith's rowdier attack inspires Burrell to lay on the funk. This performance opens with a gunshot blast from the drums and Smith's signature organ squawk, delaying the actual theme, which has a faded nursery school quality in melody and lyrics ("Who's that coming down the street? / Good old organ grinder Pete"). The trio ignores the lyrics, but Smith inserts a couple of amusing vocal breaks that consist of well-timed mumbles. When he goes into the main theme, note the bagpipe feeling suggested by the full timbre, a good example of his use of the drawbars. At 1:48 and 1:56, he employs, albeit for only a few seconds, his trademark gambit of repeating a note or a tremolo. In concert, Smith would hold a chord while soloing over it for several choruses, until the audience begged for mercy.

THE ORGAN GRINDER'S SWING

Jimmy Smith

Jimmy Smith, Hammond B3 organ; Kenny Burrell, electric guitar; Grady Tate, drums

LABEL: *Organ Grinder Swing*, Verve V(6)8628; *Organ Grinder Swing* (Verve 731454383127)
DATE: 1965
STYLE: soul jazz
FORM: 12-bar blues

Chorus 1

0:00   A short blast from the drums leads directly into the opening chorus, marked (as each chorus is) by a loud, squawking organ chord. Smith plays rhythmically tricky riffs on the organ, connected by a simple rocking back and forth between two notes. He's supported by his own walking bass line and the guitar's steady, syncopated two-chord comping.

0:12	The organ holds out simple blues chords, falling from V (0:12) to IV (0:13), reinforced by the drums.
0:14	On the last beat of the measure, the harmony resolves to I. During the two-bar break that follows, Smith quietly mumbles an inaudible phrase.

Interlude

0:18	Over a pedal point, Smith plays a portion of the well-known children's melody popularized in the 1932 song "The Organ Grinder." Behind him, the drum plays a syncopated pattern on the cymbals.
0:27	The band stops for a two-bar break while Smith continues playing.
0:30	The band reenters. As in the blues, the harmonic progression moves to IV, resolving to I at 0:33.
0:35	Once again the harmony moves to IV, in preparation for a half cadence on V.
0:40	A shorter one-bar break announces the entrance of the guitarist (Burrell), who begins with a high-pitched blue note.

Chorus 2

0:41	Burrell keeps his solo simple, remaining largely in a pentatonic blues scale.
0:53	As the harmony changes, he shifts to a more dissonant scale.
0:55	A two-bar break leaves his line exposed; after a short pause, it ascends in triplets.

Chorus 3

0:59	Burrell's second chorus begins with a high note, nearly obscured on the downbeat by Smith's chord.
1:13	During another two-bar break, Smith returns. His melodic line is frequently doubled by additional notes.

Chorus 4

1:16	Beginning of chorus.
1:23	Smith builds a short rhythmic motive, placing it polyrhythmically against the background beat. Underneath, we can hear his voice in a wordless mumbling, which has both a comic and rhythmic effect.
1:31	He's more aggressive during this two-bar break, entering almost immediately with an active line.

Chorus 5

1:34	Smith's second chorus begins with a phrase accented sharply on the backbeat.
1:38	For a time, he reduces his line to a tremolo between the tonic and a blue note.

1:42	Moving much faster now, he spills a short bluesy phrase against the beat.
1:48	The break during this chorus lasts for four bars, filled in (once again) by Smith's vocalized and rhythmic mutterings.

Chorus 6

1:54	Beginning of chorus.
1:56	As before, another tremolo yields to an irregular fast bluesy phrase (2:00), finally resolving to a more beat-oriented polyrhythm (2:03).
2:07	As the harmony changes, Smith returns to his simple blues chords. When he resolves to the tonic, the tune simply stops.

SINGERS IN THE MAINSTREAM

The 1950s are often described as a golden age for singers of the classic American songbook. The claim is justified on several counts, and may be attributed to at least four factors. First, the number of gifted vocalists was remarkable; most of them had apprenticed with big bands and were now aiming for solo careers. After the war, tens of thousands of returning servicemen whose musical tastes had been conditioned by prewar band styles and the singers who dominated V-Discs (recordings made expressly for the armed forces) provided a made-to-order audience, looking for a link between the present and a fondly recalled past. Second, in addition to new songs constantly ground out for movies, theater, and record sessions, a huge repertory of songs written between the 1920s and 1950s had become part of the country's musical diet. Key composers and lyricists were still alive and available to promote their catalogs; some (Irving Berlin, Richard Rodgers, Duke Ellington, Hoagy Carmichael, Johnny Mercer, Harold Arlen, and others) were as well known to the public as the performers. Third, the 45-rpm single furthered the careers of rising stars and encouraged novelty songs and other "one-hit wonders." At the same time, the 33-rpm album attracted an older and more affluent audience, as an ideal forum for mature performers like Ella Fitzgerald and Frank Sinatra. Finally, the rise of television in the 1950s helped sustain the careers of established performers, particularly singers. Variety shows, combining music and comedy, were broadcast nearly every day, in the afternoon as well as during prime time, and most were initially built around singers who had become famous during the war. The TV audience had limited patience for instrumental music, jazz or classical, but it never tired of singers.

As they supplanted bandleaders as music industry stars, many singers maintained a connection to jazz or swing, as Bing Crosby had done in the 1920s and 1930s, because that was the music they had grown up with. They weren't necessarily jazz singers, but they were products of the Swing Era, and when their appeal to young listeners faltered in the years of rock and roll, they returned to their jazz roots. To choose one of many examples, Rosemary Clooney was a best-selling recording artist between 1951 and 1954. Her biggest hit, a nonsense song about food, "Come On-a My House," was so popular it put her on the cover of *Time* and led to a film and television career. She had recorded it under duress: it was a novelty number—an Armenian tune, sung in an Italian accent, accompanied by harpsichord—and she considered it beneath her. Its phenomenal success, however, allowed her to record more personally rewarding LPs, like the 1956 collaboration with Duke Ellington *Blue Rose*. During the last thirty years of her career, she performed almost exclusively with jazz musicians, singing the classic American songbook. Clooney was essentially an exceptional popular artist who had learned her trade touring with a big band.

In contrast, Nat "King" Cole was an accomplished jazz pianist who enjoyed an unexpected triumph as one of the most successful pop singers of all time. Born in Alabama, the son of a pastor, Cole sang and played in church, and began to record while still in his teens. In 1939, he formed the highly influential King Cole Trio, which popularized the combination of piano, guitar, and bass. His singing on the novelty song "Straighten Up and Fly Right" helped him achieve a commercial breakthrough in 1943, yet during the next few years he was still known primarily as an excellent pianist who occasionally sang numbers with an R&B appeal similar to that of Louis Jordan. After the war, however, Cole began recording ballads like "Mona Lisa" and "Too Young," smash hits that outsold most of his white rivals'. Although he continued to record with jazz musicians and as a pianist, he was now a pop star, usually standing at a microphone and backed by an orchestra that combined big-band instrumentation with a large string section. His popularity was so great that in 1956 he became the first African American entertainer (and the last for more than a decade) to be offered his own television show, sponsored by Revlon cosmetics. When Southern affiliates protested, though, Revlon withdrew its support, complaining that Negro women did not use cosmetics. Cole's much-quoted response was "Revlon is afraid of the dark."

Although Cole's success never waned (he recorded more than 115 charted singles between 1943 and 1964), his jazz abilities were increasingly obscured by such commercial projects as albums of country songs and Spanish songs. In the years following his death, as his early records were re-released, younger jazz fans were surprised to discover his immense talents as a jazz musician.

Frank Sinatra (1915–1998) AND
Sarah Vaughan (1924–1990)

No popular singer had a more fabled career than Frank Sinatra, universally admired by jazz artists—from classic prewar figures like Louis Armstrong, Duke Ellington, and Count Basie (all of whom he performed with) to such modernists as Miles Davis and John Coltrane, who acknowledged his influence and recorded several of the songs he introduced. Born in Hoboken, New Jersey, Sinatra started out as an imitator of his idol, Bing Crosby, but developed a deeply personal style as he listened to the way such singers as Billie Holiday and cabaret performer Mabel Mercer interpreted lyrics, turning them into statements of private anguish. Sinatra believed that every song tells a story and that a singer's phrasing should emphasize the meaning of the lyric. As a young man, he practiced holding his breath under water to increase his lung power so that, like an instrumentalist, he could sing eight-bar phrases without pausing.

Sinatra lacked the rhythmic confidence of Crosby or Holiday, but won immediate recognition as a ballad singer who could delve deeper into the emotional core of a song than anyone else. From 1939 to 1942, he received international acclaim as the "boy singer" with the big bands of Harry James and Tommy Dorsey. His debut as a star in his own right was front page news, attracting screaming female fans who fainted in his presence (some were paid to do so); newspapers called them swooners and referred to Sinatra as "Swoonatra." His more enduring nickname was "the Voice." In the early 1940s, Sinatra launched his own radio show and a film career in Hollywood. He often covered hits associated with Crosby, demonstrating particular affection for songs written in the 1920s. At the same time, he attracted prominent songwriters who were eager to write for him. In those years, he rarely recorded anything at a fast tempo.

With the end of the war, Sinatra's career fell apart. Returning servicemen who resented his failure to serve ignored his recordings and broadcasts. They preferred Crosby, who had made a more vigorous contribution to the war effort, participating in entertainment tours in America and overseas; the years 1946 to 1949 turned out to be the most successful in Crosby's career. As Sinatra's career declined, excessive drinking and smoking marred his voice, gossip columnists pursued his rocky personal life (divorces, public brawls), and a newer crop of singers, like Clooney, Cole, Tony Bennett, and especially Billy Eckstine, won the hearts of younger listeners. Under contract to Columbia Records, he no longer had the clout to choose material, and was humbled into recording dreadful novelties—on "Mama Will Bark," he barked like a dog. It still didn't sell.

In perhaps the most celebrated comeback in American show business, Sinatra set about reinventing himself. He affected a new persona: the jet-set hipster-gambler-drinker-womanizer, sporting a fedora and holding a trench coat over his shoulder. He rebuilt his film career with powerful dramatic performances, winning an Academy Award as the doomed Maggio in *From Here to Eternity*. His most profound change, however, was musical. Although he remained a nonpareil ballad singer, Sinatra focused increasingly on up-tempo swing numbers, accompanied by studio orchestras arranged by some of the finest writers in popular music—most notably the orchestrator Nelson Riddle, known for his imaginative way of expanding the big-band sound with strings, harp, flutes, and other colorful instruments.

Sinatra did not improvise as freely as a jazz singer, but he embellished the melodic line to make it more interesting. His baritone became weightier, more virile. He continued to phrase in order to accentuate meaning, no matter the tempo. If he failed to swing in the easy legato manner associated with jazz, he did create his own kind of swing: a buoyant, foot-tapping, on-the-beat style that his detractors unfairly characterized as "a businessman's bounce." Ellington got to the root of Sinatra's art when he said, "Every song he sings is understandable and, most of all, believable, which is the ultimate in theater."

Working with Riddle (who also wrote albums for Cole, Clooney, and many other singers, as well as television and film scores), Sinatra was one of the first artists to conceive of the LP as a nontheatrical opera, where the selection of songs reflected a particular concept or theme (young love, loneliness, travel, dance). By 1956, Sinatra was king of the LP—he was also the anti–Elvis Presley, who was king of the 45. Sinatra's most successful years coincided with those of Presley, who more than anyone else turned rock and roll into a national spectacle. Presley ignited his audience no less than Sinatra had the swooners, who now found in Sinatra a powerful link to the bands they had known as teenagers. He remained a major force in the entertainment industry for the rest of his life.

"THE BIRTH OF THE BLUES"

"The Birth of the Blues," recorded in 1952 with a studio orchestra consisting of big-band veterans, captures Frank Sinatra in transition: it was one of the first records to show the 1940s ballad crooner recreating himself as the 1950s swinger. The song is typical of Sinatra's repertory of the period. Written for a Broadway revue in 1926 by the thriving team of Buddy DeSylva, Lou Brown, and Ray Henderson, it was revived by Bing Crosby for a 1941 movie, *Birth of the Blues*. Although it is not a blues, the lyric poetically evokes the beginnings of jazz. The tune features an imaginative verse that, unlike most verses, is as well known as the thirty-two-bar AABA chorus and is always performed as an essential part of the song. Sinatra makes the most of its dramatic quality, as he does the bridge—reaching exciting high notes before retreating into his ballad mode, never breaking a sweat.

The purity of Sinatra's timbre is evident throughout, especially in half-time episodes (at 1:07 and 2:33), when he takes the time down to a near-rubato crawl. He also toys with his voice, using an occasional groan or croakiness to underscore feeling. He sings several melodic embellishments, including a motive introduced at the outset as he accentuates the word "blues," bending it into a two-note phrase. The arrangement by Heinie Beau (who worked with Tommy Dorsey and other bandleaders in the Swing Era and went on to arrange for singers and television shows through the 1970s) adds an introduction and a coda to resolve the main melody. Note that Beau singles out two instruments to play obbligato responses to the vocal: alto saxophone (Fred Stulce) in the verse and trumpet (Zeke Zarchy) in the chorus, imitating "the wail of a downhearted frail." Notice, too, the *wah-wah* effects played by the brasses, a jazzy sound associated with King Oliver in the 1920s, and that the piece begins and ends with the drums. The arrangement's stylistic diversity suits Sinatra's always impressive command of the material.

THE BIRTH OF THE BLUES

Frank Sinatra

Frank Sinatra, vocal; Alex Stordahl and His Orchestra, including Zeke Zarchy, trumpet; Frank Stulce, alto saxophone; Heinie Beau, arranger

LABEL: Columbia 39882; *Frank Sinatra Sings His Favorite Hits* (Columbia/Legacy 65420)
DATE: 1952
STYLE: jazz-pop fusion
FORM: 32-bar popular song (**AABA**), with verse

Introduction

0:00	After an opening drum shot, the band enters with a *fortissimo* (very loud) *soli*. On the last note, the trumpets play shakes (quick trills between two notes, in imitation of a wide vibrato).
0:03	Sinatra answers on the same melody: *"These are the blues!"*
0:06	The band repeats the melody at a lower pitch.
0:10	Sinatra again responds, ending with a long, exaggerated downward slide: *"Nothing but blues!"*
0:13	The brass play a series of short riffs, each featuring the blue (lowered) third.

Verse

0:19	Sinatra enters on a long-held note, singing slightly behind the beat: *"Oh, they say some people long ago . . ."* Behind him, a saxophone plays a bluesy countermelody.
0:29	*". . . were searching for a different tune, one that they could croon as only they can."* Sinatra sings over the walking bass and rhythm guitar. Underneath, the trombone occasionally hits the low dominant.
0:41	During a one-measure break, he starts a new section: *"They only had the rhythm, so . . ."*
0:48	*"they started swayin' to and fro."*
0:54	*"They didn't know just what to use, this is how the blues really began."*
1:03	The full band rounds off the verse with strong staccato chords.
1:07	The tempo is interrupted by a break, featuring Sinatra supported only by saxophone chords. The break uses rubato: each chord is held for an unusually long time. *"They heard the . . ."*

Chorus

1:13	**A**	*". . . breeze in the trees . . ."* Sinatra resumes the original tempo over a walking bass. The melody rises gradually by sequence.
1:19		*". . . singin' weird melodies . . ."* On *"weird,"* he bends upward with a long-held note, supported by rich, resonant saxophone chords.
1:25		*". . . and they made that the start of the blues!"* His melody is accompanied by descending chromatic chords in the saxophones.

1:37		The next line starts with a rubato break. Sinatra decorates his line with unexpected melismas. *"And from a . . ."*
1:40	**A**	*". . . jail came the wail of a downhearted frail, and they played that as a part of the blues!"* Each of Sinatra's phrases is answered by a loud, wailing trumpet.
1:59		The full brass plays a series of descending chords to round out the two **A** sections.
2:05	**B**	*"From a whip-poor-will way up on a hill, they took a new note."* At the start of the bridge, Sinatra's melodic line reaches its peak.
2:12		He cuts his line off brusquely, leaving room for the brass to answer with distorted timbre. The last note of the riff falls off.
2:17		*"Pushed it through a horn until it was worn into a blue note."*
2:24		As the horns respond again, the drums play on the backbeat.
2:28		The tempo is interrupted again by a rubato break, with Sinatra exaggerating the downward slide on each note. *"And then they . . ."*
2:33	**A**	*". . . nursed it, they rehearsed it, and then sent out that news, that the Southland gave birth to the blues."* Sinatra begins his line quietly, only to build to a climax.

Coda

2:52		As Sinatra holds out his last note, the harmony moves away from the tonic, signaling the start of the coda.
2:58		*"They nursed it . . . then they rehearsed it . . ."* His statements rise chromatically, each answered by a brass choir.
3:04		*"And they sent out that news!"* As the music moves toward its final climax, Sinatra's voice becomes emphatic.
3:08		*"That the Southland . . ."* He sings an unaccompanied held note, finally supported by the drums.
3:14		*" . . . they gave birth to the blues!"* As he sings his last phrase, he hits his highest note.
3:18		The band plays a descending bluesy line before ending with a sustained chord, finally cut off with a drum stroke.

Sarah Vaughan approached the jazz-pop fusion from the opposite vantage point. Sinatra was a pop performer steeped in the tradition of Tin Pan Alley and swing. Vaughan was a dedicated jazz singer who applied bop harmonies, rhythms, and improvisational ideas to popular music. The leading figures of bop attempted to make their music accessible (Charlie Parker's strings, Dizzy Gillespie's comical novelties), but they could never reach as far into the mainstream as Vaughan, who had one of the most admired and lustrous voices in twentieth-century music. Jazz musicians crowned her with two enduring nicknames, "Sassy" to denote her artistic temperament, and "the Divine One" to denote her art.

Vaughan was born in Newark, New Jersey, where she sang in the Mt. Zion Baptist Church, and learned piano from her mother, the church organist. At twelve, Sarah was good enough to sub for her mother at the organ. Shy and awkward at eighteen, she sang "Body and Soul" at the Apollo Theater's Amateur Night, winning the competition and an important job. In the audience that night was pianist Earl Hines, and though he was not impressed by her gawky demeanor, he was astonished by her voice. He gave her a spot in his orchestra, playing second piano to Hines and sharing vocals with Billy Eckstine, his popular ballad singer and a lifelong friend to Vaughan. Word of Vaughan's gifts quickly spread, and in 1944 she recorded one of the first bop sessions (Parker and Gillespie were sidemen). Two years later, she headlined at New York's Café Society, developing a confident stage presence that eventually became world famous: sensuous, imperious, and yet humorously self-deprecating. One of her characteristic lines, uttered midway through a set as she wiped perspiration from her brow, was "I come up here every night looking like Lena Horne, and go home looking like Sarah Vaughan." Inevitably, she was signed by a major record label, Columbia.

As an established singer, Vaughan rarely played piano in public, but she continued to play in private, exploring substitute chord changes that ultimately informed her vocal improvisations. Her greatest asset, though, was her voice, a contralto that ranged over four octaves with excellent intonation, allowing her to nail far-reaching melodic and harmonic embellishments that were usually the restricted property of instrumentalists. She had a strong feeling for the blues (reflecting her gospel training) and, in marked contrast with Sinatra, an instinctive feeling for swing: no businessman's bounce for her. By the time she signed with Columbia, in 1949, Vaughan was admired for her stunning creativity at any tempo.

The record label, however, didn't want that kind of creativity, which it felt would alienate an audience that wanted to hear familiar songs in a familiar style. During her five years with Columbia, Vaughan was allowed to record only one outright jazz session (with sideman Miles Davis, who later compared her brilliance to that of Charlie Parker), but the presence of large string orchestras could not rein in her improvised embellishments. Nor could she fake interest in the kind of novelties that governed the pop charts in the early 1950s—the era of million-sellers like "The Doggie in the Window" and "Hot Diggity, Dog Diggity." Vaughan was poised between two careers—that of an indomitable jazz creator and an exquisite pop star, a predicament that took on contractual formality when she signed with

Mercury Records in 1954. That label acknowledged her dual appeal by having her alternate between jazz and pop record dates. In her first year with Mercury, Vaughan achieved a major hit with the forgettable and forgotten "Make Yourself Comfortable," by the man who conceived "The Doggie in the Window," and also recorded an ageless jazz classic (called simply *Sarah Vaughan*) featuring trumpet player Clifford Brown. Typically, she refused to sing inferior songs in concert, no matter how well they sold.

The 1950s were the years when Ella Fitzgerald expanded her audience with her songbook series, helping to establish the pantheon of American songwriters while sustaining her jazz following with delirious flights of scat-singing. Some of Vaughan's best work similarly resulted from a fusion of jazz and pop, in theme albums like *Great Songs from Hit Shows*. Bad songs disengaged her, but sugary arrangements of good ones rarely fazed her; sometimes overwrought orchestrations that dripped with syrupy violins inspired her to bolder melodic embellishments. As long as she could work in both fields, everything was fine. But by the 1960s, a new generation of record executives was less than enchanted by her free-thinking spontaneity and rapier wit. Vaughan complained that producers handed her sheet music for new songs on the day they were to be recorded, depriving her of rehearsal time on the assumption that unfamiliarity with the material would tame her creative impulses.

By 1967, she had had enough of their attempts to market her as a middlebrow pop star. When her contract ended, she turned her back on the industry and refused to record for four years. This turned out to be the beginning of the most successful phase in her career. Like Sinatra, Vaughan reinvented herself, but not by changing her music. Instead, she modified her place in the business, working in major concert halls with a trio instead of nightclubs, although she occasionally performed with big bands, guest stars, and even symphonic orchestras. When she resumed recording, she did so on her own terms and continued to successfully combine concerts and recordings until her death in 1990.

"BABY, WON'T YOU PLEASE COME HOME?"

This song is even older than "The Birth of the Blues." The earliest recorded version dates from 1922 (sung by Eva Taylor, the wife of Clarence Williams, its composer and publisher), and it may have been written as early as 1919. Hundreds of jazz and pop performers recorded it in the 1920s and 1930s and again in the 1950s. The swing bands and bop musicians largely ignored it, however, so it was an unusual choice for Sarah Vaughan in 1962. The setting is also unusual. At a time when she usually recorded with studio orchestras, this was one of two albums Vaughan made with just guitar (Barney Kessel, a prominent and influential disciple of Charlie Christian) and bass (Joe Comfort, a big-band veteran who often worked with Sinatra and Riddle). The spare, elegant accompaniment gives the singer no place to hide; her every note adds prominently to the harmonic and rhythmic contours of the performance. Under these circumstances, most pop singers stick close to the melody. Vaughan, with infallible intonation, plays freely with the material.

The arrangement consists of an introduction, three choruses of the thirty-two-bar AA' tune, and a protracted coda. Each chorus is treated with a different rhythmic approach: cool medium tempo, followed by a funky backbeat treatment, followed by double-time swing. Notice how frequently Vaughan alters her vocal quality, from the soulfully seductive timbre of her first notes to the speech-like cadence at the end. She constantly modulates her vibrato, especially at the ends of phrases to underscore the rhythm. For example, she amplifies the word "name" (0:30) and changes the emphasis on "part," cutting it short in the first chorus and extending it with vibrato in the second; in the third chorus, she puts the emphasis instead on the preceding "heart." Unlike Sinatra, Vaughan doesn't build to climactic high notes. With her entire range at her disposal, she casually rises to high notes or dips down to low ones to highlight the melodic embellishment of the moment, taking particular liberties in the first half of the third chorus. Some of her phrases are short, playing against the support of the guitarist, and others are surprisingly long—even breathless, though she is never really short of breath. While Sinatra sings long phrases to underscore the meaning of the lyric, Vaughan uses them to extend the melodic idea of her improvisation. Although she is singing an old pop song in a way that would have been accessible to everyone, she leaves not the slightest doubt that she is a true jazz vocalist.

BABY, WON'T YOU PLEASE COME HOME?

Sarah Vaughan

Sarah Vaughan, vocal; Barney Kessel, guitar; Joe Comfort, bass

LABEL: Roulette R(S)52118; *Sarah + 2* (Blue Note 8000GPI2NG)
DATE: 1962
STYLE: jazz-pop fusion
FORM: 32-bar popular song (**AA'**)

Introduction

0:00	To introduce the song, the guitar and bass play the last eight bars of the chorus. The guitar's chords are bluesy, bending notes expressively. The bass sets a slow, shuffle groove.
0:09	The harmony comes to rest in a half cadence (on the dominant).

Chorus 1

0:10	**A**	*"Baby, won't you please come home? 'Cause your mama's all alone."* Vaughan sings the repeated notes in the melody pleadingly, each note bent slightly and dragged behind the beat.
0:14		Having started without vibrato, she relaxes and allows her voice to flourish at phrase's end.
0:21		*"I have tried in vain, never no more to call your name."*
0:31	**A′**	*"When you left, you broke my heart, because I never thought we'd part."* Displaying her voice control, Vaughan connects the new stanza (*"When you left"*) to the last in a long, continuous phrase.
0:39		At the end of the line, her voice drops off suddenly, suggesting a more speech-like sound.
0:42		*"Every hour in the day, you will hear me say, Baby, baby, won't you please come home?"* For the last two lines, Vaughan switches to a bluesier sound.
0:51		Kessel (guitar) plays a chord that signals a modulation to a higher key.

Chorus 2

0:52	**A**	*"Baby, won't you please come home? 'Cause your mama's all alone."* Kessel digs into the pulse, planting each chord solidly into each beat. Comfort suddenly plays a straightforward walking bass. Vaughan matches this rhythmic groove precisely: she turns the melody into a series of steady repeated notes, adding tiny embellishments to reinforce each beat.
0:56		As the line continues, her timbre begins to thin out, as if her breath were about to expire. And yet by the phrase's end, she has plenty of breath to complete her line with grace and style.
1:03		*"I have tried in vain never no more to call your name."* Vaughan begins to differentiate her lines with skillful syncopation.
1:08		In a sudden rise to the upper octave, she shows off her higher register.
1:13	**A′**	*"When you left, you broke my heart, because I never thought we'd part."*
1:18		Vaughan shifts to her lower register, where her timbre becomes dark and sultry.
1:24		*"Every hour in the day, you will hear me say, Baby, won't you please come home?"* For the final couplet, she sings in call and response with the guitar.
1:33		Kessel signals another modulation.

Chorus 3

1:34	**A**	*"Baby, won't you please come home? 'Cause your mama's all alone."* The groove switches to double-time: Kessel comps while Comfort plays a fast walking bass. Vaughan's voice swings hard against the beat.
1:43		*"I have tried (Lord knows I've tried) in vain never no more to call your name."* As she improvises, words appear in strange rhythmic positions.
1:47		Vaughan's line descends deep to a note implied by one of the underlying chords.
1:50		At the phrase's end, she lets her timbre broaden and her volume increase, leading seamlessly to the next couplet.
1:52	**A'**	*"When you left, you broke my heart, because I never thought we'd part."*
1:59		The tempo slows down dramatically to an approximation of the opening groove.
2:01		*"Every hour in the day, you will hear me say, Baby, won't you please come home?"* Vaughan's timbre becomes loud and brassy.

Coda

2:12	*"Baby, won't you please come home?"* For the conclusion, the band repeats the last four bars of the tune. Vaughan swoops up to her highest note.
2:17	*"Baby, won't you please . . ."* As they near the final cadence, the harmonies slow down.
2:22	*"Come on home? Come on home? Come on home?"* Vaughan sings the last words in different octaves, contrasting her lyrical high voice with a deep, resonant low one.
2:30	*"Come on home!"* Her last phrase collapses from song into speech.
2:31	A final guitar chord ends the song.

LATIN JAZZ: CUBA AND BRAZIL

The dance beats of the Caribbean, which are closely related to actual West African sources, have always exerted a powerful influence on jazz history, beginning with New Orleans. As Jelly Roll Morton counseled: "If you can't manage to put tinges of Spanish into your tunes, you will never be able to get the right seasoning, I call it, for jazz." Yet in the postwar era, the Latin "tinge," especially as developed in Cuba and Brazil, fused with jazz to create riveting new developments. The Cuban influence produced a series of exciting, highly percussive dances that swept the nation in the 1950s, while the Brazilian influence introduced a laid-back, melodious counterstatement to rock (bossa nova) that had an even bigger impact in the early 1960s.

Cuban music maintained a large following in the United States in the big-band era and after, spurring a fashionable series of dances: the rumba in the 1930s, the mambo in the 1940s, and the cha-cha-cha in the 1950s. In those years, Cuba was a popular destination for vacationing Americans, who returned with a taste for those exotic, sexy dances. The most successful of the Cuban bands working in the United States offered little in the way of jazz, but they kept ballrooms hopping and were much admired for their rhythmic vitality and colorful showmanship, which often involved extravagant costumes and beautiful dancers and singers.

The most famous of all the Latin bandleaders was Xavier Cugat, a Spanish-born violinist whose family moved to Cuba when he was a boy. He played with Havana's Grand Opera Company and the Berlin Symphony before traveling to Los Angeles, where he worked as a newspaper cartoonist specializing in celebrity caricatures. Cugat organized his first band in 1929, and quickly found success in nightclubs in Los Angeles and New York. His fame peaked in the 1940s thanks to hit records and frequent appearances on radio and in the movies—he appeared in more Hollywood musicals than any other bandleader. Cugat's band did not play jazz, but it furthered a vogue for Latin music and bandleaders, of which there were soon a great many. (Desi Arnaz popularized that image on television in *I Love Lucy*.) Their success was encouraged by the Good Neighbor Policy, initiated by the United States in the late 1930s to counter its own interventionist policies, combat Nazi propaganda, and promote better relations with countries throughout Latin America.

Another factor in the growing popularity of Latin music was the 1940 battle between ASCAP, the performing rights organization, and the recently formed Broadcast Music Incorporated (BMI). ASCAP composers didn't want their music played on radio for free, and radio broadcasters, who formed BMI, balked at paying high licensing fees. Both sides finally agreed to new rates, but before they did, ASCAP songs were taken off the air, creating a musical vacuum that South American songwriters, most notably the Brazilian composer Ary Barroso, whose songs included "Brazil" and "Bahia," helped to fill.

Walt Disney hired Barroso and others to provide music for his studio's contributions to the Good Neighbor Policy, movies that combined animation with live action: *Saludos Amigos* and *The Three Caballeros*. These films introduced several South American songs that gained tremendous popularity in North America: everyone from Bing Crosby to Charlie Parker recorded them. Hollywood also began promoting a new generation of

Latin leading men in musicals and dramas that pretended to take place in Havana or Rio, but were actually filmed on the studio lots. The most prominent Latin import was the wildly effervescent Brazilian entertainer Carmen Miranda, known for performing her songs in outrageous costumes that involved huge fruit-salad hats. Her impact in spreading Latin music was far from frivolous. Miranda's pre-Hollywood recordings helped to trigger interest in samba (a traditional dance music with African roots) in her native country. In Hollywood, she insisted on being accompanied onscreen by her own band, performing authentic sambas with wit and brio—her expressive arms and facial gestures emphasized the music's stirring rhythms.

Mario Bauzá (1911–1993), Machito (1908–1984), AND THE Dizzy FACTOR

A profound realignment of Cuban music and jazz began to take place during the war but was little noticed until the late 1940s. This brew had been fermenting for years, partly in protest against Cugat's showboating and inauthentic presentations. The new Cuban-jazz fusion was known as Cubop or Afro-Cuban jazz, and its relatively little-known godfather was the trumpet player and arranger Mario Bauzá. Born in Havana, Bauzá came to New York as a teenager and worked with important big bands, most notably that of Chick Webb. (When you recall that Webb also introduced Louis Jordan and Ella Fitzgerald, his posthumous influence beyond jazz is really quite astonishing.) Like the R&B innovators who found little recognition playing in swing bands, Bauzá bided his time—until 1939, when he attempted to form an Afro-Cuban band with Frank Grillo, soon to be known as the bandleader, singer, and maracas player Machito.

Machito was also raised in Havana, where he began performing in the 1920s. He moved to the United States in 1937, and worked with several Latin ensembles before he and Bauzá launched their first band, which was forced to fold for want of steady engagements. Bauzá joined Cab Calloway's orchestra and Machito recorded with Xavier Cugat. A year later, in 1940, everything changed: Machito formed the Afro-Cubans, a ten-piece band (two saxophonists, two trumpeters, pianist, bassist, four percussionists), and never looked back. Bauzá soon left Calloway to become Machito's music director, and hired innovative young arrangers to give the band a jazz sound. During the next few years, the two men grew closer as Bauzá married Machito's sister Estela, though their professional progress was interrupted when Machito served in the army. On his return, his ensemble created tremendous interest among modern jazz musicians. The California-based bandleader Stan Kenton, known for his embrace of orchestral modernism, later recalled that when he went to see Cugat, a member of the band told him, "Man, if you think this is good, you should go and hear Machito—he's the real thing!" In 1946, Machito and Kenton shared a bill and Kenton recorded his tribute, "Machito."

The foundation of Cuban music, and specifically of Cubop, is the clave (Spanish for "keystone"): a time-line pattern on which other rhythms may be stacked. A crucial difference between jazz and Latin rhythms is that jazz has a fairly symmetrical forward momentum (swing), charged by a strong backbeat. Clave is asymmetrical, creating tension within each measure by its fluid, constantly changing nature. It originated in West Africa and was adapted by Cuban musicians as the defining organizing rhythmic principle for their music. The most widely played clave patterns are the son clave and the rumba clave. The son clave is a two-bar phrase that can be notated as

played as shown here or with the measures reversed. The rumba clave is similar but with one important change:

That subtle rhythmic shift allows rumba clave to fit compatibly with a more Africanized 6/8 meter. In a Latin band, the rhythm section is larger than the jazz configuration of piano, bass, and drums. It consists of a team of percussionists who may outnumber the members of the reed or brass sections, as with Machito's Afro-Cubans. In addition to trap drums, the instruments played by a typical Cubop percussion team are timbales, congas, bongos, maracas, claves (short wooden sticks), and guiros.

For all the interest generated by Machito, the breakthrough for the Afro-

Cuban jazz movement was triggered by Dizzy Gillespie. Once again, the seeds had been planted by Mario Bauzá. During the two years he spent with the Cab Calloway Orchestra, Bauzá persuaded Calloway to hire the young, untested Gillespie, whom he then privately instructed in the essentials of Cuban music, including clave. In 1946, backed by a contract with RCA-Victor, Gillespie organized a big band and started working toward a fusion of jazz and Cuban music. After Bauzá introduced him to Chano Pozo, the ingeniously flamboyant congas player who occasionally worked with Machito's band, Gillespie invited Pozo and bongo player Chiquitico (Diego Iborra) to appear with his band at Carnegie Hall, marking the first public presentation of a serious jazz-Latin fusion.

Gillespie had already displayed a penchant for Afro rhythms in "A Night in Tunisia," but he now delved deeply into the arena of Cuban music, a subject about which he knew virtually nothing—in consulting Bauzá, he initially called the congas "one of those tom-tom things." He was a fast learner, eventually becoming a fair congas player himself. But in Pozo, he had a master: a tough, wiry man who had been something of an underground legend in Havana. He had limited command of English, but Gillespie gave him a free reign to instill Latin polyrhythms in his band from 1947 until the end of 1948, when Pozo's life was cut short at age thirty-four by a bullet in a Harlem bar. In December 1947, the Gillespie band recorded their major works together: "Cubana Be" and "Cubana Bop" (arranged by George Russell in an early example of modal jazz), "Algo Bueno," and the instantly influential "Manteca." Recalling the response to "Manteca," Gillespie said, "It was similar to a nuclear weapon when it burst on the scene. They'd never heard a marriage of Cuban music and American music like that before."

"MANTECA"

"Manteca" was originally Pozo's idea. The title, which literally means grease or lard in Spanish but which was also Cuban slang for marijuana, is loudly invoked by Pozo throughout the recording. We hear his conga drumming from the outset, interlocked with a Latin syncopated bass line strikingly different from the walking-bass line that characterized swing and bebop. The sections of the orchestra add riff upon riff, saturating the musical space with cross-rhythms. Pozo apparently wanted nothing but this tumultuous Latin groove, stretched out over a single tonic chord (another example of modal jazz). "If I had let it go like he wanted it," recalled Gillespie, "it would've been strictly Afro-Cuban, all the way."

Gillespie's job was to link these sensational sounds to jazz. In the introduction, his rapid-fire bebop solo ricochets past the riffs like an express train. Later on, he complements the "Manteca" tune with a sixteen-bar bridge that suddenly shifts to the distant realms of chromatic harmony. The whole piece, it seems, is in constant tension, moving from one world to another, giving the musicians a rhythmic background to challenge them and a harmonic one to comfort them. One of Gillespie's soloists, "Big Nick" Nicholas, was a hard-swinging tenor saxophonist, so the arrangement drops him into an "I Got Rhythm" chord progression with a steady four-four bass—he's so comfortable, he casually interpolates a reference to the song "Blue Moon." There is no better example of cultural fusion in mid-century America than "Manteca."

MANTECA

Dizzy Gillespie and His Orchestra

Dizzy Gillespie, Dave Burns, Elmon Wright, Benny Bailey, Lamar Wright Jr., trumpets; Bill Shepherd, Ted Kelly, trombones; Howard Johnson, John Brown, alto saxophones; Joe Gayles, George "Big Nick" Nicholas, tenor saxophones; Cecil Payne, baritone saxophone; John Lewis, piano; Al McKibbon, bass; Kenny Clarke, drums; Chano Pozo, congas and vocal

LABEL: Victor 20-3023; *Dizzy Gillespie: The Complete RCA Victor Recordings* (Bluebird 7863)
DATE: 1947
STYLE: big-band Latin jazz
FORM: 40-bar popular song (**AABA**; the bridge lasts 16 bars) with interludes

Introduction

0:00	The piece opens with an interlocking duet between the Afro-Cuban drumming of Pozo and the bassist. Pozo's repeated pattern emphasizes a strong backbeat on beat 2 (the high-pitched drum), and two drum beats that fall *just before* beat 1. The syncopated bass line falls strongly off the beat.
0:05	The drum set fills in the texture, adding its own pattern but also playing a bass drum accent firmly on the beginning of each measure. Pozo begins chanting, *"Manteca! Manteca!"*
0:08	The baritone saxophone enters with yet another polyrhythmic riff, a two-note riff in octaves.
0:13	The baritone saxophone is doubled by tenor saxophones.

0:16	The brass instruments enter: the trombone section on its own riff, the trumpet section doubling the saxophones but adding a chord at the end.
0:19	Gillespie adds his own improvised layer in bebop style.
0:24	He suddenly accelerates to a faster passage.
0:30	The full band enters with a sudden explosion on a triplet rhythm (*da*-da-da, *da*-da-da, *da*-da-da, *da*-da-da, *daaah!*).
0:32	The final note is held and allowed to decay, each instrument falling away at its own rate. The texture once again reduces to the bass-conga duet (with the drums playing quietly behind them).

Chorus 1 (head)

0:38	**A**	The saxophones play a short riff, answered by the full band. Each line ends in a shake—a rapid tremolo that marks the end of the phrase. Behind them, the bass plays various asymmetric riffs.
0:44		The conga drum adds improvised accents.
0:46		At the end of the **A** section, the full band repeats its answer, its syncopations accented by the drum set.
0:49	**A**	
1:00	**B**	Playing a sustained chord, the saxophones modulate to a new key. The congas continue their rhythm, but the bassist has shifted to a walking-bass pattern.
1:12		Gillespie takes over the melody on trumpet, the saxophones harmonizing underneath him.
1:22	**A**	

Interlude 1

1:33	We return to the bass-conga duet, with subtle changes in the bass line.
1:36	As Pozo shouts, "*Manteca!*" the trombones double the bass.
1:39	The saxophones play their octave riff.
1:42	Over a cross-rhythm, the full band enters with the high trumpets on top.

Interlude 2 ("I Got Rhythm")

1:48	**A**	With a flourish, Nicholas enters on tenor saxophone, improvising against block chords played by the full band. The chord progression is the jam-session favorite, "I Got Rhythm," with a walking bass.
1:52		The background chords, voiced at the peak of the trumpet section's range, feature intense bebop dissonances.
1:54		Nicholas's line lands strongly on the flatted fifth (a melodic dissonance).
1:59	**A**	The band is now silent, leaving Nicholas to play with the rhythm section. He quotes the opening of "Blue Moon." The congas are still heard, but they subordinate their Latin rhythms to the prevailing bebop groove.
2:05		Again, Nicholas hits the flatted fifth.

Chorus 2 (abbreviated)

2:10	**B**	The brass play a syncopated version of the melody, backed by a countermelody from the saxophones.
2:21		Entering on a stunning high note, Gillespie improvises over the second phrase.
2:31		As Gillespie reaches the end of the phrase, he throws in a series of bebop dissonances (including the flatted fifth).
2:32	**A**	The band returns to the opening riff.
2:38		Pozo bellows "*Manteca!*" over the entire band.

Coda

2:43	A conglomeration of riffs gradually declines in volume. Pozo continues to yell, changing his pitch and rhythm. The sound retreats to the bass and congas.
2:55	The bassist, now the focus of attention, plays variations on his line.
3:03	A few short drum strokes end the piece.

The fascination with Cuban rhythms quickly spread. An especially important recording following on the heels of "Manteca" came about in 1948, when, as part of a recorded survey called *The Jazz Scene*, producer Norman Granz asked Machito to contribute a selection. He chose a 1943 Bauzá composition (frequently cited as the first piece written in the Afro-Cuban idiom), "Tanga." At the center of this performance was a tenor saxophone solo by jazz star Flip Phillips (formerly of the Woody Herman band), but the context was an intricate clave developed by six percussionists. It was probably no coincidence that in Havana, *manteca* and *tanga* were both terms for marijuana: if "Manteca" approached the merger from a jazz angle, "Tanga" defined the same union from a Cuban purview. Still, as Chico O'Farrill, a principal Afro-Cuban composer hired by both Bauzá and Gillespie, noted, "I truly believe jazz ended up influencing Cuban music more than Cuban music influenced jazz."

By 1950, the Latin influence was widespread. Woody Herman had recorded the dazzling "Sidewalks of Cuba" (arranged by Ralph Burns and featuring the meteoric trumpet star Sonny Berman); Charlie Parker recorded with Machito (they connected on "Tico Tico," one of the songs introduced by Disney's *Saludos Amigos*); Bud Powell drew on clave for his trio recording of "Un Poco Loco"; Stan Kenton regularly used bongos, maracas, and other Latin devices. In the mid-1950s, Afro-Cuban jazz receded; like bop itself, Cubop had polarized the mass audience. But Machito's career continued unabated, not least at vacation resorts in places like the Catskills, where he promoted the mambo and cha-cha-cha. He made two kinds of records: those that featured jazz solos and those that did not. Soon, the Cuban style became part of a broader appreciation of Latin American styles, which included the Brazilian bossa nova, the Argentine tango, and Mexican mariachi. At the same time, Afro-Cuban music sparked another kind of fusion, between Cuba and other areas in the Caribbean, especially Puerto Rico, as blended together on New York's streets. Puerto Rican musicians named the new Afro-Caribbean merger salsa (sauce). By the 1970s, salsa was a full-blown urban tradition, with several ballrooms accommodating its orchestras and the loyal dancers and fans who followed them.

In these bands, the jazz input was not an option but a given. Every salsa group employed accomplished jazz improvisers as well as singers and rhythm sections that built disarmingly danceable clave rhythms. Many key figures in the salsa movement were born in New York and had grown up with strong ties to the twin traditions of Machito and Gillespie—among them, Tito Puente, Ray Barretto, Eddie Palmieri, and Willie Bobo. Barretto, for example, was encouraged early on by Charlie Parker, played straight jazz as often as he did salsa, and was the first to play the conga in 4/4 jazz time, with no trace of clave—on a Wes Montgomery album. Established jazz stars hired Latin rhythm sections to give their music a clave foundation. One of the most successful was a vibraphonist from St. Louis, Cal Tjader, who initially made his name in the cool school working for pianist George Shearing, whose music regularly employed Latin rhythms. In 1955, Tjader went out on his own; two years later, he was able to hire two of the prized percussionists in Tito Puente's band, Willie Bobo and Mongo Santamaria. Tjader's group enjoyed much success during the next several years, culminating in 1964, when his album *Soul Sauce* sold 100,000 copies.

In 1961, Mongo Santamaria (1922–2003) left Tjader to start his own group. Within a year, he had a top-ten hit: "Watermelon Man," an Afro-Cuban treatment of a new piece by the young pianist with Miles Davis's quintet, Herbie Hancock. *Salsa* was not yet a household term, bossa nova had only just begun to stir interest, and not even Hancock had had the opportunity to record his tune. Santamaria's single, released on a small independent label, helped pave the way for a flexible Latin-soul fusion that covered mainstream hits in addition to creating its own tunes.

Santamaria was born in Havana, where he studied violin, and turned to drums after hearing Chano Pozo. Arriving in the United States in 1950, he spent most of the next seven years working with Tito Puente. He didn't become known in the jazz world until he joined with Tjader, an association that led to his making freelance records as a leader. An innovator of *charanga*, a standard Cuban style featuring flute and violin, Santamaria added saxophones and trumpet to give the music more weight and thrust. In the wake of "Watermelon Man," he became the archetypal crossover musician whose audience encompassed fans of salsa, jazz, soul, and middle-of-the-road pop. His first name became so well known that Mel Brooks used it as a punch line in the movie *Blazing Saddles*. By then, most of his records reflected strictly commercial ambitions, but Santamaria was a versatile musician, who occasionally collaborated with Gillespie, and whose composition "Afro-Blue" remains a jazz standard, best known in a version by John Coltrane.

"WATERMELON MAN"

Santamaria instantly saw the potential of "Watermelon Man," which is a variation on the sixteen-bar blues form, moving from the tonic to the subdominant in the four-bar A sections and to the dominant in the eight-bar B section. The A sections include long rests, more than a measure each (for example, at 0:12 and 0:19), which Santamaria fills with vocal shouts and laughter. This use of space emphasizes the unchanging pulse of the rock-steady vamp. Everything about the performance, including the sculpted ensemble phrasing of the theme, is subordinate to the repetitive force of that vamp. After the second chorus, there's a brief transition before the only solo, played by Santamaria's longtime trumpet player Marty Sheller. It's a pleasant solo, but was it improvised or composed? It hardly matters, though it is interesting to note that it became a standardized part of the arrangement: in Santamaria's 1965 version of the piece, arranged by Hancock, the trumpet solo is virtually identical. This is an example of a record in which jazz feeling is maintained (in the solo and in the blending of the ensemble instruments), but not jazz substance—essentially, it is dance music.

WATERMELON MAN

Mongo Santamaria

Mongo Santamaria, congas; Marty Sheller, trumpet; Pat Patrick, Bobby Capers, flutes and tenor saxophone; Rodgers Grant, piano; Victor Venegas, bass; Frank Hernandez, Kalil Madi, drums; Kako, Chihuahua Martinez, Joseph Gorgas, Latin percussion; Martinez and La Lupe, vocal effects

LABEL: Battle 909; *Watermelon Man* (Concord, Milestone MCD-47075-2)
DATE: 1962
STYLE: Afro-Cuban jazz
FORM: 16-bar blues: **A** (4) **A** (4) **B** (8)

0:00		The tune begins with a montuno: a one-to-two-bar syncopated vamp in the piano that is repeated ad infinitum. In this case, the piano chords come straight from the original Herbie Hancock version. There are also various percussion instruments: conga drums, guiro, and woodblock.

Chorus 1 (head)

0:07	**A**	The horns sneak in, building with a *crescendo* to the first note of the phrase.
0:11		At the end of the phrase, the concluding chords are played slightly behind the beat.
0:12		The male vocalist responds with a series of distorted shouts.
0:15	**A**	The melody is repeated, with the first note played higher to adjust to the change of harmony to IV.
0:19		The vocalist's response is a high-pitched laugh.
0:23	**B**	The horns play, in block chords that oscillate back and forth between the harmonies IV and V.
0:33		As the band takes a one-measure break, the horns play the opening melody one more time.

Chorus 2 (head)

0:39	**A**	The band plays the melody again; a male vocalist responds with a single prolonged shout.
0:47	**A**	
0:51		After the second phrase, a woman responds, "That's right, baby, come on!" then laughs.
0:55	**B**	

Interlude

1:11		The band repeats the montuno one more time.

Chorus 3

1:15	**A**	Marty Sheller begins a trumpet solo. His phrases are followed by a riff, played by the saxophones.

1:23	A	As the harmony changes to IV, the background riff is transposed upward. Sheller's lines are short and simple, with some colored by a bluesy tone.
1:31	B	
1:41		The one-bar break is silent for a few beats before Sheller reenters on a syncopated riff with a tenor saxophone.

Interlude

| 1:47 | Another two-bar interlude featuring the montuno. Toward the end, a percussionist fills in space on a cowbell. |

Chorus 4

1:51	A	
1:55		After the first and second phrases, the two vocalists harmonize a response: "Watermelon man!"
1:59	A	
2:07	B	

Coda

| 2:23 | The tune fades out rapidly after the end of the chorus. |

BOSSA NOVA: Jobim, Gilberto, AND Getz

The Brazilian samba originated in the nineteenth century as an amalgam of African dances and march rhythms that laid particular emphasis on the second beat of the measure, or more specifically the eighth note leading from beat 1 to beat 2. Although it was grounded on a version of clave, samba does not use clave as an organizing rhythmic principle: the overall feeling is more relaxed than that of Cuban music. The samba found acceptance in the United States in the 1930s and 1940s through hit songs like "Brazil" and "Tico Tico" and the Hollywood stardom of Carmen Miranda, but by the 1950s it had faded into nostalgic memory, supplanted by more orderly Cuban dances, which North Americans found easier to learn.

That all changed toward the end of the decade. In 1958, the revered Brazilian singer and actress Elizete Cardoso released an album (*Canção do Amor Demais*) that created a stir in Rio de Janeiro and beyond, though not in the United States. Recorded at the request of playwright, composer, and diplomat Vinicius de Moraes, it consisted of the lyrics he wrote to melodies by a thirty-year-old unknown and untested composer, Antônio Carlos Brasileiro de Almeida (Tom) Jobim (1927–1994), and thus introduced Brazil to the most gifted songwriter it had ever produced. Of equal importance, Cardoso was accompanied on a couple of selections by Jobim's friend guitarist João Gilberto (b. 1931), whose way of playing gave Jobim's tunes a uniquely tranquil style that soon became known as bossa nova (new flair).

The Cardoso album was a culmination of several years' work that began when Vinicius hired Jobim to write music for his 1956 play *Orfeu da Conceição*, based on the legend of Orpheus and Eurydice. A year after the album's release, Vinicius helped to spur an international triumph when his Orpheus play was adapted by a French filmmaker, Marcel Camus, as *Orfeo Negro* (*Black Orpheus*), a classic film with an irresistible score by the guitarist-composer Luiz Bonfá plus a couple of new tunes by Jobim. Those songs were more in the traditional style of the boisterous samba than the "new flair," but they brought worldwide attention to the melodically infectious music of Brazil. Still, it was Camus's rejection of most of the songs Vinicius and Jobim had written for the stage version that prompted the Cardoso album, which brought together the key figures in a new movement: Vinicius de Moraes, who had published his first samba in 1953; Tom Jobim, often cited as the finest composer of popular music since the golden age of Gershwin, Berlin, and Porter; and João Gilberto, who recorded a series of albums over the next couple of years (*Chega de Saudade* has been called the Brazilian *Kind of Blue*) that cemented his stature as the definitive interpreter of bossa nova. Often concertizing alone, sometimes for ninety minutes or two hours at a stretch, Gilberto accompanied his spare, unemotional yet strangely moving vocals with infallibly soft rhythmic guitar.

Although detractors insisted that they were merely reinterpreting the traditional samba, Jobim and company insisted that bossa nova represented a break with tradition no less meaningful than bop's break with swing. The public agreed. Bossa nova incarnated a young, innovative attitude with poetic, sometimes self-mocking lyrics and melodies that, though occasionally melancholy, were almost invariably as gentle as a summer's breeze. Rhythmically, bossa nova seemed to sway rather than swing. Harmonically, it delighted in intricate chord changes not unlike those of bop, favoring seventh and ninth chords and melodic dissonances. The title of one of Jobim's best-known songs, "Desafinado," is Portuguese for "out of tune"; its melody makes bold use of bop's signature interval, the flatted fifth, and its lyric uses the phrase that he initially coined to describe Gilberto's innovative style—bossa nova.

————

As of 1960, bossa nova was a phenomenon largely confined to Brazil. Two factors brought it north. First, as far as the United States was concerned, the 1959 Cuban Revolution put a damper on celebrating anything Cuban, from cigars to music. Brazil was now the logical place to turn to for South American rhythms. Second, touring jazz musicians—often sponsored by the State Department—discovered Jobim's songs and embraced them. Not surprisingly, the first American to seriously study Jobim's music was Dizzy Gillespie, during a visit in 1961. He added such bossa nova benchmarks as "Desafinado" and "Chega de Saudade" to his repertory and recorded them shortly after returning. Then he made the commercially disastrous decision to postpone releasing his Brazilian album *New Wave!*, which left the field open to other musicians who were also visiting Brazil in 1961.

One of those musicians was guitarist Charlie Byrd, who toured South America for three months with his trio. Born in Virginia, Byrd was one of the few modern guitarists who concentrated on the acoustic rather than electric guitar—a reflection of his admiration for Django Reinhardt and studies with the classical guitarist Andres Segovia. By 1961, he was an established jazz player in the Washington, D.C., area. Meetings with Jobim and João Gilberto raised his sights, and made him realize that the "texture and volume" of bossa nova was more conducive than other kinds of Latin music to the guitar. Byrd recalled:

◆ ◆ ◆

There was a noticeable difference from the Cuban approach, for example, from the Xavier Cugats and those kinds of things—a more delicate and light way of playing. Also appealing were the ingenious melodies of Jobim and Bonfá and those people. They emulated American popular songs to some extent, but they had a lot of innovation in their own tradition, and they were very inventive people themselves.

◆ ◆ ◆

Byrd could not interest an American label in recording bossa nova until he recruited Stan Getz for the project. Getz (1927–1991), one of the most influential tenor saxophonists of the 1950s, along with Dexter Gordon, Sonny Rollins, and John Coltrane, was born in Philadelphia and demonstrated a prodigious talent while in high school. At seventeen, he became a member of Stan Kenton's band, and then worked with Benny Goodman and other prominent bandleaders. Woody Herman hired him in 1947, placing him in what quickly evolved into the distinctive bebop reed section famously known as the "Four Brothers." Getz's brief solo on Herman's "Early Autumn" made him an overnight jazz star—his firmly gentle timbre had a cool, romantic, otherworldly quality that was instantly recognizable. His reputation soared in the 1950s until problems with narcotics forced him to decamp for Europe. In 1961, intent on reestablishing himself in the United States, he completed a pioneering album with composer Eddie Sauter (*Focus*), which fused jazz and classical techniques and proved his artistry if not his commercial potential. When Getz, who worked with Machito during the Afro-Cuban jazz vogue, listened to recordings Byrd brought back from Brazil, he was sold on bossa nova.

Joining with Byrd's trio (plus a second drummer), Getz recorded *Jazz Samba* early in 1962. Byrd wisely realized that Getz would dominate the album. A record plugger convinced his bosses at Verve Records to issue a single of "Desafinado," edited down to two minutes from the nearly six-minute album version, highlighting Getz's solo. That single became the kind of hit that drives album sales: *Jazz Samba* reached the No. 1 spot on the pop music charts. Within a year, more than two dozen jazz and pop albums claiming to have something to do with bossa nova were released, including creative ventures by Gillespie, Sonny Rollins, Cal Tjader, and Sarah Vaughan. There had been nothing like it in American pop since Elvis Presley triggered rock and roll—and nothing like it in jazz since the Swing Era. In 1963, Getz, aiming for greater authenticity, collaborated with the Brazilians who created bossa nova and had begun performing in New York. The million-selling *Getz / Gilberto* comprised eight songs by Jobim (who played piano), including the track that became emblematic of the bossa nova fad, "The Girl from Ipanema." For these recording sessions, Getz asked Gilberto's wife Astrud, who was present, to translate some of the song lyrics. Although she had never sung professionally, Getz liked the wispy innocence of her thin voice and persuaded Gilberto to let her sing on this track—which became a milestone in the globalization of the jazz–bossa nova fusion.

"SAMBA DEES DAYS"

As the punning title suggests, "Samba Dees Days" is not a Brazilian bossa nova. It was written by Charlie Byrd for the *Jazz Samba* session, in an attempt to meet what he considered the challenge of composing a samba. His piece catches the rhythmic excitement of Brazilian jazz but also the more wistful elements, as in the interval of a third at 0:03 and 0:05 and in subsequent A sections, and the blues feeling in the last half (0:26) of the sixteen-measure bridge. The first half of the bridge uses a familiar device in the songs of Tom Jobim, also commonplace in jazz: the repetition of one note. Indeed, one of the Jobim songs included on *Jazz Samba* is "Samba de Una Nota Só" ("One-Note Samba"), which Byrd recalled as "the most recorded [song] of all" in Brazil.

The star of the performance is Stan Getz, whose effortless phrasing, combined with the understated playing of the two drummers, captures the music's easygoing polyrhythms. His playing has an irresistibly offhand confidence as he alternates long and short phrases, bounces along on the one-note idea of the bridge, and rises to a couple of high-note climaxes (1:54, 3:11) that were something of a Getz specialty—increasing not only his range but also the power of his timbre. His fluid attack is especially noteworthy as he navigates the turnarounds, the measures that end one chorus and lead to another; his manner of moving from one chorus to the next emphasizes the cumulative drama and overall coherence of the perfor-mance. Even his final chorus contributes to that unity by echoing aspects of Byrd's solo. In Getz's most penetrating playing, we have the convergence of a uniquely glowing timbre, tender but forceful; an immense gift for melodic invention; and the ability to lucidly communicate his ideas and emotions, which made him the ideal musician to establish Brazil's bossa nova as a major North American event.

SAMBA DEES DAYS

Stan Getz and Charlie Byrd

Stan Getz, tenor saxophone; Charlie Byrd and Gene Byrd, acoustic guitars; Keeter Betts, bass; Buddy Deppenschmidt, Bill Reichenbach, percussion

LABEL: *Jazz Samba,* Verve MGV8432; *Jazz Samba* (Verve 731452141323)
DATE: 1962
STYLE: Latin jazz
FORM: 40-bar popular song (**AA'BA'**

Introduction

0:00   Getz plays a series of lazy unaccompanied arpeggios, which establish the key of the piece.

Chorus 1 (head)

0:02 **A**   Getz plays the melody—a series of short phrases, discreetly doubled in thirds by Byrd's guitar. Behind the melody, the accompaniment (includ-ing maracas) keeps a quiet Latin rhythm.

0:08		The first eight-bar section ends with a half cadence on the dominant chord.
0:10	**A'**	The next eight-bar phrase begins on the same chord, but ends (0:17) with a full cadence on the tonic.
0:18	**B**	The bridge (lasting 16 bars instead of 8) begins with Getz and Byrd playing a single syncopated note.
0:22		Getz and Byrd repeat the gesture, this time ending with a bluesy phrase.
0:26		As the harmonic progression changes, the melody slowly sinks back to the dominant (at 0:33).
0:35	**A'**	
0:41		The arrival on the tonic signals a two-bar break.

Chorus 2

0:43	**A**	Getz begins with a simple, riff-like rhythmic figure.
0:47		Many of his phrases end early, leaving a great deal of open space.
0:51	**A'**	As he warms up, his melodic ideas begin to cohere into longer and longer phrases.
0:59	**B**	On the bridge, Getz opens up the repeated note to a full octave, complementing it with bluesy phrases.
1:07		As the harmonies change, his phrases become more active, moving rapidly in arpeggios.
1:14	**A'**	

Chorus 3

1:22	**A**	As Getz plays a long phrase, he accents the backbeat (coinciding with the background maracas).
1:30	**A'**	
1:38	**B**	Getz builds a longer, highly decorated phrase around the single note.
1:50		As the phrases increase in intensity, his volume rises.
1:54	**A'**	The last phrase begins with his highest note (a D-sharp).

Chorus 4

2:02	**A**	Byrd begins his solo quietly, playing single-note lines on guitar. Behind him, the details of the Latin rhythmic background are more clearly audible.
2:10	**A'**	
2:18	**B**	At the beginning of the bridge, Byrd switches to a series of chords.
2:26		He plays a phrase polyrhythmically against the beat, adjusting the notes to match the underlying harmony.
2:33	**A'**	
2:37		To signal the end of his solo, Byrd plays a bluesy gesture.

Chorus 5

| 2:41 | **A** | Getz begins his second solo mimicking the rhythms and phrases of Byrd's improvised melody. |

2:49	A'	As Getz suggests the melody of the head, he reduces the rhythm to even quarter notes.
2:57	B	Once again, Getz's bridge focuses on a single note, embedding it within an ornate, complex line.
3:02		His bluesy response is played with particular intensity.
3:05		He plays a series of ascending arpeggios, each culminating in a high note; the last of these high notes (at 3:11) is the dominant.
3:13	A'	He returns to the head.

Coda

3:19		Getz improvises unaccompanied for two bars. After a sharp drum stroke, Byrd follows with his own two-bar phrase.
3:23		Getz and Byrd exchange another two bars. Each of their lines remains largely within the blues scale.
3:27		Switching to the major scale, the two musicians play a composed-out line.
3:30		The piece concludes with two quick strokes.

As the initial excitement over bossa nova waned, it continued to enjoy popularity as easy-listening lounge music, devoid of most of the features that had made it so captivating to jazz musicians. The Brazilian pianist Sergio Mendes, for example, first made his mark with a deft fusion of Brazilian rhythms and hard bop jazz solos, underscored by his own Horace Silver–influenced keyboard style. But he didn't become an international celebrity until he leached out the jazz content, added cooing voices, and covered American Top Forty tunes.

Still, bossa nova never completely lost its bite, as became evident in 2008 when its fiftieth anniversary was celebrated in Brazil with festivals, concerts, panels, articles, and books. By now it had fused with rock and classical music. The samba received a forceful jolt in the 1990s and early twenty-first century in the music of young singer-songwriters like Marisa Monte and Adriana Calcanhotto, who created a repertory that drew on bossa nova in the context of jazz, rock, and soul music. Born in Rio de Janeiro and trained in opera, Monte became a leading figure in a style known as MPB (*Música Popular Brasileira*: Brazilian Popular Music). Calcanhotto, born in Porto Alegre and the daughter of a jazz drummer, reinterprets bossa classics, accompanying herself on guitar and cello and supported by a rhythm section with two drummers. At the same time, a more faithful development of bossa nova was maintained by Rosa Passos, a native of Bahia who began on piano but took up guitar after hearing João Gilberto. At eleven, she sang on local television, and soon developed into a premier interpreter of Jobim and other Brazilian songwriters while contributing to the repertory as a prolific lyricist. After disappearing from public view for several years to raise a family, Passos began a busy recording career in 1996, touring the world—sometimes in tandem with the classical cellist Yo-Yo Ma, who called her voice "the most beautiful in the world."

MASS MEDIA JAZZ

As the gap widened between modern jazz and an increasingly uncomprehending public, jazz began to embody four very different cultural clichés—each far removed from the optimistic "Let's Dance" status that buoyed the music during the Swing Era. The use of jazz on TV in the late 1950s and early 1960s tells the story. In one cliché, jazz was associated with urban mavericks, especially beatniks, treated with comical disdain or hysterical fear. These depictions emphasized jive talk, eccentric haircuts and goatees, and aimless scat-singing or crime. The stereotype had nothing to do with music (though a few characters carried around bongo drums) and underscored the idea that jazz musicians and enthusiasts were cultural outsiders and probably not very bright.

The second cliché, though musical, also fostered a negative image: jazzy sounds—particularly sultry high notes played on alto saxophone—served as cues in dozens of shows to introduce women of doubtful virtue or bad parts of town. Detective shows almost always featured jazz scores, most famously *Peter Gunn* (1958–61), with a theme by Henry Mancini that became a big hit. *M Squad* (1957–60) had music by Count Basie and Benny Carter, while Nelson Riddle scored *The Untouchables* (1959–63) and *Route 66* (1960–64: one memorable episode featured Ethel Waters, Coleman Hawkins, and Roy Eldridge), and Dave Brubeck wrote themes for the rapidly canceled *Mr. Broadway* (1964).

The third cliché was largely positive though no less tiresome, and possibly did more damage than the others. This one postulated that jazz was the exclusive property of the super-hip. If you didn't qualify, you were a square or "out to lunch." Jazz embodied the sleek, affluent, postwar adult world of sexy people with expensive hi-fi's; it was the antidote to rock and roll, regarded as kids' music. Cutting-edge comedians like Lenny Bruce revered jazz; stylish writers like Jack Kerouac and Norman Mailer pondered its meaning. This sort of jazz lover disappeared in the middle 1960s, as the Beatles, Bob Dylan, and others certified rock's adult bona fides.

The fourth role was the most positive and realistic: the actual presentation of jazz musicians on variety shows, late-night gabfests, and arts programming like *Omnibus* (1953–57), which hired Leonard Bernstein to explain "What Is Jazz?" Several isolated one-shot programs were devoted entirely to jazz, including the justly acclaimed *The Sound of Jazz*, which aired live on a Sunday at 5:00 P.M., in 1957. The overall portrait, however, was severely circumscribed by mass taste and racial imperatives: singers were favored, blacks were limited to guest appearances, and true modernists were rarely welcome. Even so, more jazz was seen on television in the 1950s and 1960s than in the past thirty years of cable TV—it was too much a part of the cultural landscape to ignore.

17
CHAPTER

Fusion II: Jazz, Rock, and Beyond

BARBARIANS AT THE GATE

I n the middle 1950s, a revolution occurred outside the gates of jazz and popular music. A new sound, rock and roll, was unsettling the music industry by attracting a sizable and ever-growing body of white teenagers to a compelling fusion of the fluid rhythms of black race records and the insistent plaintiveness of white "hillbilly" music. Its leaders included Elvis Presley, a Memphis truck driver who added pelvic gyrations and sensual poses to his mixture of blues, country, and Tin Pan Alley pop;

◀ Keith Jarrett, shown playing with bassist Cecil McBee, burst onto the jazz scene in the late 1960s with the Charles Lloyd Quartet. He's one of the most electrifying pianists active today.

Chuck Berry, a St. Louis bluesman who mimicked white country music, duck-walked through his guitar solos, and showed an uncanny knack for writing songs about adolescents; and Little Richard, a gospel singer from Georgia who had begun recording boogie-woogie-style R&B in 1951 but didn't let loose until five years later, performing in mascara and whooping his way onto the pop charts.

In retrospect, it seems that jazz musicians should have been paying attention to this new music; but few did. Early rock and roll was marketed and viewed as music for undemanding teenagers, created by amateurs and catering to untutored tastes. As far as most adults were concerned, it was at best errant nonsense, at worst a juvenile plague—"the martial music of every side-burned delinquent on the face of the earth," as Frank Sinatra arrogantly remarked. Jazz, by contrast, was firmly part of an adult sensibility that surely would triumph over such rubbish. When Presley joined the army in 1958, sacrificing his pompadour for a crisply pressed uniform, it seemed that youthful rebellion had indeed been contained. That illusion crumbled in the 1960s, when rock overwhelmed popular music, and jazz musicians (and just about every other kind of musician) found themselves struggling for survival in a world not of their making. The eventual result was a new jazz-rock fusion, which many assumed was simply the next phase of jazz, a fashion that would, at least for a while, displace all that had come before. For several years, it seemed like no one could escape it. Even bebop legends like Dizzy Gillespie and John Lewis allowed their sideburns to grow and opted for electric bass or electric piano. But *fusion* soon fell from favor, replaced by market-driven, fiendishly inaccurate terms like *smooth jazz* and *contemporary jazz*.

The immediate changes that transformed a generation of jazz musicians can be traced back to the popularity of white rock and roll in the late 1950s, which initially had no connection to jazz. Its success was intertwined with a new generation of songwriters working in the Brill Building on Broadway in New York City. There, Otis Blackwell (a black former blues performer who struck gold writing hits and making demos for Presley, Jerry Lee Lewis, and other white rock and roll stars), Carole King, Neil Sedaka, Neil Diamond, and others churned out hundreds of tunes aimed at the youth market. Few of these songs, with their puerile lyrics (Sedaka's "Stupid Cupid," for example), appealed to jazz musicians still attuned to the sophisticated harmonies and lyrics of Gershwin, Porter, Berlin, and

Rodgers. But they provided an alternative pop repertory that appeared to shun the adult world.

In the same period, a different signal was sent by the collegiate Kingston Trio, which sold 6 million copies of their glossy version of an old folk song, "Tom Dooley," in 1958; it went on to win, implausibly enough, the first-ever Grammy Award for Best County & Western Performance. Within a few years, a folk revival brought a new and tougher aesthetic: austere, simple, and moralistic. Veterans like Pete Seeger and Odetta and fresh-faced singers like Bob Dylan and Joan Baez became the lodestars for politically active youth, who felt it better to make their own music with harmonicas and guitars than to sully themselves with music devised for mass tastes. Yet in 1963, Dylan's "Blowin' in the Wind," as sung by Peter, Paul and Mary, sold a million copies, rising toward the top of both *Billboard*'s pop and easy listening charts.

In 1964, the rock revolution went into full swing with the British invasion led by the Beatles and the Rolling Stones. Shunning some aspects of the button-down and condescending qualities of corporate rock and roll while retaining others, they brought back into circulation pop styles from the 1950s that had struck the mainstream as obscure or extreme—those of Chuck Berry and Little Richard, rockabilly pioneers Carl Perkins and Gene Vincent, and Chicago blues artists Bo Diddley and Muddy Waters. Indeed, the Rolling Stones, who derived their name from a Muddy Waters song, originally labeled themselves a blues band. If the Beatles made audiences feel safe, with matching suits and haircuts and a cheerful demeanor and repertory (including "Till There Was You," from *The Music Man*), the Stones introduced a note of surly defiance. The Beatles wanted to "hold your hand"; the Stones couldn't "get no satisfaction." Yet the Beatles soon proved even more irreverent than the Stones, comparing their popularity to that of Jesus and writing songs that celebrated drugs. The British artists turned pop aesthetics on its head. They made an anti-establishment attitude synonymous with youth culture.

The British invasion also brought its own music, requiring little if any help from Brill Building professionals. The Beatles were gifted songwriters: to the initial surprise of American record labels, John Lennon and Paul McCartney created an astonishing catalog of tunes that were melodic, harmonically fresh, and instantly popular. They triggered a shift in the music industry that favored singer-songwriters over "mere" performers. Recording artists were expected to create their own songs, infusing them through performance with an aura of authenticity. When Bob Dylan went electric in 1965, bringing his heightened, expressive poetry into rock (to the horror of folk purists), it became clear that rock and roll—or rock, as it was now known—needed no outside interpreters. This transformation left jazz musicians out in the cold. Throughout the 1960s, they tried giving what they considered the more sophisticated of the new rock tunes their own interpretive spin, but the results (the 1966 *Basie's Beatles Bag* and similar efforts) were meaningless—not because the performances were inept, but because the jazz-rock enterprise seemed suspect.

To be sure, the music business did not change overnight. Mainstream pop songs in the old tradition continued to be written by the likes of Burt Bacharach (his inventive "Alfie" and the unavoidable "Raindrops Keep Falling on My Head"). There were new musicals, supplying a steady if narrow stream of hit songs and profits for record companies: *My Fair Lady* (1956, filmed in 1964) sold 5 million albums, and *The Sound of Music* (1959, filmed in 1965) and *Camelot* (1960, filmed in 1967) each sold 2 million. Jazz musicians continued to mine them for new material: the 1964 season of musicals generated jazz versions by Cannonball Adderley (of *Fiddler on the Roof*), Duke Ellington (of *Mary Poppins*), and Louis Armstrong (of "Hello, Dolly!"). As the decade went on, even this material dried up. Executives at the major labels nervously watched as soundtrack albums—their bread and butter—declined in sales. The end of an era was in sight.

Record sales overall, however, skyrocketed. Beginning in 1955—as rock and roll records began to appear—sales increased by about 36 percent per year, reaching $600 million in 1959. In the 1960s, the growth was unparalleled. Sales broke the $1 billion mark in 1966 and the $2 billion mark by 1972. These staggering increases, obviously due to rock, indicated a greater than ever disparity between pop sales and jazz or classical sales. Record companies that had been indifferent to 1950s rock and roll, despite Presley's astronomical sales for RCA (like bebop, early rock and roll was documented mostly by small, independent labels), quickly adjusted, filling their staffs with business-savvy rock enthusiasts. Rock became a sprawling business, swallowing up opera and musicals (*Jesus Christ Superstar, Tommy, Hair*), bluegrass and country music (the folk-rock movement), the avant-garde (Frank Zappa, Captain Beefheart), and race music (Motown, soul). It even collided with world music: after the Indian virtuoso Ravi Shankar took a place of honor at the 1969 Woodstock concert in Bethel, New York, fans began to expect virtuoso rock musicians, like guitarist Eric Clapton, to improvise over long stretches of time.

THE CHALLENGE TO JAZZ AND
THE RENEWAL OF FUNK

In the late 1960s, rock groups began to shift away from the tight pop format of 45-rpm singles in favor of album-oriented improvisation, signaled by the shift from AM to FM radio. Groups like Cream, which teamed Eric Clapton with bassist Jack Bruce and drummer Ginger Baker (all of them jazz or blues fans from England), featured a freewheeling, blues-based style that was occasionally characterized as electrified jazz. In San Francisco, Jerry Garcia's Grateful Dead similarly favored jams that embedded improvisation in a broad context, including bluegrass, gospel, country, and blues. In the guitarist, singer, and songwriter Jimi Hendrix, rock had its most formidable virtuoso improviser, stunning audiences with the intensity of his solos.

Within the more traditional pop sphere, groups like Blood, Sweat and Tears enjoyed enormous success by adding saxophones and trumpets to their electric guitar, keyboard, and bass, and drawing on their affinity for jazz improvisation. Two of the most talented jazz trumpet players of the era, Randy Brecker and Lew Soloff, initially became known through their work with Blood, Sweat and Tears; soon, they would be playing with the likes of Horace Silver and Gil Evans. For its second album (1967), Blood, Sweat and Tears dipped into jazz repertory, creating an eclectic reworking of Billie Holiday's "God Bless the Child" on a disc that sold 3 million copies. Their later albums featured bits of Thelonious Monk mixed with Prokofiev.

Jazz musicians who coveted commercial success now faced several obstacles. Despite its growing appeal to adults, rock remained primarily the music of youth. The word "teenager" had been in existence only since the 1940s, but two decades later it denoted the huge demographic known as the baby boomer generation. As a group, teenagers had affluence and access to what the historian Eric Hosbawm described as "an unprecedented share of middle-class parents' prosperity." And they were permanent: thirteen-year-olds grew up, but new ones took their place, and the musicians they preferred were invariably young or youngish. The phrase "Don't trust anyone over thirty" made it difficult for older jazz musicians, who had spent their lives mastering their idiom, to believe they could ever again be accepted by that audience.

Baby boomers not only looked, dressed, and spoke unlike their parents, but also developed an attachment to musical electronics that went far beyond anything dreamed of by Charlie Christian. Rock was built on the electric guitar and remained indebted to the blaring power of amplification. Thanks to the stacks of amplifiers that now lined every rock stage, an electric guitarist could drown out an entire big band with one chord. Rock musicians brought unbridled enthusiasm to new technologies: their *wah-wah* pedals, phasers, feedback, electric keyboards, and synthesizers produced a dramatically new range of timbres. Jazz, though long familiar with technological advances, struggled to keep up with the rapid changes, especially as they affected the process of making records. Rock musicians depended far more on the studio than on live performance—initially, in some cases, to compensate for weak-voiced singers. But technology turned the studio into a wonderland of possibilities. Multitracking opened the way to startling sonic landscapes. A handful of artists like the Beatles and Brian Wilson of the Beach Boys broke down the barriers keeping rock musicians out of the engineer's booth, and made studio production part of their creative process. Jazz musicians had made efforts to master editing, but remained trapped in the belief that recordings should transparently demonstrate what a band sounds like in person.

To the degree that early rock and roll grew out of rhythm and blues, it employed loose rhythms similar to jazz—as Chuck Berry's "Rock and Roll Music" declared, "It's got a backbeat, you can't lose it." Countless rock and roll records of the 1950s used jazz drummers, most frequently the swing veteran Panama Francis and the bop veteran Connie Kay. But by the 1960s, the rock groove had shifted away from swing toward a steady, pounding, even-eighth-note 4/4. Jazz musicians who had grown up on the more flexible patterns of uneven eighth notes found it hard to adjust, frequently refusing to do so for aesthetic reasons.

Another change involved the emphasis on bands that submerged individual musicians into a collective sound, not unlike the ballroom dance bands and early New Orleans ensembles. The loose combos of modern jazz focused on the contribution of each musician—not only soloists, but the interactive spontaneity of rhythm players. By bebop standards, it would take a revolution in thought for jazz to return to a group-oriented aesthetic. Yet this happened twice in the 1960s: in the avant-garde at the beginning of the decade, and in fusion at the end of the decade. In the area of virtuoso musicianship, however, it was rock that had to change to meet jazz standards. Virtually every respectable jazz musician was capable of instrumental feats far beyond the norm. Rock had little patience with that kind of technique. Through the "do-it-yourself" ethos of the folk or blues revival and the naive primitivism of the teenage garage band, rock shifted attention toward other qualities—the band, the song, the singer. Not until rock moved toward instrumental virtuosity, in the work of players like Hendrix and Clapton, would jazz musicians find a place at its table.

Ultimately, the fusion of the late 1960s was designed to meet each of these obstacles. It was electronic music, created in a studio by younger musicians, often in groups; it fused a strong dance-beat rhythm with a modified cult of jazz virtuosity. The vocabulary that allowed jazz musicians to create this fusion came not from mainstream rock but from a different source: the contemporary version of race music, generally known as soul or funk.

Although soul music dated back to the 1950s, when Ray Charles redefined black music by dragging religious grooves into the secular marketplace, and instrumentalists like Horace Silver and Jimmy Smith emphasized backbeat rhythms, a new and more intense kind of funk was born in the pop world. Specifically, it was the revolutionary music created by James Brown when he entered the national spotlight in 1965 with crossover hits like "I Got You (I Feel Good)" and "Papa's Got a Brand New Bag." Brown felt it first in the recording studio: "I had discovered that my strength was not in the horns, it was in the rhythm. I was hearing everything, even the guitars, like they were drums. On playbacks, when I saw the speakers jumping, vibrating a certain way, I knew that was it." Brown spawned an entire section of black pop, infusing it with an African polyrhythmic intensity.

Funk used rhythmic contrast in innovative ways. Unlike rock, where the 4/4 rhythmic groove dominated the texture, each layer in a funk or soul tune was independent rhythmically, allowing greater possibilities for inventive bassists, guitarists, and drummers to offer fresh support. Jazz drummers interested in this music had to learn to switch from a swing feeling to a new funk groove—but the best of them understood that there was freedom as well as responsibility in this way of playing. Bassists shifted from walking-bass lines to more asymmetric, syncopated lines. Soloists understood that their phrases were only one part of the overall texture, contributing to but not dominating the groove.

Funk offered an opportunity for jazz musicians to continue to draw on their mastery of chromatic harmony. Unlike rock, which often reduced its chords to their most basic forms, funk was harmonically sophisticated, supporting denser, jazz-oriented harmonies and opening the door for chromatically based semi-atonal sounds, including modal improvisation. In

James Brown's hands, a funk tune was flexible and open-ended, typically featuring lengthy stretches on a single harmony. The band would move to a contrasting bridge only on a cue from the vocalist. Funk was a new dance groove, based like rock on the steady eighth note. Young people could relate to it—as could young musicians eager to find a way to link jazz to the dance music of their generation. This dance groove was not opposed to harmonic improvisation: one of the most surprising and stimulating things fusion musicians discovered is that a steady beat was enough to hold their audience even when they ventured into extremely dissonant harmonies.

By 1967, jazz was in a state of crisis. Coltrane had died, leaving the free jazz movement without its most charismatic leader. The music was losing its audience, as nightclubs began closing and concerts drying up. Critics had started to take rock artists seriously, lifting the Beatles to new heights (with the Rolling Stones as a scruffy alternative). Even *Down Beat*, which had become the leading trade magazine for modern jazz, remembered its roots in swing and pop and started featuring articles on rock. Seeing the writing on the wall, young jazz musicians started forming groups, like the Free Spirits and the 13th-Floor Elevators, that had the look and feel of rock bands. Something needed to be done to bridge the gap between jazz and pop. "Everybody was dropping acid and the prevailing attitude was 'Let's do something different,'" recalled guitarist Larry Coryell. "We were saying, 'We love Wes, but we also love Bob Dylan. We love Coltrane but we also love the Beatles. We love Miles but we also love the Rolling Stones.'"

The first groups to begin to break down the barriers found opportunities in the California jam-band scene. John Handy, the former alto saxophonist with Charles Mingus, hooked up with electric violinist Michael White and released an album of extended improvisations recorded at the 1965 Monterey Jazz Festival that enjoyed formidable sales. More successful was Charles Lloyd, a Coltrane-influenced tenor saxophonist who had worked with cool jazz drummer Chico Hamilton and soul jazz star Cannonball Adderley. Born in 1938, Lloyd moved from Memphis to Los Angeles to study composition at the University of Southern California, and became known as a skillful arranger. He formed his own group in 1965, and, under the shrewd management of George Avakian, landed a prominent spot at the 1966 Monterey Jazz Festival, where his music was suddenly labeled "psychedelic jazz"—an idea Lloyd was only too happy to play up ("I play love vibrations," he told the press). Lloyd's quartet did not sound strikingly different from other jazz bands of the time, though it had a killer rhythm section with the then-unknown pianist Keith Jarrett and drummer Jack DeJohnette. Lloyd benefited from the loose cultural boundaries on the San Francisco scene, where jazz drifted into a melting pot with many kinds of music. On radio, he later recalled, "They would play my music alongside Jimi Hendrix or the Grateful Dead, or Ravi Shankar. . . . All the San Francisco groups loved our music." On one San Francisco gig in 1966, Elvin Jones and the Joe Henderson Quartet appeared on the same stage as Jimi Hendrix, Big Mama Thornton, and the Jefferson Airplane.

In 1968, Tony Williams, the dazzling drummer who had recently left the Miles Davis Quintet, formed the groundbreaking trio Emergency, with the electric guitarist John McLaughlin, whom he brought over from the U.K., and organist Larry Young. The band sought to revive the spirit of Williams's organ trio roots in Boston in the early 1960s, but with a sonically forceful edge. As an organ trio playing electric music, it was caustic, hard-driving, dissonant, and given to extended improvisations. The group lasted only a few years, producing a handful of exciting but uneven records that failed to capture the band's intensity in live performance. Still, they pointed the way toward a style of group improvisation that would form the basis for fusion. Williams, who joined Davis's band at seventeen, had grown up in the rock era and felt he was connecting with his own generation. More surprising fusion pioneers were Gil Evans and Sun Ra, who at fifty-seven and fifty-five respectively, began using synthesizers and other electric instruments in 1969. Evans made a challenging record that year, fusing his orchestral style with rock rhythms and colors, but because it was for a one-shot label, few people heard it—yet it signaled a switch in his thinking that would dominate the music he played for the rest of his life.

MILES AHEAD: THE BREAKTHROUGH

The true insurrection of fusion happened only when it captured the attention of the biggest name in jazz—Miles Davis. In 1968, Davis, an old man by baby boomer standards (forty-two), expressed dissatisfaction with the direction taken by his postbop quintet, and by his steadily decreasing record sales, a situation his label harped on. At the same time, a change in his personal life inclined him to take a closer look at youth culture. His young wife, Betty Mabry, had studied fashion design and worked as a model for youth-oriented magazines like *Jet* and *Seventeen*. Mabry understood the new look and embodied it with her outsized Afro and miniskirts; one musician remembered her as "walking eye-candy." She was also a musician who wrote pop arrangements, occasionally sang, and counted Jimi Hendrix and Sly Stone among her friends. A reviewer who came to the Davis apartment was startled to find piled on the coffee table albums by the Fifth Dimension, which had just had a hit with "Up, Up, and Away," and the daring funk group Sly and the Family Stone.

Davis had been searching for something to rescue him from the tired routines of modern jazz. He thought he heard it in the music of Chicago's preeminent bluesman, Muddy Waters, which offered the power of basics in "the $1.50 drums and the harmonicas and the two-chord blues. . . . I had to get back to that now because what we had been doing was just getting really abstracted." Rock put that kind of simplicity back into the spotlight, and Davis wanted a piece of it. He began changing the instrumentation of his group, pushing his rhythm section to go electric. Ron Carter didn't like the electric bass, so Davis replaced him with a young British player, Dave Holland. Electric music was in the air: Cannonball Adderley had introduced Joe Zawinul's electric piano (borrowed in turn from Ray Charles). Davis similarly put a Fender Rhodes in front of Herbie Hancock for a series of loosely conceived recording sessions. When Hancock failed to return on time from a honeymoon in Brazil, he hired Chick Corea as his replacement at one of those sessions. He also brought in Gil Evans to help arrange the music and forestall imminent chaos.

These experiments produced the 1968 *Filles de Kilimanjaro,* a scintillating yet deliberately repetitive blend of modal jazz and abstracted soul rhythm, with the harmonies floating over ostinato bass lines. Tony Williams's drum parts don't sound like rock, but they are clearly influenced by it, and provide a firm foundation for the shifting bass riffs that underscore most of the pieces. Davis realized that by maintaining a steady beat, Williams could hold together complicated textures, retaining the sought-for simplicity no matter how dense and complicated the harmonies became. "Mademoiselle Mabry" is based in part on Jimi Hendrix's "The Wind Cried Mary." On the jacket, above the title *Filles de Kilimanjaro,* in tiny letters, Davis insisted on the legend "Directions in music by Miles Davis," making it clear that his music could no longer be contained by a single idiom. In case anyone missed the point, he told an interviewer that calling his music jazz was "old fashioned"—"like calling me colored."

More dramatic changes came with his next album, *In a Silent Way.* Among the musicians at this session was John McLaughlin, who added the crucial missing ingredient to the jazz-rock mix: the distorted sound of electric guitar. On the title track, Davis drastically pared down a tune by

Joe Zawinul; in place of Zawinul's carefully crafted harmonic progression, Davis asked McLaughlin to play an E major chord, the most basic sound on the guitar. The musicians thought it was a rehearsal, but Davis and his producer, Teo Macero, kept the tapes running, and the musicians' spontaneous interaction over this static harmonic background became part of the finished album.

Increasingly, Davis came to rely on studio post-production. This was hardly new to jazz, but Davis took full advantage of the new technologies firmly in place at Columbia Records. Whatever happened in the studio was now raw material for future editing. In Macero, Davis had a producer who did for him what the producer George Martin did for the Beatles. At day's end, Macero cut and spliced the session tapes into new patterns: "I had *carte blanche* to work with the material," he later said. "Shhh/Peaceful" was stitched together from hours of performing, interwoven into shapes that underscored and made coherent the drama at the largely improvised sessions. Davis's musicians were often surprised and pleased to hear how their work was ultimately combined and recombined. The overall effect sacrificed the purposeful intensity of earlier jazz for a deeper sense of groove. *In a Silent Way* consisted of two long tracks, each taking up a full side of the LP, a startling change for a jazz stalwart. As Davis acknowledged in an interview, "This one will scare the shit out of them."

Scarier stuff was to follow. Davis's leadership was sparse and intermittent, leaving plenty of room for his musicians. "He'd go out and play, and you'd follow," said Chick Corea. "Whenever he'd stop playing, he never told the group what to do, so we all went and did whatever." Earlier in the 1960s, his rhythm section had learned to take advantage of what they called Davis's "controlled freedom." By the end of the decade, Davis was gathering much larger groups of musicians: two drummers, two bassists, two percussionists, a bass clarinet, an electric guitar, and the three electric keyboards of Hancock, Corea, and Zawinul. The texture was dense but light: while the musicians "had egos," Zawinul remembered, their respect for each other meant that "nobody stepped on anybody's feet." The musicians were a full generation younger than Davis and often looked the part, sporting casual hippie clothing and long hair. Yet Davis justly insisted that his music drew less from conventional rock than from the new currents in African American music: "I don't play rock, I play *black*." During this time, Miles remained under contract to Columbia Records, which kept a few major jazz and classical stars for their cultural capital, even as the label as a whole moved solidly toward rock. When a Columbia executive complained of his static sales, Davis retorted, "If you stop calling me a *jazz* man, I'll sell more." He proved his point with his next album, *Bitches Brew.*

Bitches Brew, recorded at three sessions in 1969 and released the following year, looked and sounded nothing like a typical jazz album. "It was loose and tight at the same time," said Davis. "Everybody was alert to different possibilities that were coming up in the music." Some of the tunes came from his then-current band's repertory, but others took shape only after the fact through ingenious editing. Because each song was long—the title track lasted twenty-seven minutes—*Bitches Brew* was a sprawling double album, decorated with an elaborate drawing by the Israeli artist Mati Klarwein. No one in their right mind would have considered it a commercial product: it was dissonant, texturally dense, and radio-unfriendly (although "Spanish Key" was released, in highly abbreviated form, as a single). Nevertheless, *Bitches Brew* found a niche in the new album-oriented rock of the day, selling a half million copies during its first year. Davis never looked back. Neither did the music industry, which now loudly trumpeted the new category, marketed in the record store as "Fusion."

Mahavishnu, Return to Forever, AND Weather Report

Bitches Brew may have been the revolutionary album that launched fusion, but it could not serve as a model for other musicians. It was too idiosyncratic and too reliant on the unmistakable sound of Miles Davis's trumpet. Instead, fusion as a style found its template in the intense yet disciplined electric-guitar sound of the Mahavishnu Orchestra, the creation of John McLaughlin (b. 1942), an English guitarist from Yorkshire. Like many young guitarists of the period, he was inspired by the playing of American blues musicians such as Muddy Waters and Lead Belly. But McLaughlin also mastered aspects of flamenco guitar, which showed him how the blues could be linked to blindingly fast passagework and constantly shifting cross-rhythms. Records by Django Reinhardt and Tal Farlow inspired him toward becoming a jazz musician; but he retained openness to music of all kinds—including 1960s rock. Working with the influential Graham Bond Organization, he interacted with future Cream members Ginger Baker and Jack Bruce. At the same time, he recorded an album with avant-garde jazz players, drummer Tony Oxley (who later worked extensively with Cecil Taylor) and saxophonist John Surman.

An invitation from Tony Williams brought McLaughlin to New York in 1969. After a year of playing with Williams and Miles, he was ready to strike out on his own. Fascinated by Eastern religion, McLaughlin studied the teachings of Sri Chinmoy, an Indian "New Age" guru who also counted rock guitarist Carlos Santana among his disciples. As a result, he immersed himself in Indian classical music, which offered the improviser a bewildering variety of unusual meters, or *tala*. Chinmoy suggested that McLaughlin call his band Mahavishnu Orchestra. By 1970, fusion was hot, and Mahavishnu was signed by Columbia Records to a large advance. The band's first two albums, *The Inner Mounting Flame* (1972) and *Birds of Fire* (1973), sold 700,000 copies—proof that a so-called jazz band could compete in the same commercial league as the rock bands.

Mahavishnu Orchestra was an ideal band for the times. It played loud, fast, intensely distorted music, better suited to concert dates with ZZ Top and Emerson, Lake and Palmer than to the confined quarters of a jazz club. McLaughlin was out in front, playing an electric guitar with two necks— one with six strings, the other with twelve. With lengthy solos, played at sledgehammer volume, McLaughlin raised the level of virtuosity associated with rock guitarists like Hendrix to a new level. Yet he was also part of a band. A typical Mahavishnu tune featured McLaughlin playing seamlessly alongside the amplified violin of Jerry Goodman, the electric keyboard of Jan Hammer (who had to be convinced that a jazz group wouldn't damage his reputation), and drummer Billy Cobham, a powerhouse who, like McLaughlin, had recently worked with Miles.

Although one observer compared Mahavishnu to "a car that could only function at 100 miles per hour," the group's inventiveness was undeniable. Its reliance on *talas* produced rhythmic groupings reminiscent of Dave Brubeck—five, seven, or nine—but could be more complicated: "Birds of Fire" asks the musicians to improvise in a meter of eighteen, while "The Dance of Maya" somehow squeezes a hard-driving boogie-woogie into a meter of twenty. Harmonically, the band played chords that had little in common with the harmonies of popular song, including slash chords— triads sitting precariously on top of completely unrelated bass roots. (The term reflects fake-book notation: an E major triad over a C bass is shown as E/C, pronounced "E slash C.") These chords aren't atonal—the triads offer points of stability—but they propel harmony into greater realms of dissonance. Mahavishnu's music relished such harmonically tricky combinations.

Looking for a band that would prove artistically satisfying and commercially successful, Chick Corea (b. 1941) was among the most influential musicians to adopt the Mahavishnu Orchestra's approach as a prototype to enter fusion. Before that, he had proved himself an uncommonly gifted acoustic jazz player. Born in Boston, Corea studied jazz by transcribing the harmonic voicings of Horace Silver and learning to play Bud Powell's solos. He had broad tastes and could fit into any setting. His first important job was with Mongo Santamaria; within the next few years, he toured with Sarah Vaughan, recorded with Stan Getz, and piloted his own adventurous recordings, before taking Hancock's place with Davis. In 1968, Corea recorded the classic trio album *Now He Sings, Now He Sobs*, which, much to his vexation, is still regarded as his finest work by musicians who studied his playing on it as assiduously as he had studied Bud Powell's.

For all his mastery of bop, Corea was also drawn to free improvisation. Shortly after leaving Davis in 1970, he joined with saxophonist Anthony Braxton and bassist Dave Holland in Circle, an avant-garde group that recorded six albums in one year. Then, just as suddenly, he found this kind of improvisation alienating. "It was like group therapy, just getting together and letting our hair down," he said later. "Everybody yelled and screamed. Then after a while nobody cared." Religion forced a change in his attitude. After seeking help in Scientology, he formed the first of his groups known as Return to Forever in 1972. This band dabbled in fusion, mixing the Brazilian stylings of vocalist Flora Purim and her husband, the percussionist Airto Moreira, with Corea's electric piano and the mainstream saxophone and flute playing of Joe Farrell. Within a few years, though, after hearing Mahavishnu, Corea reconsidered his goals. "More than my experience with Miles," he recalled, "John's band led me to want to turn the volume up and write music that was more dramatic and made your hair move." Jan Hammer's use of the synthesizer as a fluid, singing solo voice inspired him to take up an entire rack of synthesizers. To capture McLaughlin's lead, he hired guitarist Bill Connors, who was replaced a year later by Al DiMeola, a pyrotechnic soloist who once proclaimed that his goal was "to be the fastest guitarist in the world." Corea continued to call his group Return to Forever, but by the mid-1970s, it was a vehicle for Corea's disciplined compositions in the context of Mahavishnu's crowd-pleasing volume and intensity.

The most artistically and commercially successful fusion group of the 1970s was Weather Report, yet another band with roots in the Miles Davis experience: its founders, Joe Zawinul (albeit briefly) and Wayne Shorter, were 1960s Davis sidemen. Shorter's previous experience had been almost exclusively with acoustic jazz—with Art Blakey and Davis, and on his own much-admired series of ten Blue Note albums. While other fusion bands came and went, Zawinul and Shorter's partnership lasted uninterrupted for a decade and a half, evolving from its loose, experimental playing in the early 1970s to a propulsive funk in the 1980s, topping the charts, selling out stadiums, and maintaining for most of its tenure the support of the critics. Yet Shorter's role in the group was controversial. He continued to write melodically elliptical and harmonically inventive compositions, but some listeners felt that the band's opulent textures submerged his solo voice. Jack DeJohnette summed up that attitude in one of his tunes, "Where or Wayne."

The dominant force in the group was Zawinul, who grew up in Austria, where he had survived the war in countryside music camps that sheltered talented youngsters. There he experimented with his first instrument, the accordion, by gluing felt onto the soundboard, creating a pungent nasal timbre that prefigured his later synthesizer style. He came to America in 1959, on a scholarship from the Berklee College of Music in Boston, and had no trouble finding work, touring with the Maynard Ferguson big band, accompanying singer Dinah Washington, recording with Ben Webster, and becoming an unlikely member of the Cannonball Adderley quintet, which was largely associated with soul jazz. For the next decade, he was the only white musician in the group—a mutual decision that reflected Adderley's conviction that he played "black," and Zawinul's love of black music and entertainment, cultivated in Austria as he watched, over and over, movies like the 1942 *Stormy Weather* (featuring Bill "Bojangles" Robinson, Lena Horne, Cab Calloway, Fats Waller, and the amazing dance team the Nicholas Brothers). "To me," he later said, African Americans "are the easiest to understand, the closest to my environment."

Weather Report became a laboratory for new sounds made possible by technology. Inspired by Ray Charles, Zawinul took up electric piano in the mid-1960s, and made it pay off handsomely when he used it to compose and perform Adderley's biggest hit, "Mercy, Mercy, Mercy." He soon mastered the synthesizer, using it extensively on Weather Report's third album, *Sweetnighter*. But he despised the preset sounds on his instruments, and burrowed deep into the equipment to create his own timbres, sometimes detuning the intervals to mimic non-Western instruments. Taking charge of the ARP 2600 even required him to play "backward," using an inverted keyboard with the top notes starting on the left-hand side.

Over time, Weather Report moved from expansive jazz improvisations toward straight-ahead Afro-pop rhythmic grooves. "We were a black band," Zawinul explained. "In spite of me not being black, it was always a black band, more or less." The albums became funkier: the title track on *Black Market* (1975) is a percussive, riff-based tune that rolls along on its syncopated, pentatonic bass line. But the band did not find its center of gravity until it drafted a new member. Zawinul was standing outside Miami's Gusman Theater when a youthful-looking twenty-three-year-old walked up and introduced himself: "My name is John Francis Pastorius III, and I am the greatest bass player in the world." Zawinul replied, "Get the fuck out of here!" But a year later, after he heard Jaco Pastorius's first album and Weather Report's bassist Alphonso Johnson decided to leave, Zawinul arranged an audition for him.

Jaco was the first jazz bassist who did not play acoustic. He was born the same year as the electric bass (1951), which for two decades had been used primarily in small dance bands—a poor relation to its delicate and expensive acoustic cousin. Musicians put up with its muddy sound only because they could easily increase the volume with a knob. But they soon found a way to make the instrument speak: James Jamerson used his electric bass to create the lively, dancing figures that energized dozens of Motown hits in the 1960s. Pastorius's virtuosity showed that the same creative intensity could be applied to jazz. He grew up in Fort Lauderdale, Florida, where he learned his craft in local rhythm and blues bands. He loved electric bass, creating his own version with the frets removed (the holes sealed with wood filler), flying over the soundboard with extraordinary speed. By manipulating the controls on his amplifier, he developed a rich, singing sound: "that ballad voice," Zawinul called it. His skills astonished the jazz community. On his first album, *Jaco Pastorius,* he sealed his claim on the jazz tradition by playing an unaccompanied version of the bebop standard "Donna Lee," a notoriously difficult piece even for its composer, Miles Davis, who wrote it for Charlie Parker.

Pastorius became Weather Report's "warhead," grounding its rhythm section while playing fluid melodic lines one might normally expect from a guitarist. (In concert, he played feedback solos à la Hendrix.) "Jaco . . . brought the white kids in," Zawinul remembered. "He was all of a sudden a real white All-American folk hero." Tragically, his fall was as steep as his climb. A few years after joining Weather Report, he surrendered to drugs, almost daring himself to perform his convoluted solos in states of extreme intoxication. He left the group in 1982, and was soon living on the streets. In 1987, he was beaten by a bouncer as he tried to break into a nightclub in his hometown of Fort Lauderdale. He never recovered from his injuries, and died a week later at thirty-five. Yet with Jaco as its foundation, Weather Report had reached its commercial and some would say artistic zenith, especially with the 1976 album *Heavy Weather*, featuring Zawinul's catchy "Birdland," a tribute to the jazz club named after Parker. Although its overall texture is driving funk, it evokes a genial, big-band feeling in its refrain. Zawinul's compositional skill is evident throughout: the piece is built on the most basic musical elements, the G major scale and the G blues scale, but in a way that leaves us hanging until the climactic refrain brings us home.

"TEEN TOWN"

Named after a neighborhood in Miami, "Teen Town" is a Pastorius showcase. He plays two roles: the electric bass soloist and the substitute drummer. The tune features a peculiar chord progression, cycling through four major triads. The chords are simple but ambiguous: no one key can contain them all. Over this shifting background, Pastorius plays a melody line that snakes its way through different rhythms with unexpected accents. It sounds improvised but is composed, as becomes clear when it begins to repeat. Still, there are moments when Pastorius the improviser trumps Pastorius the composer, adjusting his line to the heat of performance. While Pastorius is clearly in front, the tune also works as a dialogue—sometimes with Shorter, who plays brief solos that hint at his remarkable melodic invention, but more often with Zawinul. By the end of the performance, the dialogue is wide open. In live performance, Weather Report would extend this last section, allowing room for Shorter and Zawinul to trade melodic and harmonic ideas with Pastorius before the final lick closed the tune off.

TEEN TOWN

Weather Report

Joe Zawinul, Fender Rhodes piano, melodica, Oberheim polyphonic synthesizer, ARP 2600; Wayne Shorter, soprano saxophone; Jaco Pastorius, electric bass, drums; Manolo Badrena, congas

LABEL: *Heavy Weather,* Columbia CK 65108; *X2 (Heavy Weather/Black Market)*
(Columbia/Legacy 886973301128)
DATE: 1976
STYLE: fusion
FORM: eight-measure cycle

Introduction

0:00   A series of rapid-fire snare drum hits opens the tune.

0:01   Shorter on soprano saxophone and Zawinul on synthesizer play the
         melody harmonized in thirds (Zawinul on top, Shorter below). Behind
         them, the drummer begins a rapid, steady pattern, with high-hat cym-
         bal accents on the backbeat and the snare falling on the third beat of
         the measure. Distantly in the background, the percussionist adds Latin
         rhythms.

0:03   The drummer punctuates the space in between melody phrases with
         loud bass drum accents.

Chorus 1

0:08   An accented pair of high notes announces the first chorus. Pastorius
         begins a lightning-fast line on electric bass, accompanied by the synthe-
         sizer. The chords in the background are major triads from different keys:
         each new chord cancels out the previous one.

Chorus 2

0:16   The chords begin to repeat, establishing an eight-bar cycle. Pastorius
         continues his line, changing the rhythm and pitches.

Chorus 3

0:23   Pastorius's line bridges the boundary between one chorus and the next.
         Underneath, Shorter emerges from the background with long-held
         saxophone notes.

0:27   Pastorius's line rises in volume and pitch.

0:29   A short bluesy phrase is followed by bass drum accents.

Chorus 4

0:31   On this chorus, Pastorius plays the pair of accented high notes, this time
         doubled by the drums.

0:34   His line becomes intensely syncopated. In its wake, the drummer
         answers with his own snare drum and bass drum accents.

0:38   Pastorius plays the repeated high notes again, linking them to a longer
         melody line.

Chorus 5

0:39   Pastorius repeats the line from the first chorus note for note, making it
         clear that the solo is a composed piece, not an improvisation.

0:41   The first phrase is answered by short decorative passages by Shorter.

0:45   After the next phrase, the drummer lays a loud bass drum accent right on the downbeat.

Chorus 6

0:46   Pastorius repeats the line from the second chorus.

0:49   The end of his line is doubled by sharp snare drum accents.

Chorus 7

0:53   Pastorius's line disappears, replaced by the synthesizer. Unlike Pastorius's rapid-fire solo, it's slow, drawing attention to the increasingly dissonant synthesizer chords behind.

0:59   Pastorius reenters.

Chorus 8

1:01   After playing only a single phrase, Pastorius drops out again. In the absence of melodic activity, the bass and snare drums add syncopated fills.

Interlude (introduction)

1:08   Zawinul and Shorter play the introductory melody again, this time with the synthesizer on a softer and more resonant timbre.

1:23   At the end of the second phrase, the harmony suddenly shifts into a new direction: the piece has modulated to a new key.

Chorus 9

1:24   Doubled by synthesizer, the bass plays a mighty ascending line. Each phrase is answered by a loud "boom" from the drums.

Chorus 10

1:31   Over the bass line, the synthesizer adds a slow line that rises chromatically.

Chorus 11

1:39   The synthesizer line rises until it disappears into the upper range. The background chords, now played by an ethereal electric piano, become more extended and dissonant.

Chorus 12

1:47   Shorter plays a few tentative notes on saxophone before retreating to silence. In his absence, the drummer fills in with syncopated accents.

Chorus 13

1:54   The chord progression is doubled by a slow synthesizer line.

Chorus 14

| 2:02 | Pastorius begins improvising in the style of the opening chorus. His line is dissonant against the background chords. |

Chorus 15

2:09	Pastorius begins with the phrase that opened the fifth chorus, but sends it off into an unexpected direction.
2:13	Shorter sneaks in with a descending line.
2:16	Pastorius ends the chorus with a closing phrase: a rhythmically catchy lick using just two notes.

Chorus 16

| 2:17 | The texture thins out. It becomes easier to hear the conga drums improvising alongside the drumming. |
| 2:23 | Pastorius repeats the closing phrase from the end of the last chorus. |

Chorus 17

| 2:24 | Shorter plays another short solo. |
| 2:30 | Pastorius repeats the closing phrase. |

Coda

2:31	The harmony suddenly comes to a stop on a sustained chord. The drumming continues.
2:38	The drummer adds ferocious bass drum accents, culminating in a cymbal crash.
2:40	The sound of the drummer becomes distant, as if heard from far away.
2:42	The synthesizer enters with the opening of the introduction.
2:46	The harmony shifts in unexpected directions. The final chord is heard over the accented pair of high notes.

CHAMELEONS: Herbie Hancock (B. 1940) AND Keith Jarrett (B. 1945)

One of the ironies of the 1970s is that two of its most popular jazz stars were extraordinarily sophisticated musicians who found success by creating sounds of disarming simplicity. If this approach recalls Count Basie's achievement in the 1930s, the comparison is not inapt. Basie reduced the mechanics of stride piano to emphasize rhythm, economy, and space. Herbie Hancock and Keith Jarrett put their own virtuosity on hold with similar goals in mind. During his years with Miles Davis, Hancock established himself as a postbop composer of subtlety and captivating complexity, while also showing a talent for writing tunes built on funky vamps, like "Watermelon Man" and "Cantaloupe Island." Yet by the early 1970s, under the name Headhunters, he created a far more elemental mixture of funk and jazz that consisted of little more than syncopated bass lines repeated and extended ad infinitum. He once observed: "We jazz listeners tend, 90% of the time, to like clever, complex treatments of simple ideas. That's what we respect. . . . But what I found out is that . . . there's a much more subtle kind of challenge in going towards the simple." Jarrett seemed even less likely to break through with the public—he despised rock and rejected its electronic paraphernalia ("I can get toys in a toy shop"), preferring to play his unamplified acoustic piano in hushed silence. Yet his biggest-selling album, *The Köln Concert*, mesmerized listeners with extended repetitions of gospel grooves and ostinatos.

The title of Hancock's most lucrative recording, "Chameleon," indicates his career-long ability to adapt to new surroundings in an instant. Hancock has balanced several careers simultaneously, sustaining his reputation as a superb modern jazz pianist while also composing film scores and achieving stardom as a pop star in 1970s funk, 1980s hip-hop, and diverse collaborations with performers like Sting, Christina Aguilera, Josh Groban, and Norah Jones. In concert, he will play a Steinway grand and then switch to a "keytar" (a keyboard he slings around his neck like a guitar), playing acoustic jazz as well as contemporary R&B. Widely respected, he refuses to be pinned down. His 2007 album *River: The Joni Letters*, an inventive interpretation of songs by Joni Mitchell (and a couple by Wayne Shorter and Duke Ellington), was the first jazz recording to win the Grammy Award as album of the year since the 1964 *Getz / Gilberto*.

Born in Chicago, Hancock grew up playing classical music well enough to win a competition at age eleven, leading to a performance of a Mozart concerto with the Chicago Symphony. He also played rhythm and blues and turned toward jazz, listening to Bill Evans and Oscar Peterson and learning to play in a bluesy style by "clinically," as he put it, replaying their recordings. Still, he entered Iowa's Grinnell College with the idea of majoring in engineering—and dropped out when trumpet player Donald Byrd offered him a chance to tour with his band. By this time, he had developed an extraordinary ear for harmony: how to voice it to emphasize his expressive needs, how to work it into every fabric of his compositions. As soon as he arrived in New York, in 1961, Hancock found work with master musicians ranging from Coleman Hawkins to Eric Dolphy. He made his first album as a leader, *Takin' Off*, in 1962, with Dexter Gordon as a sideman and "Watermelon Man" as its lead track. That piece, which had already been popularized by Mongo Santamaria, evoked for Hancock the vendors on Chicago's summer streets, but its title entailed a risk: thanks to minstrel shows, watermelon symbolized decades of racist stereotypes as the favorite, often purloined fruit of plantation "darkies." Hancock remembered, "I looked at myself in the mirror. 'Now wait a minute, man. You are projecting something from the black experience, tell what the thing is. What are you ashamed of?'" His follow-up albums, especially *Maiden Voyage*, with its title track suspended on cool ambiguous harmonies and the innovative use of slash chords on "Dolphin Dance," appealed to jazz fans of every stripe and became texts for study by countless young musicians.

Once the rock revolution was underway, Hancock found new uses for the electrical engineering he had studied as an undergraduate. After leaving Davis in 1970, he formed a highly experimental group, combining his complex postbop jazz impulses with textures created by an array of synthesizers (helped out by electronics wizard Patrick Gleeson). This was an exciting band for him, one in which everyone had adopted an African name: bass clarinetist Bennie Maupin was Mwile, trumpeter Eddie Henderson was Mganga, and Hancock was Mwandishi—Swahili for composer. The group struggled, though, and Hancock began to feel he had made a mistake. He was now practicing Nichiren Shoshu Buddhism and chanting daily. Through his meditations, he came to realize he had been a "jazz snob." The music he *really* admired was the heightened funk of James Brown, Sly and the Family Stone, and Tower of Power. "I decided that it was now time to try some funky stuff myself and get me some cats who could play that kind of music."

Hancock recast his band as the Headhunters, finding new musicians with little jazz experience but with a background in funk: the drummer Harvey Mason, who could improvise expertly within a strong funk groove; Paul Jackson, a master of syncopated bass lines; and percussionist Bill Summers, who brought with him an education in the traditional West African music he had studied at the University of California in Berkeley. The music on their 1974 album of similar name spoke a new language: beguiling (or tedious, depending on your taste) in its simplicity, yet intensely polyrhythmic. The big hit, "Chameleon," was little more than a bass line locked into a steady clave rhythm that cycled back and forth between two chords. On this foundation, Hancock added layer upon layer, recreating the web of sounds that energized a James Brown recording, using electronic keyboards instead of guitars. Although the piece lasts fifteen minutes—shifting midway to a different bass ostinato that allows Hancock to explore subtler harmonizations—it was the minimalism of the piece that won him a mass audience.

Some people disliked *Head Hunters*, feeling that in trying to combine jazz and funk, Hancock was doing neither. "I don't even think this is well-done funk," Lester Bowie complained in a Blindfold Test in 1979. "They were basically jazz cats—they don't know nothing about funk, that's why they sound so funny. They ain't been on the road up and down doing that stuff. . . . It's beat-your-head-into-the-concrete type music." Hancock was hurt by this criticism, but not by the distinction between jazz and funk. "Some of the dance music I do," he once said, "is not done for art." When he balanced his inventive complexity with the demands of straightforward funk, the results could be illuminating. Albums like *Thrust* (1974) and *Man-Child* (1975) wove a jazz sensibility into modern funk grooves. But not every album worked. Hancock's disco efforts in the late 1970s were marred by excessive repetition, as Hancock conceded: "We thought it would be hypnotic rather than monotonous." His work in that period was not helped by the Vocoder, a device invented by Wendy Carlos and Walter Moog that transformed his spoken voice into an electronically modified keyboard sound.

He rebounded quickly enough: in the early 1980s, in Los Angeles, Hancock listened to tapes sent to him by Bill Laswell and Michael Beinhorn, then working with the Brooklyn hip-hop group Material, which used the scratching sounds of the turntablist Grand Mixer DXT. Intrigued, Hancock added his own melody on top. The result, "Rockit" (1983), emerged as an underground success and an MTV video—with robots banging their heads in time to the music. Typically, he toured that same year with an acoustic jazz quartet featuring the young Wynton Marsalis. Hancock has gone back and forth between jazz and pop, and mergers of the two, ever since.

Keith Jarrett is a no less idiosyncratic musician, but in a different way. He grunts and yowls when he improvises, and his body—despite the perfect balance his hands maintain on the keyboard—seems possessed, gyrating and twisting, rising off the bench or kneeling below it. His fans debate as to whether this is show business or genuine musical possession. But even his fans can be less tolerant of his boorish behavior in concert, interrupting performances to berate audiences for inattention, coughing, latecoming, and, in stadium settings, photography. At one outdoor event, he launched into a lecture declaring that music is fluid and that still photographs are antithetical to that. Someone shouted, "Is it okay, then, to use a camcorder?" He stormed off the stage, but soon returned. Audiences have come to expect such outbursts, and his longtime trio partners—bassist Gary Peacock and drummer Jack DeJohnette—stand or sit mutely by as they run their course. Nevertheless, Jarrett has built and sustained a wide following because he is one of the most resourceful and exciting pianists in jazz.

Jarrett was born in Allentown, Pennsylvania, and, like Hancock, emerged as a musical prodigy with classical training. Along the way he learned to improvise, a skill that earned him a spot at the Berklee College of Music. After a brief stint in Art Blakey's Jazz Messengers, he played in the Charles Lloyd Quartet, where his extravagant, gospel-tinged improvisations caught public attention. For a few years, he survived a stint with Miles Davis, a remarkable feat for someone who thought fusion was a mistake. "The main reason I joined the band was that I didn't *like* the band," he explained. "I liked what Miles was playing very much and I hated the rest of the band playing together." He tolerated electric pianos out of a desire to help Davis achieve his artistic goals, later writing about the recordings the band made at the Cellar Door, in Washington, D.C.: "You don't usually see this kind of comet go by more than once or twice in a lifetime."

Jarrett's best-known music is restricted to the piano. His improvisations range from the quietly meditative to the blindingly aggressive, but almost always reflect a powerful melodic sensibility. His 1970s recitals were known not least for their marathon length: a series recorded in Japan, *The Sun Bear Concerts*, stretched out to ten LPs. More famous and more accessible is *The Köln Concert* (1975), a double LP that, having sold more than 4 million copies, ranks among the top-selling jazz albums of all time. According to Jarrett, everything about the concert was wrong: "It was the wrong piano; we had bad food in a hot restaurant; and I hadn't slept for two days. . . . But I knew something special was happening when I started playing." Recorded live in Cologne, *The Köln Concert* brought his music to people who were not jazz fans but who were attracted by another kind of fusion, known as New Age. (Masseuses, to this day, use tepid examples of New Age to relax or irritate clients.) In Jarrett's hands, such freewheeling improvisation brought jazz into a compelling real-time mix with gospel, folk music, and whatever else captured his attention in the spur of the moment. "I was trying to get rid of all the way of playing that was normal," he explained, "and just leave a giant hole to jump into when I finally went there." The slew of New Age pianists and guitarists who imitated him often settled for making easy-listening trance music, free of swing, dissonance, and creative suspense. For Jarrett, playing is a genuinely spiritual experience, more intent on stimulating an audience than calming its nerves.

In the 1970s, Jarrett divided his time between two quartets, American and European. The American group pitted him firmly within the cutting-edge jazz of the day, surrounded by bassist Charlie Haden, tenor saxophonist Dewey Redman (a Texas-born former educator who made a terrific splash in New York working with Ornette Coleman and in Haden's Liberation Music Orchestra), and drummer Paul Motian. In this heady company, Jarrett created a wide spectrum of pieces, blending gospel and free jazz, often with him doubling on soprano saxophone or bass recorder. His European group paired him with the Norwegian saxophonist Jan Garbarek and two other Scandinavian musicians: drummer Jon Christensen and bassist Palle Danielsson. This group was equally far-ranging but less abrasive in its basic approach. Manfred Eicher, who recorded the group for his ECM records, said of Scandinavian musicians that they "play a different blues. It's not of urban America . . . they know isolation and they know stillness and they know tranquility because that is all around them." Jarrett's subsequent work has been vast and diffuse, ranging from classical music (some of it recorded on pipe organ and clavichord) to avant-garde improvisations to divine inspirations (he dedicated *Hymns* to the Sufis), though most of his performances during the past quarter-century have involved his nonpareil "standards" trio.

"LONG AS YOU KNOW YOU'RE LIVING YOURS"

Jarrett's "different blues" can be heard on "Long as You Know You're Living Yours," recorded in Oslo, and cited by Jarrett as a favorite among his own recordings. It's one of his ebullient gospel pieces, a romp in F major introduced by an open-ended vamp. The melody seems more straightforward than it is. The harmonies shift unpredictably back and forth, and the rhythm is slippery, never pausing before launching off on another tangent. The piece has no form to speak of: it unfolds phrase after phrase, over a sprawling thirty measures. It's a surprise, then, when the tune suddenly shifts into different territory. The bass moves up to a new note and becomes stuck on a pedal point. Jarrett's harmonies move away to dissonant chords but obsessively return again and again. Over the drummer's increasingly agitated accompaniment, Jan Garbarek's tenor saxophone plays a wonderfully engaging modal improvisation, starting low before inching his way upward to his highest register. We hold our breath, waiting to hear how it will turn out—and the answer, once again, is deceptively simple: a return to the opening melody, now heard as the triumphant answer to all the turmoil of the interlude.

LONG AS YOU KNOW YOU'RE LIVING YOURS

Keith Jarrett

Keith Jarrett, piano; Jan Garbarek, tenor saxophone; Palle Danielsson, bass; Jon Christensen, drums

LABEL: *Belonging*, ECM 1050 (829115)
DATE: 1974
STYLE: acoustic jazz-pop fusion
FORM: free-form gospel

Vamp

0:00	Jarrett plays a few chords on the upbeat to introduce the vamp—a short, repeated chord progression that precedes the main melody.
0:01	Jarrett's chords cycle back and forth between the tonic and the sub-dominant, creating a gospel flavor. The bassist plays a syncopated line, landing solidly on the tonic on virtually every downbeat. The drummer plays in straight eighth notes, accenting strongly on the main beat of each measure while adding syncopated fills in between.
0:16	Jarrett adds a chord that increases the tension by ratcheting up the level of dissonance.
0:33	After playing the tonic in the bass, Jarrett sounds as though he's abandoning the chordal vamp for the main melody. Yet a few notes later, he quickly retreats.
0:49	Again, he intensifies the sense of harmonic movement by adding an extra chord.

Head

0:59	Garbarek (saxophone) finally enters with the main melody, doubled by Jarrett's piano—a simple diatonic melody, with unpredictable syncopations.
1:05	The harmony moves to a new chord, suggesting a half cadence on the dominant; the tune doesn't pause, but continues in its syncopated way.
1:10	The harmony returns to the tonic.
1:17	A new phrase begins on the dominant chord.
1:28	New chords lead to a strong cadence, which comes a few seconds later.
1:32	A new phrase of the melody begins and remains on the tonic.
1:39	The melody becomes more wide-ranging, soaring to the upper tonic and spreading out rhythmically in triplets.

Head

1:52	The melody ends; but Jarrett immediately begins it again, prompting Garbarek to follow after just a few notes. The melody follows the same pattern as before.

Interlude

2:45	The bass unexpectedly moves up from the tonic to a new note, A—the same note that Garbarek sustains on the saxophone. The bass will remain on this note for the next minute and a half.
2:47	Jarrett's first chords are sharply dissonant; in a few seconds, they resolve back to the main chord (A7). Throughout this passage, Jarrett moves back and forth between the stability of the main chord and his highly inventive dissonances.
2:53	Garbarek rises from the A by a half step, creating a sharply dissonant note that resolves a few seconds later.
2:59	By way of contrast, Garbarek descends to a lower-pitched melody, which will eventually resolve to a lower note.
3:13	Surprising us by jumping in ahead of the beat, Garbarek soars upward to a new high note (C-sharp); he gradually descends to a low point by 3:21.
3:21	The line soars upward to the same note before descending once again.
3:26	The drummer's improvisation becomes more unpredictable, his intense accents disturbing the previously steady 4/4 accompaniment.
3:39	Garbarek fastens onto a three-note rhythmic motive (short-short-long).
3:44	He rises to a new high note, rocking ecstatically back and forth on a polyrhythmic rhythm with distorted timbre.
3:50	Sounding a bit like Coltrane, Garbarek ascends yet higher, straining with distorted timbre.
3:56	Having reached a note several octaves above the place where he started, Garbarek pushes the limit of his playing abilities.
4:01	Somehow, he manages to move up *slightly* higher.
4:05	The climax is over: a steadier rhythm in the drums signals that the band will draw a close to this episode. Garbarek steadily descends.
4:12	As the snare drum marks time, Garbarek settles on a lower note. Jarrett plays the basic A7 clearly on the downbeat.

Vamp

4:26	The harmony suddenly relaxes to the tonic. The bass, now free from its pedal point, plays ecstatic glissandos.
4:32	For a brief moment, we can hear Jarrett's voice in the background.
4:41	The piano stops for a few measures; this makes it easier to hear the drummer accenting the main beats on the cymbals.
4:51	Jarrett adds a brief but intense dissonance to the vamp.
4:56	He begins hinting at the head, playing a few of its melodic ideas lightly and leaving lots of space to be filled in by the bass.

| 5:04 | Yet another opportunity to hear Jarrett's voice in the texture. |

Head

| 5:09 | Jarrett and Garbarek return to the opening melody. For the next minute, the band joyfully plays through the head with renewed intensity. |
| 6:02 | The piece finally ends on the tonic, slowly decaying in volume. |

FROM HARD FUSION TO SMOOTH JAZZ

Fusion entered a new phase when it passed from veterans like Miles Davis and even Herbie Hancock to a generation of musicians who no longer treated rock as an exotic seasoning or worried about maintaining jazz purity. These players had absorbed fusion as the music of their own generation. None achieved a more devoted fan base than guitarist Pat Metheny (b. 1954), originally of Lee's Summit, Missouri, near the very center of the continent. Like most would-be jazz guitarists growing up in the 1960s, Metheny was infatuated with Wes Montgomery, whose *Smokin' at the Half Note* (1965) he called "the absolute greatest jazz guitar album ever made. It's also the record that taught me how to play." Listening repeatedly to Montgomery's solos, he learned how to play in octaves and to use his thumb instead of a pick. But he also listened to Bob Dylan, the Beatles, Waylon Jennings, and bossa nova, embracing it all, his guitar drawing jazz into an ongoing dialogue with the whole landscape of pop music.

Metheny entered the jazz field professionally as a teenager. By 1975, he had played with vibraphonist Gary Burton (an early aficionado of fusion) and recorded his first album, *Bright Size Life,* with Jaco Pastorius. His sound was already fully formed on this album: a warm tone from a hollow-bodied guitar, spread out through two amplifiers and a decay unit to achieve a rich and ringing voice. His phrases are broad and melodic, and his tunes, often explicitly geographical ("Missouri Uncompromised," "Omaha Celebration"), betray a country-like openness. He found a composing partner in Lyle Mays, an introverted pianist whose musical ideas fused with Metheny's lyricism. The two formed the Pat Metheny Group in 1977, launching the long-haired guitarist as the fresh face of fusion jazz.

Jazz had struggled to be heard against the dominant rock guitar of the 1960s. Metheny evened the playing field as the first musician of his generation to reclaim the guitar as a solo jazz instrument. His slightly older contemporary Bill Frisell also spurred the reclamation, blending jazz with rock sounds and songs that suggested a comprehensive immersion in twentieth-century Americana, but Frisell stayed closer to the jazz tradition and made his mark a few years later, in the wake of Metheny's initial impact. Each of them achieved an instantly recognizable sound. Metheny maintains his individualism despite his use of electronic accoutrements such as the guitar synthesizer. At times, he verges into pop, with backgrounds generated by sequencers spinning out loops created in advance. But he prizes the jazz element most, having familiarized himself with the tradition, from Louis Armstrong to Ornette Coleman. On *80/81*, he recorded with Coleman's former bassist Charlie Haden and Dewey Redman, testing his fusion style against the free-floating challenge of Coleman's tunes. In 1985, on the triumphant *Song X*, he recorded with Coleman himself (and his band Prime Time, with his son Denardo Coleman on drums). Metheny extends the openness and optimism of Coleman's music by adding his own ecstatic layer to the harmolodic texture.

A different type of fusion pulls in music not only from outside the jazz tradition, but outside the United States, producing what is generally referred to as world music. In this realm, not surprisingly, European players have a powerful role, but unlike the musicians of Django Reinhart's generation who, though they drew on local idioms, aimed chiefly at mastering the American jazz style, these younger musicians use jazz as a platform for exploring their own musical cultures. Jan Garbarek's career offers a paradigm. He was born a displaced person, to a Polish father who had been sent to Norway during the war to build Nazi railroad lines. Growing up in Norway, he found his musical idol in John Coltrane, especially for his use of Third World scales and percussion. Musicians visiting Norway brought similarly impressive juxtapositions. Don Cherry, part black and part Native American, dressed in African garb, recited Indian philosophy, and insisted that his Norwegian audience take its folk heritage seriously. George Russell moved to Oslo, bringing with him a capacious theoretical approach that embraced Indonesian gamelan music, European classical music, and bebop. Garbarek became a jazz ethnomusicologist, learning to sing various folk traditions and infusing his improvisations with them, recording a long series of albums over thirty years. He refuses to call his distinctive music jazz (he refuses to call *anything* after *Bitches Brew* jazz). It is simply Norwegian music. You could multiply his example by a hundred and not take into account all the music that fuses jazz with overseas traditions.

Another way for jazz to go global was exemplified by Paul Winter, who took on stewardship of the entire earth. He began as a straight-ahead saxophonist who served as cultural ambassador in Latin America and Brazil, where he soaked up local folk traditions. By 1967, his band had morphed into the Paul Winter Consort, a term he borrowed from Elizabethan music to evoke the idea of diversity. Winter soon began to widen his sphere of influence: he drew on the cry of the wolf and the singing of humpbacked whales—he even performed for whales in the North Pacific. Ranging from high-pitched squeals to earth-rattling depths, whale songs became the basis for recordings marketed through the Winter Consort, including *Common Ground* (1978). Subsequent projects took him from New York's Cathedral of St. John the Divine to the Grand Canyon.

The Consort's theme, "Icarus," an arching, folk-like melody set against advanced jazz harmony, was composed by Ralph Towner, who, in 1970, left the Consort with other members to form a group called Oregon. Each musician in Oregon has a primary instrument, but the fluid nature of the band allows them to experiment with other instruments: Ralph Towner was originally a trumpet player and pianist who turned to acoustic guitar at twenty-two. He became a virtuoso on the six-string and twelve-string guitar, though he occasionally played French horn and returned to piano. Bassist Glen Moore also played violin and flute. Paul McCandless specialized in the oboe, an exceedingly rare instrument in jazz. Percussionist Colin Walcott (who never played the trap set) was the group's firmest link to world traditions, as a former student of Alla Rakha on tabla and of Ravi Shankar on sitar. Oregon is closely associated with New Age jazz—quiet, reflective, serene. But its intricate compositions and musicianship warrant attention and respect.

To some observers, however, Oregon comes perilously close to the kind of jazz that isn't jazz. When Bill Clinton was asked early in his presidency to name his favorite saxophonists, he replied: "Lester Young and Kenny G," a pairing most of us find as inconceivable as a jazz musician saying his favorite presidents are Abraham Lincoln and Calvin Coolidge. But if Clinton wanted to drop a name that would have resonance with the largest number of voters, he was probably obliged to name the king of "smooth jazz." That invidious term first appeared in the late 1980s, when the label *fusion* had run out of steam. But the idea behind it—an innocuous, listener-friendly blending of jazz with an upbeat, celebratory brand of R&B and funk—dates back to the 1960s, when producer Creed Taylor helped Wes Montgomery break through with cover versions of the Beatles. Taylor's label, CTI, took off in the early 1970s, offering recordings by George Benson, Freddie Hubbard, Herbie Mann, Antonio Carlos Jobim, and other accomplished musicians in the context of unruffled rhythms and easy-listening atmospherics, often arranged for a large studio orchestra by Don Sebesky. Sometimes the backgrounds were created first; then the soloists were brought in to dub their parts. Smooth jazz found a mass audience of those who liked the superficial sounds of jazz, but not the bother of digging past them.

In time, the music grew funkier. It remained light and easy, but the rhythms took on a kick and the timbres of the soloists took on grit. It was mood music you could dance to, reflecting a laid-back affluence that appealed especially to black professionals who were turned off by the blaring volume of fusion and the apparent incoherence of the avant-garde. For conservative tastes, this music suggested a parallel to early rhythm and blues; it was their music, and it created its own stars. The Philadelphia saxophonist Grover Washington became a star with *Mister Magic*, in 1975, achieving greater success in 1980 with *Winelight*, featuring "Just the Two of Us." Guitarist George Benson, who had struggled for years to escape the shadow of Wes Montgomery, hit it big with *Breezin'*, featuring "This Masquerade," a remake of a Leon Russell tune with Benson singing in tandem with his guitar improvisation. Musicians like Donald Byrd, a competent hard bop trumpet player, abandoned acoustic jazz for fusion with the 1972 *Black Byrd*. Some groups dropped the word "jazz" when it threatened to limit their appeal—the Jazz Crusaders, a hard bop group in the Art Blakey tradition, became the Crusaders, performing jazz-influenced dance music.

Significantly, this music was radio driven. While record companies prefer broad categories (corresponding to sections of a record store), radio searches for finer and finer divisions of taste. By the late 1980s, a new category had emerged, variously known as "new adult contemporary," "jazz lite," "quiet storm," or "smooth jazz." The music was pioneered by such stations as KTWV in Los Angeles, known as The Wave, and monitored by marketing companies like Broadcast Architecture. The target audience was the "money" demographic, ages twenty-five to fifty-four: adults who had "graduated" from rock to a less abrasive music, but were still shy of embracing jazz. Smooth jazz was supposed to be the perfect soundtrack for their lifestyle. In 1987, *Billboard* amended its charts, placing jazz in the category "traditional jazz," while dubbing its pop-oriented spinoff as "contemporary jazz." As smooth jazz ricocheted back to a predominantly white demographic, the funk receded.

Enter President Clinton's saxophone hero, Kenny G, or Kenneth Gorelick. A saxophonist from Seattle, he made his mark with the Jeff Lorber band; but it was as a solo performer that he ascended from the ranks of mere musicians into the pop stratosphere. He is currently ranked No. 25 of all performers by the Recording Industry Association of America—having sold 48 million recordings, including 12 million for *Breathless,* undoubtedly the highest total ever for anyone associated, however fitfully, with jazz. His name has evoked howls of derision from jazz musicians, especially when he dubbed his solos—which Pat Metheny memorably described as "his lame-ass, jive, pseudo bluesy, out-of-tune noodling"—over Louis Armstrong's "What a Wonderful World."

There are many things to dislike about smooth jazz—for example, everything. Jazz has always depended on real-time interaction, live or in the studio. Pop recordings long ago dispensed with the concept of live performance. Tunes are constructed in layers, with each musician recorded separately, often wearing headphones, listening and performing with tracks created days or weeks before. The sound may be beautiful, even precise (thanks to digital sampling and synthesized drum tracks), but it comes at the cost of the interaction central to jazz. We can't blame technology per se: many jazz pieces, including "Teen Town" and "Tutu," have been recorded in this way. But technology aside, jazz of every school and era is about spontaneous expression, risk-taking, improvisational resourcefulness, rhythmic excitement, and the promise of the unforeseen, all of which is absent from smooth jazz, which exists primarily as musical wallpaper for the Weather Channel, exercise classes, and presumably the Clinton home.

JAM BANDS, ACID JAZZ, AND HIP-HOP

If smooth jazz is chiefly a commodity, other types of fusion are inescapable from the sweat and toil of contemporary life and music. The jam band concept has its roots in 1960s rock bands like the Grateful Dead, which rejected commercial dictates in favor of communal improvisation. The Dead was not terribly concerned with recordings, although a surprising number of performances were taped by loyal "Deadheads." The band became an international phenomenon, devoted to the freedom of the moment. Along with so many other independent-minded musicians, its leader Jerry Garcia recorded with Ornette Coleman. Phish, an improvisational rock group led by guitarist Trey Anastasio, continued the jam band approach in the early 1980s as a pick-up band playing gigs in its home state of Vermont; by the time it disbanded in 2004, it had reached an audience astronomically larger than anything jazz could muster (hundreds of thousands attended its concerts). Like the Dead, Phish could not be construed as a jazz band; but its enthusiasm for open-ended improvisation encouraged jazz-oriented bands to follow in its footsteps.

One such band was founded by Charlie Hunter, a guitarist from the San Francisco Bay area who uses an eight-string guitar. On the lower two strings, he plays bass lines, separately amplified for the proper mix; the rest of his hand is free for guitar licks synchronized with the overall groove. Another group, Medeski, Martin and Wood, got a direct boost from Phish, which played their tapes between sets. John Medeski, a pianist who said he rejected his training in classical music because of its social pretensions ("all these rich people in fur coats"), studied at the New England Conservatory, where he began playing with the bassist Chris Wood. On one of their early gigs, they discovered the drummer Billy Martin, a New Yorker who brought "that more danceable element" to their music. They came to New York as a conventional piano trio, but in the early 1990s they embarked on a road tour in a van and camper, booking gigs along the way—including bills with alternative rock bands like Los Lobos and the Dave Matthews Band. Although Medeski was an acoustic pianist, he found electric instruments more suitable to the band's peripatetic existence, and became expert on the Hammond B3 organ, the Clavinet, the Wurlitzer electric piano, the Mellotron (another Wurlitzer instrument), the ARP String Ensemble, and the Yamaha synthesizer. Each instrument has its own amplifier. He has said, "I can hit three notes on any of my keyboards, and each will sound different."

Medeski finds the term *jam band* "demeaning." Yet the music of Medeski, Martin and Wood is very much part of that scene, better suited to coffeehouses and rock clubs than jazz nightclubs where organ trios build on customs pioneered by Jimmy Smith. Inevitably, their audiences affect what they create—in part because each night's show is taped, digitized, and loaded onto the Internet for everyone's free use. Much of their music seems retro, aimed at a camp audience that enjoys hearing modern versions of older soul-jazz styles. But it is also sufficiently modern to incorporate the work of hip-hop artists like DJ Logic and Scott Harding, both of whom help the band conceive of their music as a whole, not just as a collection of individual soloists.

"CHANK"

In 1998, Medeski, Martin and Wood received a phone call from an important fan, jazz guitarist John Scofield, who had played with Miles Davis in the early 1980s. Over the years, Scofield had earned a reputation as a skillful composer as well as a performer equally at home within straight jazz and the neo-funk movement. His playing combines a searing, distorted blues timbre with a deep knowledge of postbop scales. His command of chord progressions guaranteed his acceptance within mainstream jazz, but—like most of Miles's children—he yearned for a change of groove. "I'm at a point now where I'm bebopped out," he complained. Scofield arranged for Medeski, Martin and Wood to play on his next album, *A Go Go*. Scofield wrote the tunes, keeping them basic, often little more than a few guitar licks set against a funk rhythm. But the rhythmic flow was designed for improvisation. "I'm not a huge fusion fan per se," Scofield said. "I like swing. But some grooves make you want to play, if you're a jazz musician."

"Chank" was written as a tribute to Jimmy "Chank" Nolen, a guitarist in James Brown's stellar rhythm section. Scofield's part was basically a rhythm line—not usually the role jazz guitarists hanker for. But the line was essential in setting up the overall mood. Scofield remembers the bass line as reminiscent of James Brown's seminal "Cold Sweat" (1967): on the offbeat, except for the first beat of the measure. "[Saxophonist] Maceo Parker and [trombonist] Fred Wesley describe funk as 'about the one,' and on that tune, everything comes back to it. It was a whole way of breaking up the bass and drum rhythm." The form is also derived from a James Brown idea: an A section over a single chord, used for modal improvisation, followed by a bridge. The bridge is cued by each soloist, who can play as long as he wants: "On 'Chank,' you play four-bar phrases, not choruses." The musicians, who had played together only three times in rehearsal, mesh beautifully, and the album sparked Scofield's career, selling 100,000 copies—nowhere near as much as, say, Hancock's *Head Hunters*, but a quantum leap by jazz standards.

CHANK

John Scofield

John Scofield, electric guitar; John Medeski, Hammond B3 organ; Chris Wood, electric bass; Billy Martin, drums

LABEL: *A-Go-Go*, Polygram 539979
DATE: 1998
STYLE: jam band fusion
FORM: AABA (AB during the solos)

Introduction

0:00	Scofield (electric guitar) plays a dissonant chord in a syncopated rhythm.
0:02	After a brief pause, he follows with a brief pentatonic lick.
0:04	Scofield repeats the guitar chord, this time following with a rhythmically tricky passage.
0:08	Having established the pattern, Scofield plays it repeatedly.
0:15	On an upbeat, the drums enter, followed by the electric bass.
0:16	The drums and bass add their own rhythmic layers, sometimes reinforcing Scofield's syncopations, at other times creating new patterns. The bass begins squarely on the downbeat before shifting to the offbeat.

Head

0:32	A	Medeski (organ) plays a melody with strong, sustained blue notes, in a simple repetitive pattern that contrasts with the syncopated accompaniment.
0:38		The last note of the line dissolves in a bluesy glissando.
0:48		Having completed two complete phrases, the organ rests, giving the drums, bass, and guitar room to continue the groove for another eight bars.
0:57	A	The melody is repeated in a higher register.
1:05		Medeski begins the melody harmonized in thirds.
1:13	B	The bass note moves to IV. After a few beats, the guitar and organ play syncopated chords, followed by a riff.
1:21		The band reaches a half cadence (on the dominant chord).
1:22		A brief drum solo closes the bridge after only five bars.
1:24	A	Medeski returns to the opening melody, again harmonized in thirds.

Solo 1

1:40	A	Medeski plays a few staccato chords.
1:42		Scofield enters for his guitar solo with a forceful electric sound. Some of his phrases are loud, others suddenly quiet.
1:49		As Scofield plays, Medeski comps quietly in the background.
1:56		Scofield's lick begins quietly on the downbeat with fast repeated notes.
2:08		Scofield plays a line with expressive, upward-bending blue notes.
2:16		He stitches together several short ideas into a long continuous phrase.
2:28		In the background, the organ holds out sustained notes.
2:44		Scofield returns to the repeated-note idea, interacting aggressively with Medeski's comping.
2:50		As Scofield ends his phrase with a short, distorted passage, the organ plays a brief riff.
2:53		Scofield echoes the riff, adding brief rhythmic decorations.
2:56		His guitar sound becomes more distorted.

3:00	With a change in the timbre of his guitar, Scofield repeats a simple four-note riff, playing it in call and response with a lower-pitched blues line.
3:06	At times, his lines become blurred in pitch and rhythm.
3:16	Scofield begins to suggest the tune's opening melody.
3:20	He follows this with a rapid repeated riff.
3:24	By referring once more to the opening melody, he signals the bridge.
3:32	**B**

Solo 2

3:43	**A**	Medeski begins his organ solo with a fiercely repeated riff, placed poly-rhythmically against the bar.
3:47		In the background, Scofield plays a variant of the line he introduced at the beginning of the tune.
4:00		Medeski's next line is a string of fast notes, moving "outside" the main chord until it descends into the bass register.
4:07		His licks become shorter, interacting more with Scofield's syncopated accompaniment.
4:14		Medeski focuses on a single bluesy note.
4:24		He begins a simple four-note riff, then repeats it at different pitch levels, some dissonant against the prevailing harmony.
4:31		He starts a longer and faster melody that once again moves into disso-nant territory.
4:46		To signal the bridge, Medeski plays the opening melody, which quickly disintegrates into polyrhythmic improvisation.
5:01	**B**	

Head (abbreviated)

| 5:12 | **A** | Medeski leads a version of the head that's reduced to two phrases. |

Coda

5:28	The band moves to a composed passage (lasting nine and a half mea-sures). As the bass slowly ascends, the guitar and organ play a bizarre melody, harmonized in dissonant intervals that fall just short of octaves.
5:32	The melody is repeated, with the bass slightly higher and the intervals slightly more dissonant.
5:40	The melody moves in faster note values.
5:43	The passage comes to rest on a half cadence, followed by a brief drum solo.
5:47	The passage is repeated exactly.
6:06	As the passage is repeated one more time, the guitar begins playing a solo over harmonies played by the organ.
6:24	The bass shifts down chromatically to a new harmony; the organ lingers on a fragment of the melody, repeated polyrhythmically against the bass.

6:28	A strange synthesized sound fills up the melody space, gradually growing louder.
6:31	Suddenly the bass rises in pitch as it speeds up, as if the tape were being run faster.
6:40	The bass finally stops, ending the piece.

The term *acid jazz* comes from England's "rave" scene, in dance clubs of the 1980s and early 1990s. Late at night (so late that the events often took place in secret locations to avoid curfew regulations), DJs would draw crowds of dancers with electronic music enhanced by light shows and artificial fog. The music was known as "acid house," and it was relentlessly repetitive, powered by a sturdy bass line. One night, DJ Chris Bangs, tired of the usual selections, offered an alternative woven together from soul jazz tracks in his record collection. He called it acid jazz, and the term spread. Dancers heard the music as retro, a chic evocation of now-forgotten fashions from the 1960s, available only on LPs. For many young people, it was their pathway into the jazz tradition—albeit a tradition quite different from the usual modernist narrative.

The acid jazz craze brought back to life styles that had been shunted to the fringes. During a time when giants like Coltrane, Mingus, and Coleman roamed the earth, soul jazz received little critical attention, much of it derisory. Some critics saw it as trite, monotonous, and shamelessly commercial—the worst sort of "regression," to be spurned by serious jazz lovers. Yet soul jazz survived, through the few bands that continued to play it and in private record collections. As DJs hungry for new beats combed through piles of used vinyl looking for material, they discovered boatloads of these albums and recycled them back into dance music. Acid jazz was, in fact, jazz pastiche.

Most groups associated with acid jazz have only a tenuous connection to jazz. Some, like the Brand New Heavies, do little more than regurgitate the styles of 1970s soul bands. Others lie more securely on the jazz-pop borderline, notably the Groove Collective, a band of roughly a dozen instrumentalists that performed at the Giant Step, a Manhattan dance club. The Groove Collective uses a DJ to blend its sounds and borrows rhythms from hip-hop dance music. But the band also features fine jazz soloists, including saxophonist Jay Rodriguez and trombonist Josh Roseman. The music has a bohemian feeling, but it is hardly out of touch with the modern scene. As one member said, "Groove Collective has the energy of a rock band.

We are not cool dudes with a beatnik feel and berets and dark glasses."
The first minute of "Rentstrike," from their first album, has the faint and
scratchy recording quality of a bebop 78 from the 1940s. Then the music
switches into a contemporary dance groove, cycling between two chords,
slightly out of tonal kilter. The bebop tune was, of course, "faked"—but it
was worked into the main theme of the piece, giving the jazz musicians a
way to take solos that don't disturb the group's groove.

The latest area to be affected by the fusion impulse is black hip-hop, which
arose from the streets of the Bronx in the 1970s and by the 1980s had
spread throughout the country and beyond to make an indelible mark on
the entire world. Few jazz musicians had any involvement with it (Herbie
Hancock's "Rockit" is a memorable exception, with its turntable scratching), and by the 1990s it had become a symbol of everything jazz was
not: young, countercultural, and in touch with the reality of the streets
in black communities. Two things had to happen for jazz/hip-hop fusion
to work. First, hip-hop artists had to discover jazz. Musicians from bands
like A Tribe Called Quest and Digable Planets began raiding their parents'
cabinets, finding old Blue Notes and pulling cuts to use as samples on
their own records. The results surprised almost everyone. In 1994, Us3
transformed Herbie Hancock's "Cantaloupe Island" into a new mix called
"Cantaloop (Flip Fantasia)," which made it into the top twenty. Blue Note
enjoyed unanticipated prosperity as sales of its classics rose dramatically,
thanks to their use on hip-hop records. So many artists were sampling
Blue Note records that the company—figuring if it couldn't beat them, it
might as well join them—opened up its vaults to hip-hop DJ Madlib to
plunder at will.

The second thing was that jazz musicians had to find a way to use hip-
hop that went beyond adding spoken rhymes to conventional jazz numbers. The financial incentives were obvious: embracing hip-hop opened up
a new, young audience for their music. But yielding older swing grooves
for new ones presented a challenge. Hip-hop fans were no more likely to
be enticed by instrumental jazz gerrymandered to a hip-hop beat than
1960s rock fans were to Count Basie playing the Beatles. That didn't stop
jazz musicians from trying their damnedest. *Stolen Moments*—a 1994 tribute album designed to fight AIDS—included Lester Bowie mixed in with
Digable Planets, Herbie Hancock with Me'Shell NdegéOcello, and Ron
Carter with MC Solaar.

The nature of fusion depends on who's in charge. Recordings controlled by hip-hop artists tend to keep jazz well in the background, reduced to short sampled loops or buried in the mix. Such was the case with *Jazzmatazz,* an album by Guru (aka Keith Elam), who honored Roy Ayers and Donald Byrd but kept them distinctly behind his rapping. Jazz artists, for their part, are willing to absorb just enough hip-hip to make their own music more stylish. Branford Marsalis's fusion band, Buckshot LeFonque (after one of Cannonball Adderley's pseudonyms), adds a rapper and a turntablist to an otherwise conventional electric jazz ensemble. A more promising approach is suggested by pianist Jason Moran, who in his version of "Planet Rock" and original compositions honestly uses musical elements of hip-hop (rhythms, loops, dubs) to spark his jazz improvisations.

MILES TO GO

Miles Davis's immersion in fusion did not end with *Bitches Brew.* In the 1970s, he turned forcefully toward contemporary black pop with *On the Corner.* The cover art suggests an unlikely environment for the son of a wealthy dental surgeon: a comical, colorful street life populated by pimps, hustlers, a book-laden customer, and teenagers wearing "Vote Miles" shirts, all of them wearing platform shoes. Determined to reach a young black audience, Davis introduced dense, interlocking, bass-heavy rhythmic layers. Critics panned the album, finding it simplistic and formless. But the intended audience responded with enthusiasm, and older jazz lovers, who were used to Davis's studied bandstand indifference, were amazed to see him ending concerts by walking to the stage apron and slapping palms with his new fans. The critics came around, too: in 2007, the complete *On the Corner* sessions were released to rapturous reviews. They were seen as an auguring of techno music's ambient rhythms.

Even more controversial were the albums he released after going into seclusion in 1975: two double albums recorded in Osaka on the same day, *Agharta,* released in the United States, and *Pangaea,* released abroad. *Agharta,* in particular, was damned as a profound decline, as Davis's trumpet playing on it is sporadic and unmistakably weak. He had begun to spend more stage time in front of a bank of electric keyboards. (In 1974, to mark the passing of Duke Ellington, Davis recorded a thirty-minute threnody based on an organ drone with no trumpet whatsoever.) Yet taken whole, this was among the most thrilling recordings he had ever released, with most of the solo space divided between two inspired if outwardly disparate musicians: the jazz alto saxophonist Sonny Fortune (another graduate of Mongo Santamaria's band) and the elusive, Chicago-based, Hendrix-influenced guitarist Pete Cosey, whose earlier experiences had included the AACM and R&B. *Agharta* proved that Davis's magic no longer depended on his trumpet; he had devised an open-ended music that he controlled through instrumental gestures, on trumpet or keyboards, and verbal and physical signals as he wandered the stage.

As Davis's self-imposed exile continued year after year, he suffered from sickle-cell anemia, degeneration of his hips, ulcers, and walking pneumonia—all of which he treated, by his own account, with nonstop cocaine and sex. Then in 1980, incredibly, he began to record and tour again. He gradually found an approach that suited his temperament, allowing him to extend his interest in black pop while reviving his signature lyricism, occasionally playing standard tunes he had abandoned more than a decade earlier. His trumpet technique improved markedly, though he continued to focus on keyboards. It wasn't easy for older jazz fans to accept the aging Miles. Martin Williams described him as a man nearing sixty dressed "in what looked like a left-over Halloween fright-suit, emitting a scant handful of plaintive notes." For young musicians, on the other hand, playing with Miles was still the ultimate credential. He employed funk musicians and outstanding jazz talents, including John Scofield and saxophonist Kenny Garrett, as well as his longtime drummer Al Foster; he even reunited with Gil Evans, though the one major work they discussed (an adaptation of *Tosca*) never materialized. His repertory included expected funk tunes and such unexpected pop as Cyndi Lauper's "Time After Time." His aura had dimmed not at all, and his concerts invariably sold out.

"TUTU"

In 1985, irritated by the company's lackluster support for his recent albums, Davis terminated his long-standing contract with Columbia Records and signed with Warner Bros. for an enormous advance—compensated in part by their appropriating half the copyrights to his compositions. Fascinated by the singer-songwriter Prince ("the new Duke Ellington of our time"), Davis wanted to feature him on his next album along with electronic samples and overdubs. Warner Bros. put him in touch with Marcus Miller, a bassist, producer, and arranger. "Wow," he said, "if Miles is willing to start using drum machines and stuff, let me show my take on that." For the album's opening track, Miller devised as a backdrop a brooding, shuffling sound that was intended to evoke Miles's standing as the Prince of

Darkness. The voicings were influenced by the darting chromatic chords of Herbie Hancock, which suggest harmonies while undermining them at the same time.

TUTU

Miles Davis

Miles Davis, trumpet; Marcus Miller, soprano saxophone, synthesizer, electric bass, drums; Paulinho DaCosta, percussion

LABEL: *Tutu,* Warner Brothers 25490
DATE: 1986
STYLE: jazz-pop fusion
FORM: chorus (**AAB**) with solo improvisation over a vamp (ostinato)

Introduction

0:00	A short bass drum hit leads to a loud orchestral chord in the synthesizer. As the sound slowly decays, we hear a quiet pulse and a few strikes on the conga drum.
0:03	A second orchestral chord is followed by more aggressive drumming.
0:08	Davis enters with a muted trumpet, playing a descending line.

Vamp

0:13	The bass plays a simple, loping ostinato, doubled by the synthesizer. Its continually repeated asymmetric rhythm locks in with the driving percussive groove, featuring the ride cymbal. Above the ostinato, Davis plays simple lines, circling around a blue note.
0:21	As Davis reaches for a high note, his sound becomes distorted.
0:25	As if responding to Davis's rhythms, the ostinato temporarily adds a few notes.
0:30	The bass breaks briefly away from the ostinato to play a short lick.

Head

0:33	A	Davis plays the main melody, supported by the synthesizers and the bass line: an eight-bar phrase, voiced with modern quartal chords. The ostinato continues as accompaniment.
0:47		For a few bars, the melody is silent. Davis hits a long held note before completing his phrase with a flourish and then dissolving into the lower register.
0:54	A	
1:08	B	The melody (now doubled by the bass line) descends in a syncopated phrase. The harmony is ambiguous, drifting outside the main key.
1:13		A quiet ascending line in the synthesizer brings us back to the tonic, signaled by an orchestral chord.

Solo

1:14		The ostinato is silent, opening up the texture. Davis interacts with Miller's improvisations on bass, with quiet synthesizer chords and massive orchestral hits.

Head

1:28	A	Davis leads the return to the main melody.
1:38		Over the melody's last held note, he improvises new patterns.
1:41	A	
1:51		Again, he adds brief improvised lines.
1:55	B	

Solo

2:01		Again, the ostinato is silent. Miller plays another descending bass run, echoed by Davis, who squeezes a few notes into spaces left by the synthesizer.
2:09		Davis is quiet while the percussion takes over with a strong backbeat.
2:15		A delicate wash of synthesizer sound precedes Davis's reentrance with a repeated two-note motive.
2:26		His expressive high note is undercut by a deep sagging sound in the bass.
2:29		Davis suddenly inserts a faster, more nervous phrase.
2:34		After he hits a high note, the whole background bends slightly in pitch.
2:36		As Davis enters on the downbeat, the bass ostinato begins again. Over a percussion background featuring the ride cymbal, Davis plays repeatedly with two notes, hitting them in unpredictable rhythmic patterns.
2:49		The overall rhythmic texture intensifies with bass licks and percussive hits.
3:00		A wash of synthesizer sound leads us back to the main melody.

Head

3:03	A	A return to the main melody, with more frequent improvised comments by Davis and Miller.
3:13		Davis's line suddenly ascends to a perilously high note.
3:16	A	He now begins to add to his version of the melody—sometimes doubling the synthesizer, but at other times departing from it with improvised comments.
3:30	B	

Solo

3:37		Davis's playing becomes sparser. Interacting with the conga drum, he makes the most of a few intense notes.
3:44		He threads a piercing line through an increasingly dense intersection of sounds.

| 3:50 | | A loud synthesizer hit silences Davis's line, opening up the texture. |
| 3:59 | | A faint background chord grows in volume, leading us once again back to the main melody. |

Head

4:04	**A**	Davis plays against the main melody, nearly obliterating it with harsh high notes.
4:12		As the melody nears the end of its phrase, he plays a steady descending line over it.
4:18	**A**	Davis's improvisation focuses on a short bluesy phrase, repeated with ever varying rhythmic nuances.
4:31	**A**	Instead of moving to the bridge, the melody continues, punctuated by Davis's commentary.

Solo (coda)

| 4:45 | | Davis plays short phrases in call and response with the bass ostinato. |
| 4:59 | | The track begins to fade out. |

Davis's working band did not appear on the recording. His role was simply to respond as trumpet soloist to the studio-created synthesizer textures and drum machine tracks (augmented by a few musicians, including Miller and keyboardist Adam Holzmann). The idea may seem artificial and stilted, but this was essentially the process by which Davis made his classic recordings with Gil Evans: Davis's trumpet surrounded by sumptuous textures. His sound on "Tutu" is as individual as on *Sketches of Spain*: no one could mistake his use of the Harmon mute, his plaintive wail, his elliptical phrasing. "As soon as Miles walked into the studio and played his first three notes," Miller said, "it became his." "Tutu" was recorded in one take, with a few trumpet clams edited out. If the album, which Davis decided to name in praise of Desmond Tutu, has not worn well in its entirety, the title track stands as an expression of Davis's stubborn genius. The stark cover photographs by Irving Penn show an emotionally blank close-up of Davis and an arresting profile of his hands, frozen as if playing one of his favorite notes.

18 CHAPTER

Historicism: Jazz on Jazz

THE WEIGHT OF HISTORY

n 1925, shortly after joining Fletcher Henderson's big band in New York, Louis Armstrong showed Henderson's arranger, Don Redman, a handbook containing music that he and his mentor, King Oliver, had composed in Chicago. Armstrong encouraged Redman to select a piece for the purpose of orchestrating it. Redman decided on "Sugar Foot Stomp," which Oliver had recorded as "Dippermouth Blues," and wrote an arrangement in which Armstrong was asked to perform Oliver's famous cornet solo.

◄ John Lewis, who believed in jazz education, helped launch the Lenox School in the year that he brought the Modern Jazz Quartet to Paris, 1957.

"Sugar Foot Stomp" helped put Henderson's band on the map: it was a startling example of a modern New York recording based on written and improvised material taken from a traditional New Orleans (by way of Chicago) jazz recording, and the piece quickly became a favorite among dancers and musicians. This was not the first nor last time Henderson looked to jazz history for inspiration. A year earlier, he had recorded "Copenhagen," a piece introduced only months before by Chicago's Wolverines (the white band that featured Bix Beiderbecke); Henderson's records served as critiques, showing that New York was paying attention to Chicago even as it moved in a new direction. Then in 1926, Henderson recorded "King Porter Stomp," based on the third strain of a Jelly Roll Morton piano piece; a decade later, that arrangement would be embraced as a Swing Era anthem.

The two narratives that have dominated our chronicling of jazz thus far are suitable and necessary for a music busy being born. The first presented jazz as an art-for-art's-sake tradition whose masters move the music along with radical leaps of creativity, and the second viewed jazz as a fusion tradition in which jazz evolves in response to contemporary pop culture. The Henderson recordings suggest the foundation for a third way of interpreting jazz history, a historicist narrative, which begins with the precept that jazz creativity is inextricably bound to its past. It's particularly useful in considering today's jazz. In its current phase, where jazz—having already explored most of the known musical options—continues to develop but in more incremental, less radical advances, historicism helps to explain how it became increasingly self-conscious about its status, and why twenty-first-century jazz is plagued with countless tributes, recreations, and variations on its past.

Historicism originated in the nineteenth century as an alternative theory to the notion that great men and women and their works arise independently of history. Instead, it connects each new undertaking to its predecessors, emphasizing historical evolution over individual genius, positing an exchange between past and present that Friedrich Hegel called a dialectic. For artists, the dialectic means never having to say you're sorry for borrowing, rejecting, satirizing, and appropriating time-honored accomplishments. In the 1980s, critical theorists put forth a New Historicism, which says that a work of art must be viewed within the context of the place and time of its creation. Rejecting the New Criticism, which analyzes works of art as sufficient unto themselves, the New Historicists look beyond a work to the historical and social conditions that determined it. These two schools of criticism were never really at war in jazz; on the contrary, they complemented each other.

Perhaps the leading advocate of the New Criticism as applied to jazz was the writer and producer Martin Williams, who always focused on the particularity of a musical work, analyzing a piece by breaking down its chorus structure and examining the components that went into making it a success or failure. Williams paid relatively little attention to historical details that might have furnished a different kind of interpretation. In the 1970s, while working at the Smithsonian Institution, he created *The Smithsonian Collection of Classic Jazz*, an anthology that revolutionized the teaching of jazz. Yet as an example of pitfalls inherent in the New Criticism, consider that Williams included Jelly Roll Morton's "Dead Man Blues" while excising its comic introduction, which he considered irrelevant, dated, and rather embarrassing. A historicist, on the other hand, finds value in that bit of tomfoolery: it tells us something of Morton's times and of his background, intentions, and attitude. Williams was by no means opposed to historical inquiry or interpretation. But neither did he subscribe to the historicist idea, popularized in the 1940s, that familiarity with the personalities and backgrounds of musicians was necessary to appreciate the quality of their music. From the 1950s until the 1970s, his art-centric approach predominated.

In the twenty-first century, we are awash in countless instances of writers, filmmakers, composers, choreographers, painters, architects, and others attempting to energize the present by mining the past. We live in an age of homage and interpretation. In the 1950s and 1960s, jazz musicians strove to create new and original works of art; today, musicians are as likely to perform or pay tribute to those same works. The ways in which they apply historicist principles tend to fall into three categories: the revival of entire idioms, such as traditional jazz or swing, which usually involves an immersion in jazz repertory and the faithful reproduction of classic or neglected works; original music that celebrates music of the past, and may range from expansive tributes to playful parodies; and modernist interpretations of jazz classics as a way of using the past to spur the present. These principles have found favor throughout jazz history, but largely as a sideshow to the main action. That began to change in the late 1930s, when jazz chroniclers decried the loss of historical perspective and of musical styles subsumed by present-day fashions.

RECLAIMING AND DEFINING THE PAST: FROM BUNK TO THE ACADEMY

The first genuine movement to counter prevailing musical tastes in favor of an older, neglected jazz style did not take place until (and in response to) the height of the Swing Era. The kick-off came with the 1939 publication of *Jazzmen*, edited and partly written by Frederick Ramsey Jr. and Charles Edward Smith. A serious if faultily researched work, *Jazzmen* argued that true jazz was an essentially New Orleans–derived, African American, blues-based music—hardly a controversial position. But in romanticizing jazz's traditional roots while ignoring modern swing stylists (Lester Young, Roy Eldridge, Billie Holiday, and Lionel Hampton are mentioned only in passing or not at all), it created a nostalgic longing for early jazz and raised questions of authenticity to banish those who didn't heed the party line. In the course of researching a section on New Orleans for *Jazzmen*, the writer William Russell discovered a New Orleans trumpet player of uncertain years named Willie "Bunk" Johnson (1889–1949), and made him one of the book's heroes.

Johnson, who predated the actual year of his birth by a decade, claimed to have played with Buddy Bolden in 1895 (he would have been six at the time) and to have influenced Louis Armstrong—a boast that Armstrong gently debunked. In 1942, fitted with a new set of teeth, Johnson recorded for the first time in his career; he continued to record over the next five years, while touring the country from San Francisco to New York and spurring a major revival of traditional jazz. Bunk Johnson was exhibited as a musician of Arcadian purity: an uncompromised purveyor of the "real" jazz. Though beset by technical limitations, he was at his best an intriguing musician. He had a rosy, glowing tone and an undeniable predilection for the blues and a studied lyricism. Still, he rarely measured up to the great established figures from New Orleans, like Sidney Bechet (with whom he recorded), and was as frequently ridiculed by young musicians as he was idolized by his fan base, which consisted chiefly of conservative white men. As a result, a schism gradually developed between two mutually scornful camps: revivalists and modernists.

To their credit, Johnson and his admirers forced a reconsideration of early jazz, which was so remote to most swing fans that King Oliver and Jelly Roll Morton died broke and forgotten. Bunk also introduced a clique of veteran New Orleans musicians, born at the turn of the century, who accompanied him on tour and in the studio. They interpreted a narrow traditionalist repertory with sincerity and emotional candor, and they revived elemental musical pleasures—resolute backbeats and polyphonic elation— that had fallen by the wayside. The best known among them, clarinetist George Lewis, later played an important role in reestablishing the French Quarter in New Orleans as a destination for tourists. His plaintive sound sustained an international following well into the 1960s, long after the Bunk Johnson phenomenon ended, offering honest refuge for those unable or disinclined to tackle modern jazz, middle-of-the-road pop, or rock.

Bunk died in the summer of 1949, around the same time that Miles Davis led the Birth of the Cool sessions and Dave Brubeck made his first records; even if he paid attention to bop, which isn't likely, he can have had no idea of how many jazz schools were about to shop their wares in the years ahead—cool, hard bop, Third Stream, soul, avant-garde. The 1950s offered a nonstop parade of new styles, ingenious improvisers, and innovative composers. Not surprisingly, this creative commotion also instigated historical inquiry into older schools seemingly left in the dust. Diehard traditionalists had circled their wagons around Bunk Johnson during the Swing Era. In the postbop era, it was the swing generation that required critical resuscitation.

In 1958, the critic Stanley Dance coined the term *mainstream* to describe that giant swath of jazz situated between reactionary traditionalism and radical modernity—in short, all those musicians, from Louis Armstrong and Duke Ellington to Benny Goodman and Lester Young, who played in prebop styles. Dance, who despised bebop, sought to renew interest in musicians who were still relatively young (not yet fifty, for the most part) but were treated in the jazz press as dinosaurs. He succeeded, but in the 1960s, to his dismay, with the avant-garde at center stage, mainstream came to encompass bop musicians. Then in the 1970s, when fusion or jazz-rock dominated the spotlight, the mainstream was said to include just about everyone who played acoustic jazz. The important thing, however, is that mainstream now represented the ongoing language of jazz creativity while holding it at a distance from the latest trends.

Jazz eventually began making inroads into academia and the arts establishment, but this was an exceedingly slow process. In the unsympathetic atmosphere that would deny Duke Ellington the Pulitzer Prize, jazz activists took matters into their own hands, creating schools and exploring jazz history in books, magazines, and public discussions. Jazz had begun to look at itself as a historical phenomenon with distinct roots and a proud lineage. At the same time, musicians were crossing stylistic divides. Unlike the 1940s, when jazz musicians were swing players, modernists, or traditionalists, musicians in the 1950s practiced a new rapprochement. Louis Armstrong and Dizzy Gillespie, who feuded in the early years of bop, played together on television. In the tradition of Ellington's musical portraits, modernists composed tributes to jazz pioneers. John Lewis helped launch the Modern Jazz Quartet with his cortege for Django Reinhardt, while Charles Mingus created a threnody for Lester Young ("Goodbye Pork Pie Hat"). Dave Brubeck composed "The Duke."

Much of the historical and educational activity was stimulated in an area rarely singled out in jazz histories: Massachusetts, its eastern (Boston) and western (Lenox) borders. The first dedicated jazz curriculum was launched in 1957 as the Lenox School of Jazz, in the Berkshires near the classical music festival at Tanglewood. Never before had a faculty been convened for the exclusive purpose of teaching jazz; never before had an integrated but largely black faculty been recruited to teach whites anything. The Lenox School, under the direction of John Lewis, offered a star-studded roster of musicians and composers to a small, international selection of students who had submitted audition tapes through the mail. Lenox invented jazz pedagogy as it went along. The staff included Dizzy Gillespie, Oscar Peterson, Ray Brown, Jimmy Giuffre, George Russell, Max Roach, Gunther Schuller, J. J. Johnson, and Ornette Coleman (who, although registered as a student, also taught), along with several ensembles. In the first year, there were thirty-four instructors for forty-five students; as the number of students doubled, the staff also increased. For the educators, some of whom continued to teach at other institutions, the experience was a revelation; most of them had learned by doing—now they were at the frontier of discovering how to pass on their knowledge.

Lenox's goal was to combine chronological history with musical technique, and to rid jazz of semi-mystical notions of racial or "natural" talent. The courses ranged from writer Marshall Stearns's "The History of Jazz" to Schuller's "The Analytical History of Jazz." The school had grown out of public discussions of folk music and jazz that had taken place in the city of Lenox since 1950, under the aegis of a jazz club called the Music Inn. Each summer the Music Inn sponsored jazz workshops organized by Stearns, an English professor who later wrote an important jazz history and founded the Institute of Jazz Studies at Rutgers University. These discussions inspired the Third Stream movement and led directly to the creation of the Lenox School, which lasted four years, closing after the 1960 season.

By the time Lenox folded, jazz studies had begun to make headway in accredited schools. The most important of these were the Berklee College of Music in Boston and the University of North Texas in Denton. North Texas offered the first degree in jazz studies in 1947, and accumulated one of the largest libraries of American music; its big-band workshop has served as the training ground for a legion of gifted players. Berklee began to offer undergraduate degrees in jazz performance and composition in the middle 1960s, and continues to boast the best-known jazz department in American education. By 2000, countless musicians could claim an undergraduate background in jazz studies. Jazz players now served their apprenticeships not on the road, but in classes and school bands.

Boston probably made its most influential contribution to jazz history with the impresario George Wein, who founded the Newport Jazz Festival, across the state line in Rhode Island. Musicians knew Wein, a pianist and occasional bandleader, primarily as the proprietor of two Boston jazz clubs, Storyville and Mahogany Hall, which specialized in Dixieland and swing—though Storyville broadened its menu to include Charlie Parker, Stan Getz, and other modernists. In 1954, Wein answered the call of socialites Elaine and Louis Lorillard, who wanted him to program a jazz festival in one of the least likely, most insular settings imaginable: a tennis and croquet court in Newport, patronized by old money. The shutters of many mansions closed in outrage, but Wein prevailed, and jazz found acceptance as a symbol of postwar social enlightenment and good times. Within two years Hollywood appropriated the Newport Jazz Festival as the setting for the movie *High Society,* and in 1958 an independent production company visited Newport to shoot the much-imitated Bert Stern documentary *Jazz on a Summer's Day.*

Taking a cue from the scholarly events at Music Inn, Wein programmed panels and workshops along with the concerts, which presented every major jazz star from Armstrong and Ellington to Miles and Monk. He also invited the participation of musicians not always accepted in the jazz world; his motive may have been commercial, but his choices (including gospel singer Mahalia Jackson, Frank Sinatra, Ray Charles, and Chuck Berry) reflected both the historicist idea of placing jazz in the wider context of contemporary music and the fusion idea of showing how jazz and other music interact. Audience insurrections in the late 1960s caused a suspension of the festival in Newport, but Wein quickly relocated his operation in New York, where it grew far larger, establishing him as the most powerful producer in jazz. He later created festivals in France, New Orleans, and elsewhere, and even rebuilt summer events in Newport. By the time he stepped down in 2006, panels and lectures had generally disappeared from his presentations, though the Jazz Journalists Association, founded in the 1980s by writer Howard Mandel, had successfully reinstated them at Newport and elsewhere. Meanwhile, jazz festivals had become annual events on the cultural calendars of six continents.

AVANT-GARDE HISTORICISM AND NEOCLASSICISM

Historicism all but vanished during the avant-garde 1960s, when the emphasis in jazz was on pushing boundaries. But it made a major and apparently permanent comeback in the 1970s, as the second generation avant-garde looked to the past in order to vary its music. The boundless eclecticism favored by New York's loft scene coincided with a significant surge in jazz education, as influenced by Williams's *Smithsonian Collection of Classic Jazz* and similar compilations designed to examine jazz from a historical perspective. Record companies in that period released comprehensive boxed sets encompassing entire careers, movements, and label catalogs.

At the same time, great jazz artists whose careers had faltered during the all-consuming rise of rock in the late 1960s and early 1970s returned to jazz, creating tremendous interest in musicians of all eras. Some players had shifted their focus to studio work, the academy, and Broadway or Las Vegas pit bands; others relocated to Europe or simply kept low profiles. Now they were greeted as "living legends." Suddenly you could see long-absent musicians who had started out in the 1920s, like Benny Carter and Doc Cheatham, or in the bop era, like Dexter Gordon, Red Rodney, and James Moody. In this atmosphere, musicians experimented with the very nature of style, and the audiences seemed ready for almost anything.

Few musicians in this period proved more startling or prolific than Anthony Braxton (b. 1945), who initially made his mark on alto saxophone but eventually appeared in concerts and on records playing every instrument in the saxophone and clarinet family, plus flute and piano. Born in Chicago, Braxton began on clarinet at eleven; after three years in the army, he attended Roosevelt University as a philosophy major. At the same time, he joined the AACM, and in 1967 launched the Creative Construction Company, a trio with violinist Leroy Jenkins and trumpet player Leo Smith. In 1969, Braxton released a two-disc album, *For Alto*, consisting of unaccompanied alto saxophone solos. The sheer audacity of the venture generated a firestorm, with a by-then-familiar response: he was either a genius or a fraud. Some critics argued that the album was not jazz, but most had to concede that it demonstrated Braxton's thoroughgoing mastery of the saxophone. It also showed his knowledge of avant-garde classical music as well as cutting-edge jazz—he was interested equally in free improvisations and structural blueprints. Braxton kept his listeners guessing through the variety of his associations, including sideman duties with Chick Corea, Dave Holland, and Dave Brubeck, and duets with Max Roach. He issued dozens of recordings under his own name, with instrumentation ranging from synthesizer to twin orchestras.

Braxton's historicism caused more controversy than accord. In 1974, he formed a quartet, In the Tradition, to present jazz and pop standards (originally it confined itself to pieces by Charlie Parker), but the band performed in ways that undermined the feeling of the original works. His choice of instruments (like the huge contrabass saxophone), harmonies, and rhythms often seemed to counter the traditions he promised to explore. He was criticized for not swinging, for ignoring chord progressions, and for titling his pieces with drawings that resembled circuit diagrams. Ultimately, his music proved so varied and touched on so many idioms and styles (from brass band marches to atonal big-band swing) that the word *jazz*—as Duke Ellington had warned long ago of jazz in general and of his own music in particular—could not contain it. Braxton eventually found a home in academia as a professor of music. In 1994, he created the Tri-Centric Foundation to present multimedia and interdisciplinary concerts in New York.

"PIECE THREE"

Braxton released one of his most widely noted albums, *Creative Orchestra Music*, in 1976. It was his first work with a large ensemble, and the selection of musicians emphasized the stylistic sweep that characterized the Loft Era; here were musicians associated with swing (Seldon Powell), bebop (Jon Faddis), fusion (Dave Holland), Euro modernism (Kenny Wheeler), and every kind of avant-garde music in and out of jazz. Each of the album's six selections illustrated a different type of composition, employing aspects of big-band jazz, parade music, and free improvisation. "Piece Three" remains unique in attempting to construct and deconstruct the sort of march that James Reese Europe's regimental band might have played during the First

World War. The title simply means that it's the album's third track (it's also designated by one of Braxton's mathematic diagrams). As a composition, it represents the kind of wry, transgressive gambit he does best.

From the very beginning, the music startles with its authenticity: whoever heard of a march on a jazz album? Yet for all the jubilance of the opening four strains, the last of which suggests the kind of music heard in an old German beer garden more than it does a military cadence, we soon realize that the composer has other things on his mind. The *oompahs* are suddenly stuck in a repetitive rut, as though the melody had been wrung out. Dissonant chords signal the entrance of trumpeter Leo Smith, playing pitches of no use in a march. Yet the bass lines, harmonies, and rhythms are controlled and deliberate. No less surprising is the appealing ostinato for reeds and flute that sets up the droll, tailgate trombone playing by George Lewis, and the brief spot of parade drumming that introduces Braxton's quizzical clarinet solo. Such touches of contrast and humor occur throughout the piece, as does the persistent echoing and harmonizing of the glockenspiel. When the march is reconstructed for the finale (6:34), the harmonies approach those of an ordinary march, to the point of cliché. Yet in this context, they have the effect of an ironic wink, as the piece waddles off in the sunshine.

PIECE THREE

Anthony Braxton

Kenny Wheeler, Cecil Bridgewater, Leo Smith, trumpets; Jon Faddis, trumpet and piccolo trumpet; George Lewis, Garrett List, trombones; Jack Jeffers, bass trombone; Jonathan Dorn, tuba; Anthony Braxton, alto saxophone and clarinet; Seldon Powell, alto saxophone and flute; Ronald Bridgewater, tenor saxophone; Bruce Johnstone, baritone saxophone and bass clarinet; Roscoe Mitchell, bass saxophone; Dave Holland, bass; Karl Berger, glockenspiel; Warren Smith, Barry Altschul, snare drums; Frederick Rzewski, bass drum; Philip Wilson, marching cymbals

LABEL: *Creative Orchestra Music 1976*, Arista 4080; *The Complete Arista Recordings of Anthony Braxton* (Mosaic Box)
DATE: 1976
STYLE: avant-garde historicist
FORM: idiosyncratic

Introduction

| 0:00 | The piece begins with the band playing standard introductory material for a march: a thunderous line in octaves that snakes its way upward to a half cadence on the dominant chord. |

Strain A

0:03   The trumpets play the melody, doubled by the glockenspiel, over a steady two-beat accompaniment in the tuba and percussion. The saxophones answer with riff figures. Underneath, the trombones play simple supporting lines.

Strain B

0:17   After a brief pause, the new strain begins. The instrumentation remains the same, while the harmony begins not on the tonic but on the dominant.

Strain C

0:31   The third strain begins on yet another chord. The tune in the trumpets continues as before, while the saxophone riffs become more elaborate.

Strain D

0:45   The melody shifts to the tuba, doubled by the bass drum, and falls on the downbeat. The upbeats are filled with chords played crisply by the brass. The harmony shifts back and forth between the tonic and the dominant.

Solo 1

0:59   Suddenly, the bass line moves to a new, dissonant note. The harmony on the upbeat sounds as though it ought to resolve—but it doesn't.

1:03   The bass line and chords, which had been alternating in simple duple meter, suddenly switch to a new meter in groups of three. Adding to the confusion, we hear a caterwauling trumpet sound in the uppermost register.

1:06   The harmony remains stuck on the dissonance. The trumpet player, Smith, descends to a more normal register, but his choice of notes remains decidedly "outside."

1:11   The bass line and chords now change meter unpredictably: sometimes in groups of two, sometimes in three, four, or even five.

1:21   Smith's melodic line occasionally contains fragments of melody, but the overall impression is of a *sound*, hovering dissonantly above the constantly changing accompaniment.

1:33   As if to stabilize his line, Smith leans into a single sustained note. This, too, eventually disintegrates into higher unstable pitches.

1:50   The trumpet sounds as if it were mimicking human speech.

2:16   Struggling to read their parts, the accompaniment players occasionally miss some of Braxton's relentlessly changing meters.

Solo 2

2:33   The solo and accompaniment suddenly come to a stop. In their place we hear a simple five-note line, played by the clarinets in octaves. They continue to repeat it as an ostinato.

2:41	A saxophone joins the ostinato.
2:48	A flute adds a part of its own, creating a thin harmony.
2:55	With a dramatic glissando, Lewis enters on trombone. He begins with simple, idiomatic trombone gestures, but soon adds stratospheric assaults on the upper register and extraordinarily quick passages.
3:03	In the background, another flute begins to improvise.
3:09	The glockenspiel and clarinet join the ostinato.
3:15	Using the trombone's slide, Lewis punctuates his solo with loud glissandos.
3:40	As Lewis finishes his solo, the snare drum interrupts the texture with a faster rhythmic figure that displaces the ostinato.

Solo 3

3:43	A cymbal crash introduces the next section. While a percussionist keeps time on the side of his instrument, brass instruments play chords in a steady short-short-long rhythmic gesture. Braxton starts a disjointed solo on clarinet.
3:47	More and more instruments continue to join the chords, making them heavier and more dissonant. Each instrument adds its own note, and several begin to drop by half step.
3:59	The saxophones interrupt with a long, low-pitched dissonant chord.
4:08	As Braxton continues improvising, the glockenspiel adds notes above him.
4:13	The saxophones play another dissonant chord. After a brief pause, they play two more dissonant chords, one immediately following the other.
4:25	Faddis on piccolo trumpet adds notes that complicate the rhythm. Another dissonant chord follows.
4:37	After reaching a peak of intensity, the background chords quiet down.
4:40	A higher-pitched dissonant chord is followed by a new burst from the piccolo trumpet.
4:51	The dissonant chords begin to increase in number, each emphasized by the crash of a cymbal.
4:58	Yet another dissonant chord. As Braxton reaches the climax of his solo, his tone becomes shrill and distorted.
5:09	A loud cymbal announces three more dissonant chords, augmented by crazy decoration from the glockenspiel.
5:27	Three more dissonant chords, each with its own cymbal crash.

Interlude

5:42	A few strokes of the snare drum dissipate the previous section.
5:44	The saxophones enter with a chromatic unison line.
5:46	As with the interlude to Sousa's "Stars and Stripes Forever," the entire band descends on a chromatic scale.
5:48	The gesture is repeated twice, each time at a higher pitch (a sequence).

| 5:54 | The phrases become shorter, each ending with a half-step dissonance. |
| 5:59 | As the clarinet trills wildly, the band inexorably moves toward a big cadence. |

Strain E

| 6:04 | In a slower, grander tempo, the band triumphantly returns to the opening mood of the piece. The cymbal plays on every beat, while the piccolo trumpet improvises a countermelody on top. |
| 6:20 | A descending line signals a repetition. |

Strain E

6:22	As the band plays the strain one more time, the snare drums cement the groove with press-rolls.
6:34	To signal the end, Braxton adds a slight intensification to the harmonic progression.
6:40	One last blast ends the piece.

The Loft Era musicians borrowed from old styles as resources: they combined swing, funk, and free rhythms to create an independent music seasoned with humor, irony, nostalgia, sarcasm, and deep feelings. For them, the aging battle cry of "free jazz" meant the freedom to play whatever they liked—even ragtime, even a march. In the manner of Hegel's dialectic, however, that thesis invariably triggered an antithesis in the early 1980s. The ensuing movement involved a more conservative approach toward historicism, which may be characterized as neoclassical. This approach was predicated on fidelity to a specific canon of masterpieces. Instead of looking at marches or swing or bop as generic styles that could be interpreted and reinterpreted, it paid homage to particular musicians and works, infusing them with a contemporary luster—at best. Yet neoclassicists also argued that jazz must swing in a certain way, that harmonies and melodies had to conform to traditional practices, that jazz had clear-cut borders imposed by its key artists.

This kind of traditionalism found acceptance for several reasons, not least the conservative temper of the time. Ronald Reagan had just been elected president, promising to implement (despite his own messy personal life) traditional American values, a harsh approach toward law and order, and a rollback of 1960s Great Society programs, including welfare and civil rights. He represented a backlash against the excesses associated with a period roiled by an unnecessary war, political assassinations, and student rebellion. Reagan, who frequently referred to the allegedly golden age of his youth, sometimes confused real life with movie plots, and his popularity reflected both a pragmatic yearning for a steadying hand at the tiller of government and a purely sentimental longing for a paradise lost. He precipitated a storm of anti-intellectualism and hostility toward the arts, especially those thought to appeal to an *elitist* (still a prominent code word on the right) audience. Arts funding was reduced, while books and other art works were censored or removed from public display. In this atmosphere, nostalgia for an orderly, swinging style of jazz was practically a given.

Established players who had been alienated by the avant-garde and fusion began to explore jazz history by paying homage to deceased or neglected musicians. At first the trend seemed novel, but it grew into a tidal wave of tributes on records and in concerts. Joe Henderson recorded albums of music by Billy Strayhorn and Miles Davis; Kenny Barron and musicians associated with Thelonious Monk formed a quartet, Sphere, to play his music. Philly Joe Jones organized a big band to play music by Tadd Dameron. Steve Lacy focused on works by the overlooked pianist-composer Herbie Nichols. Keith Jarrett, who almost always played original music as a bandleader, now launched a standards trio to reinvestigate classic pop and jazz tunes.

The most expansive tribute bands were orchestras designed to examine big-band jazz, either by performing original arrangements or by commissioning new versions of classic works. The jazz repertory movement got its start in the middle 1970s, with the debuts of two groups. The New York Jazz Repertory Company, launched by George Wein, produced two seasons of concerts at Carnegie Hall by rotating music directors: Cecil Taylor led a large orchestra that included former students; George Russell conducted a revised version of his expansive *Living Time*; Paul Jeffrey conducted orchestral versions of music by Thelonious Monk with Monk playing piano; and so forth. By contrast, the National Jazz Ensemble, a solitary orchestra with stable personnel, directed by bassist Chuck Israels, played new versions of venerable jazz works. By the middle 1980s, those organizations had long since departed, but the neoclassical sentiment whetted the appetite for more ambitious jazz repertory concerts. At first these were isolated events, presenting large bands and small. Duke Ellington's music was frequently revived. Other presentations recreated famous events, like the 1938 Benny Goodman Carnegie Hall concert and the 1924 Paul Whiteman Aeolian Hall concert.

In 1986, the American Jazz Orchestra debuted, conducted by John

Lewis, who had managed to create one of the most successful small ensembles of his time, the Modern Jazz Quartet, while pioneering jazz education. In addition to music by Ellington, Goodman, Count Basie, Jimmie Lunceford, Mary Lou Williams, Woody Herman, Dizzy Gillespie, and Gil Evans, the orchestra performed arrangements that had rarely if ever been heard, including Ellington's *Black, Brown, and Beige*, conducted by Maurice Peress with a revised ending based on instructions Ellington dictated to Peress shortly before his death. Several composers from various eras of jazz history—Benny Carter, Jimmy Heath, Muhal Richard Abrams, Henry Threadgill, Bob Brookmeyer, David Murray—were invited to present new works during the orchestra's seven years. Similar orchestras were created in San Diego, Washington, D.C. (at the Smithsonian), and elsewhere.

From 1992 to 2002, Jon Faddis, a high-note trumpet virtuoso and former protégé of Dizzy Gillespie, led the Carnegie Hall Jazz Band, which premiered new versions of classic jazz works, creating such unexpected transformations as an arrangement for full orchestra of John Coltrane's *A Love Supreme*, and recovered neglected works like Lalo Schifrin's suite *Gillespiana*. But the most durable of the new repertory orchestras debuted in 1987 at New York's leading cultural institution. The Lincoln Center Jazz Orchestra, under the direction of Wynton Marsalis, achieved outstanding successes, musically and in the frequently neglected area of fundraising: an independent jazz wing was built for the center, including a multiplex that houses concert halls, a night club, and educational facilities. Encouraged by the Jazz at Lincoln Center program, university and high school music departments introduced jazz repertory in their student orchestras.

Some performers took a more nostalgic attitude. Singer-pianists Harry Connick Jr. and Diana Krall demonstrated popular appeal by resurrecting performance styles of the 1940s and 1950s. Connick was the first of several male singers to invoke the manner of Frank Sinatra, though he also spiced his performances with piano playing that reflected Monk's percussive wit. Krall initially made her name with a trio that echoed the instrumentation (piano, guitar, bass) and songs of Nat King Cole. She later recorded ballads with lush studio orchestras in the manner of mainstream 1950s singers. Less rewarding were a cluster of retro-swing orchestras that triggered a revival of ballroom dancing. These bands were fine for dancing but not for listening, as they usually performed in a generic style that lacked the individuality at the core of the great swing bands. They appealed to a nostalgic desire for the world as it was, and soon faded away. Jazz nostalgia even found its way into such movies as Bertrand Tavernier's *'Round*

Midnight, in which tenor saxophonist Dexter Gordon created a character based on Bud Powell and Lester Young; Clint Eastwood's *Bird*, a fictionalized biography of Charlie Parker, with Parker's saxophone solos grafted to a modern rhythm section; and Robert Altman's *Kansas City*, in which 1930s musicians were viewed as a positive counterstatement to the city's appalling crime and corruption.

The young neoclassical musicians of the 1980s found an unmistakable leader in Wynton Marsalis (b. 1961), an audacious trumpet virtuoso who loudly denied that avant-garde music and fusion had anything to do with jazz. Marsalis also sought to alter the personal styles of musicians. Ridiculing the dashikis, occasional facial paint, and general informality in the way musicians appeared onstage, he insisted on a suit-and-tie dress code that reinstated the elegance of Swing Era bands. Marsalis was the ultimate Reagan-era jazz musician. He launched his recording career with simultaneous jazz and classical releases, winning Grammy Awards in both categories. Highly intelligent, impeccably groomed, and fiercely outspoken, he changed the discussion in jazz from one of progressive modernism—with its liberal borrowings from world, popular, and classical music—to the strict interpretation of mainstream jazz parameters, insisting that jazz had to swing with a particular regularity.

Though lambasted as divisive by many musicians, Marsalis was quickly accepted by the popular culture, frequently appearing in televised concerts, in magazine articles, and as a key voice in Ken Burns's television miniseries *Jazz*. He was the first straight-ahead jazz musician to achieve that degree of renown in more than a decade. Yet Marsalis was as hard on himself as he was on everyone else, making his mark with all kinds of jazz historicism. As the artistic director of Jazz at Lincoln Center, he conducted dozens of jazz repertory concerts, interpreting composers from Ellington and Armstrong to Mingus and Gil Evans. He recorded fanciful interpretations of Morton and Monk. He created a massive body of original work that probes African American history, tradition, and music in such formats as jazz ensembles, chamber groups, and ballet.

Marsalis was born in New Orleans to a musical family; his father, Ellis Marsalis, a well-known pianist and educator, instilled in him and his gifted brothers a sense of dedication and discipline. Yet only Wynton insisted on establishing an exclusive circle around his particular view of jazz. His older brother, the equally skilled saxophonist Branford Marsalis, seemed to take particular pleasure in violating that concept by playing in diverse musical contexts, including a tour with Sting, and creating a band that uses techniques borrowed from hip-hop. Wynton did not begin as a purist. At fourteen, he played Haydn's Trumpet Concerto with the New Orleans Philharmonic, and his early taste in jazz ran to funk and fusion. In 1980, while studying at Juilliard, Marsalis auditioned for Art Blakey and won a much-coveted position with Blakey's Jazz Messengers. After making a dynamic showing on Blakey's *Album of the Year*, he toured with a Herbie Hancock quartet and then organized his own quintet with Branford—a group loosely modeled on the 1963–68 Miles Davis Quintet. Many people found his deliberate turn to the musical past, along with his dark suits and sober demeanor, a delightful return to jazz sanity. If he hadn't used his celebrity to attack less well-placed musicians, setting off a windstorm of petty feuds, his success might have proved even more widespread.

Unfortunately, the mass media that accepted Marsalis as an engaging personality and musical spokesman was no longer responsive to jazz itself. It could absorb Marsalis as a celebrity, but could not roll the clock back to a time when musicians appeared on radio and television and when record releases by its most creative players were well-publicized events. Marsalis's exacting historicism underscored the fact that jazz now competed less with pop or classical music than with its own past. Young fans were challenged with a choice: do you buy a new tribute to Monk, or do you buy Monk? As jazz record sales plummeted, even Marsalis—despite his Grammys and a 1997 Pulitzer Prize for his oratorio *Blood on the Fields*—was dropped by his label, Columbia Records, which turned its corporate back on jazz altogether.

Marsalis, nothing daunted, worked as busily as ever, devoting his energies to tours, education, and star-studded (if jazz shy) fundraising events to ensure the success of Jazz at Lincoln Center. His music became increasingly eclectic, combining references to earlier forms of jazz in a manner that could only be described as pastiche. For a while, his trumpet playing turned from the Miles Davis approach to an earlier style that employed mutes and vocalized sounds, à la Ellington. In time, however, he also developed greater clarity in his improvisations, making the most of long phrases and high-note gambits, and perfecting his highly personal timbre. He also loosened his strictures, though not about the avant-garde, and collaborated on mainstream Americana and vocal projects, including a popular recording with Willie Nelson.

"PROCESSIONAL"

Marsalis's *In This House, On This Morning,* recorded during 1992 and 1993, represented his most ambitious work to date. Written for his septet, it chronicles a Sunday in the life of a religious congregation, from devotional prayers through the sermons and hymns of the church service to the "Pot Blessed Dinner." It is structured in three movements, each of which is made up of smaller units. "Processional," from the first part, follows "Devotion" and "Call to Prayer" and precedes "Representative Offerings" and "The Lord's Prayer."

"Processional" introduces a gospel theme that's every bit as credible as Anthony Braxton's march. But where Braxton bulldozes his march before reconstituting it, Marsalis uses subtler touches to give his take on gospel music a modernist affect, mostly through odd structural changes that slightly distort our expectations. These alterations have a historical accuracy in that Southern black rural music tended to be less precise and codified than city music. Marsalis's interpretation also owes a great deal to Stravinsky's approach to metrical shifts in his early ballets, especially *The Rite of Spring.* (Marsalis recorded Stravinsky's *L' histoire du soldat* as *Fiddler's Tale* in 1999.) In "Processional," phrases come up a bit short (2:14) or long (2:37) or peculiar (the "threes" at 3:49). Such oddities, thoroughly rehearsed, give the piece its spry whimsy. Other references to the past are also in evidence. The A theme is in the style of folk songs and hymns like "Down by the Riverside" and "I've Been Working on the Railroad," and consequently recalls Horace Silver's similar piece, "The Preacher." The harmonies underlying the C theme suggest those of "Sweet Georgia Brown" (1:04). The use of tambourine is as evocative of gospel traditions as Braxton's glockenspiel is of march tradition. Ellington's influence is apparent in the blending of bowed bass and horns (0:42), the superbly vocalized trombone playing by Wycliffe Gordon (throughout), and Marsalis's half-valve trumpet effects (2:53). Each detail emphasizes the literalness of Marsalis's approach to the past.

PROCESSIONAL

Wynton Marsalis Septet

Wynton Marsalis, trumpet; Wycliffe Gordon, trombone; Wessell Anderson, alto saxophone; Todd Williams, tenor saxophone; Eric Reed, piano; Reginald Veal, bass; Herlin Riley, drums

LABEL: *In This House, On This Morning,* Columbia C2K-53220
DATE: 1993
STYLE: historicist
FORM: AABA, with contrasting C section and interludes

Introduction (transition)

0:00	The band moves out of the preceding movement, "Call to Prayer" (echoes of which can be heard in the first few seconds). A hoarse-sounding trombone leads with a descending glissando into this new movement.

A (16 bars)

0:03	The trombonist (Gordon) plays a pair of four-bar phrases. The groove solidly evokes the gospel church: the tambourine accents on the back-beat, while the bass bounces fluidly between a syncopated two-beat pattern and a walking bass. The piano plays simple, churchy chords.
0:13	The second eight-bar phrase echoes the first, moving to a more extended cadence, backed by a walking-bass pattern.

A

0:23	Behind the trombone, a choir of trumpet, alto saxophone, and tenor saxophone plays a riff in block-chord harmony.
0:33	As Gordon plays the second phrase, the horn choir moves its accompanying harmonies to a simpler rhythmic pattern.

Interlude

0:42	The trombone's melody is interrupted by a simple four-note, descending pentatonic riff, played by the three horns and the bowed bass. After a short pause, Gordon begins to play.
0:44	He's cut short by a two-bar break, in which the bass bows a simple variation of the descending riff. Once again, Gordon restarts his line.

B (8 bars)

0:47	As the harmony moves to IV, the horns play a rhythmically intricate riff.
0:49	At the end of the first phrase, a bar is deliberately cut short (it lasts for only two beats instead of four).
0:54	The second phrase is interrupted by a return of the descending riff (harmonized). This time, the line is cut short after its third note.

A (abbreviated)

0:56	The opening melody returns; but by inserting a few strategic rests, Marsalis forces it into unexpected rhythmic shapes. The tambourine continues to play the backbeat, but its position within the meter is continually changing.

C (16 bars)

1:04	After a short break, the tenor and alto saxophones play simple quarter-note melodies. Each line is designed to fit within the new harmony, but they often clash with sharp dissonances. Riley (drums) enters, displacing the tambourine with a firm backbeat on the snare drum.
1:14	As the harmony shifts to more distant chords, the melody lines become more rhythmically independent. In response, Riley plays more complex polyrhythms.

A

1:24	With a plunger mute, Gordon returns us to the mood of the opening, playing in between the tambourine backbeats with an intensely distorted timbre.
1:28	After his first phrase, a band member responds with an appreciative grunt.
1:34	In the second eight-bar phrase, Gordon shows his command of the instrument, playing soulful yet rhythmically intricate lines.

A

1:44	As the horns return to their riff, Gordon improvises in response to their call.

Interlude

2:04	In a two-bar break, the horns and bass play the four-note pentatonic riff.

B

2:06	Behind the trombone, the horns play increasingly complicated harmonies and rhythms.
2:14	Once again, the phrase is interrupted by the descending riff—this time only three notes (which means a bar and a *half*).

A

2:16	Gordon returns to the main melody.
2:25	The bass and the pianist's left hand set up a counterrhythm—three eighth notes against the prevailing quarter-note pulse. Against this, we can hear two lines: one played by the trombone and the trumpet, the other by the saxophones. Riley improvises his own accompaniment on the tambourine.
2:35	In a two-bar break, the bass enters with a plucked version of the descending riff.

B

2:37	Over the harmony of the bridge, the horns combine on a complex block-chord figure. The concluding drum figure adds an extra measure, making the phrase five bars long.

2:43	The second measure of the next phrase is slightly longer, pushing the downbeat arrival (at 2:46) one beat late.

C

2:48	The rhythmic groove suddenly shifts away from gospel toward a modern jazz sound. The bass plays a walking-bass line, while the piano voices the chords as postbop harmonies. Marsalis takes a solo.
2:53	Marsalis squeezes out several notes through half-valving.

C

3:08	Anderson begins a four-bar solo on alto saxophone.
3:12	His improvisation is matched by four bars by Williams on tenor: the two are trading fours.
3:17	Anderson's and Williams's lines become increasingly complicated as they play off each other's ideas.

C

3:27	As the saxophones continue trading fours, the accompaniment by the drums and piano heats up in intensity.
3:41	Williams begins playing rapid passages in double-time.

C

3:46	Anderson mimics Williams's rapid passage before returning to a normal groove.
3:49	Williams's response comes in after only three bars: the soloists are now "trading *threes*."
4:00	The two horns enter on a set of composed lines, moving in steady quarter notes (reminiscent of 1:04).
4:03	In the background, Gordon begins a trombone glissando, starting softly but growing in intensity.

A

4:05	The glissando pulls us back into the gospel groove: the trombone is in the lead, the horns playing riffs behind.

Coda

4:12	In a two-bar break, the piano and bass interrupt with a rising line that modulates to an unfamiliar key a half step higher.
4:14	The main melody of the **A** section is repeated in the new key.
4:21	The band stops on a blue note, holding it out as if deliberately slowing the tempo to prepare for a final cadence. After a slight pause, though, the melody line continues as before.
4:24	An unexpected missing downbeat masks a sudden modulation to the original key. The missing beat forces the tambourine's backbeat to fall on the downbeat.

4:27	As it approaches the cadence, the band disorients us further by playing a melodic figure in three different rhythmic shapes.
4:31	Finally, the band lands on its final cadence.
4:35	As the piece is ready to move on to the next movement, the track cuts off.

ALTERNATIVE ROUTES TO HISTORY

Between Wynton Marsalis's historicist fidelity and Anthony Braxton's historicist revisionism, less extreme ways of dealing with the past won the hearts of most jazz musicians. Some continued to devote concerts and albums to the works of major figures, like Ellington or Monk, while others wandered so far afield from jazz traditions that they opened up what was, in effect, virgin territory—rock songs, country blues, classical themes, folk idioms. Jazz in the twenty-first century may be characterized, to a degree, by the number and variety of these projects. They tend to be more conventional than the loft generation's radical interpretations, while ignoring strictures favored by the neoclassicists. A very short list of examples can also serve as an introduction to some of the most gifted and influential jazz musicians on the current scene:

Clarinetist Don Byron (b. 1958) has interpreted the works of Mickey Katz, a Jewish musical satirist and composer of klezmer dance music; novelty composer Raymond Scott, whose pieces were often adapted for Looney Tune cartoons; and 1930s jazz bassist John Kirby, known for "swinging the classics." Guitarist Bill Frisell (b. 1951) plays freely improvised concert sets that range over every kind of American music, in a kind of stream-of-consciousness that ties Monk to Aaron Copland to Bob Dylan to Charles Ives to traditional folk and country tunes. Singer Cassandra Wilson (b. 1955) has expanded the vocalist's repertory by reaching back to Delta blues singers like Son House and Robert Johnson and to recent pop performers like Joni Mitchell, Dylan, and the Monkees. Singer Dee Dee Bridgewater (b. 1950) has recorded albums of instrumental pieces by Horace Silver, outfitted with new lyrics, and French chanson; she expanded her reach as a singer-actress on and off Broadway. The Bad Plus Trio, consisting of pianist Ethan Iverson (b. 1973), bassist Reid Anderson (b. 1970), and drummer Dave King (b. 1970), plays a unique repertory that includes Nirvana, Blondie, Aphex Twin, Queen, Radiohead, and Ornette Coleman.

Guitarist Marc Ribot (b. 1954) has adapted melodies of Albert Ayler to solo guitar, collaborated with punk rock groups, and created the band Los Cubanos Postizos to explore Afro-Cuban compositions. Trumpet player Nicholas Payton (b. 1973) has performed tributes to Cannonball Adderley, Herbie Hancock, and 1930s Kansas City swing; performed solos by Louis Armstrong and King Oliver; and recorded duets with ninety-year-old trumpeter Doc Cheatham. Pianist Uri Caine (b. 1956) combines classical, rock, electronica, and jazz techniques in predominantly jazz settings to interpret the music of Mahler, Bach, and Mozart; he created a musical montage to reproduce the ethnic complexity of early Tin Pan Alley. Trumpet player Dave Douglas (b. 1963) has formed discrete bands to pay homage to Wayne Shorter, Mary Lou Williams, and Booker Little; he has also played klezmer music and introduced the band Tiny Bell Trio to interpret Baltic folk tunes. Italian alto saxophonist Francisco Cafiso (b. 1989), who began recording at fourteen, has recreated the entire body of Charlie Parker's recordings with strings, accompanied by the thirteen-piece chamber orchestra I Solisti di Perugia. Trumpet player Wallace Roney (b. 1960) has participated in Chick Corea's Bud Powell tribute band and Gerry Mulligan's recreation of the "birth of the cool" sessions, and performed in concert a faithful rendition of Miles Davis's *Kind of Blue*.

These projects (the tip of the iceberg) suggest some of the ways the historicist outlook links modern jazz to its own past and that of other kinds of music. They underscore the degree to which jazz has been liberated from the relatively orthodox repertory that governed the postbop era, which focused almost exclusively on standards by pantheon songwriters, new tunes based on the harmonies of those standards, and original modernist works of various quality. The historical eclecticism that has predominated since the 1980s has more in common with the repertory of the Swing Era bands, which routinely adopted pop songs as well as an occasional classical theme and even a few ethnic styles, from Cuban to Yiddish.

Two unpredictable stylists of the new historicism, representing different generations, found mutual inspiration in conflating the new with the old. The drummer Ronald Shannon Jackson (b. 1940) and the saxophonist James Carter are known for aggressive virtuoso skills and a willingness to look beyond musical parameters that led them to explore the avant-garde, fusion, and funk, as well as traditional jazz, separately and together. Jackson was born in Fort Worth, where his mother played church piano and his father stocked jukeboxes and ran a record store. He listened to everything: records by Howlin' Wolf and B. B. King alongside those of Charlie Parker and Erroll Garner; he heard hillbilly and rhythm and blues on radio and classical music in school. Jackson studied piano, then switched to drums, and began playing professionally at fifteen. He enrolled at Lincoln University in Pennsylvania, but dropped out to pursue his career. After resuming his education at the University of Bridgeport, he studied sociology and history. He received a 1967 scholarship from the New York College of Music.

Over the next three years, Jackson backed singer Betty Carter, played timpani for Charles Mingus, and toured with Albert Ayler. But jazz was in the economic doldrums, and for five years he played mostly weddings and bar mitzvahs. In 1975, as Jackson ate breakfast in a Greenwich Village restaurant, Ornette Coleman walked in and mentioned he was looking for a drummer for his band Prime Time. Jackson's subsequent recordings with Coleman, *Dancing in Your Head* and *Body Meta*, aroused much interest. He combined tensile attentiveness with a heavily jubilant rhythmic feeling; in effect, he brought funk to avant-garde jazz. This was reaffirmed in 1978, when he recorded with Cecil Taylor: on *3 Phasis,* Jackson, without warning, infused the climax of the piece with a backbeat rhythm that inspired Taylor and the ensemble to a rigorous finish.

Soon Jackson was leading his own band, which he called the Decoding Society because it sought to find the common denominator that brought various musical forces into harmony:

♦ ♦ ♦

The thing I'm trying to do is organize the music, and you have to rehearse constantly, because we're talking about putting together all the musical ideas of the past 30 years. It's got to swing—swing is the egg in the meatloaf— but it can be bop, reggae, rock, classical. It has to be a total experience for everyone involved, like going to a Buddhist meeting, where we deal in our energies, not in egos or who we are or what we do.

♦ ♦ ♦

In 1994, the Decoding Society recorded an exemplary quartet album, *What Spirit Say*, featuring James Carter on tenor and soprano saxophones. At twenty-five, Carter (b. 1969, the year Braxton recorded *For Alto*) already had an impressive resume. Along with Joshua Redman, a tenor and soprano saxophonist born the same year, he was considered by some to be the representative musician for an era in which historicism simultaneously boosted involvement with the past and knocked down borders in the present. Both men comfortably straddled the bounding line between bop and avant-garde, worked in funk, and developed unrestricted repertories. But as Redman focused on increasingly personal, complex compositions and a saxophone style that emphasized timbre and restraint, Carter pursued a ferocious improvisational enthusiasm. Born in Detroit, he began on saxophone at eleven, and five years later toured Scandinavia with a student ensemble. While still in his teens, he worked with Wynton Marsalis and Lester Bowie, the two trumpet players who incarnated the divide in 1980s jazz, publicly feuding with each other after Marsalis declared that Bowie and the Art Ensemble of Chicago weren't jazz musicians. Even so, they apparently agreed on Carter's overwhelming musicianship, revealed in his mastery of saxophones from soprano to baritone. Carter later played in Marsalis's Lincoln Center Jazz Orchestra, but his inclinations ran to the open-endedness of Loft Era freemen; after moving to New York in 1990, he enlisted in two of Bowie's ensembles, including a fusion group centered on the Hammond B3 organ.

Carter recorded his first album, *JC on the Set,* in 1993, a dramatic debut that led to a series of quartet albums. He defied categorization, playing with harmonic sophistication on one number and in gritty funk mode on the next—equally comfortable with blues, ballads, and free improvisation. He soon became involved in a series of historicist projects, including Robert Altman's film *Kansas City,* in which he helped recreate the musical and social atmosphere of the 1930s, chiefly in a rousing tenor saxophone duel with Joshua Redman intended to recreate the fabled combats between Coleman Hawkins and Lester Young. For his 1996 album *Conversin' with the Elders,* Carter recruited an unparalleled quartet of musicians from two jazz eras: tenor saxophonist Buddy Tate and trumpeter Harry Edison from Count Basie's 1930s orchestra, and Bowie and baritone saxophonist Hamiet Bluiett from the Loft Era cooperatives. In 2000, Carter simultaneously released two albums: *Chasin' the Gypsy,* a thoughtful, scrupulously arranged interpretation of music by Django Reinhardt, and *Layin' in the Cut,* a set of improvisations with a fusion rhythm section. A few years later, he returned to the fusion tradition that had captivated Bowie, and formed a trio with organ, tenor saxophone, and drums.

"NOW'S THE TIME"

Compared with modernist resurrections of nineteenth-century jazz precursors, as in Braxton's march and Marsalis's church service, Ronald Shannon Jackson's "Now's the Time" may seem like a dip into the recent past: a fusion version of the classic Charlie Parker bebop blues, first released in 1946. Parker's theme had already picked up fusion associations with the rhythm and blues steal "The Hucklebuck." Jackson's take is highly sophisticated (it's more harmonically dissonant than any of Parker's versions), and yet it partakes of the partying sensibility associated with pop music. Structurally, the performance is simplicity itself: the theme, consecutive solos by James Carter's soprano saxophone and Jef Lee Johnson's guitar, return of the theme, and a coda. The primary interest stems from the quartet's collective effort: we are always aware of each of the four musicians.

The first chorus is striking: Jackson introduces a variation on the melody by playing a shalmei, thought to be the oldest reed instrument and a predecessor of the double-reed oboe. The jarring guitar chords add to a sense of strangeness, but as the blues changes kick in, we approach familiar ground. The repetitiveness of the blues chords—through twelve choruses—gives the performance a quality of inevitability, but the constant contrariness of discordant harmonies and contrapuntal melodies renders the piece as unmistakably contemporary. The change-ups, syncopations, and other contributions by bass, drums, and guitar, particularly in support of the saxophone solo, have the effect of keeping the piece on edge and flush with small surprises. Compare this group activity with the 1953 Parker recording, where the rhythm section is relatively unified in support of his solo. Despite dissonances and melodic eruptions, including Carter's high-note squawks, the integrity of the blues harmony is never threatened. We always know where we are.

NOW'S THE TIME

Ronald Shannon Jackson

Ronald Shannon Jackson, drums and shalmei; James Carter, soprano saxophone; Jef Lee Johnson, electric guitar; Ngolle Pokossi, electric bass

LABEL: *What Spirit Say,* DIW 895
DATE: 1994
STYLE: avant-garde historicist
FORM: 12-bar blues

Chorus 1 (introduction)

0:00	Jackson plays a riff on the shalmei, answered by dissonant and strangely timed chords from Johnson on electric guitar.
0:07	The guitar arrives on IV. Jackson plays syncopations (sudden accents on the offbeat) that mirror the original melody to "Now's the Time."

| 0:18 | By the time the harmony returns to I in the tenth bar, Pokossi enters on electric bass. |

Chorus 2 (head)

0:21	Carter enters with the head to "Now's the Time" on soprano saxophone, the melody roughly doubling Jackson's ongoing shalmei riff. The guitar comps behind them.
0:29	The harmony arrives on IV.
0:32	The guitar begins improvising a complementary melody in the background.
0:38	Jackson drops out, leaving Carter alone on saxophone.
0:42	Carter begins the next chorus with an ascending riff.

Chorus 3

0:43	Carter's riff ends with a blue note that coincides with a cymbal crash as Jackson reenters on the drums. The guitar breaks his chords into gentle arpeggios.
0:51	As the harmony turns to IV, the bass abandons his walking-bass line, playing simple, syncopated patterns.
0:58	Carter plays a riff, then lowers it a half step.
1:02	The chorus ends with a simple, melodic bluesy phrase.

Chorus 4

1:05	Carter suddenly plays his ascending riff an octave higher.
1:09	As the bass plays ascending octaves, Jackson ratchets up the intensity of his drumming while Carter increases the speed of his line to fast bebop-style notes.
1:12	When the harmony arrives on IV, the bass continues playing simple syncopations. In the background, the guitar adds its own melody.
1:25	Carter begins the next chorus with an even higher riff.

Chorus 5

1:26	Playing with intensely distorted timbre, Carter begins two octaves above where his solo began in chorus 3.
1:28	With an extra effort, he reaches yet another octave higher—well above what a soprano saxophonist would normally try to play.
1:33	Arriving on IV, the bass plays only the root of the chord.
1:37	Carter's improvised line begins to descend.
1:43	His last phrase sounds relaxed and bluesy.

Chorus 6

| 1:47 | The bass switches to a pedal point, freezing the harmony on the tonic for the next eight measures. Against this neutral backdrop, Carter toys with a two-note motive. |

1:55   Carter accelerates to double-time.

2:00   As the bass begins walking again, Carter returns to his high register, tooting out a repeated note.

2:05   An extremely high-pitched squawk warns us that he's ready to make yet another assault on his high register.

Chorus 7

2:07   For the next eight measures, Carter plays notes even he can't fully control. The first note he hits wavers uncertainly in pitch. The next note is higher still, but lasts for only a split second.

2:10   He begins once again on the lower pitch, getting it under better control before moving upward again. Having found the higher note, he holds it for several seconds.

2:13   For a second, he achieves his highest note: B, four octaves above middle C.

2:17   A disorienting squawk brings him down to his normal register.

Chorus 8

2:27   On guitar, Johnson begins his solo with a simple two-note riff that he transposes and plays in a variety of rhythmic positions.

2:46   His last phrase ends on an unsettling dissonance.

Chorus 9

2:48   Johnson starts with a three-note motive, heard against the background of another pedal point in the bass.

2:54   As the bass returns to walking over the IV chord, Johnson improvises a line that will run uninterrupted through the entire chorus—and beyond.

Chorus 10

3:08   Johnson's line becomes simpler, coinciding with yet another pedal point in the bass.

3:16   As the harmony becomes more intense, Johnson plays a rapid series of chords. For the remainder of the chorus, his improvisation blurs unsteadily between melody and chords.

Chorus 11 (head)

3:27   Carter returns to play the head. In response, Johnson repeats the riff, distorting it into new shapes.

3:32   The horn and guitar now play the riff in harmony.

3:34   Over the IV chord, the harmony takes on a peculiar tone as Carter moves to other modes.

3:43   Carter plays an elaborate, repeating blue note, prompting Johnson to imitate him.

Chorus 12 (head)

3:47	Over a rapidly repeated bass note, the two instruments play the riff in harmony.
3:51	Carter takes his line "outside" into uncharted harmonic territory.
3:54	Over the IV chord, Carter inserts sudden high-pitched shrieks into his line.

Coda

4:08	The guitar and saxophone come to rest on a single note. Jackson keeps the tension going with a quiet roll on the snare drum.
4:10	Johnson plays a descending bluesy line.
4:12	Carter answers with an ascending line. His last few notes are underscored by cymbal crashes.

When musicians get together and talk about the current state of jazz, they frequently grouse about the ceaseless outpouring of tributes that too often have the stale odor of desperation about them, bordering on imitation and signifying creative haplessness rather than a genuinely illuminating historicist inquiry. There are indications that this fashion may be finally in recession, but in 2008 the Grammy Awards, which have always treated jazz as a very, very poor relation, awarded its most coveted prize to Herbie Hancock's *River: The Joni Letters*. Putting aside the merit of its adaptations, which do, in fact, ring new changes on old tunes (especially when performed by a quintet with no fewer than three Miles Davis alums: Hancock, Wayne Shorter, Dave Holland), could anyone imagine the prize going to a jazz album that *didn't* offer either a fusion with pop or a tribute to the past? *Getz/Gilberto*, the previous jazz album-of-the-year winner, had explored what in 1964 was a relatively new idiom in jazz and pop. With *River*, Hancock brought off a jazz-pop fusion *and* a memorial to another era. How long jazz can continue gazing into a rear-view mirror while gliding forward is anyone's guess. As Hotspur said with his dying breath, "And time, that takes survey of all the world, / Must have a stop."

CHAPTER

Jazz Today

PARADIGMS LOST AND FOUND

I n the 1990s, a new term became fashionable: *post-historical*. Intended to convey the essentially insupportable idea that history is somehow over, that the great political and cultural movements are behind us, it was applied to every aspect of modern life, including jazz. The concept's appeal lies in the two liberating illusions it fosters: first, that our generation is perched atop the historical mountain, looking down at the past, like gods; and second, that history's afterlife is a clean slate, upon which we are free to scrawl our own blueprints for the future.

◀ Jason Moran is a representative jazz musician for the early years of the twenty-first century, at home with classic jazz, hip-hop, and everything between.

A cursory glance at post-post-historical history suggests that (as through-out human history) such arrogance leads to military debacles and moral chaos. No surprise there.

Even so, the post-historical perspective may provide a helpful way of sorting through the three narratives we have already examined in order to define jazz in the twenty-first century. So let's pretend we are looking down from the mountain crest. The art-for-art's-sake account, in which jazz is seen to have evolved in a vacuum of inspired innovations, from Buddy Bolden's slow blues to Ornette Coleman's free jazz, would seem to be at an impasse if not necessarily at an end (there's no way of knowing). After the avant-garde era, musicians freely mined the idioms of jazz's past, but the next movement, neoclassicism, represented a retrenchment—away from the avant-garde, not a continuation toward another frontier.

The fusion narrative takes us beyond the avant-garde into diverse attempts to combine the practices of jazz with those of rock, soul, hip-hop, and other kinds of pop music, domestic and international. But that also now seems a dead end, as the farther pop departs from melody and harmony, the less it offers as source material for jazz. Some would argue that the pinnacle of jazz-rock fusion was created by Miles Davis nearly forty years ago. When a modern jazz group plays a song by, say, Radiohead, it's an isolated stunt, not a meeting of minds. The historicist model is very much alive, as jazz musicians continue to measure themselves against pre-vious achievements without merely copying them. Yet it fails to describe the overall state of jazz in today's world. No matter how many instances of historicist jazz we compile, we are simply collating individual interpreta-tions and tributes, which can hardly define an era in which those instances account for a small percentage of overall jazz performances.

So while each of these paradigms gives us a way of understanding jazz history, none provides us with a satisfactory label with which to describe contemporary jazz. Still, this is far from a period of chaos: a live-and-let-live conformity has taken over in the absence of warring factions. If jazz is in a post-historical phase, it's a relatively peaceful one—traditionalists and modernists have declared a truce. A different and broader narrative may offer a better sense of the present situation. Some commentators have described jazz as America's classical music, but what exactly does that mean? The dictionary definitions of *classical* have changed over the past hundred years, largely in response to the existence of jazz. In 1885, the American musicologist J. C. Fillmore offered a simple and influential definition of *classic* as applied to music: "having permanent interest and value." The 1933 *Oxford English Dictionary* upheld the inclusiveness of that general description: "of the first rank or authority; constituting a standard or model." The 1969 *American Heritage Dictionary* limited the definition: "any music in the educated European tradition, as distinguished from popular or folk music." In 1972, the *OED* added a new restriction: "opp. JAZZ," followed by supporting extracts, including this one from a 1947 magazine: "The lowbrow, of course, divides all music into 'classical' and 'jazz'."

The lowbrow needn't detain us. Let us raise our sights to encompass the original meaning—"having permanent interest and value." No one can deny that a survey of twentieth-century music shows that jazz has proved as lasting as the most admired classical works of the same period. Only the most rigorous standards of excellence, applied ecumenically, can give *classical* real meaning. Throughout this book, we refer to classical music as the European tradition of composed music that produced the great symphonic, chamber, and operatic repertories. Here we let *classical* represent not one tradition as opposed to another, but rather the status to which all serious and lasting kinds of music (including rock) aspire. Bach, after all, was not considered classical in his day; time and semantics created the tradition in which we place him.

In this formulation, jazz has undergone four phases of development. These phases are not stylistic schools, like swing and bop, but broader stages that mark its overall place in the cultural world. The first phase (1890s–1920s) was the period of genesis. Every musical idiom begins in, and reflects the life of, a specific community where music is made for pleasure and to strengthen social bonds. In jazz, the primary breeding ground was the black South, especially New Orleans, where a mixture of musical and cultural influences combined to create a freewheeling, largely improvised, blues-based music that suited every social gathering, entertaining the living and commemorating the dead. The strength and originality of this music allowed it to spread beyond geographical, racial, and cultural boundaries.

In the second phase (1920s–1950s), jazz was transformed from a community-based phenomenon to an authentic art of unlimited potential. Speedily spreading around the world, it revolutionized musical performance and conception, extending its influence into the classical and popular fields, spurred by remarkable individuals who could express singular artistic visions within its generally stable yet constantly shifting param-

eters. Within twenty years, jazz achieved popular acceptance as a generation's dance music, and immediately thereafter spurred intellectual interest
through the modernist reformation of bebop and its various offshoots.

The third phase (1950s–1970s) was defined by the limits of modernism,
which increased artistic possibilities while alienating the general public.
Jazz had become primarily a listener's music. It continued to sustain a large
following (in particular, the years 1954 to 1964 were extraordinarily flush),
but passed from center stage in favor of newer, more popular styles (rhythm
and blues, rock and roll) that fulfilled the unchanging social needs of the
overall community—music that suited dancing and singing and required
little in the way of virtuoso technique or imaginative concentration on the
past of listeners. In this period, jazz also moved into the classroom.

The fourth stage (1970s–), at which jazz presently finds itself, may be
defined by its classical status on two counts. First, jazz has moved so far
from center stage that its survival is largely dependent on an infrastructure
of academic study and institutional support, including public and private
grants. Its limited presence in the marketplace guarantees a circumscribed
international audience. In some—perhaps most—areas of the United
States, people can live their entire lives without encountering jazz on television or radio, let alone movies and jukeboxes. It is a specialty interest, like
European classical music. Second, jazz and its musicians are weighed down
by the accomplishments of its past. Virtually every jazz artist who comes
along is measured to some degree by the presumed influences of his or her
predecessors. Young musicians are also obliged to compete with the past
in a way that did not exist in jazz before the 1990s. The commercial ramifications are familiar, because they replicate the struggle of European classical music during the same period, as listeners continued to support the
performances of famous nineteenth-century masterworks while neglecting
modern composers as either too difficult or simply too new.

On the other hand, the classical status is liberating for upcoming jazz
artists, who range freely between past and present, creating their own narratives as they attempt to forge new techniques, or to fuse jazz techniques
with those of popular and classical music, or to elaborate on acknowledged
jazz masterworks. What's more, the classical stage offers a more reasonable
way of anchoring jazz in history than the post-historical analysis: it assumes
evolving growth within its new status, leaving open the promise of waves of
performers, some of whom will be merely accomplished while others will
continue to forge daring explorations.

LINGUA FRANCA

If the present era is not dominated by a single jazz school, it does offer something akin to a universal *lingua franca*—a useful term from seventeenth-
century Europe, coined to describe the hybrid language that developed, per
necessity, between different nationalities that interacted in Mediterranean
seaports. Whatever their stylistic preferences, today's jazz musicians can all
speak the same language, a consequence of jazz education: a musical patois
grounded in bebop, with respect for previous jazz schools and knowledge of
later ones. In the past, musicians learned by doing. They traveled in bands
or memorized solos from recordings, and almost always leaned toward the
style that was dominant at the time they came of age. When apprentice
work is largely limited by undergraduate studies, however, musicians are
less likely to pick up the latest chord changes by ear than to learn them as
homework.

At a time when pop squeezes every other kind of music into the slim-
mest margin of commercial significance, jazz students are motivated to
master the shared pool of styles and techniques to survive as professional
musicians. Yet neither education nor the marketplace has succeeded in
making them assembly-line performers—a fact that, perhaps more than
any other, testifies to jazz's inviolable fortitude. Something at the heart
of jazz, and every kind of art worth its name, rejects slavish imitation; it
thrives only on acute individualism. Jazz in the twenty-first century may
seem no longer rife with the kind of innovators of earlier eras (only time
can tell if that's true), yet it has unquestionably produced one of the best-
equipped musical generations ever, which has sustained jazz as a singular,
stirring, and still surprising art.

Consider, for example, the state of jazz piano. Following is a list of fifty
pianists (with year and place of birth) who have influenced jazz in the
years since 1990. They are by no means alone. Many established pianists
also distinguished this period with the renewed vitality of their work, from
bop masters like Hank Jones and Tommy Flanagan to avant-garde pioneers like Cecil Taylor and Andrew Hill to 1980s neoclassicists (all born in
the middle 1950s) like Geri Allen, Fred Hersch, Mulgrew Miller, and Uri
Caine. This list, on the other hand, is limited to pianists born no earlier
than 1960, which means they were all raised in the "classical" era, long
after the stylistic wars of the past were resolved. A paradox is immediately
apparent: although almost any one of them could effectively sit in on a job
if another one was called away, this group represents a comprehensive vari-

ety of musical approaches. They all know the lingua franca, but are highly particular in the way they develop it.

✦ ✦ ✦

Helio Alves (1966, São Paulo)

Frank Amsallem (1961, Algeria)

Django Bates (1960, England)

Jonathan Batiste (1986, New Orleans)

Stefano Bollani (1972, Italy)

Michael Cain (1966, Los Angeles)

Marc Cary (1967, New York)

Bill Charlap (1966, New York)

Cyrus Chestnut (1963, Maryland)

George Colligan (1969, Baltimore)

Xavier Davis (1971, Grand Rapids)

Eliane Elias (1960, São Paulo)

Orrin Evans (1975, Philadelphia)

Antonio Faraò (1965, Italy)

Amina Figarova (1966, Azerbaijan)

Anat Fort (1970, Israel)

Robert Glasper (1978, Houston)

Aaron Goldberg (1974, Boston)

Larry Goldings (1968, Boston)

Edsel Gomez (1962, Puerto Rico)

Benito Gonzalez (1975, Venezuela)

Darrell Grant (1962, Philadelphia)

Tord Gustavsen (1970, Norway)

Kevin Hays (1968, New York)

Ethan Iverson (1973, Menomonie, Wis.)

Vijay Iyer (1971, Rochester, N.Y.)

D. D. Jackson (1967, Ottowa)

Geoffrey Keezer (1970, Eau Claire, Wis.)

Rodney Kendrick (1960, Philadelphia)

Guillermo Klein (1970, Argentina)

John Medeski (1965, Louisville)

Brad Mehldau (1970, Jacksonville, Fl.)

Jason Moran (1975, Houston)

Leszek Możdżer (1971, Gdańsk)

Junko Onishi (1967, Japan)

Danilo Pérez (1966, Panama)

Jean-Michel Pilc (1960, France)

Mika Pohjola (1971, Finland)

Eric Reed (1970, Philadelphia)

Marcus Roberts (1963, Jacksonville)

Renee Rosnes (1962, Saskatchewan)

Gonzalo Rubalcaba (1963, Havana)

Stephen Scott (1969, New York)

Matthew Shipp (1960, Wilmington)

Travis Shook (1969, Oroville, Calif.)

Edward Simon (1969, Venezuela)

Craig Taborn (1970, Minneapolis)

Jacky Terrasson (1966, Berlin)

Anthony Wonsey (1971, Chicago)

Bojan Zulfikarpašić (1968, Belgrade)

✦ ✦ ✦

Although Bill Evans and Cecil Taylor were born within a few months of each other in 1929, we don't think of them as sharing much common ground. Yet even the most stylistically disparate musicians listed here—from the studied lyricism of Brad Mehldau to the neoclassical proficiency of Danilo Perez to the percussive idiosyncrasy of Matthew Shipp—suggest a common grounding in jazz classicism that might allow them to cross over into each other's realms in a way that would be unthinkable for Evans and Taylor or, for that matter, Thelonious Monk and Oscar Peterson, or Earl Hines and Meade Lux Lewis, who were both born in 1905. Some of these musicians came to jazz in their late twenties or thirties after working in other fields, including European classical music, rhythm and blues, fusion, and smooth jazz. In making the leap to jazz, they brought with them aspects of those idioms, thereby increasing the pool of shared knowledge.

Note, too, the geographical diversity: Vijay Iyer, who grew up in New York State, traces his heritage to India and employs elements of Indian music (previously little explored in jazz beyond Coltrane's scales and the occasional presence of a tabla), especially in his collaborations with the alto saxophonist Rudresh Mahanthappa—who, though born in Italy and raised in Colorado, shares Iyer's heritage and his education in American universities. Jazz internationalism is a given in today's climate, fostered by constant travel to the numerous jazz festivals in Europe, Israel, Japan, Canada, Brazil, and elsewhere. The common language is exponentially enlarged through cultural exchange.

Not all of these pianists are major figures, but all are accomplished ones. Most have recorded with prominent labels, large and small, including Blue Note, ECM, Verve, BMG, Columbia, Sunnyside, Thirsty Ear, and Warner Bros. All have made recordings as leaders, though many are usually heard in sideman engagements. Some of the best-known pianists of recent years are not included here because they are primarily known as singers, though they could sustain careers as keyboard artists—among them Diana Krall (b. 1964 in British Columbia), Harry Connick Jr. (b. 1967 in New Orleans), and Norah Jones (b. 1979 in Brooklyn). These pianists are proof—similar lists can be devised around other instruments—of life after history, or rather that jazz history is in the making. Can a comparably diverse list of fifty pianists born in or after 1960 be drawn from the ranks of classical or rock musicians? Just asking.

Jason Moran (B. 1975)

For a closer look at the life of the contemporary jazz musician, one could hardly ask for a more exemplary career than that of Jason Moran. In the years since he made his first album (*Soundtrack to Human Motion*, 1998),

Moran has earned nearly unanimous acclaim, demonstrating with wit and imagination the triumphs possible in jazz despite its relatively remote standing in America's cultural life. Born in Houston, he began playing classical piano at six and continued with it, reluctantly, for seven years. He has said that he came to hate music, piano, and practicing, preferring to listen to the hip-hop records that flourished during his childhood.

Moran's attitude turned around completely when he was thirteen; at a memorial service for one of his father's friends, he heard a Thelonious Monk record, "'Round Midnight," and found himself riveted by Monk's keyboard touch, rhythmic intensity, and melodic playfulness. As he learned more about Monk, he delved deeper into jazz and particularly jazz piano—Bud Powell, Horace Silver, McCoy Tyner, Herbie Hancock. Like any young jazz lover, he allowed each musician to lead him to other musicians: soon he was also soaking up older pianists like Art Tatum and Erroll Garner and more obscure or idiosyncratic modernists like Herbie Nichols, Randy Weston, Ahmad Jamal, and Cecil Taylor. This process groomed him with a broader musical platform than that of his predecessors. It could not fail to combine elements of the avant-garde (he searched out the extremes of musical possibilities), historicism (he roamed as freely through the past as he did the present), and fusion—his increasing love of jazz by no means diminished his enthusiasm for modern pop, especially the beats of hip-hop.

After graduating from the jazz program at Houston's High School for the Performing and Visual Arts, Moran moved to New York, where in 1993 he enrolled at the Manhattan School of Music, chiefly to study with Jaki Byard (1922–1999). Over the next four years, he found "a role model for life" in Byard, the school's most distinguished jazz faculty member. Byard, a brilliant and stubbornly individual instrumentalist, was well known for his longtime association with Charles Mingus and his own records, which revealed a style that combined the techniques of stride, swing, bop, and avant-garde—an approach so far ahead of its time that some critics dismissed him as a tongue-in-cheek eclectic and audiences felt almost obliged to chuckle when he interpolated prewar styles in the course of a solo. Byard was the ideal mentor for Moran (and other young pianists, including Fred Hersch and D. D. Jackson), breaking down the various techniques and instilling a respect for their separate virtues. Moran has referred to him as "a jazz leftist," for his stylistic inclusiveness. In the same period, Moran sought out two other pianists, who had also absorbed much of the instrument's varied history but were more firmly aligned with the 1960s and 1970s avant-garde: Andrew Hill and Muhal Richard Abrams. As he developed his own style, Moran added compositions by his three primary teachers into his repertory, helping to keep alive a body of work that had been largely neglected.

In 1996, at twenty-one, Moran began appearing as a sideman with prominent musicians, including the saxophonists David Murray and Steve Coleman, who had begun to exert much influence in the 1980s. Coleman created a pan-stylistic collective centered in Brooklyn called M-Base—an acronym for Macro-Basic Array of Structured Extemporizations. It was one of the first groups to combine aspects of avant-garde and mainstream jazz with hip-hop, electronic pop, and world music. One of Coleman's most gifted associates was another alto and soprano saxophonist, Greg Osby, who used Moran on several projects, including the 1997 Blue Note album *Further Ado*, Moran's recorded debut. The next year, Blue Note signed Moran to his own contract, launched with *Soundtrack to Human Motion* and participation (along with Osby) in the label's New Directions concert tour. Osby has noted that Moran, though fascinated by avant-garde theories, hip-hop, and electronics, particularly *musique concrète*, is essentially a traditionalist. "We're like the anti young lions," Osby observed, adding, "Jason is kind of an old soul."

As Moran began to release a series of albums in 1998, one a year, it quickly became evident that he saw each one as a distinct project, with its own goals and parameters. He organized a durable trio, with bassist Tarus Mateen and drummer Nasheet Waits, that grew increasingly empathetic in the course of concert and club tours, but he planned his records to try something different every time. Even so, a few characteristics remained stable—the surprising breadth of his repertory, his love of electronic enhancements, and his humor. *Soundtrack to Human Motion* includes works based on pieces by Maurice Ravel and Alban Berg as well as a free improvisation and the first in his series of "Gangsterism" pieces. The latter is a series of thoroughly camouflaged variations on a theme by Andrew Hill, "Erato," each one discretely designed—for example, Moran describes "Gangsterism on a Lunchtable" as an attempt to "do my John Cage interpretation of hip-hop," referring particularly to Cage's use of ambient noises.

Moran's albums have included fresh yet faithful renditions of work by Byard and Ellington, movie themes (including *Godfather II* and *Yojimbo*), a collaboration with the veteran saxophonist and pianist Sam Rivers

(b. 1923), an album-length exploration of blues forms, and such idiosyncratic original works as "Ringing My Phone," in which he finds notes on the keyboard that match up with the notes of his wife and mother-in-law speaking Turkish in a taped phone conversation. In every instance, the challenge is to mesh contemporary musical ideas with tradition to create music that is recognizable yet new. This challenge was underscored when he set out to honor his first influence.

In 2007, Moran was commissioned to compose an original piece in celebration of the ninetieth anniversary of Thelonious Monk's birth. He based the work (*IN MY MIND: Monk at Town Hall, 1959*) on Monk's first big-band concert. The piece calls for an eight-piece ensemble, video projections, and recorded excerpts from Monk's Town Hall rehearsals. Moran explained: "The hard part is actually trying to unlearn what learned me. I want to reconnect with Monk, not with people talking about his 'quirky rhythms' or 'off-centered humor.' I want to get past all that and say this was a real human being who shaped the world of jazz and the world of music, partially because of what he did at the instrument but mostly because of the way he thought."

"YOU'VE GOT TO BE MODERNISTIC"

Like Monk, Moran has developed a self-sufficient approach to the piano, recognizing that playing solo piano is quite different from working with a trio. His 2002 album *Modernistic* is a benchmark achievement and a profound illustration of his capacity to combine classicism and maverick innovation. Whereas many pianists would be content simply to master James P. Johnson's 1930 "You've Got to Be Modernistic," Moran suggests its essential character while giving it a radical facelift, taking it through so many variations that by the end you suspect that you've been on a completely different trip from the one intended by Johnson. To understand Moran's interpretation, we need to recall Johnson's original piece.

"You've Got to Be Modernistic" is basically a ragtime work, made up of three sixteen-bar strains. Moran works with the original material, but adds his own variations (including new C and D strains) and frequently alters or stops the tempo. Johnson's modernism was apparent in his introduction and the first two strains (A and B), which are ornamented by augmented chords and the whole-tone scale. Although Moran is basically faithful to Johnson's primary theme, he adds incremental dissonances and extends its final melodic figure. Here and in the subsequent strains, Moran halts the flow at will, as if to look around and tweak this chord or twist that rhythm before returning to the grid.

Moran's reading suggests an asymmetrical impulsiveness that threatens the integrity of the piece, despite his frequent return to the stride under-pinning. The effect is ironic in the sense that he holds the original work at a distance, partaking of it and then rejecting it, as he lingers on passages he wants to emphasize or alters the tempo and harmonies. He defamiliarizes the piece. Passages that seem stable when Johnson plays them now seem unmoored, free to go in any direction the pianist wishes to take them, thanks to his strategically misplaced notes or wildly divergent harmonic progressions. Intermingled with his versions of Johnson's first theme are harmonic cycles that can be considered Moran's *own* strains, which, like much of his playing, are elusive and unconventional.

YOU'VE GOT TO BE MODERNISTIC

Jason Moran, piano

LABEL: *Modernistic,* Blue Note 39838
DATE: 2001
STYLE: historicist/modernist
FORM: march/ragtime with alterations

Introduction

0:00	After a sustained bass note, Moran plays a series of chords descending the whole-tone scale.

A strain

0:06	Moran faithfully plays the first four bars of James P. Johnson's "You've Got to Be Modernistic." This section (we'll call it the *theme phrase*) is his main point of contact with the original.
0:09	On its first appearance in Johnson's composition, the theme phrase ended with the left hand playing a tonic chord with a mild dissonance (we'll call it the *tonic chord passage*). Moran lingers on this passage, repeating it and gradually building in volume.
0:14	Moran defamiliarizes the theme phrase by playing a deliberately inaccurate bass note.
0:18	On its second appearance in Johnson's composition, the theme phrase was followed by chords from the whole-tone scale. Moran extends this passage, pulling it temporarily outside the meter of the piece.
0:21	On its last repetition, Moran plays the theme phrase for six bars, leading through whole-tone, or augmented, chords (made up of major thirds) to a full cadence.
0:29	He lengthens the tonic chord passage by two bars.

A strain

0:32	Moran plays the theme phrase.
0:37	The left hand suddenly drops to a remote key. Over this harmony, the right hand improvises a wild passage.
0:42	Moran repeats the theme phrase.
0:46	The left-hand chords drop once again. Moran pulls the harmony upward step by step while the right hand plays sharp dissonances.
0:51	Moran repeats the theme phrase; as before, he extends the whole-tone response.
0:57	The last repetition of the theme phrase is undistorted, coming to a full cadence.

B strain

1:06	Moran plays the opening **B** strain: descending chromatic chords divided between the hands, culminating in a bluesy phrase.
1:11	The second time through, the left hand is overwhelmed by dissonant passagework in the right hand. Not until the phrase's end (at 1:15) does the original melody and tempo return.
1:15	For four bars, Moran adheres closely to Johnson's original.
1:20	The third repetition of the opening disintegrates into harsh dissonance and free rhythm.
1:23	Suddenly, Moran returns to the original tempo and meter. Landing on the tonic, he plays the note insistently.

Interlude

1:30	Over a pedal point, Moran plays a series of descending tritones.
1:36	The phrase ends with a simple ragtime cadence, followed once again by the tonic chord passage (repeated and extended).
1:40	He repeats the descending tritones.
1:47	Suddenly he inserts a passage that sounds as though it might modulate to a new key; but it resolves quietly back to the tonic.
1:54	He repeats the tonic chord passage to support bizarre right-hand improvising.
2:10	The harmony works its way back to the descending tritones, followed by a turnaround—a short concluding chord progression. We can now recognize an eight-bar cycle: six bars of pedal point with descending tritones, followed by two bars of turnaround.

"C" strain

2:19	(cycle 1) As the left hand settles into a familiar routine, Moran begins improvising with his right hand.
2:29	(cycle 2)
2:38	(cycle 3) His left hand remains constant, but his right hand becomes increasingly wild, spreading dissonant flurries across the chord progression.

2:47	(cycle 4)
2:57	(cycle 5) He batters several notes at the top of the keyboard.
3:06	(cycle 6) The texture on the piano thickens as Moran adds complex passagework.
3:12	At the climax, we suddenly return to the simple ragtime cadence, now densely voiced at top volume. It is followed by a thunderous repetition of the tonic chord passage.

A strain

3:17	Moran returns to the theme phrase.
3:21	The left-hand chords become loosened from their moorings, moving up or down a half step in a spastic rhythm.
3:34	He repeats the theme phrase, followed by the whole-tone chords.
3:41	He again repeats the theme phrase, this time reaching a full cadence.

"D" strain

3:49	(cycle 1) The tonic chord drops down, then moves back up step-by-step in a triple meter. This establishes yet another cycle, six bars long.
3:54	(cycle 2) Moran adapts stride technique to this unusual meter: the bass line is played not on the downbeat, but in the middle of the measure (chord—bass—chord).
3:57	His right hand begins improvising within the cycle.
4:00	(cycle 3)
4:05	(cycle 4) His lines grow faster, occasionally disrupting the left-hand foundation.
4:10	(cycle 5) The right hand becomes thickened with chords, which interrupt and displace the left-hand chords.
4:15	(cycle 6) Gradually, the stride accompaniment and triple meter disappear into a complex, disjointed rhythmic flux. We still hear Moran moving slowly through the chords, however, and can recognize the end of each cycle by the return to the tonic.
4:25	(cycle 7)
4:34	(cycle 8)
4:42	(cycle 9) Finally, Moran settles back into a smooth stride accompaniment, once again in triple meter. The right hand improvises rich, mellifluous chords.
4:50	(cycle 10)
4:58	(cycle 11) The right hand begins to play behind the beat, distorting our sense of meter.
5:05	(cycle 12) The stride foundation dissolves into left-hand chords.

Coda

5:12	Before the cycle is complete, the theme phrase from strain **A** slips back in. The tempo slows down dramatically, and the piano texture is simplified.

5:16	As the phrase continues, the music becomes hushed, as if Moran were preparing for a big cadence.
5:22	He plays the upward-rising whole-tone chords quietly and slowly.
5:26	A sudden loud octave jolts us awake. Moran plays the final cadence with a certain bluesy bluntness.
5:30	He continues to fool us, however, dropping from the tonic to remote harmonies.
5:40	The piece ends on unresolved V7 chord.

"PLANET ROCK"

Moran's version of Afrika Bambaataa's "Planet Rock" is an ideal companion to "You've Got to Be Modernistic," and was recorded for the same album. One piece reclaims and reevaluates a work from the distant past, suggesting a historicist approach, while the other, drawn from contemporary pop, suggests a fusion approach. Yet the overriding impression created by both is of Moran's undeniable originality as he charts his own path through material that obviously holds great interest for him. His inventiveness is inseparable from his sense of musical tradition and his openness to the music around him. Bambaataa began as a Bronx-based disc jockey and came to be regarded as a hip-hop godfather when "Planet Rock" brought beat-box electro-funk to the dance floor, in 1982. An early and highly influential rap tune, it has a primary melody-rhythm deeply ingrained on Moran's generation.

Moran brings to his interpretation the same mixture of fidelity and independence he brought to Johnson's work, creating a riveting jazz performance that respects each component of the original: the rhythms, melodies, even the vocal timbres. He employs techniques that parallel Bambaataa's use of scratched and otherwise manipulated vinyl discs, including prepared piano strings and reverse sounds created by running a tape backward. His attempt to recreate the pitches of Bambaataa's vocal line in verse 1 entails a technique that he continued to develop in his later work, replicating speech patterns on the piano. Moran's use of reversed tapes and dubs is not itself new; Bill Evans recorded a dubbed album of solo piano, *Conversations with Myself*, in the 1960s. But where Evans used soundboard tricks to expand his harmonic and melodic options, Moran is largely concerned with rhythmic effects. He shows that hip-hop beats, which many consider anathema to jazz, are just another source for inventive music-making, and that jazz, as ever, is ultimately whatever its most creative proponents make of it.

PLANET ROCK

Jason Moran, piano and electronics

LABEL: *Modernistic,* Blue Note 3983
DATE: 2001
STYLE: historicist/fusion
FORM: verse-refrain, with a 16-bar chorus in the middle

Introduction

0:00	The piece opens with a peculiar sound—a taped piano chord played backward. It begins quietly before exploding into sound at the end.
0:02	With his left hand, Moran plays a series of pentatonic fragments. The sound of the piano is acoustically filtered, creating a distinctive timbre.
0:07	After three short phrases, Moran pauses.
0:09	He plays a more syncopated line, followed again by a pause and a repeat of the line.
0:16	He plays a single note in octaves, with a noticeable difference in timbre. By sticking foreign objects—erasers, clothespins, paper clips—into the strings, Moran has turned his keyboard into a "prepared piano."

Vamp

0:18	Moran plays the bass line from the Bambaataa recording of "Planet Rock"—a syncopated pattern alternating bass notes with a chord on the backbeat. This line, distinguished by its timbre, is recorded separately and heard throughout as a repeating track.
0:22	Every two bars, the bass line is punctuated by the sound of a left-hand chord combined with the electronically manipulated "backward" piano chord.
0:34	As the backward chord disappears, we approach the beginning of the song.

Verse 1

0:38	As painstakingly as possible, Moran matches the pitches of the original rapped vocal line to Bambaataa's version ("*Just start to chase your dreams*"). Since the original line was spoken, not sung, the pitches create strong dissonances against the repeating bass line.

Refrain

0:54	When Moran reaches the simple refrain, he plays it with literal precision.
1:02	On its repetition, he emphasizes the refrain melody in octaves.

Verse 2

1:10	Moran shifts to a different part of Bambaataa's version, again matching the pitches of the original rap ("*You're in a place where the nights are hot*") to notes on the piano. Once again, the notes clash against the bass line.

| 1:23 | To mimic a place where several voices join together on the original recording ("*hump bump bump, get bump, now let's go, house*"), Moran brings out the line with octaves. |

Refrain

| 1:26 | Moran returns to the refrain. |

Interlude

1:42	Moran moves to a line chanted by the group as a whole ("*Go rock it, don't stop it!*").
1:54	To convey the sense of call and response between group and in-studio audience on Bambaataa's recording, he pits two full, rich chords in the middle register against the same chords an octave higher.
2:06	With three chords, Moran emphasizes the dominant in a half cadence.

Chorus 1 (16 bars)

2:10	Moran plays a simple but wandering ascending melody, stretching over sixteen bars. Each note lasts two beats and is distorted at the end by a backward sound.
2:20	He begins to harmonize the melody.
2:28	As the line ascends into the upper register, another piano part (recorded as a different track with its own distinctive timbre) appears below.
2:38	The melody finally rests on a single note.

Chorus 2

| 2:42 | Moran repeats the ascending melody, clearly establishing the chorus structure. Two different layers of piano begin improvising almost immediately, adding dense, complicated chords as well as unpredictable new melodies. |
| 3:10 | The melody ends. |

Chorus 3

3:14	The timbre suddenly changes. The bass line shifts to a sinister low register (where the ringing on the backbeat chord is particularly noticeable). Moran plays the melody backward, then reverses its sound so that it appears with a distinctive timbre. All of this is used as background for more aggressive improvisation in another piano line.
3:23	In one measure, the bass line skips a backbeat.
3:42	Moran marks the end of the melody with loud chords and an insistently repeated note in the treble.

Chorus 4

| 3:46 | The sound of the melody returns to a normal timbre. This time, as it ascends, the melody is harmonized by a descending bass line (both parts are superimposed over the consistently repeating bass track). Above it, an improvised line plays increasingly dissonant patterns. |

| 3:55 | As the piece nears a climax, the improvised line switches to octaves. |
| 4:14 | The melody ends, clearly establishing the tonic, while improvisation around it continues to swirl. |

Interlude

4:18	Several different lines intersect, all rocking back and forth in a limited range and merging into a kind of rumble, augmented by a return of the backward sound.
4:27	A dissonant line begins to emerge from the mix.
4:34	Switching to octaves, the line plays with fragments from the refrain melody.
4:39	A particularly harsh chord seems to prompt the bass to drop out for a few beats.
4:43	He plays a line from the opening.

Refrain

| 4:46 | Moran returns to the refrain melody. |
| 4:50 | The timbre suddenly returns to a fuller, richer sound, doubled and even tripled by octaves. |

Coda

4:57	The melody stops; in its wake, numerous other voices emerge, chaotically echoing its motivic ideas.
5:05	As the improvisations continue, the bass line begins to slow down.
5:10	The bass line is doubled at the lower octave.
5:28	The performance disappears in a gradual fade-out.

No one has ever successfully predicted the future of jazz. It's unlikely that Buddy Bolden could have foreseen the worldwide acceptance of music he played to entertain dancers in the tenderloin district of *fin de siècle* New Orleans. Louis Armstrong helped to spur the Swing Era, but he could not have seen it arising from his Hot Five recordings of the 1920s—no more than swing musicians could have predicted bop or bop musicians the avant-garde or free jazz proponents the turn to fusion. All we can say with assurance is that jazz is here to stay. It continues to represent a way of playing and thinking about music, attracting waves of young musicians who confound, delight, and amaze discriminating music lovers around the world.

SELECTED MUSICIANS ON PRIMARY JAZZ INSTRUMENTS

Trumpet/Cornet

Nat Adderley (1931–2000)
Henry "Red" Allen (1908 -1967)
Franco Ambrosetti (b. 1941)
Louis Armstrong (1901–1971)
Chet Baker (1929–1988)
Mario Bauzá (1911–1993)
Bix Beiderbecke (1903–1931)
Bunny Berigan (1908–1942)
Sonny Berman (1925–1942)
Terence Blanchard (b. 1962)
Buddy Bolden (1877–1931)
Lester Bowie (1941–1999)
Bobby Bradford (b. 1934)
Ruby Braff (1927–2003)
Randy Brecker (b. 1945)
Clifford Brown (1930–1956)
Clora Bryant (b. 1927)
Teddy Buckner (1909–1994)
Billy Butterfield (1917–1988)
Donald Byrd (b. 1932)
Roy Campbell (b. 1952)
Conte Candoli (1927–2001)
Pete Candoli (1923–2008)
Benny Carter (1907–2003)
Doc Cheatham (1905–1997)
Don Cherry (1936–1995)
Buck Clayton (1911–1991)
Bill Coleman (1904–1981)
Johnny Coles (1926–1996)

Ted Curson (b. 1935)
Olu Dara (b. 1941)
Miles Davis (1926–1991)
Wild Bill Davison (1906–1989)
Sidney De Paris (1905–1967)
Bill Dixon (b. 1925)
Kenny Dorham (1924–1972)
Dave Douglas (b. 1963)
Harry "Sweets" Edison (1915–1999)
Roy Eldridge (1911–1989)
Don Ellis (1934–1978)
Pee Wee Erwin (1913–1981)
Jon Faddis (b. 1953)
Art Farmer (1928–1999)
Maynard Ferguson (1928–2006)
Dizzy Gillespie (1917–1993)
George Girard (1930–1957)
Bobby Hackett (1915–1976)
Tim Hagans (b. 1954)
Roy Hargrove (b. 1969)
Tom Harrell (b. 1946)
Eddie Henderson (b. 1940)
Kid Howard (1908–1966)
Freddie Hubbard (1938–2008)
Harry James (1916–1983)
Bunk Johnson (1889–1949)
Sean Jones (b. 1978)
Thad Jones (1923–1986)
Taft Jordan (1915–1981)
Freddie Keppard (1890–1933)

Ryan Kisor (b. 1973)
Nick LaRocca (1889–1961)
Yank Lawson (1911–1995)
Booker Little (1938–1961)
Brian Lynch (b. 1956)
Wingy Manone (1904–1982)
Wynton Marsalis (b. 1961)
Howard McGhee (1918–1987)
John McNeil (b. 1948)
Jimmy McPartland (1907–1991)
Bubber Miley (1903–1932)
Blue Mitchell (1930–1979)
Lee Morgan (1938–1972)
Ray Nance (1913–1976)
Fats Navarro (1923–1950)
Joe Newman (1922–1992)
King Oliver (1885–1938)
Jimmy Owens (b. 1943)
Oran "Hot Lips" Page (1908–1954)
Nicholas Payton (b. 1973)
Manuel Perez (1871–1946)
Hannibal (Lokumbe) Peterson (b. 1948)
Marcus Printup (b. 1967)
Red Rodney (1927–1994)
Shorty Rogers (1924–1994)
Wallace Roney (b. 1960)
Randy Sandke (b. 1949)
Arturo Sandoval (b. 1949)
Charlie Shavers (1920–1971)
Woody Shaw (1944–1989)
Jabbo Smith (1908–1991)
Valaida Snow (1900–1956)
Lew Soloff (b. 1944)
Muggsy Spanier (1906–1967)
Terell Stafford (b. 1966)
Bobby Stark (1906–1945)
Rex Stewart (1907–1967)
Idrees Sulieman (1923–2002)
Ira Sullivan (b. 1931)
Clark Terry (b. 1920)
Kid Thomas (1896–1987)
Malachi Thompson (1949–2006)
Charles Tolliver (b. 1942)
Warren Vache (b. 1951)

Freddie Webster (1916–1947)
Joe Wilder (b. 1922)
Cootie Williams (1910–1985)
Snooky Young (b. 1919)

Trombone
Clifton Anderson (b. 1957)
Ray Anderson (b. 1952)
Dan Barrett (b. 1955)
Eddie Bert (b. 1922)
Bob Brookmeyer (b. 1929)
Lawrence Brown (1907–1988)
George Brunis (1902–1974)
Sam Burtis (b. 1948)
Jimmy Cleveland (1926–2008)
Willie Dennis (1926–1965)
Wilbur De Paris (1900–1973)
Vic Dickenson (1906–1984)
Tommy Dorsey (1905–1956)
Eddie Durham (1906–1987)
Honoré Dutrey (1894–1935)
Robin Eubanks (b. 1955)
John Fedchock (b. 1957)
Carl Fontana (1928–2003)
Curtis Fuller (b. 1934)
Tyree Glenn (1912–1974)
Wycliffe Gordon (b. 1967)
Bennie Green (1923–1977)
Urbie Green (b. 1926)
Al Grey (1925–2000)
Slide Hampton (b. 1932)
Bill Harris (1916–1973)
Craig Harris (b. 1953)
Jimmy Harrison (1900–1931)
Conrad Herwig (b. 1959)
J. C. Higginbotham (1906–1973)
Quentin "Butter" Jackson (1909–1976)
Jack Jenney (1910–1945)
J. J. Johnson (1924–2001)
Jimmy Knepper (1927–2003)
George E. Lewis (b. 1952)
Melba Liston (1926–1999)
Albert Mangelsdorff (1928–2005)
Delfeayo Marsalis (b. 1965)

Glenn Miller (1904–1944)
Miff Mole (1898–1961)
Grachan Moncur III (b. 1937)
Benny Morton (1907–1985)
Joe "Tricky Sam" Nanton (1904–1946)
Ed Neumeister (b. 1952)
Kid Ory (1886–1973)
Benny Powell (b. 1930)
Big Jim Robinson (1892–1976)
Frank Rosolino (1926–1978)
Roswell Rudd (b. 1935)
Jack Teagarden (1905–1964)
Juan Tizol (1900–1984)
Steve Turre (b. 1948)
Bill Watrous (b. 1939)
Dicky Wells (1907–1985)
Sandy Williams (1906–1991)
Kai Winding (1922–1983)
Britt Woodman (1920–2000)
Trummy Young (1912–1984)

Saxophone
George Adams (1940–1992)
Pepper Adams (1930–1986)
Cannonball Adderley (1928–1975)
Gene Ammons (1925–1974)
Fred Anderson (b. 1929)
Albert Ayler (1936–1970)
Charlie Barnet (1913–1991)
Bill Barron (1927–1989)
Gary Bartz (b. 1940)
Sidney Bechet (1897–1959)
Tim Berne (b. 1954)
Leon "Chu" Berry (1908–1941)
Walter Blanding Jr. (b. 1971)
Jane Ira Bloom (b. 1955)
Hamiet Bluiett (b. 1940)
Arthur Blythe (b. 1940)
Earl Bostic (1913–1965)
Anthony Braxton (b. 1945)
Michael Brecker (1949–2007)
Willem Breuker (b. 1944)
Nick Brignola (1936–2002)
Tina Brooks (1932–1974)

Peter Brotzmann (b. 1941)
Pete Brown (1906–1963)
Jane Bunnett (b. 1956)
Abraham Burton (b. 1971)
Don Byas (1912–1972)
Scoops Carey (1915–1970)
Harry Carney (1910–1974)
Benny Carter (1907–2003)
James Carter (b. 1969)
Serge Chaloff (1923–1957)
Arnett Cobb (1918–1989)
Tony Coe (b. 1934)
Al Cohn (1925–1988)
George Coleman (b. 1935)
Ornette Coleman (b. 1930)
Steve Coleman (b. 1956)
John Coltrane (1926–1967)
Ravi Coltrane (b. 1965)
Junior Cook (1934–1992)
Hank Crawford (1934–2009)
Sonny Criss (1927–1977)
Eddie "Lockjaw" Davis (1921–1986)
Jesse Davis (b. 1965)
Paul Desmond (1924–1977)
Eric Dolphy (1928–1964)
Arne Domnerus (b. 1924)
Lou Donaldson (b. 1926)
Jimmy Dorsey (1904–1957)
Paquito D'Rivera (b. 1948)
Allen Eager (1927–2003)
Bill Easley (b. 1946)
Teddy Edwards (1924–2003)
Marty Ehrlich (b. 1955)
Booker Ervin (1930–1970)
Herschel Evans (1909–1939)
Joe Farrell (1937–1986)
Ricky Ford (b. 1954)
Jimmy Forrest (1920–80)
Sonny Fortune (b. 1939)
Frank Foster (b. 1928)
Bud Freeman (1906–1991)
Chico Freeman (b. 1949)
Von Freeman (b. 1922)
Jan Garbarek (b. 1947)

Kenny Garrett (b. 1960)

George Garzone (b. 1950)

Charles Gayle (b. 1939)

Stan Getz (1927–1991)

John Gilmore (1931–1995)

Jimmy Giuffre (1921–2008)

Benny Golson (b. 1929)

Paul Gonsalves (1920–1974)

Dexter Gordon (1923–1990)

Wardell Gray (1921–1955)

Johnny Griffin (1928–2008)

Gigi Gryce (1925–1983)

Lars Gullin (1928–1976)

Shafi Hadi (b. 1929)

Scott Hamilton (b. 1954)

Craig Handy (b. 1962)

John Handy (b. 1933)

Billy Harper (b. 1943)

Eddie Harris (1934–1996)

Donald Harrison (b. 1960)

Michael Hashim (b. 1956)

Antonio Hart (b. 1968)

Coleman Hawkins (1904–1969)

Tubby Hayes (1935–1973)

Jimmy Heath (b. 1926)

Julius Hemphill (1938–1995)

Joe Henderson (1937–2001)

Ernie Henry (1926–1957)

Vincent Herring (b. 1964)

Fred Ho (b. 1957)

Johnny Hodges (1906–1970)

Javon Jackson (b. 1965)

Willis "Gator" Jackson (1928–1987)

Illinois Jacquet (1922–2004)

Joseph Jarman (b. 1937)

Hilton Jefferson (1903–1968)

Budd Johnson (1910–1984)

Howard Johnson (b. 1941)

Phillip Johnston (b. 1955)

Clifford Jordan (1931–1993)

Louis Jordan (1908–1975)

Talib (T. K. Blue) Kibwe (b. 1953)

Rahsaan Roland Kirk (1936–1977)

Lee Konitz (b. 1927)

Steve Lacy (1934–2004)

Oliver Lake (b. 1944)

Ralph Lalama (b. 1951)

Harold Land (1928–2001)

Yusef Lateef (b. 1920)

Dave Liebman (b. 1946)

Charles Lloyd (b. 1938)

Joe Lovano (b. 1952)

Frank Lowe (1943–2003)

Jimmy Lyons (1931–1986)

Rudresh Mahanthappa (b. 1978)

Joe Maini (1930–1964)

Branford Marsalis (b. 1960)

Warne Marsh (1927–1987)

Jackie McLean (1931–2006)

Charles McPherson (b. 1939)

Roscoe Mitchell (b. 1940)

Hank Mobley (1930–1986)

James Moody (b. 1925)

Frank Morgan (1933–2007)

Bob Mover (b. 1952)

Gerry Mulligan (1927–1996)

David Murray (b. 1955)

Ted Nash (b. 1959)

Oliver Nelson (1932–1975)

David "Fathead" Newman (1933–2009)

Big Nick Nicholas (1922–1997)

Sal Nistico (1940–1991)

Greg Osby (b. 1960)

Harold Ousley (b. 1939)

Charlie Parker (1920–1955)

Evan Parker (b. 1944)

Leo Parker (1925–1962)

Cecil Payne (1922–2007)

Art Pepper (1925–1982)

Flip Phillips (1915–2001)

Odean Pope (b. 1938)

Chris Potter (b. 1971)

Russell Procope (1908–1981)

Ike Quebec (1918–1963)

Gene Quill (1927–1988)

Dewey Redman (1931–2006)

Joshua Redman (b. 1969)

Mario Rivera (b. 1939)

Sam Rivers (b. 1923)
Adrian Rollini (1904–1956)
Sonny Rollins (b. 1930)
Charlie Rouse (1924–1988)
David Sanborn (b. 1945)
David Sanchez (b. 1968)
Pharoah Sanders (b. 1940)
Loren Schoenberg (b. 1958)
Gene Sedric (1907–1963)
Bud Shank (1926–2009)
Archie Shepp (b. 1937)
Sahib Shihab (1925–1989)
Mark Shim (b. 1973)
Wayne Shorter (b. 1933)
Zoot Sims (1925–1985)
Buster Smith (1904–1991)
Gary Smulyan (b. 1956)
James Spaulding (b. 1937)
Sonny Stitt (1924–1982)
John Surman (b. 1944)
Lew Tabackin (b. 1940)
Buddy Tate (1913–2001)
Joe Temperley (b. 1929)
Joe Thomas (1909–1986)
Lucky Thompson (1924–2005)
Henry Threadgill (b. 1944)
Frank Trumbauer (1901–1956)
Mark Turner (b. 1965)
Stanley Turrentine (1934–2000)
Charlie Ventura (1916–1992)
Eddie "Cleanhead" Vinson (1917–1988)
David S. Ware (b. 1949)
Earle Warren (1914–1994)
Ben Webster (1909–1973)
Frank Wess (b. 1922)
Bobby Watson (b. 1953)
Rudy Williams (1919–1954)
Dick Wilson (1911–1941)
Steve Wilson (b. 1961)
Chris Woods (1925–1985)
Phil Woods (b. 1931)
Lester Young (1909–1959)
John Zorn (b. 1953)

Clarinet

Buster Bailey (1902–1967)
George Baquet (1883–1949)
Alvin Batiste (1932–2007)
Barney Bigard (1906–1980)
Peter Brötzmann (b. 1941)
Don Byron (b. 1958)
John Carter (1928–1991)
Eddie Daniels (b. 1941)
Kenny Davern (1935–2006)
Buddy DeFranco (b. 1923)
Johnny Dodds (1892–1940)
Paquito D'Rivera (b. 1948)
Irving Fazola (1912–1949)
Pete Fountain (b. 1930)
Jimmy Giuffre (1921–2008)
Benny Goodman (1909–1986)
Edmond Hall (1901–1967)
Jimmy Hamilton (1917–1994)
Stan Hasselgard (1922–1948)
Woody Herman (1913–1987)
George Lewis (1900–1968)
Joe Marsala (1907–1978)
Matty Matlock (1909–1978)
Mezz Mezzrow (1899–1972)
Don Murray (1904–1929)
Albert Nicholas (1900–1973)
Jimmy Noone (1895–1944)
Ken Peplowski (b. 1959)
Alphonse Picou (1878–1961)
Perry Robinson (b. 1938)
Leon Roppolo (1902–1943)
Pee Wee Russell (1906–1969)
Louis Sclavis (b. 1953)
Tony Scott (1921–2007)
Artie Shaw (1910–2004)
Larry Shields (1893–1953)
Omer Simeon (1902–1959)
Wilbur Sweatman (1882–1961)
Frank Teschemacher (1906–1932)
Dr. Michael White (b. 1954)
Putte Wickman (1924–2006)
Bob Wilber (b. 1928)
Lester Young (1909–1959)

Flute

George Adams (1940–1992)
Jane Bunnett (b. 1956)
Wayman Carver (1905–1967)
Buddy Collette (b. 1921)
Eric Dolphy (1928–1964)
Joe Farrell (1937–1986)
Sonny Fortune (b. 1939)
Holly Hoffman (b. 1956)
Paul Horn (b. 1930)
Rahsaan Roland Kirk (1936–1977)
Moe Koffman (1928–2001)
Yusef Lateef (b. 1920)
Hubert Laws (b. 1939)
Herbie Mann (1930–2003)
James Moody (b. 1925)
Sam Most (b. 1930)
David "Fathead" Newman (1933–2009)
James Newton (b. 1953)
Jerome Richardson (1920–2000)
Sam Rivers (b. 1923)
Ali Ryerson (b. 1952)
Albert Socarras (1908–1987)
Jeremy Steig (b. 1942)
Lew Tabackin (b. 1940)
Dave Valentin (b. 1952)
Frank Wess (b. 1922)
Elise Wood (b. 1952)
Leo Wright (1933–1991)

Piano/Keyboard

Muhal Richard Abrams (b. 1930)
Toshiko Akiyoshi (b. 1929)
Joe Albany (1924–1988)
Monty Alexander (b. 1944)
Geri Allen (b. 1957)
Mose Allison (b. 1927)
Chris Anderson (1926–2008)
Albert Ammons (1907–1949)
Lil Hardin Armstrong (1898–1971)
Lynne Arriale (b. 1957)
Kenny Barron (b. 1943)
Count Basie (1904–1984)
Jonathan Batiste (b. 1986)

Richie Beirach (b. 1947)
Walter Bishop Jr. (1927–1998)
Eubie Blake (1887–1983)
Ran Blake (b. 1935)
Paul Bley (b. 1932)
Stefano Bollani (b. 1972)
Joanne Brackeen (b. 1938)
Dave Brubeck (b. 1920)
Dave Burrell (b. 1940)
Joe Bushkin (1916–2004)
Henry Butler (b. 1949)
Ray Bryant (b. 1931)
Jaki Byard (1922–1999)
George Cables (b. 1944)
Michael Cain (b. 1966)
Uri Caine (b. 1956)
John Campbell (b. 1955)
Barbara Carroll (b. 1925)
Marc Cary (b. 1967)
Bill Charlap (b. 1966)
Ray Charles (1930–2004)
Cyrus Chestnut (b. 1963)
Sonny Clark (1931–1963)
Gerald Clayton (b. 1984)
Nat "King" Cole (1919–1965)
Alice Coltrane (1937–2007)
Harry Connick Jr. (b. 1967)
Marc Copland (b. 1948)
Chick Corea (b. 1941)
Eddie Costa (1930–1962)
Stanley Cowell (b. 1941)
Marilyn Crispell (b. 1947)
Albert Dailey (1939–1984)
Tadd Dameron (1917–1965)
Walter Davis Jr. (1932–1990)
Armen Donelian (b. 1950)
Kenny Drew (1928–1993)
Kenny Drew Jr. (b. 1958)
Elaine Elias (b. 1960)
Duke Ellington (1899–1974)
Bill Evans (1929–1980)
Victor Feldman (1934–1987)
Tommy Flanagan (1930–2001)
Joel Forrester (b. 1946)

Don Friedman (b. 1935)
Dave Frishberg (b. 1933)
Hal Galper (b. 1938)
Red Garland (1923–1984)
Erroll Garner (1921–1977)
Giorgio Gaslini (b. 1929)
Vince Guaraldi (1928–1976)
Al Haig (1924–1982)
Bengt Hallberg (b. 1932)
Herbie Hancock (b. 1940)
Sir Roland Hanna (1932–2002)
Barry Harris (b. 1929)
Hampton Hawes (1928–1977)
Kevin Hays (b. 1968)
Fred Hersch (b. 1955)
Eddie Heyward (1915–1989)
John Hicks (1941–2006)
Andrew Hill (1931–2007)
Earl Hines (1903–1983)
Jutta Hipp (1925–2003)
Art Hodes (1904–1993)
Elmo Hope (1923–1967)
Dick Hyman (b. 1927)
Abdullah Ibrahim (b. 1934)
Ethan Iverson (b. 1973)
Vijay Iyer (b. 1971)
D. D. Jackson (b. 1967)
Ahmad Jamal (b. 1930)
Keith Jarrett (b. 1945)
James P. Johnson (1894–1955)
Pete Johnson (1904–1967)
Hank Jones (b. 1918)
Duke Jordan (1922–2006)
Dick Katz (b. 1924)
Wynton Kelly (1931–1971)
Rodney Kendrick (b. 1960)
Dave Kikoski (b. 1961)
Kenny Kirkland (1955–1998)
Diana Krall (b. 1964)
Steve Kuhn (b. 1938)
Billy Kyle (1914–1966)
Ellis Larkins (1923–2002)
John Lewis (1920–2001)
Meade "Lux" Lewis (1905–1964)

Ramsey Lewis (b. 1935)
Harold Mabern (b. 1936)
Pete Malinverni (b. 1957)
Dodo Marmarosa (1925–2002)
Ronnie Mathews (b. 1935)
Dave McKenna (1930–2008)
Jim McNeely (b. 1949)
Marian McPartland (b. 1918)
Jay McShann (1916–2006)
John Medeski (b. 1965)
Brad Mehldau (b. 1970)
Misha Mengelberg (b. 1935)
Mulgrew Miller (b. 1955)
Thelonious Monk (1917–1982)
Tete Montoliu (1933–1997)
Jason Moran (b. 1975)
Jelly Roll Morton (1890–1941)
Marty Napoleon (b. 1921)
Phineas Newborn Jr. (1931–1989)
Herbie Nichols (1919–1963)
Walter Norris (b. 1931)
Horace Parlan (b. 1931)
Danilo Perez (b. 1966)
Oscar Peterson (1925–2007)
Michel Petrucciani (1962–1999)
Enrico Pieranunzi (b. 1949)
Bud Powell (1924–1966)
Mel Powell (1923–1998)
Clarence Profit (1912–1944)
Don Pullen (1941–1995)
Freddie Redd (b. 1928)
Eric Reed (b. 1970)
Luckey Roberts (1887–1968)
Marcus Roberts (b. 1963)
Joe Robichaux (1900–1965)
Ted Rosenthal (b. 1959)
Renee Rosnes (b. 1962)
Jimmy Rowles (1918–1996)
Gonzalo Rubalcaba (b. 1963)
Hilton Ruiz (1952–2006)
Alex Von Schlippenbach (b. 1938)
George Shearing (b. 1919)
Matthew Shipp (b. 1960)
Horace Silver (b. 1928)

Pine Top Smith (1904–1929)
Willie "the Lion" Smith (1893–1973)
Martial Solal (b. 1927)
Mark Soskin (b. 1953)
Jess Stacy (1904–1994)
Billy Strayhorn (1915–1967)
Joe Sullivan (1906–1971)
Sun Ra (1914–1993)
Ralph Sutton (1922–2001)
Horace Tapscott (1934–1999)
Art Tatum (1909–1956)
Billy Taylor (b. 1921)
Cecil Taylor (b. 1929)
Jacky Terrasson (b. 1966)
Sir Charles Thompson (b. 1918)
Bobby Timmons (1935–1974)
Lennie Tristano (1919–1978)
McCoy Tyner (b. 1938)
Mal Waldron (1925–2002)
Fats Waller (1904–1943)
Cedar Walton (b. 1934)
Michael Weiss (b. 1958)
Kenny Werner (b. 1951)
Randy Weston (b. 1926)
Gerald Wiggins (1922–2008)
James Williams (1951–2004)
Jessica Williams (b. 1948)
Mary Lou Williams (1910–1981)
Teddy Wilson (1912–1986)
Richard Waynds (b. 1928)
Jimmy Yancey (1898–1951)
Joe Zawinul (1932–2007)
Denny Zeitlin (b. 1938)

Organ
Count Basie (1904–1984)
Milt Buckner (1915–1977)
Wild Bill Davis (1918–1995)
Joey DeFrancesco (b. 1971)
Barbara Dennerlein (b. 1964)
Bill Doggett (1916–1996)
Charles Earland (1941–1999)
Larry Goldings (b. 1968)
Richard Groove Holmes (1931–1991)

Jack McDuff (1926–2001)
Jimmy McGriff (1936–2008)
Don Patterson (1936–1988)
Shirley Scott (1934–2002)
Jimmy Smith (1925–2005)
Johnny Hammond Smith (1933–1997)
Dr. Lonnie Smith (b. 1942)
Fats Waller (1904–1943)
Larry Young (1940–1978)
Joe Zawinul (1932–2007)

Bass
Mickey Bass (b. 1943)
Aaron Bell (1922–2003)
Jimmy Blanton (1918–1942)
Wellman Braud (1891–1966)
Cameron Brown (b. 1941)
Ray Brown (1926–2002)
Steve Brown (1890–1965)
Red Callender (1916–1992)
Ron Carter (b. 1937)
Paul Chambers (1935–1969)
Avishai Cohen (b. 1970)
Greg Cohen (b. 1953)
Joe Comfort (1917–1988)
Curtis Counce (1926–1963)
Bob Cranshaw (b. 1932)
Israel Crosby (1919–1962)
Bill Crow (b. 1927)
Art Davis (1934–2007)
Richard Davis (b. 1930)
Mark Dresser (b. 1952)
Ray Drummond (b. 1946)
George Duvivier (1920–1985)
Malachi (Maghostut) Favors (1927–2004)
George "Pops" Foster (1892–1969)
David Friesen (b. 1942)
Larry Gales (1936–1995)
Jimmy Garrison (1933–1976)
Eddie Gomez (b. 1944)
Larry Grenadier (b. 1966)
Henry Grimes (b. 1935)
Charlie Haden (b. 1937)

Bob Haggart (1914–1998)
Percy Heath (1923–2005)
Milt Hinton (1910–2000)
Dave Holland (b. 1946)
Major Holley (1924–1990)
Dennis Irwin (1951–2008)
Chuck Israels (b. 1936)
David Izenzon (1932–1979)
Bill Johnson (1872–1972)
Marc Johnson (b. 1953)
Sam Jones (1924–1981)
John Kirby (1908–1952)
Steve Kirby (b. 1956)
Peter Kowald (1944–2002)
Scott LaFaro (1936–1961)
Jay Leonhart (b. 1940)
Ahmed Abdul-Malik (1927–1993)
Wendell Marshall (1920–2002)
Tarus Mateen (b. 1967)
Cecil McBee (b. 1935)
Christian McBride (b. 1972)
Pierre Michelot (1928–2005)
Charles Mingus (1922–1979)
Red Mitchell (1927–1992)
Charnett Moffett (b. 1967)
George Mraz (b. 1944)
John Ore (b. 1933)
Walter Page (1900–1957)
William Parker (b. 1952)
Jaco Pastorius (1951–1987)
John Patitucci (b. 1959)
Alcide "Slow Drag" Pavageau (1888–1969)
Gary Peacock (b. 1935)
Niels-Henning Ørsted Pedersen (1946–2005)
Oscar Pettiford (1922–1960)
Tommy Potter (1918–1988)
Gene Ramey (1913–1984)
Rufus Reid (b. 1944)
Larry Ridley (b. 1937)
Curly Russell (1917–1986)
Eddie Safranski (1918–1974)
Arvell Shaw (1923–2002)

Slam Stewart (1914–1987)
Steve Swallow (b. 1940)
Jamaaladeen Tacuma (b. 1956)
Reginald Veal (b. 1963)
Leroy Vinnegar (1928–1999)
Miroslav Vitous (b. 1947)
Wilbur Ware (1923–1979)
Peter Washington (b. 1964)
Buster Williams (b. 1942)
Reggie Workman (b. 1937)

Drums/Percussion
Rashied Ali (b. 1935)
Carl Allen (b. 1961)
Barry Altschul (b. 1943)
Paul Barbarin (1899–1969)
Joey Baron (b. 1955)
Ray Barretto (1929–2006)
Louis Bellson (b. 1924)
Han Bennink (b. 1942)
Dick Berk (b. 1939)
Denzil Best (1917–1965)
Ed Blackwell (1929–1992)
Brian Blade (b. 1970)
Art Blakey (1919–1990)
Willie Bobo (1934–1983)
Roy Brooks (1938–2005)
Alvin Burroughs (1911–1950)
Candido Camero (b. 1921)
Terri Lynne Carrington (b. 1965)
Michael Carvin (b. 1944)
Sid Catlett (1910–1951)
Joe Chambers (b. 1942)
Kenny Clarke (1914–1985)
Terry Clarke (b. 1944)
Jimmy Cobb (b. 1929)
Billy Cobham (b. 1944)
Cozy Cole (1909–1981)
Denardo Coleman (b. 1956)
Jerome Cooper (b. 1946)
Jimmy Crawford (1910–1980)
Andrew Cyrille (b. 1939)
Alan Dawson (1929–1996)
Jack DeJohnette (b. 1942)

Warren "Baby" Dodds (1898–1959)

Hamid Drake (b. 1955)

Billy Drummond (b. 1959)

Frankie Dunlop (b. 1928)

Al Foster (b. 1944)

Vernel Fournier (1928–2000)

Panama Francis (1918–2001)

Gerry Gibbs (b. 1964)

Milford Graves (b. 1941)

Sonny Greer (1895–1982)

Chico Hamilton (b. 1921)

Jake Hanna (b. 1931)

Eric Harland (b. 1979)

Winard Harper (1962)

Beaver Harris (1936–1991)

Billy Hart (b. 1940)

Louis Hayes (b. 1937)

Roy Haynes (b. 1925)

Al "Tootie" Heath (b. 1935)

Billy Higgins (1936–2001)

Gregory Hutchinson (b. 1970)

Susie Ibarra (b. 1970)

Ronald Shannon Jackson (b. 1940)

Gus Johnson (1913–2000)

Elvin Jones (1927–2004)

Jo Jones (1911–1985)

Philly Joe Jones (1923–1985)

Tiny Kahn (1924–1953)

Connie Kay (1927–1994)

Gene Krupa (1909–1973)

Cliff Leeman (1913–1986)

Mel Lewis (1929–1990)

Victor Lewis (b. 1950)

Shelly Manne (1920–1984)

Ray Mantilla (b. 1934)

Marilyn Mazur (b. 1955)

Steve McCall (1933–1989)

Charles Moffett (1929–1997)

Airto Moreira (b. 1941)

Joe Morello (b. 1928)

Paul Motian (b. 1931)

Famoudou Don Moye (b. 1946)

Sonny Murray (b. 1936)

Lewis Nash (b. 1958)

Adam Nussbaum (b. 1955)

Tony Oxley (b. 1938)

Sonny Payne (1926–1979)

Walter Perkins (1932–2004)

Charli Persip (1929)

Ralph Peterson (b. 1962)

Chano Pozo (1915–1948)

Tito Puente (1923–2000)

Buddy Rich (1917–1987)

Dannie Richmond (1935–1988)

Ben Riley (b. 1933)

Herlin Riley (b. 1957)

Max Roach (1924–2007)

Mongo Santamaria (1922–2003)

Zutty Singleton (1898–1975)

Grady Tate (b. 1932)

Art Taylor (1929–1995)

Dave Tough (1907–1948)

Kenny Washington (b. 1958)

Freddie Waits (1943–1989)

Nasheet Waits (b. 1972)

Jeff "Tain" Watts (b. 1960)

Chick Webb (1909–1939)

Jackie Williams (b. 1933)

Tony Williams (1945–1997)

Shadow Wilson (1919–1959)

Sam Woodyard (1925–1988)

Guitar/Banjo

John Abercrombie (b. 1944)

Howard Alden (b. 1958)

Oscar Aleman (1909–1980)

Derek Bailey (1930–2005)

Danny Barker (1909–1994)

George Barnes (1921–1977)

Billy Bauer (1915–2005)

George Benson (b. 1943)

Gene Bertoncini (b. 1937)

Bobby Broom (b. 1961)

Kenny Burrell (b. 1931)

Charlie Byrd (1925–1999)

Charlie Christian (1916–1942)

Joe Cohn (b. 1956)

John Collins (1913–2001)

Eddie Condon (1905–1973)
Larry Coryell (b. 1943)
Pierre Dorge (b. 1946)
Ted Dunbar (1937–1998)
Eddie Duran (b. 1925)
Eddie Durham (1906–1987)
Herb Ellis (b. 1921)
Kevin Eubanks (b. 1957)
Tal Farlow (1921–1998)
Bill Frissell (b. 1951)
Barry Galbraith (1919–1983)
Arv Garrison (1922–1960)
João Gilberto (b. 1931)
Egberto Gismonti (b. 1947)
Freddie Green (1911–1987)
Grant Green (1935–1979)
Tiny Grimes (1916–1989)
Lonnie Johnson (1899–1970)
Robert Johnson (1911–1938)
Jim Hall (b. 1930)
Charlie Hunter (b. 1967)
Barney Kessel (1923–2004)
Carl Kress (1907–1965)
Biréli Lagrène (b. 1966)
Eddie Lang (1902–1933)
Russell Malone (b. 1963)
Pat Martino (b. 1944)
John McLaughlin (b. 1942)
Pat Metheny (b. 1954)
Wes Montgomery (1923–1968)
Joe Morris (b. 1955)
Mary Osborne (1921–1992)
Joe Pass (1929–1994)
Les Paul (b. 1915)
Bucky Pizzarelli (b. 1926)
John Pizzarelli (b. 1960)
Jimmy Raney (1927–1995)
Django Reinhardt (1910–1953)
Emily Remler (1957–1990)
Marc Ribot (b. 1954)
Emanuel "Manny" Sayles (1907–1986)
John Scofield (b. 1951)
Bolo Sete (1928–1987)
Sonny Sharrock (1940–1994)

Floyd Smith (1917–1982)
Johnny Smith (b. 1922)
Johnny St. Cyr (1890–1966)
Leni Stern (b. 1952)
Toots Thielemans (b. 1922)
Ralph Towner (b. 1940)
James "Blood" Ulmer (b. 1942)
George Van Eps (1913–1998)
T-Bone Walker (1910–1975)
Muddy Waters (1913–1983)
Chuck Wayne (1923–1997)
Mark Whitfield (b. 1966)
Jack Wilkins (b. 1944)

Vibraphone
Karl Berger (b. 1935)
Gary Burton (b. 1943)
Teddy Charles (b. 1928)
Eddie Costa (1930–1962)
Don Elliott (1926–1984)
Victor Feldman (1934–1987)
Terry Gibbs (b. 1924)
Gunter Hampel (b. 1937)
Lionel Hampton (1908–2002)
Stefon Harris (b. 1973)
Jay Hoggard (b. 1954)
Bobby Hutcherson (b. 1941)
Milt Jackson (1923–1999)
Khan Jamal (b. 1946)
Joe Locke (b. 1959)
Steve Nelson (b. 1955)
Red Norvo (1908–1999)
Warren Smith (b. 1934)
Cal Tjader (1925–1982)
Lem Winchester (1928–1961)

Violin
Svend Asmussen (b. 1916)
Billy Bang (b. 1947)
Regina Carter (b. 1966)
Johnny Frigo (1916–2007)
Stephane Grappelli (1908–1997)
Leroy Jenkins (1932–2007)
Joe Kennedy Jr. (1923–2004)

Ray Nance (1913–1976)
Jean-Luc Ponty (b. 1942)
Jenny Scheinman (b. 1973)
Stuff Smith (1909–1967)
Eddie South (1904–1962)
Joe Venuti (1903–1978)

Singers
Mose Allison (b. 1927)
Karrin Allyson (b. 1963)
Ernestine Anderson (b. 1928)
Ivie Anderson (1905–1949)
Louis Armstrong (1901–1971)
Mildred Bailey (1907–1951)
Chet Baker (1929–1988)
Tony Bennett (b. 1926)
Andy Bey (b. 1939)
Connee Boswell (1907–1976)
Boswell Sisters
    Martha (1905–1958)
    Connee
    Helvetia "Vet" (1911–1988)
Dee Dee Bridgewater (b. 1950)
Jeanie Bryson (b. 1958)
Cab Calloway (1907–1994)
Betty Carter (1929–1998)
Ray Charles (1930–2004)
June Christy (1925–1990)
Jay Clayton (b. 1941)
Rosemary Clooney (1928–2002)
Freddie Cole (b. 1931)
Nat "King" Cole (1919–1965)
Chris Connor (b. 1927)
Bing Crosby (1903–1977)
Meredith DíAmbrosio (b. 1941)
Bob Dorough (b. 1923)
Billy Eckstine (1914–1993)
Roy Eldridge (1911–1989)
Ella Fitzgerald (1917–1996)
Dave Frishberg (b. 1933)
Slim Gaillard (1916–1991)
Teddy Grace (1905–1992)
Nancy Harrow (b. 1930)
Johnny Hartman (1923–1983)

Jon Hendricks (b. 1921)
Woody Herman (1913–1987)
Al Hibbler (1915–2001)
Billie Holiday (1915–1959)
Stevie Holland (b. 1967)
Shirley Horn (1934–2005)
Helen Humes (1913–1981)
Alberta Hunter (1895–1984)
Jackie and Roy
    Jackie Cain (b. 1928)
    Roy Kral (1921–2002)
Denise Jannah (b. 1956)
Eddie Jefferson (1918–1979)
Herb Jeffries (b. 1911)
Etta Jones (1928–2001)
Louis Jordan (1908–1975)
Sheila Jordan (b. 1928)
Diana Krall (b. 1964)
Lambert, Hendricks & Ross
    Dave Lambert (1917–1966)
    Jon Hendricks
    Annie Ross
Barbara Lea (b. 1929)
Jeanne Lee (1939–2000)
Julia Lee (1902–1958)
Peggy Lee (1920–2002)
Abbey Lincoln (b. 1930)
Bobby McFerrin (b. 1950)
Carmen McRae (1920–1994)
Helen Merrill (b. 1930)
Mills Brothers
John (1882–1967)
    John Jr. (1910–1936)
    Herbert (1912–1989)
    Harry (1913–1982)
    Donald (1915–1999)
Anita O'Day (1919–2006)
Jackie Paris (1926–2004)
Rosa Passos (b. 1952)
John Pizzarelli (b. 1960)
King Pleasure (1922–1981)
Ma Rainey (1886–1939)
Dianne Reeves (b. 1956)
Annie Ross (b. 1930)

Jimmy Rushing (1903–1972)
Kendra Shank (b. 1958)
Daryl Sherman (b. 1949)
Nina Simone (1933–2003)
Frank Sinatra (1915–1998)
Carol Sloane (b. 1937)
Bessie Smith (1894–1937)
Clara Smith (1894–1935)
Mamie Smith (1883–1946)
Jeri Southern (1926–1991)
Jo Stafford (1917–2008)
Kay Starr (b. 1922)
Maxine Sullivan (1919–1987)
Sister Rosetta Tharpe (1921–1973)
Big Joe Turner (1911–1985)
Sarah Vaughan (1924–1990)
Eddie "Cleanhead" Vinson (1917–1988)
Fats Waller (1904–1943)
Dinah Washington (1924–1963)
Ethel Waters (1896–1977)
Leo Watson (1898–1950)
Lee Wiley (1908–1975)
Joe Williams (1918–1999)
Cassandra Wilson (b. 1955)
Nancy Wilson (b. 1937)

Composers/Arrangers/Leaders

Muhal Richard Abrams (b. 1930)
Manny Albam (1922–2001)
Van Alexander (b. 1915)
David Baker (b. 1931)
Bob Belden (b. 1956)
Carla Bley (b. 1938)
Francy Boland (1929–2005)
Anthony Braxton (b. 1945)
Bob Brookmeyer (b. 1929)
Dave Brubeck (b. 1920)
Ralph Burns (1922–2001)
Benny Carter (1907–2003)
Bill Challis (1904–1994)
Al Cohn (1925–1988)
Ornette Coleman (b. 1930)
Al Cooper (1911–1981)
Chick Correa (b. 1941)

Tadd Dameron (1917–1965)
Miles Davis (1926–1991)
Eddie Durham (1906–1987)
Duke Ellington (1899–1974)
Mercer Ellington (1919–1996)
James Reese Europe (1881–1919)
Gil Evans (1912–1988)
Bill Finegan (1917–2008)
Frank Foster (b. 1928)
Gil Fuller (1920–1994)
Dizzy Gillespie (1917–1993)
Gil Goldstein (b. 1950)
Benny Golson (b. 1929)
Gigi Gryce (1925–1983)
George Handy (1920–1997)
Herbie Hancock (b. 1940)
Neal Hefti (1922–2008)
Fletcher Henderson (1897–1952)
Horace Henderson (1904–1988)
Bill Holman (b. 1927)
Budd Johnson (1910–1984)
Sy Johnson (b. 1930)
Quincy Jones (b. 1933)
Thad Jones (1923–1986)
Louis Jordan (1908–1975)
Stan Kenton (1911–1979)
Andy Kirk (1898–1992)
Bill Kirchner (b. 1953)
Papa Jack Laine (1873–1966)
Michel Legrand (b. 1932)
John Lewis (1920–2001)
Abbey Lincoln (b. 1930)
Jimmie Lunceford (1902–1947)
Teo Macero (b. 1925)
Machito (1912–1984)
Johnny Mandel (b. 1925)
Wynton Marsalis (b. 1961)
Gary McFarland (1933–1971)
Tom McIntosh (b. 1927)
Jim McNeely (b. 1949)
Glenn Miller (1904–1944)
Lucky Millinder (1900–1966)
Charles Mingus (1922–1979)
Thelonious Monk (1917–1982)

Butch Morris (b. 1947)

Jelly Roll Morton (1890–1941)

Bennie Moten (1894–1935)

Gerry Mulligan (1927–1996)

Jimmy Mundy (1907–1983)

David Murray (b. 1955)

Oliver Nelson (1932–1975)

Red Nichols (1905–1965)

Chico OíFarrill (1921–2001)

Sy Oliver (1910–1988)

Hall Overton (1920–1972)

Marty Paich (1925–1995)

Charlie Parker (1920–1955)

Duke Pearson (1932–1980)

Hannibal (Lokumbe) Peterson (b. 1948)

Bud Powell (1924–1966)

Boyd Raeburn (1913–1966)

Don Redman (1900–1964)

Johnny Richards (1911–1968)

Nelson Riddle (1921–1985)

Sonny Rollins (b. 1930)

Pete Rugolo (b. 1915)

George Russell (b. 1923)

Luis Russell (1902–1963)

Edgar Sampson (1907–1973)

Heikkie Sarmanto (b. 1939)

Eddie Sauter (1914–1981)

Lalo Schifrin (b. 1932)

Maria Schneider (b. 1960)

Gunther Schuller (b. 1925)

Wayne Shorter (b. 1933)

Don Sickler (b. 1944)

Horace Silver (b. 1928)

Billy Strayhorn (1915–1967)

Cecil Taylor (b. 1929)

Claude Thornhill (1909–1965)

Henry Threadgill (b. 1944)

Charles Tolliver (b. 1942)

Fats Waller (1904–1943)

Randy Weston (b. 1926)

Paul Whiteman (1890–1967)

Ernie Wilkins (1922–1999)

Clarence Williams (1898–1965)

Mary Lou Williams (1910–1981)

Gerald Wilson (b. 1918)

John Zorn (b. 1953)

GLOSSARY

I chord chord built on the first degree of the scale; known as the *tonic.*

IV chord chord built on the fourth degree of the scale; known as the *subdominant.*

V chord chord built on the fifth degree of the scale; known as the *dominant.*

AABA form the most common 32-bar *popular song* form, referring to melody and harmonic progression (but not text). Each portion is eight bars long, with B, the *bridge,* serving as the point of contrast. A = statement, A = repetition, B = contrast, A = return.

ABAC form the second most common 32-bar *popular song* form, referring to melody and harmonic progression (but not text). Each portion is eight bars long, with the A section returning in the song's middle. Can also be considered A A9 form.

accelerando a gradual speeding up of *tempo.*

acid jazz a form of contemporary music created by DJs in the 1990s, relying heavily on samples taken from jazz recordings from the 1950s and 1960s.

alto saxophone one of the most common saxophones used in jazz performance, smaller and higher-pitched than the tenor.

arpeggio the notes of a chord played in quick succession rather than simultaneously.

arrangements composed scores for big bands, with individual parts for each musician.

arco a stringed instrument (such as the string bass) played with a bow.

art music a form of music with high aesthetic standards and social prestige, created by professional artists for a well-educated public and insulated from the commercial world.

atonal music with no key center.

augmented chord an unstable chord made up of two major thirds; found in the whole-tone scale.

avant-garde jazz a modernist style of jazz exploring new methods that radically oppose existing traditions; among the elements of jazz undermined by the avant-garde are rhythm, harmony, melody, structure, instrumentation, manner of presentation, and politics.

backbeat a simple *polyrhythm* emphasizing beats 2 and 4 of a 4/4 measure (rather than 1 and 3).

ballad (1) a slow, romantic *popular song;* (2) a long, early type of folk song that narrated a bit of local history.

bar see *measure.*

baritone saxophone the largest and deepest saxophone used in jazz performance.

bass in the *rhythm section* of a jazz band, an instrument—*string bass, electric bass,* or *tuba*—that supports the harmony and plays a basic rhythmic foundation.

bass clarinet a *wind instrument* pitched lower than a standard *clarinet.*

bass drum the large drum front and center in a jazz *drum kit,* struck with a mallet propelled by a *foot pedal;* it produces a deep, heavy sound.

bebop A style of modern jazz pioneered in the mid-1940s; it has become the basis for most contemporary jazz.

bell the flared opening at the end of a brass instrument.

bent notes see *blue notes.*

big bands large jazz orchestras featuring sections of saxophones, trumpets, and trombones, prominent during the Swing Era (1930s).

block chords a *homophonic texture* in which the chordal accompaniment moves in the same rhythm as the main melody.

blue notes notes in which the pitch is bent expressively, using *variable intonation;* also known as bent notes.

blues a musical/poetic form in African American culture, created c. 1900 and widely influential around the world.

blues form a twelve-bar *cycle* used as a framework for improvisation by jazz musicians.

blues scale the melodic resources for the *blues;* includes simple *pentatonic* and *diatonic* scales combined with *blue notes.*

blue third the lowered third degree of the scale, featured in the *blues.*

bongos in *Latin percussion,* an instrument with two drumheads, one larger than the other, compact enough to sit between the player's knees.

boogie-woogie a blues piano style in which the left hand plays a rhythmic *ostinato* of eight beats to the bar.

bossa nova "new flair"; Brazilian form of *samba* music.

bottleneck guitar *guitar* played with a glass slide over the finger to create a *glissando* effect.

bow a string instrument, such as a *string bass,* played by drawing a bow with horsehair across the strings; also known as *arco.*

brass instruments *wind instruments,* some of which are indeed made of brass, that use a cuplike *mouthpiece* to create the sound.

break a short two- or four-bar episode in which the band abruptly stops playing to let a single musician solo with a *monophonic* passage.

bridge (release) the middle part (or B section) of 32-bar *AABA form,* which connects, or "bridges," between the A sections; it typically ends with a *half cadence.*

broken octaves a form of left-hand piano accompaniment that alternates the lower note of an octave with the higher one.

cadence stopping places that divide a *harmonic progression* into comprehensible *phrases*. See *half cadence, full cadence.*

cadenza a classical-music word for a monophonic solo passage that showcases the performer's virtuosity.

cakewalk ragtime dancing featuring *syncopated* rhythms.

call and response a pervasive principle of interaction or conversation in jazz: a statement by one musician or group of musicians is immediately answered by another musician or group.

changes jazz slang for a harmonic progression. See *rhythm changes.*

Charleston rhythm a dance rhythm from the 1920s, consisting of two emphatic beats followed by a rest.

chart a shorthand musical score that serves as the point of reference for a jazz performance, often specifying only the melody and the harmonic progression; also known as a lead sheet.

Chicago style style of jazz in the 1920s that imitated the New Orleans style, combining expansive solos with *polyphonic* theme statements.

chord a combination of notes performed simultaneously.

chord clusters *dissonant* chords with closely spaced notes.

chorus (1) a single statement of the harmonic and rhythmic jazz *cycle* defined by the musical form (e.g, 12-bar blues, 32-bar popular song); (2) the repeated portion of

a *popular song,* often introduced by its *verse.*

chromatic harmony complex harmony based on the *chromatic scale.*

chromatic scale the scale containing twelve *half steps* within the *octave,* corresponding to all the keys (black and white) within an octave on the piano (e.g., from C to C).

clarinet a *wind instrument* consisting of a slim, cylindrical, ebony-colored wooden tube that produces a thin, piercing sound.

classic blues see *vaudeville blues.*

classical music *art music* from the European tradition.

clave a Latin *time-line pattern.*

clusters see *chord clusters.*

coda Italian for "tail": a concluding section to a musical performance.

collective improvisation method of improvisation found in New Orleans jazz in which several instruments in the *front line* improvise simultaneously in a dense, *polyphonic* texture.

comping a rhythmically unpredictable way of playing chords to accompany a soloist; typically one of the *variable layers* in the *rhythm section.*

congas in *Latin percussion,* two tall drums of equal height but different diameters, with the smaller one assigned the lead role.

consonant the quality of a harmony that's stable and doesn't need to *resolve* to another chord.

contrapuntal adjectival form of *counterpoint.*

cool jazz a style of modern jazz in the 1950s that used a "cool," relaxed approach to timbre and experimented with such basic elements as form, texture, instrumentation, and meter.

coon song an early form of *ragtime* popular song that yoked polyrhythmic accompaniments to grotesque racial stereotypes.

cornet a partially conical *brass instrument* used often in early jazz and eventually supplanted by the *trumpet.*

countermelody in *homophonic texture,* an accompanying melodic part with distinct, though subordinate, melodic interest; also known (especially in classical music) as obbligato.

counterpoint *polyphonic texture,* especially when composed.

counterrhythm see *cross-rhythm.*

country blues an early style of blues, first recorded in the 1920s, featuring itinerant male singers accompanying themselves on guitar.

crash cymbal a cymbal that produces a splashy, indeterminate pitch, not unlike a small gong, used for dramatic punctuations.

crescendo an increase in volume.

cross-rhythm a rhythmic layer that conflicts with the underlying meter.

cup mute an orchestral *mute* with an extension that more or less covers the *bell* of a *brass instrument.*

cycle a fixed unit of time, repeated indefinitely, that's used as the framework for improvisation in jazz.

cymbals broad-rimmed, slightly-convex circular plates that form part of the jazz *drum kit.* See also *crash cymbal, high-hat,* and *ride cymbal.*

decrescendo a decrease in volume.

degree individual notes in a scale (e.g., the first note of a scale is the first degree).

diatonic scale the seven-note scale most commonly used in Western music. See *major scale, minor scale, Dorian mode.*

diminished (or diminished-seventh) chord an unstable chord made up entirely of minor thirds.

discography the science of record classification.

dissonant the quality of an unstable harmony that *resolves* to another chord.

dominant a chord built on the fifth degree of the scale that demands resolution to the tonic chord.

Dorian mode a diatonic scale with an arrangement of half and whole steps (found on the piano white keys from D to D) that falls between major and minor.

double (1) to play more than one instrument; (2) to reinforce a melody with one or more different instruments.

double bass see *string bass.*

double stop on a bowed string instrument (violin, bass), two strings played at the same time.

double time a technique in which a jazz ensemble, especially the *rhythm section,* plays twice as fast without changing the length of the overall cycle.

downbeat the first beat of a *measure,* or bar.

dropping bombs a technique devised in *bebop* in which the bass drum plays strong accents.

drum kit (or drum set, trap set, traps) a one-man percussion section within the rhythm section of a jazz band, usually consisting of a *bass drum, snare drum, tom-toms,* and *cymbals.*

duple meter the most common form of *meter,* grouping beats into patterns of twos or fours; every *measure,* or bar, in duple meter has either two or four beats.

dynamics volume, or loudness.

electric bass a four-stringed guitar used in popular music, amplified through an electric speaker.

electric piano an electrically amplified keyboard, such as the Fender Rhodes, capable of producing piano sounds.

Ellingtonians musicians who played with Duke Ellington for years or even decades.

embouchure the shaping and positioning of the lips and other facial muscles when playing wind instruments.

extended chords *triads* to which additional pitches, or *extensions,* have been added.

extensions notes added to extend a chord beyond the triad (such as the sixth, seventh, ninth, or thirteenth).

fake book a collection of *charts* or lead sheets used by jazz musicians (so-called because jazz musicians improvise, or "fake," their way through a performance).

false fingerings on a reed instrument (especially the saxophone), playing the same note with different fingers, often producing unusual timbres or slight pitch differences.

field holler an unaccompanied, rhythmically loose vocal line sung by a field worker.

fill a short drum solo performed to fill in the spaces in an improvised performance.

fixed intonation a tuning system that fixes pitches at precise frequencies. See *variable intonation.*

flat a musical symbol (♭) that lowers a note by a half step.

flatted third the lowered third degree of the scale, typically found in the blues.

flatted fifth see *tritone.*

flatted scale degree note played a half step lower.

flugelhorn brass instrument with a fully conical bore, somewhat larger than a trumpet and producing a more mellow, rounded timbre.

folk music a form of music created by ordinary people for their own use, insulated from the commercial world and the world of social elites.

foot pedal the mechanism that propels the mallet to hit a *bass drum.*

form the preconceived structures that govern improvisation in jazz. These may include *cycles* of various kinds, popular song (like *AABA*), or compositional forms such as *march/ragtime.*

forte a loud dynamic.

foundation layers continuous, unchanging patterns whose very repetition provides a framework for a musical piece.

free improvisation improvisation in an atonal context, where the focus shifts from harmony to other dimensions of music: timbre, melodic intervals, rhythm, and the interaction between musicians.

free rhythm music that flows through time without regularly occurring pulses.

frequency the vibrations per second of a musical note.

front the nominal star of a jazz band, but not really its leader or music director.

front line in *New Orleans jazz,* the melody instruments: trumpet (or cornet), trombone, and clarinet.

full cadence a musical stopping point on the *tonic* that marks the end of a phrase.

funk a type of groove with a highly sycopated bass line and multiple contrasting rhythmic layers, favored by jazz musicians after about 1970.

fusion the joining of two types of music, especially the mixing of jazz and rock in the 1970s.

ghosting playing notes so lightly that they are almost inaudible.

glissando sliding seamlessly from one note to another, as exemplified on the trombone; also known as smear.

grace note a short, decorative note sounded either immediately before or simultaneously with a longer melodic note.

groove a general term for the overall rhythmic framework of a performance. Grooves include *swing, funk, ballad,* and *Latin.*

guiro in *Latin percussion,* a scraped gourd with ridges.

guitar a plucked string instrument with waisted sides and a fretted fingerboard; the acoustic guitar was part of early jazz *rhythm sections,* while the electric guitar began to be used in the late 1930s and came to dominate jazz and popular music in the 1960s.

half cadence a musical stopping point on the *dominant.* Half cadences sound incomplete; they serve like a comma or a semicolon in punctuation, providing a stop but not signaling full closure.

half-valving depressing one or more of the valves of a brass instrument only halfway, producing an uncertain pitch with a nasal sound.

half step the smallest interval possible in Western music.

hard bop a *bebop* style of the 1950s that refused the experiments of *cool jazz* and linked its aesthetic with African American culture; included the more populist *soul jazz* and was played by great bebop artists of the day.

Harlem Renaissance an artistic movement of the 1920s that attempted to display African American abilities in painting, drama, literature, poetry, criticism, and music; jazz was usually not included by critics of the time, although in retrospect the music of Duke Ellington seems central.

harmonic improvisation a new melodic line created with notes drawn from the underlying *harmonic progression;* also known as running the changes.

harmonic progression a series of chords placed in a strict rhythmic sequence; also known as changes.

harmonic substitution the substitution of one chord, or a series of chords, for harmonies in a progression.

Harmon mute a hollow mute, originally with a short extension but usually played without it, leaving a hole in the center and creating a highly concentrated sound.

head a composed section of music that frames a small-combo performance, appearing at the beginning and again at the end.

head arrangement a flexible, unwritten arrangement created by a band.

high-hat two shoulder-level *cymbals* on an upright pole with a foot pedal at its base; the pedal brings the top cymbal crashing into the lower one with a distinct *thunk*.

hip-hop a form of contemporary music that arose in the 1970s, featuring rapping, turntable styling, and the dance and fashion of inner-city youth.

Historicism the theory that artistic works do not rise independently of history but must be understood in relation to the past.

homophony a *texture* featuring one melody supported by harmonic accompaniment.

horns jazz slang for *wind instruments*.

inside see *playing inside*.

interval the distance between two different pitches of a scale.

irregular meter a meter featuring beats of unequal size (some are divided into twos, others into threes). A meter of five, for example, features two beats—one divided into three notes, the other divided into two notes (as in Dave Brubeck's "Take Five"). Similar combinations of seven, nine, and eleven are possible.

jam session an informal gathering at which musicians create music for their own enjoyment.

Jazz Age the 1920s; the era in which jazz became a popular, prominent form of music.

jazz repertory a movement that arose in the mid-1970s to critically examine and perform jazz from earlier eras.

keeping time playing the *foundation layers* for a musical piece.

klezmer a Jewish dance music.

Latin music dance grooves from the Caribbean, Central America, or South America (such as rumba, samba, mambo, bossa nova, or merengue) that feature syncopated bass lines and lively polyrhythm.

Latin percussion a wide variety of instruments including congas, bongos, timbales, maracas, and guiro.

legato a smooth, unbroken connection between notes.

licks short melodic ideas that form a shared basic vocabulary for jazz improvisers.

mainstream term first coined for music during the 1950s that was neither modernist (bebop, cool jazz, hard bop) or historicist (New Orleans jazz); today, it refers to styles that are neither aggressively innovative nor backward-looking, but falling in the center of the tradition.

major scale or mode the most common scale in Western music, sung to the syllables *do, re, mi, fa, sol, la, ti do*. The pattern of whole and half steps is W W H W W W H.

major second a whole step, or an interval made up of two half steps.

major triad a triad featuring a major third between the two lower notes.

maracas in *Latin percussion,* a gourd filled with beans and shaken.

march form a musical form exemplified by composers like John Philip Sousa, consisting of a series of sixteen-bar *strains,* usually repeated once and not brought back; for example, AABBCCDD; the third strain, or *trio, modulates* to a new key (usually *IV*) and is often twice as long.

march/ragtime form *march form* as adopted by ragtime composers like Scott Joplin.

measure (or bar) a rhythmic unit lasting from one downbeat to the next.

melismatic several notes sung to a single syllable.

melodic paraphrase a preexisting melody used as the basis for improvisation.

meter the organization of recurring pulses into patterns. See also *duple meter, irregular meter,* and *triple meter.*

microtones melodic intervals smaller than a half step.

minor scale or mode a diatonic scale similar to the *major scale,* but with a different pattern of half steps and whole steps (W H W W H W W); normally used in Western music to convey melancholy or sadness.

minor triad a triad featuring a minor third between the two lower notes.

modal improvisation the process of using a scale as the basis for improvisation.

modal jazz a style of jazz devised in the 1950s that relied heavily on *modal improvisation.*

modulate to move from one key (B-flat, G, D minor, etc.) to another.

monophony a *texture* featuring one melody with no accompaniment. See also *break, stop-time.*

montuno a syncopated *vamp* that serves as a rhythmic foundation in Latin music.

motive a short melodic or rhythmic idea.

mouthpiece on a brass instrument, a cuplike rest for the musician's lips, into which air is blown; on a reed instrument, the piece of hard plastic to which a reed is attached.

multiphonics complicated sounds created on a wind instrument (through intense blowing) that contain more than one pitch at the same time; used often in avant-garde jazz.

mutes physical devices inserted into the bell of brass instruments to distort the timbre of the sounds coming out. See *cup mute, Harmon mute, pixie mute, plunger mute,* and *straight mute.*

neighbor note a note one half or whole step away; neighbor notes leave and return to a note by step.

New Criticism criticism that emphasizes close examination of a work of art with little concern for the cultural or biographical circumstances under which it was created.

New Orleans jazz the earliest jazz style, developed early in the twentieth century and popularized after 1917 in New York and Chicago; native to New Orleans, it features *collective improvisation.*

ninth an interval a step larger than an octave, used to create *extended chords.*

obbligato see *countermelody.*

octave two notes with the same letter name; one pitch has a frequency precisely twice the other (in a ratio of $2:1$).

offbeat a note that falls in between the basic beats of a measure.

organ in jazz, an electrically amplified keyboard with *pedals* that imitates the sound of a pipe organ; used in *soul jazz* in the 1950s and 1960s.

ostinato (Italian for "obstinate") a repeated melodic or rhythmic pattern.

ostinato riff a riff that's repeated indefinitely.

outside see *playing outside.*

pedals the bass notes on an *organ,* played on a keyboard with the feet.

pedal point a passage in which the bass note refuses to move, remaining stationary on a single note.

pedal tone the bass note that creates a *pedal point.*

pentatonic scale a scale of five notes; for example, C D E G A.

percussion in the *rhythm section* of a jazz band, the drums, cymbals, congas, and other instruments that are struck to provide the music's rhythmic foundation.

phrase a musical utterance that's analogous to a sentence in speech.

phrasing the manner of shaping phrases: some musicians play phrases that are short and terse, while others are garrulous and intense.

piano a stringed keyboard instrument on which a pressed key triggers a hammer to strike strings; a standard part of the *rhythm section.*

piano a soft dynamic.

pickup a small microphone attached to the bridge of a *string bass* or to an acoustic *guitar* to amplify its sound.

pitch the vibrations per second, or *frequency,* of a sound.

pixie mute a small mute inserted into the bell of a brass instrument; players like Cootie Williams and "Tricky Sam" Nanton modified its sound further with a *plunger mute.*

pizzicato the technique of playing a string instrument by plucking the strings with the fingers; usually the preferred method in jazz for playing the *string bass.*

playing inside improvising within the structure of a *tonal* harmonic progression

playing outside improvising outside the structure of a *tonal* harmonic progression.

plunger mute the bottom end of a sink plunger (minus the handle), used as a mute for a brass instrument.

polyphony *texture* in which two or more melodies of equal interest are played at the same time.

polyrhythm the simultaneous use of contrasting rhythms; also known as rhythmic contrast.

popular song a type of song created by professional songwriters, especially in the period from the 1920s to the 1960s; usually falls into one of the basic song forms, such as *AABA* or *ABAC.*

press-roll an intense rumbling on the *snare drum.*

programmatic music that attempts to link itself to specific places, people, or events.

quartal chords (or harmonies) chords built using the interval of a fourth (rather than a third).

quarter tone a *microtone* that divides the half step into equal parts.

ragtime a style of popular music in the early twentieth century that conveyed African American polyrhythm in notated form; includes popular song and dance, although it's primarily known today through compositions written for the piano.

reed instruments *wind instruments* whose *mouthpieces* are inserted between the lips, with the player blowing a stream of air into a passageway between a thin, limber reed and the hard part of the mouthpiece.

refrain in *popular song* or *folk music,* a musical section that returns regularly.

register the range of an instrument or voice: upper register means its highest notes, lower register its lower notes.

resolve what an unstable (or *dissonant*) note or chord does when it moves to a stable (or *consonant*) note or chord.

rest a moment of silence, indicated by a sign in musical notation; for example, ♩ indicates a quarter rest (a quarter note's duration of silence).

retro-swing a form of dance music popular toward the end of the twentieth century that appropriated dances from the Swing Era with musical accompaniment from 1940s rhythm and blues.

rhythm changes a harmonic progression based on the George Gershwin tune "I Got Rhythm."

rhythmic contrast see *polyrhythm.*

rhythmic layers in the repetitive cyclic structures of jazz, highly individualized parts that contrast with one another, even as they create a unified whole. See also *polyrhythm.*

rhythm section instruments that provide accompaniment for jazz soloing: harmony instruments (piano, guitar), bass instruments (string bass, tuba), and percussion (drum set).

ride cymbal a cymbal with a clear, focused timbre that's played more or less continuously.

ride pattern a steady pulsation played on the ride cymbal that forms one of the foundations for modern jazz.

riff a short, catchy, and repeated melodic phrase.

ring shout an African American religious dance, performed in a circle moving counterclockwise; often cited as the earliest and most pervasive form of African survival in the New World.

rip a strong *glissando* rising to the top of a note, especially on a trumpet.

ritard a gradual slowing down of *tempo.*

rock and roll a form of contemporary music, combining rhythm and blues with elements from popular song and country music and marketed at white teenagers; since the 1960s, when it became known simply as rock, it has been the dominant form in the music industry.

root the bottom note of a *triad*.

rubato (Italian for "stolen") an elastic approach to rhythm in which musicians speed up and slow down for expressive purposes; rubato makes musical time unpredictable and more flexible.

rumba clave a slight variation of the *clave* pattern, used in the rumba.

salsa a form of Latin popular music, founded in the 1970s.

samba a traditional Latino music with African roots.

saxophone invented by Adophe Sax in the 1840s, a family of single-reed *wind instruments* with the carrying power of a brass instrument. See *alto saxophone, tenor saxophone, soprano saxophone,* and *baritone saxophone.*

scale a collection of *pitches* within the *octave,* forming a certain pattern of whole and half steps, from which melodies are created.

scat-singing improvising by a vocalist, using nonsense syllables instead of words; popularized by Louis Armstrong.

secondary ragtime a pattern of *polyrhythm* in which a short motive of three pitches, implying a meter of three, is superimposed on a duple meter.

send-off riffs ensemble *riffs* played in the first few bars of a *chorus* by the entire band. They interrupt or immediately precede a solo, "sending" the soloist off on his way; the soloist then completes the rest of the chorus.

sequence a short melodic pattern repeated on different pitches. See also *transpose.*

seventh an *interval* one step smaller than an *octave,* often used as an *extension* for chords.

shake for *brass instruments,* a quick *trill* between notes that mimics a wide *vibrato,* often performed at the end of a musical passage.

sharp a music symbol (♯) that raises a note a half step.

shuffle rhythms slow, powerfully syncopated rhythms derived from *boogie-woogie.*

sideman any musician employed by a bandleader; often used to describe members of a swing band.

singer-songwriter in contemporary popular music, a perfomer who creates his or her own music; this contrasts with the practice in the music industry before the 1960s that set songwriters apart from performers.

single reed a *reed instrument,* such as the *clarinet* or *saxophone,* that uses only one reed; in jazz, double-reed instruments such as the oboe or bassoon are rarely used.

slash chords complex *extended chords* in which the root is a note not normally part of the *triad* (e.g., an A major chord with an F root, written as A/F and spoken as "A-slash-F").

slide an elongated trombone tube that adjusts the length of a column of air when the player slides it.

small combo the standard small group for jazz, combining a few *soloists* with a *rhythm section.*

smear see *glissando.*

smooth jazz a highly popular form of contemporary jazz, featuring inoffensive soloing and digitally processed rhythm tracks, favored on some radio stations.

snare drum smaller drum in a jazz *drum kit,* either standing on its own or attached to the *bass drum,* and emitting a penetrating, rattling sound.

soli a passage for a section of a jazz band (saxophones, trumpets, trombones) in block-chord texture.

soloist any instrument in the jazz ensemble whose improvisation is featured in a performance.

son clave the standard version of the *clave* pattern.

soprano saxophone the smallest and highest-pitched saxophone used in jazz performance.

soul jazz a popularized form of *hard bop* that employs a strong backbeat, an aggressive urban sound, and gospel-typechords.

spiritual African American religious song.

staccato a short, detached way of playing notes or chords.

standard a popular song that has become part of the permanent repertory for jazz musicians.

stepwise in melody, moving from one note in the scale to the next.

stock arrangements standard arrangements of popular songs made available by publishing companies for swing bands.

stop-time a technique in which a band plays a series of short chords a fixed distance apart (e.g., a measure), creating spaces for an instrument to fill with monophonic improvisation; often used in early jazz.

straight mute a standard orchestral mute that dampens the sound of a brass instrument without much distortion.

strain in *march form,* a 16- or 32-bar section.

stride piano a style of jazz piano relying on a left-hand accompaniment that alternates low bass notes with higher chords.

string bass the most common bass used in jazz, the same acoustic instrument found in symphony orchestras; also known as double bass.

subdominant the fourth degree of the scale, or the chord built on that scale degree.

swing (1) jazz from the period 1935–1945, usually known as the Swing Era; (2) a jazz-specific feeling created by rhythmic contrast within a particular rhythmic framework (usually involving a walking bass and a steady rhythm on the drummer's ride cymbal).

swing eighth notes a jazz soloist's flexible division of the beat into unequal parts.

symphonic jazz a form of jazz popular in the 1920s that attempted to elevate the music through symphonic arrangements.

syncopation an occasional rhythmic disruption, contradicting the basic meter.

synthesizer an electronically amplified keyboard that creates its own sounds through computer programming.

tailgate trombone (or smears) exaggerated *glissandos.*

tempo the speed of a piece of music.

tenor saxophone a common type of saxophone, larger and deeper than the alto.

territory bands in the 1920s and early 1930s, dance bands that serviced a "territory," defined by a day's drive from an urban center.

texture the relationship between melody and harmony: a melody supported by harmonic accompaniment (*homophony*), a melody by itself (*monophony*), or two or more melodies played at the same time, creating their own harmonies (*polyphony*).

third the basic interval for tonal harmony; in a major scale, it's formed by skipping over a scale degree (e.g., moving from *do* to *mi*).

thirty-two-bar popular song a standard song form, usually divided into shorter sections, such as AABA (each section eight bars long) or AA′ (each section sixteen bars long).

timbales in *Latin percussion,* two drums mounted on a stand along with a cowbell, played with sticks by a standing musician.

timbre the quality of sound, as distinct from its pitch; also known as tone color.

timbre variation the use of a wide range of *timbres* for expressive purposes.

time-line pattern a repeated, asymmetric pattern that serves as a basic foundation layer in African (and, to a lesser extent, African American) music.

tom-toms cylindrical drums with no snare used in a *drum kit,* typically tuned to different pitches.

tonal music music characterized by an overall tonal center (the *tonic*) that serves as the center of gravity: all other harmonies are more or less dissonant in relation to this tonal center.

tonic the first degree of the scale, or the chord built on the first scale degree.

tonic triad the chord built on the first scale degree.

trading fours in a jam session, "trading" short (usually four-bar) solos back and forth between the drums and the soloists, or between soloists.

transpose to shift an entire musical phrase to a higher or lower pitch. See also *sequence.*

traps see *drum kit.*

trap set see *drum kit.*

tremolo the speedy alternation of two notes some distance apart; on a piano, this action imitates a brass vibrato.

triad the standard three-note chord (e.g., C-E-G) that serves as the basis for tonal music.

trill the rapid alternation of two adjacent notes.

trio (1) the third, or C section of *march* or *march/ragtime form,* usually twice as long (32 bars), *modulating* to a new key, and offering contrast; (2) a group with three members.

triple meter a *meter* that groups beats into patterns of threes; every *measure,* or bar, of triple meter has three beats.

triplet a note divided into three equal parts.

tritone a dissonant *interval* made up of three *whole steps* (e.g., C to F-sharp), also known as flatted fifth.

trombone a low-pitched *brass instrument* that uses a *slide* to adjust the column of air. See also *valve trombone.*

trumpet the most common *brass instrument;* its vibrating tube is completely cylindrical until it reaches the end, where it flares into the instrument's *bell.*

tuba a large, low-pitched *brass instrument* with an intricate nest of tubing ending in an enormous bell; often used in early jazz groups as a bass instrument because of its powerful volume.

turnaround (or turnback) a faster, more complex series of chords used in the last two bars of a blues or the last A section of an AABA form, leading back to the beginning of the chorus.

twelve-bar blues see *blues form.*

unison the "interval" formed by two different instruments performing the same pitch.

upbeat note or notes that precede the *downbeat.*

valve trombone a *trombone* that uses valves rather than a *slide* to change the length of the tube.

valves controls in *brass instruments* that shunt air into a passageway of tubing, altering a pitch.

vamp a short, repeated chord progression, usually used as the introduction to a performance.

variable intonation a tuning system that allows for certain pitches to fluctuate by microtones, thus creating *blue notes.*

variable layers contrasting parts played above the *foundation layers* in a piece.

vaudeville blues an early theatrical form of the blues featuring female singers, accompanied by a small band; also known as classic blues.

verse the introductory portion of a *popular song,* preceding the *chorus;* usually omitted by jazz musicians.

vibraphone (vibraharp) an amplified metallophone (metal xylophone) with tubes below each slab; a disc turning within each tube helps sustain and modify the sound.

vibrato a slight wobble in pitch produced naturally by the singing voice, often imitated by wind and string instruments.

voicing distributing the notes of a chord on a piano, or to different instruments in an arrangement.

walking bass a bass line featuring four equal beats per bar, usually used as a rhythmic foundation in jazz.

whole note the longest possible rhythmic note; in a four-beat *duple meter,* it would fill up an entire *measure.*

whole step an interval made up of two half steps; the distance between *do* and *re.*

whole-tone chord an *augmented chord* made up of *intervals* (major thirds) from the *whole-tone scale.*

whole-tone scale a six-note *scale* made up entirely of *whole steps;* because it avoids the *intervals* of a perfect fourth or fifth (the intervals normally used to tune instruments), it has a peculiar, disorienting sound.

wind instruments in jazz, instruments that are played by blowing air into a tube; also known in jazz as horns.

wire brushes drumsticks—actually hollow handles with thin wire strands—used to strike or brush the drumheads.

work song a type of folk song used during work to regulate physical activity or to engage the worker's attention.

COLLECTING JAZZ RECORDINGS

Notes for Beginners and Prompts for Connoisseurs

The process of collecting music or anything else tends to combine dedication (as in "I'm going to acquire every record Dinah Washington ever made") and serendipity (as in "While searching for Dinah Washington, I discovered a really obscure and wonderful singer named Teddy Grace"). This book—with its Listening Guides and passing references to other works—should serve as a fairly comprehensive beginning, whether you find yourself drawn to particular pieces, and the styles and eras they represent, or have a more capacious interest in confronting jazz whole. Jazz is a blend of art and entertainment, and its first objective is to give pleasure. In pursuing it, trust your instincts and go with what you like. If Artie Shaw's "Star Dust" makes you want to look more deeply into bands of the Swing Era, you're not required to give equal time to the avant-garde. And if Albert Ayler's "Ghosts" blows your mind, you don't have to feign a love of soul jazz. Even those of us who are seemingly enamored of every facet of jazz are likely to roll our eyes at a facet or two. On the other hand, everyone has to venerate Louis Armstrong; it's a law, punishable by loss of affect.

Tastes change, and if you are lucky, yours will expand rather than diminish in its curiosity and receptiveness. We subscribe to the advice of Sidney Bechet, this book's sole epigram: "You got to be in the sun to feel the sun. It's that way with music, too." That means listen to everything with empathy. On the other hand, don't be intimidated into letting go of your bullshit detector—this applies to arts and to arts criticism, including this book, which only pretends to be objective. Jazz criticism and reference works are a good way to expand knowledge and find recommendations for recordings. Monthly magazines like *Jazz Times, Down Beat, Jazziz,* various online sites, and a very few urban newspapers have reviewers who are dedicated and opinionated listeners. After reading the same bylines again and again, you find yourself trusting some more than others, either because their tastes prove similar to yours or you find their perspectives and styles of articulation companionable and persuasive. You know soon enough whose passions and discontents ring true.

Unhappily, criticism has a larger role in introducing jazz records and reissues than it should, owing to jazz's low (almost nonexistent in many places) profile on radio and television. Record stores have listening apparatuses, and just about every online music service allows you to sample tracks, but part of the fun of collecting jazz is occasionally taking a flyer because you like the cover design or have heard someone mention the artist's name or you recognize a few of the tunes or just want to hear something new. It is now a sad reality that retail stores have disappeared from the musical landscape in many areas. Most of us buy records online, as CDs or MP3s, sacrificing the pleasure of shuffling through bins and racks and coming across a gem we didn't know existed. Yet the advantages of online shopping are obvious, not the least of which is that we can buy a single track before investing in an album. In doing that, we are replicating the experience of our ancestors, who bought 78s: those primitive discs consisting of a hit side and a flip side.

Almost all records made before 1948 were sold as single discs, so it is logical—especially when looking for music from that era—to sample a selection or two by an artist before springing for a collection of two dozen or so tracks. From the early 1950s until the middle 1980s, the industry was dominated by the LP; many of those albums ought to be considered as integrated works. If a track may be compared to a short story or bagatelle, an album may be thought of as a novel or symphony. Works such as Miles Davis's *Sketches of Spain,* Duke Ellington's *Far East Suite,* and John Coltrane's *A Love Supreme,* among hundreds more, should be experienced in their entirety—no less than a Beethoven symphony or a Verdi opera or *Sgt. Pepper's Lonely Hearts Club Band.*

The album concept remained in force in the CD era, but its hold began to slacken, especially in jazz. Why? For one thing, the playing time got so long that it surpassed the average listener's attention span, and musical dullness spread. In introducing CDs, the recording industry elected to *double* the price of vinyl LPs, even though the digital audio quality was initially much inferior to analog engineering and despite the fact that CDs were far less costly to manufacture. The record companies hoped to compensate for this shameless flimflam with semantic pomp and extended playing time. They even devised a laughably devious euphemism for those crappy plastic CD cases: "jewel boxes." In an exercise akin to price-fixing, they settled on an arbitrary CD playing time of about seventy-five minutes.

Extended play is a good thing for an opera, symphony, jazz suite, or anthology of short selections, but it isn't a virtue when it's turned into a rule. As the producers of jazz albums felt increasingly obliged to offer maximum-time discs (critics actually grumbled about discs that played under an hour), they achieved their goal by encouraging long individual tracks. The art of economy, the philosophy of less-is-more, the goal of improvising a perfect solo in one or two choruses, the showbiz adage of "Always leave them wanting more," gave way to long improvisations that were motivated not by the fever of inspiration but by the need to fill up the disc. Not surprisingly, a later generation of listeners preferred to download tracks rather than albums.

Meanwhile, the record labels began offering elaborate boxes, dumping material onto discs, including rejected takes, false starts, unedited session tapes, and random recording session chatter. One notorious knucklehead even restored to classic concert recordings longer applause interludes and the sounds of roadie labor, as a chair was pushed around or another mike brought to the stage. Some of these makeshift documentary recordings are extremely interesting, others are simply annoying. Gerry Mulligan, confronted with a boxed set of his "complete" sessions (the tracks arranged in the order they were recorded rather than as they were sequenced for the original album), was appalled: "Do you know how much time we spent arranging the tunes so they would be fun to listen to? They've turned it into homework."

Special editions are for specialist interests. For one artist, you may be satisfied with a greatest-hits type collection; for another, you may want everything the artist ever released; for yet another, you may want the released stuff plus those newly excavated alternate takes and false starts. Bigger is not necessarily better. Some classics have been rendered virtually unlistenable by the addition of scraps from the cutting-room floor. To pick one of many examples, in 1959 Verve released the beloved album *Gerry Mulligan Meets Ben Webster.* In 1997, that same label issued *The Complete Gerry Mulligan Meets Ben Webster,* a two-disc CD in which the original tracks are cluttered with twenty rejected takes. Only a truly obsessed fan is likely to enjoy four consecutive versions of the same tune. One of Ellington's great late-period triumphs, the 1967 ". . . *and his mother called him Bill,*" a tribute to Billy Strayhorn, ended with an unplanned Ellington piano rendition of Strayhorn's "Lotus Blossom," played quietly at the end of a session as the other musicians packed up; it serves as an emotionally devastating *l'envoi.* A CD producer, noting that "Lotus Blossom" was played at the end of a middle session, mindlessly programmed it midway on the CD.

You need to examine an album's contents, even in the case of a genuine classic, before buying it. Are you getting the original work, or the original work with new tracks, and are the new tracks added at the end (a bonus that no one is likely to complain about) or scattered throughout? On the list below, we intended to include Bill Evans's 1961 album *Waltz for Debby,* recorded live at the Village Vanguard, and were saddened to find that the only versions presently in print are an admirable but expensive "complete" three-disc set of the Vanguard engagement, or a single-disc version with consecutive performances of the same tunes, destroying the concentrated beauty of the original LP. In this book, we discuss the original version of Charles Mingus's "Boogie Stop Shuffle," which Mingus approved for release. That track is difficult to find now, because after Mingus's death a producer spliced back the passages that Mingus had edited out (in his approved release, the saxophone solo begins with a shout rather than a warm-up chorus). You may prefer the longer version, but we believe the record label also ought to offer the album as initially conceived. We've included the false start to Charlie Parker's "Ko Ko" because it provides fascinating insight into how that masterpiece was created. We've used the rejected take of Jelly Roll Morton's "Dead Man Blues" because, despite the flawed trumpet solo, we think it a more effective performance than the one chosen for release in 1926. (The Morton album in the list below offers both takes.) The point is that there is a sensible way to program reissues, and as sensibleness is in short supply, the consumer is obliged to do some digging to learn exactly what is being offered.

One way to check recording information is by consulting a discography—a book or site that lists all of an artist's record sessions (and surviving concert performances) chronologically, with the recording dates, band personnel, and catalog numbers. A discography for all of jazz, collating tens of thousands of sessions, is expensive, but dozens of individual jazz artists are represented by free online discographies (see the indispensable website www.jazzdisco.org). Ellington recorded several performances of "Mood Indigo," and if you are looking for a particular one, you need to know the label (he recorded five versions in 1930 alone, for Victor, OKeh, and Brunswick), the present owner of the labels (Victor and OKeh now belong to Sony, Brunswick to Polygram), the full date, and the matrix or catalog number to be certain of getting the desired take.

For the most part, however, buying jazz records is a straightforward business. Reliable mail-order companies often have people who can answer questions, as retail stores once did. The best and easiest way to get advice is to solicit it from the large and passionate circle of fellow jazz enthusiasts. A few decades ago, this would have presented a challenge—many jazz lovers, especially in small towns, were as isolated as atheists or gays or gourmands or readers of Homeric Greek. Yet cyberspace is rich in jazz sites (including allaboutjazz.com, jerryjazzmusician.com, and jazzcorner.com) and chat groups. The population of dedicated jazz fans may be small, and at times cranky, but it is also ardent and helpful—most jazz lovers love to be in touch with other jazz lovers. It's them against the world.

Go for Broke

Meanwhile, here is a list of 101 albums by 101 artists. Two things make this discography unusual and potentially useful beyond the recommendation of good records. First, it is not a 101-best list. No artist is represented by more than a single work as a leader—a serious library of recorded jazz would include many recordings by central figures like Ellington and Miles Davis, whose influence and achievement represent artistic growth over decades. In fact, by sticking to our rule, which favors variety over prominent individuals and acknowledged masterworks, we were obliged to exclude some of our favorite records, some of which figure as Listening Guides.

With this list, we offer a way to look at the jazz map from several perspectives; all these albums are excellent, and each one may lead you—through sidemen, arrangers, songs—to others, in an ever-expanding web that touches on most of the major avenues and side streets that make up the jazz world of the past century. (Admittedly, some areas are underrepresented, most conspicuously foreign jazz.) Each entry represents a way to explore a part of jazz and, with it, your own emotional and intellectual responses to it. In keeping with that idea, the second unusual aspect of this list is that it's alphabetical rather than chronological. The idea here is to distract you from the customary tendency to pigeonhole musical works according to the eras that produced them. It is one thing, for example, to study 1950s jazz and listen to Art Blakey as an example of hard bop, and another to encounter him on his own, possibly in tandem with Bix Beiderbecke and Arthur Blythe, who are connected to him on this list through the juxtapositions of alphabetical serendipity.

Not that you ought to start at number one and work down the list. Start anywhere you like. The point is to create a fourth narrative for jazz, unique to your experience. Unlike the first three—jazz as artistic progression, fusion, and historicism—this narrative is as random as life, and may well provide the most rewards. Included with each entry on the list is the year in which it was recorded, so that if you find yourself favoring a particular period, you can pursue it by reading the list from the right rather than the left. Note that this list includes no catch-all collections, like Martin Williams's *Smithsonian Collection of Classic Jazz* or *Ken Burns's Jazz: The Story of American Music*. In fact, there are no boxed sets and no items with more than two discs. Our selections, especially in cases where the same music is available in various formats from multiple labels, were influenced by audio quality, price, and availability. They are intended to encourage you to investigate the market on your own. If you search for the single-disc Dizzy Gillespie compilation of his 1940s RCA recordings, you will discover that a superior two-disc edition exists for those who would rather get the complete works.

Some of these albums survey entire careers, while others are classic LPs. Some capture the early work that established an artist's reputation, while others exemplify autumnal maturity (see, for example, Ornette Coleman, Stan Getz, Sonny Rollins). All these items were available in one form or another in the early months of 2009. (A few, like Lee Konitz's *Motion* and Roy Eldridge's *Uptown*, no longer exist as domestic CDs, but can be purchased as MP3s from iTunes.) By the time you read this, it is certain that some of these recordings will *not* be readily available, while others, left off the list, will be back in catalog. The record business has never been more volatile than it is now, when technology and changes in ownership have brought it to a point of crisis. At this moment, the entire Black Saint catalog of loft jazz from the 1970s and 1980s is out of print but has recently been purchased by a company that will soon rerelease it; also missing is the Commodore catalog of 1930s and 1940s swing and Dixieland classics, and no one knows when or how it will reemerge. We were astonished that we could not find—as CDs or MP3s—suitable anthologies or classic albums by Jack Teagarden, Randy Weston, Henry Threadgill, Anthony Braxton, and, most incredibly, the prewar Lester Young (though his major solos are collected on the Count Basie, Billie Holiday, and Jimmy Rushing discs). Yet record company executives complain when jazz fans trade and download favorite recordings! They have made us that way. Every jazz lover is a sleuth. Your sleuthing may as well begin here.

1. Muhal Richard Abrams: *Blu Blu Blu* (Black Saint), 1990

2. Cannonball Adderley: *Mercy, Mercy, Mercy!* (Capitol), 1966

3. Gene Ammons and Sonny Stitt: *Boss Tenors* (Polygram), 1961

4. Louis Armstrong: *The Complete Hot Five & Hot Seven Recordings*, vol. 3 (Columbia), 1928

5. Albert Ayler: *Spiritual Unity* (ESP-Disk), 1964

6. Count Basie: *One O'Clock Jump: The Very Best of Count Basie* (Sony), 1936–42

7. Mildred Bailey: *The Rockin' Chair Lady* (Verve), 1931–50

8. Sidney Bechet: *The Legendary Sidney Bechet* (RCA), 1932–41

9. Bix Beiderbecke: *At the Jazz Band Ball* (ASV Living Era), 1924–28

10. Art Blakey: *Mosaic* (Blue Note), 1961

11. Arthur Blythe: *Focus* (Savant), 2002

12. Lester Bowie: *The Great Pretender* (ECM), 1981

13. Clifford Brown and Max Roach: *Clifford Brown and Max Roach* (Polygram), 1954

14. Dave Brubeck: *Time Out* (Columbia), 1959

15. Jaki Byard and Roland Kirk: *The Jaki Byard Experience* (Prestige), 1968

16. Don Byron: *Tuskegee Experiments* (Nonesuch), 1992

17. Benny Carter: *Further Definitions* (Impulse!), 1961

18. James Carter: *Chasin' the Gypsy* (Atlantic), 2000

19. Bill Charlap: *Live at the Village Vanguard* (Blue Note), 2007

20. Charlie Christian: *The Benny Goodman Sextet Featuring Charlie Christian* (Sony), 1939–41

21. Nat King Cole: *After Midnight: The Complete Session* (Blue Note), 1956

22. Ornette Coleman: *Sound Grammar* (Sound Grammar), 2006

23. John Coltrane: *A Love Supreme* (Impulse!), 1964

24. Chick Corea: *Now He Sings, Now He Sobs* (Blue Note), 1968

25. Sonny Criss and Horace Tapscott: *Sonny's Dream* (Prestige OJC), 1968

26. Bing Crosby: *Jazz Singer* (Retrieval), 1931–41

27. Miles Davis: *Kind of Blue* (Columbia), 1959

28. Eric Dolphy: *Out There* (Prestige), 1960

29. Roy Eldridge: *Roy Eldridge with the Gene Krupa Orchestra Featuring Anita O'Day Uptown* (Sony), 1941–49

30. Duke Ellington: *The Essential Duke Ellington* (Sony), 1927–60

31. Bill Evans: *The Paris Concert, Edition One* (Blue Note), 1979

32. Gil Evans: *Out of the Cool* (Impulse!), 1960

33. Ella Fitzgerald: *Something to Live For* (Verve), 1937–66

34. Erroll Garner: *Concert by the Sea* (Sony), 1955

35. Stan Getz and Kenny Barron: *People Time* (Polygram), 1992

36. Dizzy Gillespie: *A Night in Tunisia: The Very Best of Dizzy Gillespie* (RCA), 1946–49

37. Benny Goodman: *Carnegie Hall Jazz Concert* (Sony), 1938

38. Dexter Gordon: *Go!* (Blue Note), 1962

39. Herbie Hancock: *Maiden Voyage* (Blue Note), 1965

40. Roy Hargrove: *Habana* (Polygram), 1997

41. Johnny Hartman: *John Coltrane and Johnny Hartman* (Impulse!), 1963

42. Coleman Hawkins: *Ken Burns Jazz Collection* (Polygram), 1926–63

43. Roy Haynes: *Roy Haynes Trio Featuring Danilo Perez and John Pattitucci* (Polygram), 2000

44. Fletcher Henderson: *Ken Burns Jazz Collection* (Sony), 1924–40

45. Woody Herman: *Blowin' Up a Storm: The Columbia Years* (Sony), 1945–47

46. Andrew Hill: *Point of Departure* (Blue Note), 1964

47. Billie Holiday: *Lady Day: The Best of Billie Holiday* (Sony), 1935–42

48. Dave Holland: *Conference of the Birds* (ECM), 1972

49. Keith Jarrett: *Whisper Not* (ECM), 1999

50. Stan Kenton: *Contemporary Concepts* (Blue Note), 1955

51. Lee Konitz: *Motion* (Verve), 1961

52. George Lewis: *Jazz in the Classic New Orleans Tradition* (Riverside OJC), 1950

53. Abbey Lincoln: *You Gotta Pay the Band* (Polygram), 1991

54. Joe Lovano: *Joyous Encounter* (Blue Note), 2005

55. Jimmie Lunceford: *Rhythm Is Our Business* (ASV Living Era), 1933–40

56. Rudresh Mahanthappa: *Kinsmen* (PI), 2008

57. Wynton Marsalis: *Standards & Ballads* (Sony), 1983–97

58. John McLaughlin: *Live at the Royal Festival Hall* (Polygram), 1989

59. Brad Mehldau: *Live* (Nonesuch), 2008

60. Charles Mingus: *The Black Saint & the Sinner Lady* (Impulse!), 1963

61. Roscoe Mitchell: *Sound* (Delmark), 1966

62. Modern Jazz Quartet: *Django* (Prestige), 1953–54

63. Thelonious Monk: *The Best of the Blue Note Years* (Blue Note), 1947–52

64. Wes Montgomery: *Smokin' at the Half Note* (Verve), 1965

65. Jason Moran: *Modernistic* (Blue Note), 2002

66. Lee Morgan: *The Sidewinder* (Blue Note), 1963

67. Jelly Roll Morton: *Birth of the Hot* (RCA Bluebird), 1926–27

68. Gerry Mulligan: *The Concert Jazz Band at the Village Vanguard* (Verve), 1960

69. David Murray: *Shakill's Warrior* (Sony), 1991

70. Fats Navarro and Tadd Dameron: *The Complete Blue Note and Capitol Recordings* (Blue Note), 1947–49

71. Oliver Nelson: *The Blues and the Abstract Truth* (Impulse!), 1961

72. King Oliver: *Off the Record: The Complete Jazz Band Recordings* (Archeophone), 1923

73. Charlie Parker: *Best of the Complete Savoy and Dial Studio Recordings* (Savoy), 1944–48

74. Bud Powell: *Jazz Giant* (Verve), 1949–50

75. Joshua Redman: *Back East* (Nonesuch), 2007

76. Django Reinhardt: *The Best of Django Reinhardt* (Blue Note), 1936–48

77. Sam Rivers: *Fuchsia Swing Song* (Blue Note), 1964

78. Sonny Rollins: *Road Shows*, vol. 1 (Doxy), 1980–2007

79. Jimmy Rushing: *Mr. Five by Five* (Pearl), 1929–42

80. George Russell: *Ezz-Thetics* (Riverside), 1961

81. John Scofield and Pat Metheny: *I Can See Your House from Here* (Blue Note), 1994

82. Artie Shaw: *Begin the Beguine* (RCA), 1938–41

83. Archie Shepp: *Fire Music* (Impulse!), 1965

84. Wayne Shorter: *Footprints Live!* (Verve), 2002

85. Horace Silver: *Song for My Father* (Blue Note), 1964

86. Bessie Smith: *The Essential Bessie Smith* (Sony), 1923–33

87. Jimmy Smith: *The Sermon* (Blue Note), 1958

88. Art Tatum: *Piano Starts Here* (Columbia), 1933–49

89. Cecil Taylor: *Unit Structures* (Blue Note), 1966

90. Lennie Tristano: *The New Tristano* (Atlantic), 1955–62

91. Joe Turner: *The Boss of the Blues* (Atlantic/Collectables), 1956

92. Sarah Vaughan: *Sarah Vaughan with Clifford Brown* (Polygram), 1954

93. Fats Waller: *The Very Best of Fats Waller* (RCA), 1929–42

94. David S. Ware: *Go See the World* (Columbia), 1998

95. Dinah Washington: *The Essential Dinah Washington* (Polygram), 1952–59

96. Weather Report: *Heavy Weather* (Sony), 1977

97. Chick Webb: *Stompin' at the Savoy* (ASV Living Era), 1934–39

98. Ben Webster and Oscar Peterson: *Ben Webster Meets Oscar Peterson* (Verve), 1959

99. Cassandra Wilson: *Belly of the Sun* (Blue Note), 2002

100. World Saxophone Quartet: *Revue* (Black Saint), 1980

101. Lester Young and Teddy Wilson: *Pres and Teddy* (Verve), 1956

JAZZ ON FILM

In 1981, a British researcher, David Meeker, published his second edition of *Jazz in the Movies,* listing 3,724 feature films, short subjects, television shows, and documentaries with jazz content, however little it might be. That was thirty years ago, and even then his work had dozens of unavoidable lapses. Hardly a year goes by when significant jazz footage, unknown to the most zealous collectors, isn't discovered—often from long forgotten television programs languishing in European broadcasting archives. Here is an introductory guide to jazz-related movies, divided into four categories: feature films with jazz as the subject; feature films with jazz scores; documentaries and performance films; and television series. Most of these films have been available on one or more home video formats over the years, usually on DVD. Those that are not presently in catalog may be found in libraries or are likely to be reissued.

Feature Films with Jazz Stories

Jazz has had a rather twisted relationship with Hollywood dating back to the silent era, when jazz, blues, and ragtime themes were often used to indicate wayward flappers, dissolute roués, and other lost souls. During the Swing Era, Hollywood imported jazz orchestras to suggest optimism and good times. As bandleaders achieved national recognition, it was good business to banner them on movie marquees. After the war, jazz usually signified the denizens of urban blight. Some of the movies listed here are unintentionally hilarious, but they all have savory musical moments.

The Benny Goodman Story (1955, Valentine Davis): Cliché-ridden idiocy at every turn and a stupefying lead performance, but worthy music makes it endurable.

Bird (1988, Clint Eastwood): A powerful, partly factual and partly imagined telling of the Charlie Parker story with much music and an eye-popping studio recreation of New York's 52nd Street.

Birth of the Blues (1941, Victor Schertzinger): One of several films reflecting the historicist New Orleans revival, with Bing Crosby, Jack Teagarden, and a game Mary Martin inventing jazz as only Hollywood Caucasians could.

Black Orpheus (1959, Marcel Camus): A visually and musically thrilling version of the Orpheus legend told against the Brazilian Carnival and introducing several of the sambas that helped to launch bossa nova.

Blues in the Night (1941, Anatol Litvack): A Warner Bros. gangster film from the perspective of white jazz musicians, inspired by authentic Negro "misery"; this is a revealing curio, briskly directed, with a cameo appearance by Jimmie Lunceford's band.

Cabin in the Sky (1942, Vincente Minelli): A brilliant all-black musical with production numbers featuring Ethel Waters, Duke Ellington, Lena Horne, Eddie "Rochester" Anderson, the wickedly cool tap dancer John Bubbles, and a funny cameo by Louis Armstrong.

The Connection (1961, Shirley Clarke): The garrulous junkies waiting for their connection, in this film version of Jack Gelber's play, include the Freddie Redd Quartet, playing a celebrated score and featuring saxophonist Jackie McLean.

The Gig (1985, Frank Gilroy): A smart, realistic comedy about a group of white professionals who play jazz for fun, until they get a gig at a Catskills resort working with a pro.

The Glenn Miller Story (1953, Anthony Mann): A nostalgic fabrication in which Miller explains his radical musical ideas: "To me, music is more than just one instrument. It's a whole orchestra playing together!" Louis Armstrong and Gene Krupa drop by.

Hollywood Hotel (1937, Busby Berkeley): This is the way Hollywood packaged swing for the masses, salvaged by Benny Goodman's integrated quartet at its absolute peak.

Jazzman (1983, Karen Shakhnazarov): Hard to find, but keep an eye out for this superb Russian film about musicians risking their freedom to play hot jazz in the Soviet Union of the 1920s.

A Man Called Adam (1966, Leo Penn): Sammy Davis Jr. plays an overwrought trumpet player in an overwrought film made memorable by Louis Armstrong, in a straight acting role, and a musical score by Benny Carter.

Murder at the Vanities (1934, Mitchell Leisen): A backstage murder mystery immortalized by Duke Ellington playing his take on Liszt (classical musicians mow his band down with machine guns) and the production number "Sweet Marijuana"—those were the days.

New Orleans (1947, Arthur Lubin): More New Orleans revivalism, purportedly from the black perspective, as Louis Armstrong leads his people in an exodus from Storyville and Billie Holiday shows up as a maid who sings as she dusts.

Orchestra Wives (1942, Archie Mayo): Underrated, surprisingly well-written story in which Glenn Miller's band hits the road (look sharp for Bobby Hackett), and the great Nicholas Brothers steal his thunder with acrobatic jazz dancing.

Passing Through (1977, Larry Clark): Difficult to see, this stunning student film, with a musical score by Horace Tapscott along with records by Charlie Parker and

Eric Dolphy, captures the dilemma of the Los Angeles jazz avant-garde struggling to survive.

Pennies from Heaven (1936, Norman Z. McLeod): A Depression fable that may strike a relevant note today, with Bing Crosby in excellent voice and Louis Armstrong making his first feature film appearance performing "A Skeleton in the Closet."

Paris Blues (1961, Martin Ritt): Not much plot animates this soap opera, but when Paul Newman and Sidney Poitier shut up, Duke Ellington's all-star orchestra takes over, including sequences featuring Louis Armstrong.

Pete Kelly's Blues (1955, Jack Webb): A splendidly photographed and scored saga of Kansas City in the 1920s, in which a white jazz band battles racketeers while Ella Fitzgerald operates a speakeasy, Peggy Lee goes insane, and Lee Marvin plays clarinet and is punched out by little Jack Webb.

A Song Is Born (1948, Howard Hawks): A remake of the comedy *Ball of Fire* (which has a Gene Krupa solo played on a matchbox) in which cloistered professors, led by Danny Kaye, investigate jazz with the help of Benny Goodman, Louis Armstrong, Lionel Hampton, Tommy Dorsey, and others.

Ray (2004, Taylor Hackford): Jamie Foxx's uncanny imitation of Ray Charles traces his career from swing to gospel-infused R & B to his unique amalgamation of jazz, R & B pop, and rock—interrupted by narcotics, sex, and other domestic interludes.

'Round Midnight (1986, Bertrand Tavernier): Dexter Gordon's performance, in a role based on the lives of Bud Powell and Lester Young, is astonishing; Bobby Hutcherson, Herbie Hancock, Wayne Shorter, and others also appear.

Stormy Weather (1943, Andrew L. Stone): This all-black musical loosely touches on the early years of jazz, including James Reese Europe, but is best savored for performances by Bill Robinson, Lena Horne, Fats Waller, Cab Calloway, and the Nicholas Brothers.

Sweet Love, Bitter (1966, Herbert Danska): Melodrama of a black genius, thinly based on Charlie Parker (he's called Eagle), as experienced by his concerned white friend; score by Mal Waldron, alto saxophone solos by Charles McPherson.

Sweet Smell of Success (1957, Alexander Mackendrick): A dark, caustic classic that involves an incestuous columnist framing a jazz musician for marijuana use; Elmer Bernstein's score is complemented by the on-screen Chico Hamilton Quintet.

Tap (1989, Nick Castle): The modest story is an excuse to gather several of the greatest jazz or tap dancers assembled in a Hollywood film, including star Gregory Hines, Sandman Sims, Bunny Briggs, Sammy Davis Jr., and the young Savion Glover.

The Tic Code (2000, Gary Winick): A young boy suffering from Tourette's syndrome learns to express himself through jazz, with Gregory Hines as a jazz star who learned to cover-up his own TS and a score by pianist Michael Wolff.

Feature Films with Jazz Scores

Hollywood soundtracks often employed jazz or jazzy touches, but not until the 1950s did composers start using jazz as the governing style for film scores. Not surprisingly, the plots of most of these films concern junkies, sexual deviants, and murderers. In the late 1950s and 1960s, genuine jazz composers were also hired. Here are a few benchmarks in chronological order.

A Streetcar Named Desire (1951): Often cited as the first film to use a jazz-style score for a nonjazz-themed story, fittingly set in New Orleans, and composed by Alex North.

The Man with the Golden Arm (1955): Elmer Bernstein's score is mostly pseudo-jazz, but it conveys a kick as the basic blues theme comes up during the opening credits. Frank Sinatra is the junkie who wants to play drums with the on-screen Shorty Rogers band.

Elevator to the Gallows (*Ascenseur pour l'echafaud*, 1957): For Louis Malle's first thriller, one of the most piquant and influential film scores of all time was entirely improvised by Miles Davis, during an all-night session.

I Want to Live! (1958): Director Robert Wise hired former big-band composer Johnny Mandel to write the first true jazz score in a Hollywood feature, a brilliant achievement, underscored by on-screen performances by an all-star Gerry Mulligan band—the film opens with four minutes of music before a line of dialog is spoken.

Touch of Evil (1958): The prolific Henry Mancini is best known for his movie ballads, like "Moon River" (from *Breakfast at Tiffany's*), but he used ingenious jazz scoring in several 1950s works, including this Orson Welles classic and the TV series *Peter Gunn*.

Anatomy of a Murder (1959): Director Otto Preminger made a counterintuitive decision in hiring Duke Ellington to score a film about a Midwestern trial lawyer; Ellington wrote a superb score, and appears on-screen as the local pianist, Pie Eye.

Odds Against Tomorrow (1959): Robert Wise's race-conscious heist film is luminously scored by the Modern Jazz Quartet's John Lewis, including his tender ballad "Skating in Central Park"—Bill Evans and Jim Hall play in the soundtrack orchestra.

Shadows (1961): Charles Mingus never completed his score for John Cassavetes's film about racial conflict in New York, so the director created a soundtrack out of Mingus's bass solos and Shafi Hadi alto saxophone solos.

Mickey One (1961): Arthur Penn's surreal showbiz fantasy boasts an Eddie Sauter score with improvised solos by Stan Getz—a musical sequel to their renowned album *Focus*.

The Cincinnati Kid (1965): Lalo Schifrin, the former pianist for Dizzy Gillespie, wrote more than 200 film scores; this one uses Ray Charles on the title song and various New Orleans traditionalists—Cab Calloway has an acting role.

In the Heat of the Night (1967): One of the best of Quincy Jones's many scores employs Ray Charles on the title song, and bassist Ray Brown and flutist Roland Kirk throughout.

The Young Girls of Rochefort (1968): Michel Legrand, a French jazz pianist and songwriter, scored several New Wave classics by Jean Luc Godard, Agnes Varda, and Jacques Demy—his swinging take on the MGM musical in this Demy film is irresistible.

The Gauntlet (1977): Clint Eastwood used jazz in most of his films, never more memorably than in this Jerry Fielding score, with expansive solos by trumpeter Jon Faddis and alto saxophonist Art Pepper.

Naked Lunch (1991): For David Cronenberg's adaptation of William Burroughs's novel, Howard Shore wrote a suitably mind-bending score constructed around improvisations by the Ornette Coleman Trio.

Documentaries and Performance Films

Although the market for jazz documentaries is small, the field has attracted dozens of filmmakers. Many of their films were made initially for television, a few had theatrical releases, some were conceived for educational purposes, and others went directly to home video. Note that the following list, the tip of a rapidly expanding iceberg, excludes all but a few short subjects: many early jazz bands were filmed for one-reelers by Vitaphone and other movie companies. Anthologies of these films occasionally appear (see *The Best of Jazz and Blues* below), and individual shorts are often included as extras on DVDs of classic movies—especially by Warner Bros. Also worth noting are cartoons of the 1930s and 1940s. Warner Bros. (Looney Tunes and Merrie Melodies), Disney, and other studios frequently used jazz—none as cannily as Fleischer Studio, which produced the great Betty Boop series: "Snow-White," "I Heard," "I'll Be Glad When You're Dead You Rascal You," and "The Old Man of the Mountain" (1932–33) are among the best of the risqué Bettys, using on-screen and traced (rotoscoped) images of Cab Calloway, Don Redman, and Louis Armstrong.

"After Hours" and "Jazz Dance" (1961/1954): The former was created as a television pilot but never broadcast, probably because of inane narration and a terrible singer. But Roy Eldridge and especially Coleman Hawkins *kill*.

Art Blakey: The Jazz Messenger (1987): A documentary of the drummer whose band became a graduate school for young musicians, by Dick Fontaine and Pat Hartley.

The Art Ensemble of Chicago (1981): A live performance at Chicago's Jazz Showcase.

Artie Shaw: Time Is All You've Got (1985): Brigitte Berman's Oscar-winning life of a great clarinetist and bandleader who gave up music because he hated being a celebrity.

Barry Harris: The Spirit of Bebop (2000): Interviews, performances, classic footage.

Benny Carter: Symphony in Riffs (1989): Harrison Engle's life of a musician for all seasons.

The Best of Jazz & Blues (2001): An indispensable Kino Video compilation of short films from 1929–41, including Bessie Smith's *St. Louis Blues* and others featuring Duke Ellington, Louis Armstrong, Fats Waller, Cab Calloway, and more.

Billie Holiday: The Long Night of Lady Day (1984): Though hard to find, this BBC film by John Jeremy remains the best biographical portrait of the singer.

Bix: Ain't None of Them Play Like Him Yet (1981): Brigitte Berman's detailed biographical portrait of Bix Beiderbecke.

Buena Vista Social Club (1999): Wim Wenders's multiple-prize-winning and hugely popular study of Cuban music as seen through some of its aging masters.

Celebrating Bird: The Triumph of Charlie Parker (1987): Gary Giddins's biographical portrait includes Parker's 1952 television performance (with Dizzy Gillespie) of "Hot House."

Ella Fitzgerald: Something to Live For (1999): Charlotte Zwering's PBS documentary, narrated by Tony Bennett, traces the First Lady of Song's career from her discovery at the Apollo Theater.

Erroll Garner in Performance (1964): Two sets initially broadcast by the BBC.

Fred Anderson, Timeless (2005): The avant-garde saxophonist leading his trio in concert in Chicago.

A Great Day in Harlem (1995): Jean Bach's Oscar-nominated documentary, centered on a celebrated 1958 photograph, is a treasure brimming with anecdotes; it's improved on a two-disc DVD with hours of added footage.

Imagine the Sound (1981): Ron Mann's beautifully photographed film includes uninterrupted performances by Cecil Taylor, Bill Dixon, Paul Bley, and Archie Shepp.

Jammin' the Blues (1941): The best ten minutes of jazz ever filmed—a Vitaphone short with Lester Young and other swing greats (including drummers Jo Jones and Sid Catlett)—can be found as an extra on the DVD of *Blues in the Night* (see above).

Jazz '34 (1996): Robert Altman's superior companion piece to his film *Kansas City* focuses on music, as such modernists as Joshua Redman, James Carter, and Geri Allen revisit 1930s swing.

The Jazz Master Class Series (2007): Seven double-disc sets explore the lives and artistry of Barry Harris, Jimmy and Percy Heath, Hank Jones, Cecil Taylor, Clark Terry, Toots Thielemans, and Phil Woods through extensive interviews and master class sessions with student musicians.

Jazz on a Summer's Day (1958): The first great music video, exquisitely photographed by Bert Stern at the 1958 Newport Jazz Festival, capturing classic performances by Louis Armstrong, Anita O'Day, Mahalia Jackson, Gerry Mulligan, and others.

Jazz (2001): Ken Burns's PBS epic, written by Geoffrey C. Ward, is the most ambitious film ever made about jazz (nineteen hours long, more than 2,000 film clips); criticized for cutting the story off in the 1960s, it remains a remarkable, matchless achievement.

John Hammond: From Bessie Smith to Bruce Springsteen (1990): Hart Perry's Peabody-winning film, written by Gary Giddins, traces the life of jazz's most influential talent scout and record producer.

Last Date: Eric Dolphy (1991): Hans Hylkema's life of the great and tragic saxophonist and flutist.

Last of the Blue Devils (1979): Bruce Ricker's expansive look at the history and ongoing influence of Kansas City jazz, focusing on Jay McShann, Count Basie, and Big Joe Turner.

Norman Granz Presents Improvisation (2007): Long-suppressed material from the 1940s and 1950s, including Jazz at the Philharmonic sequences and previously unknown footage of Charlie Parker and Coleman Hawkins.

Ornette: Made in America (1985): Shirley Clarke's study of Ornette Coleman, with recreations of his early years and extensive interviews with Coleman.

The Miles Davis Story (2001): A lively documentary by Mike Dibb with interviews of more than a dozen of Davis's associates.

Mingus (1968): A controversial, riveting film by Thomas Reichman, capturing Mingus at home, on the bandstand, and in the process of being evicted from his studio.

Satchmo (1989): Gary Giddins's award-winning PBS documentary on Louis Armstrong, based on his book, with much rare footage.

Sonny Rollins: Saxophone Colossus (1986): Robert Mugge's film features archival footage and interviews but is best remembered for the concert footage in which Rollins suddenly leaps from a precipice, finishing his solo lying on the ground with a sprained ankle.

The Sound of Jazz (1957): The best hour of jazz ever broadcast on American television (on a Sunday afternoon), with an all-star cast, including a legendary Billie Holiday blues with Lester Young, Coleman Hawkins, Ben Webster, Gerry Mulligan, and Roy Eldridge.

Thelonious Monk: Straight, No Chaser (1988): Peerless concert footage shot by Charlotte Zwerin is edited, with many interviews, into a gripping portrait of an enigmatic genius on tour.

Television Series

Jazz Casual: In the 1960s, critic Ralph J. Gleason produced twenty-eight half-hour shows, all issued on DVD. They include performances by and interviews with John Coltrane, Sonny Rollins, Louis Armstrong, Dizzy Gillespie, Carmen McRae, Jimmy Rushing, the Modern Jazz Quartet, and Dave Brubeck.

Jazz Icons: A magnificent, ongoing series of concert performances, shot live or in the studio for European television between the late 1950s and the early 1970s; these broadcasts were largely unknown here, and include first-class work by such figures as Dizzy Gillespie, Louis Armstrong, Sonny Rollins, Art Blakey, Bill Evans, Thelonious Monk, Buddy Rich, Dexter Gordon, Sarah Vaughan, Dave Brubeck, Wes Montgomery, Charles Mingus, Roland Kirk, and Nina Simone.

Jazz Scene USA: A short-lived 1962 series, shot in California, with two half-hour segments on each DVD, including shows with Cannonball Adderley, Jimmy Smith, Teddy Edwards, and Stan Kenton.

END NOTES

Chapter 1 Musical Orientation: Elements and Instruments

2. "You got to be in the sun": Sidney Bechet, *Treat It Gentle* (Hill and Wang, 1960), p. 2.

Chapter 3 The Roots of Jazz

44. Jazz is an "art form": Robert Walser, ed., *Keeping Time* (Oxford University Press, 1999), p. 333.

45. "Great reward can be used": Tony Bennett with Will Friedwald, *The Good Life* (Pocket Books, 1998), epigraph.

46. The "mulatto" nature: Albert Murray, *The Omni-Americans: Black Experience and American Culture* (Vintage, 1970), p. 22.

46. The blasting of a railroad tunnel: Scott Reynolds Nelson, *Steel Drivin' Man: John Henry—The Untold Tale of an American Legend* (Oxford University Press, 2006).

47. "The Buzzard Lope" is a spiritual dance: Mark Knowles, *Tap Roots: The Early History of Tap Dancing* (McFarland, 2002), p. 320.

50. African American society had shifted: Lawrence Levine, *Black Culture and Black Consciousness* (Oxford University Press, 1978), pp. 222–23.

50. "I wasn't making money": liner notes to *Long Way from Home: The Blues of Fred McDowell* (Milestone MSP 93003, 1966).

54. "They were led by a long-legged chocolate boy": W. C. Handy, *Father of the Blues: An Autobiography* (Collier, 1941), pp. 80–81.

61. "distort a sentimental, simple": Eileen Southern, *The Music of Black Americans*, 2nd ed. (Norton, 1983), p. 108.

62. "We get our dances": Lewis A. Erenberg, *Steppin' Out: New York Nightlife and the Transformation of American Culture* (Greenwood Press, 1981), pp. 163–64.

62. "When a good orchestra": ibid., p. 153.

64. "a town without its brass band": Raoul Camus, "Band," in *The New Grove Dictionary of American Music,* ed. H. Wiley Hitchcock and Stanley Sadie (Macmillan, 1986), vol. 1, p. 133.

70. "Sweatman was my idol": Garvin Bushell (as told to Mark Tucker), *Jazz from the Beginning* (University of Michigan Press, 1988), p. 18.

Chapter 4 New Orleans

77. A consequence of a large African population: Jerah Johnson, *Congo Square in New Orleans* (Louisiana Landmarks Society, 1995), p. 43.

79. The jazz guitarist Danny Barker: Alan Lomax, *Mister Jelly Roll* (Duell, Sloan and Pearce, 1950), p. 61.

83. "Everybody got up quick": *Down Beat,* December 15, 1940.

83. "He was one of the sweetest trumpet players": Donald M. Marquis, *In Search of Buddy Bolden* (Louisiana State University Press, 1978), p. 100.

84. "You never had to figure": Nat Shapiro and Nat Hentoff, *Hear Me Talkin' to Ya: The Story of Jazz as Told by the Men Who Made It* (Rinehart, 1955), pp. 66–67.

88. "He played practically the same way": Sidney Bechet, *Treat It Gentle* (Twayne, 1960), p. 84.

97. "Even if a tune": Lomax, *Mister Jelly Roll,* p. 63.

101. "I was sitting at the piano": Shapiro and Hentoff, *Hear Me Talkin' to Ya,* pp. 45–46.

106. "He was standing there": Richard Merryman, *Louis Armstrong—A Self-Portrait* (Eakins Press, 1971), pp. 48–49.

107. "I wish to set down": Ralph de Toledano, ed., *Frontiers of Jazz* (Durrell, 1947, trans. and rev.), p. 122.

Chapter 5 New York in the 1920s

117. "Negroes playing it": *San Francisco Examiner,* April 11, 1928, p. 6.

124. "[Fletcher's] was the band": Duke Ellington, *Music Is My Mistress* (Doubleday, 1973), p. 49.

132. J. A. Rogers celebrated jazz: Alain Locke, *The New Negro* (Albert and Charles Boni, 1925), pp. 216–24.

Chapter 6 Louis Armstrong and the First Great Soloists

145. "had the potential capacity": Gunther Schuller, *Early Jazz* (Oxford University Press, 1968), p. 89.

148. "She never envied no one": Louis Armstrong, *Satchmo: My Life in New Orleans* (Prentice-Hall, 1954), p. 9.

Chapter 7 Swing Bands

174. In 1939, two-thirds of the public: Russell B. Nye, *The Unembarrassed Muse: The Popular Arts in America* (Dial, 1970), p. 384.

175. "the abandon of a crowd": David W. Stowe, *Swing Changes: Big-Band Jazz in New Deal America* (Harvard University Press, 1994), p. 24.

176. "fancy wall decorations all over": Clyde Bernhardt, *I Remember: Eighty Years of Black Entertainment, Big Bands, and the Blues* (University of Pennsylvania Press, 1986), pp. 149–50.

176. "For the dancer, you know what will please him": Howard Spring, *American Music* 1997 (15:2), p. 191.

177. "to observe the Lindy Hop": ibid., p. 210.

177. "If you were on the first floor": Count Basie (with Albert Murray), *Good Morning Blues: The Autobiography of Count Basie* (Random House, 1985), p. 120.

178. "a lot of kids playing": Dickie Wells, quoted in Jeffrey Magee, *The Uncrowned King of Swing: Fletcher Henderson and Big Band Jazz* (Oxford University Press, 2005), p. 171.

182. "get a Harlem book": James Maher, transcript from *Ken Burns's Jazz* (http://www.pbs.org/jazz/about/pdfs/Maher.pdf).

183. "These were our songs": ibid.

184. "I have always been Mr. Showmanship": Lionel Hampton and James Haskins, *Hamp: An Autobiography* (Warner, 1989), p. 36.

187. "There was no white pianist": John Hammond, *John Hammond on Record: An Autobiography* (Penguin, 1977), pp. 68, 32–33.

187. "Hammond in action": Stowe, *Swing Changes,* p. 57.

187. "vapid and without the slightest": John Hammond, "The Tragedy of Duke Ellington," in *The Ellington Reader,* ed. Mark Tucker (Oxford University Press, 1993), p. 120.

189. "one of the foremost jazz conservatories": Artie Shaw, *The Trouble with Cinderella: An Outline of Identity* (Farrar, Straus, and Young, 1952), pp. 196–97, 203.

189. "I was actually living": ibid., p. 228.

190. "They won't even let me play": Richard M. Sudhalter, *Lost Chords: White Musicians and Their Contribution to Jazz, 1915–1945* (Oxford University Press, 1999), p. 581.

190. "We arrived in one town": Nat Shapiro and Nat Hentoff, *Hear Me Talkin' to Ya: The Story of Jazz as Told by the Men Who Made It* (Rinehart, 1955), pp. 328–30.

193. "Until I met Jimmie": Sy Oliver, quoted in Alyn Shipton, *A New History of Jazz* (Continuum, 2001), p. 299.

194. "They would come out and play a dance routine": Eddie Durham, National Endowment for the Arts/Smithsonian Institution Jazz Oral History Project.

198. One musician remembers: Albert McCarthy, *Big Band Jazz: The Definitive History of the Origins, Progress, Influence and Decline of Big Jazz Bands* (Berkley, 1974), p. 211.

199. "The only difference": Cab Calloway and Bryant Rollins, *Of Minnie the Moocher and Me* (Crowell, 1976), p. 42.

Chapter 8 Count Basie and Duke Ellington

203. "the colored patrons": Dave Dexter, quoted in Frank Driggs, *Kansas City Jazz: From Ragtime to Bebop—A History* (Oxford University Press, 2005), pp. 130–31.

208. Sometimes they were paid: Linda Dahl, *Morning Glory: A Biography of Mary Lou Williams* (Pantheon, 1999), p. 85.

209. "She'd be sitting": Andy Kirk (as told to Amy Lee), *Twenty Years on Wheels* (University of Michigan Press, 1989), p. 73.

209. "I listened to how a pianist": Dahl, *Morning Glory,* pp. 87, 77.

209. While touring with the Count Basie band: Billie Holiday (with William Dufty), *Lady Sings the Blues* (Abacus, 1975), p. 56.

210. "What does a jacket": Anita O'Day (with George Eells), *High Times, Hard Times* (Putnam, 1981), pp. 101–2.

214. "I had never heard": Count Basie (with Albert Murray), *Good Morning Blues: The Autobiography of Count Basie* (Random House, 1985), pp. 4–5.

214. "Whenever we wanted to do something": Driggs, *Kansas City Jazz,* p. 121.

214. The band finally dissolved: Nathan W. Pearson Jr., *Goin' to Kansas City* (University of Illinois Press, 1987), p. 75.

215. "the poor, the black": Pearson, *Goin' to Kansas City,* p. 84.

215. "might as well have been": Roy Wilkins, quoted in Douglas Henry Daniels, *Lester Leaps In: The Life and Times of Lester "Pres" Young* (Beacon Press, 2002), p. 182.

215. This tiny, L-shaped salon was so small: Basie, *Good Morning Blues,* p. 164.

215. "I don't think we had": ibid.

215. "It wasn't unusual": Nat Shapiro and Nat Hentoff, *Hear Me Talkin' to Ya: The Story of Jazz as Told by the Men Who Made It* (Rinehart, 1955), p. 291.

216. "revival meetings": Gene Ramey, National Endowment for the Arts/Smithsonian Institution Jazz Oral History Project.

217. "just like you were mixing": Stanley Dance, *The World of Count Basie* (Scribner, 1980), p. 103.

219. "did not aspire to live": Gerald Early, *Tuxedo Junction: Essays on American Culture* (Ecco Press, 1989), p. 279.

219. "I don't think I even knew": Basie, *Good Morning Blues,* p. 137.

219. "By the time you read this": ibid., p. 180.

220. "It was like the Blue Devils": ibid., p. 199.

222. "You know, don't you": Albert McCarthy, *Big Band Jazz: The Definitive History of the Origins, Progress, Influence and Decline of Big Jazz Bands* (Berkley, 1974), p. 207.

223. "Negro folk music": Richard Boyer, "The Hot Bach," in *The Ellington Reader,* ed. Mark Tucker (Oxford University Press, 1993), p. 218.

223. "beyond category": Edward Kennedy Ellington, *Music Is My Mistress* (Doubleday, 1973), p. 237.

224. "Perhaps a musician": Boyer, "The Hot Bach," p. 233.

224. "I'm supposed to remember": Dizzy Gillespie (with Al Fraser), *To Be, or Not . . . to Bop* (Doubleday, 1979), p. 184.

225. "at the height of his creative powers": Irving Townsend, "When Duke Records," in *The Ellington Reader,* p. 320.

225. "You can't write music right": Boyer, "The Hot Bach," p. 228.

226. "a sort of majestic folk quality": ibid., p. 231.

226. "Those were my two ways of being": Stanley Dance, *The World of Duke Ellington* (Scribner, 1970), p. 106.

228. "Duke merely lifts a finger": *Down Beat,* November 5, 1952, p. 18.

230. "It's a primitive instinct": Archie Bell, "The Ellington Orchestra in Cleveland," in *The Ellington Reader,* p. 53.

230. "This band has no boss": Boyer, "The Hot Bach," p. 217.

230. "It was a happy day": Duke Ellington, "We, Too, Sing 'America,'" in *The Ellington Reader,* p. 146.

231. "Where in the white community": Ralph Ellison, "Homage to Duke Ellington on his Birthday," in *The Ellington Reader,* pp. 96–97.

231. "take Uncle Tom out of the theater": Ellington, *Music Is My Mistress,* p. 175.

231. "I guess serious is a confusing word": "Why Duke Ellington Avoided Music Schools," in *The Ellington Reader,* p. 253.

232. "I don't feel the pop tunes": Boyer, "The Hot Bach," p. 231.

232. Playing by ear: Mercer Ellington, in Dance, *The World of Duke Ellington,* p. 39.

237. "That was the last thing": David Hajdu, *Lush Life: A Biography of Billy Strayhorn* (Farrar, Straus and Giroux, 1996), p. 253.

238. "His greatest virtue, I think": ibid., p. 257.

Chapter 9 A World of Soloists

243. "the man for whom Adolphe Sax": Jon Hendricks on the album *Lambert, Hendricks, & Bavan at Newport '63* (RCA-Victor, 1964).

243. "People always say I invented the jazz tenor": Hawkins on the album *Coleman Hawkins: A Documentary* (Riverside Records, 1956).

248. "so-called Southwest tenor style": Martin Williams, *The Jazz Tradition* (Oxford University Press, rev. ed., 1993), p. 75.

248. "During his early period": Rex Stewart, *Jazz Masters of the 30's* (Macmillan, 1972), p. 128.

249. "Man, this cat ain't playing harsh": Gary Giddins, *Visions of Jazz* (Oxford University Press, 1998), p. 191.

252. "I'm looking for something soft": Francois Postif, "Lester Paris 59," in *Jazz Hot* (Paris), April 1959.

256. "it's most improbable that anyone will ever know": Duke Ellington on the album *The Afro Eurasian Eclipse* (Fantasy Records, 1976).

Chapter 11 Modern Jazz: Bebop

296. "entirely separate and apart": Charlie Parker, "No Bop Roots in Jazz: Parker," *Down Beat,* September 9, 1942, p. 12.

297. "Everybody would get up there": Trummy Young, National Endowment for the Arts/Smithsonian Institution Jazz Oral History Project.

297. "Man, is that cat crazy?": Nat Shapiro and Nat Hentoff, *Hear Me Talkin' to Ya: The Story of Jazz as Told by the Men Who Made It* (Rinehart, 1955), p. 356.

298. "Stop that crazy boppin'": ibid., p. 351.

299. "That's what I've been hearing": Ira Gitler, *Jazz Masters of the Forties* (Collier, 1974), p. 20.

300. "With bop, you had to know": Scott DeVeaux, "Conversation with Howard McGhee," *Black Perspective in Music* 25 (September 1987), p. 73; italics added.

301. "Bird couldn't play much": Gene Ramey, National Endowment for the Arts/Smithsonian Institution Jazz Oral History Project.

302. "real advanced New York style": Leonard Feather, *Inside Be-Bop* (Robbins, 1949), p. 15.

303. "I worked hard": Dizzy Gillespie (with Al Fraser), *To Be, or Not . . . to Bop* (Doubleday, 1979), p. 218.

304. "head and hands": Miles Davis (with Quincy Troupe), *Miles: The Autobiography* (Simon and Schuster, 1989), p. 64.

304. "Charlie Parker brought the rhythm": Gillespie (with Fraser), *To Be, or Not,* p. 232.

305. "As we walked in": Marshall Stearns, *The Story of Jazz* (Oxford University Press, 1956), pp. 224–25.

307. "I had never heard": DeVeaux, interview with Howard McGhee, December 20, 1980.

308. "Naming-day at Savoy": Douglass Parker, in *The Bebop Revolution in Words and Music,* ed. David Oliphant (University of Texas Press, 1994), p. 165.

314. "The one was jazz": Teddy Reig (with Edward Berger), *Reminiscing in Tempo: The Life and Times of a Jazz Hustler* (Scarecrow Press, 1990).

317. "All we wanted to do": Davis (with Troupe), *Miles,* p. 114.

320. "I listened to bebop after school": Imanu Amiri Baraka, *The Autobiography of LeRoi Jones/Amiri Baraka* (Freundlich, 1984), pp. 57–58, 60.

322. "He had to stop and think": Gitler, *Jazz Masters,* p. 125.

322. "one with the music itself": ibid., p. 110.

327. "When Pres appeared": ibid., p. 205.

328. "There'd be a lot of cats on the stand": ibid., p. 209.

332. "Since I've been over here": Dan Morgenstern, *Living with Jazz* (Pantheon, 2004), p. 375.

332. "There was no such thing": Gillespie (with Fraser), *To Be, or Not,* p. 343.

334. "nervous jazz": Whitney Balliett, "Pandemonium Pays Off," in *Collected Works: A Journal of Jazz, 1954–2000* (St. Martin's Press, 2000), p. 8.

334. "They rarely move from their seats": ibid.

Chapter 12 The 1950s: Cool Jazz and Hard Bop

338. "gave up jazz": Hugues Panassie and Madeleine Gautier, *Guide to Jazz* (Houghton Mifflin, 1956), p. 210.

339. "One countered racial provocation": Ralph Ellison, *The Collected Essays of Ralph Ellison* (Modern Library, 1995), p. 631.

342. "Diz and Bird play a lot of real fast notes": Miles Davis (with Quincy Troupe), *Miles: The Autobiography* (Simon and Schuster, 1989), pp. 219–20.

349. "We had a hard time": author interview, Gary Giddins, *Visions of Jazz* (Oxford University Press, 1998), p. 384.

353. "We used to jam together": Giddins, *Visions of Jazz,* p. 331.

Chapter 13 Jazz Composition in the 1950s

381. "I say play your own way": Grover Sales, "I Wanted to Make It Better: Monk at the Blackhawk," in *Jazz: A Quarterly of American Music* 5 (Winter 1960).

383. "I used to have a phobia": Nat Hentoff, *The Jazz Life* (London: P. Davies, 1962), p. 203.

384. "I always had to be alert": Nat Hentoff, liner notes to *Giant Steps* (Atlantic Records, 1959).

390. "I am Charles Mingus": *Mingus,* a film by Thomas Reichman, 1968.

404. "It's not like when you base stuff on chords": Miles Davis (with Quincy Troupe), *Miles: The Autobiography* (Simon and Schuster, 1989), p. 225.

405. "The challenge here": ibid.

405. "I thought that Kind of Blue": Eric Nisenson, *The Making of "Kind of Blue"* (St. Martin's Press, 2000), p. 177.

408. "Such men must be guarded": Leonard Feather, "The Jazz Workshop," in *Down Beat Jazz Record Reviews,* vol. 2 (Maher, 1958), p. 169.

Chapter 14 Modality: Miles Davis and John Coltrane

412. "My ultimate culture hero": William C. Banfield, *Black Notes* (Scarecrow Press, 2004), p. 148.

426. "It took that long": Ralph J. Gleason, liner notes to *Coltrane's Sound* (Atlantic Records, 1960).

432. "He gets a very personal sound": Ian Carr, Digby Fairweather, and Brian Priestley, *Jazz: The Essential Companion* (London: Grafton, 1987), p. 510.

432. "the turning point": ibid., p. 182.

433. "musical nonsense": John Tynan, "Take Five," *Down Beat,* November 23, 1961.

438. "The main thing a musician would like to do": John Coltrane, liner notes to *Crescent* (Impulse Records, 1964).

Chapter 15 The Avant-Garde

449. "Musicians tell me, if what I'm doing": Ornette Coleman at World Jazz Scene, Great Quotes of and About Musicians, http://www.worldjazzscene.com/quotes.html.

449. "Bebop is like playing scrabble": Duke Ellington, *Look Magazine,* August 10, 1954.

450. "It's like not having anything to do with what's": Charles Mingus, quoted in Gary Giddins, *Visions of Jazz* (Oxford University Press, 1998), p. 445.

451. "You can always reach into the human sound": Ornette Coleman, quoted in Nat Hentoff, liner notes to Coleman's *Something Else!!!!* (Contemporary Records, 1958).

451. Hale Smith . . . observed: interview with Gary Giddins, 1978.

451. "Jazz is the only music in which": Ornette Coleman, quoted in Wilfrid Mellers, *Music in a New Found Land* (Hillstone, 1975), p. 346.

459. "The eyes are really not to be used": Cecil Taylor, quoted in Gary Giddins, *Riding on a Blue Note* (Oxford University Press, 1981), pp. 281–82.

460. "We had a magical dialogue": Andrew Cyrille, quoted in *Cecil Taylor,* an interview by Ted Panken, 2005.

468. "screaming the word 'FUCK'": Ted Joans, review of Albert Ayler in *Coda Magazine* (Canada), 1971.

468. "coonish churchified chuckle tunes": Leroi Jones (Amiri Imamu Baraka), *Black Music* (Morrow, 1968), p. 126.

468. "Salvation Army band on LSD": Dan Morgenstern, "Concert Review: Newport '67," *Down Beat,* August 10, 1967.

474. "We were not in the business of showcasing standards": Muhal Richard Abrams, quoted in Giddins, *Riding on a Blue Note,* p. 194.

475. "Until I had the first meeting": Joseph Jarman, quoted in J. B. Figi, liner notes to Jarman's *Song For* (Delmark Records, 1967).

483. "exhibits a disciplined disregard": unsigned statement, Vision Festival website, http://www.visionfestival.org/literature.php.

Chapter 16 Fusion I: R&B, Singers, and Latin Jazz

486. "Jazz is an octopus": Dexter Gordon, quoted in Gary Giddins, *Visions of Jazz* (Oxford University Press, 1998), p. 330.

489. "He really was a great musician": Sonny Rollins, interview with Gary Giddins, City University of New York, Graduate Center, 2008.

493. "When finally I got enough money": Jimmy Smith, quoted in Leonard Feather, liner notes to *The Sounds of Jimmy Smith* (Blue Note Records, 1957).

500. "Every song he sings is understandable": Duke Ellington, *Music Is My Mistress* (Doubleday, 1973), p. 239.

508. "If you can't manage to put tinges": Jelly Roll Morton, in *The Complete Library of Congress Recordings,* 1938 (released in 2005 by Rounder Records).

512. "It was similar to a nuclear weapon": Dizzy Gillespie, in *Routes of Rhythm,* PBS series (telecast 1997).

513. "If I had let it go": Dizzy Gillespie (with Al Fraser), *To Be, or Not . . . to Bop* (Doubleday, 1979), p. 321.

515. "I truly believe jazz ended up influencing": Chico O'Farrill, quoted in Giddins, *Visions of Jazz,* p. 325.

521. "There was a noticeable difference": Charlie Byrd, quoted in John Litweiler, liner notes to *Jazz Samba: Stan Getz: Charlie Byrd* (Verve Records, 1996).

Chapter 17 Fusion II: Jazz, Rock, and Beyond

533. "an unprecedented share": Eric Hobsbawm, *The Jazz Scene* (Pantheon, 1993), p. xxviii.

535. "I had discovered that my strength": James Brown (with Bruce Tucker), *James Brown: The Godfather of Soul* (Thunder's Mouth, 1997), p. 158.

536. "Everybody was dropping acid": *Down Beat,* May 1984, p. 16.

537. "They would play my music": Stuart Nicholson, *Jazz Rock: A History* (Schirmer, 1998), p. 79.

537. "walking eye candy": Michael Henderson, quoted in *Jazziz,* February 2004, p. 37.

538. "the $1.50 drums and the harmonicas": Miles Davis (with Quincy Troupe): *Miles: The Autobiography* (Simon and Schuster, 1989), p. 288.

538. "like calling me colored"; interview, *Village Voice,* 1969.

539. "He'd go out and play": *Down Beat,* March 28, 1974, p. 15.

539. "nobody stepped on anybody's feet": Joe Zawinul, liner notes to *Forecast: Tomorrow* (Columbia, 2006).

540. "If you stop calling me a *jazz* man": Clive Davis, *Clive: Inside the Record Business* (Morrow, 1975), p. 260.

540. "It was loose and tight at the same time": Davis (with Troupe), *Miles,* p. 299.

542. "It was like group therapy": *Down Beat,* October 21, 1976, p. 14.

542. "More than my experience with Miles": *Down Beat,* September 1988, p. 19.

542. "to be the fastest guitarist": Nicholson, *Jazz Rock,* p. 203.

543. "To me," he later said: *Down Beat,* June 15, 1978, p. 21.

544. "We were a black band": *Down Beat,* April 1988, p. 17.

544. "Jaco . . . brought the white kids in": ibid.

549. "We jazz listeners tend": Herbie Hancock, in *Down Beat,* September 8, 1977, p. 56.

549. "I can get toys in a toy shop": *Down Beat,* August 2005, p. 43.

550. "I looked at myself in the mirror": *Down Beat,* October 24, 1974, p. 44.

550. "I decided that it was now time": *Time,* July 8, 1974.

551. "I don't even think this is well-done funk": *Down Beat,* May 17, 1979, p. 33.

552. "The main reason I joined the band": *Down Beat,* October 24, 1974, p. 17.

552. "You don't usually see": *Down Beat,* August 2005, p. 43.

552. "It was the wrong piano": *Jazz Times,* June 2001, p. 73.

552. "I was trying to get rid of all": *Down Beat,* September 2003, p. 50.

553. "play a different blues": *Jazz Times,* June 2001, p. 73.

556. "the absolute greatest jazz guitar album": James Isaacs, liner notes to *Wes Montgomery: The Verve Jazz Sides* (Verve, 1995).

557. He was born a displaced person: *Jazziz,* April 2005, p. 36.

561. "all these rich people in fur coats": *Electronic Musician,* September 2005, pp. 85–86ff.

561. "that more danceable element": *Down Beat,* November 2000, p. 28.

561. "I can hit three notes on any of my keyboards": *Electronic Musician,* September 2005, pp. 85–86ff.

562. "I'm at a point now": *Guitar Player,* June 1998, p. 40.

565. "Groove Collective has the energy": *Rolling Stone,* June 16, 1994, p. 21.

568. "in what looked like a leftover": Martin Williams, *Jazz In Its Time* (Oxford University Press, 1989), pp. 48–49.

568. "Wow," he said, "if Miles": Paul Tingen, *Miles Beyond: The Electric Explorations of Miles Davis, 1967–1991* (Billboard, 2001), p. 232.

571. "As soon as Miles walked into the studio": ibid., p. 235.

Chapter 18 Historicism: Jazz on Jazz

596. "The thing I'm trying to do": Gary Giddins, *Rhythm-a-ning* (Oxford University Press, 1985), p. 99.

Chapter 19 Jazz Today

611. "We're like the anti young lions": Greg Osby, press release, 1999.

612. "The hard part is actually trying to unlearn": Jason Moran, press release, 2007.

CREDITS

Photo Credits

Chapter 4: Frank Driggs Collection
Chapter 17: Frank Driggs Collection
Chapter 19: © Jimmy Katz
All other chapters: © Herman Leonard Photography LLC/CTSIMAGES.COM

Music Credits

INDEX

Page numbers in *italics* indicate illustrations.